HOUSING LAW:
CASES, MATERIALS AND COMMENTARY

AUSTRALIA
The Law Book Company
Sydney

CANADA
The Carswell Company
Toronto, Ontario

INDIA
N. M. Tripathi (Private) Ltd.
Bombay
and
Eastern Law House (Private) Ltd.
Calcutta
M.P.P. House
Bangalore
Universal Book Traders
Delhi

ISRAEL
Steimatzky's Agency Ltd.
Tel-Aviv

PAKISTAN
Pakistan Law House
Karachi

HOUSING LAW:
CASES, MATERIALS AND
COMMENTARY

by

MARTIN PARTINGTON, B.A., LL.B.
of the Middle Temple, Barrister,
Professor of Law and Dean of the Faculty of Law,
University of Bristol

JONATHAN HILL, LL.B., LL.M.
Lecturer in Law, University of Bristol

LONDON
SWEET & MAXWELL
1991

Published in 1991 by
Sweet & Maxwell Limited of
South Quay Plaza,
183 Marsh Wall, London E14 9FT
Laserset by
P.B. Computer Typesetting, N. Yorks.
Printed by
Richard Clay Limited, Bungay, Suffolk

*A CIP catalogue record
for this book is available
from The British Library*

PREFACE

This book has been developed from the cases and materials text, *Landlord and Tenant* by Martin Partington, published by Weidenfeld and Nicolson in their *Law in Context* series (1st ed. 1975, 2nd ed. 1980).

To some extent this new work still reflects both the structure and philosophy of those earlier works. We hope that those who study housing law will be able not only to acquire knowledge of those areas of law which seek to regulate the operation of the housing market, but also, through the provision of other relevant materials, to acquire some understanding of the social context within which this law operates.

While the underlying educational purposes of this text may be based in earlier work, we have nonetheless sought to ensure that full account is taken of the profoundly important changes to housing law that have occurred over the last decade. All those who provide housing — whether public authorities, housing associations, a private landlord — are required to operate within a legal and policy context that is in many respects substantially different from that existing in 1980.

We hope that the publication of this work will come at an opportune time. The need for more legal practitioners to be aware of and offer services in the area of housing law is becoming increasingly recognised, not least within the Law Society. Amongst housing practitioners, as well, there has been increased recognition of the importance of understanding the legal context within which they must operate; this has been reflected in important changes to the curriculum for professional qualifications that have been adopted by the Institute of Housing. Introductory texts, such as Andrew Arden's *Manual of Housing Law* (Sweet & Maxwell, 4th ed. 1989), provide an outline of the basic law, and major practitioners' texts, especially the *Encyclopedia of Housing Law & Practice* (Sweet & Maxwell), provide detailed coverage of the area. This book, however, aims to fill a gap. Students of housing law — whether legally qualified or not — who plan to go on and practise in the area of housing law must have understanding of the main issues and access to the relevant legal materials. This is what we have sought to provide.

In the preparation of this book we have each had the benefit of help from numerous quarters. In particular thanks are due to Ruth Annand (of the Faculty of Law, University of Bristol), Andrew Arden (who has

v

collaborated on much work with Martin Partington, and has had a major influence in developing Housing Law, both as a subject for study and as an important area of legal practice), Sheila Hill (for support and understanding) and Jackie Williams (who typed the text of Chapters 1 and 7). We also acknowledge the encouragement of a number of colleagues associated with the Institute of Housing, particularly Peter Williams, now Professor of Town Planning at the University of Wales, Cardiff, and Mike Williams, Director of the Gwalia Housing Association.

The Bristol University Law Faculty Research Fund provided some financial support for research assistance, for which we are most grateful.

Primary responsibility for preparing Chapters 1 and 7 has laid with Martin Partington; Jonathan Hill has been responsible for the rest of the text and made a major contribution to the planning of the overall structure of the work. We have, however, read and commented upon successive drafts and have taken joint responsibility for checking the proofs. Equally, we are jointly responsible for errors and omissions.

The law is stated as at January 1, 1991.

University of Bristol   MARTIN PARTINGTON
January 1991   JONATHAN HILL

ACKNOWLEDGMENTS

Grateful acknowledgment is made to the following for permission to quote from their works:

BBC Enterprises Ltd.: Extracts from The Home Front by Patrick Nuttgens.

Butterworth Law Publishers Ltd.: Extracts from the All England Law Reports and from The County Court Practice 1990 ed. Thompson.

The Estates Gazette Ltd.: Extracts from Estates Gazette Law Reports.

HMSO: Extracts from Law Commission Report No. 174, DOE Circular 3/89, Housing and Construction Statistics 1978–1988 and the Government Review of Homelessness Legislation 1989 reproduced with the permission of the Controller of Her Majesty's Stationery Office.

The Housing Corporation: Extracts from the Housing Corporation 1979 survey; Tenant's Choice: How it works; Tenant's Choice: Criteria for Landlord Approval © Housing Corporation.

The Incorporated Council of Law Reporting for England and Wales: Extracts from the Law Reports and Weekly Law Reports

The Legal Action Group: Extracts from A. Jessup and S. Burrage — Landlord and Tenant Act 1987 (1988) Legal Action, November; Luba — Repairs: Tenant's Rights (1991); Madge and Luba — Recent Developments in Housing Law Legal Action (June 1989).

Megarry: Extracts from The Rent Acts (Eleventh Edition) Sweet and Maxwell.

Megarry and Wade: The Law of Real Property (Fifth Edition) Sweet and Maxwell.

Extracts from Housing Acts 1985, 1988; Local Government and Housing Act 1989; Rent Act 1977 and extracts from various statutes © Crown Copyright.

CONTENTS

1. SETTING THE CONTEXT

2. OUTLINE OF THE LAW OF LANDLORD AND TENANT

3.   THE SCOPE OF STATUTORY PROTECTION

5. SECURITY OF TENURE II: PROBLEMS ARISING FROM ASSIGNMENT AND SUB-LETTING, SUCCESSION, RELATIONSHIP BREAKDOWN, AND MORTGAGE OR SALE OF THE REVERSION

6. REPAIRS AND IMPROVEMENTS

7. RENT AND OTHER TERMS

8. THE PRIVATISATION OF PUBLIC SECTOR HOUSING

9. HOMELESSNESS

TABLE OF CASES

TABLE OF STATUTES

TABLE OF STATUTORY INSTRUMENTS

TABLE OF RULES AND ORDERS

CHAPTER 1

SETTING THE CONTEXT

I INTRODUCTION

"Housing Law" is, potentially, a subject of vast scope. Taken literally, it covers all that body of law that relates to the operation of the housing market.[1] This book has, however, been conceived and planned as a *student* textbook. For a whole variety of reasons, both of principle and pragmatism, we have had to limit the scope of this work.

For example, we have assumed that insofar as this work will be used by law students, they are likely also to be studying in other parts of their course the basic principles of land law and equity which provide the legal foundations for the ownership of land, and other rights in land. Save for a consideration of basic principles of landlord and tenant law, we have not sought to repeat material likely to be found elsewhere in the legal syllabus. Insofar as the text might be of value to students studying for professional housing examinations, we did not want to incorporate large amounts of legal material that would not really be relevant to their needs.

Instead, our aim in this work is to provide our readers with the chance to explore and analyse *aspects* of the law relating to the operation of the housing market, with special reference to the landlord-tenant relationship, and to ask a range of questions about the effectiveness of that law in relation to the apparent aims and objectives of housing policy.

(A) THE BASIC FEATURES OF HOUSING POLICY

In order to do this, we must offer some definition, however rudimentary, of the nature and purpose of housing policy. Our starting point is very simple:

Shelter is essential for human survival. The central features of housing policy must, therefore, be to ensure that there is an adequate quantity of housing accommodation, located where people need it, to satisfy demand; that the accommodation stock should be of a reasonable

---

[1] See, *e.g.* Arden & Partington, *Housing Law* (2nd ed. forthcoming); also the massive *Encyclopaedia of Housing Law and Practice* (ed. Arden) (4 vols.).

1

quality; that the price people are required to pay for their housing should also be reasonable, taking into account both the individual's ability to pay and the nature and quality of the accommodation provided; that people should be able to live in their accommodation in reasonable security; and that those who provide housing do so on terms that enable them to remain financially viable.

For a large proportion of the population, these criteria are satisfied. But, for a minority they clearly are not. They pay large sums for poor quality accommodation; or, worse still, have nowhere to live at all. The focus of this work, therefore, is on those aspects of the interaction of law and policy which are of particular significance to the minority of the population living in unsatisfactory conditions and/or on unsatisfactory terms.

The basic question, underlying the text, is: to what extent can the *law* protect those whose place in the housing market is weak?

Given this perspective, the materials in this book concentrate on those areas of law that seek to regulate the relationship of landlord and tenant in the housing market, for it is here that the problems of inequality are most apparent and where the focus of much regulatory law is most obvious.

We recognise that this concentration on the position of the more vulnerable in the housing market can be distorting. Focusing on the problems of the poor and weak may divert attention from the problems caused by the rich and the strong. Also, concentrating on the landlord and tenant relationship does mean that a number of analogous matters in the owner-occupied sector, in particular those relating to the relationship between mortgagors and mortgagees, are not discussed as fully as perhaps they should be, particularly given the shift towards owner-occupation as the primary form of housing tenure.

Nonetheless, for all the emphasis in the media and in political circles on owner-occupation as the preferred form of housing tenure,[2] a significant section of the population of the country still lives in rented accommodation, and it is in this sector of the housing market that many of the most difficult questions of the interaction of the law and social policy arise. For these reasons, therefore, we feel justified in continuing to focus primarily on the rented sector of the housing market.

(B)   REGULATING THE LANDLORD-TENANT RELATIONSHIP

The bulk of the law analysed in this book seeks to regulate the landlord-tenant relationship. This very fact raises some initial and interesting questions. Why is it necessary to have such a body of law at all? Is not the landlord-tenant relationship merely an example of the rights of

---

[2] For discussion as to whether or not this is sensible see, *e.g.* Whitehead & Kleinman *Private Rented Housing in the 1980's and 1990's* (1986) esp. Chapter 5.

landowners to enter into contracts to dispose of interests in their land as they wish—in this case for limited periods of time? The landlord-tenant relationship is based on two of the most potent "verbal symbols"[3] which the common law seeks to uphold: "property rights" and "freedom of contract". Are these not part of the fundamental values on which our law is founded?[4]

These very values are, however, also the source of further difficulties. For example, the very notion of "rights" highlights the fact that those without property have no rights. The apparent "freedom" to contract may be distorted by inequality of bargaining power. The history of the landlord-tenant relationship and the law regulating that relationship, is studded with examples of attempts both by the courts and more recently by Parliament to strike some balance between the interests of the landlord and the interests of the tenant. It is not at all clear that the balance which has been struck has been successful; but there is widespread agreement on the need to make the attempt.

(C) SOME HISTORICAL NOTES

The legal concept of the lease developed at least as early as the twelfth century, though outside the feudal systems of land tenure.[5] It was designed to enable landowners to use their land in a more commercial fashion.[6] At first, tenants only had a personal action for damages were they to lose possession of their land. By 1499, however, there was a decision of the Court of Common Pleas, confirmed by Kings Bench, which settled that a lessee had a right to recover possession against ejectors (including the land owner).[7] Thus the courts had recognised the inadequacy of damages as a remedy.

This important legal development apparently encouraged the use of the lease as the basis on which agricultural land was held and farmed.[8] But while the landlord-tenant relationship *could* work admirably,[9] it could also be extremely exploitative, for example in the way English landowners treated their tenants in Ireland.[10] From the nineteenth century onwards, successive Parliaments intervened in attempts to control abuse.[11]

---

[3] See Kahn-Freund, *Labour and the Law* (2nd ed., 1977), p. 13.
[4] Stein & Shand, *Legal Values in Western Society* (1974), Chapter 9.
[5] Holdsworth, *History of English Law* (1908) Vol. 3, p. 213.
[6] Bean,*The Decline of English Feudalism 1215–1540* (1968), pp. 20–25.
[7] Holdsworth, *ibid.* pp. 216–217; see also Milsom, *Historical Foundations of the Common Law* (2nd ed. 1981), pp. 152–157.
[8] Simpson, *Introduction to the History of Land Law* (1961), pp. 233 ff.
[9] For examples of the use of leases in early town planning, see Chalklin, Urban Housing Estates in the 18th Century (1968) 5 *Urban Studies* 67–85.
[10] Simpson, *ibid.* See also Chambers & Mingay, *The Agricultural Revolution, 1750–1880* (1966), pp. 17 et seq.
[11] Abuse was not always direct; mass evictions of tenant farmers by landlords in Wales following the General Election in 1868 played an important part in the introduction of electoral ballots in 1872 Douglas, *Land People and Politics: A History of the Land Question 1878–1952* (1976), p. 97; see also Thompson, *English Landed Society in the Nineteenth Century* (1963), pp. 201 et seq.

With the increasing urbanization of the country, attention turned from the problems surrounding agricultural and farming leases to new tensions that were developing as a result of appalling urban housing conditions. During the nineteenth century there were numerous examples of conflict between landlords and tenants.[12] The development of policy responses in the nineteenth century, though initially somewhat tentative in scope and permissive rather than compulsory in character, did nevertheless provide the basis from which more positive interventions occured in the twentieth century.[13] The history of the Rent Acts is discussed below (pp. 110–116).

Interpreting the nature of the response of the courts and governments to these questions in the specific context of the landlord-tenant relationship is inevitably a matter of considerable debate. Some have argued that these interventions have amounted to an effective destruction of private property. Others suggest that property has been re-structured so that ownership of land is no longer a source of rights, but of social obligations as well. Yet others say that to look at changes in legal forms is misleading; that the imbalance of power inherent in landlord-tenant relationships remains and will not be removed until the capitalist system has been destroyed and the social relationships based on capitalism are replaced by social relationships founded on different political-economic structures.

It is not the purpose of this book to resolve these debates, which in any event cannot be adequately summarized here. However, two specific points may be made:

The first is that although the landlord-tenant relationship was often regarded as beneficial to both sides, especially in the context of agricultural holdings, nonetheless there was often the possibility, and sometimes the reality of conflict resulting from an imbalance of power in the landlord-tenant relationship. This conflict might take the form of direct exploitation of tenants; or be indirect, based on the political control landlords might have over their tenantry.

Secondly, the landlord-tenant relationship did not emerge as an efficient way of ensuring that the very poorest were given opportunities for access to decent quality housing. This became a source of increasing social tension, and is a key factor in understanding how housing law and housing policy developed in the twentieth century.

II   THE LANDLORD-TENANT RELATIONSHIP: SELECTED CONTEMPORARY DATA

The overall effect of the legislative interventions that began in the middle-to-late nineteenth century, and which have continued to the

---

[12] See, *e.g.* Englander, *Landlord and Tenant in Urban Britain, 1838–1918* (1983); Stedman-Jones, *Outcast London* (1976) Part II.

[13] See, *e.g.* Gauldie, *Cruel Habitations* (1974).

present day, is the subject of considerable debate; the materials later in this book, which discuss the mix between traditional common law and more recent statute law, are presented with the view of encouraging readers to think about how, if at all, the nature of the landlord-tenant relationship has changed over the years. One point to be made here is that, unlike other areas of social policy, such as education, health or social insurance, where what was originally provided privately came to be taken over predominantly by government, housing has remained the one area of social policy in which the private sector of the economy has continued to dominate. Although approaching a quarter of all homes are now provided by local authorities,[14] the ideology of private property, and those whose interests were protected by that ideology, have helped to ensure that there would be no serious challenge to the dominance of the private sector in the provision of housing generally.

The following paragraphs set out and comment on some basic statistical information about recent trends in the housing market, which has particular relevance to the matters to be discussed in this work.

(A) CHANGES IN TENURE PATTERNS

The decline in the size of the private rented sector is well known and documented. In 1914 it was estimated that nearly 90 per cent. of dwellings were rented from private landlords; 10 per cent. were owner occupied and only a negligible quantity was provided by local authorities. The total number of dwellings at that time was 7.9 million.

By 1951, 52 per cent. of the then total of 12.5 million dwellings were still rented from private landlords; owner occupation had increased to 31 per cent. and local authorities (including new towns) then provided 17 per cent. In 1976, the balance had changed again. Local authority and new town rentals had increased to 29 per cent. of the total (now 18.1 million dwellings); owner occupation was over half, at 56 per cent. the private rented sector had declined to 15 per cent. of the total.[15]

(B) CURRENT TENURE PATTERNS

Over the last decade, there have been further substantial shifts in tenure patterns. Between December 1979 and March 1990 the total stock of dwellings rose from 20.7 million to 22.6 million.[16] Within these totals, owner-occupied dwellings rose from 55 per cent. of the total in 1979 to 66 per cent. of the total in 1990. Local authority (including new

---

[14] The precise overall average figure is 23 per cent.; there are substantial regional variations—in particular Scotland, where the figure is 44 per cent. See *Housing and Construction Statistics*, (1990) Vol. 41, Table 2.22.

[15] Figures derived from Ginsburg, *Class Capital and Social Policy* (1979), p. 113.

[16] *Housing & Construction Statistics* (1990), Vol. 41, Table 2.22.

town) rented accommodation dropped from 31.4 per cent. of the total in 1979 to 23 per cent. of the total in 1990. Private sector rentals dropped from 11 per cent. of the total in 1979 to 7.2 per cent. in 1990. Dwellings rented from housing associations increased more modestly in percentage terms from 2 per cent. of the total in 1979 to nearly 3 per cent. in 1990.[17]

Despite the obvious rise in owner occupation, where trends existing in the 1970's were given a substantial boost by the "right to buy" policy introduced by the Conservative Government in 1980,[18] two points need to be stressed.

First, renting as a form of tenure still applies to approximately a *third* of all dwellings. The average figures set out above also disguise very marked regional variations; in Scotland, for example, owner occupation is still only at 48 per cent. of the total housing stock. In East Anglia, 10 per cent. of dwellings are still privately rented (and the figure is nearly the same in the south west region). Rentals from local authorities are as low as 15 per cent. in the South West, but 30 per cent. in the North of England.[19]

Secondly, despite the considerable emphasis being given to the development of housing associations as an alternative form of "social" housing tenure, outside local authority control, and while the total number of dwellings actually provided by housing associations nearly doubled between 1976 and 1990, such numbers nevertheless remain a very small percentage of the total stock of dwellings. It is most unlikely that without dramatic new policy initiatives local authorities, as substantial landlords, will disappear in the near future, despite recent ministerial predictions to the contrary.[20]

(C) LANDLORDS

(1) Public Sector Landlords

We have already noted that local authorities are now by far the largest providers of rented accommodation. As this sector of the housing market grew from the 1920's to the 1970's, policy was based on two fundamental assumptions: that local authorities would be "model" landlords; and that local authorities would be "social" landlords.

Behind the notion of "model" landlordism is the idea that local authorities will behave towards their tenants in a benevolent, even paternalistic way. The arbitrary evictions, the poor quality of

---

[17] *Ibid.* Percentages and figures have been rounded.
[18] See pp. 506–533.
[19] *Ibid.* Table 2.24.
[20] One proposed means of hastening the demise of local authority control, the Housing Action Trusts which were provided for in the 1988 Housing Act, have notably failed to attract tenant support. See pp. 556–559.

accommodation, the failure to do repairs, the charging of extortionate rents that were said to be characteristics of the private sector, were all to be removed from public sector housing. In more recent years, however, many attacks have been made on the role of local authorities as landlords. The discretions that they formerly had regarding their choice of tenants and allocation of accommodation, their policies for management of estates and defining the terms of lettings, and the fixing of rent levels have all been subject to criticism and in many cases have been replaced or supplemented by measures of statutory control.

For example, although 60 per cent. of local authority housing allocation in 1987-1988 was to those on council waiting lists, the freedom to make such allocations has been reduced by such measures as the Housing (Homeless Persons) Act 1977 (now Part III of the Housing Act 1985) which provides duties towards the homeless in priority need.[21] As a consequence, during the same period, 26 per cent. of the local authorities' allocations were to the homeless.[22] Freedom to set rent levels has been substantially reduced.[23] The Housing Act 1980 gave local authority tenants statutory rights to security of tenure,[24] and other rights collectively known as the "tenants' charter."[25] Local authorities are now subjected to a body of regulatory legislation that is much more analogous to that which applies to the private sector than was the case 10 years ago.

Insofar as local authorities were to be "social" landlords, the assumption was that they would offer housing opportunities to those who were hardest hit by the operation of the free market in housing. One of the predicted outcomes of measures such as the "right to buy" is that the social mix of local authority tenants will be reduced as the better-off purchase their dwellings, leaving rented council estates as "residual" housing, the exclusive preserve of the poor and destitute.

(2) Housing Associations[26]

Housing associations come in a bewildering variety of forms. They have long been regarded as a potentially very important source of accommodation. Some have argued that they may ultimately replace the private landlord; others are heard to argue that they should replace public sector landlords: this potential has yet to be fully realised.

---

[21] See below, Chapter 9.
[22] See *Social Trends* (1991), Table 8.7. The figures for 1981–82 were, respectively 67 per cent. and 16 per cent.: *ibid.*
[23] See below, Chapter 7 p. 459.
[24] See below, Chapter 4 p. 249.
[25] It cannot be said that this particular measure has had much impact on local authority management practice: see Kay, Legg and Foot, *The 1980 Tenants' Rights in Practice* (1983?: City University); also the unpublished Ph.D. thesis by Brennan *The Illusion of the Gap: A Case Study of the Implementation of the Consultation Provisions of the Tenants' Charter* (Brunel University, 1989).
[26] See generally, Alder & Handy, *Housing Association Law* (1987).

Since the Housing Act 1974[27] came into effect, housing associations wishing to receive grants and loans from public funds have been required to register with the Housing Corporation.[28] The Corporation has extensive powers to provide dwellings itself, to acquire land and to develop it.[29] But in practice its most important tasks are the promotion and regulation of the activities of housing associations.[30]

On the promotion side, it is given substantial borrowing powers, including the power to borrow abroad and from the European Investment Bank and the Commission of the EEC[31]; and it can therefore lend money to housing associations.[32] Further the Corporation makes grants, subject to Treasury consent.[33]

As regards regulation, the Corporation has broad powers to inquire into the affairs of housing associations and act for their protection.[34]

Associations vary considerably in type. Their housing stock consists of both purpose-built accommodation and older properties which have been improved. Their use of the stock relates to the crucial distinction between "specialist associations," which allocate more than 50 per cent. of their available accommodation to a particular type of tenant, and general-purpose associations. Specialist associations may offer sheltered accommodation for the elderly, hostels for single people, accommodation for the socially or economically vulnerable—*e.g.* one-parent families, ex-psychiatric patients, the handicapped, ex-offenders—or groups identified by a job or activity, such as nurses or students. A particular recent interest is housing in rural areas.[35] The general-purpose associations are self-explanatory; they are for all categories of tenant who may apply for housing by the association in question.

(3) Private Sector

Landlords in the private sector are even more varied. The *Report of the National Dwelling & Housing Survey, 1978*[36] distinguished between the following categories of landlord: property companies, employers, relatives, other persons and others. Individual landlords were further divided between resident landlords and non-resident landlords.[37] It was clear from this survey that a clear majority of privately rented dwellings were rented from individual private landlords. Paley's study, *Attitudes to Letting in 1976*[38] showed that these individual landlords tended to let a

[27] Now repealed and replaced by the Housing Associations Act 1985.
[28] Housing Associations Act 1985, s.5.
[29] s.89.
[30] s.75.
[31] ss.92 and 93.
[32] ss.79 *et seq.*
[33] s.87.
[34] ss.28 *et seq.*
[35] See *Housing Corporation Corporate Plan* (1985).
[36] (1978).
[37] See Tables 40 and 41.
[38] (1978).

small number of dwellings only; corporate residential landlords had larger numbers of units of accommodation available for letting.[39]

There has regrettably been no recent official, national survey of private sector landlords, and none that takes into account the new forms of tenure created by the Housing Act 1988. A useful critique of the classification of landlords in social surveys, such as those used in the reports just cited, has recently been developed by Allan and McDowell.[40] They argue that the structure of private landlordism, can only be understood using what they call a "realist account." This offers a classification under the following heads:

— "traditional" landlords such as the Church, Charitable Trusts and the Crown Estate who, although in the private sector, have social considerations very much in mind; although they are interested in the rental income for other purposes (*e.g.* the payment of clergy salaries), they may not be so interested in profit maximisation through high rent levels;

— employer landlords who provide accommodation to ensure the availability of labour but who again are not usually seeking to maximise direct rental yields;

— informal landlords—typically resident or small landlords willing to make spare accommodation available, often using any rental income to service mortgage debt payments, but again not interested in maximising profits;

— "investor" landlords who predominated in the first half of this century but who have increasingly disappeared from the market;

— "commercial" landlords who see rented housing as a commodity to be traded in like other commodities; and

— "financial" investors—big property companies and financial institutions that may have some residential accommodation as a small part of larger investment portfolios.

Unfortunately this classification was developed for a detailed study of landlords in the London Boroughs of Hackney and Islington; it has not been tested nationally. It might however prove a useful basis for analysis since it offers a new framework within which to consider the types of regulatory provisions that have been enacted by Parliament. It may also assist in predicting the outcomes of initiatives in legislative reform. For example, present legislation makes no effective distinction between different categories of landlord (with the exception of resident landlords[41]). If the objective of legislative reform, however, is to create a revival of the private rented sector of the housing market and if this aim is to be taken seriously, the need to target legislation on particular landlord groups may be an important precondition for success.

---

[39] *Ibid.* p. ii.
[40] Allen & McDowell, *Landlords and Property* (1989).
[41] See p. 148.

(D) TENANTS

(1) Local Authority Tenants

Finding official data on the characteristics of local authority tenants is by no means straightforward.

The *General Household Survey* for 1987 suggests that there has been an increase in the average age of council tenants: 31 per cent. were aged 65 or more in 1981; this had gone up to 39 per cent. by 1987.[42] One possible explanation for this trend is the movement out of this form of tenure by the younger, more economically active groups, who have taken advantage of the "right to buy."

The same source suggests that the average weekly income of those council tenants who are economically active is considerably lower than that for the economically active population as a whole.[43] A recent survey showed that 62 per cent. of local authority tenants were in receipt of housing benefit.[44]

Social Trends provides information on the marital status of the head of households: over 40 per cent. of divorced or separated women rent from public sector landlords[45]; and nearly 40 per cent. of both widows and widowers rent in the public sector.[46] This confirms the trend noted in 1977[47] for local authorities increasingly to cater for widowed, divorced and deserted women with children.

The preceding paragraphs demonstrate that the broad objective of local authorities in providing housing on more of a "social policy" basis rather than a completely "market" basis to groups in the community who are relatively disadvantaged as compared with other groups in the community has to a considerable extent worked. Certain groups, in particular single people, are not however catered for by local authorities as well as other groups.

There is also some evidence that, in the allocation of housing, families from ethnic minority groups do not fare as well as might be expected, leading to the conclusion that there may be discrimination, albeit unconscious, in the operation of housing allocation policies.[48]

(2) Housing Association Tenants

A useful "profile" of housing association tenants was provided by the Housing Corporation in 1979. It surveyed new housing association tenants in a two week period in May 1978 and found:

---

[42] *General Household Survey 1987* (1989) Fig. 3C. The information in the 1988 survey is presented in a different format: see Chapter 11.
[43] *Ibid.* Table 3.12.
[44] *The Nature & Effectiveness of Housing Management in England* (H.M.S.O., 1989) Table 3.3.
[45] *Social Trends, 1990* (1990) Table 8.23.
[46] *Ibid.*
[47] *Housing Policy* (1977) Vol. 3, p. 12.
[48] See, *e.g.* Commission for Racial Equality, *Race and Council Housing* (1984); MacEwan, *Housing, Race and Law* (1991).

Of the 1,775 new housing association tenants identified in the survey, 125 (seven per cent.) were occupying older properties purchased for rebuilding or modernisation ... These sitting tenants did not become tenants because of associations' selection policies, but because of the type of development being undertaken. The remaining 1,650 tenants were allocated housing as a result of deliberate procedures on the part of the housing associations ... In comparison with the household structure and characteristics of the population in England and Wales as a whole, new tenants are significantly more likely to be:

> "single persons of all ages; small families with children under 16, and particularly single parent families; retired from full time employment; employed in junior and other non-manual, skilled and semi-skilled manual occupation; unemployed."

As a consequence of the relatively high proportion of retired or unemployed household heads, gross incomes tended to be low, with a median for all new tenants of £2,080 per annum (£40 per week) compared with a national median for household heads working full-time in all tenures of between £4,000 and £4,100 (about £78 per week).

Almost one third of the new tenants had rented accommodation from a private landlord previously, about 25 per cent. had shared with relatives or friends, and 18 per cent. had been tenants of a local authority. Eleven per cent. had been owner-occupiers. For about 10 per cent. of the new tenants, the grant of a housing association tenancy was the first time they had lived as separate households.

Twelve per cent. of the new tenants had lacked one or more of the basic amenities in their previous accommodation, slightly above the national average. Thirty-eight per cent. of new tenants had shared one of the basic amenities, compared with only two per cent. nationally. Eighteen per cent. of new tenants said that they had been overcrowded in their previous home, while 9 per cent. had found their previous accommodation too large.

Unsatisfactory or unsuitable housing was the reason given most frequently by association staff for allocating accommodation to new tenants (43 per cent. of cases). Other common reasons given for allocating accommodation were that the tenant had been nominated for housing by a local authority and a variety of reasons connected with homelessness or insecurity. Reasons connected with the lack of alternative housing solutions were frequently given.

Over half the new tenants were housed as a result of making a direct application to an individual housing association, while over a quarter were housed as a result of being nominated by a local authority. The characteristics of tenants housed as a result of these two practices were very similar. Eight per cent. of the new tenants were referred to housing associations by other agencies.

Referred tenants were more likely to be families with children compared with tenants from other sources, and household heads were likely to be manual workers on low wages. Rates of unemployment amongst household heads who were economically active were 38 per cent., almost 10 times the national average. Referred tenants were also more likely to have been sharing accommodation with relatives or friends, or to have been living in a hostel or institution than other groups of tenants. Two thirds of them had shared one or more of the basic amenities in their previous accommodation, compared with under one third of the direct applicants and nominated tenants.

Sitting tenants were more likely to be elderly single people, almost all of whom rented their accommodation from a non-resident private landlord. Two thirds of the sitting tenants had lacked one or more of the basic amenities in their previous accommodation, and over half mentioned other deficiencies including damp, rot and faulty wiring, and under occupation of the space.

One fifth of the new tenants were allocated accommodation by specialist associations, which comprised 46 per cent. of the associations taking part in the survey. The range of housing needs being met by these associations was wide, but two groups of people in particular were more highly represented amongst new tenants of specialist associations than amongst new tenants of general purpose associations. The first group were elderly single people, two thirds of whom were housed by three large national associations. The second significant group were single people of working age, 85 per cent. of whom were housed by small specialist associations with fewer than 250 dwellings.

Four fifths of the new tenants were housed by general purpose housing associations who housed a wider range of people overall; and significantly more families with children, who formed over half the new tenants of these associations.

Tenants housed by specialist associations were more likely to have applied direct for housing than in general purpose associations and over half the new tenants in specialist associations were allocated sheltered housing. Almost half the new tenants of general purpose associations also applied direct, and a third were nominated by local authorities. Only six per cent. of general purpose association tenants were allocated sheltered housing, and over a quarter of the new tenants were allocated improved older housing.

Tenants housed in Greater London were more likely to be single people of working age, whereas those in metropolitan or non-metropolitan areas were more likely to be over retirement age. However, within each area, major differences were observed between those by general purpose associations, and it is clear from the survey data that it is the type of association rather than the type of area of operation which has the determining influence on who is housed.

A more recent study, *The Nature and Effectiveness of Housing Management in England*[49] indicated, as might be expected, that housing association tenants were (like council tenants) markedly poorer than the population as a whole, with some 60 per cent. of tenants being in receipt of housing benefits. The same study also suggested that housing associations may house rather more single people than local authorities.[50] Apart from this, the general profile of housing association tenants was very similar to that of local authority tenants.

(3) Private Sector Tenants

Tenants in the private rented sector have rather more varied characteristics.[51] First the sector does have many elderly people, whose tenure dates back to the time when private renting was much more common. Secondly, the sector caters for the young and mobile. Thirdly, the sector provides much housing related to employment. Fourthly, the

---

[49] (1989), p. 34.
[50] *Ibid.*
[51] The following is adapted from Kemp "Private Renting: An Overview" Chapter 1 in *The Private Provision of Rented Housing* (ed. Kemp) (1988), pp. 6–7. These generalizations are derived from statistical reports prepared by the Office of Population Censuses & Surveys, based, in turn, on 1981 Census data.

private sector now provides some "residual" housing, especially for single people, who cannot obtain access to local authority and housing association tenancies, but who cannot afford to own a dwelling. Finally, there is a small "luxury" subsector, particularly in London.

III THE FUNCTION OF HOUSING LAW

In the final section of this chapter, we wish to raise for discussion some questions about the function of housing law as a method of regulating the landlord-tenant relationship.

(A)   THE 'GAP' PROBLEM

The body of law that is discussed in the following chapters may be seen to have a number of quite different objectives:

   (i)   it may *prescribe procedures* for effecting certain transactions, for example in relation to the creation of a lease;

  (ii)   it may attempt to *create rights* to protect certain groups, *e.g.* security of tenure for tenants, or certain duties regarding the homeless;

 (iii)   it may offer *modes of enforcement* which underpin those rights, *e.g.* in the law on harassment and unlawful eviction;

 (iv)   it may have a *constitutional function*, for example authorising the expenditure of public funds on housing provision;

  (v)   it may attempt to *lay down standards*, for example by providing definitions of unfitness of certain accommodation for human habitation.

But as we shall also see, the "success" of the law in achieving those apparent objectives is extremely mixed. Rights go by default or are not enforced; standards are not met; procedures are ignored. So it is important to ask why there is this apparent gap between the objectives of the law and its achievements.[52] (This problem is not, of course, unique to housing law, but is one of the general issues raised by the study of law.) A number of explanations may be suggested.

(1) The Imbalance of Political Strength

One of the important lessons to be drawn from the data presented in the previous section of this chapter is that, taken as a whole, tenants are relatively poor, or otherwise disadvantaged. Many are elderly; others

---

[52] Studies carried out for the Civil Justice Review suggest that, possession proceedings and rent assessment committee hearings apart, less than 1,700 cases were brought in the county court in 1986, despite, for example, the English Housing Condition Survey of 1981 showing that over two and three quarters of a million dwellings needed repairs costing in excess of £1,000. (Cm. 394, 1988) para. 704.

are highly mobile. These factors may help to explain why tenants' organisations, especially in the private sector and housing association sector, have tended to be politically ineffective.

Amongst council tenants there is a longer tradition of tenants' organisation. The fact that most council tenants live on council estates has eased the problems of organisation and communication, as compared with the tenants in the private sector. While tenants' organisations have on occasion been very active and effective in fighting particular issues, their overall impact has however been somewhat limited.

This is not to say that the tenants' case has been wholly unrepresented. Charitable pressure groups such as Shelter have been extremely active in putting forward the claims of tenants to government. But these groups have not generally been able to claim massive "grassroot" support.

One development which might have had some impact in raising the collective consciousness and strength of council tenants' organisations was the creation of the tenants' charter. The Housing Act 1980 gave many council tenants security of tenure and required local authorities to consult with their tenants about various aspects of housing management. Sceptics anticipated, however, that, far from encouraging genuine tenant participation, the concept would be used by local authorities as an additional method of controlling the lives of tenants. Research shows that the tenant's charter has not achieved any substantial redress in the balance of political power.[53]

By contrast, landlords are relatively well organised. Local authority landlords have developed powerful pressure groups, both at the political level (for example, the Association of Metropolitan Authorities, the Association of District Councils) and at official level (for example, the Institute of Housing). Most housing associations belong to the National Federation of Housing Associations, an "independent" body funded by the Department of the Environment. The Federation and its parent body, the Housing Corporation, obviously represent another powerful group. In the private sector, there are still a number of substantial company landlords in business. The British Property Federation spends much of its time advancing the claims of these larger landlords. There is also the Small Landlords' Association, whose purpose is clear from its title, and around the country there are a number of local landlords' representative bodies.

The influence of these groupings on the development of particular policies, and any consequent legislation, is hard to assess. Despite the apparent political weakness of tenants, a number of measures have been passed designed to protect the interests of tenants. In parliamentary terms, tenants' interests have been represented with some success.

[53] See research cited above, note 25.

Nonetheless, as has already been remarked, the laws that have been enacted have by no means always operated as intended. Does the apparent political imbalance between landlords and tenants help to explain this? Is it possible to assess the extent to which laws are effective as a means of controlling the economically or politically powerful?

(2) Judicial Attitudes

Another suggestion as to why laws in the housing area do not appear to operate as intended is that this is due to judicial attitudes, which are said to be hostile to the aims of the legislation. The difficulty with this line of argument is that although it may be possible to detect apparently hostile remarks in the pages of particular reported cases in housing law, this does not prove that all judges—in particular those county court judges and registrars (now district judges) who deal with the bulk of cases in this area—share the same attitudes. Casual empiricism may suggest that this is the case; but the lower courts have not been adequately studied for the validity of the hypothesis to be sustained.

One case that is worth considering in this context is the House of Lords decision in *Johnson* v. *Moreton*[54] in which the issue under discussion was whether a landlord and an agricultural tenant could (by clause 27 of the lease) contract out of the statutory protection contained in section 24 of the Agricultural Holdings Act 1948. Consider the following remarks of Lord Salmon (at 52–53):

During the last war, the submarine menace was such that it would have been virtually impossible to import into this country any more goods vital for our survival than we in fact did. Accordingly, it is extremely doubtful whether we could have survived had it not been for the food produced by our own farms. Even in 1947 when the Agriculture Act of that year was passed, food rationing was still in existence. It must have been clear to all that it was then and always would be of vital importance, both to the national economy and security, that the level of production and the efficiency of our farms should be maintained and improved. This could be achieved only by the skill and hard work of our farmers and the amount of their earnings which they were prepared to plough back into the land from which those earnings had been derived. A very large proportion of those farmers were tenant farmers. They were tenants because they did not have the necessary capital to buy land or could not find any land they wanted that was for sale, or for sale at a price which they could afford. In spite of sections 23 and 25 of the [Agriculture] 1923 Act which had put them in a somewhat better position than did the common law, the sword of Damocles was always hanging over their heads. If they were tenants for a term of years, they might receive an effective notice to quit on the date when the term expired, and this term was rarely for more and usually for less than ten years. If they were tenants from year to year, and very many of them were, they might in any year receive an effective notice to quit at the end of the next ensuing year.

[54] [1980] A.C. 37.

Accordingly there was no great inducement for these farmers to work as hard as they could, still less to plough money back into land which they knew they might well lose sooner or later.

The security of tenure which tenant farmers were accorded by the 1947 Act was not only for their own protection of the weak against the strong; it was for the protection of the nation itself. This is why section 31(1) of the 1947 Act, reproduced by section 24(1) of the 1948 Act, gave tenant farmers the option to which I have referred and made any agreement to the contrary void. If any clause such as clause 27 was valid landlords might well insist on a similar clause being introduced into every lease; and prospective tenants, having no money with which to buy the land they wanted to farm, would, in reality, have had a little choice but to agree. Accordingly, if clause 27 is enforceable the security of tenure which Parliament clearly intended to confer, and did confer on tenant farmers for the public good would have become a dead letter ...

Lord Hailsham said (at 58–61):

It seems to me that the whole validity of the landlords' argument depends on his being able to establish, to borrow the words of Lord Westbury L.C. in *Hunt v. Hunt*, 4 De G.F. & J. 221 that the remedy and right conferred on the tenant by section 24(1) of the 1948 Act is "nothing more than a private remedy and a private right," or, to use the phrase of Lord Simon of Glaisdale quoted above, that the procedure prescribed by section 24(1) is one entirely in the favour of a particular tenant, without any element of public policy ... I myself am satisfied that this is not so on at least two separate but closely connected heads.

The first is the nature of farming itself. At least since the 1880s successive Parliaments have considered the fertility of the land and soil of England and the proper farming of it as something more than a private interest. Fertility is not something built up as the result of a mere six months' activity on the part of the cultivator, which was all the period of notice given by the common law to to the individual tenant, by whom in the main the land of England was cultivated then, as now, mainly under a yearly tenancy. It takes years (sometimes generations) of patient and self-abnegating toil and investment to put heart into soil, to develop and gain the advantage of suitable rotations of crops, and to provide proper drains, hedges and ditches. Even to build up a herd of dairy cattle, between whose conception and first lactation at least three years must elapse, takes time and planning, whilst to disperse the work of a lifetime of careful breeding is but the task of an afternoon by a qualified auctioneer. Even within the space of a single year the interval between seed time and harvest, between expenditure and return with all the diverse dangers and chances of weather, pest or benignity of climate is sufficient to put an impecunious but honest cultivator at risk without adding to his problems any uncertainty as to his next year's tenure. At first Parliament was concerned simply with compensation for cultivation, manuring and improvement. But it never regarded these as matters simply for private contract, or something wholly unconnected with any public interest. From the first, Parliament was concerned with the management of the soil, the land of England which had grown gradually into its present fertility by the toil of centuries of husbandmen and estate owners. By the 1920s Parliament similarly concerned itself with the length of notice to which the yearly tenant was entitled. Such provisions are now to be found in sections 3 and 23 of the 1948 Act. But they date from this time. In 1947 a new and momentous step was taken. The landlord's notice to quit, save in certain specified instances, was at the option of the tenant to be subject to consent, at first of the Minister, but latterly of a quasi-judicial tribunal, the agricultural land tribunal, whose jurisdiction clause 27 of this lease seeks by its express terms to eliminate and oust. Even the consent of the agricultural land tribunal is carefully regulated by section 25 of the 1948 Act (consolidating and amending the 1947 provisions). The circumstances in which its consent may be accorded are thus defined and limited by objective and justiciable criteria. These are not simply matters of private contracts from which the landlord can stipulate that the tenant can deprive himself as if it were a 'jus pro se introductum.' It is a public interest introduced for the sake of the soil and husbandry of England of which both landlord and tenant are in a moral, though not of course a legal, sense the trustees for posterity. Silence is not an argument, particularly when the words are prima facie mandatory, for excusing a term in a contract introduced for the purpose of annulling the protection given to the tenant by section 24.

But there is another ground, closely related to the first, for disagreeing with the landlords' contention. It is not only the tenants of agricultural holdings that Parliament has increasingly sought to protect by statute from an improvident use of their contractual powers. The policy of the law has been repeatedly used to protect the weaker of two parties who do not contract from bargaining positions of equal strength. The protection given to minors by the courts is, of course, immemorial but has been reinforced by statute. The exigencies of war have provided a whole bundle of interferences with contractual obligations, and these have often developed into permanent features of peace-time legislation. The Rent Restriction Acts are an example. We were referred to the momentous decision of Astbury J., under the 1915 Act in *Artizans, Labourers and General Dwellings Co. Ltd.* v. *Whitaker*, [1919] 2 K.B. 301, 304, subsequently embodied by Parliament in the 1920 Act....

There was also the line of cases beginning with *Salford Union of Guardians* v. *Dewhurst* [1926] A.C. 619 ... which fortified the robust treatment by Farwell J. of the war time emergency legislation of 1939 in *Soho Square Syndicate Ltd.* v. *E. Pollard & Co.* [1940] Ch. 638, 644, 655. Farwell J.'s reasoning was subsequently endorsed by the Court of Appeal in *Bowmaker Ltd.* v. *Tabor* [1941] 2 K.B. 1. ... The truth is that it can no longer be treated as axiomatic that, in the absence of explicit language, the courts will permit contracting out of the provisions of an Act of Parliament where that Act, though silent as to the possibility of contracting out, nevertheless is manifestly passed for the protection of a class of persons who do not negotiate from a position of equal strength, but in whose well-being there is a public as well as a private interest. Such acts are not necessarily to be treated as simply 'jus pro se introductum,' a 'private remedy and a private right' which an individual member of the class may simply bargain away by reason of his freedom of contract. It is precisely his weakness as a negotiating party from which Parliament wishes to protect him ... I would not have it supposed that the examples I have given of the policy of recent Parliaments to limit freedom of contract in the interest of the weaker party to contracts of a particular class are limited to the examples I have given. Almost every session of Parliament provides fresh examples in the field, for instance, of consumer protection, or employer and employee. I have limited myself, however, to classes of legislation examples of which were cited in argument in the instant case. It is not for the courts to decide whether the policy underlying these statutes is always wise or productive of the results intended. The point is that, once the court has identified the point of such legislation, it should be cautious about permitting 'contracting out' ...

Lord Simon said (at 65–69):

The appellants rely on the principle of law expressed in the maxim 'quilibet potest renunciare juri pro se introducto' ('anyone may, at his pleasure, renounce the benefit of a stipulation or other right introduced entirely in his own favour'). The right to serve a counter-notice was, the landlords argue, a statutory provision entirely in favour of the agricultural tenant (it is completely up to him whether or not he serves a counter-notice) and he can therefore contract not to do so. In argument this has been referred to as 'contracting out of the statute' ...

   The maxim exemplifies Maine's famous observation that the movement of progressive societies had thitherto been a movement from status to contract, that is, from on the one hand societies where legal relationships between persons arise from their membership of classes to which the law ascribes ¨eculiar rights and obligations, capacities and incapacities, to on the other hand societies where those relationships arise from private agreements between the parties which will be enforced by the law. It was natural for Maine, writing in the middle of the 19th century, to discern such a movement. The laissez-faire laissez-aller ideology was dominant. Human felicity, it was argued, was best promoted by leaving to every person to seek his own maximum advantage in competition with his fellows. A free market, including a free labour market, would ensure that the individual's effort was directed to anticipating and satisfying with maxium efficiency the wants of his fellow. The most powerful motive force in the universe, man's pursuit of his own interest, would thus be harnessed to drive a whole society forward. 'Man's selfishness is God's providence,' they said.

   The development of the law, as so often, reflected the dominant ideology. Freedom and sanctity of contract tended to be considered as pre-eminent legal values. It is unnecessary to expatiate after Dicey's classic study: it is sufficient to note, for example, equity's increasing reluctance to relieve against contractual forfeitures and Jessel M.R.'s representative pronouncement in *Printing and Numerical Registering Co.* v. *Sampson* (1875) L.R. 19 Eq. 462, 465:

   " ... if there is one thing which more than another the public requires
   it is that men of full age and competent understanding shall have the
   utmost liberty of contracting, and that their contracts when entered into
   freely and voluntarily shall be held sacred and shall be enforced by courts
   of justice."

But well within the lifetimes of Maine and Jessel M.R. the ideology which lay behind their juristic views was questioned. By some it was directly attacked: society's objective should be not wealth but welfare (with the implication that the pursuit and achievement of wealth were destructive of welfare), which was best promoted by the direct intervention of the organ of the state and could not be left to the bargain of the market-place. 'Competition' came to have the cliché 'cut-throat' attached to it. Others, more subtly, argued that, for the laissez-faire system to work felicitously as claimed, there must be a genuinely free, open and abundant market in which there is equality of bargaining power: equality of knowledge of the market and of staying-power in holding out for a bargain. This called for at least a limited intervention by the state to prevent or counteract rigging of the market by monopolies or oligopolies and to redress inequalities of the bargaining power. And consonantly, even in the 19th century, the law began to back-pedal. The 'quilibet' maxim was held to be inapplicable to a matter in which the public had an interest.

There was one economic and social relationship where it was claimed that there were palpably lacking the prerequisites for the beneficent operation of laissez-faire, that of the landlord and tenant. The market was limited and sluggish: the supply of land could not expand immediately and flexibly in response to demand, and even humble dwellings took more time to erect than those in want of them could spare. Generally, a man became a tenant rather than an owner-occupier because his circumstances compelled him to live hand-to-mouth; the landlord's purse was generally longer and his command of knowledge and counsel far greater than the tenant's. In short, it was held, the constriction of the market and the inequality of bargaining power enabled the landlord to dictate contractual terms which did not necessarily operate to the general benefit of society. It was to counteract this described constriction of the market and to redress this described inequality of bargaining power that the law, specifically, in the shape of legislation, came to intervene repeatedly to modify freedom of contract between landlord and tenant. Since Maine the movement of many 'progressive' societies has been reversed. The holding of a statutory or a protected tenancy is rather status than a pure creature of contract. The Agricultural Holdings Act 1948 exemplifies such legislative activity specifically where the tenancy is of agricultural land.

The movement from status to contract was largely a creature of the common law. The reverse movement has been largely a creature of legislation. As result lawyers sometimes tend to regard freedom and sanctity of contract as still of special and supervening juristic value. But freedom of contract and its consequences are quite likely to be 'mischiefs' as that word is used in statutory construction. Courts of law do not nowadays hold themselves out to judge public policy in the light of ideologies. But since statutory construction almost always calls for consideration of the statutory objective, it is incumbent to hold in mind the palpable objective of section 24(1), namely, to vouchsafe to the good tenant-husbandman a security of tenure which went beyond the lease he had bargained for ...

The principle which, in my view, emerges from this line of authority is as follows. Where it appears that the mischief which Parliament is seeking to remedy is that a situation exists in which the relations of parties cannot properly be left to private contractual regulation, and Parliament therefore provides for statutory regulation, a party cannot contract out of such statutory regulation (albeit exclusively in his own favour), because so to permit would be to reinstate the mischief which the statute was designed to remedy and to render the statutory provision a dead letter.

I think that this principle applies to section 24(1) of the 1948 Act.

Comment

Do you regard these as statements of principle that should be clearly applied to the residential landlord-tenant relationship as well? Or are they expressions of liberal sentiment that should not be applied more widely? To what extent should the kinds of consideration that appear to have influenced their Lordships in this case be applied in other contexts discussed in this book? To what extent have they been applied?

One suggestion that has been made is that housing law would be more sensitively applied if there were to be created a specialist housing court or housing tribunal. This idea was rejected by the Civil Justice Review though new procedures relating specifically to the handling of housing cases are likely to be developed consequent upon the enactment of the Courts and Legal Services Act 1990. Certainly the need for judicial training in housing matters has been recognised. Will specially trained judges and district judges be more likely to understand the underlying social issues in housing cases? Would such reforms result in a closing of the gap between the law in the books and the law in practice?

(3) Lack of Legal and Other Advisory Services

Another suggested reason for the failure of the law to meet its apparent objectives is the fact that there are insufficient lawyers prepared to understand the relevant legislation and to take on cases in this area. Two particular points may be noted. First, in so far as empirical evidence is available, it does seem that, in general, solicitors in private practice do not do much work in the landlord-tenant area. Secondly, in those areas where neighbourhood law centres have been established housing issues have tended to dominate case-loads. These two points, taken together, suggest that there is extensive unmet need for additional legal services on such issues. It is therefore suggested that, were such services available, the apparent 'gap' between the letter of the law and its use would be narrowed. An extension of this argument suggests that if housing advice services were more generally available this could result in more effective use of the legislation. But what general impact would massive increases in such services have? How far is it likely that there will ever be adequate services to advise all those potentially affected by landlord-tenant law?

(4) Complexity of the Law

A further argument as to why the law has failed to achieve its apparent objectives is that it is far too complex for the layman to comprehend. The complexity of the law will, no doubt, be conceded by anyone who has studied the contents of this book. However, although calls to simplify the law are frequently made, it must be asked to what extent this is a realistic possibility. Is not the law attempting to balance a complex and varied range of interests? If that is so, is it not inevitable that the legal provisions required to achieve this political objective will be somewhat complicated? Is there not a danger that simpler laws may result in unacceptably rough justice?

(B)   LIMITS OF THE LAW

Whatever response is made to the issues raised above, the inherent limits of the law must also be appreciated.

First, however much protective legislation may exist, this cannot guarantee that private landlords in particular will wish to continue renting accommodation. It is frequently asserted that the decline in the availability of privately rented accommodation is exclusively attributable to the passing of the Rent Acts. This crude hypothesis is simply not sustainable; the decline in the size of the private rented sector appears to have begun even before the first Rent Act was passed in 1915, and many other factors have encouraged the shift to owner-occupation (availability of mortgage finance, tax concessions, better rates of return on investments than housing and so on). (In some respects what is surprising is that there are still private landlords left at all.) However, it cannot be denied that the enactment of protective legislation has contributed to the decline of this sector of the market. So another limitation on the function of landlord-tenant law is that landlords may vote with their feet and abandon this form of enterprise.

Secondly, and more importantly, whether there are enough houses of adequate standard, at a price people can afford, is essentially the result of political and economic decisions relating to the distribution of resources in society. The law may assist in very many cases to prevent tenants being arbitrarily evicted, or to improve housing conditions, but whatever functions the law may have in regulating the landlord-tenant relationship and providing forums for the settlement of disputes, these crucial questions relating to the availability of accommodation must not be regarded as exclusively legal issues.

Bibliographical note

There is a substantial literature on housing and housing policy in the United Kingdom. For a general overview, see P. Malpass and A. Murie, *Housing Policy and Practice* (3rd ed., 1990, Macmillan).

There are a number of valuable histories of housing policy: see, *e.g.* J. Burnett, *A Social History of Housing, 1815–1970* (1980, Methuen); E. Gauldie, *Cruel Habitations* (1974, Croom Helm); D. Englander, *Landlord and Tenant in Urban Britain, 1838–1918* (1983, Clarendon Press); A.E. Holmans, *Housing Policy in Britain: A History* (1987, Croom Helm); S. Merrett, *State Housing in Britain* (1979, Routledge and Kegan Paul).

The best account of the impact of recent policy initiatives on public sector housing is R. Forrest and A. Murie, *Selling the Welfare State: The Privatisation of Council Housing* (1990, Routledge). A new review of the place of housing associations is H. Cope's *Housing Associations: Policy and Practice* (1990, Macmillan).

Up-to-the minute discussion of policy issues relating to housing is found in the excellent bi-monthly journal, *ROOF*, published by Shelter. The Institute of Housing publishes a wide variety of housing news in its weekly, *Inside Housing*. More substantial articles appear in the monthly journal, *Housing*. Regular discussion of developments in housing law is to be found in *Legal Action*, published monthly by the Legal Action Group. This includes a regular quarterly up-date.

CHAPTER 2

OUTLINE OF THE LAW OF LANDLORD AND TENANT

Introduction

The starting point for any discussion of housing law (as we have defined it) in England and Wales must be the traditional common law and equitable principles which govern the relationship between landlord and tenant. This chapter provides a basic account of the relevant principles. First, however, it is important to look at the legal vocabulary which is used in this area.

Lawyers, like other professional groups, have developed an extensive vocabulary of technical terms to describe the concepts they employ. Such vocabulary consists partly of words or phrases, (*e.g.* fee simple) which are obviously incomprehensible without further explanation; partly of words and phrases, (*e.g.* year, term of years) which look straightforward but are in fact used in a specialist sense, often quite different from ordinary use. In some instances concepts which at one time could be understood literally have become positively misleading because of changes in the law. Perhaps the most notorious example of this phenomenon in housing law is "notice to quit": as a result of statutory intervention the issuing of a notice to quit does not usually have the effect of requiring the tenant to leave.

Furthermore, there is the more general issue, but one that is of great importance in the context of housing law, of the complexity of language to be found in legislation. Such complexity is largely the product of the conventional rules under which statutes are drafted (though the legislation does also reflect the complexity of the issues with which it has to deal). As a consequence law tends to be inaccessible and mysterious. The following section attempts to make the basic vocabulary used in the law of landlord and tenant more accessible and less mysterious. An understanding of the terminology is an essential prerequisite to making any sense of this area of the law.

I BASIC VOCABULARY

(A) ESTATES IN LAND

The doctrine of estates (the word "estate" derives from the Latin *status*) has been used since feudal days to refer to the period of time during which a person's property rights are to last. Section 1(1) of the Law of Property Act 1925 provides:

The only estates in land which are capable of subsisting or of being conveyed or created at law are—

(a)   An estate in fee simple absolute in possesion;

(b)   A term of years absolute.

The estate in fee simple absolute in possession is a freehold estate. It is the most extensive estate which can be created in English law, and for almost all practical purposes can be equated with absolute ownership of land.

The term of years is the leasehold estate. Although the phrase "term of years" appears self-explanatory, section 205(1)(xxvii) of the Law of Property Act 1925, defines it in a far from obvious way to include "a term for less than a year, or for a year or years and a fraction of a year or from year to year." Therefore, all kinds of arrangement, from weekly tenancies to 999-year leases, fall within the definition.

(B)   LEASE: TENANCY: DEMISE

A term of years is more commonly known as a tenancy or lease. Under conventional usage, tenancy usually refers to relatively short-term landlord-tenant relationships; lease to more formal, longer-term re-lationships. They are not, however, terms of art, and there are no hard and fast rules. Demise is a more technical term, frequently appearing in conveyancing documents, which also means lease.

(C)   LANDLORD: TENANT

The person who grants a lease is the landlord/lessor; the person to whom the lease is granted is the tenant/lessee.

(D)   REVERSION

When a tenancy is created, the landlord who has granted the tenancy always retains an interest in the land, known as a reversion. The reversion is that part of the lessor's estate in the land of which he has not disposed when granting the tenancy. In the most straightforward situation—where a tenancy is granted by the owner of an estate in fee simple absolute in possession—the landlord retains the freehold reversion. When the tenancy ends, the land reverts to the grantor.

(E) ASSIGNMENT

It is possible both for the landlord to assign his reversion and for the tenant to assign his lease. The effect of this is that a new landlord or a new tenant steps into the shoes of the original landlord or tenant. Frequently the tenant's right to assign is restricted or even excluded by a covenant against assignment.[1]

(F) SUB-LETTING

Instead of assigning, the tenant may create a sub-lease (or under-lease), whereby a new letting for a shorter period than that held by the original tenant, is created. The original tenancy is sometimes called the "mesne" tenancy. Again, the power to sub-let is commonly curtailed.[2]

Megarry & Wade, *The Law of Real Property* (5th edition, 1984)[3]

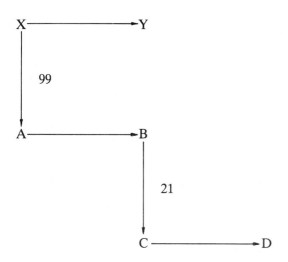

This diagram is the usual way of representing the following events. X grants a 99-year lease to A and then assigns the reversion to Y. B takes an assignment of A's lease and grants a sub-lease to C for 21 years, and C assigns his sub-lease to D. As to the 99–years lease, X is the "lessor," and Y is the "assignee of the

[1] See pp. 280–301.
[2] *Idem.*
[3] pp. 631–632.

reversion" or "landlord," and A is the "lessee". B is in a dual position: as to the 99–years lease, he is the "assignee" or "tenant"; as to the 21–years lease, he is the "sub-lessor" or "landlord". The 99–years lease is then called the "head lease," so as to distinguish if from the sub-lease. C is the "sub-lessee," and D the "assignee" of the sub-lease, or the "sub-tenant'.

It will be appreciated that it is possible for very extensive chains of leases to be created. In 1979 the Royal Commission on Legal Services noted:

In parts of Lancashire in particular there are tiers of leases comprising one or more houses. At one and the same time there may exist leases for 999 years, for 999 years less 10 days, for 990 years, for 990 years less 10 days, for 99 years, for 99 years less 10 days and so on until eventually at the bottom of the ladder there is an actual tenant in occupation.[4]

(G) LEASEHOLD COVENANTS

Covenants are promises made by the parties to the lease. Covenants commonly found in leases are those to pay rent and to carry out repairs. Covenants may be express—that is, specifically agreed by the parties—or implied by statute or by the common law. For example, the Landlord and Tenant Act 1985 implies into short leases of residential premises covenants imposing certain repairing obligations on landlords.[5] Similarly, the landlord's covenant for quiet enjoyment will be implied if not specifically mentioned in the lease.[6]

(H) PRIVITY OF CONTRACT: PRIVITY OF ESTATE

As between the original parties to a lease, all the covenants are enforceable under normal contractual principles based on privity of contract.

Where either the lease or the reversion is assigned there is no privity of contract between the parties who stand for the time being in the relationship of landlord and tenant. However, certain covenants continue to be enforceable by virtue of the doctrine of privity of estate. Where the lease is assigned (but not sub-let), those covenants which "touch and concern" the land are enforceable between the lessor and the assignee of the lease (*i.e.* the new tenant).[7] Similarly, when the reversion is assigned the covenants, which have "reference to the

---

[4] *Report of the Royal Commission on Legal Services* (1979), p. 283, para. 4.
[5] See pp. 361–363.
[6] See p. 274.
[7] *Spencer's case* (1583) 5 Co.Rep. 16a.

subject-matter of the lease,"[8] are enforceable between the assignee of the reversion, (*i.e.* the new landlord) and the tenant.

A covenant is regarded as touching and concerning the land or having reference to the subject-matter of the lease (the two formulations are regarded as being synonymous) if it "affects the landlord *qua* landlord and the tenant *qua* tenant."[9]

The test for determining whether a covenant touches and concerns the land was recently discussed by the House of Lords in *P. & A. Swift Investments* v. *Combined English Stores Group plc.*[10] Lord Oliver, without claiming to provide an exhaustive guide, suggested that:

the following provides a satisfactory working test for whether, in any given case, a covenant touches and concerns the land: (1) the covenant benefits only the reversioner for the time being, and if separated from the reversion ceases to be of benefit to the covenantee; (2) the covenant affects the nature, quality, mode of user or value of the land of the reversioner; (3) the covenant is not expressed to be personal (that is to say neither being given only to a specific reversioner nor in respect of the obligations only of a specific tenant); (4) the fact that a covenant is to pay a sum of money will not prevent it from touching and concerning the land so long as the three foregoing conditions are satisfied and the covenant is concerned with something to be done on, to or in relation to the land.[11]

Law Commission Report No. 174 *Landlord and Tenant Law—Privity of Contract and Estate* (1989)[12]

2.23 The rules concerning covenants which run with the land were criticised some 50 years ago as "purely arbitrary, and the distinctions, for the most part, quite illogical". ... [T]here are a number of difficult borderline cases from which it is hard to discern a clear guiding principle. To take a few examples. A landlord's covenant to renew a lease runs with the land, but a covenant that a landlord will make a payment to the tenant at the end of the lease, or in default will grant a new lease does not. A covenant not to employ a named person on business premises binds the tenant's successors; a covenant not to employ a particular class of people on the property does not. ...

2.25 In *Hua Chiao Commercial Bank Ltd.* v. *Chiaphua Industries Ltd*[13] the lease provided that the tenant should pay to the landlord at the commencement of the term a substantial security deposit on the basis that it would be repayable at the end of the term if there was no breach of the tenant's covenants. The Privy Council, overruling the Court of Appeal of Hong Kong, held that the landlord's obligation to return the security deposit at the end of the term did not touch and

---

[8] Law of Property Act 1925, s.141(1) and s.142(1).
[9] Megarry & Wade, *The Law of Real Property* (5th ed., 1984), p. 744.
[10] [1989] A.C. 632.
[11] At 642.
[12] Citations from the text are omitted.
[13] [1987] A.C. 99.

concern the land. It was merely a personal covenant between the original parties to the lease. Accordingly, the landlord's assignee, who had not received the deposit, was not obliged to return it to the tenant, who had not broken his covenants and who was left without a remedy as the original landlord was in liquidation. Lord Oliver of Aylmerton, giving the judgment of the Board, made it clear that not every covenant which is related to some obligation which touches and concerns the land itself necessarily has the same character.

2.26 In *Kumar* v. *Dunning*[14] the Court of Appeal did not regard the Privy Council decision as ruling out the possibility that a covenant "closely connected and bound up" with a covenant which does touch and concern the land can itself touch and concern the land. It was held, overruling earlier recent decisions at first instance, that a covenant by a surety, guaranteeing performance of covenants by a tenant which touch and concern the land, itself has the same character and is therefore automatically enforceable by an assignee of the reversion. This decision has recently received the approval of the House of Lords.[15]

Under the present law the original lessee remains liable on the covenants throughout the term of the lease, even though after assignment those covenants which touch and concern the land may be enforced by the landlord against the assignee. So, if an assignee fails to pay the rent the landlord may recover the unpaid rent from the lessee. A lessee who is made liable in this way for the default of an assignee has a right to indemnify himself against either the person to whom he has assigned the lease, or, where the lease has been assigned more than once, against the assignee in possession.

In practice, the landlord will generally only sue the lessee if the tenant in possession is unable to perform the covenants (for example, as a result of insolvency). Accordingly, the lessee's right of indemnity will often be entirely worthless. It has recently come to be recognised that the continuing liability of the original lessee after assignment of the lease may produce substantial injustice, and the Law Commission has proposed that where a tenant assigns his interest he should be released from the covenants of the tenancy.[16]

II CATEGORIES OF OCCUPATION

(A) LICENSEES AND TRESPASSERS

The simple fact that a person occupies residential premises, the freehold of which is owned by someone else, does not automatically mean that the occupier is a tenant. For a tenancy to be created certain basic conditions must be satisfied.[17] Where these legal requirements are

---

[14] [1989] Q.B. 193.
[15] In *P. & A. Swift Investments* v. *Combined English Stores Group plc* [1989] A.C. 632. See also *Coronation Street Properties* v. *Ingall Industries plc* [1989] 1 W.L.R. 304.
[16] Law Commission Report No. 174 *Landlord and Tenant Law—Privity of Contract and Estate* (1989).
[17] See pp. 49–84.

not met, the occupier may be a trespasser (commonly referred to as a squatter), or a licensee.

(1) Trespassers

A trespasser is someone who occupies land without the permission of the landowner. The occupation of land by a trespasser is, however, precarious. The landowner may bring possession proceedings, and the law provides for a summary procedure which allows the landowner to recover possession swiftly. In relation to the High Court the summary procedure was established by the Rules of the Supreme Court Order 113. It is available:

Where a person claims possession of land which he alleges is occupied solely by a person or persons (not being a tenant or tenants holding over after the termination of the tenancy) who entered into or remained in occupation without his licence or consent or that of any predecessor in title of his, the proceedings may be brought by originating summons in accordance with the provisions of this Order.

An identical jurisdiction was created for the county court, and is now to be found in Order 24, Part I.

The County Court Practice 1990 (Thompson (ed.)) (1990)[18]

Availability of procedure.—A summary order for possession may be made against a person who has entered into occupation with the consent of the person entitled to possession but remains in occupation without such consent or licence: *Bristol Corpn.* v. *persons unknown* [1974] 1 All E.R. 593, [1974] 1 W.L.R. 365. See also *Greater London Council* v. *Jenkins* [1975] 1 All E.R. 354, [1975] 1 W.L.R. 155, C.A. In *Moore Properties (Ilford) Ltd* v. *McKeon* [1977] 1 All E.R. 262, [1976] 1 W.L.R. 1278, H.C., it was held that R.S.C. Ord. 113 was available to a head landlord against unlawful sub-tenants. So, too, the procedure may be used by a tenant against a person who during his absence, has been let into occupation with the consent of the landlord: *Borg* v. *Rogers* (1981) 132 N.L.J. 134, C.A.; but it cannot be used by a landlord against a person whom the tenant has allowed into the premises, unless the tenancy has been determined or surrendered: *Auto Finance Ltd.* v. *Pugh* (1985) CAT, 10 June; the mere fact that the tenant has left the premises owing rent does not justify the inference of surrender: *Preston Borough Council* v. *Fairclough* (1982) 8 H.L.R. 70, 10 June; C.A. ...

A county council which failed to fulfil its statutory duty to provide adequate accommodation for gypsies was held to be disentitled to an order for possession against them under this rule: *West Glamorgan County Council* v. *Rafferty* [1987] 1 All E.R. 1005, [1987] 1 W.L.R. 457, C.A.

The procedure is more appropriate to proceedings for the eviction of squatters than for a highly complicated claim as to title: *Cudworth* v. *Masefield* (1984) *The Times*, May 16, C.A. or, where it is arguable whether or not a purported licence agreement is a sham: *Markou* v. *Da Silvaesa*; *Crancour Ltd.* v. *Merola* (1986) 52

---

[18] p. 326.

P. & C.R. 204, 278 Estates Gazette 618, 733, C.A., or whether or not facts relied upon by the landlord are capable of amounting to a surrender of a tenancy by operation of law: *Cooper* v. *Varzdari* (1986) 18 H.L.R. 300, C.A.

In a period of housing shortage people may resort to trespassing simply in order to have somewhere to live. Homelessness is not, however, a defence to trespass.

McPhail v. *Persons* (*Names Unknown*) [1973] Ch. 447

Lord Denning M.R. said (at 455–458):

1. Introduction

Mr. McPhail is the owner of a leasehold house, no. 4, Thornhill Square, Islington. There was some furniture in it, but otherwise it seems to have been unoccupied. On Friday, April 13, 1973, the premises were left locked and secured. On Sunday, April 15, 1973, some persons, then unknown, made entry. They got in by the front door and put a new lock on. On Monday, April 16, 1973, Mr. McPhail went with a detective inspector, and asked them their names. They did not give them. So he took proceedings for possession under R.S.C., Ord, 113. These were served on them some time on Thursday, April 19 for hearing on April 25. They then gave their names. They said they believed that the house had been empty for at least two years, and, as they had nowhere to live, they decided to make their home there. On April 25, Phillips J. made an order that Mr. McPhail do recover possession . . .

[The squatters] admit that they have no defence in law, but they ask the court to give them time. They only asked for four weeks, or so. Can the court give it to them? The case raises this question: when the owner of the house asks for an order for possession, is the judge bound to make an order which is enforceable forthwith or can he suspend it for a while?

2. The law as to squatters

What is a squatter? He is one who, without any colour of right, enters on an unoccupied house or land, intending to stay there as long as he can. He may seek to justify or excuse his conduct. He may say that he was homeless and that this house or land was standing empty, doing nothing. But this plea is of no avail in law. As we said in *Southwark London Borough Council* v. *Williams* [1971] Ch. 734, 744:

"If homelessness were once admitted as a defence to trespass, no one's house could be safe. . . . So the courts must, for the sake of law and order, take a firm stand. They must refuse to admit the plea of necessity to the hungry and the homeless: and trust that their distress will be relieved by the charitable and the good."

(i) *The remedy of self-help*

Now I would say this at once about squatters. The owner is not obliged to go to the courts to obtain possession. He is entitled, if he so desires, to take the remedy into his own hands. He can go in himself and turn them out without the aid of the courts of law. This is not a course to be recommended because of the disturbance which might follow. But the legality of it is beyond question. The squatters were themselves guilty of the offence of forcible entry contrary to the Statute of 1381 (4 Ric. 2, stat. 1, c. 7). When they broke in, they entered "with strong hand" which the statute forbids. They were not only guilty of a criminal offence. They were guilty of a civil wrong. They were trespassers when they entered, and they continued to be trespassers so long as they remained there. The owner never acquiesced in their presence there. So the trespassers never gained possession. The owner, being entitled to possession, was entitled forcibly to turn them out: see *Browne* v. *Dawson* (1840) 12 Ad. & El. 624. As Sir Frederick Pollock put it in his book on Torts:

> "A trespasser may in any case be turned off land before he has gained possession, and he does not gain possession until there has been something like acquiescence in the physical fact of his occupation on the part of the rightful owner": see *Pollock on Torts*, 15th ed. (1951), p. 292.

Even though the owner himself should use force, then so long as he uses no more force than is reasonably necessary, he is not himself liable either criminally or civilly. He is not liable criminally (1) because it was said in the old times that none of the statutes of forcible entry apply to the expulsion by the owner of a tenant at will (see *Anonymous* (1670) 1 Vent. 89; *Rex* v. *Dorny* (1700) 1 Salk 260; *Rex* v. *Bathurst* (1755) Say. 225); but, even if this is no longer true, (2) in any case the statutes only apply to the expulsion of one who is in possession: see *Reg.* v. *Child* (1846) 2 Cox C.C. 102. They do not apply to the expulsion of a trespasser who has no possession. The owner was not civilly liable because the owner is entitled to turn out a trespasser using force, no more than is reasonably necessary: see *Hemmings* v. *Stoke Poges Golf Club* [1920] 1 K.B. 720.

(ii) *The remedy by action*

Although the law thus enables the owner to take the remedy into his own hand, that is not a course to be encouraged. In a civilised society, the courts should themselves provide a remedy which is speedy and effective: and thus make self-help unnecessary. The courts of common law have done this for centuries. The owner is entitled to go to the court and obtain an order that the owner "do recover" the land, and to issue a writ of possession immediately. That was the practice in the old action of ejectment which is well described by Sir William Blackstone in his *Commentaries*, 8th ed. (1778), vol. III, pp. 200–205 and Appendix No. II; and by Maitland in his *Equity* (1909), pp. 352–354. So far as I can discover, the courts of common law never suspended the order for possession. Once the order was made, the owner could straightaway get a writ of possession for the sheriff to cause the owner to be put into possession. Sometimes the owner, although he got an order, might not wish to get the sheriff to turn out the trespassers, because the sheriff was known to charge extortionate fees. In that case the owner was entitled to take possession at once by his own hand: see *Harris* v. *Austen* (1615) 1 Rolle 210, 213, *per* Coke C.J., *Lacy* v. *Berry* (1659) 2 Sid. 155, 156 and *Aglionby* v. *Cohen* [1955] 1 Q.B. 558.

Seeing that the owner could take possession at once without the help of the courts, it is plain that, when he does come to the courts, he should not be in any worse position. The courts should give him possession at once, else he would be tempted to do it himself. So the courts of common law never suspended the order for possession.

It was suggested by Mr. Harper that, although the courts of common law never suspended the order for possession, nevertheless, the courts of equity might do so: because they had power to issue an injunction to restrain the owner from proceeding with his action at law or with the enforcement of his order. In support of his argument, Mr. Harper cited a passage from *Gilbert's History and Practice of Chancery* (1758) pp. 195–196, which was repeated afterwards in *Harrison, Chancery Practice*, 7th ed. (1790), vol. 11, p. 247 and *Bacon's Abridgement*, 6th ed. (1807), vol. III, p. 654; 7th ed. (1832), vol. IV, p. 432. But the passage is obscurely worded. And I am satisfied that a court of equity would never intervene in aid of a wrongdoer. In *Grafton* v. *Griffin* (1830) 1 Russ. & M. 336, where some claimants had wrongfully turned a widow out of a house and got possession of it, Lord Lyndhurst L.C. said, at p. 337: "This court will not interfere to support a possession so acquired."

By the Supreme Court of Judicature Act 1875 [38 & 39 Vict. c. 77], the old action of ejectment was replaced by an action for the recovery of land: but the practice remained the same, although the machinery was different: see *Gledhill* v. *Hunter* (1880) 14 Ch.D. 492, 498–500. The judgment was, as before, that the plaintiff "do recover" possession. No time was mentioned. No date was given. The plaintiff could at once issue a writ of possession which was executed against the premises themselves. The sheriff's officers turned out everyone who was there. If there was some one else there, in addition to the defendant, he too would be turned out unless he applied to come in and defend: see *Minet* v. *Johnson* (1890) 6 T.L.R. 417 and *Leicester Permanent Building Society* v. *Shearley* [1951] Ch. 90.

(iii) *The remedy by summons*

So the matter rested until some difficulties were discovered recently. When some squatters entered on vacant land belonging to the Manchester Corporation, this court granted an injunction against them, but held that it could not make an order for recovery of possession except in a final judgment: see *Manchester Corporation* v. *Connolly* [1970] Ch. 420. And when some squatters occupied houses in Brighton, Stamp J. held that no proceedings could be taken for recovery of possession unless they were named as defendants: see *In re Wykeham Terrace, Brighton, Sussex, Ex parte Territorial Auxiliary and Volunteer Reserve Association for the South East* [1971] Ch. 204. The result was that if the squatters did not give their names, or if one squatter followed another in quick succession, no order for possession could be made. I must confess that I doubt the correctness of that decision. But it does not matter. The position was soon put right by new rules of court. R.S.C., Order 113, of the High Court and Ord. 26[19] in the county court are quite clear. A summons can be issued for possession against squatters even though they cannot be identified by name and even though, as one squatter goes, another comes in. Judgment can be obtained summarily. It is an order that the plaintiffs "do recover" possession. That order can be enforced by a writ of possession immediately. It is an authority under which any one who is squatting on the premises can be turned out at once. There is no provision for giving any time. The court cannot give any time. It must, at the behest of the owner, make an order for recovery of possession. It is then for the owner to give such time as he thinks right to the squatters. They must make their appeal to his goodwill and consideration, and not to the courts. I think that the judgment of Goulding J. in *Department of the Environment* v. *James* [1972] 1 W.L.R. 1279 was correct.

---

[19] Now Order 24.

Notes

(i)   The Criminal Law Act 1977 repealed the Forcible Entry Acts 1361 and 1623[20] and established the new offence of using or threatening violence for securing entry to premises. Section 6 provides:

(1) Subject to the following provisions of this section, any person who, without lawful authority, uses or threatens violence for the purpose of securing entry into any premises for himself or for any other person is guilty of an offence, provided that—

(a)   there is someone present on those premises at the time who is opposed to the entry which the violence is intended to secure; and

(b)   the person using or threatening the violence knows that that is the case.

(2) The fact that a person has any interest in or right to possession or occupation of any premises shall not for the purposes of subsection (1) above constitute lawful authority for the use or threat of violence by him or anyone else for the purpose of securing his entry into those premises.

(3) In any proceedings for an offence under this section it shall be a defence for the accused to prove—

(a)   that at the time of the alleged offence he or any other person on whose behalf he was acting was a displaced residential occupier of the premises in question; or

(b)   that part of the premises in question constitutes premises of which he or any other person on whose behalf he was acting was a displaced residential occupier and that the part of the premises to which he was seeking to secure entry constitutes an access of which he or, as the case may be, that other person is also a displaced residential occupier.

(4) It is immaterial for the purposes of this section—

(a)   whether the violence in question is directed against the person or against property; and

(b)   whether the entry which the violence is intended to secure is for the purpose of acquiring possession of the premises in question or for any other purpose.

(5) A person guilty of an offence under this section shall be liable on summary conviction to imprisonment for a term not exceeding six months or to a fine not exceeding level 5 on the standard scale or both.[21]

---

[20] s.13(1).

[21] The standard scale of maximum fines on a conviction of a summary offence is to be found in s.37 of the Criminal Justice Act 1982:

level 1	£50
level 2	£100
level 3	£400
level 4	£1,000
level 5	£2,000

The Secretary of State is empowered by s.48 of the Criminal Justice Act 1982 to vary the maximum amount of fines.

(6) A constable in uniform may arrest without warrant anyone who is, or whom he, with reasonable cause, suspects to be guilty of an offence under this section.

For the purposes of section 6(3) a displaced residential occupier is defined as "any person who was occupying any premises as a residence immediately before being excluded from occupation by anyone who entered those premises as a trespasser. ... so long as he continues to be excluded from occupation of the premises by the original trespasser or a subsequent trespasser,"[22] subject to the proviso that the occupier was not "himself occupying the premises in question as a trespasser immediately before being excluded from occupation."[23] Accordingly, the remedy of self-help may not be as straightforward as Lord Denning M.R. suggested.

(ii) Notwithstanding the insecure nature of a trespasser's occupation, the law recognises that the landowner's right to recover possession from a squatter does not continue indefinitely: after 12 years' adverse possession the former owner's rights are extinguished. Thus, a person who enters land as a trespasser may acquire title to that land by adverse possession.

Adverse possession is a technical concept, which involves more than simple occupation. It must be shown that there was discontinuance of possession by the owner followed by possession by the squatter, or dispossession of the owner by the squatter. The squatter must not only show factual possession, but also an *animus possidendi*, that is an "intention of excluding the owner as well as other people."[24] In view of the length of time required to extinguish the owner's rights to recover possession, and the legal remedies which are available to a dispossessed owner, it is rare—in the housing context—for a trespasser to acquire title to land by adverse possession.

(2) Licences

A licence arises where a tenancy is not created but the occupier has the landowner's permission to occupy the land. The traditional definition of a licence is that offered by Vaughan C.J. in *Thomas* v. *Sorrell*:

A dispensation or licence properly passeth no interest, nor alters or transfers property in any thing, but only makes an action lawful, which without it had been unlawful.[25]

---

[22] s.12(3).
[23] s.12(4).
[24] Lindley L.J. in *Littledale* v. *Liverpool College* [1900] 1 Ch. 19 at 23.
[25] (1673) Vaugh. 330 at 351.

In other words, acts which would otherwise constitute trespass are legitimated. Licences arise in many different factual situations: guests at a party are licensees, as are lodgers and occupiers of hotel rooms.

Although a licensee of residential premises will have rights of occupation as defined by the terms of the licence (either express or implied), the law conceptualises a licence as a personal right and not a proprietary interest; by contrast, a tenancy passes an interest in the land to the tenant.

(B)   THE IMPORTANCE OF THE LEASE/LICENCE DISTINCTION

In the context of private residential accommodation whether or not a given set of facts gives rise to a tenancy or a licence has been an issue of central importance. This is a consequence of the structure of housing legislation in the private sector. Broadly speaking, the existence of a tenancy is an essential precondition for the application of the Rent Act 1977 or the Housing Act 1988. The schemes of protection established by these statutes do not apply unless there is a "tenancy under which a dwelling-house is *let* as a separate dwelling."[26] As a result licensees do not enjoy the rent control or security of tenure which the law provides for regulated and assured tenants.[27]

It is necessary to stress that the importance of the lease/licence distinction is a private sector phenomenon. In relation to public sector housing a licensee enjoys the same degree of statutory protection as a tenant.[28]

Although the most important consequence of a finding that a licence, rather than a lease, has been created is that the arrangement falls outside the scope of the Rent Act 1977 and the Housing Act 1988, there are other consequences which can be discussed under two heads:

(1)   Relationship Between Licensee and Licensor

The problem here is to know when a licence may be validly terminated. In the residential context the law recognises various kinds of licence.

(i) A *gratuitous* (or bare) licence can be revoked, at any time, at the will of the licensor, subject to the licensor giving the licensee a reasonable time in which to leave the premises.[29]

(ii) A *contractual* licence can only be brought to an end according to the terms of the contract. Many contractual licences expressly address the question of revocation (for example, stating that the licence may be terminated by either party at one month's notice). Where, on the other

---

[26] Rent Act 1977, s.1; Housing Act 1988, s.1(1). The full significance of this definition is discussed in Chapter 3.
[27] There is an exception to this general proposition: a licensee under a restricted contract (governed by the Rent Act 1977) can apply to have a fair rent registered in the same way as a regulated tenant.
[28] Housing Act 1985, s.79(3). See p. 175.
[29] *Minister of Health* v. *Bellotti* [1944] K.B. 298.

hand, the contract does not stipulate the circumstances in which the licence may be revoked, if a dispute arises, the court will have to imply terms into the contract.

Where a licence to occupy land is granted for a limited period, the courts may imply into the contract an obligation on the part of the licensor not to revoke the licence during this period.[30] On the other hand, when the licence is created for an indefinite period the courts are likely to imply a term into the contract whereby the licensor may lawfully revoke the licence on giving a specified period of notice.[31]

Whenever the contract expressly or impliedly restricts the licensor's right to revoke the licence, the licensee may seek to obtain an injunction from the court to prevent revocation in breach of contract.[32] Where an injunction is not obtained and there is wrongful revocation by the licensor, the licensee is entitled to damages.[33]

(iii) In certain situations a licensee may be protected by the doctrine of *proprietary estoppel*. In general terms, a licence by estoppel (also sometimes referred to as an equitable licence) will arise if two conditions are satisfied. First, the licensee must have an expectation (either encouraged by or known to the licensor) that he has or is to be given a right in the property in question. Secondly, the licensee must have acted to his detriment (for example, through the expenditure of money on the land) in reliance on this expectation.

Where a licence by estoppel arises the courts will not allow the licensor to insist on his strict legal rights if to do so would be inconsistent with the licensee's expectations. Not only may the courts grant an injunction to prevent the licensor from revoking the licence,[34] in certain circumstances the courts may order the licensor to compensate the licensee for his expenditure on the land,[35] or even require the licensor to transfer the property itself to the licensee.[36]

In the celebrated case of *Pascoe* v. *Turner*[37] the plaintiff and the defendant lived together as man and wife in a house owned by the plaintiff. Later, the plaintiff purchased another house, and he told the defendant that this house and its contents were hers. In reliance on this gratuitous promise, she expended some of her own money on repairs and improvements. Subsequently, when the relationship between the parties came to an end, the plaintiff sought to terminate the defendant's licence on giving two months' notice. The Court of Appeal held that the facts gave rise to an estoppel in the defendant's favour. Furthermore, it was decided that the appropriate remedy was to compel the plaintiff to

---

[30] *Hurst* v. *Picture Theatres Ltd.* [1915] 1 K.B. 1.
[31] In *Chandler* v. *Kerley* [1978] 1 W.L.R. 693 it was held that 12 months' notice was appropriate.
[32] *Winter Garden Theatre (London) Ltd.* v. *Millennium Productions Ltd.* [1948] A.C. 173.
[33] *Tanner* v. *Tanner* [1975] 1 W.L.R. 1346.
[34] *Inwards* v. *Baker* [1965] 2 Q.B. 29; *Williams* v. *Staite* [1979] Ch. 291.
[35] *Dodsworth* v. *Dodsworth* (1973) 228 E.G. 1115.
[36] *Dillwyn* v. *Llewelyn* (1862) 4 De G.F. & J. 264.
[37] [1979] 1 W.L.R. 431.

give effect to his promise and her expectations by transferring legal and beneficial ownership of the house to the defendant.

From this example it should be apparent that the doctrine of proprietary estoppel gives rise to difficult legal problems. Perhaps somewhat predictably, it has also provoked considerable controversy.

(2) Effect of Licences on Third Parties

A lease is classified as a proprietary interest. One of the consequences of this classification is that the tenant may enforce the rights conferred by the lease against a new landlord (including someone who purchases the reversion from the original lessor). A licence, on the other hand, is traditionally regarded as a personal right rather than a proprietary right. According to the orthodox view a licensee cannot assert his rights against a subsequent purchaser of the land; he is left with his contractual remedy against the licensor for damages.

In recent years, however, the orthodox view has come under attack from the judiciary and academics both in relation to contractual licences and licences by estoppel.

(a) It has come to be accepted in many quarters that an estoppel licence is capable of binding a third party purchaser who has notice of the licensee's interest, and the case of *E. R. Ives Investment Ltd.* v. *High*[38] is commonly cited in support of this proposition.[39] The issue is not, however, free from doubt.

(b) As for contractual licences, their effect on third parties has been the subject of extended controversy. Following the lead given by Denning L.J. in 1952 in the case of *Errington* v. *Errington & Woods*,[40] the courts reconsidered the extent to which contractual licences may be capable of binding third parties.[41] On the basis of these developments it seemed as though contractual licences were destined to be recategorised as proprietary rights.[42] More recently, however, the Court of Appeal reaffirmed the orthodox view—namely, that contractual licences are, in principle, personal to the parties.

Ashburn Anstalt v. *Arnold* [1989] Ch. 1

The case concerned an action for possession brought against the defendants, who were occupiers of commercial premises. The plaintiffs,

---

[38] [1967] 2 Q.B. 379.
[39] *e.g.* Megarry & Wade, *The Law of Real Property* (5th ed., 1984), p. 806.
[40] [1952] 1 K.B. 290.
[41] *Binions* v. *Evans* [1972] Ch. 359; *D.H.N. Food Distributors* v. *Tower Hamlets L.B.C.* [1976] 1 W.L.R. 852; *Re Sharpe* [1980] 1 W.L.R. 219; *Midland Bank* v. *Farmpride Hatcheries* (1980) 260 E.G. 493.
[42] In the fifth edition of *The Law of Real Property* (1984) Megarry and Wade expressed the following opinion (p. 808):
"All the indications now are that contractual licences are capable of binding successors in title as equitable interests."

who had purchased the property, argued that since the defendants occupied the premises as licensees, they were not bound by the defendants' rights. The defendants submitted, *inter alia*, that they were tenants and therefore the plaintiffs were bound by their interest. The Court of Appeal accepted this argument.[43] However, Fox L.J. (at 13–26) also went on to consider (*obiter*) what the position would have been had the defendants been contractual licensees:

It is Arnold & Co.'s case that even if the 1973 agreement created no tenancy after February 28, 1973, so that its occupancy thereafter is that of a contractual licensee only, its rights are nevertheless binding upon a purchaser for value with notice of the licence. Lord Templeman in *Street* v. *Mountford* [1985] A.C. 809, 814 said:

"A licence in connection with land while entitling the licensee to use the land for the purposes authorised by the licence does not create an estate in the land."

That was not challenged on behalf of Arnold & Co., but it was said that a contractual licence does give rise to an interest (as opposed to an estate) in the land; we must assume for this purpose that the rights are of sufficiently certain duration to be capable of subsisting as an interest in land. If they are not, the point does not arise. The question then is whether Arnold & Co.'s proposition is correct in law. Until comparatively recently it would, we think, have been rejected. As long ago as 1674, in *Thomas* v. *Sorrell* (1674) Vaug. 330, 351, Vaughan C.J. said:

"A dispensation or licence properly passeth no interest, nor alters or transfers property in any thing, but only makes an action lawful, which without it had been unlawful."

A number of cases in this century support that view.

Daly v. *Edwardes* (1900) 83 L.T. 548 was concerned with "front of house" rights in a theatre. In 1894 Edwardes granted to Daly a licence of two theatres for a term of years. The lease contained a covenant by the lessee not, inter alia, to part with any estate or interest in the premises. Daly granted to Warr:

"the free and exclusive licence or right to the use of the refreshment rooms and bars in the theatre together with the free right of access thereto."

The lessor claimed that this was a breach of the covenant against disposing of any estate or interest in the premises. That claim failed. Rigby L.J. said, at p. 551:

"On the whole, I think that the proper conclusion is that Frank Warr and Co. took no estate or interest in land, but that they were entitled for all reasonable purposes, to consider themselves as having an exclusive licence to provide refreshments and all that follows from that privilege, and nothing else."

Vaughan Williams L.J. said, at p. 551, that the agreement was "really a grant of a privilege and licence merely masquerading as a lease." The case went to the

---

[43] See pp. 80–83.

House of Lords as *Edwardes* v. *Barrington* (1901) 85 L.T. 650, and the decision of the Court of Appeal was affirmed.

In *Frank Warr & Co. Ltd.* v. *London County Council* [1904] 1 K.B. 713, the London County Council compulsorily acquired the Globe Theatre. At the time of the acquisition Warr had front of house rights at the theatre under a subsisting agreement with the lessee. Compensation was only payable to persons having an interest in the land acquired. The claim failed. Collins M.R. said, at p. 722:

> "Do those parts of the agreement amount merely to a licence properly so called, or to a grant of an interest in, or something arising out of, the land? To my mind it is clear that they create nothing more than a licence properly so called."

These cases, it seems to us, clearly proceed on the basis that a contractual licence creates no interest in land.

The next is *King* v. *David Allen and Sons (Billposting) Ltd.* [1916] 2 A.C. 54. King owned premises in Dublin. David Allen had for many years under an agreement between the predecessors of King and David Allen, enjoyed the right to exhibit posters on the wall of the premises. King wished to let the premises to a third party; David Allen had no objection provided its rights were preserved. In July 1913 King and David Allen agreed that David Allen should have exclusive permission to fix posters to the flank wall of a cinema which it was proposed to build on the site. In August 1913 King agreed with F., a trustee for a company to be formed, that a lease should be granted to the company. King was to assign to F., as a trustee for the company, his interest in the 1913 agreement, and F. agreed that the company would accept the lease and ratify the 1913 agreement. The company, when formed, duly did so. The cinema was built. The July agreement was not referred to in the lease and King did not assign his interest under that agreement to the company. David Allen attempted to post advertisements on the flank wall but the company, despite opposition from King (a director), prevented it. David Allen then sued King alleging that he was in breach of the July agreement by putting it out of his power to perform it. The claim succeeded. The company was not a party to the action but the effect of the licence vis-à-vis the company was in issue because King would not have been liable to David Allen in damages had the licence which he agreed to grant been binding on the company, which had notice of it. The House of Lords regarded the contract as creating nothing but a personal obligation. Earl Loreburn said, at p. 62:

> "Well, if the agreement of July 1, which purports to be on the face of it a licence, was equivalent to creating an incoporeal hereditament or a sufficient interest in land, Mr. King did not break his contract in making the lease, and would not be responsible for any trespasses that were committed by his licensees. But we must look at the document itself, and it seems to me that it does not create any interest in the land at all; it merely amounts to a promise on the part of Mr. King that he would allow the other party to the contract to use the wall for advertising purposes, and there was an implied undertaking that he would not disable himself from carrying out his contract."

Lord Buckmaster L.C. said, at pp. 59–60:

> "There are two circumstances to which attention has been quite properly called by the appellant's counsel, which are no doubt important in considering what the agreement effected. The first is the fact of the rent reserved, and the next that there is a term of years granted and that arrangements are introduced into the agreement to prevent other people having competing

rights with Messrs. David Allen and Sons upon this wall. Those considerations do not, in my opinion, necessarily conflict with the view that this is
nothing but a licence—a licence for a fixed term of years, but a licence which
creates no estate or interest in the land ... "

We are unable to reconcile the approach of the House of Lords in *King* v.
David Allen with the submission, on behalf of Arnold & Co., that a mere
contractual licence is an interest in land binding on a purchaser with notice. The
two front of house rights cases to which we have referred are to the same effect.
    The next case of consequence is *Clore* v. *Theatrical Properties Ltd.* [1936] 3
All E.R. 483, which was again concerned with front of house rights. The
agreement provided:

> "the lessor does hereby demise and grant unto the lessee the free and
> exclusive use of all the refreshment rooms ... of the theatre ... for the
> purpose only of the supply to and accommodation of the visitors to the
> theatre and for no other purpose ... "

The definition clause provided that the terms "lessor" and "lessee" should
include their executors, administrators and assigns. The assignee of the lessor
sought to prevent an assignee of the lessee from exercising any of the rights
under the agreement. It was held that the agreement was not a lease but a
licence, and was not binding upon a third party. The court, as we read the
judgments, regarded the case as falling within the examples of *Daly* v. *Edwards*,
83 L.T. 548 and *Frank Warr & Co. Ltd.* v. *London County Council* [1904] 1
K.B. 713. The licensee had sought to rely upon *De Mattos* v. *Gibson* (1859) 4
De G. & J. 276 and *Lord Strathcona Steamship Co. Ltd.* v. *Dominion Coal Co.
Ltd.* [1926] A.C. 108. That was not accepted. Lord Wright M.R. regarded these
authorities as confined to charterparties and said, at p. 491: "I do not think that
a personal covenant as in the present case can be binding on a third party with
notice ... "
    Down to this point we do not think that there is any serious doubt as to the
law. A mere contractual licence to occupy land is not binding on a purchaser of
the land even though he has notice of the licence.
    We come now to a case which is of central importance on the present issue.
That is *Errington* v. *Errington and Woods* [1952] 1 K.B. 290. A father, wishing
to provide a home for his son who had recently married, bought a house with
the help of a building society mortgage. He paid a lump sum towards the
purchase price, the remainder of which was provided by the building society's
loan. The loan was repayable by instalments. He retained the conveyance in his
own name and paid the rates, but he promised that if the son and daughter-in-
law continued in occupation and duly paid all the instalments, he would then
transfer the property to them. The father died and by his will left the house to
his widow. Up to that time the son and his wife had lived in the house and paid
the instalments. The son then separated from his wife and left the house. The
daughter-in-law continued to pay the mortgage instalments. The widow then
sought possession of the house from the daughter-in-law. The county court
judge dismissed the action. He held that the daughter-in-law was a tenant at will
and that the claim against her was statute-barred. That reasoning was rejected
by the Court of Appeal, though the actual decision of the judge was upheld.
Denning L.J., whose reasons for dismissing the appeal were concurred in by
Somervell L.J., said, at pp. 298–299:

> "it seems to me that, although the couple had exclusive possession of the
> house, there was clearly no relationship of landlord and tenant. They were
> not tenants at will but licensees. They had a mere personal privilege to

remain there, with no right to assign or sub-let. They were, however, not bare licensees. They were licensees with a contractual right to remain. As such they have no right at law to remain, but only in equity, and equitable rights now prevail. I confess, however, that it has taken the courts some time to reach this position. At common law a licence was always revocable at will, notwithstanding a contract to the contrary: *Wood* v. *Leadbitter* (1845) 13 M. & W. 838. The remedy for a breach of the contract was only in damages. That was the view generally held until a few years ago: see, for instance, what was said in *Booker* v. *Palmer* [1942] 2 All E.R. 674, 677 and *Thompson* v. *Park* [1944] K.B. 408, 410. The rule has, however, been altered owing to the interposition of equity. Law and equity have been fused for nearly 80 years, and since 1948 it has been clear that, as a result of the fusion, a licensor will not be permitted to eject a licensee in breach of a contract to allow him to remain: see *Winter Garden Theatre (London) Ltd.* v. *Millennium Productions Ltd.* [1946] 1 All E.R. 678, 680, *per* Lord Greene, and in the House of Lords *per* Lord Simon; nor in breach of a promise on which the licensee has acted, even though he gave no value for it: see *Foster* v. *Robinson* [1951] 1 K.B. 149, 156, where Sir Raymond Evershed M.R. said that as a result of the oral arrangement to let the man stay, he was entitled as licensee to occupy the premises without any payment of rent for the rest of his days. This infusion of equity means that contractual licences now have a force and validity of their own and cannot be revoked in breach of the contract. Neither the licensor nor anyone who claims through him can disregard the contract except a purchaser for value without notice."

It is not in doubt that the actual decision was correct. It could be justified on one of three grounds. (i) There was a contract to convey the house on completion of the payments giving rise to an equitable interest in the form of an estate which would be binding on the widow: see *Megarry & Wade, The Law of Real Property*, 5th ed. (1984), p. 806. The widow was not a purchaser for value. (ii) The daughter-in-law had changed her position in reliance upon a representation binding on the widow as a privy of the representor: see *Spencer Bower and Turner, Estoppel by Representation*, 3rd ed. (1977), p. 123. (iii) The payment of the instalments by the son or the daughter-in-law gave rise to direct proprietary interests by way of constructive trust, though it is true that, until *Gissing* v. *Gissing* [1971] A.C. 886, the law relating to constructive trusts in this field was not much considered.

Accordingly, it does not appear to have been necessary, in order to produce a just result, to have accepted the broad principle stated, at p. 299, in the passage which we have quoted, that "Neither the licensor nor anyone who claims through him can disregard the contract except a purchaser for value without notice." That statement itself is not supported by any citation of authority, and indeed we do not think it could have been supported on the authorities. None of the cases prior to *Errington* v. *Errington and Woods* to which we have referred, except *Thomas* v. *Sorrell*, Vaugh. 330, is mentioned in the judgments and it does not appear that any was cited.

The decision of the House of Lords in *Winter Gardens Theatre (London) Ltd.* v. *Millennium Productions Ltd.* [1948] A.C. 173 does not advance the matter. It was the first occasion on which a licensee was held entitled to an injunction restraining the licensor from revoking a licence in breach of contract. The case was concerned with contract only. In our view it is not an authority for the proposition that a contractual licence creates an interest in land capable of binding third parties.

National Provincial Bank Ltd. v. *Hastings Car Mart Ltd.* [1965] A.C. 1175 was the case in which the House of Lords, reversing the majority decision of the

Court of Appeal [1964] Ch. 665, rejected the deserted wife's equity. Russell L.J. who dissented in the Court of Appeal, stated, at pp. 696–697:

"It is therefore necessary to consider what is the law in connection with title to unregistered land relating to rights such as those now in question. For this purpose, I consider that the deserted wife's right cannot be greater than that of a person in occupation under a contractual licence from the owner to occupy, which licence is by its terms not revocable for a period, and breach of which would be restrained by injunction against the licensor. What is the position of such a licensee in the case of unregistered land? Has he a right capable of enforcement not only against the licensor but also against a purchaser or mortgagee from the licensor?

"On authority it seems to me that the answer is that he has not such a right against a purchaser for value even with actual notice of the licence. I do not propose to discuss the question exhaustively. I am content to refer generally to the article on this question on Licences and Third Parties by Professor H. W. R. Wade (68 L.Q.R. 337), and the cases there discussed of *King* v. *David Allen and Sons (Billposting) Ltd.* [1916] 2 A.C. 54 in the House of Lords, and *Clore* v. *Theatrical Properties Ltd.* [1936] 3 All E.R. 483 in the Court of Appeal, and to add some comments.

"I am regretfully aware that this view runs counter to much that has been said, particularly by the present Master of the Rolls, especially in *Bendall* v. *McWhirter* [1952] 2 Q.B. 466 and is in conflict with an instructive article on Licences to Live in Houses by Mr. L. A. Sheridan (The Conveyancing and Property Lawyer, N.S., vol. 17, p. 440). But the decision of the House of Lords in *King's* case necessarily involved a decision that a contractual licence to post advertisements on a wall for a period of years was not binding upon a purchaser from the licensor with actual notice of the licence, because it created a mere personal obligation on the licensor and not an estate or interest in the land. I cannot accept that that decision depends for its validity on the fact that the licence had not yet been acted upon. In this connection, I venture to repeat that the actual occupation is not the right; it is a form of notice of a right; the right must be sought elsewhere. Since in *King's* case there was actual notice of the licence which conferred the right, the question of occupation would not seem to affect the matter. The licence rights would (or would not) affect the purchaser with actual notice of them whether or not they had been partly exercised. The *Clore* case seems plainly a case in which this court held that a personal licence to occupy, which had been acted upon for many years, was not enforceable against a purchaser with actual notice, expressly for the same reason that it created no interest in the land. I do not think that its binding authority can be properly undermined by saying that this court mistakenly assumed that as between the contracting parties revocation in breach of contract would not be restrained by injunction in accordance with what Lord Uthwatt in *Winter Garden Theatre (London)* v. *Millennium Productions Ltd.* [1948] A.C. 173, 202 described as 'the settled practice of the courts of Equity ... to do what they can by an injunction to preserve the "sanctity of a bargain." ' I do not, with respect, think that the *Clore* case can be described as one in which the licensee was not in actual occupation. The grant was of the free and exclusive use of substantial and defined parts of the premises for the purpose of exercising front of the house rights. Surely the licensee was in actual occupation of, for example, the wine cellars. And the judgment appealed from in terms declared that the defendant had 'no right to the use and occupation' of those parts referred to in the licence.

"In *In re Webb's Lease* [1951] Ch. 808, in this court, the question whether the lessee could refuse to recognise the licence by the lessor to fix advertisements was not in issue for determination; counsel for the lessee conceded that he could not; but the lessee did not want to; he simply wanted as against the lessor to be entitled to receive the licence payments from the licensee. In that context the remarks of Lord Evershed M.R. [1951] Ch. 808, 821 and of Jenkins L.J. [1951] Ch. 808, 830, 831 cannot be taken as binding authority.

"I desire to add on *Errington* v. *Errington and Woods* [1952] 1 K.B. 290, in this court, nothing to the comments in Professor Wade's article, save that I find it not easy to see, on authority, how that which has a purely contractual basis between A and B is, though on all hands it is agreed that it is not to be regarded as conferring any estate or interest in property on B, nevertheless to be treated as producing the equivalent result against a purchaser C, simply because an injunction would be granted to restrain A from breaking his contract while he is still in a position to carry it out."

When the case reached the House of Lords the observations of Russell L.J. were not expressly accepted, but nor were they rejected. Lord Hodson said, at pp. 1223–1224:

"To describe a wife as a licensee, unless that overworked word is merely used to describe a person lawfully on land and not a trespasser, is not only uncomplimentary but inaccurate. She is not a person who needs any licence from her husband to be where she has a right to be as a wife. *Thomas* v. *Sorrell* (1674) Vaugh. 330, 351 contains the classic definition of a licence propounded by Vaughan C.J.: 'A dispensation or licence properly passeth no interest, nor alters or transfers property in any thing, but only makes an action lawful, which without it had been unlawful.' This shows the fallacy of the analogy for the wife would not be a trespasser in her husband's house in the absence of a licence from her husband."

Lord Upjohn also considered the position of a licence, at p. 1239:

"Your Lordships heard much interesting discussion as to the rights of contractual licensees to remain in occupation as against third parties. As I emphatically decline to equate the deserted wife with a contractual licensee or to draw any analogy between the two I shall be very brief on this subject. The cases of *Foster* v. *Robinson* [1951] 1 K.B. 149 and *Errington* v. *Errington and Woods* [1952] 1 K.B. 290 were much canvassed before your Lordships. In the latter case the licensees were in exclusive occupation upon the terms of paying off the mortgage instalments and after the matrimonial rupture the wife continued to do so. This, I would have thought, would have given the spouses an interest in the land, in accordance with a well-known line of authority starting with *Webb* v. *Paternoster* (1619) Pop. 151, valid against all except a purchaser for value without notice.

"The more interesting and really text-book case is *Foster* v. *Robinson*. Whether the right (undoubtedly contractual against the owner of the property) of Robinson the retired servant to remain in exclusive occupation of his cottage rent-free for the rest of his life will by judicial decision one day be held to create an equitable estate or interest binding all except purchasers for value without notice, or whether, as Russell L.J. thinks, statutory legislation is required to bring about that result is a matter upon which I propose to express no opinion. On the other hand, Roxburgh J. in *Thompson* v. *Earthy* [1951] 2 K.B. 596, 599, may have taken the view that an exclusive licensee may thereby have an interest in the land, and Professor Cheshire supports this view in a very interesting article on this matter in The Modern Law Review, vol. 16, p. 1. He does, I think, in that article, underestimate the difficulties created by *King* v. *David Allen and Sons* (*Billposting*) *Ltd.* and *Clore* v. *Theatrical Properties Ltd.* But if it is later decided that a licensee having an irrevocable licensee to remain in occupation of the land for a defined period creates an interest in land and is valid against subsequent purchasers with notice that would not affect my view that the purely personal, evanescent and changeable rights exerciseable against her husband by the deserted wife cannot affect a purchaser from the husband."

Lastly, we refer to the observations of Lord Wilberforce, at pp. 1250–1251:

"1. *The licence theory.* One main line of argument, for conferring upon the deserted wife an interest binding her husband's successors in title, has been to this effect: the wife is a licensee in the house under, so it is sometimes said, an irrevocable licence, or at least a licence which is only revocable by the court: some licences which are irrevocable are binding on purchasers with notice: ergo the wife's rights are binding on purchasers with notice. I hope that I do justice to the argument by this brief summary. I confess that I find it far from helpful. In the first place, I doubt the utility of describing the wife as a licensee. If all that is done by this is to place some descriptive label on the capacity in which the wife remains in the house, I suppose that the word 'licensee' is as good as any other, though I would think that most wives would consider this description a strange one. But what is achieved by the description? After she has been so described, the incidents of the description have to be ascertained, and the only correct process is surely to analyse what the nature of the wife's rights are, the answer being that they are rights of co-habitation and support and the right to resist dispossession by her husband if that would interfere with marital rights. What is not surely legitimate is to start by describing the wife as a licensee, and then to ascribe to her rights which are defined by reference to other kinds of licences: that is an argument per saltum. The second comment which must be made on the argument is that even if one accepts the leap from the wife as licensee to other (*e.g.* contractual) licensees, one has not reached a solution, for the legal position of contractual licensees, as regards 'purchasers,' is very far from clear. The Court of Appeal has attempted to reach a generalisation by which licences, or at least licences coupled with occupation, are binding upon 'purchasers' but I note that the members of that court are not wholly agreed as to this doctrine. No doubt the time will come when this whole subject will have to be reviewed; this is not the occasion for it and I think that it would be undesirable now to say anything which might impede the development of this branch of the law. Neither contractual licences nor those licences where money has been expended by the licensee in my view afford any useful analogy or basis upon which to determine the character of the wife's rights.

"I would only add, with reference to the authorities (1) that I must not be taken as accepting the arguments placed before the Court of Appeal whereby such cases as *King* v. *David Allen and Sons* (*Billposting*) *Ltd.* and *Clore* v. *Theatrical Properties Ltd.* are put on one side as not, or no longer, relevant authorities; (2) that, while accepting the actual decision I do not find that the case of *Errington* v. *Errington and Woods*, even if reconcilable with the two cases I have mentioned, is of assistance as to the transmissibility of contractual licences. The Court of Appeal in that case seem to have treated it simply as one of contract and not to have focused their argument on the precise legal position of the plaintiff, *i.e.* whether she was the legal personal representative or the successor in title of the licensor."

These cases were the subject of consideration by Goff J. in *In re Solomon, A Bankrupt, Ex parte Trustees of the Property of the Bankrupt* v. *Solomon* [1967]

Ch. 573, Goff J. concluded that the wife in that case was not a contractual licensee, and accordingly he did not have to decide which authority he should follow. But he expressed a preference for the reasoning of Russell L.J. in the *Hastings Car Mart* case [1964] Ch. 665 and was hesitant to recognise the existence of a new species of equitable right.

It is convenient to pause at this point because, although there are later cases in what may be regarded as this series, there is none in which a contractual licence is held to bind a third party in the absence of a finding that the third party took the land as a constructive trustee. It is therefore appropriate to review how the law stands, or ought to stand, in the absence of such a finding.

Young v. *Bristol Aeroplane Co. Ltd.* [1944] K.B. 718 establishes the familiar rule that this court is bound to follow its own decisions save that (relevantly to this case) it is entitled and bound to decide which of two conflicting decisions of its own it will follow, and it is bound to refuse to follow a decision of its own which, though not expressly overruled, cannot in its opinion stand with a decision of the House of Lords.

It must, we think, be very doubtful whether this court's decision in *Errington* v. *Errington and Woods* [1952] 1 K.B. 290 is consistent with its earlier decisions in *Daly* v. *Edwardes*, 83 L.T. 548; *Frank Warr & Co.* v. *London County Council* [1904] 1 K.B. 713 and *Clore* v. *Theatrical Properties Ltd.* [1936] 3 All E.R. 483. That decision cannot be said to be in conflict with any later decision of the House of Lords, because the House expressly left the effect of a contractual licence open in the *Hastings Car Mart* case. But there must be very real doubts whether *Errington* can be reconciled with the earlier decisions of House of Lords in *Edwardes* v. *Barrington*, 85 L.T. 650, and *King* v. *David Allen and Sons (Billposting) Ltd.* [1916] 2 A.C. 54. It would seem that we must follow those cases or choose between the two lines of authority. It is not, however, necessary to consider those alternative courses in detail, since in our judgment the House of Lords cases, whether or not as a matter of strict precedent they conclude this question, state the correct principle which we should follow.

Our reasons for reaching this conclusion are based upon essentially the same reasons as those given by Russell L.J. in the *Hastings Car Mart* case [1964] Ch. 665, 697 and by Professor Wade in the article, "Licences and Third Parties" (1952) 68 L.Q.R. 337, to which Russell L.J. refers. Before *Errington* the law appears to have been clear and well understood. It rested on an important and intelligible distinction between contractual obligations which gave rise to no estate or interest in the land and proprietary rights which, by definition, did. The far-reaching statement of principle in *Errington* was not supported by authority, not necessary for the decision of the case and per incuriam in the sense that it was made without reference to authorities which, if they would not have compelled, would surely have persuaded the court to adopt a different ratio. Of course, the law must be free to develop. But as a response to problems which had arisen, the *Errington* rule (without more) was neither practically necessary nor theoretically convincing. By contrast, the finding on appropriate facts of a constructive trust may well be regarded as a beneficial adaptation of old rules to new situations.

The constructive trust principle, to which we now turn, has been long established and has proved to be highly flexible in practice. It covers a wide variety of cases from that of a trustee who makes a profit out of his trust or a stranger who knowingly deals with trust properties, to the many cases where the courts have held that a person who directly or indirectly contributes to the acquisition of a dwelling house purchased in the name of and conveyed to another has some beneficial interest in the property. The test, for the present purposes, is whether the owner of the property has so conducted himself that it would be inequitable to allow him to deny the claimant an interest in the property: see *Gissing* v. *Gissing* [1971] A.C. 886, 905, *per* Lord Diplock.

In *Bannister* v. *Bannister* [1948] 2 All E.R. 133, on the plaintiff's oral undertaking that the defendant continue to live in a cottage rent free for as long as she wished, the defendant agreed to sell to him that and an adjacent cottage. The conveyance contained no reference to the undertaking. The plaintiff thereafter occupied the whole cottage save for one room which was occupied by the defendant. The plaintiff after a time sought to expel the defendant. The Court of Appeal (Scott and Asquith L.JJ. and Jenkins J.) held that he was not entitled to. Scott L.J., giving the judgment of the court, said, at p. 136:

> "It is, we think, clearly a mistake to suppose that the equitable principle on which a constructive trust is raised against a person who insists on the absolute character of a conveyance to himself for the purpose of defeating a beneficial interest, which, according to the true bargain, was to belong to another, is confined to cases in which the conveyance itself was fraudulently obtained. The fraud which brings the principle into play arises as soon as the absolute character of the conveyance is set up for the purpose of defeating the beneficial interest. ... Nor is it, in our opinion, necessary that the bargain on which the absolute conveyance is made should include any express stipulation that the grantee is in so many words to hold as trustee. It is enough that the bargain should have included a stipulation under which some sufficiently defined beneficial interest in the property was to be taken by another."

In *In re Schebsman, decd.* [1944] Ch. 83, 89, Lord Greene M.R. said:

> "It is not legitimate to import into the contract the idea of a trust when the parties have given no indication that such was their intention."

Du Parcq L.J. said, at p. 104, that "the court ought not to be astute to discover indications of such an intention." We do not, however, regard either of these observations as differing from what Scott L.J. said in *Bannister* v. *Bannister*. It is, we think, in every case a question of what is the reasonable inference from the known facts.

We come then to four cases in which the application of the principle to particular facts has been considered.

In *Binions* v. *Evans* [1972] Ch. 359, the defendant's husband was employed by an estate and lived rent free in a cottage owned by the estate. The husband died when the defendant was 73. The trustees of the estate then entered into an agreement with the defendant that she could continue to live in the cottage during her lifetime as tenant at will rent free; she undertook to keep the cottage in good condition and repair. Subsequently the estate sold the cottage to the plaintiffs. The contract provided that the property was sold subject to the tenancy. In consequence of that provision the plaintiffs paid a reduced price for the cottage. The plaintiffs sought to eject the defendant, claiming that she was tenant at will. That claim failed. In the Court of Appeal Megaw and Stephenson L.JJ. decided the case on the ground that the defendant was a tenant for life under the Settled Land Act 1925. Lord Denning M.R. did not agree with that. He held that the plaintiffs took the property subject to a constructive trust for the defendant's benefit. In our view that is a legitimate application of the doctrine of constructive trusts. The estate would certainly have allowed the defendant to live in the house during her life in accordance with their agreement with her. They provided the plaintiffs with a copy of the agreement they made. The agreement for sale was subject to the agreement, and they accepted a lower purchase price in consequence. In the circumstances it was a proper inference that on the sale to the plaintiffs, the intention of the estate and the plaintiffs was that the plaintiffs should give effect to the tenancy agreement. If they had failed to do so, the estate would have been liable in damages to the defendant.

In *D.H.N. Food Distributors Ltd.* v. *Tower Hamlets Borough Council* [1976] 1 W.L.R. 852, premises were owned by Bronze Investments Ltd. but occupied by an associated company (D.H.N.) under an informal agreement between them— they were part of a group. The premises were subsequently purchased by the council and the issue was compensation for disturbance. It was said that Bronze was not disturbed and that D.H.N. had no interest in the property. The Court of Appeal held that D.H.N. had an irrevocable licence to occupy the land. Lord Denning M.R. said, at p. 859:

"It was equivalent to a contract between the two companies whereby Bronze granted an irrevocable licence to D.H.N. to carry on their business on the premises. In this situation Mr. Dobry cited to us *Binions* v. *Evans* [1972] Ch. 359 to which I would add *Bannister* v. *Bannister* [1948] 2 All E.R. 133 and *Siew Soon Wah* v. *Young Tong Hong* [1973] A.C. 836. Those cases show that a contractual licence (under which a person has a right to occupy premises indefinitely) gives rise to a constructive trust, under which the legal owner is not allowed to turn out the licensee. So, here. This irrevocable licence gave to D.H.N. a sufficient interest in the land to qualify them for compensation for disturbance."

Goff L.J. made this a ground for his decision also.

On that authority, Browne-Wilkinson J. in *In re Sharpe (A Bankrupt), Ex parte Trustee of the Bankrupt's Property* v. *The Bankrupt* [1980] 1 W.L.R. 219 felt bound to conclude that, without more, an irrevocable licence to occupy gave rise to a property interest. He evidently did so with hesitation. For the reasons which we have already indicated, we prefer the line of authorities which determine that a contractual licence does not create a property interest. We do not think that the argument is assisted by the bare assertion that the interest arises under a constructive trust.

In *Lyus* v. *Prowsa Developments Ltd.* [1982] 1 W.L.R. 1044, the plaintiffs contracted to buy a plot of registered land which was part of an estate being developed by the vendor company. A house was to be built which would then be occupied by the plaintiffs. The plaintiffs paid a deposit to the company, which afterwards became insolvent before the house was built. The company's bank held a legal charge, granted before the plaintiffs' contract, over the whole estate. The bank was under no liability to complete the plaintiffs' contract. The bank, as mortgagee, sold the land to the first defendant. By the contract of sale it was provided that the land was sold subject to and with the benefit of the plaintiffs' contract. Subsequently, the first defendant contracted to sell the plot to the second defendant. The contract provided that the land was sold subject to the plaintiffs' contract so far, if at all, as it might be enforceable against the first defendant. The contract was duly completed. In the action the plaintiff sought a declaration that their contract was binding on the defendants and an order for specific performance. The action succeeded. This again seems to us to be a case where a constructive trust could justifiably be imposed. The bank were selling as mortgagees under a charge prior in date to the contract. They were therefore not bound by the contract and on any view could give a title which was free from it. There was, therefore, no point in making the conveyance subject to the contract unless the parties intended the purchaser to give effect to the contract.

Further, on the sale by the bank a letter had been written to the bank's agents, Messrs. Strutt & Parker, by the first defendant's solicitors, giving an assurance that their client would take reasonable steps to make sure the interests of contractual purchasers were dealt with quickly and to their satisfaction. How far any constructive trust so arising was on the facts of that case enforceable by the plaintiffs against owners for the time being of the land we do not need to consider.

In re Sharpe [1980] 1 W.L.R. 219 seems to us a much more difficult case in which to imply a constructive trust against the trustee in bankruptcy and his successors, and we do not think it could be done. Browne-Wilkinson J. did not, in fact, do so. He felt (understandably, we think) bound by authority to hold that an irrevocable licence to occupy was a property interest. In *In re Sharpe* although the aunt provided money for the purchase of the house, she did not thereby acquire any property interest in the ordinary sense, since the judge held that it was advanced by way of a loan, though, no doubt, she may have had some rights of occupation as against the debtor. And when the trustee in bankrupty, before entering into the contract of sale, wrote to the aunt to find out what rights, if any, she claimed in consequence of the provision of funds by her, she did not reply. The trustee in bankruptcy then sold with vacant possession. These facts do not suggest a need in equity to impose constructive trust obligations on the trustee or his successors.

We come to the present case. It is said that when a person sells land and stipulates that the sale should be "subject to" a contractual licence, the court will impose a constructive trust upon the purchaser to give effect to the licence: see *Binions* v. *Evans* [1972] Ch. 359, 368, *per* Lord Denning M.R. We do not feel able to accept that as a general proposition. We agree with the observations of Dillon J. in *Lyus* v. *Prowsa Developments Ltd.* [1982] 1 W.L.R. 1044, 1051:

> "By contrast, there are many cases in which land is expressly conveyed subject to possible incumbrances when there is no thought at all of conferring any fresh rights on third parties who may be entitled to the benefit of the incumbrances. The land is expressed to be sold subject to incumbrances to satisfy the vendor's duty to disclose all possible incumbrances known to him, and to protect the vendor against any possible claim by the purchaser. ... So, for instance, land may be contracted to be sold and may be expressed to be conveyed subject to the restrictive covenants contained in a conveyance some 60 or 90 years old. No one would suggest that by accepting such a form of contract or conveyance a purchaser is assuming a new liability in favour of third parties to observe the covenants if there was for any reason before the contract or conveyance no one who could make out a title as against the purchaser to the benefit of the covenants."

The court will not impose a constructive trust unless it is satisfied that the conscience of the estate owner is affected. The mere fact that that land is expressed to be conveyed "subject to" a contract does not necessarily imply that the grantee is to be under an obligation, not otherwise existing, to give effect to the provisions of the contract. The fact that the conveyance is expressed to be subject to the contract may often, for the reasons indicated by Dillon J., be at least as consistent with an intention merely to protect the grantor against claims by the grantee as an intention to impose an obligation on the grantee. The words "subject to" will, of course, impose notice. But notice is not enough to impose on somebody an obligation to give effect to a contract into which he did not enter. Thus, mere notice of a restrictive covenant is not enough to impose upon the estate owner an obligation or equity to give effect to it: *London County Council* v. *Allen* [1914] 3 K.B. 642.

Note

In the years between the Court of Appeal's decisions in *Errington* v. *Errington & Woods* and *Ashburn Anstalt* v. *Arnold* there were various academic attempts to explain the legal character of licences, their classification and their effect on third parties: H. W. R. Wade, Licences and third parties (1952) 68 L.Q.R. 337; A. Briggs, Licences: back to basics? [1981] Conv. 212; M. P. Thompson, Licences: questioning the basics [1983] Conv. 50; A. Briggs, Contractual licences: a reply [1983] Conv. 285; A. Everton, Towards a concept of quasi-property [1982] Conv. 118 & 177; S. Moriarty, Licences and land law: legal principles and public policies (1984) 100 L.Q.R. 376; J. Dewar, Licences and land law: an alternative view (1986) 49 M.L.R. 741.

Although Fox L.J.'s judgment in *Ashburn Anstalt* v. *Arnold* deals (*obiter*) with the central issue of the effect of contractual licences vis-à-vis third parties, it would be wrong to think that all potential problems in this area have been resolved. See J. Hill, Leases, licences and third parties (1988) 51 M.L.R. 226; A. J. Oakley, Leases and licences—a return to orthodoxy [1988] C.L.J. 353; P. Sparkes, Leasehold terms and contractual licences (1988) 104 L.Q.R. 175; M. P. Thompson, Leases, licences and the demise of Errington [1988] Conv. 201; G. Battersby, Contractual and estoppel licences as proprietary interests in land [1991] Conv. 361.

III ESSENTIAL PREREQUISITES FOR THE CREATION OF A LEASE

Introduction: The Role of the Courts

Not surprisingly legislation which provides protection for private sector tenants tends to be unpopular with private landlords. Rent control and security of tenure combine to reduce the capital value of rented accommodation and limit the income which can be derived from it. Landlords have, therefore, sought to avoid the impact of the legislation by creating licences rather than leases. In this way, landowners hope to maximise their economic return and escape the consequences of the security of tenure provisions.

Until quite recently the courts tended to adopt a sympathetic attitude towards attempts by private sector landlords to avoid the impact of the statutory schemes of protection through the use of licence agreements.[44] However, in the 1980s members of the judiciary (at least in the House of Lords) have adopted a more interventionist approach. In certain circumstances the courts will strike down a licence agreement on the basis that it is "sham." That is to say, although an agreement relating to residential occupation superficially looks like a licence, it may be decided that—in reality—the substance of the agreement is a tenancy.

---

[44] See, *e.g. Somma* v. *Hazelhurst* [1978] 1 W.L.R. 1014.

(A) EXCLUSIVE POSSESSION

For a lease to be created the right to exclusive possession of the premises must be given to the tenant. A lease is an estate in land, and therefore a tenant has the right to exclude all other persons from the premises—including the landlord—during the period of the lease.

However, as the following materials illustrate, it is not always easy to determine whether or not an occupier enjoys exclusive possession. Furthermore, the fact that an occupier does enjoy exclusive possession does not necessarily lead to the conclusion that the occupier is a tenant.

Street v. *Mountford* [1985] A.C. 809

Lord Templeman said (at 814–827):

My Lords, by an agreement dated March 7, 1983, the respondent Mr. Street granted the appellant Mrs. Mountford the right to occupy the furnished rooms numbers 5 and 6 at 5, St. Clements Gardens, Boscombe, from March 7, 1983 for £37 per week, subject to termination by 14 days' written notice and subject to the conditions set forth in the agreement. The question raised by this appeal is whether the agreement created a tenancy or a licence.

A tenancy is a term of years absolute. This expression, by section 205(1)(xxvii) of the Law of Property Act 1925, reproducing the common law includes a term from week to week in possession at a rent and liable to determination by notice or re-entry. Originally a term of years was not an estate in land, the lessee having merely a personal action against his lessor. But a legal estate in leaseholds was created by the Statute of Gloucester 1278 and the Act of 1529 21 Hen. VIII, c. 15. Now by section 1 of the Law of Property Act 1925 a term of years absolute is an estate in land capable of subsisting as a legal estate. In the present case if the agreement dated March 7, 1983 created a tenancy, Mrs. Mountford having entered into possession and made weekly payments acquired a legal estate in land. If the agreement is a tenancy, the occupation of Mrs. Mountford is protected by the Rent Acts.

A licence in connection with land while entitling the licensee to use the land for the purposes authorised by the licence does not create an estate in the land. If the agreement dated March 7, 1983 created a licence for Mrs. Mountford to occupy the premises, she did not acquire any estate in the land. If the agreement is a licence then Mrs. Mountford's right of occupation is not protected by the Rent Acts. Hence the practical importance of distinguishing between a tenancy and a licence.

In the course of argument, nearly every clause of the agreement dated March 7, 1983 was relied upon by the appellant as indicating a lease and by the respondent as indicating a licence. The agreement, in full, was in these terms:

"I Mrs. Wendy Mountford agree to take from the owner Roger Street the single furnished room number 5 and 6 at 5 St. Clements Gardens, Boscombe, Bournemouth, commencing March 7, 1983 at a licence fee of £37 per week.

"I understand that the right to occupy the above room is conditional on the strict observance of the following rules:

"1. No paraffin stoves, or other than the supplied form of heating, is allowed in the room.

"2. No one but the above-named person may occupy or sleep in the room without prior permission, and this personal licence is not assignable.

"3. The owner (or his agent) has the right at all times to enter the room to inspect its condition, read and collect money from meters, carry out maintenance works, install or replace furniture or for any other reasonable purpose.

"4. All rooms must be kept in a clean and tidy condition.

"5. All damage and breakages must be paid for or replaced at once. An initial deposit equivalent to two weeks' licence fee will be refunded on termination of the licence subject to deduction for all damage or other breakages or arrears of licence fee, or retention towards the cost of any necessary possession proceedings.

"6. No nuisance or annoyance to be caused to the other occupiers. In particular, all music played after midnight to be kept low so as not to disturb occupiers of other rooms.

"7. No children or pets allowed under any circumstances whatsoever.

"8. Prompt payment of the licence fee must be made every Monday in advance without fail.

"9. If the licence fee or any part of it shall be seven days in arrear or if the occupier shall be in breach of any of the other terms of this agreement or if (except by arrangement) the room is left vacant or unoccupied, the owner may re-enter the room and this licence shall then immediately be terminated (without prejudice to all other rights and remedies of the owner).

"10. This licence may be terminated by 14 days' written notice given to the occupier at any time by the owner or his agent, or by the same notice by the occupier to the owner or his agent.

"Occupier's signature

"Owner/agent's signature

"Date March 7, 1983

"I understand and accept that a licence in the above form does not and is not intended to give me a tenancy protected under the Rent Acts.

"Occupier's signature."

On August 12, 1983 on Mrs. Mountford's application a fair rent was registered. Mr. Street then made application under section 51(*a*) of the County Courts Act 1959 for a declaration that Mrs. Mountford's occupancy was a licence and not a tenancy. The recorder in the county court held that Mrs. Mountford was a tenant entitled to the protection of the Rent Acts and made a declaration accordingly. The Court of Appeal held that Mrs. Mountford was a licensee not entitled to the protection of the Rent Acts. Mrs. Mountford appeals.

On behalf of Mrs. Mountford her counsel, Mr. Hicks Q.C., seeks to reaffirm and re-establish the traditional view that an occupier of land for a term at a rent is a tenant providing the occupier is granted exclusive possession. It is conceded on behalf of Mr. Street that the agreement dated March 7, 1983 granted exclusive possession to Mrs. Mountford. The traditional view that the grant of exclusive possession for a term at a rent creates a tenancy is consistent with the elevation of a tenancy into an estate in land. The tenant possessing exclusive possession is able to exercise the rights of an owner of land, which is in the real sense his land albeit temporarily and subject to certain restrictions. A tenant armed with exclusive possession can keep out strangers and keep out the landlord unless the landlord is exercising limited rights reserved to him by the tenancy agreement to enter and view and repair. A licensee lacking exclusive possession can in no sense call the land his own and cannot be said to own any estate in the land. The licence does not create an estate in the land to which it relates but only makes an act lawful which would otherwise be unlawful.

On behalf of Mr. Street his counsel, Mr. Goodhart Q.C., relies on recent authorities which, he submits, demonstrate that an occupier granted exclusive possession for a term at a rent may nevertheless be a licensee if, in the words of Slade L.J. in the present case [1985] 49 P. & C.R. 324, 332:

> "there is manifested the clear intention of both parties that the rights granted are to be merely those of a personal right of occupation and not those of a tenant."

In the present case, it is submitted, the provisions of the agreement dated March 7, 1983 and in particular clauses 2, 4, 7 and 9 and the express declaration at the foot of the agreement manifest the clear intention of both parties that the rights granted are to be those of a personal nature and not those of a tenant.

My Lords, there is no doubt that the traditional distinction between a tenancy and a licence of land lay in the grant of land for a term at a rent with exclusive possession. In some cases it was not clear at first sight whether exclusive possession was in fact granted. For example, an owner of land could grant a licence to cut and remove standing timber. Alternatively the owner could grant a tenancy of the land with the right to cut and remove standing timber during the term of the tenancy. The grant of rights relating to standing timber therefore required careful consideration in order to decide whether the grant conferred exclusive possession of the land for a term at a rent and was therefore a tenancy or whether it merely conferred a bare licence to remove the timber.

In *Glenwood Lumber Co. Ltd.* v. *Phillips* [1904] A.C. 405, the Crown in exercise of statutory powers "licensed" the respondents to hold an area of land for the purpose of cutting and removing timber for the term of 21 years at an annual rent. Delivering the advice of the Judicial Committee of the Privy Council, Lord Davey said, at pp. 408–409:

> "The appellants contended that this instrument conferred only a licence to cut timber and carry it away, and did not give the respondent any right of occupation or interest in the land itself. Having regard to the provisions of the Act under the powers of which it was executed and to the language of the document itself, their Lordships cannot adopt this view of the construction or effect of it. In the so-called licence itself it is called indifferently a licence and a demise, but in the Act it is spoken of as a lease, and the holder of it is described as the lessee. It is not, however, a question of words but of substance. If the effect of the instrument is to give the holder an exclusive right of occupation of the land, though subject to certain reservations or to a restriction of the purposes for which it may be used, it is in law a demise of the land itself. By [the Act] it is enacted that the lease shall vest in the lessee the right to take and keep exclusive possession of the lands described therein subject to the conditions in the Act provided or referred to, and the lessee is empowered (amongst other things) to bring any actions or suits against any party unlawfully in possession of any land so leased, and to prosecute all trespassers thereon. The operative part and habendum in the licence is framed in apt language to carry out the intention so expressed in the Act. And their Lordships have no doubt that the effect of the so-called licence was to confer a title to the land itself on the respondent."

This was a case in which the court after careful consideration of the purposes of the grant, the terms of the grant and the surrounding circumstances, came to the conclusion that the grant conferred exclusive possession and was therefore a tenancy.

A contrary conclusion was reached in *Taylor* v. *Caldwell* (1863) 3 B. & S. 826 in which the defendant agreed to let the plaintiff have the use of the Surrey Gardens and Music Hall on four specified days giving a series of four concerts and day and night fetes at the gardens and hall on those days, and the plaintiff agreed to take the gardens and the hall and to pay £100 for each day. Blackburn J. said, at p. 832:

> "The parties inaccurately call this a 'letting,' and the money to be paid a 'rent,' but the whole agreement is such as to show that the defendants were to retain the possession of the hall and gardens so that there was to be no demise of them, and that the contract was merely to give the plaintiffs the use of them on those days."

That was a case where the court after considering the purpose of the grant, the terms of the grant and the surrounding circumstances came to the conclusion that the grantee was not entitled to exclusive possession but only to use the land for limited purposes and was therefore a licensee.

In the case of residential accommodation there is no difficulty in deciding whether the grant confers exclusive possession. An occupier of residential accommodation at a rent for a term is either a lodger or a tenant. The occupier is a lodger if the landlord provides attendance or services which require the landlord or his servants to exercise unrestricted access to and use of the premises. A lodger is entitled to live in the premises but cannot call the place his own. In *Allan* v. *Liverpool Overseers* (1874) L.R. 9 Q.B. 180, 191–192 Blackburn J. said:

> "A lodger in a house, although he has the exclusive use of rooms in the house, in the sense that nobody else is to be there, and though his goods are stowed there, yet he is not in exclusive occupation in that sense, because the landlord is there for the purpose of being able, as landlords commonly do in the case of lodgings, to have his own servants to look after the house and the furniture, and has retained to himself the occupation, though he has agreed to give the exclusive enjoyment of the occupation to the lodger."

If on the other hand residential accommodation is granted for a term at a rent with exclusive possession, the landlord providing neither attendance nor services, the grant is a tenancy; any express reservation to the landlord of limited rights to enter and view the state of the premises and to repair and maintain the premises only serves to emphasise the fact that the grantee is entitled to exclusive possession and is a tenant. In the present case it is conceded that Mrs. Mountford is entitled to exclusive possession and is not a lodger. Mr. Street provided neither attendance nor services and only reserved the limited rights of inspection and maintenance and the like set forth in clause 3 of the agreement. On the traditional view of the matter, Mrs. Mountford not being a lodger must be a tenant.

There can be no tenancy unless the occupier enjoys exclusive possession; but an occupier who enjoys exclusive possession is not necessarily a tenant. He may be owner in fee simple, a trespasser, a mortgagee in possession, an object of charity or a service occupier. To constitute a tenancy the occupier must be granted exclusive possession for a fixed or periodic term certain in consideration of a premium or periodical payments. The grant may be express, or may be inferred where the owner accepts weekly or other periodical payments from the occupier.

Occupation by service occupier may be eliminated. A service occupier is a servant who occupies his master's premises in order to perform his duties as a servant. In those circumstances the possession and occupation of the servant is treated as the possession and occupation of the master and the relationship of landlord and tenant is not created; see *Mayhew* v. *Suttle* (1854) 4 El. & Bl. 347. The test is whether the servant requires the premises he occupies in order the better to perform his duties as a servant:

"Where the occupation is necessary for the performance of services, and the occupier is required to reside in the house in order to perform those services, the occupation being strictly ancillary to the performance of the duties which the occupier has to perform, the occupation is that of a servant"; *per* Mellor J. in *Smith* v. *Seghill Overseers* (1875) L.R. 10 Q.B. 422, 428.

The cases on which Mr. Goodhart relies begin with *Booker* v. *Palmer* [1942] 2 All E.R. 674. The owner of a cottage agreed to allow a friend to install an evacuee in the cottage rent free for the duration of the war. The Court of Appeal held that there was no intention on the part of the owner to enter into legal relationships with the evacuee. Lord Greene M.R., said, at p. 677:

"To suggest there is an intention there to create a relationship of landlord and tenant appears to me to be quite impossible. There is one golden rule which is of very general application, namely, that the law does not impute intention to enter into legal relationships where the circumstances and the conduct of the parties negative any intention of the kind. It seems to me that this is a clear example of the application of that rule."

The observations of Lord Greene M.R. were not directed to the distinction between a contractual tenancy and a contractual licence. The conduct of the parties (not their professed intentions) indicated that they did not intend to contract at all.

In the present case, the agreement dated March 7, 1983 professed an intention by both parties to create a licence and their belief that they had in fact created a licence. It was submitted on behalf of Mr. Street that the court cannot in these circumstances decide that the agreement created a tenancy without interfering with the freedom of contract enjoyed by both parties. My Lords, Mr. Street enjoyed freedom to offer Mrs. Mountford the right to occupy the rooms comprised in the agreement on such lawful terms as Mr. Street pleased. Mrs. Mountford enjoyed freedom to negotiate with Mr. Street to obtain different terms. Both parties enjoyed freedom to contract or not to contract and both parties exercised that freedom by contracting on the terms set forth in the written agreement and on no other terms. But the consequences in law of the agreement, once concluded, can only be determined by consideration of the effect of the agreement. If the agreement satisfied all the requirements of a tenancy, then the agreement produced a tenancy and the parties cannot alter the effect of the agreement by insisting that they only created a licence. The manufacture of a five-pronged implement for manual digging results in a fork even if the manufacturer, unfamiliar with the English language, insists that he intended to make and has made a spade.

It was also submitted that in deciding whether the agreement created a tenancy or a licence, the court should ignore the Rent Acts. If Mr. Street has succeeded, where owners have failed these past 70 years, in driving a coach and horses through the Rent Acts, he must be left to enjoy the benefit of his ingenuity unless and until Parliament intervenes. I accept that the Rent Acts are irrelevant to the problem of determining the legal effect of the rights granted by the agreement. Like the professed intention of the parties, the Rent Acts cannot alter the effect of the agreement.

In *Marcroft Wagons Ltd.* v. *Smith* [1951] 2 K.B. 496 the daughter of a deceased tenant who lived with her mother claimed to be a statutory tenant by succession and the landlords asserted that the daughter had no rights under the Rent Acts and was a trespasser. The landlords expressly refused to accept the daughter's claims but accepted rent from her while they were considering the position. If the landlords had decided not to apply to the court for possession but to accept the daughter as a tenant, the moneys paid by the daughter would have been treated as rent. If the landlords decided, as they did decide, to apply for possession and to prove, as they did prove, that the daughter was not a statutory tenant, the moneys paid by the daughter were treated as mesne profits. The Court of Appeal held with some hesitation that the landlords never accepted the daughter as tenant and never intended to contract with her although the landlords delayed for some six months before applying to the court for possession. Roxburgh J. said, at p. 507:

> "Generally speaking, when a person, having a sufficient estate in land, lets another into exclusive possession, a tenancy results, and there is no question of a licence. But the inference of a tenancy is not necessarily to be drawn where a person succeeds on a death to occupation of rent-controlled premises and a landlord accepts some rent while he or the occupant, or both of them, is or are considering his or their position. If this is all that happened in this case, then no tenancy would result."

In that case, as in *Booker* v. *Palmer* the court deduced from the conduct of the parties that they did not intend to contract at all.

Errington v. *Errington and Woods* [1952] 1 K.B. 290 concerned a contract by a father to allow his son to buy the father's house on payment of the instalments of the father's building society loan. Denning L.J. referred, at p. 297, to the judgment of Lord Greene M.R. in *Booker* v. *Palmer* [1942] 2 All E.R. 674, 677 where, however, the circumstances and the conduct of the parties negatived any intention to enter into legal relationships. Denning L.J. continued, at pp. 297–298:

> "We have had many instances lately of occupiers in exclusive possession who have been held to be not tenants, but only licensees. When a requisitioning authority allowed people into possession at a weekly rent: ... when a landlord told a tenant on his retirement that he could live in a cottage rent free for the rest of his days: ... when a landlord, on the death of the widow of a statutory tenant, allowed her daughter to remain in possession, paying rent for six months: *Marcroft Wagons Ltd.* v. *Smith* [1951] 2 K.B. 496; when the owner of a shop allowed the manager to live in a flat above the shop, but did not require him to do so, and the value of the flat was taken into account at £1 a week in fixing his wages: ... in each of those cases the occupier was held to be a licensee and not a tenant. ... The result of all these cases is that, although a person who is let into exclusive possession is prima facie to be considered a tenant, nevertheless he will not be held to be so if the circumstances negative any intention to create a tenancy. Words alone may not suffice. Parties cannot turn a tenancy into a licence merely by calling it one. But if the circumstances and the conduct of the parties show that all that was intended was that the occupier should be granted a personal privilege, with no interest in the land, he will be held to be a licensee only."

In *Errington* v. *Errington and Woods* [1952] 1 K.B. 290 and in the cases cited by Denning L.J. at p. 297 there were exceptional circumstances which negatived the prima facie intention to create a tenancy, notwithstanding that the occupier enjoyed exclusive occupation. The intention to create a tenancy was negatived if the parties did not intend to enter into legal relationships at all, or where the relationship between the parties was that of vendor and purchaser, master and service occupier, or where the owner, a requisitioning authority, had no power to grant a tenancy. These exceptional circumstances are not to be found in the present case where there has been the lawful, independent and voluntary grant of exclusive possession for a term at a rent.

If the observations of Denning L.J. are applied to the facts of the present case it may fairly be said that the circumstances negative any intention to create a mere licence. Words alone do not suffice. Parties cannot turn a tenancy into a licence merely by calling it one. The circumstances and the conduct of the parties show that what was intended was that the occupier should be granted exclusive possession at a rent for a term with a corresponding interest in the land which created a tenancy.

In *Cobb* v. *Lane* [1952] 1 T.L.R. 1037, an owner allowed her brother to occupy a house rent free. The county court judge, who was upheld by the Court of Appeal, held that there was no intention to create any legal relationship and that a tenancy at will was not to be implied. This is another example of conduct which negatives any intention of entering into a contract, and does not assist in distinguishing a contractual tenancy from a contractual licence.

In *Facchini* v. *Bryson* [1952] 1 T.L.R. 1386, an employer and his assistant entered into an agreement which, inter alia, allowed the assistant to occupy a house for a weekly payment on terms which conferred exclusive possession. The assistant did not occupy the house for the better performance of his duty and was not therefore a service occupier. The agreement stipulated that "nothing in this agreement shall be construed to create a tenancy between the employer and the assistant." Somervell L.J. said, at p. 1389:

> "If, looking at the operative clauses in the agreement, one comes to the conclusion that the rights of the occupier, to use a neutral word, are those of a lessee, the parties cannot turn it into a licence by saying at the end 'this is deemed to be a licence'; nor can they, if the operative paragraphs show that it is merely a licence, say that it should be deemed to be a lease."

Denning L.J. referred to several cases including *Errington* v. *Errington and Woods* and *Cobb* v. *Lane* and said, at pp. 1389–1390:

> "In all the cases where an occupier has been held to be a licensee there has been something in the circumstances, such as a family arrangement, an act of a friendship or generosity, or such like, to negative any intention to create a tenancy. ... In the present case, however, there are no special circumstances. It is a simple case where the employer let a man into occupation of a house in consequence of his employment at a weekly sum payable by him. The occupation has all the features of a service tenancy, and the parties cannot by the mere words of their contract turn it into something else. Their relationship is determined by the law and not by the label which they choose to put on it: ... "

The decision, which was thereafter binding on the Court of Appeal and on all lower courts, referred to the special circumstances which are capable of negativing an intention to create a tenancy and reaffirmed the principle that the professed intentions of the parties are irrelevant. The decision also indicated that in a simple case a grant of exclusive possession of residential accommodation for a weekly sum creates a tenancy.

In *Murray Bull & Co. Ltd.* v. *Murray* [1953] 1 Q.B. 211 a contractual tenant held over, paying rent quarterly. McNair J. found, at p. 217:

> "both parties intended that the relationship should be that of licensee and no more ... The primary consideration on both sides was that the defendant, as occupant of the flat, should not be a controlled tenant."

In my opinion this case was wrongly decided. McNair J. citing the observations of Denning L.J. in *Errington* v. *Errington and Woods* [1952] 1 K.B. 290, 297 and *Marcroft Wagons Ltd.* v. *Smith* [1951] 2 K.B. 496 failed to distinguish between first, conduct which negatives an intention to create legal relationships, secondly, special circumstances which prevent exclusive occupation from creating a tenancy and thirdly, the professed intention of the parties. In *Murray Bull & Co. Ltd.* v. *Murray* the conduct of the parties showed an intention to contract and there were no relevant special circumstances. The tenant holding over continued by agreement to enjoy exclusive possession and to pay a rent for a term certain. In those circumstances he continued to be a tenant notwithstanding the professed intention of the parties to create a licence and their desire to avoid a controlled tenancy.

In *Addiscombe Garden Estates Ltd.* v. *Crabbe* [1958] 1 Q.B. 513 the Court of Appeal considered an agreement relating to a tennis club carried on in the grounds of a hotel. The agreement was:

"described by the parties as a licence ... the draftsman has studiously and successfully avoided the use either of the word 'landlord' or the word 'tenant' throughout the document" *per* Jenkins L.J. at p. 522.

On analysis of the whole of the agreement the Court of Appeal came to the conclusion that the agreement conferred exclusive possession and thus created a tenancy, Jenkins L.J. said, at p. 522:

"The whole of the document must be looked at; and if, after it has been examined, the right conclusion appears to be that, whatever label may have been attached to it, it in fact conferred and imposed on the grantee in substance the rights and obligations of a tenant, and on the grantor in substance the rights and obligations of a landlord, then it must be given the appropriate effect, that is to say, it must be treated as a tenancy agreement as distinct from a mere licence."

In the agreement in the *Addiscombe* case it was by no means clear until the whole of the document had been narrowly examined that exclusive possession was granted by the agreement. In the present case it is clear that exclusive possession was granted and so much is conceded. In these circumstances it is unnecessary to analyse minutely the detailed rights and obligations contained in the agreement.

In the *Addiscombe* case Jenkins L.J. referred, at p. 528, to the observations of Denning L.J. in *Errington and Errington and Woods* to the effect that "The test of exclusive possession is by no means decisive." Jenkins L.J. continued:

"I think that wide statement must be treated as qualified by his observations in *Facchini* v. *Bryson* [1952] 1 T.L.R. 1386, 1389; and it seems to me that, save in exceptional cases of the kind mentioned by Denning L.J. in that case, the law remains that the fact of exclusive possession, if not decisive against the view that there is a mere licence, as distinct from a tenancy, is at all events a consideration of the first importance."

Exclusive possession is of first importance in considering whether an occupier is a tenant; exclusive possession is not decisive because an occupier who enjoys exclusive possession is not necessarily a tenant. The occupier may be a lodger or service occupier or fall within the other exceptional categories mentioned by Denning L.J. in *Errington* v. *Errington and Woods* [1952] 1 K.B. 290.

In *Isaac* v. *Hotel de Paris Ltd.* [1960] 1 W.L.R. 239 an employee who managed a night bar in a hotel for his employer company which held a lease of the hotel negotiated "subject to contract" to complete the purchase of shares in the company and to be allowed to run the nightclub for his own benefit if he paid the head rent payable by the company for the hotel. In the expectation that the negotiations "subject to contract" would ripen into a binding agreement, the employee was allowed to run the nightclub and he paid the company's rent. When negotiations broke down the employee claimed unsuccessfully to be a tenant of the hotel company. The circumstances in which the employee was allowed to occupy the premises showed that the hotel company never intended to accept him as a tenant and that he was fully aware of that fact. This was a case, consistent with the authorities cited by Lord Denning in giving the advice of the Judicial Committee of the Privy Council, in which the parties did not intend to enter into contractual relationships unless and until the negotiations "subject to contract" were replaced by a binding contract.

In *Abbeyfield (Harpenden) Society Ltd.* v. *Woods* [1968] 1 W.L.R. 374 the occupier of a room in an old people's home was held to be a licensee and not a tenant. Lord Denning M.R. said, at p. 376:

> "The modern cases show that a man may be a licensee even though he has exclusive possession, even though the word 'rent' is used, and even though the word 'tenancy' is used. The court must look at the agreement as a whole and see whether a tenancy really was intended. In this case there is, besides the one room, the provision of services, meals, a resident housekeeper, and such like. The whole arrangement was so personal in nature that the proper inference is that he was a licensee."

As I understand the decision in the *Abbeyfield* case the court came to the conclusion that the occupier was a lodger and was therefore a licensee, not a tenant.

In *Shell-Mex and B.P. Ltd.* v. *Manchester Garages Ltd.* [1971] 1 W.L.R. 612 the Court of Appeal after carefully examining an agreement whereby the defendant was allowed to use a petrol company's filling station for the purposes of selling petrol, came to the conclusion that the agreement did not grant exclusive possession to the defendant who was therefore a licensee. At p. 615 Lord Denning M.R. in considering whether the transaction was a licence or a tenancy said:

> "Broadly speaking, we have to see whether it is a personal privilege given to a person (in which case it is a licence), or whether it grants an interest in land (in which case it is a tenancy). At one time it used to be thought that exclusive possession was a decisive factor. But that is not so. It depends on broader considerations altogether. Primarily on whether it is personal in its nature or not: see *Errington* v. *Errington and Woods* [1952] 1 K.B. 290."

In my opinion the agreement was only "personal in its nature" and created a "a personal privilege" if the agreement did not confer the right to exclusive possession of the filling station. No other test for distinguishing between a contractual tenancy and a contractual licence appears to be understandable or workable.

Heslop v. *Burns* [1974] 1 W.L.R. 1241 was another case in which the owner of a cottage allowed a family to live in the cottage rent free and it was held that no tenancy at will had been created on the ground that the parties did not intend any legal relationship. Scarman L.J. cited with approval, at p. 1252, the statement by Denning L.J. in *Facchini* v. *Bryson* [1952] 1 T.L.R. 1386, 1389:

> "In all the cases where an occupier has been held to be a licensee there has been something in the circumstances, such as a family arrangement, an act of friendship or generosity, or such like to negative any intention to create a tenancy."

In *Marchant* v. *Charters* [1977] 1 W.L.R. 1181 a bedsitting room was occupied on terms that the landlord cleaned the rooms daily and provided clean linen each week. It was held by the Court of Appeal that the occupier was a licensee and not a tenant. The decision in the case is sustainable on the grounds that the occupier was a lodger and did not enjoy exclusive possession. But Lord Denning M.R. said, at p. 1185:

"What is the test to see whether the occupier of one room in a house is a tenant or a licensee? It does not depend on whether he or she has exclusive possession or not. It does not depend on whether the room is furnished or not. It does not depend on whether the occupation is permanent or temporary. It does not depend on the label which the parties put upon it. All these are factors which may influence the decision but none of them is conclusive. All the circumstances have to be worked out. Eventually the answer depends on the nature and quality of the occupancy. Was it intended that the occupier should have a stake in the room or did he have only permission for himself personally to occupy the room, whether under a contract or not? In which case he is a licensee."

But in my opinion in order to ascertain the nature and quality of the occupancy and to see whether the occupier has or has not a stake in the room or only permission for himself personally to occupy, the court must decide whether upon its true construction the agreement confers on the occupier exclusive possession. If exclusive possession at a rent for a term does not constitute a tenancy then the distinction between a contractual tenancy and a contractual licence of land becomes wholly unidentifiable.

In *Somma* v. *Hazelhurst* [1978] 1 W.L.R. 1014, a young unmarried couple H. and S. occupied a double bedsitting room for which they paid a weekly rent. The landlord did not provide services or attendance and the couple were not lodgers but tenants enjoying exclusive possession. But the Court of Appeal did not ask themselves whether H. and S. were lodgers or tenants and did not draw the correct conclusion from the fact that H. and S. enjoyed exclusive possession. The Court of Appeal were diverted from the correct inquiries by the fact that the landlord obliged H. and S. to enter into separate agreements and reserved power to determine each agreement separately. The landlord also insisted that the room should not in form be let to either H. or S. or to both H. and S. but that each should sign an agreement to share the room in common with such other persons as the landlord might from time to time nominate. The sham nature of this obligation would have been only slightly more obvious if H. and S. had been married or if the room had been furnished with a double bed instead of two single beds. If the landlord had served notice on H. to leave and had required S. to share the room with a strange man, the notice would only have been a disguised notice to quit on both H. and S. The room was let and taken as residential accommodation with exclusive possession in order that H. and S. might live together in undisturbed quasi-connubial bliss making weekly payments. The agreements signed by H. and S. constituted the grant to H. and S. jointly of exclusive possession at a rent for a term for the purposes for which the room was taken and the agreement therefore created a tenancy. Although the Rent Acts must not be allowed to alter or influence the construction of an agreement, the court should, in my opinion, be astute to detect and frustrate sham devices and artificial transactions whose only object is to disguise the grant of a tenancy and to evade the Rent Acts. I would disapprove of the decision in this case that H. and S. were only licensees and for the same reason would disapprove of the decision in *Aldrington Garages Ltd*. v. *Fielder* (1978) 37 P. & C.R. 461 and *Sturolson & Co*. v. *Weniz* (1984) 272 E.G. 326.

In the present case the Court of Appeal, 49 P. & C.R. 324 held that the agreement dated March 7, 1983 only created a licence. Slade L.J., at p. 329 accepted that the agreement and in particular clause 3 of the agreement "shows that the right to occupy the premises conferred on the defendant was intended as an exclusive right of occupation, in that it was thought necessary to give a special and express power to the plaintiff to enter. ... " Before your Lordships it was conceded that the agreement conferred the right of exclusive possession on Mrs. Mountford. Even without clause 3 the result would have been the same. By the agreement Mrs. Mountford was granted the right to occupy residential accommodation. The landlord did not provide any services or attendance. It was plain that Mrs. Mountford was not a lodger. Slade L.J. proceeded to analyse all the provisions of the agreement, not for the purpose of deciding whether his finding of exclusive possession was correct, but for the purpose of assigning some of the provisions of the agreement to the category of terms which he thought are usually to be found in a tenancy agreement and of assigning other provisions to the category of terms which he thought are usually to be found in a licence. Slade L.J. may or may not have been right that in a letting of a furnished room it was "most unusual to find a provision in a tenancy agreement obliging the tenant to keep his rooms in a 'tidy condition' " (p. 329). If Slade L.J. was right about this' and other provisions there is still no logical method of evaluating the results of his survey. Slade L.J. reached the conclusion that "the agreement bears all the hallmarks of a licence rather than a tenancy save for the one important feature of exclusive occupation": p. 329. But in addition to the hallmark of exclusive occupation of residential accommodation there were the hallmarks of weekly payments for a periodical term. Unless these three hallmarks are decisive, it really becomes impossible to distinguish a contractual tenancy from a contractual licence save by reference to the professed intention of the parties or by the judge awarding marks for drafting. Slade L.J. was finally impressed by the statement at the foot of the agreement by Mrs. Mountford "I understand and accept that a licence in the above form does not and is not intended to give me a tenancy protected under the Rent Acts." Slade L.J. said, at p. 330:

> "it seems to me that, if the defendant is to displace the express statement of intention embodied in the declaration, she must show that the declaration was either a deliberate sham or at least an inaccurate statement of what was the true substance of the real transaction agreed between the parties; ... "

My Lords, the only intention which is relevant is the intention demonstrated by the agreement to grant exclusive possession for a term at a rent. Sometimes it may be difficult to discover whether, on the true construction of an agreement, exclusive possession is conferred. Sometimes it may appear from the surrounding circumstances that there was no intention to create legal relationships. Sometimes it may appear from the surrounding circumstances that the right to exclusive possession is referable to a legal relationship other than a tenancy. Legal relationships to which the grant of exclusive possession might be referable and which would or might negative the grant of an estate or interest in the land include occupancy under a contract for the sale of the land, occupancy pursuant to a contract of employment or occupancy referable to the holding of an office. But where as in the present case the only circumstances are that residential accommodation is offered and accepted with exclusive possession for a term at a rent, the result is a tenancy.

The position was well summarised by Windeyer J. sitting in the High Court of Australia in *Radaich* v. *Smith* (1959) 101 C.L.R. 209, 222, where he said:

"What then is the fundamental right which a tenant has that distinguishes his position from that of a licensee? It is an interest in land as distinct from a personal permission to enter the land and use it for some stipulated purpose or purposes. And how is it to be ascertained whether such an interest in land has been given? By seeing whether the grantee was given a legal right of exclusive possession of the land for a term or from year to year or for a life or lives. If he was, he is a tenant. And he cannot be other than a tenant, because a legal right of exclusive possession is a tenancy and the creation of such a right is a demise. To say that a man who has, by agreement with a landlord, a right of exclusive possession of land for a term is not a tenant is simply to contradict the first proposition by the second. A right of exclusive possession is secured by the right of a lessee to maintain ejectment and, after his entry, trespass. A reservation to the landlord, either by contract or statute, of a limited right of entry, as for example to view or repair, is, of course, not inconsistent with the grant of exclusive possession. Subject to such reservations, a tenant for a term or from year to year or for a life or lives can exclude his landlord as well as strangers from the demised premises. All this is long established law: see *Cole on Ejectment* (1857) pp. 72, 73, 287, 458."

My Lords, I gratefully adopt the logic and the language of Windeyer J. Henceforth the courts which deal with these problems will, save in exceptional circumstances, only be concerned to inquire whether as a result of an agreement relating to residential accommodation the occupier is a lodger or a tenant. In the present case I am satisfied that Mrs. Mountford is a tenant, that the appeal should be allowed, that the order of the Court of Appeal should be set aside and that the respondent should be ordered to pay the costs of the appellant here and below.

Lords Scarman, Keith, Bridge and Brightman agreed.

Notes

Although *Street* v. *Mountford* went some way towards providing a simple test for the courts of first instance to apply Lord Templeman's speech presents a number of problems.

(i) Lord Templeman states that "[a]n occupier of residential accommodation at a rent for a term is either a lodger or a tenant."[45] The courts have had some difficulty applying this formula where shared residential accommodation is involved.[46] Furthermore, the formula is plainly not very useful in the context of commercial premises.[47] One commentator has suggested that the introduction of the notion of lodger into the discussion was "a quite unnecessary complication."[48]

[45] At 817–818.
[46] See *Brooker Settled Estates* v. *Ayers* (1987) 19 H.L.R. 246; *Hadjiloucas* v. *Crean* [1988] 1 W.L.R. 1006; and *A.G. Securities* v. *Vaughan*; *Antoniades* v. *Villiers* [1988] A.C. 417 (pp. 63–77).
[47] See *London & Associated Investment Trust* v. *Calow* (1987) 53 P. & C.R. 340; *Dellneed* v. *Chin* (1987) 53 P. & C.R. 112; *University of Reading* v. *Johnson-Houghton* [1985] 2 E.G.L.R. 113; *Dresden Estates* v. *Collinson* (1988) 55 P. & C.R. 47; *Smith* v. *Northside Developments* (1988) 55 P. & C.R. 164; *Essex Plan Ltd.* v. *Broadminster* [1988] 43 E.G. 84.
[48] Anderson, Licences: Traditional Law Revived? (1985) 48 M.L.R. 712 at 713.

(ii) Lord Templeman notes that "exclusive possession is not decisive because an occupier who enjoys exclusive possession is not necessarily a tenant"[49]; there are a number of "exceptional categories" in which an occupier who has exclusive possession is a licensee. It appears that the "exceptional categories" listed by Lord Templeman are illustrative rather than exhaustive.[50]

(iii) In *Street* v. *Mountford* the facts were very simple: there was a single agreement between the owner and the occupier, and crucially it was conceded that the occupier had exclusive possession. However, there are two reasons why it is not always easy to determine whether or not an agreement confers exclusive possession on a residential occupier. First, many agreements relating to residential accommodation contain clauses which purport to negative the grant of exclusive possession. For example, in *Crancour* v. *Da Silvaesa*[51] the agreement contained the following provision:

The licensor may for any reason and at any time require the licensee forthwith to vacate the flat and move to any other flat of comparable size in the building which the licensor may offer the licensee.

If a clause which is designed to avoid the grant of exclusive possession is regarded by the courts as genuine, a tenancy cannot arise.

Secondly, complications arise where residential accommodation is shared and each occupier enters a separate agreement with the owner. In the context of shared accommodation, depending on the precise circumstances, the courts may analyse the facts in one of a number of different ways:

— none of the occupiers may have exclusive possession of any part of the accommodation, in which case the occupiers are licensees; or

— each occupier may have exclusive possession of part of the accommodation (such as a bed-sitting room), in which case each occupier is a tenant; or

— the occupiers may collectively have exclusive possession of the whole of the shared accommodation, in which case they are joint tenants.

In view of the practical significance of the lease/licence distinction in the private rented sector there was little likelihood that the House of Lords' decision in *Street* v. *Mountford* would staunch the flow of litigation in

---

[49] At 818.
[50] See *Sharp* v. *McArthur* (1986) 19 H.L.R. 364 (*cf. Bretherton* v. *Paton* (1986) 18 H.L.R. 257); *Ogwr BC* v. *Dykes* [1989] 1 W.L.R. 295 (although this case was doubted by the Court of Appeal in *Family Housing Association* v. *Jones* [1990] 1 W.L.R. 779).
[51] (1986) 18 H.L.R. 265.

this area. In 1987 the Law Commission took the view that *Street* v. *Mountford* was "not likely to have ended the battle; rather it settled a series of skirmishes and moved the front line."[52] Indeed, in the sphere of the lease/licence distinction each new decision of the higher courts, rather than bringing about major substantive changes, has tended merely to cause landlords to redraft their standard-form agreements with a view to exploiting gaps in the courts' reasoning (or other loopholes in the legislation[53]). Accordingly, it was only to be expected that in due course the House of Lords would be given another opportunity to consider this area of the law.

A.G. Securities v. *Vaughan*; *Antoniades* v. *Villiers*
[1990] A.C. 417

Lord Templeman said (at 454–466):

My Lords, in each of the two appeals now under consideration, the question is whether the owner of residential accommodation granted a tenancy or granted licences.

In the first appeal, the appellant company, A.G. Securities, owned a block of flats, Linden Mansions, Hornsey Lane, London. Flat No. 25 consists of six living-rooms in addition to a kitchen and bathroom. The company furnished four living-rooms as bedrooms, a fifth as a lounge and a sixth as a sitting-room. In 1974 furnished lettings became subject to the Rent Acts. If the company granted exclusive possession of the flat to one single occupier or to two or more occupiers jointly in consideration of periodical payments, the grant would create a tenancy of the flat. If the company granted exclusive possession of one bedroom to four different occupiers with joint use of the lounge, sitting-room, kitchen and bathroom, each of the four grants would create a tenancy of one bedroom. Exclusive possession means either exclusive occupation or receipt of rent and profits.

The company entered into separate agreements with four different applicants. Each agreement was in the same form, and was expressed to be made between the company as "the owner" and the applicant as "licensee." The agreement contained, inter alia, the following relevant clauses:

"1. The owner grants to the licensee the right to use in common with others who have or may from time to time be granted the like right the flat known as 25, Linden Mansions, Hornsey Lane, N.6 but without the right to exclusive possession of any part of the said flat together with the fixtures furniture furnishings and effects now in the said flat for six months from the ——— day of ——— 19— and thereafter until determined by either party giving to the other one month's notice in writing to take effect at any time.

"2. The licensee agrees with the owner as follows: (1) To pay the sum of £—— per month for the right to share in the use of the said flat such sum to

[52] Law Commission Report No. 162, *Landlord and Tenant: Reform of the Law* (1987), para. 4.8.
[53] See *e.g.* pp. 126–132.

be payable by equal monthly instalments on the first day of each month ...
(3) To share the use of the said flat peaceably with and not to impede the use
of the said flat by such other persons not exceeding three in number at any
one time to whom the owner has granted or shall from time to time grant
licence to use the said flat in common with the licensee and not to impede the
use by such other persons of the gas electricity and telephone services
supplied to the flat provided that each shares the cost of such services. (4) If
at any time there shall be less than three persons authorised by the owner to
use the said flat in common with the licensee upon reasonable notice given by
the owner to meet with any prospective licensee nominated by the owner at
the flat to provide an opportunity to such prospective licensee to agree terms
for sharing the cost of services in accordance with clause 2(3). (5) Not to
assign this agreement nor permit any other person except as licensed by the
owner to sleep or reside in or share occupation of the said flat or any part of
it at any time."

The flat was kept fully occupied; whenever one agreement was terminated the
company invited applications to fill the vacancy. The company's agent produced
a draft of the agreement to an applicant. The monthly sum payable by the
applicant was not necessarily the same as the monthly sum payable by any of the
continuing occupiers of the flat because inflation and other factors caused the
value of an agreement to fluctuate. The company and its agent gave no
directions or explanations about the manner in which the applicant and other
persons not exceeding three in number would use the flat in common. The
applicant was sent off to the flat to agree terms with the three continuing
occupiers. There he would be offered a vacant bedroom and the use of the
lounge, sitting-room, kitchen and bathroom with the other occupiers each of
whom had his own bedroom. It was the practice that whenever a bedroom fell
vacant upon termination of an agreement, each of the three continuing
occupiers, in order of seniority, decided whether to change his bedroom. The
applicant for the vacancy was then offered the bedroom which the other three
least coveted. The applicant, if content, signed his agreement and moved into
his bedroom. If he were unable to share the use of the common parts of the flat
peaceably he could terminate his agreement, or the other three occupiers could
terminate their agreements or prevail upon the company to terminate the
agreement of the unpopular occupier.

The respondent, Mr. Vaughan, signed an agreement in 1982 to pay £86.66 per
month. The respondent, Mr. Lyons, signed an agreement dated March 2, 1984
to pay £99 per month. The respondent, Mr. Russell, signed an agreement dated
August 1, 1984 to pay £125 per month, and the respondent, Mr. Cook, signed
an agreement dated January 28, 1985 to pay £104 per month. From January 28,
1985 onwards, each of the four respondents occupied one bedroom and shared
the use of the lounge, sitting-room, kitchen and bathroom.

The respondents claim that under and by virtue of the four agreements signed
by them respectively, they became tenants of the flat. The company contends
that each respondent is a licensee.

In the second appeal, the appellant, Mr. Antoniades, is the owner of the
house, 6, Whiteley Road, Upper Norwood. The attic was converted into
furnished residential accommodation comprising a bedroom, a bed sitting-room,
kitchen and bathroom. The furniture in the sitting-room consisted of a bed-
settee, a table-bed, a sideboard and a chair.

The appellants, Mr. Villiers and Miss Bridger, spent three months looking for
a flat where they could live together. In February 1985 they were shown the
attic flat. The bedroom lacked a bed; the appellants expressed a preference for a
double bed which Mr. Antoniades agreed to provide. Mr. Antoniades and Mr.
Villiers entered into an agreement dated February 9, 1985. The agreement was

described as a licence, Mr. Antoniades was described as "the licensor" and Mr. Villiers was described as "the licensee." The agreement recited that

"the licensor is not willing to grant the licensee exclusive possession of any part of the rooms hereinafter referred to" and that "the licensee is anxious to secure the use of the rooms notwithstanding that such use be in common with the licensor and such other licensees or invitees as the licensor may permit from time to time to use the said rooms."

The material provisions of the agreement were as follows:

"By this licence the licensor licences the licensee to use (but not exclusively) all those rooms (hereinafter referred to as 'the rooms') on the top flat (1 bedroom, 1 bed-sitting-room, the kitchen and bathroom) of the building ... 6, Whiteley Road, S.E.19 ... together with the use of the furniture fixtures and effects now in the rooms (more particularly set out in the schedule of contents annexed hereto) from February 14, 1985 for the sum of £87 per calendar month on the following terms and conditions: (1) The licensee agrees to pay the said sum of £87 (on the 14th of each month) monthly in advance. ... (3) The licensee shall use his best endeavours amicably and peaceably to share the use of the rooms with the licensor and with such other licensees or invitees whom the licensor shall from time to time permit to use the rooms and shall not interfere with or otherwise obstruct such shared occupation in any way whatsoever. ... (10) The licensee shall not do or suffer to be done in the rooms any act or thing which may be a nuisance cause of damage or annoyance to the licensor and the other occupiers or users of the rooms ... (12). The licensee ... will not use the rooms in any illegal or immoral way. ... (16) The licensor shall be entitled at any time to use the rooms together with the licensee and permit other persons to use all of the rooms together with the licensee. ... (17) This licence is personal to the licensee and shall not permit the use of the rooms by any person whatsoever and only the licensor will have the right to use or permit the use of the rooms as described in clause 16. The licensee under no circumstances will have the right to allow any other people of his choice to use the rooms in any way. ... (22) The licensee (occupier) declares that he is over 18 years old and understands this licence. ... (23) The real intention of the parties in all surrounding circumstances is to create this licence which is not coming under the Rent Acts and is binding as written. (24) This licence represents the entire agreement of the parties and no oral or other agreements were made and no different explanations or representations were made and only agreements in writing will be legally binding. (25) The licensee read and understood this licence and received copy and the licensee understands that all rooms and all parts of the dwelling will be shared and no exclusive possession of any part of the whole will be allowed to the licensees by the licensor under any circumstances."

There then followed the schedule of furniture and then a new clause as follows:

"26. Subject to clause 21 this licence may be terminated by one month's notice in writing given by either party at any time and the licensor reserves the right of eviction without court order."

That agreement was signed by Mr. Villiers in five places and each of his signatures was witnessed.

Either then or thereafter, Mr. Villiers signed an addendum to the agreement whereby Mr. Villiers:

"Agrees that the licence signed on February 9, 1985 does not come under the Rent Acts and the flat is for single people sharing and if Mr. Villiers marries any occupier of the flat then Mr. Villiers will give notice and vacate the flat at 6, Whiteley Road, London S.E.19. The owner Mr. Antoniades did not promise any other accommodation in any way. No persons will have exclusive possession of the above flat as agreed."

Mr. Antoniades entered into a separate agreement and a separate addendum with Miss Bridger. The agreement and the addendum were in the same form, bore the same date, were executed on the same day and were signed and witnessed in the same way as the agreement and addendum entered into by Mr. Villiers.

Thereupon Mr. Villiers and Miss Bridger entered into occupation of the rooms comprised in the agreement. Mr. Antoniades has never attempted to use any of the rooms or authorised any other person to use the rooms.

The appellants, Mr. Villiers and Miss Bridger, claim that they became tenants of the whole of the attic flat. Mr. Antoniades contends that each appellant is a licensee.

My Lords, ever since 1915 the Rent Acts have protected some tenants of residential accommodation with security of tenure and maximum rents. The scope and effect of the Rent Acts have been altered from time to time and the current legislative protection is contained in the Rent Act 1977. Section 1 of the Act of 1977, reproducing earlier enactments, provides:

"Subject to this Part of this Act, a tenancy under which a dwelling-house (which may be a house or part of a house) is let as a separate dwelling is a protected tenancy for the purposes of this Act."

Parties to an agreement cannot contract out of the Rent Acts; if they were able to do so the Acts would be a dead letter because in a state of housing shortage a person seeking residential accommodation may agree to anything to obtain shelter. The Rent Acts protect a tenant but they do not protect a licensee. Since parties to an agreement cannot contract out of the Rent Acts, a document which expresses the intention, genuine or bogus, of both parties or of one party to create a licence will nevertheless create a tenancy if the rights and obligations enjoyed and imposed satisfy the legal requirements of a tenancy. A person seeking residential accommodation may concur in any expression of intention in order to obtain shelter. Since parties to an agreement cannot contract out of the Rent Acts, a document expressed in the language of a licence must nevertheless be examined and construed by the court in order to decide whether the rights and obligations enjoyed and imposed create a licence or a tenancy. A person seeking residential accommodation may sign a document couched in any language in order to obtain shelter. Since parties to an agreement cannot contract out of the Rent Acts, the grant of a tenancy to two persons jointly cannot be concealed, accidentally or by design, by the creation of two documents in the form of licences. Two persons seeking residential accommodation may sign any number of documents in order to obtain joint shelter. In considering one or more documents for the purpose of deciding whether a tenancy has been created, the court must consider the surrounding circumstances including any relationship between the prospective occupiers, the course of negotiations and the nature and extent of the accommodation and the intended and actual mode of occupation of the accommodation. If the owner of a one-bedroomed flat granted a licence to a husband to occupy the flat provided he shared the flat with his wife and nobody else and granted a similar licence to the wife provided she shared the flat with the husband and nobody else, the court would be bound to consider the effect of both documents together. If the licence to the husband required him to pay a licence fee of £50 per month and the licence to the wife required her to pay a further licence fee of £50 per month, the two documents read together in the light of the property to be occupied and the obvious intended mode of occupation would confer exclusive occupation on the husband and wife jointly and a tenancy at the rent of £100.

Landlords dislike the Rent Acts and wish to enjoy the benefits of letting property without the burden of the restrictions imposed by the Acts. Landlords believe that the Rent Acts unfairly interfere with freedom of contract and exacerbate the housing shortage. Tenants on the other hand believe that the Acts are a necessary protection against the exploitation of people who do not own the freehold or long leases of their homes. The court lacks the knowledge and the power to form any judgment on these arguments which fall to be considered and determined by Parliament. The duty of the court is to enforce the Acts and in so doing to observe one principle which is inherent in the Acts and has been long recognised, the principle that parties cannot contract out of the Acts.

The enjoyment of exclusive occupation for a term in consideration of periodical payments creates a tenancy, save in exceptional circumstances not relevant to these appeals: see *Street* v. *Mountford* [1985] A.C. 809, 826–827. The grant of one room with exclusive occupation in consideration of a periodic payment creates a tenancy, although if the room is not a dwelling, the tenant is not protected by the Rent Acts: see *Curl* v. *Angelo* [1948] 2 All E.R. 189. The grant of one room with exclusive occupation as a dwelling creates a tenancy but if a tenant shares some other essential living premises such as a kitchen with his landlord or other persons, the room is not let as a separate dwelling within the meaning of section 1 of the Rent Act 1977: see *Neale* v. *Del Soto* [1945] K.B. 144 and *Cole* v. *Harris* [1945] K.B. 474. Section 21 of the Act of 1977 confers some rights on a tenant who shares essential living premises with his landlord, and section 22 confers protection on a tenant who shares some essential living premises with persons other than the landlord.

If, under an agreement, the owner of residential accommodation provides services or attendance and retains possession for that purpose the occupier is a lodger and the agreement creates a licence. Under an agreement for the exclusive occupation of a room or rooms consisting of a dwelling for periodic payments then, save in the exceptional circumstances mentioned in *Street* v. *Mountford* [1985] A.C. 809, 826–827, a single occupier, if he is not a lodger, must be a tenant. The agreement may provide, expressly or by implication, power for the owner to enter the dwelling to inspect or repair but if the occupier is entitled to the use and enjoyment of the dwelling and is not a lodger he is in exclusive occupation and the agreement creates a tenancy.

Where residential accommodation is occupied by two or more persons the occupiers may be licensees or tenants of the whole or each occupier may be a separate tenant of part. In the present appeals the only question raised is whether the occupiers are licensees or tenants of the whole.

In the first appeal under consideration the company entered into four separate agreements with four separate persons between 1982 and 1985. The agreements were in the same form save that the periodical sum payable under one agreement did not correspond to the sum payable pursuant to any other agreement. The company was not bound to make agreements in the same form or to require any payment. The agreement signed by Mr. Vaughan in 1982 did not and could not entitle or compel Mr. Vaughan to become a joint tenant of the whole of the flat with Mr. Cook in 1985 on the terms of Mr. Vaughan's agreement or on the terms of Mr. Cook's agreement or on the terms of any other agreement either alone with Mr. Cook or together with any other persons. In 1985 Mr. Vaughan did not agree to become a joint tenant of the flat with Mr.

Cook or anybody else. In 1985, in the events which had happened, the company possessed the right reserved to the company by clause 2(3) of Mr. Vaughan's agreement to authorise Mr. Cook to share the use of the flat in common with Mr. Vaughan. In 1985 Mr. Vaughan orally agreed with Mr. Cook that if the company authorised Mr. Cook to use the flat in common with Mr. Vaughan, then Mr. Vaughan would allow Mr. Cook to occupy a specified bedroom in the flat and share the occupation of the other parts of the flat excluding the other three bedrooms. Mr. Vaughan's agreement with the company did not prevent him from entering into this oral agreement with Mr. Cook. Under the standard form agreement the company did not retain power to allocate the four bedrooms but delegated this power to the occupiers for the time being. If the occupiers had failed to allocate the bedrooms the company would have been obliged to terminate one or more of the agreements. The respondents claim that they are joint tenants of the flat. No single respondent claims to be a tenant of a bedroom.

The Court of Appeal, ante. p. 422c, (Fox and Mustill L.JJ., Sir George Waller dissenting), concluded that the four respondents were jointly entitled to exclusive occupation of the flat. I am unable to agree. If a landlord who owns a three-bedroom flat enters into three separate independent tenancies with three independent tenants each of whom is entitled to one bedroom and to share the common parts, then the three tenants, if they agree, can exclude anyone else from the flat. But they do not enjoy exclusive occupation of the flat jointly under the terms of their tenancies. In the present case, if the four respondents had been jointly entitled to exclusive occupation of the flat then, on the death of one of the respondents, the remaining three would be entitled to joint and exclusive occupation. But, in fact, on the death of one respondent the remaining three would not be entitled to joint and exclusive occupation of the flat. They could not exclude a fourth person nominated by the company. I would allow the appeal.

In the first appeal the four agreements were independent of one another. In the second appeal the two agreements were interdependent. Both would have been signed or neither. The two agreements must therefore be read together. Mr. Villiers and Miss Bridger applied to rent the flat jointly and sought and enjoyed joint and exclusive occupation of the whole of the flat. They shared the rights and the obligations imposed by the terms of their occupation. They acquired joint and exclusive occupation of the flat in consideration of periodical payments and they therefore acquired a tenancy jointly. Mr. Antoniades required each of them, Mr. Villiers and Miss Bridger, to agree to pay one half of each aggregate periodical payment, but this circumstance cannot convert a tenancy into a licence. A tenancy remains a tenancy even though the landlord may choose to require each of two joint tenants to agree expressly to pay one half of the rent. The tenancy conferred on Mr. Villiers and Miss Bridger the right to occupy the whole flat as their dwelling. Clause 16 reserved to Mr. Antoniades the power at any time to go into occupation of the flat jointly with Mr. Villiers and Miss Bridger. The exercise of that power would at common law put an end to the exclusive occupation of the flat by Mr. Villiers and Miss Bridger, terminate the tenancy of Mr. Villiers and Miss Bridger, and convert Mr. Villiers and Miss Bridger into licensees. But the powers reserved to Mr. Antoniades by clause 16 cannot be lawfully exercised because they are inconsistent with the provisions of the Rent Acts.

When Mr. Antoniades entered into the agreements dated Februay 9, 1985 with Mr. Villiers and Miss Bridger and when Mr. Antoniades allowed Mr. Villiers and Miss Bridger to occupy the flat, it is clear from the negotiations which had taken place, from the surrounding circumstances, and from subsequent events, that Mr. Antoniades did not intend in February 1985, immediately or contemporaneously, to share occupation or to authorise any other person to deprive Mr. Villiers and Miss Bridger of exclusive occupation of the flat. Clause 16, if genuine, was a reservation by a landlord of a power at some time during the currency of the tenancy to share occupation with the tenant. The exclusive occupation of the tenant coupled with the payment of rent created a tenancy which at common law could be terminated and converted into a licence as soon as the landlord exercised his power to share occupation. But under the Rent Acts, if a contractual tenancy is terminated, the Acts protect the occupiers from eviction.

If a landlord creates a tenancy under which a flat is let as a separate dwelling the tenancy is a protected tenancy under section 1 of the Rent Act 1977. After the termination of a protected tenancy the protected tenant becomes a statutory tenant under section 2 of the Act. By section 3(1):

"So long as he retains possession, a statutory tenant shall observe and be entitled to the benefit of all the terms and conditions of the original contract of tenancy, so far as they are consistent with the provisions of this Act."

By section 98 a court shall not make an order for possession of a dwelling house which is subject to a protected tenancy or a statutory tenancy unless the court considers that it is reasonable to make such an order and is satisfied either that alternative accommodation is available or that certain other conditions are satisfied. The landlord cannot dispense with an order of the court and enter into possession in exercise of his common law powers.

Where a landlord creates a tenancy of a flat and reserves the right to go into exclusive occupation at any time of the whole or part of the flat with or without notice, that reservation is inconsistent with the provisions of the Rent Acts and cannot be enforced without an order of the court under section 98. Where a landlord creates a tenancy of a flat and reserves the right to go into occupation of the whole or part of the flat with or without notice, jointly with the existing tenants, that reservation also is inconsistent with the provisions of the Acts. Were it otherwise every tenancy agreement would be labelled a licence and would contract out of the Rent Acts by reserving power to the landlord to share possession with the tenant at any time after the commencement of the term.

Clause 16 is a reservation to Mr. Antoniades of the right to go into occupation or to nominate others to enjoy occupation of the whole of the flat jointly with Mr. Villiers and Miss Bridger. Until that power is exercised Mr. Villiers and Miss Bridger are jointly in exclusive occupation of the whole of the flat making periodical payments and they are therefore tenants. The Rent Acts prevent the exercise of a power which would destroy the tenancy of Mr. Villiers and Miss Bridger and would deprive them of the exclusive occupation of the flat which they are now enjoying. Clause 16 is inconsistent with the provisions of the Rent Acts.

There is a separate and alternative reason why clause 16 must be ignored. Clause 16 was not a genuine reservation to Mr. Antoniades of a power to share the flat and a power to authorise other persons to share the flat. Mr. Antoniades did not genuinely intend to exercise the powers save possibly to bring pressure to bear to obtain possession. Clause 16 was only intended to deprive Mr. Villiers and Miss Bridger of the protection of the Rent Acts. Mr. Villiers and Miss Bridger had no choice in the matter.

In the notes of Judge Macnair, Mr. Villiers is reported as saying that: "He [Mr. Antoniades] kept going on about it being a licence and not in the Rent Act. I didn't know either but was pleased to have a place after three or four months of chasing." The notes of Miss Bridger's evidence include this passage: "I didn't understand what was meant by exclusive possession or licence. Signed because so glad to move in. Had been looking for three months."

In *Street* v. *Mountford* [1985] A.C. 809, 825, I said:

"Although the Rent Acts must not be allowed to alter or influence the construction of an agreement, the court should, in my opinion, be astute to detect and frustrate sham devices and artificial transactions whose only object is to disguise the grant of a tenancy and to evade the Rent Acts."

It would have been more accurate and less liable to give rise to misunderstandings if I had substituted the word "pretence" for the references to "sham devices" and "artificial transactions." *Street* v. *Mountford* was not a case which involved a pretence concerning exclusive possession. The agreement did not mention exclusive possession and the owner conceded that the occupier enjoyed exclusive possession. In *Somma* v. *Hazelhurst* [1978] 1 W.L.R. 1014 and other cases considered in *Street* v. *Mountford*, the owner wished to let residential accommodation but to avoid the Rent Acts. The occupiers wished to take a letting of residential accommodation. The owner stipulated for the execution of agreements which pretended that exclusive possession was not to be enjoyed by the occupiers. The occupiers were obliged to acquiesce with this pretence in order to obtain the accommodation. In my opinion the occupiers either did not understand the language of the agreements or assumed, justifiably, that in practice the owner would not violate their privacy. The owner's real intention was to rely on the language of the agreement to escape the Rent Acts. The owner allowed the occupiers to enjoy jointly exclusive occupation and accepted rent. A tenancy was created. *Street* v. *Mountford* reasserted three principles. First, parties to an agreement cannot contract out of the Rent Acts. Secondly, in the absence of special circumstances, not here relevant, the enjoyment of exclusive occupation for a term in consideration of periodic payments creates a tenancy. Thirdly, where the language of licence contradicts the reality of lease, the facts must prevail. The facts must prevail over the language in order that the parties may not contract out of the Rent Acts. In the present case clause 16 was a pretence.

The fact that clause 16 was a pretence appears from its terms and from the negotiations. Clause 16 in terms conferred on Mr. Antoniades and other persons the right to share the bedroom occupied by Mr. Villiers and Miss Bridger. Clause 16 conferred power on Mr. Antoniades to convert the sitting-room occupied by Mr. Villiers and Miss Bridger into a bedroom which could be jointly occupied by Mr. Villiers, Miss Bridger, Mr. Antoniades and any person or persons nominated by Mr. Antoniades. The facilities in the flat were not suitable for sharing between strangers. The flat, situated in an attic with a sloping roof, was too small for sharing between strangers. If clause 16 had been genuine there would have been some discussion between Mr. Antoniades, Mr. Villiers and Miss Bridger as to how clause 16 might be operated in practice and in whose favour it was likely to be operated. The addendum imposed on Mr. Villiers and Miss Bridger sought to add plausibility to the pretence of sharing by forfeiting the right of Mr. Villiers and Miss Bridger to continue to occupy the flat if their double-bedded romance blossomed into wedding bells. Finally and significantly, Mr. Antoniades never made any attempt to obtain increased income from the flat by exercising the powers which clause 16 purported to reserve to him. Clause 16 was only designed to disguise the grant of a tenancy and to contract out of the Rent Acts. In this case in the Court of Appeal, *ante,* p. 446C–D, Bingham L.J. said:

"The written agreements cannot possibly be construed as giving the occupants, jointly or severally, exclusive possession of the flat or any part of it. They stipulate with reiterated emphasis that the occupants shall not have exclusive possession."

My Lords, in *Street* v. *Mountford* [1985] A.C. 809, this House stipulated with reiterated emphasis that an express statement of intention is not decisive and that the court must pay attention to the facts and surrounding circumstances and to what people do as well as to what people say.

In *Somma* v. *Hazelhurst* [1978] 1 W.L.R. 1014, a young unmarried couple applied to take a double bedsitting-room in order that they might live together. Each signed an agreement to pay £38.80 per month to share the use of the room with the owner and with not more than one other person at any one time. The couple moved into the bedsitting-room and enjoyed exclusive occupation. In terms the owner reserved the right to share living and sleeping quarters with the two applicants. If the couple parted and the youth moved out, the owner could require the damsel to share her living and sleeping quarters with the owner and with a stranger or with one of them or move out herself. The couple enjoyed exclusive occupation until the owner decided to live with them or until one of their agreements was terminated. The right reserved to the owner to require the applicants or one of the applicants to share with the owner or some other third party was contrary to the provisions of the Rent Acts and, in addition was, in the circumstances, a pretence intended only to get round the Rent Acts.

In *Aldrington Garages Ltd.* v. *Fielder* (1978) 37 P. & C.R. 461, Mr. Fielder and Miss Maxwell applied to take a self-contained flat in order that they might live together. Each signed an agreement to pay £54.17 per month to share the use of the flat with one other person. The couple moved into the flat and enjoyed exclusive occupation. In terms if the couple parted and Mr. Fielder moved out, the owner could require Miss Maxwell to share her living and sleeping quarters with a stranger or move out herself. Mr. Fielder and Miss Maxwell enjoyed exclusive occupation unless and until one of their agreements was terminated. The right reserved to the owner to require Miss Maxwell to share with a third party if Mr. Fielder's agreement was terminated and to require Mr. Fielder to share with a third party if Miss Maxwell's agreement was terminated was contrary to the provisions of the Rent Acts and in addition was, in the circumstances, a pretence intended only to get round the Rent Acts.

In *Sturolson and Co.* v. *Weniz* (1984) 17 H.L.R. 140, the defendant and a friend applied to take a self-contained flat for the occupation of the defendant, his wife and the friend. The defendant and his friend signed agreements to pay £100 per month to share the flat with such other persons as might be nominated or approved by the owner from time to time. The defendant, his wife and the friend, moved into the flat and enjoyed exclusive occupation. In terms the defendant and the friend paid between them £200 per month for a flat which could be invaded by one or more strangers at any time. The owner's agent gave the game away by saying that the owner was happy so long as he received £200 per month from the flat. The defendant and the friend enjoyed exclusive occupation. The right reserved to the owner to require them to share with others was contrary to the provisions of the Rent Acts and was in any event a pretence intended only to get round the Rent Acts.

In *Street* v. *Mountford* [1985] A.C. 809, 825, this House disapproved of the decisions of the Court of Appeal in *Somma* v. *Hazelhurst* [1978] 1 W.L.R. 1014, *Aldrington Garages Ltd.* v. *Fielder*, 37 P. & C.R. 461 and *Sturolson and Co.* v. *Weniz*, 17 H.L.R. 140, which held that the occupiers were only licensees and not tenants.

In *Crancour Ltd.* v. *Da Silvaesa* (1986) 18 H.L.R. 265, 276 in which leave was given to defend proceedings under R.S.C., Ord. 113, Ralph Gibson L.J. referring to the disapproval by this House in *Street* v. *Mountford* [1985] A.C. 809, 825, of the decision of the Court of Appeal in *Somma* v. *Hazelhurst*, said:

"As I understand the reference to the 'sham nature of the obligation,' namely that of sharing the room in common with other persons nominated by the landlord, the House of Lords is there saying, first, that the agreement in that case constituted the grant of exclusive possession; secondly, that the written obligation to share the room was not effective to alter the true nature of the grant; and, thirdly, that, on the facts of the case, it should have been clear to the Court of Appeal that the landlord cannot have intended the term as to sharing occupation to be a true statement of the nature of the possession intended to be enjoyed by the 'licensees.' "

I agree with this analysis.

In *Hadjiloucas* v. *Crean* [1988] 1 W.L.R. 1006, two single ladies applied to take a two-roomed flat with kitchen and bathroom. Each signed an agreement to pay £260 per month to share the use of the flat with one other person. The two ladies moved into the flat and enjoyed exclusive occupation. In terms, if the agreement of one lady was terminated, the owner could require the other to share the flat with a stranger. The judge in the county court decided that the agreements only created licences. The Court of Appeal ordered a retrial in order that all the facts might be investigated. Since, however, the two ladies applied for and enjoyed exclusive occupation unless and until one of their agreements was terminated, the ladies acquired a tenancy protected by the Rent Acts. The reservation to the owner of the right at common law to require one of the ladies to share the flat with a stranger was a pretence.

My Lords, in each of the cases which were disapproved by this House in *Street* v. *Mountford* [1985] A.C. 809, and in the second appeal now under consideration, there was, in my opinion, the grant of a joint tenancy for the following reasons. (1) The applicants for the flat applied to rent the flat jointly and to enjoy exclusive occupation. (2) The landlord allowed the applicants jointly to enjoy exclusive occupation and accepted rent. A tenancy was created. (3) The power reserved to the landlord to deprive the applicants of exclusive occupation was inconsistent with the provisions of the Rent Acts. (4) Moreover in all the circumstances the power which the landlord insisted upon to deprive the applicants of exclusive occupation was a pretence only intended to deprive the applicants of the protection of the Rent Acts.

The Court of Appeal, *ante*, p. 438E, (Bingham and Mann L.JJ.) decided in the second appeal under consideration that Mr. Villiers and Miss Bridger were licensees. I would restore the order of Judge MacNair who declared that Mr. Villiers and Miss Bridger were tenants protected by the Rent Acts.

Lord Oliver said (at 466–472):

My Lords, since lettings of residential property of an appropriate rateable value attract the consequences of controlled rent and security of tenure provided by the Rent Acts, it is not, perhaps, altogether surprising that those who derive their income from residential property are constantly seeking to attain the not always reconcilable objectives on the one hand of keeping their property gainfully occupied and, on the other, of framing their contractual arrangements with the occupants in such a way as to avoid, if they can, the application of the Acts. Since it is only a letting which attracts the operation of the Acts, such endeavours normally take the form of entering into contractual arrangements designed, on their face, to ensure that no estate is created in the occupant for the time being and that his occupation of the land derives merely from a personal and revocable permission granted by way of licence. The critical question, however, in every case is not simply how the arrangement is presented to the outside world in the relevant documentation, but what is the true nature of the arrangement. The decision of this House in *Street* v. *Mountford* [1985] A.C. 809 established quite clearly that if the true legal effect of the arrangement entered into is that the occupier of residential property has exclusive possession of the property for an ascertainable period in return for periodical money payments, a tenancy is created, whatever the label the parties may have chosen to attach to it. Where, as in that case, the circumstances show that the occupant is the only occupier realistically contemplated and the premises are inherently suitable only for single occupation, there is, generally, very little difficulty. Such an occupier normally has exclusive possession, as indeed she did in *Street* v. *Mountford*, where such possession was conceded, unless the owner retains control and unrestricted access for the purpose of providing attendance and services. As my noble and learned friend, Lord Templeman, observed in that case, the occupier in those circumstances is either a lodger or a tenant. Where, however, the premises are such as, by their nature, to lend themselves to multiple occupation and they are in fact occupied in common by a number of persons under different individual agreements with the owner, more difficult problems arise. These two appeals, at different ends of the scale, are illustrations of such problems.

The relevant facts have been fully set out in the speech of my noble and learned friend, Lord Templeman, which I have had the advantage of reading in draft, and I reiterate them only to the extent necessary to emphasise the points which appear to me to be of critical importance.

ANTONIADES *v.* VILLIERS AND ANOTHER

The appellants in this appeal are a young couple who at all material times were living together as man and wife. In about November 1984 they learned from a letting agency that a flat was available in a house at 6, Whiteley Road, London S.E.19, owned by the respondent, Mr. Antoniades. They inspected the flat together and were told that the rent would be £174 per month. They were given the choice of having the bedroom furnished with a double bed or two single beds and they chose a double bed. So, right from the inception, there was never any question but that the appellants were seeking to establish a joint home and they have, at all material times, been the sole occupants of the flat.

There is equally no question but that the premises are not suitable for occupation by more than one couple, save on a very temporary basis. The small living-room contains a sofa capable of being converted into a double bed and also a bed-table capable of being opened out to form a narrow single bed. The appellants did in fact have a friend to stay with them for a time in what the trial judge found to be cramped conditions, but the size of the accommodation and the facilities available clearly do not make the flat suitable for multiple occupation. When it came to drawing up the contractual arrangements under which the appellants were to be let into possession, each was asked to and did sign a separate licence agreement in the terms set out in the speech of my noble and learned friend, Lord Templeman, under which each assumed an individual, but not a joint, responsibility for payment of one half of the sum £174 previously quoted as the rent.

There is an air of total unreality about these documents read as separate and individual licences in the light of the circumstance that the appellants were together seeking a flat as a quasi-matrimonial home. A separate licensee does not realistically assume responsibility for all repairs and all outgoings. Nor in the circumstances can any realistic significance be given to clauses 16 and 17 of the document. It cannot realistically have been contemplated that the respondent would either himself use or occupy any part of the flat or put some other person in to share accommodation specifically adapted for the occupation by a couple living together. These clauses cannot be considered as seriously intended to have any practical operation or to serve any purpose apart from the purely technical one of seeking to avoid the ordinary legal consequences attendant upon letting the appellants into possession at a monthly rent. The unreality is enhanced by the reservation of the right of eviction without court order, which cannot seriously have been thought to be effective, and by the accompanying agreement not to get married, which can only have been designed to prevent a situation arising in which it would be quite impossible to argue that the "licensees" were enjoying separate rights of occupation.

The conclusion seems to me irresistible that these two so-called licences, executed contemporaneously and entered into in the circumstances already outlined, have to be read together as constituting in reality one single transaction under which the appellants became joint occupiers. That of course does not conclude the case because the question still remains, what is the effect?

The document is clearly based upon the form of document which was upheld by the Court of Appeal as an effective licence in *Somma* v. *Hazelhurst* [1978] 1 W.L.R. 1014. That case, which rested on what was said to be the impossibility of the two licensees having between them exclusive possession, was overruled in *Street* v. *Mountford* [1985] A.C. 809. It was, however, a case which related to a single room and it is suggested that a similar agreement relating to premises containing space which could, albeit uncomfortably, accommodate another person is not necessarily governed by the same principle. On the other hand, the trial judge found that apart from the few visits by the respondent (who, on all but one occasion, sought admission by knocking on the door) no one shared with the appellants and that they had exclusive possession. He held that the licences were "artificial transactions designed to evade the Rent Acts," that a tenancy was created and that the appellants occupied as joint tenants.

His decision was reversed by the Court of Appeal, *ante*, p. 438E, on, broadly, the grounds that he had erred in treating the subsequent conduct of the parties as admissible as an aid to construction of the agreements and that in so far as the holding above referred to constituted a finding that the licences were a sham, that was unsupported by the evidence inasmuch as the appellants' intention that they should enjoy exclusive possession was not shared by the respondent. The licences could not, therefore, be said to mask the real intention of the parties and fell to be construed by reference to what they said in terms.

If the documents fall to be taken seriously at their face value and to be construed according to their terms, I see, for my part, no escape from the conclusion at which the Court of Appeal arrived. If it is once accepted that the respondent enjoyed the right—whether he exercised it or not—to share the accommodation with the appellants, either himself or by introducing one or more other persons to use the flat with them, it is, as it seems to me, incontestable that the appellants cannot claim to have had exclusive possession. The appellants' case therefore rests, as Mr. Colyer frankly admits, upon upholding the judge's approach that the true transaction contemplated was that the appellants should jointly enjoy exclusive possession and that the licences were mere sham or window-dressing to indicate legal incidents which were never seriously intended in fact, but which would be inconsistent with the application to that transaction of the Rent Acts. Now to begin with, I do not, for my part, read the notes of the judge's judgment as showing that he construed the agreement in the light of what the parties subsequently did. I agree entirely with the Court of Appeal that if he did that he was in error. But though subsequent conduct is irrelevant as an aid to construction, it is certainly admissible as evidence on the question of whether the documents were or were not genuine documents giving effect to the parties' true intentions. Broadly what is said by

Mr. Colyer is that nobody acquainted with the circumstances in which the parties had come together and with the physical lay-out and size of the premises could seriously have imagined that the clauses in the licence which, on the face of them, contemplate the respondent and an apparently limitless number of other persons moving in to share the whole of the available accommodation, including the bedroom, with what, to all intents and purposes, was a married couple committed to paying £174 a month in advance, were anything other than a smoke-screen; and the fact the respondent, who might be assumed to want to make the maximum profit out of the premises, never sought to introduce anyone else is at least some indication that that is exactly what it was. Adopting the definition of a sham formulated by Purchas L.J. in *Hadjiloucas* v. *Crean* [1988] 1 W.L.R. 1006, 1013, Mr. Colyer submits that the licences clearly incorporate clauses by which neither party intended to be bound and which were obviously a smoke-screen to cover the real intentions of both contracting parties. In the Court of Appeal, *ante*, pp. 446H–447A, Bingham L.J. tested the matter by asking two questions, *viz*.: (1) on what grounds, if one party had left the premises, could the remaining party have been made liable for anything more than the £87 which he or she had agreed to pay, and (2) on what ground could they have resisted a demand by the respondent to introduce a further person into the premises? For my part, however, I do not see how this helps. The assumed negative answers prove nothing, for they rest upon the assumption that the licences are not sham documents, which is the very question in issue.

If the real transaction was, as the judge found, one under which the appellants became joint tenants with exclusive possession, on the footing that the two agreements are to be construed together, then it would follow that they were together jointly and severally responsible for the whole rent. It would equally follow that they could effectively exclude the respondent and his nominees.

Although the facts are not precisely on all fours with *Somma* v. *Hazelhurst* [1978] 1 W.L.R. 1014, they are strikingly similar and the judge was, in my judgment, entitled to conclude that the appellants had exclusive possession of the premises. I read his finding that, "the licences are artificial transactions designed to evade the Rent Acts" as a finding that they were sham documents designed to conceal the true nature of the transaction. There was, in my judgment, material on which he could properly reach this conclusion and I, too, would allow the appeal.

A. G. SECURITIES *v*. VAUGHAN AND OTHERS

The facts in this appeal are startlingly different from those in the case of *Antoniades*. To begin with the appeal concerns a substantial flat in a mansion block consisting of four bedrooms, a lounge, a sitting-room and usual offices. The trial judge found, as a fact, that the premises could without difficulty provide residential accommodation for four persons. There is no question but that the agreements with which the appeal is concerned reflect the true bargain between the parties. It is the purpose and intention of both parties to each agreement that it should confer an individual right on the licensee named, that he should be liable only for the payment which he had undertaken, and that his agreement should be capable of termination without reference to the agreements with other persons occupying the flat. The judge found that the agreements were not shams and that each of the four occupants had arrived independently of one another and not as a group. His finding was that there was never a group of persons coming to the flat altogether. That has been challenged because, it is said, the evidence established that initially in 1977 and 1978 there was one occupant who was joined by three others who, although they came independently and not as a trio, moved in at about the same time. Central heating was then installed, so that the weekly payments fell to be increased and new agreements were signed by the four occupants contemporaneously. Speaking for myself, I cannot see how this can make any difference to the terms upon which the individuals were in occupation. If they were in as licensees in the first instance, the mere replacement of their agreements by new agreements in similar form cannot convert them into tenants, and the case has, in my judgment, to be approached on the footing that agreements with the occupiers were entered into separately and individually. The only questions are those of the effect of each agreement vis-à-vis the individual licensee and whether the agreements collectively had the effect of creating a joint tenancy among the occupants of the premises for the time being by virtue of their having between them exclusive possession of the premises.

Taking first, by way of example, the position of the first occupier to be let into the premises on the terms of one of these agreements, it is, in my judgment, quite unarguable, once any question of sham is out of the way, that he has an estate in the premises which entitles him to exclusive possession. His right, which is, by definition, a right to share use and occupation with such other persons not exceeding three in number as the licensor shall introduce from time to time, is clearly inconsistent with any exclusive possession in him alone even though he may be the only person in physical occupation at a particular time. He has no legal title which will permit him to exclude other persons to whom the licensor may choose to grant the privilege of entry. That must equally apply to the additional licensees who join him. None of them has individually nor have they collectively the right or power lawfully to exclude a further nominee of the licensor within the prescribed maximum.

I pause to note that it has never been contended that any individual occupier has a tenancy of a particular room in the flat with a right to use the remainder of the flat in common with the tenants of other rooms. I can envisage that as a possibility in cases of arrangements of this kind if the facts support the marking out with the landlord's concurrence of a particular room as the exclusive domain of a particular individual. But to support that there would, I think, have to be proved the grant of an identifiable part of the flat and that simply does not fit with the system described in the evidence of the instant case.

The real question—and it is this upon which the respondents rely—is what is the position when the flat is occupied concurrently by all four licensees? What is said then is that the licensor has now exhausted, for the time being, his right of nomination, the four occupants collectively have exclusive possession of the premises because they can collectively exclude the licensor himself. Because, it is argued, (1) they have thus exclusive possession and, (2) there is an ascertainable term during which all have the right to use and occupy, and (3) they are occupying in consideration of the payment of periodic sums of money. *Street* v. *Mountford* [1985] A.C. 809 shows that they are collectively tenants of the premises. They are not lodgers. Therefore they must be tenants. And because each is not individually a tenant, they must together be joint tenants.

My Lords, there appear to me to be a number of fallacies here. In the first place, the assertion of an exclusive possession rests, as it seems to me, upon assuming what it is sought to prove. If, of course, each licence agreement creates a tenancy, each tenant will be sharing with other persons whose rights to be there rest upon their own estates which, once they have been granted, they enjoy in their own right independently of the landlord. Collectively they have the right to exclude everyone other than those who have concurrent estates. But if the licence agreement is what it purports to be, that is to say, merely an agreement for permissive enjoyment as the invitee of the landlord, then each shares the use of the premises with other invitees of the same landlord. The landlord is not excluded for he continues to enjoy the premises through his invitees, even though he may for the time being have precluded himself by contract with each from withdrawing the invitation. Secondly, the fact that under each agreement an individual has the privilege of user and occupation for a term which overlaps the term of user and occupation of other persons in the premises, does not create a single indivisible term of occupation for all four consisting of an amalgam of the individual overlapping periods. Thirdly, there is no single sum of money payable in respect of use and occupation. Each person is individually liable for the amount which he has agreed, which may differ in practice from the amounts paid by all or some of the others.

The respondents are compelled to support their claims by a strange and unnatural theory that, as each occupant terminates his agreement, there is an implied surrender by the other three and an implied grant of a new joint tenancy to them together with the new incumbent when he enters under his individual agreement. With great respect to the majority in the Court of Appeal, this appears to me to be entirely unreal. For my part, I agree with the dissenting judgment of Sir George Waller in finding no unity of interest, no unity of title, certainly no unity of time and, as I think, no unity of possession. I find it impossible to say that the agreements entered into with the respondents created either individually or collectively a single tenancy either of the entire flat or of any part of it. I agree that the appeal should be allowed.

Lords Bridge, Jauncey and Ackner delivered concurring speeches.

Notes

There are two particularly important aspects to *AG Securities* v. *Vaughan* and *Antoniades* v. *Villiers.*

(i) The cases reveal that not all shams are of the same type. In fact, three different types of sham can be distinguished, all three of which arose in *Antoniades* v. *Villiers.* First, the terminology employed in an agreement may misrepresent the true legal category into which the arrangement falls. Secondly, documents may include clauses by which neither party intends to be bound and which are obviously a smokescreen to cover the real intentions of both contracting parties. Thirdly, where there are a number of transactions creating a composite whole the court may look at the overall result of what is achieved rather than considering the individual transactions in isolation. So, where a number of occupiers enter separate licence agreements the courts may treat the occupiers as joint tenants.

(ii) There are within the speeches of their Lordships certain ambiguities as to what constitutes exclusive possession—and whether exclusive possession is different from exclusive occupation. Lord Templeman seems to employ the terms possession and occupation indiscriminately, and for the most part it seems that he regards them as synonymous. However, consider the following passage from Lord Templeman's speech:

Clause 16, if genuine, was a reservation by a landlord of a power at some time during the currency of the tenancy to share occupation with the tenant. The exclusive occupation of the tenant coupled with the payment of rent created a tenancy which at common law could be terminated and converted into a licence as soon as the landlord exercised his power to share occupation. But under the Rent Acts, if a contractual tenancy is terminated, the Acts protect the occupiers from eviction.[54]

This passage is not easy to reconcile with the following part of Lord Oliver's speech:

If the documents fall to be taken seriously at their face value and to be construed according to their terms, I see, for my part, no escape from the conclusion at which the Court of Appeal arrived. If it is at once accepted that the respondent enjoyed the right—whether he exercised it or not—to share the accommodation with the appellants, either himself or by introducing one or more other persons to use the flat with them, it is, as it seems to me, incontestable that the appellants cannot claim to have had exclusive possession.[55]

(ii) Notwithstanding the efforts of the House of Lords to clarify the distinction between a lease and a licence there seems to be no end to the litigation on this difficult issue.[56] In particular, the courts have not always been willing to construe separate, but identical licence agreements as giving rise to a joint tenancy. In *Mikeover Ltd.* v. *Brady*,[57] for example, the issue was similar to that which arose in *Antoniades* v. *Villiers*: an unmarried couple took a flat, signing separate agreements in identical terms. The Court of Appeal held that they were not joint tenants on the basis that they were not jointly liable for the rent. Slade L.J., giving the judgment of the court, said:

[I]t appears to us that unity of interest imports the existence of joint rights and joint obligations. We therefore conclude that the provisions for payment contained in these two agreements (which were genuinely intended to impose and did impose on each party an obligation to pay no more than the sums reserved to the plaintiffs by his or her separate agreement) were incapable in law of creating a joint tenancy, because the monetary obligations of the two

[54] At 461.
[55] At 468–469.
[56] *Aslan* v. *Murphy* (*Nos. 1 & 2*) [1990] 1 W.L.R. 776; *Nicolaou* v. *Pitt* (1989) 21 H.L.R. 487; *Nunn* v. *Dalrymple*, (1990) 59 P. & C.R. 231; *Stribling* v. *Wickham* (1989) 21 H.L.R. 381; *Family Housing Association* v. *Jones* [1990] 1 W.L.R. 779; *Ward* v. *Warnke* (1990) 22 H.L.R. 497.
[57] [1989] 3 All E.R. 618.

parties were not joint obligations and there was accordingly no complete unity of interest.[58]

Bibliographical note

There is an enormous amount of legal literature on the lease/licence distinction. For a synthesis of the recent case law see J. E. Martin, *Residential Security* (1989, Sweet & Maxwell) Chapter 2.

The leading cases which have been reproduced in this section have been discussed in numerous journals:

Street v. *Mountford*

S. Anderson, Licences: traditional law revived? (1985) 48 M.L.R. 712; S. Bridge, *Street* v. *Mountford*—no hiding place [1986] Conv. 344; D. N. Clarke, *Street* v. *Mountford*: the question of intent—a view from down under [1986] Conv. 39; D. C. Hoath, [1986] J.S.W.L. 46; R. Street, Coach and horse trip cancelled?: Rent Act avoidance after *Street* v. *Mountford* [1985] Conv 328; S. Tromans, Leases, licences and the Lords [1985] C.L.J. 551; P. Vincent-Jones, Exclusive possession and exclusive control of private rented housing: a socio-legal critique of the lease-licence distinction (1987) 14 Journal of Law and Society 445.

A.G. Securities v. *Vaughan*; *Antoniades* v. *Villiers*

C. Harpum, Leases, licences, sharing and shams [1989] C.L.J. 19; J. Hill, Shared accommodation and exclusive possession (1989) 52 M.L.R. 408; P. F. Smith, Those who do not remember the past [1989] Conv. 128; D. C. Hoath, [1989] J.S.W.L. 246; P. Sparkes, Breaking flat sharing licences [1989] J.S.W.L. 293.

Some other cases on the lease/licence distinction referred to in the preceding pages have also been commented upon: A. J. Waite, Leases and licences: the true distinguishing test (1987) 50 M.L.R. 226 (*Crancour* v. *Da Silvaesa*); P. T. Evans [1990] J.S.W.L. 128 (*Aslan* v. *Murphy* (*No. 1*); J. Warburton, Leases, licences and "an object of charity" [1990] Conv. 397 (*Family Housing Association* v. *Jones*).

The exploitation of the lease/licence distinction represents merely one of a number of possible ways in which landlords may seek to avoid the impact of protective legislation.[59] For a discussion of the courts' approach to avoidance (not only in the context of housing law) see A. Nicol, Outflanking protective legislation—shams and beyond (1981) 44 M.L.R. 21.

---

[58] At 627.
[59] Other avoidance possibilities are discussed in Chapter 3; company lets (pp. 126–132); holiday lets (pp. 144–148); the provision of board and attendance (pp. 157–162).

(B) CERTAIN TERM

It is an old principle that the term for which a lease is made must be certain. This principle can be easily applied where the duration of the lease is fixed in the agreement. During World War II a problem arose because the courts held that a lease "for the duration of the war" was void at common law since the term of the lease was uncertain in duration.[60] As a result the Validation of War-Time Leases Act 1944 was hurriedly passed, converting such tenancies into leases for a fixed period of 10 years, determinable after the end of the war, usually on one month's notice.

The principle that a tenancy is void for uncertainty of duration is more difficult to apply in the case of periodic tenancies. Nevertheless, the courts have, somewhat pragmatically, reached the conclusion that a tenancy—although of uncertain duration at the outset—will be valid at common law if it can be rendered certain by one of the parties.

Ashburn Anstalt v. *Arnold* [1989] Ch. 1

In May 1973 Matlodge, the freehold owners of commercial premises, entered into an agreement with Arnold, the defendants. Clause 5 of the agreement provided:

From and after completion Arnold shall be at liberty to remain at the property as Licensee and to trade therefrom until September 29, 1973 without payment of rent or any other fee to Matlodge save that Arnold shall pay all outgoings so long as it is in occupation of the property from and after September 29, 1973 Arnold shall be entitled as Licensee to remain at the property and trade therefrom on the like terms save that it can be required by Matlodge Limited to give possession on not less than one quarter's notice in writing upon Matlodge certifying that it is ready at the expiration of such notice forthwith to proceed with the development of the property and the neighbouring property involving inter alia the demolition of the property.

The plaintiffs were successors in title to Matlodge, having acquired the freehold in 1985. Less than a month after completion the plaintiffs wrote to the defendants informing them that they were required to vacate the premises. The defendants refused, and the plaintiffs brought an action for possession. As part of their defence the defendants argued that clause 5 of the agreement created a tenancy which was binding on the plaintiffs.[61]

Fox L.J. said (at 10–13):

It is the plaintiff's case that clause 5 created no term sufficiently identifiable to be capable of recognition by the law, and that accordingly no tenancy was

---

[60] *Lace* v. *Chantler* [1944] K.B. 368.
[61] Under Land Registration Act 1925, s.70(1)(g).

created. For that, the plaintiff relies upon *Lace* v. *Chantler* [1944] K.B. 368. In that case a house was let "for the duration of the war." The Court of Appeal held that a leasehold interest was not created. The basis of that decision was stated by Lord Greene M.R., at p. 370:

"A term created by a leasehold tenancy agreement must be expressed either with certainty and specifically or by reference to something which can, at the time when the lease takes effect, be looked to as a certain ascertainment of what the term is meant to be. In the present case, when this tenancy agreement took effect, the term was completely uncertain. It was impossible to say how long the tenancy would last."

The ambit of the decision in *Lace* v. *Chantler* was limited by the further decision of this court, *In re Midland Railway Co.'s Agreement* [1971] Ch. 725. Russell L.J., giving the judgment of the court in that case, said, at p. 732:

"Now it appears to us that that decision is confined to a case in which that which was purported to be done was simply to create a leasehold interest for a single and uncertain period. The applicability of this matter of certainty to a periodic tenancy was not under consideration."

In the *Midland Railway* case the grant was for a period of six months from June 10, 1920, "and so on from half year to half year until the said tenancy shall be determined." Clause 2 of the agreement provided for the termination of the agreement by three months' written notice given by either party to the other, but subject to a proviso that the landlords should not exercise that right unless they required the premises for their undertaking. The court observed that, in the ordinary case of a periodic tenancy, for example, a yearly tenancy, it was plain that, in one sense at least, it was uncertain at the outset what would be the maximum length of the tenancy; the term would grow from year to year as a single term springing from the original grant. Accordingly, the simple statement of the law that the maximum duration of a term must be certainly known in advance of its taking effect could not have direct reference to periodic tenancies. It had been argued that the reason why the principle of avoidance through uncertainty was not applicable to a periodic tenancy was because either party could at any time define the maximum period of the term by giving notice of determination: neither party was left in a state of unknowing as to his maximum commitment. But it was said that where, by the terms of the agreement, either party was deprived of that power until some event the occurrence of which was uncertain, then that person was in such a state of unknowing. On that argument the conclusion of the court, at p. 733, was:

"In the course of the argument we found this approach logically attractive. Here is one term growing period by period and there is no knowing (on one side) its maximum length, if (on that side) there is no power to determine save in an event the occurrence of which is in point of time uncertain. Why logically should that differ from a lease directly for a term of which the maximum duration is uncertain? But in the end we are persuaded that, there being no authority to prevent us, it is preferable as a matter of justice to hold parties to their clearly expressed bargain rather than to introduce for the first time in 1971 an extension of a doctrine of land law so as to deny the efficacy of that bargain."

In the present case there was an initial term from the date of the agreement of February 28, 1973 until September 29, 1973, the Michaelmas Quarter Day. Thereafter, the term would continue until (a certificate of readiness to proceed having been given) Matlodge should give not less than one quarter's notice to give up possession. It may be that the notice has to take effect on a quarter day calculated from the date of the commencement of the term rather than on one of the usual quarter days: see *Kemp* v. *Derrett* (1814) 3 Camp. 510 and *King* v. *Eversfield* [1897] 2 Q.B. 475; but, as Cotton L.J. said in *In re Threlfall* (1880) 16 Ch.D. 274, 281:

> "I know of no law or principle to prevent two persons agreeing that a yearly tenancy may be determined on whatever notice they like."

We see no reason to limit that approach to yearly tenancies.

So far as *Lace* v. *Chantler* [1944] K.B. 368 is concerned, the present case, it seems to us, is distinguishable. In *Lace* v. *Chantler* the duration of the war could not be predicted and there was no provision for either party to bring the tenancy to an end before the war ended, and that event might itself be very hard to pinpoint. In the present case the arrangement, so far as Matlodge was concerned, would continue until Matlodge determined it by giving not less than a quarter's notice, upon Matlodge giving the required certificate. The event entitling Matlodge to give the certificate might not, of course, occur. But the same applies to the qualifying event for the giving of the landlord's notice in the *Midland Railway Co.'s Agreement* [1971] Ch. 725. The plaintiff says, however, that in this case (unlike the *Midland Railway* case) there is no provision for determination by Arnold & Co. It was said, therefore, that in the absence of notice by Matlodge, the term was uncertain in duration. We do not agree with that. As a matter of construction of the document, the possibilities are as follows.

(i) Arnold & Co. was not entitled to determine the arrangement at all. We reject that entirely. Bearing in mind that Arnold & Co. was not required to pay any rent, such a construction is quite unreal in business terms; Arnold & Co. was not obliged to occupy the premises, and, if it did not occupy, the outgoings would be nil or negligible, so there was no benefit to Matlodge in continuing the relationship.

(ii) Arnold & Co. was required to give more than a quarter's notice. That seems to us equally unreal.

(iii) Arnold & Co. was required to give a quarter's notice. If that is right, the case in substance is really indistinguishable from the *Midland Railway Co.'s Agreement*. The occupancy continues from quarter to quarter until determined.

(iv) Arnold & Co. was required to give notice of less than a quarter or no notice at all—it could simply walk out. Apart, possibly, from the need of some short notice to enable Matlodge to make the premises secure, the latter would do no harm to Matlodge since no rent was payable.

It is not necessary to determine which of the possibilities under heads (iii) and (iv) above is correct. The matter would be capable of resolution by the court. Whatever the correct answer, the position would be free from uncertainty.

The result, in our opinion, is that the arrangement could be brought to an end by both parties in circumstances which are free from uncertainty in the sense that there would be no doubt whether the determining event had occurred. The vice of uncertainty in relation to the duration of a term is that the parties do not know where they stand. Put another way, the court does not know what to enforce. That is not the position here. It seems to us therefore that, as in the *Midland Railway Co.'s Agreement* there is no reason why the court should not hold the parties to their agreement. That is so even though the tenancy is not (or may not be) an ordinary periodic tenancy. The rights of the parties are no more subject to uncertainty than those in the *Midland Railway* case. We do not see why the mere absence of a formula referring to a periodic tenancy or occupancy should alter the position. The nearest one comes to uncertainty is the circumstance that Matlodge might not be able to give a certificate. A similar circumstance existed in the *Midland Railway* case, in that the lessor might not have been able to establish that it needed the premises for its undertakings. The Court of Appeal stated expressly that it did *not* decide the case on the basis that the grantor might have been able to tailor the requirements of its undertaking to satisfy the provisions. The result, in our opinion, is that, contrary to the view of the deputy judge, the agreement of February 28, 1973 conferred upon Arnold & Co. possession of the premises for a term which was not uncertain. Consistently with the statement of principle in *Radaich* v. *Smith*, 101 C.L.R. 209, 222, that creates a tenancy. We appreciate that, as pointed out by the deputy judge, clause 5 is drafted in terms of a licence. But the parties' description of their transaction cannot affect the substance of it: see *Street* v. *Mountford* [1985] A.C. 809, 819F and *Radaich* v. *Smith*, 101 C.L.R. 209, 222.

(C)   IS THE PAYMENT OF RENT NECESSARY?

Ashburn Anstalt v. *Arnold* [1989] Ch. 1

Fox L.J. said (at 9–10):

In *Street* v. *Mountford* [1985] A.C. 809 Lord Templeman, who gave the leading speech, regarded three hallmarks as decisive in favour of a tenancy of residential accommodation, namely exclusive possession, for a term, at a rent: see pp. 826E, 825C and 826G. In the present case it is common ground that Arnold & Co. was always in exclusive occupation of the premises from February 28, 1973, as it was before that date. As regards rent, Arnold & Co. was not required to pay a rent under the provisions of clause 5, nor did it do so. It may be that the sum paid to Arnold & Co. for its leasehold interest took account of the freedom from rent under clause 5. There is, however, no evidence of that. We treat the case as one where no rent was payable. Did that prevent the provisions of clause 5 from creating a tenancy? We do not think so. We are unable to read Lord Templeman's speech in *Street* v. *Mountford* as laying down a principle of "no rent, no lease." In the first place, that would be inconsistent with section 205(1)(xxvii) of the Law Property Act 1925, which defines "Term of years absolute" as "a term of years (taking effect either in possession or in reversion whether or not at a rent) ... " Secondly, it would be inconsistent with the judgment of Windeyer J. in *Radaich* v. *Smith* (1959) 101 C.L.R. 209, 222, which was expressly approved by Lord Templeman in *Street* v. *Mountford*, at p. 827:

" 'What then is the fundamental right which a tenant has which distinguishes his position from that of a licensee? It is an interest in land as distinct from a personal permission to enter the land and use it for some stipulated purpose or purposes. And how is it to be ascertained whether such an interest in land has been given? By seeing whether the grantee was given a legal right of exclusive possession of the land for a term or from year to year or for a life or lives. If he was, he is a tenant.' "

Windeyer J. in this passage makes no reference to a rent.

In the circumstances I conclude that the reservation of a rent is not necessary for the creation of a tenancy. That conclusion involves no departure from Lord Templeman's proposition in *Street* v. *Mountford*, at p. 825:

"If exclusive possession at a rent for a term does not constitute a tenancy then the distinction between a contracutal tenancy and a contractual licence of land becomes wholly unidentifiable."

We are saying only that we do not think that Lord Templeman was stating the quite different proposition that you cannot have a tenancy without a rent.

This approach was followed in *Birrell* v. *Cary*.[62]

Although a rent-free arrangement may constitute a tenancy, a tenant who does not pay rent will not enjoy the benefit of statutory protection. Where no rent is payable the tenant cannot be an assured tenant,[63] nor a protected or statutory tenant,[64] and he falls outside the protective ambit of section 3 of the Protection from Eviction Act 1977.[65]

IV   THE CLASSIFICATION OF TENANCIES

The law recognises a great range of tenancies and gives different names to different types. A fundamental distinction exists between fixed-term tenancies which are granted for a fixed period and periodic tenancies which, at common law, continue until brought to an end by one of the parties.

(A)   FIXED TERM TENANCIES: DIFFERENT TYPES

(1) Tenancy for a Term of Years

This is self-explanatory.

(2) Tenancy Determinable With Life

At common law it was possible to create a tenancy for the period of one's life or, indeed, *pur autre vie*, during the lifetime of another. This used to be a legal estate. Section 1(1) of the Law of Property Act 1925, however, has changed this rule. By section 149(6) of the Act such a lease is converted into one for a fixed period of 90 years, determinable after the death by at least one month's notice in writing, if the lease is granted at a rent.[66]

(3) Reversionary Lease

It is possible to create a lease that takes effect at some future date. Before 1926 this was not possible because of the doctrine of *interesse termini* which meant that actual entry on to the property was usually

---

[62] (1989) 58 P. & C.R. 184.
[63] Housing Act 1988, s.1(2); Sched. 1, para. 3.
[64] Rent Act 1977, s.5(1).
[65] Protection from Eviction Act 1977, s.3A(7)(b).
[66] This type of arrangement must be distinguished from a tenancy for life which operates under the Settled Land Act 1925, but which has nothing to do with the law of landlord and tenant.

necessary before the lease could be effective. This doctrine was, however, abolished by section 149(1) of the Law of Property Act 1925. Section 149(3) imposes limits on the validity of reversionary leases:

A term, at a rent or granted in consideration of a fine, limited after the commencement of this Act to take effect more than 21 years from the date of the instrument purporting to create it, shall be void. . . . [67]

(4) Perpetually Renewable Lease

A lease which gives the tenant the right to renew it as often as it expires is converted by section 145 of the Law of Property Act 1922 into a term of 2,000 years determinable by the lessee but not the lessor.[68] It seems that the courts will try to avoid construing a lease as being perpetually renewable unless there is a clear covenant to this effect.[69] A sub-lease which is perpetually renewable is converted into a lease of 2,000 years less one day.[70]

(5) Concurrent Leases

It is even possible to have leases of the same premises, at the same time, to different lessees. There is little evidence on how much these are used, and little case law.

(B)   USE OF FIXED-TERM TENANCIES

Long fixed-term tenancies are often referred to as "building leases." Under such an arrangement, the lessee pays a low ground rent to his landlord for a period of (say) 99 years; in addition he covenants to erect on the site and keep in repair specified buildings. This form of lease may be used by a landowner who wishes to lease the land to a property developer who will come on to the land and build accommodation. It is sometimes also used where the lessee is to be the occupier of premises already built on the site. Using a "building lease" in these circumstances is of course a fiction but is the result of conveyancing practice in different parts of the country.

Use of leases as the form of tenure for owner-occupation varies significantly in different parts of the country.

---

[67] See *Re Strand and Savoy Properties* [1960] Ch. 582; *Weg Motors* v. *Hales* [1962] Ch. 49.
[68] *Caerphilly Concrete Products Ltd.* v. *Owen* [1972] 1 W.L.R. 372.
[69] *Marjorie Burnett Ltd.* v. *Barclay* (1980) 125 S.J. 199.
[70] *Northchurch Estates* v. *Daniels* [1947] Ch. 117.

Short fixed-term tenancies (say for 7, 14 or even 21 years) are often referred to as "occupation leases." A major difference between these and "building leases" is that a full market rent will more often be paid.

(C)   PERIODIC TENANCIES: DIFFERENT TYPES

(1) Tenancy From Year To Year

This type of tenancy can be created expressly by the grant of a lease to run "from year to year" or "as yearly tenancy." In addition, such a tenancy may be implied from the surrounding circumstances. This may happen, for example, when a fixed term of years comes to an end, and the tenant holds over with the landlord's consent.[71] Whether or not such a tenancy can in fact be inferred may be a difficult question of fact.

A feature of a yearly tenancy, as opposed to other periodic tenancies, is that the common law period of notice to bring it to an end is half a year (rather than a full period) unless there is an express arrangement to the contrary.

(2) Tenancies for Less Than a Year

These may be quarterly, monthly or weekly. The best way of distinguishing these short, periodic tenancies is to consider the period by reference to which rent is paid. If weekly, then the arrangement is a weekly tenancy and so on. In the absence of express agreement, the period of notice to terminate such a tenancy is the full period of the tenancy. This principle is, however, subject to section 5(1) of the Protection from Eviction Act 1977.[72] The possibility of a daily tenancy has been doubted.[73]

Periodic tenancies for periods of less than a year, in particular weekly and monthlytenancies, are the most commonly used in Britain for residential premises.

(3) Tenancy for Discontinuous Periods

There is no requirement that a lease should be for a continuous period.[74] Discontinuous leases are becoming more common as they are being used in the context of the time-sharing of holiday homes (for example, where each time-share owner purchases, for a lump sum, a lease to occupy premises for one week per year for 80 years[75]).

---

[71] *Tickner* v. *Buzzacott* [1965] Ch. 426.
[72] See p. 199.
[73] *Appah* v. *Parncliffe Investments* [1964] 1 W.L.R. 1064.
[74] In *Smallwoods* v. *Sheppards* [1895] 2 Q.B. 627 a lease for three successive bank holidays was regarded as valid.
[75] In *Cottage Holiday Associates Ltd.* v. *Customs & Excise Commissioners* [1983] Q.B. 735 a lease of this type was held not to be for "a term certain exceeding 21 years."

(D) OTHER TENANCIES

(1) "Tenancy at Will"

This concept was originally developed to cover "tenant" farmers who had no fixed term or formal lease. Here, the occupier of the land has no defined estate: he holds the land for no fixed period, but at "at will." The owner of the land can put him out at any time. A tenancy at will may arise by express grant or by implication.[76]

(2) "Tenancy at Sufferance"

This arises where someone who was previously in lawful possession of the land, holds over after his tenancy has expired, without the landlord's consent. In effect, this is similar to squatting,[77] except that a squatter enters the land without the landlord's consent. The interpretation of a situation as giving rise to a tenancy at sufferance is a legal device to prevent the tenant being regarded as a trespasser. (The distinction between a tenancy at will and a tenancy at sufferance is discussed by Viscount Simonds in *Wheeler* v. *Mercer*.[78])

At common law it was well established that both these categories of tenancy could be expanded to become periodic tenancies where rent was paid and accepted. The length of the tenancy would be related to the period in respect of which rent was paid.[79] One result of this principle was that a tenant at sufferance could not be sued for rent; if the landlord acknowledged that rent was owing, this would amount to recognition of a new tenancy. Instead, the landlord would have to bring an action for possession, together with a claim for "mesne profits" for the use and occupation of the property.

In the case of tenancies falling within the scope of statutory schemes of protection it appears that these principles have been modified. In cases governed by the Rent Acts or Housing Acts, the landlord normally has no option but to permit the tenant to remain in possession when the contractual tenancy comes to an end—whether the contractual tenancy is determined by notice to quit or by the expiry of a fixed term. In these circumstances, the court will not infer the creation of a new tenancy even where there is payment and acceptance of rent after the contractual tenancy comes to an end.[80]

Scott L.J. in *Morrison* v. *Jacobs*[81] explained the position in the following terms:

---

[76] *Heslop* v. *Burns* [1974] 3 All E.R. 406; *Cardiothoracic Institute* v. *Shrewdcrest Ltd.* [1986] 1 W.L.R. 368; *Javad* v. *Aqil* [1991] 1 All E.R. 243.

[77] See pp. 29–34.

[78] [1957] A.C. 416 at 426.

[79] *Dougal* v. *McCarthy* [1893] 1 Q.B. 736; *Young* v. *Hargreaves* (1963) 186 E.G. 355.

[80] *Harvey* v. *Stagg* (1978) 247 E.G. 463.

[81] [1945] K.B. 577 at 580.

It is erroneous, I think, to hold, in the case of a dwelling-house to which the Rent Restrictions Acts apply, that where the tenant has remained in possession after a term of years and the landlord has accepted rent from the tenant, any such inference of a consensus *ad idem* between the parties to a new common law tenancy arises, because before the passing of those Acts, in certain circumstances such an inference could be drawn. The relevant consideration is that in the case of a dwelling-house to which the Rent Restrictions Acts apply, where a term of years, has expired, the landlord cannot obtain possession of the house unless he brings himself within the terms of certain provisions of those Acts ...

(3) "Tenancy by Estoppel"

The basis of this type of tenancy has been described by leading commentators in the following terms:

Estoppel is a principle of the law of evidence which precludes parties who have induced others to rely upon their representations from denying the truth of the facts represented. In this context it means that the landlord cannot question the validity of his own grant, nor can the tenant question it once he is in possession and has the benefit of the lease, "for so long as a lessee enjoys everything which his lease purports to grant, how does it concern him what the title of the lessor, or the heir or assignee of his lessor, really is?". ...

Where the landlord's title is defective but the parties are bound by the estoppel just described, there is said to be a tenancy by estoppel. Even though the landlord's want of title is apparent to the parties, both they and their successors in title will be estopped from denying that the grant was effective to create the tenancy that it purported to create. Thus, in effect, there is brought into being a tenancy under which the parties and their successors in title have (as against one another) most of the rights and liabilities of a legal estate.

... If after creating a tenancy by estoppel the landlord later acquires a legal estate out of which the tenancy could be created (as where he purchases the fee simple), this is said to "feed the estoppel": the tenant then at once acquires a tenancy based upon the newly acquired estate in place of his tenancy by estoppel.[82]

A tenant by estoppel is protected by any applicable statutory scheme *vis-à-vis* the landlord by estoppel, but not against the true owner of the land.[82a]

(E)   STATUTORY PROTECTION

The introduction of statutory schemes of protection which provide extensive security of tenure for various categories of tenant has made

---

[82] Megarry & Wade *The Law of Real Property* (5th ed., 1984) pp. 660–662 (notes omitted).
[82a] See Megarry, *The Rent Acts* (11th ed., 1988) p. 67.

the distinction between periodic and fixed-term tenancies less significant than was once the case. In practical terms, a periodic tenancy may provide the same degree of security as a lease granted for 21 years.

It is important to stress at this stage that there is a plethora of schemes of statutory protection, each one being governed by separate legislative provisions. Depending on the precise circumstances of the case a tenancy may be classified as one (or more) of the following:

— an assured tenancy (or assured shorthold tenancy) under the Housing Act 1988;
— a regulated tenancy under the Rent Act 1977 (which may be a protected tenancy, a protected shorthold tenancy or a statutory tenancy);
— a secure tenancy under the Housing Act 1985;
— a housing association tenancy governed by Part VI of the Rent Act 1977.

Each of the statutory schemes lays down certain conditions which a tenancy has to satisfy if the tenant is to qualify for protection.[83] Of course, not all tenancies of residential premises fall within the ambit of any of the protective legislation.

In outline the position is as follows (assuming that the necessary conditions are satisfied):

(1) The Private Sector

A tenancy granted on or after January 15, 1989 (the date of the entry into force of the relevant provisions of the Housing Act 1988) will be an *assured tenancy* or an *assured shorthold tenancy* (governed by the Housing Act 1988). An assured shorthold tenancy must be granted for a fixed-term of at least six months and the landlord must serve a notice in prescribed form on the tenant before the commencement of the tenancy.

A tenancy created before January 15, 1989 will generally be a *protected tenancy*—under the Rent Act 1977. On the expiry or termination of a protected tenancy the tenant becomes a *statutory tenant*. However, after the entry into force of the relevant provisions of the Housing Act 1980 it became possible for landlords to grant *protected shorthold tenancies* (which are tenancies for a fixed-term of one to five years), and certain approved landlords were entitled to grant *assured tenancies*. However, assured tenancies created before January 15, 1989 are now assured tenancies within the terms of the Housing Act 1988.

A tenancy which is not a protected tenancy (for example, because the landlord is also resident in the building which is occupied by the tenant) may be a *restricted contract*. Restricted contracts are also governed by the Rent Act 1977 (as amended).

---

[83] The scope of the various statutory schemes is discussed in detail in Chapter 3.

(2) The Public Sector

Tenancies granted by local authorities and other designated public bodies are *secure tenancies* governed by the Housing Act 1985 (as amended).

(3) The Independent Sector

Housing associations, housing trusts and the Housing Corporation are quasi-public bodies; they are neither like local authorities nor private companies. The law prior to January 15, 1989 reflected this hybrid nature. The Housing Act 1988, however, has brought new lettings by these quasi-public bodies into the private sector scheme.

Tenancies granted before January 15, 1989 by the Housing Corporation, housing trusts and many housing associations are *secure tenancies* under the Housing Act 1985. However, tenancies granted by housing associations which are not secure tenancies may be *protected tenancies* within the Rent Act 1977. Futhermore, since 1980, if approved by the Secretary of State, Housing associations could grant *assured tenancies* under the Housing Act 1980. Assured tenancies granted by housing associations under the Housing Act 1980 are now assured tenancies under the Housing Act 1988.

Part VI of the Rent Act 1977 provides rent control for *housing association tenancies*. A housing association tenancy must be granted by a housing association, a housing trust or the Housing Corporation and must not be a protected tenancy. (A tenancy granted by a housing association, a housing trust or the Housing Corporation before January 15, 1989 can be both a secure tenancy and a housing association tenancy.)

From January 15, 1989 tenancies granted by housing associations (other than fully mutual housing associations), housing trusts and the Housing Corporation are *assured tenancies* or *assured shorthold tenancies* under the Housing Act 1988.

Note

As a result of the Housing Act 1988 housing associations are destined to play an ever increasing role in the provision of rented accommodation. An account of the voluntary housing movement—out of which housing associations have grown—is to be found in P. N. Balchin, *Housing Policy: An Introduction* (2nd ed., 1989, Routledge) Chapter 7.

For a thorough account of all aspects of the law relating to housing associations see J. Alder & C. R. Handy, *Housing Association Law* (1987, Sweet & Maxwell). A brief overview of the area (which, in the words of the author, is "complex, technical and can only be discovered by collecting obscure provisions from different statutes") is provided by J. Alder, Housing associations—the third world of housing policy [1983]

J.S.W.L. 222. The special position of co-operative housing associations is discussed by the same author: Co-operative housing associations—alternative tenure [1988] Conv. 187 & 254.

V CREATION OF LEASES

(A) GENERAL FORMAL REQUIREMENTS

The Law of Property Act 1925 provides:

52.—(1) All conveyances of land or of any interest therein are void for the purpose of conveying or creating a legal estate unless made by deed.

(2) This section does not apply to:
. . . . . .
(d) leases or tenancies . . . not required by law to be made in writing.

54.—(2) Nothing in the foregoing provisions . . . shall affect the creation by parol of leases taking effect in possession for a term not exceeding three years (whether or not the lessee is given power to extend the term) at the best rent which can be obtained without taking a fine.[84]

205.—(1)(ii) "Conveyance" includes . . . lease . . .

As a result of these provisions, while a deed is necessary to create legal leases for a term of three years or more, there is no such requirement for short-term tenancies (including periodic tenancies). Indeed, tenancies falling within the scope of section 54(2) need not satisfy any formal requirements at all.[85]

There are, however, advantages to the creation of any tenancy by written agreement. First, the mere fact that a lease is in written form goes some way towards ensuring that both parties to the leasehold relationship have given thought to their mutual rights and obligations. Secondly, a written agreement provides clear evidence of the tenancy. Where there is no writing, a tenant (or landlord) may be put at a severe disadvantage if the landlord (or tenant) wishes to alter unilaterally the terms which have been orally agreed. In such a situation there is scope for abuse by the more powerful side of the landlord-tenant relationship. Although oral periodic tenancies are legally binding, lack of written evidence of the terms of the agreement may cause problems if cases come to court and a judge is required to decide which party is telling the truth.

(B) REGISTRATION OF TITLE

It is worth noting that by the end of 1990 the whole of England and Wales had become a compulsory area for the purposes of registration of

---

[84] See *Kushner* v. *Law Society* [1952] 1 K.B. 214.
[85] See Law of Property (Miscellaneous Provisions) Act 1989, s.2(5)(a).

title under the Land Registration Act 1925. Not all leases, however, need to be registered.

The situations in which registration is compulsory, and the effects of failure to register, are set out in sections 8 and 123 of the Land Registration Act 1925:

8.—(1) Where the title to be registered is a title to a leasehold interest in land—

    (a)   any estate owner (including a tenant for life, statutory owner, personal representative, or trustee for sale, but not including a mortgagee where there is a subsisting right of redemption), holding under a lease for a term of years absolute of which more than 21 are unexpired, whether subject or not to incumbrances, or

    (b)   any other person (not being a mortgagee as aforesaid and not being a person who has merely contracted to buy the leasehold interest) who is entitled to require a legal leasehold estate held under such a lease as aforesaid (whether subject or not to incumbrances) to be vested in him,

may apply to the registrar in respect of such estate, or in the case of a person not being in a fiduciary position to have registered in his stead any nominee, as proprietor ...

(1A) An application for registration in respect of leasehold land held under a lease in relation to the grant or assignment of which section 123(1) of this Act applies (whether by virtue of this Act or any later enactment) may be made within the period allowed by section 123(1), or any authorised extension of that period, notwithstanding that the lease was granted for a term of not more than 21 years or that the unexpired term of the lease is not more than 21 years.

(2) Leasehold land held under a lease containing a prohibition or restriction on dealings therewith inter vivos shall not be registered under this Act unless and until provision is made in the prescribed manner for preventing any dealing therewith in contravention of the prohibition or restriction by an entry on the register to that effect, or otherwise.

123.—(1) In any area in which an Order in Council declaring that registration of title to land within that area is to be compulsory on sale is for the time being in force, every conveyance on sale of freehold land and every grant of a term of years absolute of more than 21 years from the date of delivery of the grant, and every assignment on sale of leasehold land held for a term of years absolute having more than 21 years to run from the date of delivery of the assignment shall (save as hereinafter provided), on the expiration of two months from the date thereof or of any authorised extension of that period, become void so far as regards the grant or conveyance of the legal estate in the freehold or leasehold land comprised in the conveyance, grant, or assignment, or so much of such land as is situated within the area affected, unless the grantee (that is to say, the person who is entitled to be registered as proprietor of the freehold or leasehold land) or his successor in title or assign has in the meantime applied to be registered as proprietor of such land:

Provided that the registrar, or the court on appeal from the registrar, may, on the application of any persons interested in any particular case in which the registrar or the court is satisfied that the application for first registration cannot be made within the said period, or can only be made within that period by incurring unreasonable expense, or that the application has not been made within the said period by reason of some accident or other sufficient cause, make an order extending the said period; and if such order be made, then, upon the registration of the grantee or his successor or assign, a note of the order shall be endorsed on the conveyance, grant or assignment:

In the case of land in an area where, at the date of the commencement of this Act, registration of title is already compulsory on sale, this subsection shall apply to every such conveyance, grant, or assignment, executed on or after that date.

Registration of title (where applicable) is an additional formal requirement, not a substitute to the formal requirements of the Law of Property Act 1925. In registered land a legal lease for a term not exceeding 21 years will bind other persons dealing with the freehold reversion as an "overriding interest,"[86] notwithstanding the fact that it is not protected by an entry on the register.

(C) INFORMAL LEASES

Although there may be good reasons for requiring written documentation and registration for the creation of legal interests in land—to prevent fraud, define the obligations of the parties and so on—practical reality shows that there are always people who have attempted to create leases but who do not, for one reason or another, comply with the formal rules. Obviously great hardship could be caused if the law were wholly to deny the validity of such informal arrangements. There are, however, two ways in which the courts will give effect to a lease notwithstanding the fact that the necessary formalities are not satisfied.

First, although an oral or written agreement for a term of three years or more is ineffective to create a legal estate, a tenancy might arise independently of the express agreement. Where the tenant goes into possession of the premises with the landlord's consent and pays rent periodically, the courts will construe this factual situation as giving rise to a legal periodic tenancy. So, if the tenant pays rent on a monthly basis, a monthly periodic tenancy arises.

Secondly, through the application of the doctrine of the courts of equity, a contract for a lease may be given validity despite the failure of the parties to execute a deed (or, in the context of registered land, the parties' failure to complete the transaction by registration). However in order for an agreement to be given effect to in equity certain conditions must be satisfied.

When a long-term lease is being negotiated, conveyancing practice is that the parties will usually reach a point where they exchange contracts before they complete the conveyance of the legal interest in the property.[87] The courts of equity decided that such exchange of contracts

---

[86] Land Registration Act 1925, s.70(1)(k).

[87] Prior to the exchange of contracts all negotiations are conducted "subject to contract." Except in exceptional circumstances, any document stated to be "subject to contract" does not create a contract: *Tiverton Estates Ltd.* v. *Wearwell Ltd.* [1975] Ch. 146.

conferred on the lessee an equitable interest in the property, with the result that the terms of the lease could be enforced between the parties.

In order for the lease to be enforceable in equity two essential conditions must be satisfied. First, the agreement must conform to the basic law of contract. There must be an offer which has been accepted, and consideration. In addition, certain essential terms must be agreed: the identity of the parties; the premises to be let; the date of commencement and length of the term; and the rent or other consideration to be paid. Secondly, the agreement must satisfy the requirements of section 2 of the Law of Property (Miscellaneous Provisions) Act 1989 which provides:

2.—(1) A contract for the sale of land or other disposition of an interest in land can only be made in writing and only by incorporating all the terms which the parties have expressly agreed in one document or, where contracts are exchanged, in each.

(2) The terms may be incorporated in a document either by being set out in it or by reference to some other document.

(3) The document incorporating the terms or, where contracts are exchanged, one of the documents incorporating them (but not necessarily the same one) must be signed by or on behalf of each party to the contract.
. . . . . .

(5) This section does not apply in relation to—

(a)   a contract to grant a lease as is mentioned in section 54(2) of the Law of Property Act 1925 (short leases);
. . . . . .

(7) Nothing in this section shall apply to in relation to contracts made before this section comes into force.[88]

(8) Section 40 of the Law of Property Act 1925 (which is superseded by this section) shall cease to have effect.

If these conditions are satisfied, two remedies are available. Although an action for damages is the normal remedy for breach of contract, in the context of land transactions a disappointed party may not be particularly interested in receiving compensation. The lessee would often rather have the use of the land for which he was negotiating. Land is immovable; one piece of land in a particular location may have special attributes which another piece does not.

---

[88] This section came into force on September 27, 1989. For the law prior to the commencement of the Act see, Megarry & Wade, *The Law of Real Property* (5th ed., 1984) p. 571 *et seq.*

Because of the uniqueness of individual pieces of land, the courts of equity developed the remedy of specific performance to help those who might otherwise be harmed by the breaking of contracts affecting land. This remedy is based on the principle that "equity regards as done that which ought to be done."[89] Specific performance consists of an order from the court ordering the party in breach of the contract to perform specifically that contract, *i.e.* in this context to complete the conveyance (thereby transferring a legal estate to the plaintiff).

Specific performance is in principle a discretionary remedy, but it will usually be issued as long as certain conditions are fulfilled. In essence these are as follows:

— the contract must be complete and definite and have no terms which are incapable of performance[90];
— the plaintiff must come to the court "with clean hands"[91];
— the lessor must have good title;
— specific performance will not be ordered if it would cause serious hardship.

Because of the availability of specific performance it is sometimes said that "a contract for a lease is as good as a lease." However, whereas between the parties to the agreement this may be more or less true, the owner of an equitable interest in unregistered land will not be able to enforce his interest against a third party (such as a purchaser or mortgagee of the landlord's reversion) unless the equitable lease is registered as an estate contract.[92] In relation to land subject to the system of registered conveyancing, an estate contract should be protected on the register (at the Land Registry) by the entry of a notice or caution.[93] If an estate contract is not protected on the register, it will nevertheless be binding on a purchaser of the landlord's reversion as an "overriding interest" if the owner of the interest is in actual occupation of the land.[94]

VI OTHER FORMAL REQUIREMENTS

(A) RENT BOOKS

The purpose of much of the legislation relating to the residential landlord-tenant relationship discussed in this book is to create a "poor man's lease" defining the rights and obligations of landlords and tenants, and, in some cases, overriding the express obligations agreed by the parties. One of the major reasons why the law is not relied upon more

---

[89] See *Walsh* v. *Lonsdale* (1882) 21 Ch.D. 9.
[90] See *Johnson* v. *Agnew* [1980] A.C. 347.
[91] *Coatsworth* v. *Johnson* (1886) 55 L.J.Q.B. 220.
[92] Land Charges Act 1972, ss.2(4)(iv) and 4(6).
[93] Land Registration Act 1925, ss.48 and 54.
[94] Land Registration Act 1925, ss.20(1) and 70(1)(g).

by tenants is that they are often ignorant of their legal rights. Further, many prospective tenants fail to seek legal advice on their legal rights. While acquisition of knowledge does not necessarily lead to its use, it is nonetheless an essential prerequisite for its use. It is, therefore, necessary to devise effective means of passing on this information.

The law on rent books is one of the methods that has been adopted. The Landlord and Tenant Act 1985 provides:

4.—(1) Where a tenant has a right to occupy premises as a residence in consideration of a rent payable weekly, the landlord shall provide a rent book or similar document for use in respect of the premises.

(2) Subsection (1) does not apply to premises if the rent includes payment in respect of board and the value of that board to the tenant forms a substantial proportion of the whole rent.

The Act then provides that the name and address of the landlord be given in the rent book, and gives the Secretary of State powers to require other information to be incorporated into rent books relating to tenancies covered by the Rent Act 1977 and the Housing Act 1988.[95] It is a criminal offence to fail to comply with the obligations imposed by these provisions, the maximum penalty being a fine not exceeding level 4 on the standard scale.[96]

The required information for assured tenancies falling within the Housing Act 1988 and for regulated tenancies governed by the Rent Act 1977 is contained in the Rent Book (Forms of Notice) Regulations 1982.[97]

FORM FOR RENT BOOK FOR ASSURED TENANCY OR ASSURED AGRICULTURAL OCCUPANCY

IMPORTANT–PLEASE READ THIS

If the rent for the premises you occupy as your residence is payable weekly, the landlord must provide you with a rent book or similar document. If you have an assured tenancy, including an assured *shorthold* tenancy (*see* paragraph 7 below), or an assured agricultural occupancy, the rent book or similar document must contain this notice, properly filled in.

---

[95] s.5.
[96] s.7.
[97] S.I. 1982 No. 1474 as amended by the Rent Book (Forms of Notice) (Amendment) Regulations 1988 (S.I. 1988 No. 2198) and the Rent Book (Forms of Notice) (Amendment) Regulations 1990 (S.I. 1990 No. 1067).

1. Address of premises ....

....

* 2. Name and address of landlord ....

....

* 3. Name and address of agent (if any) ....

....

* 4. The rent payable including/excluding† rates is £ ...... per week.

* 5. Details of accommodation (if any) which the occupier has the right to share with other persons ....

....

6. The other terms and conditions of the tenancy are ....

....
....
....

7. If you have an assured tenancy or an assured agricultural occupancy you have certain rights under the Housing Act 1988. These include the right not to be evicted from your home unless your landlord gets a possession order from the courts. Unless the property is let under an assured *shorthold* tenancy, the courts can only grant an order on a limited number of grounds. Further details regarding assured tenancies are set out in the Department of the Environment and Welsh Office booklet "Assured Tenancies" no. 19 in the series of housing booklets. These booklets are available from rent officers, council offices and housing aid centres, some of which also give advice.

8. You may be entitled to get help to pay your rent through the housing benefit scheme. Apply to your local council for details.

9. It is a criminal offence for your landlord to evict you without an order from the court or to harass you or interfere with your possessions or use of facilities in order to force you to leave.

10. If you are in any doubt about your legal rights or obligations, particularly if your landlord has asked you to leave, you should go to a Citizens' Advice Bureau, housing aid centre, law centre or solicitor. Help with all or part of the cost of legal advice from a solicitor may be available under the Legal Aid Scheme.

* These entries must be kept up-to-date.
† Cross out whichever does not apply.

FORM FOR RENT BOOK FOR PROTECTED OR STATUTORY TENANCY

INFORMATION FOR TENANT

IMPORTANT−PLEASE READ THIS

If the rent for the premises you occupy as your residence is payable weekly, the landlord must provide you with a rent book or similar document. If you have a protected or statutory tenancy (see paragraph 9 below), the rent book or similar document must contain this notice, properly filled in.

---

1. Address of premises ....

....

*2. Name and address of landlord ....

....

*3. Name and address of agent (if any) ....

....

*4. The rent payable including/excluding† rates is £ .... per week.

If a fair rent is registered paragraph 5 and, where it applies, paragraph 6 must be filled in, otherwise they should be crossed out.

---

*5. The registered rent (which excludes rate) is £ .... per week, effective from .... (date).

If the rent is registered as variable (because it includes service charges which vary), this should be indicated by placing a tick in the box □.

*6. In addition to the registered rent, £ .... per week is payable to cover rates paid by the landlord or superior landlord.

7. Details of the accommodation (if any) which the occupier has the right to share with other persons ....
....
....

8. The other terms and conditions of the tenancy are ....
....
....

9. You are protected by the Rent Act 1977 and known as a "regulated tenant." The Rent Act contains important rules concerning the amount of rent you have to pay and your rights to stay in your home. Details of these rules are set out in the Department of the Environment and Welsh Office booklets "Regulated Tenancies" and "Notice That You Must Leave", nos. 25 and 22 in the series of housing booklets. These booklets are available from rent officers, council offices and housing aid centres, some of which also give advice.

10. Either you or your landlord may apply to the rent officer for a fair rent to be registered. It is wise to get advice before doing so. Whether or not your rent is registered by the rent officer there are rules about how and when it can be increased. You cannot be evicted from your home unless your landlord gets a possession order from the courts, and the courts can grant an order only in special circumstances.

11. If you have a protected shorthold tenancy or your tenancy was formerly a controlled one, special rules apply.

13. You may be entitled to get help to pay your rent through the housing benefit scheme. Apply to your council for details.

14. It is a criminal offence for your landlord to evict you without an order from the court or to harass you or interfere with your possessions or use of facilities in order to force you to leave.

15. If you are in any doubt about your legal rights or obligations, particularly if your landlord has asked you to leave, you should go to a Citizens' Advice Bureau, housing aid centre, law centre or solicitor. Help with all or part of the cost of legal advice from a solicitor may be available under the Legal Aid Scheme.

These provisions raise a number of questions, in particular the extent to which the prescribed information is exprssed in a way which is readily comprehensible. It is interesting to note that the current forms are considerably shorter and less complex than those which formerly were prescribed by the 1976 regulations.[98]

So far rent books have been discussed as a medium of education. But they have other functions as well. They can be useful evidence in cases of dispute about payment of rent, and tenants who have applied for a council tenancy can use them to show their reliability as tenants.

Despite their potential usefulness, a careful look at the provisions of the Act shows that the scope of the legislation is severely limited. Landlords may simply evade the law by requiring the rent to be paid fortnightly or monthly. And there are many gaps in the information that has to be provided. As long ago as 1971 the Francis Committee suggested that the law relating to rent books should be amended in the following respects:

(a) The provision of a rent book (or similar document) should be made obligatory not only where the rent is payable weekly, but whenever the rent is payable at intervals not exceeding two months.

(b) The rent book should be supplied to and remain in the custody of the tenant, without prejudice to the right of the landlord to keep a duplicate, and subject to the right of the landlord to call for production of it where necessary, *e.g.* to make any proper entry therein or amendment thereto.

(c) A rent book (or similar document) relating to a furnished tenancy should contain an inventory of the furniture (including fixtures and fittings) supplied by the landlord for the use of the tenant at the commencement of the tenancy.[99]

Local authorities should have a general power to call for production of rent books, and should from time to time, through an appropriate officer carry out spot checks, especially in furnished multi-occupied houses, for the purpose of ascertaining whether the law is being complied with.

It has also been suggested that the landlords should be required to make it clear whether rent is payable in advance or arrear; where services are provided, these should be specified; and a summary of the landlord's repairing obligations under what is now the Landlord and Tenant Act 1985 should be given.[1] Notwithstanding these suggestions, reform appears to be a low priority. There are no plans for major alterations to the rent book rules.

Even if the rules were changed, the problem of their enforcement would remain. Given that breach of the rules is a criminal offence, one

---

[98] Rent Book (Forms of Notice) Regulations 1976 (S.I. 1976 No. 378). For a text of the form prescribed by the 1976 regulations for a regulated tenancy see Partington, *Landlord and Tenant: Text and Materials on Housing and Law* (2nd ed., 1980), pp. 59–62.

[99] *Report of the Committee on the Rent Acts* (1971) Cmnd. 4609, pp. 226–227.

[1] Hoath, Rent books: the law, its uses and abuses [1978–9] J.S.W.L. 3 at 12.

possible sanction (if local authorities will not use their powers of prosecution) would be to deny landlords their right to rent while they are committing an offence. This argument was raised, but rejected, in *Shaw* v. *Groom*.[2]

It has been suggested that many complaints of harassment begin with a tenant's request for a rent book. Accordingly, "a tenant who likes his accommodation and gets on well with his landlord should consider whether he really needs a rent book."[3] However, if the rules are followed, it has been seen that they would provide tenants with certain information regarding their legal rights. While the law on rent books may be a less crucial issue than some other issues discussed in this book, it should be regarded as symptomatic of the seriousness, or otherwise, of official attempts to demystify the law by making sure that knowledge of legal rights is accessible to lay people.

(B) OTHER INFORMATION

The Landlord and Tenant Act 1985 and Part VI of the Landlord and Tenant Act 1987 make provision concerning information which must—in certain circumstances—be supplied to tenants.

The Landlord and Tenant Act 1985 provides:

1.—(1) If the tenant of premises occupied as a dwelling makes a written request for the landlord's name and address to—

(a) any person who demands, or the last person who received, rent payable under the tenancy, or

(b) any other person for the time being acting as agent for the landlord, in relation to the tenancy,

that person shall supply the tenant with a written statement of the landlord's name and address within the period of 21 days beginning with the day on which he receives the request.

2.—(1) Where a tenant is supplied under section 1 with the name and address of his landlord and the landlord is a body corporate, he may make a further written request to the landlord for the name and address of every director and of the secretary of the landlord.

(2) The landlord shall supply the tenant with a written statement of the information requested within the period of 21 days beginning with the day on which he receives the request.

---

[2] [1970] 2 Q.B. 504.
[3] Cutting, *A Housing Rights Handbook* (1979), p. 126.

(3) A request under this section is duly made to the landlord if it is made to—

(a)   an agent of the landlord, or

(b)   a person who demands the rent of the premises concerned;

and any such agent or person to whom such a request is made shall forward it to the landlord as soon as may be.

3.—(1) If the interest of the landlord under a tenancy of premises which consist of or include a dwelling is assigned, the new landlord shall give notice in writing of the assignment, and of his name and address, to the tenant not later than the next day on which rent is payable under the tenancy or, if that is within two months of the assignment, the end of that period of two months.

(2) If trustees constitute the new landlord, a collective description of the trustees as the trustees of the trust in question may be given as the name of the landlord, and where such a collective description is given—

(a)   the address of the new landlord may be given as the address from which the affairs of the trust are conducted, and

(b)   a change in the persons who are for the time being the trustees of the trust shall not be treated as an assignment of the interest of the landlord.

. . . . . .

(3A) The person who was the landlord under the tenancy immediately before the assignment ("the old landlord") shall be liable to the tenant in respect of any breach of any covenant, condition or agreement under the tenancy occurring before the end of the relevant period in like manner as if the interest assigned were still vested in him; and where the new landlord is also liable to the tenant in respect of any such breach occurring within that period, he and the old landlord shall be jointly and severally liable in respect of it.

(3B) In subsection (3A) "the relevant period" means the period beginning with the date of the assignment and ending with the date when—

(a)   notice in writing of the assignment, and of the new landlord's name and address, is given to the tenant by the new landlord (whether in accordance with subsection (1) or not), or

(b)   notice in writing of the assignment, and of the new landlord's name and last-known address, is given to the tenant by the old landlord,

whichever happens first.

A landlord, who without reasonable excuse, fails to supply the requested information commits an offence,[4] punishable by a fine not exceeding level 4 on the standard scale.

These provisions (which in substance originated in the Housing Act 1974) have been supplemented by Part VI of the Landlord and Tenant

---

[4] Landlord and Tenant Act 1985, s.1(2), s.2(4) and s.3(3).

Act 1987. In addition to adding subsections (3A) and (3B) to section 3 of the 1985 Act, the 1987 Act provides:

48.—(1) A landlord of premises to which this Part applies[5] shall by notice furnish the tenant with an address in England and Wales at which notices (including notices in proceedings) may be served on him by the tenant.

(2) Where a landlord of any such premises fails to comply with subsection (1), any rent or service charge otherwise due from the tenant to the landlord shall (subject to subsection (3)) be treated for all purposes as not being due from the tenant to the landlord at any time before the landlord does comply with that subsection.

(3) Any such rent or service charge shall not be so treated in relation to any time when, by virtue of an order of any court, there is in force an appointment of a receiver or manager whose functions include the receiving of rent or (as the case may be) service charges from the tenant.

(C) STAMP DUTY REQUIREMENTS

Stamp duty is one of this country's oldest taxes, having been originally introduced in 1694. Stamp duty is a tax on documents, rather than transactions or persons. Accordingly, stamp duty is not payable where a periodic tenancy is created by oral agreement. Details can be found in standard text books on taxation.

It seems likely that many tenancy agreements relating to residential premises never get to the relevant authorities for stamping. Although failure to stamp a document is not a criminal offence, and an instrument which is not stamped is still effective, failure to stamp may in certain circumstances have serious consequences. An instrument which is not duly stamped in accordance with the law in force at the time when it was executed "shall not, except in criminal proceedings, be given in evidence, or be available for any purpose whatsoever ... "[6]

Notwithstanding the formal position, it seems that failure to comply with stamping provisions does not inhibit rent officers and rent assessment committees. Lord Goddard in *R. v. Fulham etc. Rent Tribunal ex p. Zerek*[7] said:

There is one other matter which, though immaterial for the purpose of the decision, cannot be passed over without notice. The document produced by the landlord, and on which he relied as a memorandum of agreement, was improperly stamped. It may be that he required the tenant to sign over a stamp with a view to impressing on him that it was a formal document, but the document would in any event have required a sixpenny stamp. Had he attempted to put it in before a court of law, an arbitrator, or a referee, it could not have been looked at without requiring him to pay the proper stamp duty and a penalty of £10. These tribunals cannot be described as courts of law ...

---

[5] Part VI of the 1987 Act applies to "premises which consist of or include a dwelling and are not held under a tenancy to which Part II of the Landlord and Tenant Act 1954 applies" (s.46(1)).

[6] Stamp Act 1891, s.14(4).

[7] [1951] 2 K.B. 1 at 7–8.

nor are its members arbitrators or referees. We could not say, therefore, that they were not entitled to look at the document, and, as we have to consider whether their decision was within their jurisdiction, it is necessary for us to look at the same evidence as was before them. It will be for the Commissioners of Inland Revenue to determine what, if any, action they should take in view of what appears to be a deliberate understamping of the document, and it will be sent to them by the court.

VII   TERMS OF THE LEASE: COVENANTS

(A)   EXAMPLES OF TENANCY AGREEMENTS AND LEASES

It has been seen when written documentation is required, and when not, and how the courts have developed remedies to cope with failure to conform to the rules. This section looks more closely at the content of some of the conditions that may be found in written tenancy agreements or leases.

One point of some sociological importance should be stressed at the outset. Although lawyers may think it quite proper that the terms of a tenancy should be written down, the parties involved may not adopt a legalistic approach to the landlord-tenant relationship.

A landlord-tenant relationship that is proceeding smoothly may not need to be finalised; but, if it begins to break down a written record of the terms of letting may be helpful. There are a number of standard forms on the market which are widely used, and precedents are available from a variety of sources. Below is reproduced a short modern form suitable for an assured tenancy of furnished accommodation.[8]

TENANCY AGREEMENT made   198   between the Landlord   of
and the Tenant   .

1. The Landlord lets to the Tenant

   (a)   the furnished room(s) numbered   in the building known as

   (b)   the furniture and equipment listed in the inventory signed by the Tenant and attached.

[Together with the shared use of the bath-room and lavatory on the floor.]

2. The tenancy runs from   19   to   19   and then from month to month but the Landlord may end it immediately if any rent is in arrear for two weeks (without the need for formal demand) or if the Tenant breaks any of the Tenant's obligations in this Agreement.

3. The tenant must pay the rent by instalments of £   per month in advance on the   day of the month by Bank Order to Account   at   Bank,   Branch (or any other Account later notified in writing) and must also pay a surcharge of £3 for each week (or part of week) the rent is in arrear. The rent may be revised in accordance with Clause 10 below.

---

[8] *Precedents for the Conveyancer*, No. 5–101, pp. 2998/136—2998/138.

4. The Tenant must

(a)   occupy the room(s) personally and not assign sub-let share or part with possession nor permit use or occupation by anyone else

(b)   keep the room(s) clean and in reasonable condition allowing for fair wear and tear

(c)   keep the furniture and equipment in as good condition as at the start of the tenancy allowing for fair wear and tear

(d)   leave the room(s) clean and free of all items (except the listed furniture and equipment) and rubbish at the end of the tenancy

(e)   report any damage loss or malfunction to the Landlord's Agents

(f)   abide by the fire regulations for the buidling.

5. The Tenant must not

(a)   except with consent
    (i)   carry out redecorations or alterations to the room(s)
    (ii)   move any furniture and equipment out of the room(s)
    (iii)   change the locks or instal additional locks
    (iv)   instal or use additional heaters
    (v)   keep any pets

(b)   create any nuisance in the room(s) or anywhere else in the building nor permit the Tenant's visitors to do so

(c)   play radios TV sets tape machinery record players or musical instruments to cause annoyance or in any event after 11.00 p.m.

(d)   do anything to invalidate the Landlord's insurance on the room(s) the furniture and equipment of the building.

6. The Landlord must keep in repair the structure and exterior of the room(s) and the building and the installations in the room(s) and the building for the supply of water, gas and electricity and for sanitation but subject to the provisions of section 11, Landlord and Tenant Act 1985.

7. The Landlord may

(a)   enter the room(s) at any time for inspection or to carry out work to the room and the furniture and equipment or the building

(b)   use the deposit of £   made by the Tenant to cover rent arrears or to make good the Tenant's responsibilities for any loss or damage to the room(s) or to any part of the building damaged by the Tenant or the Tenant's visitors or to the furniture and equipment or to clean the room(s) if left dirty on leaving (any balance to be refunded within two weeks after the amount of deductions is established).

8. "Consent" means written consent before the act or event in question, and a reference to "the room(s)" includes any part of the rooms(s).

9. For the purposes of section 48, Landlord and Tenant Act 1987, the Landlord's address for the service of notices is that given above.

10. [*Rent adjustment provision, for example Form 5—99, 5—100, 5—103 or 5–104.*]
Signed by or for the Landlord
Signed by the Tenant

(B)   ABSENCE OF WRITTEN TERMS

Where a lease arises informally, there will be no written terms, and even where the parties do conclude a written agreement certain issues may not be addressed by the express terms. However, the law has developed means whereby terms will be incorporated into the parties' agreement in these situations. Indeed, certain implied covenants cannot be excluded by the express agreement of the parties.

The landlord's covenant for quiet enjoyment, which is implied at common law, is one of the most important of the landlord's implied obligations.[9] Furthermore, in certain circumstances a landlord will be subject to obligations implied by statute, such as repairing obligations.[10] At common law, the tenant is also subject to implied obligations: for example, the tenant's covenant to pay rent, and to use the premises in a tenant-like manner.[11] Where the tenancy is governed by one of the statutory schemes of protection, there may also be statutorily implied covenants. For example, in relation to a statutory periodic assured tenancy there will be an implied covenant by the tenant not to assign or sub-let without the consent of the landlord.[12]

Note

Detailed discussion of particular covenants (for example, on rent, repair, quiet enjoyment and assignment) will follow. On a more general level it is worth considering whether certain of the clauses incorporated into tenancies are too restrictive of the tenants' activities in their accommodation. This point was taken up by the National Consumer Council in 1976 which—after a survey of local authority tenancy agreements—was very critical of the often absurd and detailed rules contained in such agreements.[13] The tenants' charter which was introduced in the Housing Act 1980 (and is now to be found in Part IV of the Housing Act 1985) was devised in order to meet some of these criticisms. It is also provided that all council tenants should be provided with a copy of the terms of their tenancy.[14] There is, however, no equivalent to the tenants' charter in the private rented sector. Furthermore, despite proposals for reform in this area,[15] the number of covenants implied by law into tenancy agreements remains strictly limited.

VIII JURISDICTION

The county court is the forum for the resolution of the majority of housing disputes. Jurisdiction is expressly conferred on the county court

---

[9] See p. 274.
[10] See pp. 361–363.
[11] See pp. 429–431 and 356–358.
[12] Housing Act 1988, s.15(1). See pp. 288–289.
[13] *Tenancy Agreements* (1976).
[14] Housing Act 1985, s.104(2).
[15] *e.g.* see Law Commission, *Obligations of Landlords and Tenants* (1975).

in relation to most matters involving regulated tenancies,[16] secure tenancies,[17] and assured tenancies.[18]

There are, however, certain issues relating to rents under the Rent Act 1977 which are within the jurisdiction of rent fixing agencies,[19] and some questions which may arise under the Housing Act 1988 are referred to rent assessment committees.[20]

There are also significant types of case (such as situations involving major repairs) which may be dealt with by the High Court. The Crown Court and the magistrates' courts have criminal jurisdiction relating to harassment, illegal eviction and statutory nuisances. Finally, in the context of homelessness, there is no direct appeal to the courts against a decision of a local authority on the merits of the case, although an aggrieved claimant may have the possibility of seeking judicial review by virtue of Order 53 of the Rules of the Supreme Court.[21] These cases are heard by the Divisional Court (which is part of the High Court). An application for judicial review requires leave of the court.

The current system has been subjected to various criticisms, including the fact that there is no single forum which deals with all housing disputes. As a result of dissatisfaction, it has been suggested that a specialist housing court should be established.

Various jurisdictional issues relating to housing cases were considered in the Civil Justice Review.

Report of the Review Body on Civil Justice (1988, Cm. 394)

668. Complaints about the present procedures for dealing with housing cases include the following:—

  (i) Cases in the County Court take too long: landlords in particular complain about the length of time before their cases come to hearing and about the slowness of enforcement procedures which implement the court's decision that they are entitled to possession of their property.
 (ii) At the hearing cases are often disposed of without any detailed consideration of the individual circumstances of the case; possession cases are frequently disposed of at the rate of 40–50 in a morning.
(iii) Courts are unable to make consistent or adequately based decisions because of lack of information and the defendant's non-participation in the proceedings; the court is frequently quite ignorant of the family or economic situation of the tenant or of other circumstances relating to the premises, the letting or the parties.

---

[16] Rent Act 1977, s.141.
[17] Housing Act 1985, s.110(1).
[18] Housing Act 1988, s.40.
[19] See Chapter 7.
[20] Note, in particular, the statutory procedure for securing an increase in rent (s.13), the mechanism for altering the terms of an assured tenancy (s.6), and the procedure for referring excessive rents under an assured shorthold tenancy (s.22). See pp. 432–437.
[21] See p. 597.

(iv) Courts are too formal: landlords and tenants alike are said to find court proceedings forbidding. The formal language used in court and on court forms is seen as inhibiting to those least able to put their own case or pay for representation. The result is to deter those who may have a valid defence from attending to put their case.

(v) Court cases cost too much: the potentially high cost of taking or defending legal action is also said to act as a major deterrent. There are complaints that legal aid is not widely available for cases brought before the courts and not available at all for cases brought before tribunals. . . .

718. The Review Body was asked by the Lord Chancellor and the Secretary of State for the Environment to take full account of the arguments advanced for the establishment of a separate housing court or tribunal.

719. Organisations which supported a separate housing court included the Royal Institution of Charted Surveyors and the Association of Metropolitan Authorities. Organisations which advocated reforms in the handling of housing cases within the present County Court structure included the Law Society, the Bar, the Association of County Court and District Registrars, the Association of District Councils and the Housing Courts Steering Group. (The last is an umbrella group which represents a broad spectrum of organisations concerned with housing and the law, including the Legal Action Group, Shelter, SHAC, the Law Centres Federation, the London Private Tenants Workers Group, the Campaign for Bedsit Rights, the Housing Law Practitioners Association and many individual advice agencies, private practitioners and local groups. Some members of the group had initially submitted individual responses advocating a separate housing court but subsequently subscribed to the consensus view in support of reforms based on the County Court.)

720. Arguments put forward in support of a separate housing court or tribunal were based on the need to:—

(i) eliminate confusion caused by the number of courts and tribunals involved in determining housing disputes;
(ii) promote consistency in decision making and procedures;
(iii) encourage expertise in housing legislation on the part of the judiciary;
(iv) reduce formality of procedures;
(v) allow an aggrieved party easy and prompt access to a remedy at an affordable and economic cost.

721. Those who favoured reforms based on the present County Court structure considered that:—

(i) Improvements to County Court procedures would be more cost effective than the introduction of a separate court or tribunal.
(ii) The separation of housing cases from the rest of civil litigation would have a detrimental effect on the quality of justice since the general law of contract, tort, debt enforcement, divorce and land could all have relevance in housing disputes.
(iii) The disparate nature of rent assessment cases and possession cases, which together account for the great majority of housing litigation, made it unlikely that any attempt to amalgamate them would be satisfactory.
(iv) The important consequences for the parties of decisions in those housing cases now dealt with by the County Court required that such cases be dealt with in a wholly judicial context.

722. The Review Body has concluded that improvements within the existing County Court structure would meet the main criticisms which originally led to calls for a housing court. Specifically improvements should aim to:—

(i)   improve access to the courts for both landlords and tenants;
(ii) ensure proper judicial consideration of individual cases; and
(iii) encourage better management of rent arrears. . . .

R. 77 There should be no separate housing court but the systematic handling of housing cases should be actively encouraged. In particular, courts should maintain distinctive lists for housing cases.

Note

Within the context of the Civil Justice Review empirical research into housing cases was carried out by the School of Advanced Urban Studies, University of Bristol, on behalf of the Lord Chancellor's Department. The results of this study were produced as part of the consultation process prior to final report: *Consultation Paper No. 5: Housing Cases* (1987). A more detailed analysis of some of the problems relating to housing cases, and in particular to the fact that defendants are often either not present or not represented at the hearing is to be found in M. Hill and A. Mercer, Participation in housing cases: an examination of attendance and representation at county court possession hearings and rent assessment committees [1987] J.S.W.L. 237.

Chapter 12 of the National Consumer Council's *Ordinary Justice* (1989, H.M.S.O.) provides a good discussion of the issues surrounding jurisdiction in housing cases.

Proposals for changing the procedures used in housing cases are being developed. However, the draft amended rules produced by the County Court Rules Committee which aimed to introduce a new rent action have been criticised both by landlords and tenants. Accordingly, implementation of the Civil Justice Review's recommendations has been delayed.[21a]

[21a] Luba & Madge, Recent developments in housing law (1991), Legal Action, March, p. 12.

CHAPTER 3

THE SCOPE OF STATUTORY PROTECTION

I THE PRIVATE SECTOR

Until recently the series of Rent Acts passed between 1915 and 1977 was the cornerstone of legislative attempts to regulate by law the landlord-tenant relationship in the private sector of the housing market. The Rent Acts were based on the idea that if the housing market was not regulated residential tenants would be exploited by landlords. The legislative scheme introduced by the Housing Act 1988, however, represents a change of philosophy. The 1988 Act is inspired by a belief in a free market for the private rented sector.

In later chapters the substance of the protections contained in the legislation—such as rent control, security of tenure, rights of succession—will be examined. This chapter looks at the difficult questions which must be explored before any substantive issue can be dealt with, relating to what categories of tenancy fall within the sphere of legislative protection.

The structure of this chapter is complicated by the fact that since January 15, 1989 there have been two mutually exclusive schemes of statutory protection for residential tenants: regulated (*i.e.* protected and statutory) tenancies under the Rent Act 1977 and assured tenancies governed by Part I of the Housing Act 1988. While there are concepts which are common to both schemes of protection, the definition of an assured tenancy is in important respects different from that of a protected tenancy.

(A) AN OUTLINE OF THE HISTORY OF PROTECTION IN THE PRIVATE SECTOR

Rent control was first introduced in this country by the Increase of Rent and Mortgage Interest (War Restrictions) Act of 1915. The Act was seen essentially as a temporary measure, introduced as the result of agitation by munition workers who were extremely angry at proposals to raise their rents. The categories of properties which fell within the scope of the Increase of Rent and Mortgage Interest (War Restrictions) Act 1915 were those whose net rateable value (N.R.V.) was £35 or below in

London, and £26 in the rest of England and Wales. The second reading debate clearly indicates that the legislation was intended for "comparatively poor people."

In relation to the rented sector the main purpose of the legislation was (as indicated by the short title) rent control. The effect of the 1915 Act was to freeze rents at the level which existed on August 3, 1914.[1] But, since at common law a periodic tenancy can be terminated by notice to quit, any protection as to rent is likely to prove illusory unless coupled with security of tenure. Accordingly, section 1(3) of the 1915 Act provided that:

No order for possession of a dwelling-house to which this Act applies or for the ejectment of a tenant therefrom shall be made so long as the tenant continues to pay rent at the agreed rate as modified by this Act and performs other conditions of the tenancy, except on the ground that the tenant has committed waste or has been guilty of conduct which is a nuisance or annoyance to adjoining neighbouring occupiers, or that the premises are reasonably required by the landlord for the occupation of himself or some other person in his employ, or in the employ of some tenant from him, or on some other ground which may be deemed satisfactory by the court making such order. ...

Although designed as a temporary measure, the 1915 Act established a basic framework for the regulation of the private rented sector, which was effectively unchallenged until the entry into force of the Housing Act 1988. All subsequent Rent Acts centred on two fundamental principles: rent control and security of tenure.

In 1918, the Hunter Committee reported.[2] This report summarised the main themes in the continuing debate about rent controls. The majority felt that control had to end if free enterprise was ever to provide accommodation again (while conceding that ending controls could not happen at once). The minority, however, said that they saw no end to control as long as accommodation was scarce. The result of the report was that in 1919 a new Increase of Rent and Mortgage Interest (War Restrictions) Act permitted increases of 10 per cent. in rent levels, at the same time doubling the rateable value limits. However, these controls, and their subsequent amendments up to 1939, only applied to houses already in existence in April 1919, not to new building.

In 1920 following the Salisbury Committee[3] the legislation was put on a slightly more permanent footing. The rateable value limits were raised again to £105 in London and £78 elsewhere in England and Wales. In this way, all except the largest houses were made subject to control. The

---

[1] Increase of Rent and Mortgage Interest (War Restrictions) Act 1915, ss.1(1) and 2(1)(b).
[2] *Report of the Committee on the Increase of Rent and Mortgage (War Restrictions) Acts* (1918) Cmd. 9235.
[3] *Report of the Committee on the Increase of Rent and Mortgage Interest (Restrictions) Acts* (1920) Cmd. 658.

Act also authorised a further 15 per cent. rise in rents, being an estimate of the increase in return to be expected on an investment since 1914, and yet another 25 per cent. if the landlord was responsible for all repairs.

In 1923 the Onslow Report suggested decontrol on vacant possession.[4] This was condemned by Labour M.P.'s. Nevertheless, after the short but violent depression which ended the post-war boom, steps were taken towards the withdrawal of rent control. Under the Rent and Mortgage Interest Restrictions Act 1923, premises were decontrolled but only when the landlord obtained vacant possession. However, this Act had a disastrous effect on landlords since it coincided with further economic recession and tenants were able to use a number of devices to avoid paying rent increases. The tensions that this situation caused were examined, first by the Constable Committee in 1925[5] and later by the Marley Committee in 1931.[6] The Marley Committee felt that decontrol of the smaller houses had been too fast while that of the larger houses had been too slow. At the same time the Committee emphasized that the shortage of working-class housing had, since World War I, been mitigated solely by the endeavours of local authorities.

By the Rent and Mortgage Interest Restrictions (Amendment) Act 1933 controlled houses were divided into three groups: (i) Class A, where both the recoverable rent and the N.R.V. was above £45 in London and £35 elsewhere in England and Wales, was decontrolled at once; (ii) Class B, where the N.R.V. was between £20 and £45 in London and £13 and £35 elsewhere in England and Wales, continued to be decontrolled on vacant possession; (iii) Class C houses, whose N.R.V.s were below the Class B limits, ceased to be decontrollable.

In 1938 Class B was divided so that the houses with N.R.V.s of £35 or above in London and £20 elsewhere were decontrolled at once. All those with lower rateable values become permanently controlled.

The situation in August 1939 was therefore quite different from that which had existed in 1923. All pre-1914 houses with N.R.V.s above £35 in London and £20 elsewhere had been excluded from control, along with a substantial though unknown number of smaller houses. In 1945 the Ridley Committee estimated the number of those decontrolled houses at 4.5 million. In addition, there were also 4.5 million houses built after 1919 which were excluded from control. Accordingly, out of a total of about 13 million houses and flats, only about 4 million (those with N.R.V.s not exceeding £35 in London and £20 elsewhere and almost entirely owned by private landlords) were still subject to control.

On the outbreak of World War II, however, a new system of control was introduced. On September 1, 1939 all dwelling-houses not subject to

[4] *Final Report of the Departmental Committee on the Increase of Rent and Mortgage Interest (Restrictions) Act 1920* (1923) Cmd. 1803.
[5] *Report of the Committee on the Rent Restriction Acts* (1925) Cmd. 2423.
[6] *Report of the Inter-Departmental Committee on the Rent Restriction Acts* (1931) Cmd. 3911.

the old control and with N.R.V.s of not more than £100 in London and £75 elsewhere were made subject to the new system. The result was that by 1953 over 90 per cent. of the dwelling-houses in England and Wales were within the rateable value limits and generally speaking all unfurnished tenancies were subject to control.

In 1953 the Government took up a suggestion made by the Leasehold Committee[7] and recommended that some measure of protection be given to long leaseholders on the expiry of their leases. These proposals, subsequently modified, were incorporated into Part I of the Landlord and Tenant Act 1954.[8]

Also in 1954, the Housing Repairs and Rents Act, which was concerned with the encouragement of house repairs and slum clearance, provided that all new housing built for letting should be outside Rent Act control, as should houses which had been converted in order to be let. This Act was the first major effort after World War II to encourage private enterprise to provide accommodation for letting.

This policy was extended dramatically in 1957, when the Rent Act of that year proposed to decontrol all houses with rateable values above £40 in London and £30 elsewhere. Other properties would be decontrolled when the landlord obtained vacant possession. The Act was not fully implemented at once because the Landlord and Tenant (Temporary Provisions) Act 1958 (which provided that decontrolled houses could not be repossessed without a court order[9] and gave the court power to postpone the operation of an order for possession[10]) effectively postponed the full operation of the 1957 Act until August 1, 1960.

However, creeping decontrol (when property became vacant) did continue. Problems thrown up by the effects of this process were revealed by the Milner-Holland Report.[11] The result was the introduction, first, of a new Protection from Eviction Act 1964; and, second, the introduction of the "fair rent" scheme by the Rent Act 1965. Initially, the rateable value limits for this protection were set at £400 in Greater London and £200 elsewhere. They were subsequently increased by section 4 of the Rent Act 1977[12] partly to take into account the revaluation of property in 1973, and partly as a consequence of counter-inflation measures taken in 1973.

In 1974, the Labour Government extended Rent Act protection to furnished accommodation, hitherto excluded from the full range of statutory protection, but at the same time created a category of what were called "restricted contracts" (which were basically tenancies

---

[7] Uthwatt-Jenkins, *Committee on Leasehold, Final Report* (1950) Cmd. 7982.
[8] See pp. 137–138.
[9] s.1.
[10] s.3.
[11] Milner-Holland, *Report of the Committee on Housing in Greater London* (1965) Cmd. 2605.
[12] See pp. 136 and 157.

granted by resident landlords).[13] Tenants who occupied premises under a restricted contract had the benefit of rent control, but did not have security of tenure.

Soon after coming to power in 1979 the Conservative Government began to try to implement a policy of deregulation in the private sector. The White Paper which preceded the Housing Act 1988 clearly identified what the Government saw as the cause of the decline of the private rented sector:

1.3 Too much preoccupation since the War with controls in the private rented sector, and mass provision in the public rented sector, has resulted in substantial numbers of rented houses and flats which are badly designed and maintained and which fail to provide decent homes. The return to private sector landlords has been inadequate to persuade them to stay in the market or to keep their property in repair. . . .

1.8 Rent controls have prevented property owners from getting an adequate return on their investment. People who might have been prepared to grant a temporary letting have also been deterred by laws on security of tenure which make it impossible to regain their property when necessary. These factors have contributed to shortages of supply and poor maintenance.[14]

Erosion of the legal protection of tenants in private rented sector both in terms of security of tenure and rent control began with the Housing Act 1980. These developments are explained in the 1987 White Paper in the following terms:

3.5 The Housing Act 1980 created the new concept of "assured tenancies." New and substantially renovated dwellings can now be let by approved landlords at freely negotiated rents. Assured tenants have full security of tenure for the duration of their initial tenancy provided they comply with its terms. At the end of the tenancy the tenant has a right to a new one on terms which may be agreed between the parties, or, if they cannot agree, which can be fixed by the County Court. Any rent fixed by the Court will be at a market level.

3.6 The 1980 Act also created a second new tenure of shorthold lettings. This was introduced to assist those potential landlords who may be prepared to let for a period even at a restricted rent provided they can be absolutely certain of getting their property back at the end of the period. Under the shorthold provisions landlords may let on this basis for a fixed period but either landlord or tenant may apply for the registration of a fair rent.

These developments were not very successful in bringing more properties into the private rented sector.[15] Many private landlords seemed unwilling to create protected shortholds—preferring to avoid granting security of tenure by more traditional means, such as licence

[13] See pp. 168–174 and 248–249.
[14] *Housing: The Government's Proposals* (1987) Cm. 214.
[15] *Ibid.* para. 3.7.

agreements—both because the Labour Party's stated policy was to convert retrospectively shorthold tenancies into fully-fledged protected tenancies, and because protected shorthold tenancies were subject to the fair rent system.

Whereas the Housing Act 1980 involved little more than tinkering with the existing Rent Act system, the 1988 Act marked the beginning of an attempt to realise a free market solution to the problems of the private rented sector. The 1988 Act introduced two new types of tenancy: the assured tenancy (which is in many respects different from the tenancy of the same name introduced in the 1980 Act) and the assured shorthold tenancy. Although the regime for existing lettings governed by the Rent Acts was subject to relatively minor changes, tenancies created on or after January 15, 1989 are governed by the Housing Act 1988 and therefore are assured (or assured shorthold) tenancies.

The assured tenant is given a degree of security of tenure similar to that enjoyed by a protected tenant under the Rent Act 1977, but the landlord is free to charge a market rent. However, by granting an assured shorthold tenancy a landlord may effectively opt out of the security of tenure provisions which apply to assured tenancies. An assured shorthold tenancy must be for a fixed minimum period of six months and certain formalities must be complied with for its creation. Once the fixed term has expired the landlord has an automatic right to recover possession (normally) on giving two months' notice. The landlord is of course free to charge a full market rent, although the tenant may refer the rent to the rent assessment committee during the original contractual term if he thinks that it is higher than the market level. It is not inconceivable, however, that tenants will be discouraged from making such references by the knowledge that they have no security of tenure beyond the contractual term.

It can be seen from this brief account that the linchpin of the 1988 Act is the abolition of rent control. However, the widespread use of the assured shorthold tenancy would also emasculate the security of tenure provisions of the 1988 Act. The assured shorthold tenancy would appear to give the landlord the best of both worlds, since it is not subject to rent control, and once the initial term has expired the tenant does not have security of tenure. It is likely, therefore, that assured shorthold tenancies will quickly become the predominant form of tenure in the private sector.

Note

Two particular lessons may be drawn from this historical account. The first is that although Rent Act protection was initially designed to concentrate on housing occupied by the poorest tenants only, there was a gradual, if haphazard extension to more and more types of property.

Under the 1977 Rent Act very few properties were excluded on the rateable value ground. The same is true under the Housing Act 1988.[16]

The second point is that the creation of and subsequent development in this area of the law cannot be seen from the purely legal viewpoint. It must be understood that housing policy, and the law that purports to give effect to that policy, has long been a matter of acute political controversy. This is particularly evident in the recent changes heralded in by the Housing Act 1988. Suggestions that "politics should be taken out of housing" tend to be impractical if not misguided. The history of legislative protection in the private sector is just one manifestation of a much wider debate about the extent to which the social need for housing can be met by the operation of the private sector of the economy. The social significance of the Rent Acts and the Housing Act 1988 cannot be understood without some awareness of these underlying political issues.

(B) ASSURED TENANCIES

The Housing Act 1988 defines an assured tenancy in sections 1 to 4 and Schedule 1. Although these are complicated provisions, there are essentially two aspects to the definition: the basic definition and the exceptions.

(1) The Basic Definition

The basic definition of an assured tenancy is to be found in section 1(1) of the Housing Act 1988 which provides:

A tenancy under which a *dwelling-house* is *let as a separate dwelling* is for the purposes of this Act an assured tenancy if and so long as—

(a)   the tenant or, as the case may be, each of the joint tenants is an *individual*; and

(b)   the tenant or, as the case may be, at least one of the joint tenants occupies the dwelling-house as his *only or principal home*; and

(c)   the tenancy is not one which, by virtue of subsection (2) or subsection (6) below, cannot be an assured tenancy.

The formula "let as a separate dwelling"—which defines the outermost boundary of the scheme of protection for occupiers of private sector residential accommodation—was used in the Increase of Rent and Mortgage Interest (War Restrictions) Act 1915,[17] and has been reproduced in all the subsequent legislation regulating the private sector. It is perhaps not surprising that every part of this formula has been the

---

[16] The abolition of domestic rating by the Local Government Finance Act 1988 and the introduction of the community charge has required the amendment of various housing provisions as regards lettings after April 1, 1990. The limits of the assured tenancy regime under the Housing Act 1988 are now determined by annual rent levels instead of rateable values. See p. 136.

[17] s.2(2).

subject of litigation. The requirement that the premises must be a dwelling-house is also derived from the Rent Acts.

The other components which make up the basic definition—the fact that the tenant be an individual and that he should occupy the dwelling-house as his only or principal home—originate in the public sector regime (which was introduced by the Housing Act 1980 and is now to be found in the Housing Act 1985).

In view of the fact that all the important concepts which delimit the scope of the assured tenancy scheme originate in previous legislation, in the discussion which follows extensive reference is made to cases decided under the Rent Acts and the Housing Acts.

(a) "Dwelling-house"

Section 45(1) states that a "dwelling-house" may be a "house or part of a house." It is clear that under this definition a flat qualifies as a dwelling-house for the purposes of section 1(1). Although it would appear that moveable structures are intended to be excluded from the Act, a caravan might in certain circumstances fall within the scope of the legislation. In *R.* v. *Nottinghamshire Registration Area* (*Rent Officer*), *ex p. Allen*[18] some of the factors which ought to be taken into account when deciding whether or not accommodation constitutes a dwelling-house were discussed. Farquharson J. said:

> There is no doubt in my mind that there was a letting of the caravan by the applicant to Mrs. Moore and that the purpose of that letting was that she should have the use of it as a separate dwelling. As counsel has emphasised, the only issue is whether the caravan is a house.
> In my judgment, it is not possible to say that, because the subject-matter is the letting of a caravan, it cannot be within the Act. Plainly, it must depend on the circumstances of the letting. Where the caravan is let as a moveable chattel, there can be no question of it being properly described as a house. Where, on the other hand, it is rendered completely immobile, either by the removal of its wheels or by its being permanently blocked by some brick or concrete construction, then it is more likely to be regarded as a house in the same way as a bungalow or prefabricated dwelling would be. Difficulties will arise when the facts are somewhere between those two extremes. The rent officer or the county court judge, as the case may be, will have regard to the features of the caravan that may reveal elements of site permanence, on the one hand, or mobility on the other. Are the wheels still on the vehicle? Are the stabilising struts of a permanent nature or of a kind ordinarily used by a caravan when moving from site to site? Are the services attached to the caravan? If so, are they of a fixed nature or readily detachable? Is the caravan ever moved? If so, for what purpose and with what facility? Plainly, rent officers will be on their guard against landlords who rent out caravans on their estates on a permanent or long-term basis and who seek to avoid the controls of the Rent Acts by making superficial arrangements tending to show some mobility in their caravans when the reality is that they are permanently based on the site.

[18] (1985) 52 P. & C.R. 41.

If the occupancy of the caravan is such that it is plainly used by the tenant as his or her permanent home, then there is a greater likelihood of the caravan being permanently in place rather than of its being used as a temporary expedient.

The present case, on its facts, is not altogether easy to determine because the characteristics of this vehicle place it on both sides of the line, but overall, in my judgment, the movement of these caravans from time to time, as disclosed by the applicant's affidavit, and the impermanence of the connection of the various services, establish that they could not, in reality (although I am only concerned with caravan no. 22), be described as houses.

The feature of mobility is not, of course, the sole determining factor in deciding on which side of the line any particular case will fall. However, it is perhaps more significant than any other.[19]

Compare *Makins* v. *Elson*[20] where it was held on similar facts that a caravan was a dwelling-house for the purposes of section 29 of the Finance Act 1965.

(b) "Let"

As has already been noted, for section 1 to operate there must be in existence a tenancy valid according to ordinary common law principles.[21] A licensee cannot be an assured tenant. The word "let" also includes "sub-let."[22]

(c) "As"

In delimiting the scope of protection under the Housing Act 1988 not only is it important that the premises which are let are used as a dwelling, the premises must have been let as a dwelling. Three types of problem arise in this context.

First, there is the situation where although the lease stipulates that premises are not to be used for residential purposes, in fact the tenant occupies the premises as his home. The relevant principle has been stated to be: "The important matter is the rights under the lease, not the *de facto* use."[23] In a number of reported instances the courts have stressed the importance of the terms of the tenancy. As Scarman L.J. stated in *Horford Investments Ltd.* v. *Lambert*[24] (in relation to section 1 of the Rent Act 1968):

The section affords protection to the tenancy of a house only if the house is let as a separate dwelling. This section directs attention to the letting, that is to say, the terms of the tenancy. The courts have proceeded on the basis that the terms of the tenancy are the primary consideration: see *Wolfe* v. *Hogan* [1949] 2 K.B.

---

[19] At 44–45.
[20] [1977] 1 W.L.R. 221.
[21] See pp. 49–84.
[22] Housing Act 1988, s.54(1).
[23] Scrutton L.J. in *Barrett* v. *Hardy Brothers (Alnwick) Ltd.* [1925] 2 K.B. 220 at 227.
[24] [1976] Ch. 39 at 52.

194. In my opinion there is here a principle of cardinal importance; whether a tenancy of a house (or part of a house) is protected depends on the terms of the tenancy, not on subsequent events. If, as may happen, subsequent events modify or alter the terms of the tenancy, they are relevant: otherwise no.

Deciding whether premises are let as a dwelling or for business purposes has not always been easy to determine. In *Ponder* v. *Hillman*[25] Goff J. said:

This is a case in which the plaintiffs claim against their tenant and a person who alleges that he has a valid subtenancy possession of the demised premises ...

The demised premises consist of a shop and other premises which can be and are in fact being used by the second defendant as dwelling accommodation ...

[The plaintiffs] say, and I accept, that I am entitled to look at the lease referred to in the statement of claim, and they have produced a counterpart to me. The submission is that it is plain, both from the description of the property in the parcels and from the covenants in the lease—the user covenants, a covenant about advertising and a proviso in the covenant whereby the tenant agrees to permit the lessors to advertise the premises during the last three months of the term—that the contemplation of the parties at the time was a letting as a shop and not as a dwelling-house.

In my judgment, that is a fair conclusion from the terms of the lease and at all events in the absence of any evidence to the contrary by the first defendant. It is sufficient to take the case out of the Act and entitle the plaintiffs to leave to sign judgment. I think that clearly appears from the decision of the Court of Appeal in *Wolfe* v. *Hogan* [1949] 2 K.B. 194 and in particular the judgment of Evershed L.J. at p. 203, where he approved the following passage in *Megarry* on *The Rent Acts* (1967), 4th ed., p. 19:

"Where the terms of the tenancy provide for or contemplate the use of the premises for some particular purpose, that purpose is the essential factor, not the nature of the premises or the actual use made of them. Thus, if premises are let for business purposes, the tenant cannot claim that they have been converted into a dwelling-house merely because somebody lives on the premises." ...

If, of course, the plaintiffs had consented or not objected to the occupation by the second defendant, different considerations would apply. However, their case is to the contrary and is not disputed by the first defendant.

The courts have also had to consider the situation where premises are let for mixed residential and business purposes and subsequently the business user ceases. While the premises are being used for business purposes, the tenancy falls within the scope of Part II of the Landlord and Tenant Act 1954. Once the premises cease to be used for business purposes the 1954 Act no longer applies; however, the tenancy does not become subject to the scheme of protection for private sector residential tenants (unless a new tenancy can be implied) since the premises were not let *as* a separate dwelling.[26]

---

[25] [1969] 1 W.L.R. 1261 at 1262–1263.

[26] See *Pulleng* v. *Curran* (1982) 44 P. & C. R. 58; *Russell* v. *Booker* (1982) 263 E.G. 513; *Wagle* v. *Trustees of Henry Smith's Charity Kensington Estate* [1989] 2 W.L.R. 669; *Webb* v. *Barnet L.B.C.* (1989) 21 H.L.R. 228 (a case involving the same issue in the public sector).

Secondly, problems may arise where the lease is silent on the question of user. In this situation the issue is what was contemplated by the parties. The intention of the parties may be gleaned from indications in the tenancy itself—for example, where premises are described as a shop[27]—and the surrounding circumstances, including the physical nature of the premises.[28]

Thirdly, there is the situation where a house is let together with other land (such as a garden or paddocks). Section 2 of the 1988 Act provides:

(1) If, under a tenancy, a dwelling-house is let together with other land, then, for the purposes of this Part of this Act,—

    (a)   if and so long as the main purpose of the letting is the provision of a home for the tenant or, where there are joint tenants, at least one of them, the other land shall be treated as part of the dwelling-house; and

    (b)   if and so long as the main purpose of the letting is not as mentioned in paragraph (a) above, the tenancy shall be treated as not being one under which a dwelling-house is let as a separate dwelling.

(2) Nothing in subsection (1) above affects any question whether a tenancy is precluded from being an assured tenancy by virtue of any provision of Schedule 1 to this Act.

If a dwelling is a mere "adjunct" to, say, a campsite, there will be no assured tenancy[29]; but where a garden or garage is let as an "adjunct" to a dwelling-house, the whole will be an assured tenancy. In *Jelley* v. *Buckman*[30] a strip of land used as a vegetable garden was held to be part of the dwelling and thus could not be severed by a purported conveyance by the landlord to a third party.

(d) "A"

For a tenancy to qualify as an assured tenancy the premises must be let as a single unit of habitation. This issue is to be determined at the date on which the tenancy was granted.

Whitty v. *Scott-Russell* [1950] 2 K.B. 32

In 1937 premises consisting of a house known as Tower House, Wadhurst, and a cottage and the garden, were let by the predecessor in title of the present

---

[27] See *Harris* v. *Evans* (1949) 153 E.G. 306.
[28] *Wolfe* v. *Hogan* [1949] 2 K.B. 194 at 204–205.
[29] See *Feyereisel* v. *Parry* [1952] 2 Q.B. 29, a case decided under the equivalent provisions of the Rent and Mortgage Interest Restrictions Act 1939.
[30] [1974] 2 Q.B. 488.

landlords to the defendant for three years at a rent of £75 a year, payable quarterly. The house and cottage were semi-detached, but there was no internal communication between them. The garden and land extended considerably beyond the site of the house. The lease described the demised premises as 'the dwelling-house and cottage with the garden and land thereto belonging,' and the tenant covenanted 'to use the premises as and for a private dwelling-house only.' The tenant did not require the cottage for use as part of his own home, and, with the assent of the original landlord, sub-let it. At the end of the three years the tenant held over as a yearly tenant. On December 22, 1948, the original lessor having died, his executors, the present landlords, gave the tenant notice to quit expiring on June 24, 1949. The tenant failed to vacate the premises, and the landlords brought the present action, claiming possession of the house and cottage. On December 15 the judge dismissed the action, holding that the house and cottage were let as one dwelling-house within the meaning of the Rent Restriction Acts, and that the tenant was protected.

The landlords appealed.

Asquith L.J. said (at 37–40):

[Was] the 'complex' let a 'dwelling-house'? ...

The main authority relied on by the tenant on this issue is *Langford Property Co., Ltd* v. *Goldrich* ([1949] 1 K.B. 511). That was a case in which two flats, not contiguous but forming part of the same block of flats under a single roof, were held to be a 'dwelling-house' within the definition. Somervell L.J., in a judgment with which the other two members of the court concurred, says: "In my opinion, if the facts justify such a finding, two flats, or indeed so far as I can see two houses could be a separate dwelling-house within the meaning of the definition." ...

He appears to base this conclusion partly on the terms of the lease, under which the subject-matter let is expressed to be two flats; partly on the Interpretation Act, whereby the singular prima facie includes the plural, hence 'house' in the definition includes houses; but partly also (in relation to the part of the definition which reads 'let as a separate dwelling') on the fact that the tenant in that case wanted the two flats as a home for his family or its overflow, which one flat would have been unable to accommodate.

If the Interpretation Act alone were concerned, this reasoning would be open to the comment that, if the inclusion of the plural in the singular permitted us to read 'house' as including houses, it would equally permit (or perhaps require) us to read 'let as a separate dwelling' as including 'let as two separate dwellings.' An impartial application of the Interpretation Act might lead to odd results.

It is unnecessary, however, to speculate on this, since we are bound by the decision in *Langford Property Co., Ld* v. *Goldrich*, of which this was part of the ratio decidendi. It enables us to read 'house' as covering two houses. But is this (composite) 'house' in the present case 'let as a separate dwelling'? In *Langford Property Co., Ld* v. *Goldrich*, the tenant's purpose in taking two flats was that his family should occupy both, as in fact they did. 'What happened here,' says Somervell L.J. (517), 'was that the tenant wished to accommodate in his home these relatives to whom I have referred, and he wanted more accommodation than could be found or conveniently found in one flat. He ... thereupon took the two flats and made those two flats his home.' It would seem that the circumstance that the tenant intended to make the two flats—the totality of the parcels let—his home, was thought material, and indeed necessary, by Somervell L.J., to his decision that the flats were let 'as a separate dwelling.' If the flats had been let to the tenant, one to be dwelt in by him and his family, the other not to be so dwelt in, the decision might, it appears, have been different. In the present case the tenant only took the cottage along with the house because the lessor refused to let the one without the other. He never lived in, and never from the start intended to live in, the cottage .... .

In these circumstances, we are of opinion that the complex 'let' in this case was a dwelling-house within the definition, and we are fortified in that opinion by the concession, in argument, that if X took a tenancy of a house consisting of, say, three floors, and sub-let one floor at once and permanently, the fact of the sublease would not deprive the subject-matter of the head lease of its character as a dwelling-house, provided that in other respects it possessed that character. It cannot in our view make a crucial difference that in the case supposed the part sub-let and the part not sub-let possess internal inter-communication through the common stair, whereas in this case the two units, one of which is sub-let, are two houses clamped together and without such internal intercommunication.

St Catherine's College v. *Dorling* [1980] 1 W.L.R. 66

Eveleigh L.J. said (at 67–70):

[As a result of the passing of Rent Act 1977, section 8] a firm of estate agents in Oxford, Messrs. Runyards, with the co-operation of a large number of Oxford colleges, introduced a scheme by which it was envisaged that accommo-dation would more readily be made available to undergraduates. They published a booklet giving details of that scheme. The general idea was that the owner of the house would let premises to the college, who would then make the accommodation available to undergraduates. A £50 deposit was taken from undergraduates who had made an application for the accommodation, and that deposit was treated as an application fee, unless the arrangements were finally completed, when it was treated as part-payment of rent. Runyards orally guaranteed to the colleges concerned that every undergraduate would have a separate room.

In so far as 208, Headington Road is concerned, there were four under-graduates of the college who applied to Messrs Runyards for accommodation. They found a suitable house, namely, 208, Headington Road. The college was willing to take those premises under a lease.

On June 12, 1978 the undergraduates signed a document entitled 'Agreement and Indemnity,' which stated:

'In consideration of the College, through the Domestic Bursar, entering on my behalf into a Lease of 208 Headington Road, Oxford, from July 8, 1978 for one year less 7 days at a rent of £224.25 per month ... I hereby agree with the College to fulfil and observe all conditions and covenants contained in their lease and to indemnify the College against all liabilities which it may incur there under.'

The question in this case is whether the premises were let as a separate dwelling within the meaning of section 1. The important point in answering that question is to determine the contemplated use of the premises .... .

So it follows that one has to consider the terms of the lease and the surrounding circumstances at the time that the lease was granted. It may be that in some cases that assistance can be obtained from the subsequent user of the premises. But in my opinion generally speaking such assistance will be found to be a matter of last resort.

I turn to consider the terms of the tenancy agreement in this case. There is the usual habendum and reddendum, and then I turn to clause 2 (1), in which the tenant covenants:

'(i) Not to use the demised premises otherwise than for occupation by a person or persons who are as specified by Section 8 of the Rent Act 1977 pursuing or intending to pursue a course of study provided by the Tenant whether the said person or persons occupy the demised premises as sub-tenants or licensees. (ii) Not to assign sub-let part with possession or share possession or occupation of all or part of the demised premises furniture fittings or effects or any part thereof provided that there shall be no breach of this clause if the Tenant shall be a specified educational institution as defined by Section 8 of the Rent Act 1977 and either the Tenant sub-lets only to a person who is pursuing or intending to pursue a course of study provided by the Tenant or the Tenant grants a licence for the use of the demised premises to such person.'

Then clause (m), the user clause, reads:

'Not to carry on or permit to be carried on upon the demised premises any profession trade or business whatsoever or let apartments or receive paying guests in the demised premises but to use or permit the same to be used as private residence only in occupation of one person per room and not in any way to contravene the Town and Country Planning Acts and not to exhibit any notice or poster on any portion of the demised premises.'

[Counsel for the college] has submitted that here a group of students, or undergraduates, intended to occupy the premises as joint occupants of the whole, and that this was the object and purport of the tenancy granted to the college. He particularly relied on sub-clause (m) and invited the court to say that the words 'to be used as private residence only' should be read to include the indefinite article: that is to say, 'to be used as *a* private residence only' ...

[Counsel for the college] has argued, by analogy that if these premises were to be used as a private residence, the emphasis being on the indefinite article, it meant that they were not to be used as a number of different private residences, therefore they were let as a whole, with the object of their being inhabited jointly by the students. He also placed some reliance on the words of sub-clause (l)(ii), where it reads 'either the tenant sublets only to a person who is pursuing' etc. He said it was therefore contemplated that no more than one person would take, or that persons could take jointly being responsible for the whole.

On the other hand, [counsel for the respondent landlord] has contended that clause 2(m) comes to his aid. He has invited the court to construe the phrase 'as private residence' as meaning for residential purposes. I would myself accept that submission. One cannot read the words 'as private residence' without reading the words that follow, namely, 'in the occupation of one person per room.' In my opinion it is no accidental omission of the indefinite article. There is an intentional omission; and the phrase 'as private residence' is used similarly to the expression 'as business premises.' It is descriptive of the user and not of the premises themselves.

When one then sees that what is envisaged is the occupation of one person per room, using that for private purposes, and then turns to the other provision in sub-clause (l) which I have read, one sees that subletting or a licence to use is contemplated, and the words used are 'sublet only to a person'. The importance, to my mind, of the words in that sub-clause is that they show that a subletting is envisaged. That envisages as I see it (for one must read this as a whole) that the college is permitted to sublet to a person who is to occupy a single room as a private residence. If the college is to be allowed to 'sublet to a person' (to use the words of the sub-clause) any part of the building, it would follow that it should be allowed to let to more than one person, or the building would otherwise have another part unused. Quite clearly it was never contemplated that the college itself should occupy or make any particular use of the premises, other, that is to say, than as accommodation for undergraduates. Furthermore, of course, the plural is used in sub-clause (l)(i), where we see the words 'for occupation by a person or persons'.

I therefore read these two sub-clauses as saying that the college shall be in a position to sublet, and shall be in a position to sublet to 'persons'; but they must be persons 'pursuing or intending to pursue a course of study'. The use of the singular in sub-paragraph (ii) is simply because it is describing the type of person who may be a sub-tenant; and, as the college may sublet to a particular type of sub-tenant and must do so only for occupation of one person per room, it follows, in my opinion, that the purpose of this letting was that the college should be in a position to do just that. In other words, what was being granted to the college here was a tenancy of a building which contained a number of units of habitation, as they have been called. From that interpretation of this lease I would conclude that the premises were not let as separate dwellings ...

(e) "Separate"

The requirement for 'separateness' of the dwelling causes some difficulty, especially when residential premises are shared. There are a number of different factual situations which must be distinguished.

First, occupiers of shared premises may be classified as joint tenants. Where there is a written agreement, there may be an express grant of a joint tenancy to two or more persons (such as to a husband and wife or a group of friends). However, as has been seen, the courts are not bound by the labels which the parties attach to their agreements, and two or more so-called licence agreements may be construed as giving rise to a joint tenancy.[31] Similarly, a joint tenancy may arise from an oral agreement between the landlord and the occupiers of the premises.

Where a joint tenancy exists the occupiers will jointly be assured tenants and be deemed to live as a single unit in the separate accommodation. As long as one of the joint tenants occupies the premises as his only or principal home the tenancy will be assured.[32]

Secondly, accommodation may be shared by a number of individual tenants. A common arrangement is where a house is let out to a number of individual occupiers, each of which is granted exclusive possession of a bedroom and a right to share the kitchen, bathroom and other common facilities. In principle, this type of situation does not fall within the basic definition; the bedroom cannot be regarded as having been let as a separate dwelling since the ordinary activities of daily existence will be carried on in the house as a whole rather than in the room.

---

[31] *Antoniades* v. *Villiers* [1990] A.C. 417 (see pp. 63–77).
[32] Housing Act 1988, s.1(1)(b). The courts had achieved a very similar result in relation to statutory tenancies under the Rent Acts: *Lloyd* v. *Sadler* [1978] Q.B. 774.

Section 3 of the Housing Act 1988, however, ensures that where accommodation is shared the occupiers may qualify as assured tenants as long as they each have some element of "exclusive occupation":

(1) Where a tenant has the exclusive occupation of any accommodation (in this section referred to as "the separate accommodation") and—

    (a) the terms as between the tenant and his landlord on which he holds the separate accommodation include the use of other accommodation (in this section referred to as "the shared accommodation") in common with another person or other persons, not being or including the landlord, and

    (b) by reason only of the circumstances mentioned in paragraph (a) above, the separate accommodation would not, apart from this section, be a dwelling-house let on an assured tenancy,

the separate accommodation shall be deemed to be a dwelling-house let on an assured tenancy and the following provisions of this section shall have effect.

(2) For the avoidance of doubt it is hereby declared that where, for the purpose of determining the rateable value of the separate accommodation, it is necessary to make an apportionment under Part II of Schedule 1 to this Act, regard is to be had to the circumstances mentioned in subsection (1)(a) above.

(3) While the tenant is in possession of the separate accommodation, any term of the tenancy terminating or modifying, or providing for the termination or modification of, his right to the use of any of the shared accommodation which is living accommodation shall be of no effect.

(4) Where the terms of the tenancy are such that, at any time during the tenancy, the persons in common with whom the tenant is entitled to the use of the shared accommodation could be varied or their number could be increased, nothing in subsection (3) above shall prevent those terms from having effect so far as they relate to any such variation or increase.

(5) In this section "living accommodation" means accommodation of such a nature that the fact that it constitutes or is included in the shared accommodation is sufficient, apart from this section, to prevent the tenancy from constituting an assured tenancy of a dwelling-house.

It should be noted that section 3 does not apply where the tenant shares accommodation with the landlord or with the landlord and others.

Thirdly, premises may be let to a single tenant who shares the accommodation with one or more sub-tenants. Section 4 of the 1988 Act provides:

(1) Where the tenant of a dwelling-house has sub-let a part but not the whole of the dwelling-house, then, as against his landlord or any superior landlord, no part of the dwelling-house shall be treated as excluded from being a dwelling-house let on an assured tenancy by reason only that the terms on which any person claiming under the tenant holds any part of the dwelling-house include the use of accommodation in common with other persons.

(2) Nothing in this section affects the rights against, and liabilities to, each other of the tenant and any person claiming under him, or of any two such persons.

The operation of this section can be demonstrated by a simple example:

T is an assured tenant of a flat which comprises two bedrooms a kitchen and a bathroom. T sub-lets one bedroom to S, and grants S a right to share the kitchen and bathroom. As a result of section 4 T remains an assured tenant of the flat even though he shares living accommodation with S.

Fourthly, a tenant may share accommodation with his landlord. In such a situation the tenancy cannot be assured. One of the express exceptions to the assured tenancy regime relates to resident landlords.[33]

As a final point it should be noted that a number of occupiers may share accommodation by virtue of individual licence agreements. If these licence agreements are genuine, then there is no assured tenancy because the premises are not "let" within the meaning of section 1(1).[34]

(f) "Dwelling"

The premises must be let as a dwelling. This condition will generally be satisfied only if the premises are used for "all the major activities of life, particularly sleeping, cooking and feeding."[35]

In *Metropolitan Properties* v. *Barder*[36] the tenant of a flat subsequently negotiated another tenancy for a single "servant's room" which he apparently needed for an *au pair* girl. The Court of Appeal held that this second tenancy could not be regarded as a "dwelling" and was thus not protected by the Rent Acts. Edmund Davies L.J. noted:

The size of the room, its furnishing and the use to which it was being put, (*i.e.* as the au pair girl's bedroom) establish that its user was an annexe or overflow of the flat, and its entirely distinct letting on a quarterly basis was not the letting of a dwelling-house. I would stress that the present decision has no application to a case where a single room is let as the occupier's place of habitation for all purposes; to adopt the words of Lord Greene M.R. in *Curl* v. *Angelo* ([1948] 2 All ER 189, 191) the present case is totally different "from the case where the only premises demised consist of one room and that is the place where the tenant moves and has his being."[37]

(g) "Individual"

The requirement that the tenant (or where there is a joint tenancy, one of the joint tenants) must be an individual means that where residential premises are let to a company the tenancy cannot be assured.

---

[33] See pp. 148–151.
[34] See *A.G. Securities* v. *Vaughan* [1990] A.C. 417 (see pp. 63–77).
[35] Scott L.J. in *Wright* v. *Howell* (1947) 92 S.J. 26. See also *Curl* v. *Angelo* [1948] 2 All E.R. 189.
[36] [1968] 1 W.L.R. 286.
[37] At 294.

(Similarly, under the Rent Act 1977, since a statutory tenancy continues only so long as the tenant "occupies the dwelling-house as his residence,"[38] a company cannot be a statutory tenant.[39])

Potential problems arise where the "company let" is artificially employed by landlords with a view to exploiting this exception to the schemes of statutory protection.

Hilton v. *Plustitle Ltd.* [1988] 1 W.L.R. 149

Croom-Johnson L.J. (giving the judgment of the Court of Appeal) said (at 150–155):

If a dwelling house is let to a limited company, the company cannot become a statutory tenant under the terms of section 2 of the Rent Act 1977, on the termination of the tenancy. This has been so since *Hiller* v. *United Dairies (London) Ltd.* [1934] 1 K.B. 57. This rule has remained unchanged during re-enactments of the Rent Acts ever since. If a tenancy is granted to one person, *e.g.* a company, on the terms that someone else is to reside in the house, there will be no statutory tenancy in favour of that other person: *S. L. Dando Ltd.* v. *Hitchcock* [1954] 2 Q.B. 317. In *Firstcross Ltd.* v. *East West (Export/Import) Ltd.* (1980) 255 E.G. 355 the tenants' nominee was their director and was actually named in the agreement: it was held he acquired no statutory tenancy. Accordingly, if a landlord does not want to be saddled with a statutory tenant he lets on what is known as a "company let."

The plaintiff in this action, Mr. Hilton, is a civil engineer who has in recent years reconstructed a number of premises in London and therein created flats which are high quality flats. They also contain built-in furniture made in his own workshop. They are let at not excessive but market rents for flats of that quality. He is a good landlord who provides value for money. His policy is to let only as company flats, and his flats are advertised as such.

The second defendant, Miss Rose, is an actress. She saw in an evening newspaper on 8 August 1986 an advertisement referring to one of the plaintiff's flats. The advertisement made it clear that the letting was to be a company let. She knew what that meant. She got in touch with the plaintiff and saw several flats. Eventually she saw one at 45, Priory Road, London, N.W.6. Miss Rose, as an actress, had no need for a company, but the plaintiff made it clear that any letting would have to be a company let and that the rent would have to be guaranteed by a third party. He gave her the name and telephone number of his accountant, who would be able to provide her with a company which could become the tenant and then nominate her as the person who would reside in its flat. As the judge found, the plaintiff told her that the letting to the company would be for a limited period, with a possibility of renewal if everything was satisfactory. Miss Rose did not go to the accountant. She took advice from her solicitors, and went to a firm called Jordans, from whom she bought a company, the first defendant, off the shelf. It was called Plustitle Ltd. It cost her £150. She became a shareholder and a director.

On 1 September 1986 the company entered into a written agreement with the plaintiff to take the flat for an initial term of six months at a rent of £345 per month. Miss Rose signed the agreement as managing director of the company.

---

[38] Rent Act 1977, s.2(1)(a).
[39] *Carter* v. *S.U. Carburettor Co.* [1942] 2 All E.R. 228.

The agreement gave the company the right to nominate the occupiers of the property, who would pay no rent. The agreement contained all the usual tenant's covenants. The plaintiff consented to maintain the services in good condition. The rent and fees to be paid by the company were guaranteed by John Rose, who is Miss Rose's brother. Before that agreement was made, the plaintiff obtained a banker's reference for Miss Rose for an amount which was the obligation to pay the monthly rent of £345.

In February 1987 the term was by mutual agreement extended for three months till May. It was followed by an offer for a further three months' extension. There was a dispute about a slight increase in the rent and so the offer was withdrawn by the plaintiff. He asked for possession. Miss Rose sought legal advice and refused to leave. The result has been the present proceedings, in which the plaintiff has asked for an order for possession on the basis that this was a company letting. Miss Rose defends the claim on the basis that the letting to the company was a sham. That has been the only issue before the court.

The judge found the defence was not made out, and he made an order for possession. He gave a long and careful judgment. He found that Miss Rose fully understood what she was doing, and acted after obtaining legal advice. After moving in she paid the rent by her personal cheques, the company not having a bank account. After reviewing all the evidence, the judge said:

" ... I find without the slightest hesitation that it was both parties' clear intention, with all knowledge of what this involved, that the flat should be let to a company and not to Miss Rose personally. I find that as a fact, having heard the evidence, and having noted submissions made on behalf of Miss Rose in that respect."

He listed 16 items of fact, all of which indicated that Miss Rose entered into the whole transaction with the intention that this was to be a company let in the normal way, and that in the agreement there were no provisions inconsistent with the letting being to a company and not to Miss Rose. The judgment concluded:

"the reality was indeed the factual matrix that the company was the tenant and [Miss Rose] was not liable personally for anything at all. There is no disagreement between the parties that at all material times the plaintiff insisted upon a limited company as his tenant. It is quite plain upon the construction of the written agreement that its object was to create a letting to a company. [Miss Rose] has the burden of showing that this prima facie construction is either deliberately deceptive or in any way wrong. There is no evidence before me, and I mean no evidence, to support that contention. Thus, in the end, on the basis of the agreement itself and also the factual matrix, I find that this was a letting to a limited company which came to an end and that the contention that this was a sham fails in limine. At no time did the landlord purport to create or created any rights in [Miss Rose]."

Mr. Walter, for Miss Rose, says that the employment of the company was a sham in that it was a device to prevent Miss Rose from being the tenant, and so far from her being the company's nominee, the company was her agent. Accordingly, he submits, the reality of the letting was that it was to her and not to the company.

The mere fact that the purpose of the legal arrangement was to prevent the creation of the statutory tenancy is by itself not enough. In *Aldrington Garages Ltd.* v. *Fielder* (1978) 37 P. & C.R. 461, 468, Geoffrey Lane L.J. said:

"There is no reason why, if it is possible and properly done, agreements should not be entered into which do not fall within the Rent Acts, and the mere fact that those agreements may result in enhanced profits for the owners does not necessarily mean that the agreements should be construed as tenancies rather than as licences."

Roskill L.J. said, at p. 473:

"persons are entitled to arrange their affairs to their best advantage so long as the law allows it. That has long been the position in tax cases, and equally long been the position in Landlord and Tenant and Rent Acts cases."

This subject was given a detailed summary in *Antoniades* v. *Villiers* [1988] 3 W.L.R. 139, 147, by Bingham L.J., who added to the quotations from Geoffrey Lane L.J. and Roskill L.J. his own observation:

"It is not a crime, nor is it contrary to public policy, for a property owner to license occupiers to occupy property on terms which do not give rise to a tenancy."

Nevertheless, as Bingham L.J. stated, at p. 146:

"The court should be astute to detect and frustrate sham devices and artificial transactions whose only object is to disguise the grant of a tenancy and to evade the Rent Acts: *Street* v. *Mountford* [1985] A.C. 809, 825H. ... "

He went on to say:

"The court has to be especially wary and especially careful to see that things like premiums are not being used to conceal payments of rent ... "

"Shams" must be considered in many contexts. The accepted definition, to which the judge in the present case was referred, is that given by Diplock L.J. in *Snook* v. *London and West Riding Investments Ltd.* [1967] 2 Q.B. 786, 802:

"As regards the contention of the plaintiff that the transactions between himself, Auto Finance and the defendants were a 'sham,' it is, I think, necessary to consider what, if any, legal concept is involved in the use of this popular and pejorative word. I apprehend that, if it has any meaning in law, it means acts done or documents executed by the parties to the 'sham' which are intended by them to give to third parties or to the court the appearance of creating between the parties legal rights and obligations different from the actual legal rights and obligations (if any) which the parties intend to create. But one thing, I think, is clear in legal principle, morality and the authorities (see *Yorkshire Railway Wagon Co.* v. *Maclure* (1882) 21 Ch.D. 309 and *Stoneleigh Finance Ltd.* v. *Phillips* [1965] 2 Q.B. 537), that for acts or documents to be a 'sham,' with whatever legal consequences follow from this, all the parties thereto must have a common intention that the acts or documents are not to create the legal rights and obligations which they give the appearance of creating."

As Bingham L.J. expressed it in *Antoniades* v. *Villiers* [1988] 3 W.L.R. 139, 147:

"Put more shortly, a sham exists where the parties say one thing intending another: *Donald* v. *Baldwyn* [1953] N.Z.L.R. 313, 321, *per* F. B. Adams J."

In the present case the judge found as a fact that it was the intention of both parties, with all knowledge of what this involved, that the flat should be let to the company and not to Miss Rose personally. This finding has not been challenged. Directing himself in accordance with the law as stated by Diplock L.J. in the *Snook* case, he held that this transaction was not a sham. We do not find it possible to fault this reasoning.

Once the letting has been found not to be a sham, the lease has to be construed. In *Street* v. *Mountford* [1985] A.C. 809, 825, Lord Templeman said that the Rent Acts must not be allowed to alter or influence the construction of an agreement. In *Shell-Mex and B.P. Ltd.* v. *Manchester Garages Ltd.* [1971] 1 W.L.R. 612, 619, Buckley L.J. said:

> "It may be that this is a device which has been adopted by the plaintiff company to avoid possible consequences of the Landlord and Tenant Act 1954, which would have affected a transaction being one of landlord and tenant; but, in my judgment, one cannot take that into account in construing such a document to find out what the true nature of the transaction is."

In the present case, as the judge pointed out, the only construction of the lease was that the letting was to the company and not in any way to Miss Rose.

Mr. Walter has relied on the decision in *Gisborne* v. *Burton* [1988] 3 W.L.R. 921. In that case, in order to circumvent the provisions as to security of tenure conferred on the tenant of an agricultural holding under the relevant legislation, the owner of a farm, intending that it should be let to Mr. Burton, first let it to his own wife, who on the same day sublet it to Mr. Burton. When a notice to quit was served on the wife by the husband's personal representatives, she served no counter-notice. Her lease therefore came to an end, and so did the sublease in accordance with the common law. The Court of Appeal (Dillon and Russell L.JJ., Ralph Gibson L.J. dissenting) held that the head lease to the wife was a sham and that the subtenant was in reality the tenant and he was entitled to the protection of the Agricultural Holdings Acts, notwithstanding that he had fully understood that the whole purpose of the transaction was to avoid his having such security.

Dillon L.J. dealt with the facts as being analogous to those in *Johnson* v. *Moreton* [1980] A.C. 37. In *Johnson's* case the agricultural tenant had entered into a covenant not to serve a counter-notice under the Agricultural Holdings Act 1948. The House of Lords held that to allow such a covenant to be effective would be contrary to public interest as defeating the purpose for which the Act had been passed. It was not possible for tenants to contract out of the protection which Parliament had intended that they should have. The covenant was therefore unenforceable. Dillon L.J. compared *Gisborne's* case with *Johnson's* case. He concluded that the inclusion of the landlord's wife in the series of leases had the effect at the highest of making her

> "a mere nominee or agent of [the husband] to grant a tenancy to [Mr. Burton], and what actually happened was that [the husband] granted such a tenancy:" [1988] 3 W.L.R. 921, 928

In coming to that conclusion he took into account the result of *Street* v. *Mountford* [1985] A.C. 809, where Lord Templeman stated that on the true interpretation of the facts of that case the tenants obtained a tenancy and not a licence because what they received was exclusive occupation, notwithstanding that the document was called a licence. Dillon L.J. also took into account the recent tax cases based on *W. T. Ramsey Ltd.* v. *Inland Revenue Commissioners* [1982] A.C. 300, such as *Furniss* v. *Dawson* [1984] A.C. 474, where it was stated that the fiscal consequences of a series of transactions should be examined. Dillon L.J. said, at p. 927:

> "It seems to me that a similar principle must be applicable wherever there is a pre-ordained series of transactions which is intended to avoid some mandatory

statutory provision, even if not of a fiscal nature. You must look at the effect of the scheme as a whole ... "

It was in applying that test that Dillon L.J. concluded that the landlord's wife had been only the agent of the landlord.

Russell L.J. also concluded that the inclusion of the landlord's wife in the series of transactions was only in order to prevent Mr. Burton from having the right to serve a counter-notice. He concluded that since there was never any intention that the landlord's wife should farm the land, her inclusion in the transaction was tantamount to an agreement or a promise on the part of Mr. Burton not to serve a counter-notice, and so was contrary to *Johnson* v. *Moreton*.

Mr. Coney, for the plaintiff, submits that this appeal is concluded by the judge's findings of fact and that there was no "sham" within the *Snook* test [1967] 2 Q.B. 786. He submits that the real ratio of *Street* v. *Mountford* was that the finding in the agreement that the occupation was to be exclusive was crucial: after that the agreement could only be construed so as to mean that the occupation was under a tenancy. Here, looking at the substance and not only at the form, the letting was to the company, as both parties always intended that it should be. He distinguishes *Gisborne* v. *Burton* on the very ground on which the Court of Appeal decided it, that the documents were never intended to be acted on. The device of including the landlord's wife meant that she was in effect acting as her husband's agent.

In the present case, the company was not the plaintiff's agent. It was the only tenant to whom he was prepared to let the property, and the covenants in the lease were perfectly capable of being complied with by the company through its nominee, Miss Rose, and enforced against the company by the plaintiff. Unlike *Street* v. *Mountford* the transaction did represent the true position. The company obtained a protected tenancy with the benefits attached to that but neither it nor Miss Rose obtained a statutory tenancy when the protected tenancy came to an end.

We conclude that if the facts are consistent with the purported transaction, we see no reason why, by analogy with *Gisborne's* case, public policy should override the transaction which was deliberately intended to avoid, but not evade, the Rent Acts. Otherwise, public policy would be contradicting section 2 of the Rent Act 1977 and all the decisions which have preceded it. We would dismiss the appeal.

The Appeal Committee of the House of Lords refused leave to appeal.[40]

Note

The "company let" raises interesting questions from a number of angles. From the legal point of view there is a question of interpretation: is the letting to the company genuine or a sham?

Considering the various elements of the transaction between Mr Hilton and Miss Rose it is perhaps surprising that the Court of Appeal decided that the letting to Plustitle Ltd was genuine.[41] Croom-Johnson L.J. placed particular emphasis on the decision of the Court of Appeal

---

[40] [1989] 1 W.L.R. 310.
[41] Compare *Estavest Investment Ltd.* v. *Commercial Investments Ltd.* (1989) 21 H.L.R. 106.

in *Antoniades* v. *Villiers*[42] which was subsequently reversed by the House of Lords.[43] The approach adopted by Croom-Johnson L.J. is difficult to reconcile with the House of Lords' decision in *Antoniades* v. *Villiers*.

The superficially technical questions surrounding the interpretation of the agreement should not be allowed to conceal the important policy issues. The decision by the Court of Appeal in *Hilton* v. *Plustitle Ltd.* effectively allows landlords to "contract out" of statutory schemes designed to protect tenants.

The dividing line between avoidance and evasion has been the subject of extended discussion in the field of taxation (see in particular *Ramsey (W.T.) Ltd.* v. *I.R.C.*[44] and *Furniss* v. *Dawson*[45]). The potential application of the doctrines formulated in these cases to the landlord-tenant sphere has only recently come to be recognised by members of the judiciary.[46]

(h) "Only or principal home"

The requirement that the tenant must occupy the dwelling-house as his only or principal home forms part of the definition of a secure tenancy under the Housing Act 1985. Some assistance on how the courts will interpret the phrase "only or principal home" can be derived from cases decided under section 81 of the 1985 Act.[47]

Crawley Borough Council v. *Sawyer* (1988) 20 H.L.R. 98

Parker L.J. said (at 99-102):

The plaintiffs appeal from a decision of His Honour Judge MacManus in the Horsham County Court on March 16, 1987, whereby he dismissed their claim for possession of premises known as 22 Cobnor Close, Gossops Green, Crawley. The defendant was granted the tenancy of those premises on September 6, 1982, but had in fact been occupying them for some years before. He first went into occupation in 1978.

On May 20, 1986 it was reported to the plaintiffs that the premises were vacant, and on enquiry they discovered that the electricity had been cut off in June 1985 and the gas some time in 1986. It is common ground that what happened was that in 1985 the defendant had gone to live with his girlfriend at 26 Drakes Close, Horsham.

---

[42] [1990] A.C. 417.
[43] *Idem.* (pp. 63–77).
[44] [1982] A.C. 300.
[45] [1984] A.C. 474.
[46] See *Gisbourne* v. *Burton* [1989] Q.B. 390, and Rogers, Shams, subtenancies and evasion of protective legislation [1989] Conv. 196.
[47] See pp. 175–176.

In July 1986 there was a conversation between the defendant and the plaintiffs' representative, during which the defendant said that he was living with his girlfriend at Drakes Close and was purchasing it with her. ...

During the period when he was absent the defendant had paid the rent of the premises including the rates, he had visited them about once per month, and at some time had spent a week there.

On August 29, the plaintiffs gave notice to quit, expiring on September 30. By that time the defendant and his girlfriend had broken up, and the defendant had apparently ceased to make mortgage payments. He returned to the premises, according to his evidence, on October 10 and has been there ever since ...

The issue before the learned judge, on facts which to a very large extent were not disputed, was simply whether the tenant was or was not a secure tenant within the meaning of section 81 of the Housing Act. ... .

Section 81 provides:

"The tenant condition is that the tenant is an individual and occupies the dwelling-house as his only or principal home: or, where the tenancy is a joint tenancy, that each of the joint tenants is an individual and at least one of them occupies the dwelling-house as his only or principal home."

. . . .

Our attention was drawn to two cases which were said to show that there was a material difference between occupying as a residence and occupying as a home. The first is *Hampstead Way Investments Ltd.* v. *Lewis-Weare* [1985] 1 W.L.R. 164. In that case Lord Brandon made certain observations to which our attention was drawn. Only two short passages were referred to, one of which is as follows (p. 169):

" ... in order to determine this appeal, it is necessary to examine the more important cases decided between 1920 and 1968 on what is meant by the occupation of a dwelling-house by a person as his residence, or, as it is put in many of the cases (without, in my view, any difference in meaning) the occupation of a dwelling-house by a person as his home."

Then at E–F on the same page:

"Approaching the matter on that basis, it seems to me that the following propositions of general application, relevant to the present case, can be derived from the decisions concerned.

(1) A person may have two dwelling-houses, each of which he occupies as his home, so that, if either of them is let to him, his tenancy of it is protected by the Rent Act 1977."

That case does not appear to me to assist the appellants in any way. Lord Brandon quite plainly equates the two phrases as being, in effect, one and the same.

We were also referred to *Herbert* v. *Byrne* [1964] 1 All E.R. 882, and in particular to the judgment of Lord Justice Salmon. He says this (p. 887):

"In my view, if the evidence establishes, as it does here, a substantial degree of regular personal occupation by the tenant of an essentially residential nature, it would be difficult, if not impossible for a court to hold that he was not in occupation of the premises as a home within the meaning of the word as used by this court in *Skinner* v. *Geary*, and in the later authorities. In *Langford Property Co. Ltd.* v. *Athanassoglou* the evidence was that the appellant's family resided in his country home seven days a week and the appellant slept there on five days a week; that he slept two nights a week in his London flat, which was fully furnished, but very rarely took a meal there, and that the flat was used for no other purposes. This court held that he occupied the flat as a home, and that there was no evidence to support the county court judge's finding to the contrary."

It was submitted that the earlier passage which I read provides a definition. With respect, it does no such thing. It is merely giving an example of a case which was plain and which it would be impossible to upset if the learned judge were to make such a finding. For my part, it appears to me that Salmon L.J. also was taking the line pursued by Lord Brandon. It is also of interest to note, in view of a later submission made on behalf of the appellants, that at p. 886 Lord Denning M.R. says this:

"In order to be in personal occupation of a house, it is not necessary that the tenant should be there himself with his family all the time. A sea captain may be away from his house for months at a time, but it is none the less his home ... Nor does it mean that, to gain protection, the tenant must have it as his only home. A man who has a home in the country may also have a home in London, spending a couple of nights there a week, and yet be protected in respect of it."

It is quite plain that it is possible to occupy as a home two places at the same time, and indeed that is inherent in the wording of section 81. It is therefore plain that, if you can occupy two houses at the same time as a home, actual physical occupation cannot be necessary, because one cannot be physically in two places at the same time.

So far as the two cases relied upon by the learned judge are concerned, they do not appear to me to be open to criticism as cases to which he was entitled to refer. Going through the whole thread of these matters is the common principle that in order to occupy premises as a home, first, there must be signs of occupation—that is to say, there must be furniture and so forth so that the house can be occupied as a home—and, secondly, there must be an intention, if not physically present, to return to it. That is the situation envisaged in the examples given by the Master of the Rolls of, for example, the sea captain who is away for a while. His house is left fully furnished, ready for occupation, no doubt the rent paid in his absence, but he is not physically there and may not be for a very long period indeed.

In the present case the learned judge was, on the evidence, in my view well entitled to hold that throughout the period the premises the subject of the action were occupied by the defendant as a home. The only question which really arose is whether it was occupied as a principal home. The learned judge considered the question. He came to the conclusion which he did on the basis that the defendant had left to live with his girlfriend but with no intention of giving up permanent residence of Cobnor Close.

. ... The situation, which the judge was entitled to take into account, was that he had before him the evidence of the defendant, who asserted throughout that he had every intention of returning and not merely that he had not abandoned the flat. He said in his evidence-in-chief: "I accept I was not there but I had every intention to return." He again said he had every intention to return somewhat later on and that he did not intend to give up the flat. He was staying with his girlfriend helping her to buy a house. ...

The learned judge was entitled to take the view that he was there on a temporary basis and that his principal home throughout remained the premises the subject of the action. ...

O'Connor L.J. agreed.

Note

Under the Rent Act 1977 statutory tenancy continues as long as the tenant occupies the dwelling-house "as his residence."[48] There is no requirement, however, that the tenant should occupy the premises "as his only or principal home." A certain number of practical consequences flow from these different verbal formulations. In particular, the Rent Act scheme may protect the "two home tenant."[49]

(2) The Exceptions

The basic definition set out in section 1(1)(a) and (b) is subject to a number of exceptions; the fact that a dwelling-house is let as a separate dwelling which the tenant occupies as his only or principal home does not necessarily mean that the tenancy is assured. Section 1(1)(c)[50] refers to tenancies which cannot be assured tenancies by virtue of subsections (2) and (6): subsection (2) provides that "if and so long as a tenancy falls within any paragraph in Part I of Schedule I to this Act, it cannot be an assured tenancy"; subsection (6) excludes certain tenancies granted pursuant to local authorities' duties to house the homeless.

(a) Schedule 1, para. 1 (tenancies entered into before commencement)

A tenancy which is entered into before, or pursuant to a contract made before, the commencement of this Act.

This exception is subject to a number of transitional provisions.

First, by virtue of the phasing out provisions contained in Chapter V of Part I of the Housing Act 1988, on the death of a protected or statutory tenant under the Rent Acts, in certain circumstances the successor becomes an assured tenant (subject to the Housing Act 1988) and not a statutory tenant under the Rent Act 1977.[51]

Secondly, "old-style" assured tenancies (granted under the Housing Act 1980) will generally become assured tenancies governed by the 1988 Act through the operation of section 1(3):

Except as provided in Chapter V below, at the commencement of this Act, a tenancy—

    (a)   under which a dwelling-house was then let as a separate dwelling, and

    (b)   which immediately before that commencement was an assured tenancy for the purposes of sections 56 to 58 of the Housing Act 1980 (tenancies granted by approved bodies),

shall become an assured tenancy for the purpose of this Act.

---

[48] Rent Act 1977, s.2(1)(a).
[49] *Langford Property Co.* v. *Tureman* [1949] 1 K.B. 29; *Bevington* v. *Crawford* (1974) 232 E.G. 191; *Brickfield Properties Ltd.* v. *Hughes* (1988) 20 H.L.R. 108. See pp. 166–167.
[50] See p. 116.
[51] See pp. 312–313.

It should be noted that there are special provisions relating to "old style" assured tenancies which are converted into new assured tenancies by section 1(3). By virtue of section 1(4) converted assured tenancies remain subject to the 1988 Act even if they fall within the scope of paragraphs 1 to 10 of Schedule 1 to the 1988 Act. Also, where at the commencement of the 1988 Act a fully mutual housing association[52] was the landlord of an "old style" assured tenancy, the tenancy will continue to be a converted assured tenancy governed by the Housing Act 1988 as long as the association remains the landlord.[53]

(b) Schedule 1, paras. 2 and 2A (tenancies of dwelling-houses with high rateable values)

2.—(1) A tenancy—

(a) which is entered into on or after 1st April 1990 (otherwise than, where the dwelling-house had a rateable value on 31st March 1990, in pursuance of a contract made before 1st April 1990), and

(b) under which the rent payable for the time being is payable at a rate exceeding £25,000 a year.

(2) In sub-paragraph (1) "rent" does not include any sum payable by the tenant as is expressed (in whatever terms) to be payable in respect of rates, services, management, repairs, maintenance or insurance, unless it could not have been regarded by the parties to the tenancy as a sum so payable.

2A. A tenancy—

(a) which was entered into before 1st April 1990, or on or after that date in pursuance of a contract made before that date, and

(b) under which the dwelling-house had a rateable value on 31st March 1990 which, if it is in Greater London, exceeded £1,500 and, if it is elsewhere, exceeded £750.[54]

Notes

(i) Relatively few properties are excluded from the scope of the legislation as a result of these provisions. The rateable value limits in paragraph 2A also apply to certain tenancies governed by the Rent Act 1977.[55] In *Hill* v. *Rochard*[56] the premises in question fell within the scope of the Rent Act 1977 notwithstanding the fact that they comprised a handsome period house with a large number of rooms, a staff flat, outbuildings, stable and large garden.

(ii) Section 1(2A) of the Housing Act 1988 provides:

---

[52] Defined by Housing Act 1985, s.5.
[53] Tenancies granted by fully mutual housing associations on or after January 15, 1989 are excluded from the assured tenancy regime by Sched. 1, para. 12(1)(h).
[54] See also Housing Act 1988, Sched. 1, paras. 14–16.
[55] Rent Act 1977, ss.4 and 25(3). See p. 157.
[56] [1983] 1 W.L.R. 478.

The Secretary of State may by order replace any amount referred to in paragraphs 2 and 3A of Schedule 1 to this Act by such amount as is specified in the order; and such an order shall be made by statutory instrument which shall be subject to annulment in pursuance of a resolution of either House of Parliament.

(c) Schedule 1, paras. 3–3C (tenancies at a low rent)

3. A tenancy under which for the time being no rent is payable.

3A. A tenancy—

(a) which is entered into on or after 1st April 1990 (otherwise than, where the dwelling-house had a rateable value on 31st March, 1990, in pursuance of a contract made before 1st April 1990), and

(b) under which the rent payable for the time being is payable at a rate of, if the dwelling-house is in Greater London, £1,000 or less a year and, if it is elsewhere, £250 or less a year.

3B. A tenancy—

(a) which was entered into before 1st April, 1990 or, where the dwelling-house had a rateable value on the 31st March, 1990, on or after 1st April, 1990 in pursuance of a contract made before that date, and

(b) under which the rent for the time being payable is less than two-thirds of the rateable value of the dwelling-house on March 31, 1990.

3C. Paragraph 2(2) above applies for the purposes of paragraphs 3, 3A and 3B as it applies for the purposes of paragraph 2(1).

The occupiers of property on long-term leases are the typical example of tenants at a low rent. Long leaseholders will often have paid a substantial capital sum (premium) for the lease, which will provide for a ground rent of a nominal amount (for example, £10 per year). Originally, long leaseholders were wholly excluded from statutory protection. However, Part I of the Landlord and Tenant Act 1954 gave rights of security to long leaseholders at a low rent (where the tenancy was for more than 21 years). On the expiry of the contractual term the landlord can seek repossession on two broad grounds: (i) that the circumstances set out in Schedule 3 of the Act are satisfied (these are very similar to the grounds for seeking possession under the Rent Acts)[57]; (ii) that he can demonstrate to the court that he needs the property for redevelopment.[58]

The Leasehold Reform Act 1967 brought about a further significant change to the position. As regards houses,[59] tenants under long leaseholds at a low rent are given the right to enfranchise (*i.e.* to buy the landlord's reversionary interest)[60] or the right to demand an extension of the tenancy for a period of up to 50 years.[61] "Long lease"

---

[57] See pp. 231–248.
[58] The landlord's right to recover possession for development is now restricted to situations where the landlord is a body to which section 28 of the Leasehold Reform Act 1967 applies and the property is required for redevelopment within the meaning of that section. Section 28 broadly applies to public bodies (such as local authorities).
[59] s.2.   [60] s.8.   [61] s.14.

here includes leases granted for a period of 21 years or less if there is contained in the lease an option to renew which has been exercised by the tenant so as to make the tenancy longer than 21 years in fact.[62] If the tenant exercises neither his right to enfranchise nor his right to extend the lease, Part I of the Landlord and Tenant Act 1954 continues to apply.

The scope of Part I of the Landlord and Tenant Act 1954 has been limited by the Local Government and Housing Act 1989. Section 186 of the 1989 Act provides:

(1) Schedule 10 to this Act shall have effect (in place of Part I of the Landlord and Tenant Act 1954) to confer security of tenure on certain tenants under long tenancies and, in particular, to establish assured periodic tenancies when such long tenancies come to an end.

(2) Schedule 10 to this Act applies, and section 1 of the Landlord and Tenant Act 1954 does not apply, to a tenancy of a dwelling-house—

(a)   which is a long tenancy at a low rent, as defined in Schedule 10 to this Act; and

(b)   which is entered into on or after the day appointed for the coming into force of this section, otherwise than in pursuance of a contract made before that day.

(3) If a tenancy—

(a)   is in existence on 15th January 1999, and

(b)   does not fall within subsection (2) above, and

(c)   immediately before that date was, or was deemed to be, a long tenancy at a low rent for the purposes of Part I of the Landlord and Tenant Act 1954,

then, on and after that date (and so far as concerns any notice specifying a date of termination on or after that date and any steps taken in consequence thereof), section 1 of that Act shall cease to apply to it and Schedule 10 to this Act shall apply to it unless, before that date, the landlord has served a notice under section 4 of that Act specifying a date of termination which is earlier than that date.

(4) The provisions of Schedule 10 to this Act have effect notwithstanding any agreement to the contrary, but nothing in this subsection or that Schedule shall be construed as preventing the surrender of a tenancy.

Notes

(i)   Section 186 came into force on April 1, 1990.

(ii)   To qualify for protection under Schedule, the tenancy must be one which would be an assured tenancy but for the fact that the tenancy

---

[62] s.3(4).

is at a low rent.[63] Furthermore, the tenancy must be for "a term of years certain exceeding 21 years."[64]

As from January 15, 1999 long tenancies will be governed by Schedule 10, notwithstanding the fact that they were granted prior to the introduction of the assured tenancy regime.[65]

(iii) Under the 1989 Act on the expiry of a long lease the landlord has three possible courses of action. First, he can allow the tenant to continue in possession under the terms of the original tenancy.[66] Secondly, the landlord may seek to recover possession on one of a number of grounds specified in paragraph 5(1) of Schedule 10:

(a) Ground 6[67] in, and those in Part II of, Schedule 2 to the 1988 Act, other than Ground 16;

(b) the ground that, for the purposes of redevelopment after the termination of the tenancy, the landlord proposes to demolish or reconstruct the whole or a substantial part of the premises; and

(c) the ground that the premises or part of them are reasonably required by the landlord for occupation as a residence for himself or any son or daughter of his over eighteen years of age or his spouse or his spouse's father or mother and, if the landlord is not the immediate landlord, that he will be at the specified date of termination.

Thirdly, the landlord may serve a notice on the tenant proposing an assured monthly periodic tenancy.[68] There are procedures for determining the rent payable in relation to an assured tenancy created in this way.[69] Once an assured tenancy has arisen through the operation of the 1989 Act, then it can only be determined according to the terms of the Housing Act 1988.[70]

(d) Schedule 1, para. 4 (business tenancies)

A tenancy to which Part II of the Landlord and Tenant Act 1954 applies (business tenancies).

Section 23(1) of the Landlord and Tenant Act 1954 provides that Part II of the Act applies "to any tenancy where the property comprised in the tenancy is or includes premises which are occupied by the tenant and are so occupied for the purposes of a business carried on by him or for those and other purposes." It is important to emphasise that the verbal formula employed in section 23(1) is that the premises are "occupied for

[63] para. 1(1).
[64] para. 2(3).
[65] para. 1(2).
[66] para. 3.
[67] There are limits to the availability of Ground 6. Paragraph 5(2) provides that Ground 6 may not be specified if the tenancy is a former 1954 Act tenancy.
[68] para. 4(5) (a).
[69] paras. 10–12.
[70] See pp. 204–231.

the purpose of a business"; there is no requirement that the premises should have been let "as a business." This explains why premises may fall within the business tenancy scheme even though they are "let as separate dwelling."

It should be added, however, that where the tenant engages in business activity in breach of covenant the tenancy will not normally fall within the scope of the business tenancy scheme.[71] Section 23(4) of the Landlord and Tenant Act 1954 provides:

> Where the tenant is carrying on a business, in all or any part of the property comprised in a tenancy, in breach of a prohibition (however expressed) of use for business purposes which subsists under the terms of the tenancy and extends to the whole property, this Part of this Act shall not apply to the tenancy unless the immediate landlord or his predecessor in title has consented to the breach or the immediate landlord has acquiesced therein.

Deciding whether or not premises are "occupied for the purpose of a business" is potentially difficult. In *Lewis* v. *Weldcrest Ltd.*[72] the Court of Appeal had to consider whether a tenant of a five-roomed dwelling-house, who took in lodgers, was a business tenant. Although the tenant appeared to have a lease, its terms were not discussed by the court. Instead, Stephenson L.J. concentrated on the purpose of the Landlord and Tenant Act 1954:

> The purpose of that Act was primarily to give security of tenure to people who would be said, in the ordinary use of language, to be using the premises for a business, even if they were living there as well, using part as a dwelling and part as a business. When I look at the words of the definition in section 23(2) I see nothing that extends that purpose to cover such activity in providing accommodation for boarders as the applicant in the present case provided in this house.
>
> It seems to me that there is nothing in the Act, in its wording or in my understanding of its purpose, to put this lady in the category of a trader or of a person carrying on business at these premises. It is no one factor; it is all the factors—the number of lodgers, the size of the place, the sort of sums and services that were involved. I am unconvinced by Mr. Lewis's attempts, without having challenged her evidence, to show that this lady was really reaping any commercial advantage out of this activity in taking in lodgers. She was, it seems to me, doing it probably because she liked it and because the lodgers helped her to pay her way. As Mr. Lewis says, it was her only occupation. I have no doubt that she was good at it. She was rendering a service to the lodgers, and, indeed, to the public and sometimes to the welfare authorities, and she was rendering a service to the taxpayer in reducing the amount of social security that had to be paid to her. The one thing that she was not doing, however, in my judgment, was carrying on a business or trade, whether 'business' is limited to trade or whether it can have any wider connotation.[73]

---

[71] Assuming that the various conditions are satisfied, the tenancy will continue to be assured, but the landlord will be able to seek possession under Ground 12 (Sched. 2 to the Housing Act 1988). See p. 222.

[72] [1978] 1 W.L.R. 1107.

[73] At 1117–1118. See also *Gurton* v. *Parrott* [1990] E.G.C.S. 159.

Cheryl Investments v. *Saldanha*; *Royal Life Saving Society* v. *Page*
[1978] 1 W.L.R. 1329

Lord Denning M.R. said (at 1334–1337):

ROYAL LIFE SAVING SOCIETY v. PAGE

No. 14, Devonshire Street is a house with four floors. It is owned by the Howard de Walden Marylebone Estate. In 1945 they let it on a long lease to the Royal Life Saving Society for 64½ years. That society occupy most of the house themselves: but in 1960 they let the top two floors as a maisonette to a Mr. Gut for 14 years at a rent of £600 a year. There was a covenant prohibiting assignment without the landlord's consent. There was no restriction on the use which the tenant made of the premises. But it would appear that the maisonette was constructed for use as a separate dwelling: and that the letting was "as a separate dwelling" within the tests laid down in *Wolfe* v. *Hogan* [1949] 2 K.B. 194, 204–205.

In 1963 Mr. Gut made arrangements to assign the lease to the present tenant, Dr. Page. He was a medical practitioner who had his consulting rooms at no. 52, Harley Street. His major appointment was medical adviser to Selfridges and he held clinics there five days a week. Dr. Page took the maisonette in Devonshire Street so that he could live there as his home. But he thought that in the future he might possibly want to use it occasionally to see patients there. So, when he took the assignment, he asked for consent to do so. Such consent was readily given by the Royal Life Saving Society (his immediate landlords) and by the Howard de Walden Estate (the head landlords). It was a consent for Dr. Page to carry on his profession in the maisonette. After the assignment he moved in and occupied it as his home. He put both addresses (Harley Street and Devonshire Street) in the medical directory. He had separate notepaper for each address and put both telephone numbers on each. This was, of course, so that anyone who wished to telephone him could get him at one or other place. But he did very little professional work at the maisonette. Over the whole period of the tenancy, he had only seen about one patient a year there. The last patient was in distress 18 months ago. He summarised the position in one sentence: "Harley Street is my professional address, and the other is my home."

On those facts it is quite clear that no. 14, Devonshire Street was let as a separate dwelling and occupied by Dr. Page as a separate dwelling. There was only one significant purpose for which he occupied it. It was for his home. He carried on his profession elsewhere in Harley Street. His purpose is evidenced by his actual use of it. Such user as he made in Devonshire Street for his profession was not a significant user. It was only incidental to his use of it as his home. He comes within my first illustration. He is, therefore, protected by the Rent Acts as a "regulated tenancy."

The landlords later alleged that he was a business tenant and gave him notice to terminate under the Business Tenancy Act 1954. He was quite right to ignore it. He is entitled to stay on as a statutory tenant under the Rent Acts. I agree with the judge, and would dismiss the appeal.

CHERYL INVESTMENTS LTD. v. SALDANHA

Beaufort Gardens is a fine London square, in which there were in former times large houses occupied by well-to-do families and their servants. These houses have long since been converted into apartment houses. In particular nos.

46/47 Beaufort Gardens have been turned into 25 separate apartments. These are owned by a property company called Cheryl Investments Ltd., which is run by a Mr. Welcoop. In December 1975 the company advertised the apartments in the "Evening Standard" in these words: "Knightsbridge. Essex House, near Harrods, serviced flat and flatlets. Doubles from 20 guineas, Flats from 27 guineas. Short-long lets."

Mr. Roland Saldanha answered the advertisement. He had been living in Weybridge, but he wanted a permanent residence in the centre of London. He was shown one of the flats which he liked. It had a large double room with twin beds in it, a bathroom and a toilet. It had no separate kitchen, but there was an entrance hall with a cooker in it which could be used as a kitchen. The landlords provided the furniture and service in the shape of a maid to clean it and change the towels, etc. It took her half an hour a day. The charge was £36.75 a week, plus five per cent. surcharge.

Mr. Saldanha's stay there turned out to be very unhappy with quarrels between him and the landlords. Eventually on February 9, 1977, the landlords gave him notice to quit on March 26, 1977. He claimed the protection of the Rent Acts. He said: "I am a fully fledged tenant entitled to full protection under the Rent Acts." The landlords took proceedings in the county court claiming that he was not a tenant but a licensee. They relied on *Appah* v. *Parncliffe Investments Ltd.* [1964] 1 W.L.R. 1064. But the judge held that he was a tenant, and that the amount in respect of attendance did not form a substantial part of the whole rent: see section 7 of the Rent Act 1977 and *Palser* v. *Grinling* [1948] A.C. 291. So the judge decided those points in favour of Mr. Saldanha, and there is no appeal on them.

But on the day of the trial, September 27, 1977, after previous notice, the landlords amended their particulars of claim so as to assert that Mr. Saldanha occupied the flat for business purposes and was, therefore, not entitled to the protection of the Rent Acts; and they sought a declaration accordingly. The judge rejected this claim. It is from this decision that the landlords appeal to this court.

On this point the evidence was that Mr. Saldanha is an accountant by profession and a partner in a firm called Best Marine Enterprises. They carry on the business of importing sea foods from India and processing them in Scotland. The firm has no trade premises. The two partners carry on the business from their own homes. The other partner works at his home at Basildon. Mr. Saldanha works at the flat in Beaufort Gardens: and goes from there out to visit clients. When he went into the flat, he had a telephone specially installed for his own use, with the number 589 0232. He put a table in the hall. He had a typewriter there, files and lots of paper: "The usual office equipment," said the manageress. He had frequent visitors carrying brief cases. He had notepaper printed: "Best Marine Enterprises. Importers of Quality Sea-foods. Telephone 589 0232"—that is the number I have just mentioned—"P.O. Box 211, Knightsbridge, London, S.W.3."

He issued business statements on that very notepaper. A copy of one was found by the maid in a wastepaper basket showing that the firm had imported goods at a total cost of £49,903.30 and sold them for £58,152.35. The maid (whose evidence the judge explicitly accepted in preference to Mr. Saldanha's) said: "I presumed Mr. Saldanha conducted business there."

On that evidence I should have thought it plain that Mr. Saldanha was occupying the flat, not only as his dwelling, but also for the purposes of a business carried on by him in partnership with another. When he took the flat it was, no doubt, let to him as a separate dwelling. It was obviously a residential flat with just one large room with twin beds in it. No one can doubt that it was constructed for use as a dwelling and let to him as such within the test in *Wolfe*

v. *Hogan* [1949] 2 K.B. 194, 204. But as soon as he equipped it for the purposes of his business of importing sea foods—with telephone, table and printed notepaper—and afterwards used it by receiving business calls there, seeing customers there and issuing business statements from there—it is plain that he was occupying it "for the purposes of a business carried on by him." This was a significant purpose for which he was occupying the flat, as well as a dwelling. It was his only home, and he was carrying on his business from it. It comes within my second illustration.

He did it all surreptitiously. He tried to keep all knowledge of it from the landlord: but that does not alter the fact that, once discovered, his was a "business tenancy" within section 23 of the Landlord and Tenant Act 1954. Some may say: "This is a very strange result. It means that he can alter the nature of his tenancy surreptitiously without the consent of his landlord, and thus get a statutory continuation of it: with all the consequences that this entails for the landlord." That is true: but I see no escape from the words of the Acts. Section 40 of the Act of 1954 clearly contemplates that the landlord may sometimes be quite unaware of the purposes for which a tenant is occupying the premises. It enables a landlord to serve a notice on the tenant so as to find out. But, strange as the result may be, it does open a way to the landlord by which he can get possession. He can give notice of termination to the tenant and oppose any grant of a new tenancy on the ground that he has surreptitiously without the consent of the landlord changed the use of the holding: see section 30(1)(c) of the Act of 1954. I should have thought that the landlord might well be successful. It places him in a better position to evict the tenant than if the tenancy was a "regulated tenancy" protected under the Rent Acts.

The judge took a different view. He said:

> "I think [Mr. Saldanha] is carrying on some business on the premises, but of a nominal kind, and not worth even considering. It is, in my view, de minimis. It amounts to having a few files at home and making a few telephone calls at home."

It is to be noticed that the judge is there speaking of the actual "use" made of the premises: whereas the statute requires us to look at "the purpose" for which he is occupying it. A professional man may occupy premises for the "purpose" of seeing clients, but he may make little "use" of them because no clients come to see him. On the evidence it seems to me that Mr. Saldanha is in the same position as the man in my second illustration. He has only one home—the flat in Beaufort Gardens—and he is occupying it, not only for the purpose of his home, but also for the purpose of a business carried on by him; and that was a significant purpose. It cannot be dismissed by invoking the maxim de minimis non curat lex. That maxim must not be too easily invoked. A man cannot excuse himself from a breach of contract by saying that it did no damage. Nor is it permissible for a man sued in tort to say: "It was only a little wrong and did only a little damage." So here, I do not think the "purpose" of Mr. Saldanha can be excused by saying: "It was only little used."

I would ask: what is the alternative? It could only be that Mr. Saldanha would be protected by the Rent Acts and be able to stay there, using the flat for business purposes as much as he liked.

On the case of Mr. Saldanha, therefore, I take a different view from the judge. I think that at the expiry of the notice to quit Mr. Saldanha was occupying this flat for the purposes of a business carried on by him. So the landlords are entitled to a declaration to that effect. I would allow the appeal in this case.

Geoffrey Lane and Eveleigh L.JJ. agreed.

(e) Schedule 1, para. 5 (licensed premises)

A tenancy under which the dwelling-house consists of or comprises premises licensed for the sale of intoxicating liquors for consumption on the premises.

(f) Schedule 1, para. 6 (tenancies of agricultural land)

(1) A tenancy under which agricultural land, exceeding two acres, is let together with the dwelling-house.

(2) In this paragraph "agricultural land" has the meaning set out in section 26(3)(a) of the General Rate Act 1967 (exclusion of agricultural land and premises from liability for rating).

(g) Schedule 1, para. 7 (tenancies of agricultural holdings)

A tenancy under which the dwelling-house—

(a) is comprised in an agricultural holding (within the meaning of the Agricultural Holdings Act 1986); and

(b) is occupied by the person responsible for the control (whether as tenant or as servant or agent of the tenant) of the farming of the holding.

(h) Schedule 1, para. 8 (lettings to students)

(1) A tenancy which is granted to a person who is pursuing, or intends to pursue, a course of study provided by a specified educational institution and is so granted either by that institution or by another specified institution or body of persons.

(2) In sub-paragraph (1) above "specified" means specified, or of a class specified, for the purposes of this paragraph by regulations made by the Secretary of State by statutory instrument.

(3) A statutory instrument made in the exercise of the power conferred by sub-paragraph (2) above shall be subject to annulment in pursuance of a resolution of either House of Parliament.

The list of specified institutions is to be found in the Assured and Protected Tenancies (Lettings to Students) Regulations 1988.[74]

(i) Schedule 1, para. 9 (holiday lettings)

A tenancy the purpose of which is to confer on the tenant the right to occupy the dwelling-house for a holiday.

Holiday lettings fall outside the scope of the scheme of protection for residential tenants in the private sector.[75] The legislation provides no

[74] S.I. 1988 No. 2236.
[75] The holiday letting exception derives from Rent Act 1977, s.9.

definition of "holiday," though in *McHale* v. *Daneham*[76] (a case decided by Judge Edwards in the County Court) the view was expressed that a working holiday might fall within the scope of the exception.

Although it seems likely that this exception has been widely used by landlords anxious to evade the Rent Acts, what is or is not a genuine holiday letting has not received much judicial attention.

Buchmann v. *May* [1978] 2 All E.R. 993

A professional dancer from New Zealand occupied premises for two years under a number of short furnished tenancies. Then the parties entered a further written agreement, clause 6 of which stated that the tenancy was "solely for the purpose of the tenant's holiday in the London area." It was this tenancy which was the subject of the litigation.

Sir John Pennycuick said (at 998–1000):

Where parties to an instrument express their purpose in entering into the transaction effected by it, or the purposes for which, in the case of a tenancy agreement, the demised property is to be used, this expression of purpose is at least prima facie evidence of their true purpose and as such can only be displaced by evidence that the express purpose does not represent the true purpose. There is no claim here based on misrepresentation, and no claim for rectification. When I say the express purpose does not represent the true purpose, I mean that the express purpose does not correspond to the true purpose, whether the express purpose is a deliberate sham or merely a false label in the sense of a mistake in expression of intention.

In the present case, clause 6 of the agreement is perfectly unequivocal. " ... the letting hereby made is solely for the purpose of the tenant's holiday in the London area." It seems to me that that provision must stand as evidence of the purpose of the parties unless Mrs. May can establish that the provision does not correspond to the true purpose of the parties. The burden lies on her to do so. I do not doubt that in a context such as the present the court would be astute to detect a sham where it appears that a provision has been inserted for the purpose of depriving the tenant of statutory protection under the Rent Acts. But it is for the tenant to establish this, and not for the landlord to establish affirmatively that the express purpose is the true purpose.

In argument, counsel for Mrs. May used the words "absence of bona fides." But, as I understood him, he was not alleging that there had been any deliberate sham on the part of Mr. Buchmann, so much as the attachment of a label to this transaction which did not correspond to the true purpose. At any rate, there was no evidence which would justify a finding of anything resembling fraud.

We were referred to a line of cases in this court on the expression contained in the Rent Acts, "let as a dwelling or as a separate dwelling." Those decisions, although given on different words in the Act, are directly in point on the present question, namely, what is the position of an express declaration in a tenancy agreement that the letting is for the purpose of a holiday? The three cases to which we were referred are as follows. First, *Wolfe* v. *Hogan* ([1949] 2 K.B. 194), where the headnote says this:

[76] (1979) 249 E.G. 969.

"Where the terms of the tenancy provide for or contemplate the user of the premises for some particular purpose, that purpose will prima facie be the essential factor. Thus, if the premises are let for business purposes, the tenant cannot claim that they have been converted into a dwelling-house merely because someone lives on the premises. If, however, the tenancy agreement contemplates no specified user, then the actual user of the premises at the time when possession is sought by the landlord, must be considered."

Denning L.J. said ([1949] 2 K.B. 194 at 204):

"In determining whether a house or part of a house is 'let as a dwelling' within the meaning of the Rent Restriction Acts, it is necessary to look at the purpose of the letting. If the lease contains an express provision as to the purpose of the letting, it is not necessary to look further."

He was, of course, not concerned there with an allegation of sham.

In *British Land Co. Ltd.* v. *Herbert Silver (Menswear) Ltd.* ([1958] 1 Q.B. 530 at 539) Upjohn J. said:

"A long line of authorities, for the most part in this court, has established that, on the issue whether the premises are let as a separate dwelling, one looks to the bargain made between the parties and see for what purpose the parties intended the premises would be used. The first place to ascertain their intentions is in the lease itself."

Finally, in *Horford Investments Ltd.* v. *Lambert* ([1976] Ch. 39 at 52) Scarman L.J. said:

"The section affords protection to the tenancy of a house only if the house is let as a separate dwelling. The section directs attention to the letting, that is to say, the terms of the tenancy. The courts have proceeded on the basis that the terms of the tenancy are the primary consideration: see *Wolfe* v. *Hogan* ([1941] 2 K.B. 194). In my opinion there is here a principle of cardinal importance: whether a tenancy of a house (or a part of a house) is protected depends on the terms of the tenancy, not on subsequent events."

In all those cases this court laid down the principle that, in considering whether a house is let as a separate dwelling, where there is a written lease you ascertain the purpose of the parties from the terms of the lease and you do not go beyond the terms of the lease to ascertain what is the purpose of the parties. That is always so apart from the case where the terms of the lease do not correspond to the true intention of the parties.

It seems to me that on that fundamental ground the learned judge was in error in treating this as a question to be determined by reference to the oral evidence of the parties and without regard to the terms of clause 6, which would stand unless it is shown to be something in the nature of a sham or of a false label, and that on that ground his judgment cannot be supported.

What, then, is to be done? It seems to me that there was no evidence before the judge on which he could have held that clause 6 did not truly represent the common intention of the parties. Mrs. May is a Dominion national not resident in England except on a series of short residence permits, the current one of which was due to expire in December 1974. She had been out of England since the spring of 1974, leaving only some personal chattels in 24 Avenue Road. She informed Mr. Buchmann that she wished to stay in England for two months only before going abroad with her husband, who was taking up an engagement abroad. Mr. Buchmann had no reason to suspect that this was untrue. It seems to me that a stay of less than three months in such circumstances would constitute a "holiday" within the ordinary meaning of that word; and I can find no ground on which it could be properly said that the statement of purpose in clause 6 was a sham or was, without intention to deceive, an untrue statement of the purpose of the letting.

Counsel for the defendant, who has said all there was to be said on her behalf, contended, truly, that one must look at the true relation contemplated by the parties and not merely at the label. In other words, if it can be shown that the terms of this agreement do not correspond with some label in the agreement, then one can look behind the label. Then he says that here the evidence as accepted by the judge established that a holiday was not the true relation, in other words, not the true purpose for which 24 Avenue Road was being let. He said that Mrs. May's motive was to protect her right of occupation, in other words, to continue it for the benefit of Mrs. May and Mr. May together; and he said that Mrs. May did not know her rights and thought it was just one of the usual agreements. There is no evidence that Mr. Buchmann thought that was the motive of the provision as to a holiday; indeed it plainly was not his motive. Whatever Mrs. May may or may not have had in mind when she signed the agreement cannot of itself displace the effect of the express provision within the agreement. Her mere ignorance of her rights certainly could not do so.

I conclude that there is nothing in the evidence which could displace the effect of clause 6 of the agreement, and so one is left with a tenancy for a holiday, and that tenancy is withdrawn from protection by [para. 9]. Accordingly, Mr. Buchmann is now entitled to possession of the property. I would allow the appeal.

Megaw and Stephenson L.JJ. agreed.

This case was discussed—and distinguished—in *R.* v. *Rent Officer for London Borough of Camden ex p. Plant*.[77] The tenancy agreement employed by the landlord (Mr. Simon) stated that the tenant had the right to occupy and use the accommodation "for a holiday." It was, however, known to the landlord that the prospective occupiers of the premises were students. Glidewell J. said:

Prima facie this agreement of October 28, 1979 was to occupy and use this flat for a holiday, but I have clear evidence that both parties knew perfectly well in October that none of the persons who were going to occupy this flat were going to occupy it for the purposes of a holiday. I have clear evidence that all the parties knew they were going to occupy it for the purposes of their work as students. I so find and that seems to me to be conclusive of the matter.

One does not need to debate precisely what is meant by the intention of Mr. Simon. As I have already said, I am satisfied that Mr. Simon's desire was quite properly so to arrange affairs that lettings of this flat did not fall within the Rent Acts. In the particular circumstances of this case, perhaps because he found these tenants satisfactory, agreeable and respectable tenants, I know not, but for whatever reason, his letting in October 1979 failed to achieve his desire, in my view, and I find that there is clear evidence that the purpose expressed in the tenancy agreement was not the true purpose of that agreement.[78]

[77] (1980) 257 E.G. 713.
[78] At 718.

Note

Both *Buchmann* v. *May* and *R.* v. *Rent Officer for London Borough of Camden ex p. Plant* pre-date the House of Lords' decisions in *Street* v. *Mountford*[79] and *A.G. Securities* v. *Vaughan; Antoniades* v. *Villiers.*[80] The House of Lords' approach to sham "licence agreements" is equally applicable to sham "holiday lettings."

(j) Schedule 1, para. 10 and paras. 17 to 22 (resident landlords)

10.—(1) A tenancy in respect of which the following conditions are fulfilled—

(a) that the dwelling-house forms part only of a building and, except in a case where the dwelling-house also forms part of a flat, the building is not a purpose-built block of flats; and

(b) that, subject to Part III of this Schedule, the tenancy was granted by an individual who, at the time when the tenancy was granted, occupied as his only or principal home another dwelling-house which,—

   (i) in the case mentioned in paragraph (a) above, also forms part of the flat; or
   (ii) in any case, also forms part of the building; and

(c) that, subject to Part III of this Schedule, at all times since the tenancy was granted the interest of the landlord under the tenancy has belonged to an individual who, at the time he owned that interest, occupied as his only or principal home another dwelling-house which,—

   (i) in the case mentioned in paragraph (a) above, also formed part of the flat; or
   (ii) in any other case, also formed part of the building; and

(d) that the tenancy is not one which is excluded from this sub-paragraph by sub-paragraph (3) below.

(2) If a tenancy was granted by two or more persons jointly, the reference in sub-paragraph (1)(b) above to an individual is a reference to any one of those persons and if the interest of the landlord is for the time being held by two or more persons jointly, the reference in sub-paragraph (1)(c) above to an individual is a reference to any one of those persons.

(3) A tenancy (in this sub-paragraph referred to as "the new tenancy") is excluded from sub-paragraph (1) above if—

(a) it is granted to a person (alone, or jointly with others) who, immediately before it was granted, was a tenant under an assured tenancy (in this sub-paragraph referred to as "the former tenancy") of the same dwelling-house or of another dwelling-house which forms part of the building in question; and

(b) the landlord under the new tenancy and under the former tenancy is the same person or, if either of those tenancies is or was granted by two or

[79] [1985] A.C. 809. See pp. 50–61.
[80] [1988] 3 W.L.R. 1205. See pp. 63–77.

more persons jointly, the same person is the landlord or one of the landlords under each tenancy.

17.—(1) In determining whether the condition in paragraph 10(1)(c) above is at any time fulfilled with respect to a tenancy, there shall be disregarded—

(a) any period of not more than twenty-eight days, beginning with the date on which the interest of the landlord under the tenancy becomes vested at law and in equity in an individual who, during that period, does not occupy as his only or principal home another dwelling-house which forms part of the building or, as the case may be, flat concerned;

(b) if, within a period falling within paragraph (a) above, the individual concerned notifies the tenant in writing of his intention to occupy as his only or principal home another dwelling-house in the building or, as the case may be, flat concerned, the period beginning with the date on which the interest of the landlord under the tenancy becomes vested in that individual as mentioned in that paragraph and ending—

    (i) at the expiry of the period of six months beginning on that date, or

    (ii) on the date on which that interest ceases to be so vested, or

    (iii) on the date on which that interest becomes again vested in such an individual as is mentioned in paragraph 10(1)(c) or the condition in that paragraph becomes deemed to be fulfilled by virtue of paragraph 18(1) or paragraph 20 below,

whichever is the earlier; and

(c) any period of not more than two years beginning with the date on which the interest of the landlord under the tenancy becomes, and during which it remains, vested—

    (i) in trustees as such; or

    (ii) by virtue of section 9 of the Administration of Estates Act 1925, in the Probate Judge, within the meaning of that Act.

(2) Where the interest of the landlord under a tenancy becomes vested at law and in equity in two or more persons jointly, of whom at least one was an individual, sub-paragraph (1) above shall have effect subject to the following modifications—

(a) in paragraph (a) for the words from "an individual" to "occupy" there shall be substituted "the joint landlords if, during that period none of them occupies"; and

(b) in paragraph (b) for the words "the individual concerned" there shall be substituted "any of the joint landlords who is an individual" and for the words "that individual" there shall be substituted "the joint landlords."

18.—(1) During any period when—

(a) the interest of the landlord under the tenancy referred to in paragraph 10 above is vested in trustees as such, and

(b) that interest is or, if it is held on trust for sale, the proceeds of its sale are held on trust for any person who or for two or more persons of whom at least one occupies as his only or principal home a dwelling-house which forms part of the building or, as the case may be, flat referred to in paragraph 10(1)(a), the condition in paragraph 10(1)(c) shall be deemed to be fulfilled and accordingly, no part of that period shall be disregarded by virtue of paragraph 17 above.

(2) If a period during which the condition in paragraph 10(1)(c) is deemed to be fulfilled by virtue of sub-paragraph (1) above comes to an end on the death of a person who was in occupation of a dwelling-house as mentioned in paragraph (b) of that sub-paragraph, then, in determining whether that condition is at any time thereafter fulfilled, there shall be disregarded any period—

    (a)   which begins on the date of the death;

    (b)   during which the interest of the landlord remains vested as mentioned in sub-paragraph (1)(a) above; and

    (c)   which ends at the expiry of the period of two years beginning on the date of the death or on any earlier date on which the condition in paragraph 10(1)(c) becomes again deemed to be fulfilled by virtue of sub-paragraph (1) above.

19. In any case where—

    (a)   immediately before a tenancy comes to an end the condition in paragraph 10(1)(c) is deemed to be fulfilled by virtue of paragraph 18(1) above, and

    (b)   on the coming to an end of that tenancy the trustees in whom the interest of the landlord is vested grant a new tenancy of the same or substantially the same dwelling-house to a person (alone or jointly with others) who was the tenant or one of the tenants under the previous tenancy,

the condition in paragraph 10(1)(b) above shall be deemed to be fulfilled with respect to the new tenancy.

20.—(1) The tenancy referred to in paragraph 10 above falls within this paragraph if the interest of the landlord under the tenancy becomes vested in the personal representatives of a deceased person acting in that capacity.

(2) If the tenancy falls within this paragraph, the condition in paragraph 10(1)(c) shall be deemed to be fulfilled for any period, beginning with the date on which the interest becomes vested in the personal representatives and not exceeding two years, during which the interest of the landlord remains so vested.

21. Throughout any period which, by virtue of paragraph 17 or paragraph 18(2) above, falls to be disregarded for the purpose of determining whether the condition in paragraph 10(1)(c) is fulfilled with respect to a tenancy, no order shall be made for possession of the dwelling-house subject to that tenancy, other than an order which might be made if that tenancy were or, as the case may be, had been an assured tenancy.

22. For the purposes of paragraph 10 above, a building is a purpose-built block of flats if as constructed it contained, and it contains, two or more flats; and for this purpose "flat" means a dwelling-house which—

    (a)   forms part only of a building; and

    (b)   is separated horizontally from another dwelling-house which forms part of the same building.

Note

The resident landlord exception under section 12 of the Rent Act 1977 simply requires that the landlord should occupy as his residence another dwelling-house in the same building as the tenant.[81] The potential scope of the exception is considerable since a person may be regarded as having more than one home which he occupies as a residence for the purposes of the Rent Act 1977.[82] The exception under the Housing Act 1988 is more limited, however, because the test is more stringent: in order for a person to qualify as a resident landlord he must occupy another dwelling-house in the same building as his only or principal home.

(k) Schedule 1, para. 11 (Crown tenancies)

(1) A tenancy under which the interest of the landlord belongs to Her Majesty in right of the Crown or to a government department or is held in trust for Her Majesty for the purposes of a government department.

(2) The reference in sub-paragraph (1) above to the case where the interest of the landlord belongs to Her Majesty in right of the Crown does not include the case where that interest is under the management of the Crown Estate Commissioners.

(l) Schedule 1, para. 12 (local authority tenancies etc.)[83]

(1) A tenancy under which the interest of the landlord belongs to—

(a) a local authority, as defined in sub-paragraph (2) below;

(b) the Commission for the New Towns;

(c) the Development Board for Rural Wales;

(d) an urban development corporation established by an order under section 135 of the Local Government, Planning and Land Act 1980;

(e) a development corporation, within the meaning of the New Towns Act 1981;

(f) an authority established under section 10 of the Local Government Act 1985 (waste disposal authorities);

(g) a residuary body, within the meaning of the Local Government Act 1985;

(h) a fully mutual housing association; or

(i) a housing action trust established under Part III of this Act.

---

[81] This exception was considered by the Court of Appeal in *Jackson* v. *Pekic* (1990) 22 H.L.R. 9; *Wolff* v. *Waddington* (1990) 22 H.L.R. 72 and *Palmer* v. *McNamara, The Times,* November 28, 1990.

[82] *Hampstead Way Investments Ltd.* v. *Lewis-Weare* [1985] 1 W.L.R. 164.

[83] Tenancies granted by bodies listed in paragraph 12 will normally be secure tenancies which are governed by the Housing Act 1985. See pp. 175–182.

(2) The following are local authorities for the purposes of sub-paragraph (1)(a) above—

(a)   the council of a county, district or London borough;

(b)   the Common Council of the City of London;

(c)   the Council of the Isles of Scilly;

(d)   the Broads Authority;

(e)   the Inner London Education Authority; and

(f)   a joint authority, within the meaning of the Local Government Act 1985.

(m) Schedule 1, para. 13 (transitional cases)

13.—(1) A protected tenancy, within the meaning of the Rent Act 1977.

(2) A housing association tenancy, within the meaning of Part VI of that Act.

(3) A secure tenancy.

(4) Where a person is a protected occupier of a dwelling-house, within the meaning of the Rent (Agriculture) Act 1976, the relevant tenancy, within the meaning of that Act, by virtue of which he occupies the dwelling-house.

The effect of this paragraph is to preserve certain types of tenure until phased out through the operation of various provisions of the Housing Act 1988. It should be noted, however, that the phasing out of protected tenancies is likely to take at least a generation.[84]
    While there is no question that the decline of the public sector of the housing market forms part of the policy of the Housing Act 1988, it would be wrong to regard the secure tenancy as a genuine transitional case. The Housing Act 1988 brings about a change in the types of landlord which can grant secure tenancies, and introduces new mechanisms whereby housing currently in the public sector may be transferred into the private sector (notably the so-called "tenants' choice" scheme contained in Part IV of the 1988 Act).[85] However, it can hardly be envisaged that these developments will bring about the total eradication of the secure tenancy.

(n) Section 1(6) and (7):

(6) If, in pursuance of its duty under—

(a)   section 63 of the Housing Act 1985 (duty to house pending inquiries in case of apparent priority need),

(b)   section 65(3) of that Act (duty to house temporarily person found to have priority need but to have become homeless intentionally), or

---

[84] For the transitional provisions designed to phase out Rent Act tenancies see pp. 312–313.
[85] See pp. 537–553.

(c) section 68(1) of that Act (duty to house pending determination whether conditions for referral of application are satisfied),

a local housing authority have made arrangements with another person to provide accommodation, a tenancy granted by that other person in pursuance of the arrangements to a person specified by the authority cannot be an assured tenancy before the expiry of the period of twelve months beginning with the date specified in subsection (7) below unless, before the expiry of that period, the tenant is notified by the landlord (or, in the case of joint landlords, at least one of them) that the tenancy is to be regarded as an assured tenancy.

(7) The date referred to in subsection (6) above is the date on which the tenant received the notification required by section 64(1) of the Housing Act 1985 (notification of decision on question of homelessness or threatened homelessness) or, if he received a notification under section 68(3) of that Act (notification of which authority has duty to house), the date on which he received that notification.

Note

It has been suggested that these provisions have become "slightly redundant"[86] as a result of the Court of Appeal's decision in *Ogwr B.C. v. Dykes*.[87] In this case it was held that a person housed by the local authority under section 65(3) of the Housing Act 1985 was a licensee, and not a tenant, notwithstanding the fact that the occupier had exclusive possession of the premises in question and paid for the right of occupation on a periodic basis. The Court of Appeal decided that the surrounding circumstances—namely, the provision by the council of accommodation in the discharge of their functions under the homelessness legislation,[88] and the acknowledgment of that fact by the occupier—negatived any inference that a tenancy was intended. The result in this case has, however, subsequently been doubted by the Court of Appeal in *Family Housing Association v. Jones*.[88a]

(C) ASSURED SHORTHOLD TENANCIES

(1) Background: Protected Shorthold Tenancies

The Housing Act 1980 introduced the protected shorthold tenancy—a tenancy granted for a period of between one and five years' duration.[89] The key feature of the protected shorthold was that on the expiry of the contractual term the landlord had a right to recover possession under Case 19.[90] Despite the fact that protected shorthold tenants have no security of tenure beyond the stipulated contractual term, the protected shorthold tenancy was not very popular with landlords[91]: protected

---

[86] Arden & Hunter, *The Housing Act 1988* (1989), p. 25.
[87] [1989] 1 W.L.R. 295.
[88] The duties of local authorities to house the homeless are examined in Chapter 9.
[88a] [1990] 1 W.L.R. 779.
[89] ss.52 to 54.
[90] Rent Act 1977, s.98(2) and Sched. 15 (as amended by Housing Act 1980, s.55).
[91] See Balchin, *Housing Policy: An Introduction* (2nd ed., 1989), pp. 128–129.

shortholds are subject to the fair rent system, and the procedure for termination is unnecessarily complex.

(2) Assured Shorthold Tenancies

The assured shorthold tenancy builds on the basic idea of the protected shorthold, but eliminates those features which landlords found unattractive. As with assured tenancies, assured shorthold tenancies are not subject to rent control.[92] Furthermore, the procedure whereby the landlord may recover possession at the end of the contractual term is made more straightforward.[93] It should also be noted that the minimum period for an assured shorthold tenancy is six months (rather than a year) and there is no maximum period.

An assured shorthold tenancy is defined by section 20 of the Housing Act 1988 in the following way:

(1) Subject to subsection (3) below, an assured shorthold tenancy is an assured tenancy—

- (a) which is a fixed term tenancy granted for a term certain of not less than six months; and

- (b) in respect of which there is no power for the landlord to determine the tenancy at any time earlier than six months from the beginning of the tenancy; and

- (c) in respect of which a notice is served as mentioned in subsection (2) below.

(2) The notice referred to in subsection (1)(c) above is one which—

- (a) is in such form as may be prescribed;

- (b) is served before the assured tenancy is entered into;

- (c) is served by the person who is to be the landlord under the assured tenancy on the person who is to be the tenant under that tenancy; and

- (d) states that the assured tenancy to which it relates is to be a shorthold tenancy.

(3) Notwithstanding anything in subsection (1) above, where—

- (a) immediately before a tenancy (in this subsection referred to as "the new tenancy") is granted, the person to whom it is granted or, as the case may be, at least one of the persons to whom it is granted was a tenant under an assured tenancy which was not a shorthold tenancy, and

- (b) the new tenancy is granted by the person who, immediately before the beginning of the tenancy, was the landlord under the assured tenancy referred to in paragraph (a) above,

the new tenancy cannot be an assured shorthold tenancy.

---

[92] There is, however, a mechanism whereby an assured shorthold tenant may refer the rent to a rent assessment committee which may make an order reducing the rent if it is "significantly higher than the rent which the landlord might reasonably be expected to be able to obtain under the tenancy": Housing Act 1988, s.22(3)(b). See pp. 435–437.

[93] See pp. 230–231.

(4) Subject to subsection (5) below, if, on the coming to an end of an assured shorthold tenancy (including a tenancy which was an assured shorthold but ceased to be assured before it came to an end), a new tenancy of the same or substantially the same premises comes into being under which the landlord and the tenant are the same as at the coming to an end of the earlier tenancy, then, if and so long as the new tenancy is an assured tenancy, it shall be an assured shorthold tenancy, whether or not it fulfils the conditions in paragraphs (a) to (c) of subsection (1) above.

(5) Subsection (4) above does not apply if, before the new tenancy is entered into (or, in the case of a statutory periodic tenancy, takes effect in possession), the landlord serves notice on the tenant that the new tenancy is not to be a shorthold tenancy.

(6) In the case of joint landlords—

(a)   the reference in subsection (2)(c) above to the person who is to be the landlord is a reference to at least one of the persons who are to be joint landlords; and

(b)   the reference in subsection (5) above to the landlord is a reference to at least one of the joint landlords.

Notes

(i)   The tenancy must be an assured tenancy—that is to say, the tenancy must fall within the basic definition contained in section 1 and must not fall within any of the exceptions in Schedule 1.

(ii)   Reference in section 20(1)(b) to there being "no power for the landlord to determine the tenancy at any time earlier than six months from the beginning of the tenancy" does not include a standard forfeiture clause. Section 45(4) provides:

For the avoidance of doubt, it is hereby declared that any reference in this Part of this Act (however expressed) to a power for the landlord to determine the tenancy does not include a reference to a power of re-entry or forfeiture for breach of any term or condition of the tenancy.

(iii)   The prescribed form of notice required by section 20(1)(c) and (2) is set out in the Assured Tenancies and Agricultural Occupancies (Forms) Regulations 1988[94] (Form 7). The courts have no power to dispense with this requirement of notice.

(D)   REGULATED TENANCIES

Before January 15, 1989 the Rent Acts formed the core of protection for residential tenants in the private sector. It has been seen in an earlier section that the definition of the assured tenancy is largely derived from the Rent Act 1977.[95] However, in addition to a number of differences in detail, there is an important structural difference between

---

[94] S.I. 1988 No. 2203.
[95] See pp. 116–153.

the assured tenancy regime and the scheme of protection established by the Rent Act 1977. This difference emerges from the first two sections of the 1977 Act:

1.—Subject to this Part of this Act, a tenancy under which a dwelling-house (which may be a house or part of a house) is let as a separate dwelling is a protected tenancy for the purpose of this Act.

Any reference in this Act to a protected tenant shall be construed accordingly.

2.—(1) Subject to this Part of this Act—

(a)   after the termination of a protected tenancy of a dwelling-house the person who, immediately before that termination, was the protected tenant of the dwelling-house shall, if and so long as he occupies the dwelling-house as his residence, be the statutory tenant of it;. . . .

(2) In this Act a dwelling-house is referred to as subject to a statutory tenancy when there is a statutory tenant of it.

(3) In subsection (1)(a) above and in Part I of Schedule 1, the phrase "if and so long as he occupies the dwelling-house as his residence" shall be construed as it was immediately before the commencement of this Act (that is to say, in accordance with section 3(2) of the Rent Act 1968).

(4) A person who becomes a statutory tenant of a dwelling-house as mentioned in subsection (1)(a) above is, in this Act, referred to as a statutory tenant by virtue of his previous protected tenancy.

As far as the original tenant is concerned there are two aspects to protection under the Rent Act 1977. First, there must be a protected tenancy as defined by section 1. Secondly, when the protected tenancy comes to an end (for example, where a fixed term tenancy expires by effluxion of time, or where the landlord terminates a periodic tenancy by notice to quit) the tenant becomes a statutory tenant within the scope of section 2(1)(a) "if and so long as he occupies the dwelling-house as his residence."[96] This protected/statutory structure, which is not reproduced in the Housing Act 1988, is a fundamental feature of the Rent Act regime.

Protected and statutory tenancies are collectively known as regulated tenancies.

(1) Protected Tenancies

As with assured tenancies under the Housing Act 1988 there are two aspects to the definition of a protected tenancy. First, there must be a tenancy of a "dwelling-house" which is "let as a separate dwelling."[97] However, during the contractual term there is no requirement that the

---

[96] It should be noted that section 2(1)(b) and (5) provides for certain persons to become a statutory tenant by succession on the death of a protected or statutory tenant. (The succession provisions of the Rent Act 1977 have been significantly altered by the Housing Act 1988.) The transfer of tenancies on death is discussed at pp. 301–317.

[97] This formula is extensively discussed at pp. 116–126. As with the Housing Act 1988, there are special provisions dealing with the situation where a tenant has exclusive occupation of part of a dwelling-house, but shares some living accommodation with other tenants: Rent Act 1977, s.22.

tenant should occupy the premises. In *Horford Investments Ltd.* v. *Lambert*[98] Scarman L.J. stated:

A house (or part of a house) must be let as a dwelling, that is to say, a single dwelling, for the tenancy to be protected for the purposes of the Act. If it is let as a single dwelling, the fact that the tenant does not himself live there, or that he sub-lets part or the whole, or that he uses only part of the premises for habitation does not put the letting outside the Act—unless what is done either modifies the terms of the letting or brings the house within some specific exclusion stated in the Act.

Furthermore, there is no requirement that the tenant should be an individual. So, a tenancy granted to a company for five years may be a protected tenancy within section 1 of the 1977 Act as long as the premises constitute a dwelling-house which is let as a separate dwelling.[99]

Secondly, the tenancy must not fall within any of the stated exceptions: this is the significance of the phrase "Subject to this Part of this Act." The exceptions contained in sections 4 to 26 of the Rent Act 1977 are in most cases effectively the same as those to be found in Schedule 1 to the Housing Act 1988. The following situations will fall outside the scope of the Rent Act 1977: lettings of dwelling-houses above certain rateable values[1]; tenancies at a low rent[2]; dwelling-houses let with other land[3]; lettings to students by prescribed educational institutions[4]; holiday lettings[5]; agricultural holdings[6]; licensed premises[7]; cases involving resident landlords[8]; Crown lettings[9]; lettings by public sector bodies, including housing associations and housing co-operatives[10]; and business tenancies.[11]

The most important exclusion which has no direct parallel in the Housing Act 1988 relates to lettings involving payments for board and attendance. Section 7, which offered landlords another means of escaping from the Rent Act regime, provides:

(1) A tenancy is not a protected tenancy if under the tenancy the dwelling-house is bona fide let at a rent which includes payments in respect of board or attendance.

---

[98] [1976] Ch. 39 at 54.
[99] Note, however, that the fact that a tenancy is protected does not automatically mean that when the protected tenancy ends the tenant will become a statutory tenant. See pp. 162–167.
[1] ss.4 and 25 (as amended by the Reference to Rating (Housing) Regulation 1990 (S.I. 1990 No. 434) and the Local Government Finance (Repeals, Savings and Consequential Amendments) Order 1990 (S.I. 1990 No. 776)).
[2] s.5.
[3] ss.6 and 26(1).
[4] s.8. See the Assured and Protected Tenancies (Lettings to Students) Regulations 1988 (S.I. 1988 No. 2236).
[5] s.9.
[6] s.10.
[7] s.11.
[8] s.12.
[9] s.13.
[10] ss.14 to 16.
[11] s.24.

(2) For the purposes of subsection (1) above, a dwelling-house shall not be taken to be bona fide let at a rent which includes payments in respect of attendance unless the amount of rent which is fairly attributable to attendance, having regard to the value of the attendance to the tenant, forms a substantial part of the whole rent.

Notes

(i)   The requirement that the letting must be bona fide is in line with the modern approach of the courts to sham arrangements. In *Palser* v. *Grinling*[12] Viscount Simon said:

In my opinion "bona fide" in this phrase governs the whole of the words which follow. The words amount to a stipulation that the rent to be paid genuinely includes payments in respect of board [or] attendance:. ... the Act is not be evaded ... by merely colourable use of words which do not correspond with what is really provided.[13]

Scarman L.J. in *Woodward* v. *Docharty*[14] said:

Common sense considerations require the court to exercise its knowledge of the world. Today there is, as there has been since 1914, a shortage of dwelling-houses; a landlord who can on the expiry of a contractual tenancy evict his tenant has an asset incomparably more valuable than has the landlord who cannot; a man with a wife, or wife and family, who is seeking a home will accept [attendance] he does not really want in order to obtain accommodation he desperately needs, even though by accepting it he loses security of tenure which he would dearly like to have. In applying the subsection, county court judges must bear in mind general considerations such as these—considerations which can and will change with social and economic changes in our society.

(ii)   The term "board" is not defined in the Rent Act, but its meaning was recently considered by the House of Lords.

Otter v. Norman [1989] A.C. 129

Lord Bridge said (at 142–146):

The appellant was the tenant of a room in a large house in Egerton Terrace where 36 rooms on 5 floors are let as bed-sitting rooms. The appellant's weekly rent at the commencement of the tenancy in 1983 was £50; it was raised in 1985 to £70. Part of the consideration for the rent was the daily provision of a continental breakfast served in a communal dining room in the basement where there was also a large kitchen staffed by employees of the respondent landlord. The breakfast comprised two bread rolls with butter, jam and marmalade, unlimited tea or coffee with milk and sugar, additional milk for cornflakes provided by the appellant himself, and a glass of milk which the appellant took to drink in his room. No question is raised as to the bona fides of the letting to

---

[12] [1948] A.C. 291.
[13] At 310. See also *Maclay* v. *Dixon* [1944] 1 All E.R. 22.
[14] [1974] 1 W.L.R. 966 at 969.

the appellant at a rent which included payments for this daily meal. The sole question is whether it amounted to "board" under section 7(1) so as to defeat the appellant's claim to a protected tenancy. On the respondent's claim for possession, following notice to quit duly given, Mr. H. W. Burnett Q.C., sitting as an assistant recorder in the West London County Court, held that it did and gave judgment for the respondent. This judgment was affirmed by the Court of Appeal (May L.J. and Waterhouse J.) *ante*, p. 131A. The appellant now appeals by leave of your Lordships' House.

In the formal notice of appeal to the Court of Appeal three possible meanings of "board" were advanced: (a) the provision of all meals, (b) the principle of more than one meal per day, or (c) the provision of one adequate meal.

In the county court it had been argued that the appellant's continental breakfast was not an "adequate" meal which could amount to "board" if the third meaning was adopted. But this argument was not pursued in the Court of Appeal or before your Lordships. It is rightly conceded that the continental breakfast served to the appellant could not possibly be disregarded as de minimis. Again the suggestion at (a) that "board" means the provision of all meals, which I understand to imply that the requirement of section 7(1) could only be satisfied by the provision to the tenant of three meals a day, has not at any time in this litigation been seriously canvassed. We are left, therefore, with the single submission that "board" requires at least the provision of one main meal in addition to breakfast. This involves the somewhat startling proposition that if a tenant's rent entitles him to what is described in hotel literature as a "full English breakfast," his tenancy is protected but if two meals are provided in the form of, say, a continental breakfast plus either a "ploughman's lunch" or "high tea," the tenancy is not protected.

The relevant definitions of "board" in the *Shorter Oxford English Dictionary*, 3rd ed. (1944), are: "Food served at the table; daily meals provided according to stipulation; the supply of daily provisions." With the growing popularity in this country of holidays on the continent, we have grown accustomed to the use of the phrases "full board" and "half board" as corresponding no doubt to the French "pension" and "demi-pension." But if "half board" relates to breakfast plus one additional meal, I can see no reason as a matter of language or logic why breakfast by itself should not amount to partial "board," subject always to the implicit requirement that the provision of the meal to the tenant includes the ancillary services involved in preparing it and the provision of crockery and cutlery with which to eat it.

Accordingly, even if there were no relevant authority to consider, I should agree with the courts below in rejecting the appellant's contention. But my view is greatly strengthened by the only authority in point and the legislative history.

The phrase "let at a rent which includes payments in respect of board" first appeared in the proviso to section 2(2) of the Increase of Rent and Mortgage Interest (War Restrictions) Act 1915. It reappeared in proviso (i) to section 12(2) of the Increase of Rent and Mortgage Interest (Restrictions) Act 1920 as follows:

"Provided that—(i) this Act shall not ... apply to a dwelling-house bona fide let at a rent which includes payments in respect of board, attendance, or use of furniture; ... "

In *Wilkes* v. *Goodwin* [1923] 2 K.B. 86 the question at issue was whether a house let at a rent which included payments in respect of certain linoleum fell within this proviso. Bankes L.J. said, at p. 93:

"The proviso in question is introduced into the section which defines the dwelling houses to which the Act shall apply for the purpose of excluding a certain class of dwelling house from the operation of the Act. It does so by the application of two tests. The one is the bona fides of the letting and the other is that the rent includes payments in respect of board, attendance, or use of furniture. The first test depends upon a question of intention, the second is a question of fact and of degree. In some cases the tests may run the one into the other, in others they may stand independently of each other. I will take the second test first. Three quite common and well understood words are used, board, attendance, furniture. The words are used quite generally and without any limitation. The statute does not indicate whether full or partial board, complete or intermittent attendance, much or little furniture is aimed at. It uses the words quite generally, and in my opinion any amount of board, any amount of attendance, any amount of furniture, will satisfy this second test, which is not ruled out of consideration by the application of the rule 'de minimis non curat lex.' "

Scrutton L.J. said, at p. 96:

"On the rest of the proviso, in my view 'board' is not confined to the full board of an ordinary tenant, 'attendance' to full attendance, or 'furniture' to the complete furniture of a 'furnished house.' Partial board, partial attendance, or some furniture though the house is not completely furnished, will suffice to bring the proviso into operation. Parliament might have made the other provision, but have not in my opinion done so. If they did intend the other meaning, they apparently have an opportunity this year to make their meaning plain. If some furniture will do, how much will suffice?"

These two passages express the central ratio of the majority, who concurred in remitting the case to the county court judge to determine as a matter of fact and degree whether the payments in respect of linoleum, assumed to be "furniture," should be disregarded as de minimis.

Younger L.J. also concurred in the remission of the case to the county court judge, but expressed very different reasons from those of the majority. He accepted that in their literal meaning the words "attendance" and "furniture" were capable of embracing much or little, but he seems to have taken the word "board" as the touchstone for the construction of the proviso. Having referred to "attendance" and "furniture," he said, at pp. 110–111:

"As a mere matter of words each of these expressions may quite properly be taken to mean very little, although with at least equal propriety they may be taken to connote a great deal more. But in my judgment so much may not be said of the third word 'board' with which these two other expressions are associated. The word chosen is, it will be noticed, not 'food' or 'drink,' but 'board.' 'Food' may of course mean much or little; 'drink' I hope is entitled to an equally non-committal construction. 'Board,' however, is a different word altogether. It is defined, I see, in the *Oxford Dictionary* as 'daily meals provided in a lodging or boarding house according to stipulation; the supply of daily provisions.' The word without suffix or affix suggests to my mind sufficiency. It could never, I think, be satisfied by the provision, say, of an early morning cup of tea. If you wish to accentuate its abundance you may call it 'full board,' but if you would convey that it is limited then you must call it 'partial' or qualify it by the use of some other adjective of limitation. It appears to me that the natural interpretation of the word as we find it in this exception involves the conception of a provision by the landlord of such food as in the case of any particular tenancy would ordinarily be consumed at daily meals and would be obtained and prepared by a tenant for himself, if it were not provided by somebody else. ... Remembering that the Act applies to prescribed tenancies, of what I may call for brevity unfurnished and unattended houses, I think it may be properly said that a tenancy is within the exception and is outside the Act if the landlord receives payment for and provides and prepares food for his tenant's meals, which having regard to all the circumstances of the case the tenant would otherwise ordinarily provide for himself; or provides such attendance as for ordinary household purposes the tenant would in the circumstances otherwise provide for himself; or provides for the tenant's use so much furniture that when it is in place the house can no longer be fairly described as an unfurnished house."

It is not entirely clear to me whether Younger L.J. intended by these passages that the proviso should be construed as confined, in effect, to houses let fully furnished or with the provision of full board. I am inclined to think that he did, although this is hardly consistent with his concurrence in the decision to remit the case to the county court judge, rather than indicating that he would simply allow the tenant's appeal.

However, it is quite clear that these judgments, delivered on March 8, 1923, must have come to the attention of Parliament before the enactment of the Rent and Mortgage Interest Restrictions Act 1923, which received the Royal Assent on July 31, 1923. Section 10(1) of that Act seems to be a direct acceptance of Scrutton L.J.'s invitation to Parliament to make their meaning plain. It provides:

"For the purposes of proviso (i) to subsection (2) of section 12 of the principal Act (which relates to the exclusion of dwelling-houses from the principal Act in certain circumstances), a dwelling-house shall not be deemed to be bona fide let at a rent which includes payments in respect of attendance or the use of furniture unless the amount of rent which is fairly attributable to the attendance or the use of the furniture, regard being had to the value of the same to the tenant, forms a substantial portion of the whole rent."

The test of substantiality here adopted with reference to attendance and furniture has never been applied to board as the criterion of exclusion from full protection under the Rent Acts. It was, however, applied in relation to the very different control by rent tribunals first introduced by the Furnished Houses (Rent Control) Act 1946 (see section 12(3)) and which survives in the Act of 1977 in the provisions relating to restricted contracts. Thus section 19(5)(c) of the Act of 1977 provides:

"A contract is not a restricted contract if— ... (c) it is a contract for the letting of any premises at a rent which includes payment in respect of board if the value of the board to the lessee forms a substantial proportion of the whole rent; ... "

Effectively the only control imposed on restricted contracts is to subject the rents under such contracts to review by rent tribunals. One can well understand the legislative rationale for applying such a test of substantiality in relation to otherwise uncontrolled tenancies as a means of subjecting otherwise exorbitant rents to such review. However, the application of the test of substantiality in this context, contrasted with its total absence in the context of the exclusion from protection by section 7(1), seems to me quite inconsistent with the submission that nothing less than the provision of two meals daily can amount to "board" at all.

There has been no reported English decision bearing upon the point after *Wilkes* v. *Goodwin* [1923] 2 K.B. 86. But Parliament chose not to interfere in relation to "board," and it seems to have been assumed ever since that the majority view in *Wilkes* v. *Goodwin*, albeit expressed obiter, correctly stated the law, in the words of Bankes L.J., at p. 93, that "any amount of board" which is more than de minimis will suffice to exclude a tenancy from statutory protection. Thus successive editions of Sir Robert Megarry's standard text book on the Rent Acts (*Megarry, The Rent Acts*) have stated that: "In practice, the dividing line appears to fall between the early morning cup of tea on the one hand and 'bed and breakfast' on the other": see 10th ed. (1967), p. 141. The same view has been adopted in Scotland: see *Holiday Flat Co.* v. *Kuczera*, 1978 S.L.T. (Sh.Ct.) 47.

My Lords, I think we must assume that for many years many landlords and tenants have regulated their relationships on this basis, and even if I thought that a different construction could reasonably be placed on section 7(1) of the Act of 1977 I would not think it right to adopt it now and to upset existing arrangements made on the basis of an understanding of the law which has prevailed for so long.

The courts have consistently set their face against artificial and contrived devices whereby landlords have sought to deny to tenants the protection intended to be conferred by the Rent Acts. I do not believe that anything of that kind is involved here. A bona fide obligation by a landlord to serve even such a modest daily meal as the continental breakfast with which this case is concerned is hardly likely to appeal to the unscrupulous landlord as a soft option. It will necessarily involve not only the cost of the food and drink provided but also all the housekeeping chores which must be undertaken in shopping for provisions, preparation and service of meals on the premises and clearing and washing up after meals. If a landlord and a tenant genuinely contract on terms which impose such obligations on the landlord, it would, to my mind, be surprising if the legislature had provided for the perpetuation of such a contract in favour of the tenant when the landlord wishes to terminate it.

I would accordingly dismiss the appeal.

Lords Brandon, Templeman, Ackner and Oliver agreed.

(iii)   Although there is no provision in the Housing Act 1988 equivalent to section 7 of the Rent Act 1977 it must be remembered that not all occupiers of residential accommodation are tenants. In *Street* v. *Mountford* Lord Templeman stated:

The occupier is a lodger if the landlord provides attendance or services which require the landlord or his servants to exercise unrestricted access to and use of the premises.[15]

Where the provision of services or attendance is such that the occupier does not enjoy exclusive possession, the occupier is a licensee. If there is no tenancy the assured tenancy regime introduced by the Housing Act 1988 has no application.

(2) Statutory Tenancies: "if and so long as he occupies the dwelling-house as his residence"

It will be realised from the above that whether a tenancy is or is not Rent Act protected depends on considering both the definition of

---

[15] [1985] A.C. 809 at 818.

protected tenancy and the exemptions to that definition. Whether or not a protected tenancy exists is crucial to answering another question: when does a statutory tenancy exist?

When a protected tenancy comes to an end (for example, by the effluxion of time or by the landlord exercising a power of re-entry in the case of a fixed term tenancy, or by the landlord serving a notice to quit in the case of a periodic tenancy) the former protected tenant will normally become a statutory tenant. Section 2(1)(a) of the Rent Act 1977 provides that "[a]fter the termination of a protected tenancy of a dwelling-house the person who, immediately before that termination, was the protected tenant of the dwelling-house shall, if and so long as he occupies the dwelling-house as his residence, be the statutory tenant of it."

There are four points to note in relation to the requirement that a statutory tenant must occupy the dwelling-house as his residence. First, for section 2 to operate the tenant must have been Rent Act protected immediately before the termination of the tenancy[16]; and the tenant must have been occupying the dwelling as a residence.[17] Secondly, the requirement that the tenant must occupy the dwelling-house derives from case-law prior to the Rent Act 1968.

Skinner v. *Geary* [1931] 2 K.B. 546

The plaintiff, Mrs. Alice Mary Skinner, claimed from the defendant, Edward Geary, possession of a dwelling house and premises known as 26 Oxford Road, Upper Norwood, London, of which premises the defendant was a weekly tenant at 10s. a week. It was admitted that the premises came within the scope of the Rent Restriction Acts, and that on May 6, 1930, due notice to quit had been served on the defendant, who had thereby become a statutory tenant. The defendant denied that the plaintiff was entitled to possession of the premises.

For a considerable period before 1919 the defendant had been the tenant and occupier of the premises. In 1919 he went to live at a house at Tatsfield, Surrey, of which his wife was the tenant. A married sister of the defendant's wife with her husband then resided at 26 Oxford Road until June, 1930, when she left, and a sister of the defendant went to live in the house. She was residing there when proceedings were begun in the county court.

The county court judge found that the defendant was not in actual possession of the premises at the material time—namely, at the time the notice to quit was given—and that he did not retain possession within the meaning of the Rent Restriction Acts by the occupation of his wife's or his own relatives, since the purpose of that occupation was not to preserve the house as a residence for the defendant. The county court judge accordingly made an order for possession of the premises.

The defendant appealed ...

---

[16] *Smalley* v. *Quarrier* [1975] 1 W.L.R. 938.
[17] *Cove* v. *Flick* [1954] 2 Q.B. 326n.; *Dando* v. *Hitchcock* [1954] 2 Q.B. 317.

The Divisional Court affirmed the order. In the Court of Appeal, Scrutton L.J. said (at 558–564):

The history of the Rent Restriction Acts shows that there has been a very gradual feeling of its way by the Court with regard to the principles upon which these Acts are to be worked. When they were drawn there is no evidence that Parliament or the draftsman ever thought out what rights they were giving to the tenant of a house to which the Acts applied. They never considered whether they were giving him something which the tenant could assign or could leave by will, or a property which on his death intestate would pass to his administrator, or which on his bankruptcy would pass to his trustee. Consequently the Courts have had to proceed slowly and with extreme caution ...

Parliament ... [in] my opinion ... never contemplated the possibility of the tenant living somewhere else. A non-occupying tenant was in my opinion never within the precincts of the Acts, which were dealing only with an occupying tenant who had a right to stay in and not be turned out. This case is to be decided on the principle that the Acts do not apply to a person who is not personally occupying the house and who has no intention of returning to it. I except, of course, such a case as that to which I have already referred—namely, of temporary absence, the best instance of which is that of a sea captain who may be away for months but who intends to return, and whose wife and family occupy the house during his absence ...

For the reasons I have given the Act does not in my opinion apply to protect a tenant who is not in occupation of a house in the sense that the house is his home and to which, although he may be absent for a time, he intends to return. If it were to be held otherwise odd consequences would follow. The appellant in this case has contented himself with living in one house and claiming another. Suppose he had a number of houses. One object of the Acts was to provide as many houses as possible at a moderate rent. A man who does not live in a house and never intends to do so, is, if I may use the expression, withdrawing from circulation that house which was intended for occupation by other people. To treat a man in the position of the appellant as a person entitled to be protected, is completely to misunderstand and misapply the policy of the Acts. The appeal must be dismissed.

Slesser L.J. agreed; Greer L.J. also found for the plaintiff but on different grounds.

Thirdly, whether the statutory tenant is to be regarded as occupying the dwelling as a residence is a question of fact and degree.[18] "Residence" does not connote uninterrupted physical presence, and in a number of cases the courts have held that the statutory tenancy has not come to an end notwithstanding the fact that the statutory tenant has been absent from his primary residence for a prolonged period. In *Brown* v. *Brash*[18a] Asquith L.J. said:

We are of opinion that a "non-occupying" tenant prima facie forfeits his status as a statutory tenant. But what is meant by "non-occupying"? The term

---

[18] See, *e.g. Regalian Securities Ltd.* v. *Scheuer* (1982) 5 H.L.R. 48; *Hampstead Way Investments Ltd.* v. *Lewis-Weare* [1985] 1 W.L.R. 164.
[18a] [1948] 2 K.B. 247 at 254–255.

clearly cannot cover every tenant who, for however short a time, or however necessary a purpose, or with whatever intention as regards returning, absents himself from the demised premises. To retain possession or occupation for the purpose of retaining protection the tenant cannot be compelled to spend twenty-four hours in all weathers under his own roof for three hundred and sixty-five days in the year. Clearly, for instance, the tenant of a London house who spends his week-ends in the country or his long vacation in Scotland does not necessarily cease to be in occupation. Nevertheless, absence may be sufficiently prolonged or unintermittent to compel the inference, prima facie, of a cesser of possession or occupation. The question is one of fact and of degree. Assume an absence sufficiently prolonged to have this effect: The legal result seems to us to be as follows: (1.) The onus is then on the tenant to repel the presumption that his possession has ceased. (2.) In order to repel it he must at all events establish a de facto intention on his part to return after his absence. (3.) But we are of opinion that neither in principle nor on the authorities can this be enough. To suppose that he can absent himself for five or ten years or more and retain possession and his protected status simply by proving an inward intention to return after so protracted an absence would be to frustrate the spirit and policy of the Acts, as affirmed in *Keeves* v. *Dean* ([1924] 1 K.B. 685) and *Skinner* v. *Geary* ([1931] 2 K.B. 546). (4.) Notwithstanding an absence so protracted the authorities suggest that its effect may be averted if he couples and clothes his inward intention with some formal, outward, and visible sign of it; that is, instals in the premises some caretaker or representative, be it a relative or not, with the status of a licensee and with the function of preserving the premises for his own ultimate home-coming. There will then, at all events, be someone to profit by the housing accommodation involved, which will not stand empty. It may be that the same result can be secured by leaving on the premises, as a deliberate symbol of continued occupation, furniture; though we are not clear that this was necessary to the decision in *Brown* v. *Draper* ([1944] K.B. 309). Apart from authority, in principle, possession in fact (for it is with possession in fact and not with possession in law that we are here concerned) requires not merely an "animus possidendi" but a "corpus possessionis," namely, some visible state of affairs in which the animus possidendi finds expression. (5.) If the caretaker (to use that term for short) leaves or the furniture is removed from the premises, otherwise than quite temporarily, we are of opinion that the protection, artificially prolonged by their presence, ceases, whether the tenant wills or desires such removal or not. A man's possession of a wild bird, which he keeps in a cage, ceases if it escapes, notwithstanding that his desire to retain possession of it continues and that its escape is contrary thereto.

The principles enumerated in *Brown* v. *Brash* have been applied in a number of recent cases.[19] In *Brickfield Properties Ltd.* v. *Hughes*[20] (which has been described as a "borderline case"[21]) the Court of Appeal held that a statutory tenancy of a flat had not come to an end even though the flat had not been occupied by the defendant for more than a decade. Indeed, from 1978 to March 1987 the dwelling had been visited by the defendant only three times. However, the flat contained the defendant's furniture and was occupied by his adult children, and

---

[19] See, *e.g. Roland House Gardens* v. *Cravitz* (1974) 119 S.J. 167; *Colin Smith Music* v. *Ridge* [1975] 1 W.L.R. 463; *Atyeo* v. *Fardoe* (1978) 123 S.J. 97 and *Richards* v. *Green* (1984) 11 H.L.R. 1.
[20] (1988) 20 H.L.R. 108.
[21] Megarry, *The Rent Acts* (11th ed., 1988) Vol. 1, p. 247, n. 21.

the court was satisfied that the defendant had a genuine, albeit contingent, intention to return to the flat at some point in the future.[22]

Among the most difficult cases are those which involve the so-called "two-home tenant." Although the purpose of section 2 is broadly similar to that of section 1(1)(*b*) of the Housing Act 1988[23] its effect is rather different since a tenant may be regarded as having more than one residence. In some cases the courts have held that a second home may qualify for protection under the Rent Act 1977.

In *Langford Property Co.* v. *Tureman*[24] the tenant owned a cottage in the country and rented a flat in London. Although the tenant stayed in the flat on average only two nights per week the Court of Appeal held that the tenant occupied the flat as a residence. *Bevington* v. *Crawford*[25] involved a defendant who was the tenant of a flat in England which he occupied for two or three months each year; for the rest of the year he lived in France. The Court of Appeal decided that the defendant continued to qualify for protection as a statutory tenant of the flat in England. Lord Denning M.R. said:

Coming to our present case, this flat at Harrow-on-the-Hill was, in the first place, the home of both parties. Starting off as their only home is an important point. It remains their home until they give it up. They have retained the possession in law and in fact. Their furniture is there, their personal belongings and the caretaker. They retain the intention to use it as their home. It was and remains their base, the base from which they moved out and to which they return whenever they come back. It is their only home in England, though true it is they have established another in France. It looks from the evidence as though they may well be using it more in the future. At all events, the evidence is such that the judge could well form the view that they intended it to be their English home and to make such use of it as their own domestic needs and circumstances required: and that is the way they occupied it as their residence. Mr. Crawford is therefore protected by the Rent Acts. Something has been said about the wealth of Mr. Crawford; but that does not affect the application of the Rent Acts any more than the fact that Mr. Bevington bought the house as an investment to make money out of it. None of those matters affects the circumstances of this case.[26]

These cases are, however, somewhat exceptional. In a number of cases where a tenant has claimed protection of a dwelling which was not his primary home the courts have decided that the tenant did not fall within the protective ambit of section 2(1)(a) of the Rent Act 1977. In *Beck* v. *Sholz*[27] the defendant, who owned jointly with her husband a house in Luton, also rented a flat in London. The defendant stayed in the flat in London on no more than four or five times a year, and her husband

---

[22] Compare *Robert Thackray's Estate* v. *Kaye* (1989) 21 H.L.R. 160.
[23] This subsection makes it a precondition for the existence of an assured tenancy that the tenant "occupies the dwelling-house as his only or principal home." See pp. 132–134.
[24] [1949] 1 K.B. 29.
[25] (1974) 232 E.G. 191.
[26] At 191.
[27] [1953] 1 Q.B. 570.

slept in the flat about once every two months. In *Walker* v. *Ogilvy*[28] the defendant claimed to be the statutory tenant of premises (located about one and a half hour's drive from his main home) which he used for short holidays. The defendant's intention was to move into the rented accommodation on his retirement. In both of these cases it was held that the defendant was not occupying the dwelling as a residence.[29]

Fourthly, the tenant must be an individual. A corporate tenant may be protected, but a company cannot be a statutory tenant.[30]

(3) Protected Shorthold Tenancies

The protected shorthold tenancy was introduced by the Housing Act 1980.

52.—(1) A protected shorthold tenancy is a protected tenancy granted after the commencement of this section which is granted for a term certain of not less than one year nor more than five years and satisfies the following conditions, that is to say,—

(a) it cannot be brought to an end by the landlord before the expiry of the term, except in pursuance of a provision for re-entry or forfeiture for non-payment of rent or breach of any other obligation of the tenancy; and

(b) not later than the beginning of the term the landlord has given the tenant a valid notice stating that the tenancy is to be a protected shorthold tenancy;

(2) A tenancy of a dwelling-house is not a protected shorthold tenancy if it is granted to a person who immediately before it was granted, was a protected or statutory tenant of that dwelling-house.

(3) A notice is not valid for the purposes of subsection (1)(b) above unless it complies with the requirements of regulations made by the Secretary of State.

. . . . . .

(5) If a protected tenancy is granted after the commencement of this section—

(a) for such a term certain as is mentioned in subsection (1) above, to be followed, at the option of the tenant, by a further term; or

(b) for such a term certain and thereafter from year to year or some other period;

---

[28] (1974) 28 P. & C. R. 288.
[29] See also *Hampstead Way Investments Ltd.* v. *Lewis-Weare* [1985] 1 W.L.R. 164.
[30] For a discussion of the problems posed by "company lets" see *Hilton* v. *Plustitle Ltd.* [1989] 1 W.L.R. 149 (pp. 127–131).

and satisfies the conditions stated in that subsection, the tenancy is a protected shorthold tenancy until the end of the term certain.

In *Dibbs* v. *Campbell*[31] the Court of Appeal had to consider the meaning of "a person who, immediately before it was granted, was a protected or statutory tenant of that dwelling-house" for the purposes of section 52(2). In this case the landlord had sought to create a protected shorthold tenancy, but had failed to comply with the requirements of the Act. After the landlord realised the error, the parties negotiated a new agreement, whereby the tenant surrendered the original tenancy and accepted the grant of a shorthold tenancy. When the landlord sought possession under Case 19, the tenant resisted on the basis that the effect of section 52(2) of the 1980 Act was to prevent the second tenancy from being a shorthold. The Court of Appeal held (following *Foster* v. *Robinson*[32] and *Collins* v. *Claughton*[33]) that a protected tenancy can be brought to an end by surrender, and (following *Scrimgeour* v. *Waller*)[34] that a surrender can be effected without the tenant vacating the premises. In the present case, the surrender was effective and therefore the tenant was not a protected or statutory tenant immediately before the grant of the second tenancy—which was therefore a valid protected shorthold tenancy.

(E)   RESTRICTED CONTRACTS

19.—(1) A contract to which this section applies is, in this Act, referred to as a "restricted contract."

(2) Subject to section 144 of this Act, this section applies to a contract, whether entered into before or after the commencement of this Act, whereby one person grants to another person, in consideration of a rent which includes payment for the use of furniture or for services, the right to occupy a dwelling as a residence.

(3) A contract is not a restricted contract if the dwelling falls within one of the Classes set out in subsection (4) below.

(4) Where alternative rateable values are mentioned in this subsection, the higher applies if the dwelling is in Greater London and the lower applies if it is elsewhere.

Class D

The appropriate day in relation to the dwelling falls or fell on or after 1st April 1973 and the dwelling on the appropriate day has or had a rateable value exceeding £1,500 or £750.

---

[31] (1988) 20 H.L.R. 374.
[32] [1951] 1 K.B. 149.
[33] [1952] 1 W.L.R. 145.
[34] (1981) 257 E.G. 61.

Class E

The appropriate day in relation to the dwelling fell before 1st April 1973 and the dwelling—

   (a)   on the appropriate day had a rateable value exceeding £400 or £200, and

   (b)   on 1st April 1973 had a rateable value exceeding £1,500 or £750.

   (5) A contract is not a restricted contract if—

   (a)   it creates a regulated tenancy; or

  (aa)   under the contract the interest of the lessor belongs to a body mentioned in section 14 of this Act; or

   (b)   under the contract the interest of the lessor belongs to Her Majesty in right of the Crown ... or to a government department, or is held in trust for Her Majesty for the purposes of a government department; or

   (c)   it is a contract for the letting of any premises at a rent which includes payment in respect of board if the value of the board to the lessee forms a substantial proportion of the whole rent; or

  (cc)   it creates a qualifying shared ownership lease within the meaning of section 5A of this Act; or

   (d)   it is a protected occupancy as defined in the Rent (Agriculture) Act 1976; or

   (e)   it creates a tenancy to which Part VI of this Act applies except that an interest belonging to Her Majesty in right of the Crown does not prevent a contract from being a restricted contract if the interest is under the management of the Crown Estate Commissioners, or

   (f)   it creates an assured tenancy within the meaning of section 56 of the Housing Act 1980.

   (6) Subject to subsections (3) to (5) above, and to paragraph 17 of Schedule 24 of this Act, a contract falling within subsection (2) above and relating to a dwelling which consists of only part of a house is a restricted contract whether or not the lessee is entitled, in addition to exclusive occupation of that part, to the use in common with any other person of other rooms or accommodation in the house.

   (7) No right to occupy a dwelling for a holiday shall be treated for the purposes of this section as a right to occupy it as a residence.

   (8) In this section—
     "dwelling" means a house or part of a house;
     "lessee" means the person to whom is granted, under a restricted contract, the right to occupy the dwelling in question as a residence and any person directly of indirectly deriving title from the grantee; and
     "lessor" means the person who, under a restricted contract, grants to another the right to occupy the dwelling in question as a residence and any person directly or indirectly deriving title from the grantor; and
     "services" includes attendance, the provision of heating or lighting, the supply of hot water and any other privilege or facility connected with the occupancy of a dwelling, other than a privilege or facility requisite for the purposes of access, cold water supply or sanitary accommodation.

20.—If and so long as a tenancy is, by virtue only of section 12 of this Act, precluded from being a protected tenancy it shall be treated as a restricted contract notwithstanding that the rent may not include payment for the use of furniture or for services.

21.—Where under any contract—

(a)   a tenant has the exclusive occupation of any accommodation, and

(b)   the terms on which he holds the accommodation include the use of other accommodation in common with his landlord or in common with his landlord and other persons, and

(c)   by reason only of the circumstances mentioned in paragraph (b) above, or by reason of those circumstances and the operation of section 12 of this Act, the accommodation referred to in paragraph (a) above is not a dwelling-house let on a protected tenancy.

the contract is a restricted contract notwithstanding that the rent does not include payment for the use of furniture or for services.

Notes

(i)   Section 12 provides that cases involving resident landlords are outside the definition of a protected tenancy.

(ii)   Before August 14, 1974 furnished tenancies were outside the full protection of the Rent Act, though they fell within the jurisdiction of the Rent Tribunal. However, section 1 of the Rent Act 1974 provides:

(1) On and after the commencement date,—

(a)   a tenancy of a dwelling-house shall no longer be prevented from being a protected tenancy for the purposes of the Rent Act by reason only that, under the tenancy, the dwelling-house is bona fide let at a rent which includes payments in respect of the use of furniture; and

(b)   subject to the following provisions of this Act, references in the Rent Act (and in any other enactment or instrument in which those expressions have the same meaning as in that Act) to a protected tenancy, a statutory tenancy or a regulated tenancy shall be construed accordingly . . .

Despite the wording of section 19(2) of the 1977 Act, as a result of section 1(1) of the 1974 Act, furnished tenancies created between August 14, 1974 and January 14, 1989 may be protected tenancies. However, furnished contractual licences (if created before January 15, 1989) and furnished tenancies created before August 14, 1974 may fall within section 19 of the 1977 Act.[35]

---

[35] Whether premises are furnished or not is still to be determined according to principles advanced by the House of Lords in *Palser* v. *Grinling* [1948] A.C. 291, and more recently by the Court of Appeal in *Woodward* v. *Docherty* [1974] 1 W.L.R. 966.

Luganda v. *Service Hotels Ltd.* [1969] 2 Ch. 209

Lord Denning M.R. said (at 217–220):

Mr. Kasozi Luganda came to this country from Uganda in 1958. He is employed as a clerk in a company in London, but he is also a student. He is reading for the Bar and is going to take his final examinations in May. Nearly three years ago he took a furnished room in a building which is known as Queensborough Court Hotel, Queensborough Terrace, W.2. It is called a hotel, but it is very different from an ordinary hotel. It has 88 rooms which are "let" out to "tenants." But they are not strictly "let," and they are not strictly "tenants." Each "tenant" is really a contractual licensee who has the right to occupy a room in return for a weekly payment. Mr. Luganda has a Yale key for his room. It is a bed-sittingroom with a double gas ring. He gets his own meals. He provides his own towels and soap. But the company provide the bedding. The chambermaids come in every day and make his bed and clean the room: and every week they change the linen. Along the corridor there are lavatories and bathrooms which are used by all the occupants. There is, of course, a lift. There is a porter on duty down below: and there is a receptionist who puts telephone messages through to a common telephone on each floor.

Mr. Luganda has been in the same room—No. 53—for nearly three years. When he went there in April, 1966, he paid £4 14s. 0d. a week. In September, 1967, it was raised to £4 18s. 0d. a week. In January of this year, 1969, the management wanted to decorate his room—No. 53. So he went out of No. 53 into No. 4 for a fortnight while they redecorated the room. He went back into No. 53 on January 31, a Friday. On the next morning, Saturday, February 1, he received a letter from the manager telling him that his rent was to be increased by a guinea a week. It was in future to be £5 19s. 0d. a week. He did not like this increase in rent. So he went to the furnished rent tribunal and told them about it. They gave him some advice: and, in consequence, on Monday, February 3, Mr. Luganda wrote to the management saying: "I note that you have put up the rent by £1 1s 0d. a week! I am taking legal advice on this matter, but in the meantime I will continue to pay £4 18s. 0d. as in the past." The management did not like this. They went to their solicitors who wrote a letter which Mr. Luganda got on the Wednesday, February 5. They told him that he had to vacate his room by 10 o'clock on the Friday, the 7th. That was only two days' notice. Mr. Luganda did not obey their notice. He did not vacate the premises on the Friday morning. He went to work as usual. When he got back on the Friday evening, he found they had changed the lock. He could not get in. He could not even get his belongings. He had to go and spend the night with a friend nearby. Meanwhile the furnished rent tribunal wrote to him, saying his application to them had been received and would be dealt with as early as possible. They told the management also. The management did not leave room No. 53 empty for very long. They soon let it to a Turkish lady; and they told him he could not come back.

Mr. Luganda applied for an injunction. Cross J. held that Mr. Luganda had a prima facie right to remain in possession. He was within the statute which affords protection to the tenants of furnished rooms. The judge granted an injunction so as to enable him to go back to room 53; and an injunction to prevent them from stopping him having access. Now the company appeal to this court.

The statutory provisions about furnished lettings were originally contained in the Furnished Houses (Rent Control) Act, 1946, but they have now been consolidated in Part VI of the Rent Act, 1968. They were especially designed to cover a letting of furnished rooms, either under a tenancy or a contractual licence, and thus to cover such a case as the present. But Mr. Montague Waters has submitted that they do not cover it. I will take his points in order:—

First, the statute only applies to a contract relating to a "dwelling': see section 70(1)(2): and "dwelling" is defined in section 84 of the Act of 1968 as "a house or part of a house." Mr. Waters submitted that this hotel was not a "house." He referred us to a passage in *Megarry on the Rent Acts*, 10th ed. (1967), p. 50, where it is said that "premises used as an hotel may be protected if they were constructed as a dwelling-house but perhaps not if constructed as an hotel." I do not accept this submission. I am quite clear that a building which is used as a hotel is a "house," no matter whether it was purpose-built or not. As it happens, the Queensborough Court Hotel was constructed as four houses, but they have been knocked into one so as to form the hotel. It is clearly a "house": and room 53 is "part of a house."

Secondly, the statute only applies to a contract which gives to the lessee "the right to occupy as a residence" a dwelling: see section 70(1). Mr. Waters submitted that the contract here did not give Mr. Luganda the right to occupy room 53 "as a residence." He referred us again to a passage in *Megarry* at p. 505, where it is said:

"The words 'as a residence' have a limiting effect. Thus the Act does not apply to temporary accommodation of the normal hotel type, whether the Ritz or Rowton House, presumably because there is no occupation 'as a residence.' "

I agree about the Ritz or Rowton House. A person taking a room there on a short visit does not have the right to occupy it "as a residence." Mr. Waters submitted that the contract, to come within the statute, must give to the lessee, in express words, the right to occupy as a residence. But I do not think so. It is sufficient if "the lessee is within his rights in occupying the premises as a residence" even though the contract says nothing about it: see *Reg.* v. *York, Harrogate, Ripon and Northallerton Areas Rent Tribunal, Ex parte Ingle* [1954] 1 Q.B. 456, 459 by Parker J. It is plain here that Mr. Luganda was occupying room 53 as a residence. He had been there nearly three years: and he was within his rights in so occupying it. So that requirement is satisfied.

Third, in a case like the present when the lessee occupies only a part of a house (namely, one room) the contract must entitle the lessee to "exclusive occupation" of that part: see section 70(2). Mr. Waters submitted that this meant that the statute only protected a tenant, properly so called, and did not protect a contractual licensee or lodger who took a furnished room. Mr. Luganda was, of course, only a contractual licensee, and not a tenant.

Mr. Waters sought to support his submission by taking us through many provisions of earlier Rent Acts. But I do not propose to go through them now. I am quite satisfied that "exclusive occupation" in section 70(2) does not mean "exclusive possession" in the technical sense in which it is sometimes used in landlord and tenant cases. A lodger who takes a furnished room in a house is in exclusive occupation of it, notwithstanding that the landlady has a right of access at all times. It was so held 12 years ago in *Reg.* v. *Battersea, Wandsworth, Mitcham and Wimbledon Rent Tribunal, Ex parte Ambalal Parikh* [1957] 1 W.L.R. 410. Lord Goddard C.J., said, at p. 414, that, although the landlady had a right of access she has not the right "herself to come in and occupy it nor has she a right to put somebody else into that room." Mr. Waters submitted that that case was wrongly decided and should be overruled. But I think it was rightly decided. A person has a right to "exclusive occupation" of a room when he is entitled to occupy it himself, and no one else is entitled to occupy it. Even though, as here, the chambermaids come in daily to make the bed and clean the room, and change the linen each week, nevertheless, Mr. Luganda had exclusive occupation of the room, that is, the right to occupy it to the exclusion of anyone else occupying it. He has that right under the contract. This requirement too is satisfied. I would only observe that Mr. Luganda had no meals in the hotel. If he had had board in addition to lodging, to a substantial extent, he would not have come within the statute: see section 70(3)(b). But he had no board, so he is within it.

It seems to me, therefore, that prima facie at least Mr. Luganda is entitled to the protection of the statute, that is, to the protection which is afforded to lessees of furnished lettings. He was entitled to refer the contract, as he did, to the furnished rent tribunal to see what was a fair rent for him to pay; and he was given by the statute security of tenure, which might be as much as six months from the decision of the tribunal: see sections 77 and 78 of the Act of 1968.

Mr. Waters submitted that as Mr. Luganda was not now in occupation no mandatory order should be made to put him back. He suggested that such an order would require the constant superintendence of the court, which the court would not do. He cited *Ryan* v. *Mutual Tontine Westminster Chambers Association* [1893] 1 Ch. 116. I look upon the case quite differently. Mr. Luganda is prima facie entitled by statute to security to tenure of this room. It was unlawful for the management to lock him out of it: see section 30 of the Act of 1965. They were wrong to take the law into their own hands. If the management had not changed the lock—and Mr. Luganda was still in occupation—I am sure that the court would have granted an injunction to prevent the management from locking him out. They should not be in a better position by wrongfully locking him out. As Lord Uthwatt said in *Winter Garden Theatre (London) Ltd.* v. *Millennium Productions Ltd.* [1948] A.C. 173, 203: "In a court of equity, wrongful acts are no passport to favour." We must see that the law is observed. To do this, we should, I think, order that Mr. Luganda should be restored to his room. There is no difficulty about the Turkish lady. Rooms often become vacant. She can go into another room.

In my opinion the judge was quite right. An injunction should be made pending trial. But there should be an early trial. I would dismiss the appeal.

Edmund Davies and Phillimore L.JJ. agreed.[36]

(iii) Restricted contracts are being phased out by the Housing Act 1988. Section 36(1) of the 1988 Act provides that there can be no new restricted contracts:

A tenancy or other contract entered into after the commencement of this Act cannot be a restricted contract for the purposes of the Rent Act 1977 unless it is entered into in pursuance of a contract made before the commencement of this Act.

Furthermore, if the parties agree to a variation of the terms of a restricted contract (such as a new rent) this will be regarded as a new contract which therefore cannot be a restricted contract.[37] However,

---

[36] See also *Marchant* v. *Charters* [1977] 1 W.L.R. 1181 and *R.* v. *South Middlesex Rent Tribunal ex p. Beswick* [1976] 32 P.& C.R. 67.

[37] Housing Act 1988, s.36(2).

restricted contracts created before January 15, 1989 continue to be governed by the Rent Act 1977.

II THE PUBLIC SECTOR

Although private sector tenancies have been regulated by legislation for more than seventy years, tenants of council housing were not within any scheme of protection until 1980. Prior to the commencement of the Housing Act 1980 public sector tenancies were basically governed by the express terms of the tenancy agreements employed by the various local authorities and the common law. It was generally thought, however, that it was "safe and proper to give local authority landlords a complete discretion with regard to eviction of public sector tenants, and to rely on them to exercise such discretion fairly and wisely."[38]

The Housing Act 1980 introduced the concept of the "secure tenancy" and granted to secure tenants a number of rights (the so-called "tenants' charter"). One of the aims of the 1980 Act was to give to public sector tenants the sort of legal protection which had been accorded to private sector tenants for decades. Accordingly, one of the key features of the 1980 Act was the introduction of statutory security of tenure for tenants of council housing. However, the tenants' charter also had a significant political aspect: it represented the first important step of the Conservative Government's policy in relation to the public sector of the housing market. In addition to granting security of tenure, the Housing Act 1980 established the "right to buy"—whereby council tenants who satisfy certain residence conditions are entitled to buy their homes at a significant discount. Although the right to buy is no longer a subject of political controversy, at the time of its introduction it was fiercely denounced by the Opposition.

The public sector scheme introduced by the 1980 Act is now to be found in the Housing Act 1985 (as amended). Part IV of the 1985 Act sets out (a) the definition of a secure tenancy, which is the central concept in the statutory scheme of protection for tenants of public sector landlords, (b) the security of tenure provisions for secure tenants and (c) various other statutory rights of secure tenants. (The provisions relating to the right to buy are to be found in Part V of the 1985 Act.) This section deals with only the first of these topics.

Note

It is important to stress that public sector bodies are involved in housing in a variety of different ways; the direct provision of housing is only one aspect of local authorities' activity in the housing sphere. For example, under Part III of the Housing Act 1985 local authorities have

---

[38] Brandon L.J. in *Harrison* v. *Hammersmith and Fulham L.B.C.* [1981] 1 W.L.R. 650 at 661.

duties as regards the housing of homeless persons, and they have various powers under the 1985 Act to encourage the improvement of housing conditions in the private sector. These aspects of public sector endeavour are discussed in subsequent chapters.

(A) THE FRAMEWORK

Section 79 provides the framework for the definition of a secure tenancy:

(1) A tenancy under which a dwelling-house is let as a separate dwelling is a secure tenancy at any time when the conditions described in sections 80 and 81 as the landlord condition and the tenant condition are satisfied.

(2) Subsection (1) has effect subject to—
   (a)   the exceptions in Schedule 1 (tenancies which are not secure tenancies),
   (b)   sections 89(3) and (4) and 90(3) and (4) (tenancies ceasing to be secure after death of tenant), and
   (c)   sections 91(2) and 93(2) (tenancies ceasing to be secure in consequence of assignment or subletting).

(3) The provisions of this Part apply in relation to a licence to occupy a dwelling-house (whether or not granted for a consideration) as they apply in relation to a tenancy.

(4) Subsection (3) does not apply to a licence granted as a temporary expedient to a person who entered the dwelling-house or any other land as a trespasser (whether or not, before the grant of that licence, another licence to occupy that or another dwelling-house had been granted to him).

Notes

(i)   This definition involves three elements: the tenant condition, the landlord condition, and the exclusions contained in Schedule 1.[39]

(ii)   The formula "dwelling-house ... let as a separate dwelling"— which also forms one of the linchpins of the assured tenancy regime[40]— is borrowed from the Rent Acts. However, an important difference from the private sector schemes is brought about by subsection (3). This simple provision avoids the problems which the lease/licence distinction has posed in the context of private rented accommodation.[41]

(iii)   Section 79(2)(b) and (c) deals with the transfer of tenancies both *inter vivos* and on death, and sub-letting.[42]

(B) THE TENANT CONDITION

Section 81 of the Housing Act 1985 provides:

---

[39] See pp. 178–182.
[40] See pp. 116–126. For the meaning of separate see *Central Y.M.C.A. Housing Association* v. *Saunders* [1990] E.G.C.S. 153.
[41] See pp. 49–84.
[42] For further discussion, see Chapter 5.

The tenant condition is that the tenant is an individual and occupies the dwelling-house as his only or principal home; or, where the tenancy is a joint tenancy, that each of the joint tenants is an individual and at least one of them occupies the dwelling-house as his only or principal home.

Note

The requirement that the tenant should occupy the dwelling as his only or principal home has also been used by the legislature in defining the assured tenancy under the Housing Act 1988.[43]

(C) THE LANDLORD CONDITION

The landlord condition has been complicated by the Housing Act 1988, which has redrawn the dividing line between the public and private sectors. It is now important to distinguish tenancies granted before January 15, 1989 from those granted on or after that date.

Section 80 of the 1985 Act (as amended by the Housing and Planning Act 1986) provided as follows:

(1) The landlord condition is that the interest of the landlord belongs to one of the following authorities or bodies—

a local authority,
a new town corporation,
an urban development corporation,
the Development Board for Rural Wales,
the Housing Corporation,
a housing action trust which is a charity, or
a housing association or housing co-operative to which this section applies.

(2) This section applies to—

(a) a registered housing association other than a co-operative housing association, and

(b) an unregistered housing association which is a co-operative housing association.

(3) If a housing association ceases to be registered, it shall, within the period of 21 days beginning with the date on which it ceases to be registered, notify each of the tenants who thereby becomes a secure tenant, in writing, that he has become a secure tenant.

(4) This section applies to a housing co-operative within the meaning of section 27B (agreements under certain superseded provisions) where the dwelling-house is comprised in a housing co-operative agreement within the meaning of that section.

One of the consequences of this section is that a certain number of tenancies granted by housing associations (and other quasi-public bodies) before January 15, 1989 were within the public sector scheme of protection (albeit with some modifications).

---

[43] See pp. 132–134.

However, the Housing Act 1988 has the effect of excluding from the secure tenancy regime tenancies granted by housing associations and these quasi-public bodies on or after January 15, 1989. Section 80(1) has been amended so that the Housing Corporation, charitable housing trusts and housing associations are removed from the list,[44] and housing action trusts (new institutions established by Part III of the Housing Act 1988) are added.[45] So, the amended section 80(1) reads as follows:

> The landlord condition is that the interest of the landlord belongs to one of the following authorities or bodies—
>
> a local authority,
> a new town corporation,
> a housing action trust,
> an urban development corporation,
> the Development Board for Rural Wales,
> a housing co-operative to which this section applies.

Subsection (2) is repealed.[46]

Although tenancies granted by housing associations on or after January 15, 1989 may be assured tenancies within Part I of the Housing Act 1988, it should be recalled that tenancies granted by fully mutual housing associations are expressly excluded.[47]

Section 35(4) and (5) of the Housing Act 1985 contains various transitional provisions. Note in particular subsection (5) which provides:

> If, on or after the commencement of this Act, the interest of the landlord under a protected or statutory tenancy becomes held by a housing association, a housing trust, the Housing Corporation or Housing for Wales, nothing in the preceding provisions of this section shall prevent the tenancy from being a housing association tenancy or a secure tenancy and, accordingly, in such a case section 80 of the Housing Act 1985 (and any enactment which refers to that section) shall have effect without regard to the repeal of provisions of that section effected by this Act.

Note

The terminology relating to housing associations and their classification is rather complex:

"Fully mutual" in relation to a housing association means that its rules restrict membership of the association to tenants or prospective tenants and preclude the granting of tenancies to anyone who is not a member.[48]

A housing association is "registered" (for the purposes of section 80) if it is registered under the Housing Associations Act 1985.[49]

---

[44] Housing Act 1988, Sched. 18.
[45] s.83(2).
[46] Sched. 18.
[47] Sched. 1, para. 12(1)(h).
[48] Housing Act 1985, s.5(2).
[49] s.5(4).

A co-operative housing association is a fully mutual housing association which is registered under the Industrial and Provident Societies Act 1965.[50]

(A housing association may be registered both with the Housing Corporation under the Housing Associations Act 1985 and the registrar of Friendly Societies under the 1965 Act.)

(D) EXCLUSIONS

Exclusions from the secure tenancy regime are to be found in Schedule 1 to the Housing Act 1985.

(1) Schedule 1, para. 1 (long tenancies)

A tenancy is not a secure tenancy if it is a long tenancy.

Long tenancies are defined by section 115(1) of the 1985 Act as (a) tenancies granted for a term exceeding 21 years, (b) perpetually renewable leases, and (c) tenancies granted under the right to buy provisions contained in Part V of the 1985 Act. Generally speaking, however, such tenancies are not long tenancies if they are "terminable by notice after a death."[51]

(2) Schedule 1, para. 2 (premises occupied in connection with employment)

(1) A tenancy is not a secure tenancy if the tenant is an employee of the landlord or of—

> a local authority
> a new town corporation
> a housing action trust
> an urban development corporation
> the Development Board for Rural Wales, or
> the governors of an aided school,

and his contract of employment requires him to occupy the dwelling-house for the better performance of his duties.

(2) A tenancy is not a secure tenancy if the tenant is a member of a police force and the dwelling-house is provided for him free of rent and rates in pursuance of regulations made under section 33 of the Police Act 1964 (general regulations as to government, administration and conditions of service of police forces).

(3) A tenancy is not a secure tenancy if the tenant is an employee of a fire authority (within the meaning of the Fire Services Acts 1947 to 1959) and—

[50] Housing Associations Act 1985, s.5(2).
[51] Housing Act 1985, s.115(2).

    (a)   his contract of employment requires him to live in close proximity to a particular fire station, and

    (b)   the dwelling-house was let to him by the authority in consequence of that requirement.

    (4) A tenancy is not a secure tenancy if—

    (a)   within the period of three years immediately preceding the grant the conditions mentioned in sub-paragraph (1), (2) or (3) have been satisfied with respect to a tenancy of the dwelling-house, and

    (b)   before the grant the landlord notified the tenant in writing of the circumstances in which this exception applies and that in its opinion the proposed tenancy would fall within this exception,

until the periods during which those conditions are not satisfied with respect to the tenancy amount in aggregate to more than three years.

    (5) In this paragraph "contract of employment" means a contract of service or apprenticeship, whether express or implied and (if express) whether oral or in writing.

(3) Schedule 1, para. 3 (land acquired for development)

    (1) A tenancy is not a secure tenancy if the dwelling-house is on land which has been acquired for development and the dwelling-house is used by the landlord, pending development of the land, as temporary housing accommoda-tion.

    (2) In this paragraph "development" has the meaning given by section 22 of the Town and Country Planning Act 1971 (general definition of development for purposes of that Act).[52]

(4) Schedule 1, para. 4 (accommodation for homeless persons)

    (1) A tenancy granted in pursuance of—

    (a)   section 63 (duty to house pending inquiries in case of apparent priority need),

    (b)   section 65(3) (duty to house temporarily person found to have priority need but to have become homeless intentionally), or

    (c)   section 68(1) (duty to house pending determination whether conditions for referral of application are satisfied,)

is not a secure tenancy before the expiry of the period of twelve months beginning with the date specified in sub-paragraph (2), unless before the expiry of that period the tenant is notified by the landlord that the tenancy is to be regarded as a secure tenancy.

    (2) The date referred to in sub-paragraph (1) is the date on which the tenant received the notification required by section 64(1) (notification of decision on question of homelessness or threatened homelessness) or, if he received a notification under section 68(3) (notification of which authority has duty to house), the date on which he received that notification.

Paragraph 4 enables a local authority to provide temporary accommodation for homeless persons outside the secure tenancy regime.[53] Similarly, homeless persons who are temporarily housed in private sector accommodation will not acquire security of tenure: licences fall outside

---

[52] See *Attley* v. *Cherwell D.C.* (1989) 21 H.L.R. 613; *Hyde Housing Association* v. *Harrison* (1991) 23 H.L.R. 57.

[53] The duties of local authorities with respect to homelessness are examined in Chapter 9.

the assured tenancy regime, and tenancies granted by private landlords to a homeless person under an arrangement with the local authority are expressly excluded from Part I of the 1988 Act.[54]

(5) Schedule 1, para. 5 (temporary accommodation for persons taking up employment)

(1) A tenancy is not a secure tenancy before the expiry of one year from the grant if—

(a)   the person to whom the tenancy was granted was not, immediately before the grant, resident in the district in which the dwelling-house is situated,

(b)   before the grant of the tenancy, he obtained employment, or an offer of employment, in the district or its surrounding area,

(c)   the tenancy was granted to him for the purpose of meeting his need for temporary accommodation in the district or its surrounding area in order to work there, and of enabling him to find permanent accommodation there, and

(d)   the landlord notified him in writing of the circumstances in which this exception applies and that in its opinion the proposed tenancy would fall within this exception;

unless before the expiry of that year the tenant has been notified by the landlord that the tenancy is to be regarded as a secure tenancy.

(2) In this paragraph—
"district" means district of a local housing authority; and
"surrounding area", in relation to a district, means the area consisting of each district that adjoins it.

(6) Schedule 1, para. 6 (short-term arrangements)

A tenancy is not a secure tenancy if—

(a)   the dwelling-house has been leased to the landlord with vacant possession for use as temporary housing accommodation,

(b)   the terms on which it has been leased include provision for the lessor to obtain vacant possession from the landlord on the expiry of a specified period or when required by the lessor,

(c)   the lessor is not a body which is capable of granting secure tenancies, and

(d)   the landlord has no interest in the dwelling-house other than under the lease in question or as a mortgagee.

(7) Schedule 1, para. 7 (temporary accommodation during works)

A tenancy is not a secure tenancy if—

(a)   the dwelling-house has been made available for occupation by the tenant (or a predecessor in title of his) while works are carried out on the dwelling-house which he previously occupied as his home, and

(b)   the tenant or predecessor was not a secure tenant of that other dwelling-house at the time when he ceased to occupy it as his home.

(8) Schedule 1, para. 8 (agricultural holdings)

A tenancy is not a secure tenancy if the dwelling-house comprised in an agricultural holding (within the meaning of the Agricultural Holdings Act 1986) and is occupied by the person responsible for the control (whether as tenant or as servant or agent of the tenant) of the farming of the holding.

[54] Housing Act 1988, s.1(6).

(9) Schedule 1, para. 9 (licensed premises)

A tenancy is not a secure tenancy if the dwelling-house consists of or includes premises licensed for the sale of intoxicating liquor for consumption on the premises.

(10) Schedule 1, para. 10 (student lettings)

(1) A tenancy of a dwelling-house is not a secure tenancy before the expiry of the period specified in sub-paragraph (3) if—
  (a) it is granted for the purpose of enabling the tenant to attend a designated course at an educational establishment, and
  (b) before the grant of the tenancy the landlord notified him in writing of the circumstances in which this exception applies and that in its opinion the proposed tenancy would fall within this exception;
unless the tenant has before the expiry of that period been notified by the landlord that the tenancy is to be regarded as a secure tenancy.

(2) A landlord's notice under sub-paragraph (1)(b) shall specify the educational establishment which the person concerned proposes to attend.

(3) The period referred to in sub-paragraph (1) is—
  (a) in a case where the tenant attends a designated course at the educational establishment specified in the landlord's notice, the period ending six months after the tenant ceases to attend that (or any other) designated course at that establishment;
  (b) in any other case, the period ending six months after the grant of the tenancy.

(4) In this paragraph—
"designated course" means a course of any kind designated by regulations made by the Secretary of State for the purposes of this paragraph;
"educational establishment" means a university or institution which provides higher education or further education (or both); and for the purposes of this definition "higher education" and "further education" have the same meaning as in the Education Act 1944.

(5) Regulations under sub-paragraph (4) shall be made by statutory instrument and may make different provision with respect to different cases or descriptions of case, including different provision for different areas.[54a]

(11) Schedule 1, para. 11 (1954 Act tenancies)

A tenancy is not a secure tenancy if it is one to which Part II of the Landlord and Tenant Act 1954 applies (tenancies of premises occupied for business purposes).

Notes

Paragraphs 8 to 11 are derived from the Rent Act 1977. Furthermore, these provisions are mirrored in Schedule 1 to the Housing Act 1988:
(i) Paragraph 8 is derived from section 10 of the Rent Act 1977 and is in substance the same as paragraph 7 of Schedule 1 to the Housing Act 1988.

[54a] See the Assured and Protected Tenancies (Lettings to Students) Regulations 1988 (S.I. No. 2236) as amended by the Assured and Protected Tenancies (Lettings to Students) (Amendment) Regulations 1990 (S.I. No. 1825).

(ii)   Paragraph 9 operates in the same way as section 11 of the Rent Act 1977 and paragraph 5 of Schedule 1 to the Housing Act 1988.

(iii)   Paragraph 10 serves broadly the same purpose as section 8 of the Rent Act 1977 and paragraph 8 of Schedule 1 to the Housing Act 1988. It is, however, drafted slightly differently.

(iv)   Paragraph 11 is effectively the same as section 24 of the Rent Act 1977 and paragraph 4 of Schedule 1 to the Housing Act 1988.[55]

(12) Schedule 1, para. 12 (almshouses)

(1) A licence to occupy a dwelling-house is not a secure tenancy if—
(a)   the licence was granted by an almshouse charity, and
(b)   any sum payable by the licensee under the licence does not exceed the maximum contribution that the Charity Commissioners have from time to time authorised or approved for the almshouse charity as a contribution towards the cost of maintaining its almshouses and essential services in them.

(2) In this paragraph "almshouse charity" means a corporation or body of persons which is a charity and is prevented by its rules or constituent instrument from granting a tenancy of the dwelling-house.

This paragraph was necessitated by section 79(3) which includes certain licences within the definition of a secure tenancy.

Note on the allocation of council housing

The procedures for housing allocation are mostly outside direct legal regulation. Applicants for housing must, first, get onto a housing waiting list (officially known as a housing register); then, they will be subject to assessment procedures to determine their priority; finally, they will be processed through the local authority selection scheme.

Most local authorities allocate their housing stock according to some sort of points system: the speed with which an applicant on the waiting list will be housed depends on the points which he can amass. A whole range of factors (such as age, length of time on the waiting list, size of family, state of current accommodation) determine the number of points of each applicant.

An analysis of the operation of access policies and procedures is to be found in a recent study funded by the Department of the Environment: P. Prescott-Clarke, P. Allen & C. Morrissey, *Queuing for Housing: A Study of Council House Waiting Lists* (1988, HMSO). For further discussion see D. Hughes, Public Sector Housing Law (2nd ed., 1987, Butterworths), Chapter 3.

Given the largely discretionary nature of the allocation process, it is not surprising that the system has been subject to criticism. Some of the problems are discussed by N. Lewis, Council house allocation: problems

---

[55] See pp. 139–143 for a discussion of this exclusion.

of discretion and control [1976] Public Administration 147, and N. Lewis & R. Livock, Council house allocation procedures: some problems of discretion and control (1979) 2 U.L.P. 133.

However, the allocation process is not entirely free from legal control. Local authorities must have regard to section 22 of the Housing Act 1985:

A local housing authority shall secure that in the selection of their tenants a reasonable preference is given to—

(a) persons occupying insanitary or overcrowded houses,
(b) persons having large families,
(c) persons living under unsatisfactory housing conditions,
(d) persons towards whom the authority are subject to a duty under section 65 to 68 (persons found to be homeless).

An aggrieved person may seek judicial review of a housing allocation decision, and the courts may quash the local authority's decision.

R. v. *Port Talbot B.C. ex parte Jones*[56] concerned Mrs. Kingdom, a borough councillor, who applied to be housed by the local authority in July 1984. Mrs. Kingdom lived outside her ward, and one of the reasons for seeking local authority housing was so that she would be better placed to fight in the next election. In the normal course of events a person in Mrs. Kingdom's position could have expected to be given a one- or two-bedroomed flat after waiting for about four years. However, the applicant was placed on a priority list, and in April 1986 was allocated a three-bedroomed council house by the borough housing officer (largely as a result of pressure exerted by the chairman of the housing tenancy committee).

Nolan J., in the Divisional Court, on an application for judicial review by the leader of the local council, quashed the decision to allocate the house to Mrs. Kingdom. He outlined the following grounds for his judgment:

[T]he council's policy is to provide suitable accommodation for those on the waiting list. [The borough housing officer]'s duty under the standing orders was to act in accordance with that policy. He clearly did not do so. Counsel for Mrs. Kingdom argued that, whatever the normal policy might be, the decision to allocate the house to Mrs. Kingdom was authorised by the resolution of September 1984. But that resolution, whatever its other failings, did not authorise the allocation of a three-bedroomed house to Mrs. Kingdom in order that she should be the better able to fight an election, without regard to the needs of others who were on the list for housing and against the opinions of the council's officers. There could hardly be a clearer case of a decision which, to adopt the test propounded in *Associated Picture Houses Ltd.* v. *Wednesbury Corporation* [1947] 2 All E.R. 680, [1948] 1 K.B. 223, was based on an irrelevant consideration. To put it more simply, the decision was unfair to others on the housing list and was an abuse of power.[57]

[56] [1988] 2 All E.R. 207.
[57] At 214.

It is also unlawful to discriminate on grounds of sex or race.[58] In the sphere of housing allocation discrimination is prohibited (a) in relation to the terms on which premises are offered; (b) by refusing an application for premises; or (c) by treating the applicant differently from others on a waiting list for accommodation.[59] To combat racism in rented housing the Commission for Racial Equality produced a code of practice for rented housing. The code was approved by the Secretary of State and came into force on May 1, 1991.

There is a long history of racial inequality in the allocation of public housing in Britain. The fact that allocation procedures operate to the disadvantage of black families first became apparent in the late 1960s (see J. Cullingworth, *Council Housing: Purposes, Procedures and Priorities* (1969, H.M.S.O.)). It is difficult to assess whether legislation prohibiting discrimination has been successful. There is little doubt, however, that racial discrimination in the housing sphere continues to be a problem: J. Henderson & V. Karn, *Race, Class and State Housing: Inequality and the Allocation of Public Housing in Britain* (1987, Gower), M. MacEwen, *Housing, Race and Law: The British Experience* (1990, Routledge); D. Hughes & S. R. Jones, Bias in the allocation and transfer of local authority housing [1978–79] J.S.W.L. 273; and M. Bryan, Discrimination in the public provision of housing: the Commission for Racial Equality report on housing in Hackney [1984] Public Law 194.

Finally, it is interesting to note that, notwithstanding the very lengthy waiting lists, there is empty council housing. The Audit Commission's 1986 report referred to some 113,000 council owned dwellings which were vacant at the end of March 1984. This amounted to 2.4 per cent. of the total stock.[60]

III   FURTHER READING

General background

There are numerous accounts of the development of the private rented sector—in particular charting its decline. See, for example, P. N. Balchin, *Housing Policy: An Introduction* (2nd ed., 1989, Routledge), Chapter 5; P. Beirne, *Fair Rent and Legal Fiction* (1987, Macmillan), Chapter 2. For some of the background to the first Rent Act: P. Q. Watchman, The origin of the 1915 Rent Act (1980) 5 Law and State 20.

For an account of the origins and development of the local authority housing sector see S. Merrett, *State Housing in Britain* (1979, Routledge).

Assured tenancies

The Housing Act 1988 provoked a lot of discussion while it was progressing through Parliament, and not surprisingly several guides to the Act have been published, including: A. Arden & C. Hunter, *The Housing*

---

[58] Sex Discrimination Act 1975; Race Relations Act 1976.
[59] Sex Discrimination Act 1975, s.30(1); Race Relations Act 1976, s.21(1).
[60] *Managing the Crisis in Council Housing* (1986).

Act 1988 (1989, Sweet & Maxwell); G. Bennett & R. Lee, *Housing Act 1988: A Practical Guide to Private Residential Lettings* (1989, B.S.P. Professional Books); G. Bowden, *Housing Act 1988* (1989, Shaw & Sons); S. Bridge, *Blackstone's Guide to the Housing Act 1988* (1989, Blackstone Press); J. Driscoll *A Guide to the Housing Act 1988* (1989, Fourmat Publishing); C. P. Rogers, *Housing—The New Law: A Guide to the Housing Act 1988* (1989, Butterworths).

(Of course, these works are concerned not only with the definition of an assured tenancy, but also with the other aspects of the legislation, including security of tenure, reform of the law relating to unlawful eviction, the phasing out of the Rent Acts, housing action trusts and "tenants' choice".)

The legal journals also contain general accounts of the Act, notably M. Davey, The Housing Act 1988 (1989) 52 M.L.R. 661 and D. C. Hoath, The Housing Act 1988: a new regime for the private rented sector [1989] J.S.W.L. 339 & [1990] J.S.W.L. 18.

The scope of statutory protection

For a more focused discussion of the scope of statutory protection in the private sector see J. E. Martin *Residential Security* (1989, Sweet & Maxwell), Chapters 4 and 5 (regulated tenancies) and Chapters 12 and 13 (assured tenancies); A. Arden, *Manual of Housing Law* (4th ed., 1989, Sweet & Maxwell) paras. 3.01–3.36 (Rent Act tenancies); paras. 5.01–5.24 (assured tenancies). Arden's *Manual* also gives an account of the secure tenancy regime: paras. 4.01–4.18.

For a general account of the rights of secure tenants (which originated in the Housing Act 1980) see D. Yates, The public sector and the Housing Act 1980—a tenants' charter [1981] J.S.W.L. 129 & 225.

Specific aspects

(i) Residence/Only or Principal Home

As has been seen, all three of the major legislative schemes require that a tenant must live in the premises in order to have the benefits of long term security. For a discussion of some of the case law see S. Bridge, Between two stools: animus revertendi revisited [1989] Conv. 450; S. Bridge, The security of tenure of absent tenants [1988] Conv. 300 and P. F. Smith [1985] Conv. 224.

(ii) Business Lets

A dividing line has to be drawn between the scheme of protection for business tenants (Part II of the Landlord and Tenant Act 1954) and the schemes of protection for residential tenants (Rent Act 1977, Housing Act 1985, Housing Act 1988). However, as has been seen, this dividing line can be somewhat elusive. For further discussion see J. Martin, Identifying the code of protection: mixed lettings and changes of user [1984] Conv. 390.

(iii) Avoidance of the legislation

In the previous chapter the lease/licence and its possible exploitation as a method of avoiding the impact of housing legislation was discussed. In this chapter various other potential loopholes in the legislation have been considered. For further discussion of these issues see:

—*company lets*

J. E. Martin, Nominal tenants and the Rent Act [1982] Conv. 151; C. P. Rogers, Shams, subtenancies and evasion of protective legislation [1989] Conv. 196.

—*holiday lets*

T. J. Lyons, The meaning of "holiday" under the Rent Acts [1984] Conv. 286.

—*board and attendance*

P. Q. Watchman, Heartbreak hotel [1988] J.S.W.L. 147; C. P. Rogers, Making a meal out of the Rent Acts: board, attendance and the protected tenancy (1988) 51 M.L.R. 642.

CHAPTER 4

SECURITY OF TENURE I

Introduction

For a lease to exist there must be a reversion.[1] At common law, therefore, there is always the possibility that the tenant will have to give up possession of the property, either because the term of the lease has come to an end, or because the tenant has broken one or more of the covenants contained in the lease, or some other such reason. The social hardship that can result from this state of affairs has resulted in the development of an enormous body of protective law designed to assist tenants. One of the earliest developments of the law was that the courts of equity were prepared in certain circumstances to give relief against forfeiture. The Rent Acts have long given additional security of tenure to residential tenants in the private sector: a development which was extended to public sector tenants in 1980. Business tenants may have protection under Part II of the Landlord and Tenant Act 1954 and tenant farmers are protected by the Agricultural Holdings Act 1986. As noted earlier, long leaseholders are given some security of tenure by Part I of the Landlord and Tenant Act 1954 and the Local Government and Housing Act 1989, and those occupying houses were given the right to extend their tenancies or even to enfranchise themselves under the Leasehold Reform Act 1967.[2] More recently, the right to buy has been granted to local authority tenants.[3]

Discussions of housing issues in the press frequently suggest that statutory security of tenure is a unique feature of the law on housing; in fact it is a feature of the law of landlord and tenant generally. Furthermore, it often seems to be suggested that security is the main reason why owners of residential accommodation will not enter the private sector of the housing market. This opinion seems somewhat at odds with empirical studies which show that it was the low level of rents which concerned landlords much more.[4] To the extent that rent control is abolished for new tenancies granted on or after January 15, 1989, Part

---

[1] See p. 24.
[2] See pp. 137–139.
[3] See pp. 506–531.
[4] See, *e.g.*, Paley, *Attitudes to Lettings in 1976* (1978).

I of the Housing Act 1988 is clearly a response to these concerns. However, the trend since 1979 has also been to reduce the level of security of tenure for tenants in the private sector. The "protected shorthold" was introduced by the Housing Act 1980, thereby creating a potentially important exception to the basic Rent Act scheme. Similarly, the Housing Act 1988—although providing a security of tenure regime for assured tenants which is in most respects comparable to the Rent Act scheme—introduced the "assured shorthold" which is designed to enable landlords to avoid giving security of tenure beyond the original minimum term of six months. It has been argued that these developments will boost the availability of accommodation for short-term tenants, such as students and young couples waiting to buy a house. It remains to be seen what the actual social consequences of these changes will be.

This chapter deals with the security of tenure provisions as they apply to the original tenant. The problems posed by assignment of the tenancy and subletting, the death of the tenant and divorce are discussed in the next chapter.

A final point: because of the complexity of the law and the seriousness of eviction, a general requirement has been developed that, in the case of most residential occupiers, they should not be evicted without a court looking at the facts and deciding whether or not eviction is justifiable. Failure by the landlord to follow the correct procedures can lead to both civil action and criminal proceedings.

I   METHODS OF TERMINATING TENANCIES UNDER THE COMMON LAW

The common law recognises many different modes of determining tenancies, the most important of which are discussed below.

(A)   EFFLUXION OF TIME

At common law a fixed-term lease automatically determines when the period expires.

(B)   SURRENDER

A tenancy may be brought to an end by the tenant surrendering his interest to the landlord. If the landlord accepts the surrender the lease is extinguished. However, the landlord is not under any obligation to accept, and if he refuses the tenancy continues (and the tenant will continue to be bound by the terms of the lease).

Although in principle a surrender in order to be valid should be effected by deed,[5] in practice unequivocal acts by the parties—such as the landlord accepting the return of the tenant's keys—are sufficient.

(C) MERGER

A lease comes to an end when the reversion and the lease become vested in the same person (normally when the tenant buys out the landlord's interest).

(D) POWER TO DETERMINE

A fixed-term tenancy may include an express provision (commonly referred to as a "break clause") whereby either of the parties may terminate the tenancy before the term has expired, normally on the happening of some specified event. Unlike surrender and merger which are consensual modes of termination, a break clause creates a unilateral method of bringing a tenancy to an end.

To exercise a power to determine, the party wishing to end the tenancy serves a notice to determine on the other party in the form prescribed by the terms of the lease (normally the notice will have to be served a certain period of time, such as six months, before the break clause date). At common law the tenancy comes to an end on the expiry of the notice period (*i.e.* on the break clause date), regardless of the other party's wishes.

In general, break clauses are drafted in such a way that the power to determine may be exercised at specified times, but without reasons having to be given. So, where a power to determine coincides with a rent review the tenant may choose to bring the lease to an end if he feels that the new rent is likely to be more than he will be able to afford. Similarly, a long lease may include a break clause giving the landlord a power to determine at specified intervals, so that if redevelopment of the site becomes financially attractive during the contractual term the landlord can opt to end the tenancy.

(E) FORFEITURE

A landlord may forfeit a lease for breach of covenant as long as the lease contains a proviso for re-entry for breach of covenant (a forfeiture clause).[6] The normal method of enforcing forfeiture is for the landlord

---

[5] Law of Property Act 1925, s.52.
[6] The tenant's obligations may be formulated in terms of conditions rather than covenants. (For the distinction, see Megarry & Wade, *The Law of Real Property* (5th ed., 1984), p. 671.) In such a case the landlord may forfeit the lease for breach of condition even if there is no forfeiture clause.

to issue a writ for possession (in the High Court) or a summons for possession (in the county court).

(1) Waiver

The landlord's right to forfeit may be lost if he "waives" the breach of covenant. Waiver will be implied if the landlord is aware of the acts or omissions of the tenant which make the lease liable to forfeiture and the landlord does an unequivocal act recognising the continued existence of the lease.[7] The most clear-cut example of waiver is a demand for rent by the landlord, made after the breach, with knowledge of the facts constituting the breach.[8] Where the breach of covenant is a continuing one (*e.g.* failure to repair), waiver extends only to the point of time at which the landlord knew that the breaches would last; later breaches afford a new right to forfeit.[9]

(2) Forfeiture for Non-Payment of Rent

The Common Law Procedure Act 1852 regulates the process of forfeiture for non-payment of rent in the High Court. If the landlord proceeds in the county court the procedure is regulated by the County Courts Act 1984 (as amended). In either case even where the landlord has obtained judgment for possession, the tenant may apply for relief, at the court's discretion, within six months of re-entry by the landlord.[10] If relief is granted no new lease has to be granted; the parties are treated as if forfeiture has not taken place. As a general principle, relief against forfeiture will not be granted if by the time the tenant applies to the court the landlord has re-let the premises.[11]

(3) Forfeiture for Breach of Other Covenants

Section 146 of the Law of Property Act 1925 provides (in part):

(1) A right of re-entry or forfeiture under any proviso or stipulation in a lease for a breach of any covenant or condition in the lease shall not be enforceable, by action or otherwise, unless and until the lessor serves on the lessee a notice—

  (a) specifying the particular breach complained of; and

  (b) if the breach is capable of remedy, requiring the lessee to remedy the breach; and

  (c) in any case, requiring the lessee to make compensation in money for the breach;

and the lessee fails, within a reasonable time thereafter, to remedy the breach, if it is capable of remedy, and to make reasonable compensation in money, to the satisfaction of the lessor, for the breach.

---

[7] *Matthews* v. *Smallwood* [1910] 1 Ch. 777.
[8] *e.g. David Blackstone* v. *Burnett* (*West End*) [1973] 1 W.L.R. 1487.
[9] *Segal Securities Ltd.* v. *Thoseby* [1963] 1 Q.B. 887.
[10] Common Law Procedure Act 1852, s.212; County Courts Act 1984, s.138(9A) (supplied by Administration of Justice Act 1985, s.55(4)).
[11] *Stanhope* v. *Haworth* (1866) 3 T.L.R. 34.

(2) Where a lessor is proceeding, by action or otherwise, to enforce such a right of re-entry or forfeiture, the lessee may, in the lessor's action, if any, or in any action brought by himself, apply to the court for relief; and the court may grant or refuse relief, as the court, having regard to the proceedings and conduct of the parties under the foregoing provisions of this section, and to all the other circumstances, thinks fit; and in case of relief may grant it on such terms, if any, as to costs, expenses, damages, compensation, penalty, or otherwise, including the granting of an injunction to restrain any like breach in the future, as the court, in the circumstances of each case, thinks fit. . . .[11a]

It is not possible to contract out of these provisions, and a clause in a lease which has the effect of a forfeiture clause will be treated as such even if it does not look like a usual forfeiture clause.[12]

The question of whether a covenant is "capable of remedy" under section 146(1)(b) has been discussed by the courts on a number of occasions. Both positive covenants, (*e.g.* to repair) and negative covenants, (*e.g.* not to use the demised premises except as a single dwelling) pose potential problems.

Expert Clothing Service & Sales Ltd. v. *Hillgate House* [1986] Ch. 340

According to the terms of a lease dated January 23, 1978, the tenants covenanted, *inter alia*, to notify the landlords within one month if they charged the premises (clause 3(14)), and to reconstruct the premises ready for occupation by September 28, 1982 (clause 2); the landlords sought to forfeit the lease, alleging that the tenants had failed to comply with these obligations.

Slade L.J. said (at 351–358):

In a case where the breach is "capable of remedy" within the meaning of the section, the principal object of the notice procedure provided for by section 146(1), as I read it, is to afford the lessee two opportunities before the lessor actually proceeds to enforce his right of re-entry, namely (1) the opportunity to remedy the breach within a reasonable time after service of the notice, and (2) the opportunity to apply to the court for relief from forfeiture. In a case where the breach is not "capable of remedy," there is clearly no point in affording the first of these two opportunities; the object of the notice procedure is thus simply to give the lessee the opportunity to apply for relief.

Unfortunately the authorities give only limited guidance as to what breaches are "capable of remedy" within the meaning of the section. As Harman J. pointed out in *Hoffman v. Fineberg* [1949] Ch. 245, 253:

"In one sense, no breach can ever be remedied, because there must always, ex concessis, be a time in which there has not been compliance with the covenant, but the section clearly involves the view that some breaches are remediable, and therefore it cannot mean that."

[11a] For a recent case where the court granted relief see *Southern Depot Co. Ltd.* v. *British Railways Board* [1990] 33 E.G. 45.
[12] *Richard Clarke & Co.* v. *Widnall* [1976] 1 W.L.R. 845.

MacKinnon J. in *Rugby School (Governors) v. Tannahill* [1934] 1 K.B. 695 drew an important distinction in this context between positive and negative covenants. He said, at p. 701:

"A promise to do a thing, if broken, can be remedied by the thing being done. But breach of a promise not to do a thing cannot in any true sense be remedied; that which was done cannot be undone. There cannot truly be a remedy; there can only be abstention, perhaps accompanied with apology."

From this MacKinnon J. concluded that the breach of a negative covenant of this sort was not one "capable of remedy" within the section, though the lessee was not necessarily left at the lessor's mercy, since the power to grant relief remained.

The relevant breach in the *Rugby School* case consisted of the breach of a covenant not to use premises for illegal or immoral purposes. On appeal ([1935] 1 K.B. 87), the Court of Appeal, while affirming the decision of MacKinnon J. that the particular breach was not capable of remedy, did not accept without qualification the broader test suggested by him for distinguishing remediable and irremediable breaches. Greer L.J. said, at pp. 90–91:

"I think perhaps he went further than was really necessary for the decision of this case in holding that a breach of any negative covenant—the doing of that which is forbidden—can never be capable of remedy. It is unnecessary to decide the point on this appeal; but in some cases [with] the immediate ceasing of that which is complained of, together with an undertaking against any further breach, it might be said that the breach was capable of remedy. This particular breach, however—conducting the premises, or permitting them to be conducted, as a house of ill-fame—is one which in my judgment was not remedied by merely stopping this user. I cannot conceive how a breach of this kind can be remedied. The result of committing the breach would be known all over the neighbourhood and seriously affect the value of the premises. Even a money payment together with the cessation of the improper use of the house could not be a remedy."

Maugham L.J. having referred to certain authorities, said, at p. 93:

"A reasonable construction has thus been put upon the section, the object being to allow the lessee to remedy the breach or to make compensation before action is brought against him. From that two things seem to me to follow: first, the remedy which is spoken of in the section must be a complete remedy. A partial remedy is not within the section, the concluding words of subsection (1) being: 'and the lessee fails, within a reasonable time thereafter, to remedy the breach, if it is capable of remedy, and to make reasonable compensation in money, to the satisfaction of the lessor, for the breach.' The second thing to be gathered from the section is that the breach must be capable of remedy within a reasonable time. The lessor is not to be kept out of his right of action for an unreasonable time. If, for example, the breach is of such a character that many months or perhaps years must elapse before the breach can be remedied, to the satisfaction of the lessor, such a case would not be as regards remedy within the section at all."

In the present case the judge accepted that the second breach relied on by the plaintiffs was capable of remedy. As he put it:

"Not much argument has been devoted to the second breach, that is to say failure to give notice of the charge, quite rightly in my judgment. Although it is a covenant to give notice within one month, the rule is not, as I understand it, that once the stated period in the lease has gone by the covenant thereafter becomes incapable of remedy. That in itself is not sufficient to render a breach incapable of remedy, and in this case it is quite clear no damage was done to the landlord by the giving of late notice or failing to give it and the landlord finding out by other means. Accordingly, if that were the only matter on the notice then I would be quite clearly of the opinion that the breach was capable of remedy and the notice would be defective."

The plaintiffs have not sought by a respondent's notice or in argument to challenge this part of the judge's decision. However, he regarded the other breach relied on by the plaintiffs, relating to the failure to reconstruct the premises, as being of a different order. Having cited part of the passage from the judgment of Maugham L.J. in *Rugby School (Governors) v. Tannahill* [1935] 1 K.B. 87, 93, cited above, he concluded:

"That I take as guidance to the proper approach in this case, and it seems to me—and I have no real hesitation about this—that this is not such a breach, having regard to the facts as I have outlined them, as to be capable of remedy within a reasonable time. It is going to take, according to the evidence, at the very least nine months to do the necessary works. Also there is the point that was taken—and I think it is valid—that the rent review provisions are linked to the reconstructed premises and there is no ready way in which the landlord can be reinstated in that position so that at 1982 he was obtaining a rent or assenting to a rent from reconstructed premises. It seems to me that this breach lies in the area of breaches which are incapable of remedy within a reasonable time."

The nine-month period thus referred to was, I understand, the period requested by the defendants in their application for relief, so as to enable them to do the necessary works.

In supporting the judge's conclusion that the breach relating to reconstruction of the premises was irremediable, Mr. Collins, on behalf of the plaintiffs, has submitted to us three principal arguments. First, he pointed out that (as is common ground) the first defendant's failure to build by September 28, 1982 was a "once and for all" breach of the relevant covenant, and not a continuing breach: see, for example, *Stephens v. Junior Army and Navy Stores Ltd.* [1914] 2 Ch. 516, 523, *per* Lord Cozens-Hardy M.R. He submitted that the breach of a covenant such as this, which can only be broken once, is ex hypothesi in no case capable of remedy.

Some superficial support for this conclusion is perhaps to be found in the judgments in *Scala House & District Property Co. Ltd. v. Forbes* [1974] Q.B. 575, in which the Court of Appeal held that the breach of a covenant not to assign, underlet or part with possession was not a breach capable of remedy within the meaning of section 146(1). In the course of his judgment, Russell L.J., having referred to the relevant breach, said, at p. 585:

"If it is capable of remedy, and is remedied in reasonable time, the lessor is unable to prove that a condition precedent to his ability to seek to forfeit by action or otherwise has been fulfilled. Here at once is a problem. An unlawful subletting is a breach once and for all. The subterm has been created."

Russell L.J. then turned to the authorities, including the *Rugby School* case [1935] 1 K.B. 87, as to which he made these comments, at p. 585:

"this court expressed the view that breach of negative covenants might be capable of remedy, but not this one, on the ground that the stigma attaching to the premises would not be removed by mere cesser of the immoral user. I observe that it does not appear to have been considered whether the breach in that case was incapable of remedy on another ground, viz.: that the wrongful user had ceased before the section 146 notice."

After his review of the authorities, Russell L.J. continued, at p. 588:

"In summary upon the cases we have therefore a number of cases of user of premises in breach of covenant in which the decision that the breach is not capable of remedy has gone upon the 'stigma' point, without considering whether a short answer might be—if the user had ceased before the section 146 notice—that it was ex hypothesi incapable of remedy, leaving the lessee only with the ability to seek relief from forfeiture and the writ unchallengeable as such. If a user in breach has ceased before the section 146 notice (quite apart from the stigma cases) then either it is incapable of remedy and after notice there is nothing in the way of a writ: or the cesser of use has somehow deprived the lessor of his ability to seek to forfeit though he has done nothing to waive the breach, a situation in law which I find extremely difficult to spell out of section 146."

But whatever might be the position in user breach cases, Russell L.J. concluded that a breach by an unlawful subletting is not capable of remedy at all. As he put it, at p. 588:

"the introduction of such breaches into the relevant section for the first time by section 146 of the Act of 1925 operates only to confer a statutory ability to relieve the lessee from forfeiture on that ground. The subterm has been effectively created subject only to risks of forfeiture: it is a complete breach once for all: it is not in any sense a continuing breach. If the law were otherwise a lessee, when a subtenancy is current at the time of the section 146 notice, would have a chance of remedying the situation without having to apply for relief. But if the unlawful subletting had determined before the notice, the lessee could only seek relief from forfeiture."

It might well be regarded as anomalous if the once and for all breach of a negative covenant not to sublet were to be regarded as "capable of remedy" within section 146, provided that the unlawful subtenancy was still current at the date of the section 146 notice, but (as Russell L.J. considered) were not to be regarded as "capable of remedy" if the unlawful subtenancy had been determined at that date. Russell L.J. and James L.J. who agreed with his reasoning (see particularly at p. 591c–d), were clearly much influenced by this anomaly in reaching the conclusion that the breach of a covenant against underletting is never capable of remedy.

However, in the *Scala House* case [1974] Q.B. 575 this court was addressing its mind solely to the once and for all breach of a negative covenant. No corresponding anomaly arises if the once and for all breach of a positive covenant is treated as capable of remedy. While the *Scala House* decision is, of course, authority binding on this court for the proposition that the breach of a negative covenant not to assign, underlet or part with possession is never "capable of remedy," it is not, in my judgment, authority for the proposition that the once and for all breach of a positive covenant is never capable of remedy.

Mr. Neuberger, on behalf of the defendants, did not feel able to go so far as to support the view of MacKinnon J. that the breach of a positive covenant is *always* capable of remedy. He accepted, for example, that the breach of a covenant to insure might be incapable of remedy at a time when the premises had already been burnt down. Another example might be the breach of a positive covenant which in the event would be only capable of being fully performed, if at all, after the expiration of the relevant term.

Nevertheless, I would, for my part, accept Mr. Neuberger's submission that the breach of a positive covenant (whether it be a continuing breach or a once and for all breach) will ordinarily be capable of remedy. As Bristow J. pointed out in the course of argument, the concept of capability of remedy for the purpose of section 146 must surely be directed to the question whether the harm that has been done to the landlord by the relevant breach is for practicable purposes capable of being retrieved. In the ordinary case, the breach of a promise to do something by a certain time can for practical purposes be remedied by the thing being done, even out of time. For these reasons I reject the plaintiffs' argument that the breach of the covenant to reconstruct by September 28, 1982 was not capable of remedy *merely* because it was not a continuing breach.

I would add this point. If this breach was, on these grounds alone, not capable of remedy, the very same grounds would appear to render the breach of the first defendant's covenant to give notice of the charge in favour of Lloyds Bank likewise incapable of remedy. But Mr. Collins has not attempted to maintain the latter proposition, which would have been very difficult to sustain having regard to what one may suppose was the intention of the legislature in enacting section 146(1).

As his second main line of argument in this context, he submitted that the breach of the covenant to reconstruct was not capable of remedy because of the operation of the new rent review provisions incorporated in the lease by the schedule to the order of June 29, 1981. He pointed out that under these provisions the plaintiffs, on a rent review, would have an option, which they would clearly wish to exercise, to review the rent on the basis of the premises as reconstructed. He submitted that there was no ready way in which the plaintiffs could be effectively restored to the same position under the rent review clause as that in which they would have found themselves if the premises had been reconstructed by the due date.

Respectfully differing from the judge on this point, I do not think that this submission is well founded. When the rent review clause comes to be applied, the first defendant cannot rely on its own wrong (consisting of the failure to reconstruct) to reduce the rent which would otherwise have been payable as from the review date. The proper approach must be to assume for the purpose of the assessment that the required reconstruction has taken place. As Mr. Neuberger pointed out, surveyors are quite accustomed to this kind of artificial assumption in rent review valuations. With the appropriate expert advice there would be little difficulty in ascertaining the rent to which the plaintiffs would have been entitled on the first rent review, and indeed on any subsequent rent review, if the defendants had complied with their building obligations in due time. While Mr. Collins pointed out that if this had been done, the premises might have been sublet by the rent review date and this would itself have facilitated the ascertainment of a fair rack market annual rental value, there is no certainty whatever that any such subletting would have taken place. In the context of the rent review clause, any damage resulting from the relevant breach of covenant was, in my opinion, capable of being remedied simply by the payment by the defendants of an appropriate sum of money.

I therefore turn to the third, and far the most important point, relied on by Mr. Collins in support of the decision of the court below. His submissions in this context were to the following effect. The judgment of Maugham L.J. in the *Rugby School* case [1935] 1 K.B. 87, 93 and other judicial dicta indicate that if a breach is to be "capable of remedy" at all within the meaning of section 146, it

must be capable of remedy *within a "reasonable time."* As was observed by
Lord Herschell L.C. in *Hick v. Raymond & Reid* [1893] A.C. 22, 29: "there is
of course no such thing as a reasonable time in the abstract. It must always
depend upon circumstances." In the present case, it was submitted, what was a
reasonable time was a question of fact. In deciding that the breach of the
covenant to reconstruct was not capable of remedy within a reasonable time, the
judge expressed himself as "having regard to the facts as I have found them."

Mr. Collins drew attention to some of his particular earlier findings of fact.
The plaintiffs and the second defendant had first come into contact in early
1976. The second defendant had obtained his planning permission in August
1976. The first defendant had obtained possession of the premises in anticipation
of the contemplated lease in the summer of 1977. The lease had been granted in
January 1978. However, by the autumn of 1978 the defendants had abandoned
their health club project and in March 1979 they so informed the plaintiffs.
After that date nothing of practical value had been effected towards the
conversion of the premises. The defendants, in their application for relief, had
asked the judge for nine months to enable them to do the work. Having regard
to this history of default on their part there was, in Mr. Collins's submission,
ample material on which the court below could properly find that, at the date of
service of the section 146 notice, nine months was not a reasonable time and
that accordingly the relevant breach was not capable of remedy within a
reasonable time. Furthermore, he suggested, the defendants had neither the
financial resources nor the will to do the work.

Though the judge did not spell them out in this manner, I infer that these
were essentially the points which led him to conclude that the relevant breach
was not capable of remedy within a reasonable time. With great respect to him,
I have reached a different conclusion on this point for reasons which I will now
attempt to explain.

While the words "within a reasonable time" do not appear in sub-paragraph
(b) of section 146(1), I accept that a section 146 notice need not require the
tenant to remedy the breach if it is not capable of remedy within a reasonable
time after service of the notice: see, for example, the *Rugby School* case [1935]
1 K.B. 87, 93, and *Egerton v. Esplanade Hotels, London Ltd.* [1947] 2 All E.R.
88, 91, *per* Morris J. This appears to be the proper inference from the
concluding words of section 146(1) which leave the lessor at liberty to enforce
his right of re-entry if "the lessee fails, within a reasonable time thereafter, to
remedy the breach. ... " A requirement to remedy within a reasonable time is
pointless in a case where remedy within a reasonable time from the service of
the notice is impossible.

However, in my opinion, in considering whether or not remedy within a
reasonable time is possible, a crucial distinction (which I infer from the
judgment did not feature prominently in argument before the judge) falls to be
drawn between breaches of negative user covenants, such as those under
consideration in the *Rugby School* and the *Esplanade Hotels* cases, and breaches
of positive covenants. In the two last-mentioned cases, where the relevant
breaches consisted of allowing premises to be used as a brothel, even full
compliance with the covenant within a reasonable time and for a reasonable
time would not have remedied the breach. As Maugham L.J. pointed out in the
Rugby School case, at p. 94:

> "merely ceasing for a reasonable time, perhaps a few weeks or a month, to
> use the premises for an immoral purpose would be no remedy for the breach
> of covenant which had been committed over a long period."

On the facts of cases such as those, mere cesser by the tenant of the offending
use within a reasonable period and for a reasonable period of time could not

have remedied the breaches because it could not have removed the stigma which they had caused to attach to the premises. The harm had been irretrievably done. In such cases, as Harman J. pointed out in *Hoffmann v. Fineberg* [1949] Ch. 245, 257, mere cesser will not enable the tenant to "make his record clean, as he could by complying, though out of time, with a failure to lay on the prescribed number of coats of paint."

In contrast with breaches of negative user covenants, the breach of a positive covenant to do something (such as to decorate or build) can ordinarily, for practical purposes, be remedied by the thing being actually done if a reasonable time for its performance (running from the service of the section 146 notice) is duly allowed by the landlord following such service and the tenant duly does it within such time.

In the present case there is no question of the breach of the covenant to reconstruct having given rise to any "stigma" against the lessors or the premises. Significantly, the lease in 1982 still had 20 years to run. Mr. Collins has, I think, been able to suggest no convincing reasons why the plaintiffs would still have suffered irremediable damage if (i) the section 146 notice had required the lessee to remedy the breach and (ii) the lessors had then allowed a reasonable time to elapse sufficient to enable the lessee to comply with the relevant covenant, and (iii) the lessee had complied with the covenant in such reasonable time and had paid any appropriate monetary compensation. Though he has submitted that a requirement directed to the defendants to remedy the breach would have been purposeless, on the grounds that they had neither the financial means nor the will to do the necessary work, these are matters which, in my opinion, a landlord is not entitled to prejudge in drafting his notice. An important purpose of the section 146 procedure is to give even tenants who have hitherto lacked the will or the means to comply with their obligations one last chance to summon up that will or find the necessary means before the landlord re-enters. In considering what "reasonable time" to allow the defendants, the plaintiffs, in serving their section 146 notice, would, in my opinion, have been entitled to take into account the fact that the defendants already had enjoyed 15 months in which to fulfil their contractual obligations to reconstruct and to subject the defendants to a correspondingly tight timetable running from the date of service of the notice, though, at the same time, always bearing in mind that the contractual obligation to reconstruct did not even arise until June 29, 1981, and that as at October 8, 1982 the defendants had been in actual breach of it for only some 10 days. However, I think they were not entitled to say, in effect: "We are not going to allow you any time at all to remedy the breach, because you have had so long to do the work already."

In my judgment, on the remediability issue, the ultimate question for the court was this: if the section 146 notice had required the lessee to remedy the breach and the lessors had then allowed a reasonable time to elapse to enable the lessee fully to comply with the relevant covenant, would such compliance, coupled with the payment of any appropriate monetary compensation, have effectively remedied the harm which the lessors had suffered or were likely to suffer from the breach? If, but only if, the answer to this question was "No," would the failure of the section 146 notice to require remedy of the breach have been justifiable. In *Rugby School (Governors) v. Tannahill* [1935] 1 K.B. 87; *Egerton v. Esplanade Hotels, London Ltd.* [1947] 2 All E.R. 88 and *Hoffmann v. Fineberg* [1949] Ch. 245 the answer to this question plainly would have been "No." In the present case, however, for the reasons already stated, I think the answer to it must have been "Yes."

My conclusion, therefore, is that the breach of the covenant to reconstruct, no less than the breach of the covenant to give notice of charges, was "capable of remedy." In reaching this conclusion, I find it reassuring that no reported case has been brought to our attention in which the breach of a positive covenant has been held incapable of remedy, though I do not suggest that cases of this nature, albeit perhaps rarely, could not arise.

Special provisions relating to relief in respect of repairs and internal decorative repairs are discussed elsewhere.[13]

(4) The Relationship between Forfeiture at Common Law and Statutory Security of Tenure

In the context of a Rent Act tenancy, where forfeiture is ordered, that only has the effect of terminating the original contractual tenancy.[14] Thus a Rent Act protected tenancy will be converted into a statutory tenancy (by forfeiture) and the statutory tenant will have all the rights which are available under the 1977 Act.[15]

A similar position applies under the Housing Act 1985 in relation to secure tenancies. Where a public sector landlord seeks to forfeit a contractual secure tenancy in circumstances where the court would have made an order for possession at common law, the court must make an order terminating the contractual tenancy (under section 82(3) of the 1985 Act). This in itself does not entitle the landlord to possession since in these circumstances a periodic secure tenancy arises in place of the original contractual tenancy.[16] To recover possession the landlord must obtain an order of the court on one of the grounds specified by the 1985 Act.[17] It has been suggested that the power under section 82(3) "may be viewed as a cautionary 'shot across the bows,' and arguably only in the severest cases should the first exercise of the power to determine the term be accompanied by an outright order for possession."[18]

The Housing Act 1988 has reached a different solution to the problem. In relation to assured tenancies, the landlord may recover possession only by proceeding under the 1988 Act. Although a fixed-term assured tenancy should contain a forfeiture clause if the landlord wishes to be able to recover possession before the expiry of the contractual term in the event of breach of covenant by the tenant,[19] the landlord is not able to terminate an assured tenancy by forfeiture. The only way in which the landlord can recover possession is through obtaining an order of the court on one of the grounds set out in the 1988 Act.[20]

---

[13] See pp. 388–391.
[14] *Wolmer Securities Ltd.* v. *Corne* [1966] 2 Q.B. 243.
[15] See pp. 231–249.
[16] Housing Act 1985, s.86(1).
[17] *Ibid.* s.86.
[18] Arden, *The Housing Act 1985* (1986), p. 68–129.
[19] Housing Act 1988, s.7(6).
[20] For further discussion see pp. 204–231.

(5) Criminal Liability

In situations involving residential tenancies, the landlord's right to forfeit is subject to section 2 of the Protection from Eviction Act 1977 (regardless of whether the tenancy falls within the scope of any of the statutory schemes):

Where any premises are let as a dwelling on a lease which is subject to a right of re-entry or forfeiture it shall not be lawful to enforce that right otherwise than by proceedings in the court while any person is lawfully residing in the premises or part of them.

This applies to all forfeiture cases, whether relating to non-payment of rent or to breach of other covenants. Failure to observe section 2 is a criminal offence.[21]

(6) Notice to Quit

At common law either party may terminate a periodic tenancy by notice to quit. The notice period is the same period for which rent is paid (except for yearly tenancies where the period is half a year). The common law rule is that the notice should expire at the end of completed period. However, these rules are subject to the terms of the lease itself. The parties may select a different notice period (for example, a month's notice in respect of a quarterly tenancy), and a different expiry date.[22]

In the case of periodic tenancies of residential accommodation certain requirements have been laid down. (These statutory requirements were extended to residential licences by the Housing Act 1988.) Section 5 of the Protection from Eviction Act 1977[23] states:

(1) Subject to subsection (1B) below no notice by a landlord or a tenant to quit any premises let (whether before or after the commencement of this Act) as a dwelling shall be valid unless—

(a)   it is in writing and contains such information as may be prescribed, and

(b)   it is given not less than four weeks before the date on which it is to take effect. . . .

(1A) Subject to subsection (1B) below, no notice by a licensor or a licensee to determine a periodic licence to occupy premises as a dwelling (whether the licence was granted before or after the passing of this Act) shall be valid unless—

(a)   it is in writing and contains such information as may be prescribed, and

---

[21] See pp. 262–268, and *Borzak* v. *Ahmed* [1965] 2 Q.B. 320.

[22] *H. & G. Simmons Ltd.* v. *Haywood* [1948] 1 All E.R. 260. For a recent discussion see *Harler* v. *Calder* (1989) 21 H.L.R. 214.

[23] As amended by Housing Act 1988, s.32.

(b)   it is given not less than four weeks before the date on which it is to take effect.

(1B) Nothing in subsection (1) or subsection (1A) above applies to—

(a)   premises let on an excluded tenancy which is entered into on or after the date on which the Housing Act 1988 came into force unless it is entered into pursuant to a contract made before that date; or

(b)   premises occupied under an excluded licence.

Excluded tenancies and licences are defined by section 3A of the 1977 Act.[24]

The "prescribed information" referred to in section 5 is contained in the Notices to Quit, etc. (Prescribed Information) Regulations 1988[25] which provide:

1. If the tenant or licensee does not leave the dwelling, the landlord or licensor must get an order for possession from the court before the tenant or licensee can lawfully be evicted. The landlord or licensor cannot apply for such an order before the notice to quit or notice to determine has run out.

2. A tenant or licensee who does not know if he has any right to remain in possession after a notice to quit or a notice to determine runs out can obtain advice from a solicitor. Help with all or part of the cost of legal advice and assistance may be available under the Legal Aid Scheme. He should also be able to obtain information from a Citizens' Advice Bureau, a Housing Aid Centre or a rent officer.

Failure to provide this information renders the notice invalid.

The common law rules are modified in relation to tenancies which are subject to the various statutory schemes of protection. Under the Rent Act 1977 a valid notice to quit is effective to terminate the contractual protected tenancy, but it does not entitle the landlord to possession; on the expiry of the notice there arises a statutory tenancy. As regards statutory tenancies the relevant notice requirements are to be found in section 3 of the Rent Act 1977. Subsection (3) states:

Subject to section 5 of the Protection from Eviction Act 1977 (under which at least four weeks' notice to quit is required), a statutory tenant of a dwelling-house shall be entitled to give up possession of the dwelling-house if, and only if, he gives such notice as would have been required under the provisions of the original contract of tenancy, or, if no notice would have been so required, on giving not less than 3 months' notice.[26]

Section 3(4) provides:

---

[24] The text of s.3A (supplied by Housing Act 1988, s.31) is to be found at pp. 259–260.
[25] S.I. 1988 No. 2201.
[26] See *Boyer* v. *Warbey* [1953] 1 Q.B. 234 for the enforcement of this provision.

Notwithstanding anything in the contract of tenancy, a landlord who obtains an order for possession of a dwelling-house as against a statutory tenant shall not be required to give the statutory tenant any notice to quit. ...

Landlords cannot terminate secure tenancies and assured tenancies by notice to quit. Indeed, a notice to quit served by a landlord on an assured tenant or a secure tenant is of no effect.[27] However, in relation to both public and private sectors, landlords must comply with certain statutory notice requirements before starting proceedings for eviction.[28]

It is important to note that the common law rules continue to apply to the termination by notice to quit of periodic tenancies by secure tenants and assured tenants. A notice to quit given by one of several joint tenants under a periodic tenancy has the effect of bringing the tenancy to an end even if the notice is given without the authority of any other tenant.[29]

(7) Other Methods

Other methods known to the common law are: disclaimer and by the operation of the doctrine of frustration.[30]

Note

Leases may also be terminated as a result of various statutory procedures, *e.g.* compulsory purchase; enfranchisement under the Leasehold Reform Act 1967 or the Housing Act 1985; the imposition of a demolition order (or in some cases a closing order) under the Housing Act 1985.

II LAWFUL EVICTION

It has been noted above that the common law methods of bringing a lease to an end are significantly modified by the statutory schemes of protection for residential tenants. Although there are a number of features which are common to each of the schemes (for example, certain grounds for possession are to be found in the Rent Act 1977, the Housing Act 1985 and the Housing Act 1988), there are differences of structure and detail.

Before looking at the security of tenure provisions in detail, it is important to note that many thousands of lawful evictions take place each year. Many of these are taken by public sector landlords, but a substantial number of private sector tenancies are also brought to an end by the courts.

---

[27] Housing Act 1985, s.82(1); Housing Act 1988, s.5(1).
[28] See pp. 227–229 and 250–251.
[29] *Greenwich L.B.C.* v. *McGrady* (1982) 46 P. & C.R. 223; *Hammersmith & Fulham L.B.C.* v. *Monk*; *Barnet L.B.C.* v. *Smith, The Times*, November 5, 1990.
[30] *National Carriers Ltd.* v. *Panalpina (Northern) Ltd.* [1981] A.C. 675.

Housing and Construction Statistics 1978–88 (1989), Table 11.10

County Court Actions for recovery of possession of Residential Premises: 1987–1988[1]

(a) Actions commenced						Number
	1987	1988				
	All	Social landlords against tenants[2]	Agricultural tied cottages	Service tenancies	Mortgage possessions	Private landlords and all other actions[3]
Proceedings entered during period:	164,499	182,941 79,866	83	1,511	76,045	25,436
Proceedings withdrawn, settled, adjourned sine die, not serviced or otherwise disposed of:	23,869	28,015 11,405	8	254	13,703	2,645

[1] Figures are based on a sample of three individual months (February, June and October) each year.   Source: Lord Chancellor's Department.

[2] 'Social landlords' are local authorities, new towns and those housing associations and trusts whose tenancies are excluded from the Rent Act 1977 by virtue of Sections 14, 15, 16 and 19 (as amended by the Housing Act 1980) of that Act.

[3] 'Other actions' covers various actions involving rented premises which do not fall within the specific categories given e.g. matrimonial disputes, tenancies at will. It also covers all actions concerning residential premises brought, whether by private or by 'social' landlords, under Order 26 of the County Court Rules against alleged trespassers.

(b) Actions decided[4]

Number

	1987	1988 All actions	Private landlords against tenants					Agricultural tied cottages	Service tenancies	Mortgage possessions	Other types of action[3]
			Resident		Absentee						
			Pre 1980 Housing Act	Post 1980 Housing Act	Discretionary grounds	Mandatory grounds	Short hold				
England and Wales											
Orders for possession refused by Court:	1,474	1,698	25	179	116	9	..	..	3	555	311
Orders for possession made by Court: of which	98,167	114,709	2,106	10,666	7,456	323	763	268	835	50,403	41,989
Suspended up to 1 month:[5]	64,159	80,481	1,137	7,416	5,789	283	293	218	448	34,589	30,309
Suspended for over 1 month:[5]	8,376	16,291	245	974	491	27	..	12	170	10,292	4,080
Conditions imposed as to rent and/or arrears:	19,790	21,701	186	903	1,575	138	89	22	159	8,458	10,171
All applications determined:	99,642	116,407	2,131	10,845	7,572	332	763	268	738	50,958	42,800

[3] 'Other actions' covers various actions involving rented premises which do not fall within the specific categories given e.g. matrimonial disputes, tenancies at will. It also covers all actions concerning residential premises brought, whether by private or by 'social' landlords, under Order 26 of the County Court Rules against alleged trespassers.

[4] In any period some actions determined or withdrawn will have been entered in previous periods.

[5] Information not available prior to 1985.

Note: The length of time that the order is suspended for is no longer as detailed as previous returns. L.C.D. (Lord Chancellor's Dept.) say that the old method took up too much of the Court's time.

The adequacy of court procedures, as a method of reviewing cases and filtering out doubtful claims is open to question. It is also frequently claimed that delays in obtaining a hearing are extensive.

III SECURITY OF TENURE UNDER THE HOUSING ACT 1988

The security of tenure regime contained in Part I of the Housing Act 1988 borrows freely from the Rent Act scheme and the provisions which regulate the public sector. Accordingly, in the materials which follow, cases decided under earlier legislation will be used to illustrate the provisions of the 1988 Act.

The starting point for the assured tenant's security of tenure is to be found in section 5 of the Housing Act 1988 which states:

(1) An assured tenancy cannot be brought to an end by the landlord except by obtaining an order of the court in accordance with the following provisions of this Chapter or Chapter II below or, in the case of a fixed term tenancy which contains power for the landlord to determine the tenancy in certain circumstances, by the exercise of that power and, accordingly, the service by the landlord of a notice to quit shall be of no effect in relation to a periodic assured tenancy.

(2) If an assured tenancy which is a fixed term tenancy comes to an end otherwise than by virtue of—

(a) an order of the court, or

(b) a surrender or other action on the part of the tenant,

then, subject to section 7 and Chapter II below, the tenant shall be entitled to remain in possession of the dwelling-house let under that tenancy and, subject to subsection (4) below, his right to possession shall depend upon a periodic tenancy arising by virtue of this section.

(3) The periodic tenancy referred to in subsection (2) above is one—

(a) taking effect in possession immediately on the coming to an end of the fixed term tenancy;

(b) deemed to have been granted by the person who was the landlord under the fixed term tenancy immediately before it came to an end to the person who was then the tenant under that tenancy;

(c) under which the premises which are let are the same dwelling-house as was let under the fixed term tenancy;

(d) under which the periods of the tenancy are the same as those for which rent was last payable under the fixed term tenancy; and

(e) under which, subject to the following provisions of this Part of this Act, the other terms are the same as those of the fixed term tenancy immediately before it came to an end, except that any term which makes provision for determination by the landlord or the tenant shall not have effect while the tenancy remains an assured tenancy.

(4) The periodic tenancy referred to in subsection (2) above shall not arise if, on the coming to an end of the fixed term tenancy, the tenant is entitled, by virtue of the grant of another tenancy, to possession of the same or substantially the same dwelling-house as was let to him under the fixed term tenancy.

(5) If, on or before the date on which a tenancy is entered into or is deemed to have been granted as mentioned in subsection (3)(b) above, the person who is to be the tenant under that tenancy—

(a) enters into an obligation to do any act which (apart from this subsection) will cause the tenancy to come to an end at a time when it is an assured tenancy, or

(b) executes, signs or gives any surrender, notice to quit or other document which (apart from this subsection) has the effect of bringing the tenancy to an end at a time when it is an assured tenancy,

the obligation referred to in paragraph (a) above shall not be enforceable or, as the case may be, the surrender, notice to quit or other document referred to in paragraph (b) above shall be of no effect.

Notes

(i)   In section 5(1) the phrase "power for the landlord to determine the tenancy" does not refer to a forfeiture clause. Section 45(4) provides:

For the avoidance of doubt, it is hereby declared that any reference in this Part of this Act (however expressed) to a power for a landlord to determine a tenancy does not include a reference to a power of re-entry or forfeiture for breach of any term or condition of the tenancy.

It is clear, therefore, that a landlord cannot terminate a fixed term assured tenancy by forfeiture. Section 5(1) would include, however, a break clause.[31]

(ii)   When a fixed-term assured tenancy comes to an end otherwise than by virtue of an order of the court or by action by the tenant, a statutory periodic assured tenancy arises under section 5(2). So, a statutory periodic assured tenancy comes into existence where the landlord exercises a power to determine, or where the fixed-term expires.

(iii)   A landlord cannot terminate a periodic assured tenancy (whether contractual or statutory) except by an order of the court, since by, virtue of section 5(1) the service by the landlord of a notice to quit is of no effect.

(iv)   The conceptual structure established by section 5 is very different from that found in the Rent Act 1977 (which relies on a statutory tenancy arising when a contractual protected tenancy is brought to an

---

[31] See p. 189.

end by the landlord).[32] The 1988 Act structure—which is much neater—
is a modified version of that employed in the Housing Act 1985.[33]

(A) RECOVERING POSSESSION FROM AN ASSURED TENANT

(1) Grounds for Possession

The circumstances in which the court may grant an order for possession
are set out in section 7 and Schedule 2 to the 1988 Act.

7.—(1) The court shall not make an order for possession of a dwelling-house let
on an assured tenancy except on one or more of the grounds set out in Schedule 2
to this Act; but nothing in this Part of this Act relates to proceedings for
possession of such a dwelling-house which are brought by a mortgagee, within the
meaning of the Law of Property Act 1925, who has lent money on the security of
the assured tenancy.

(2) The following provisions of this section have effect, subject to section 8
below, in relation to proceedings for the recovery of possession of a dwelling-
house let on an assured tenancy.

(3) If the court is satisfied that any of the grounds in Part I of Schedule 2 to this
Act is established then, subject to subsections (5A) and (6) below, the court shall
make an order for possession.

(4) If the court is satisfied that any of the grounds in Part II of Schedule 2 to
this Act is established, then, subject to subsections (5A) and (6) below, the court
may make an order for possession if it considers it reasonable to do so.

(5) Part III of Schedule 2 to this Act shall have effect for supplementing
Ground 9 in that Schedule and Part IV of that Schedule shall have effect in
relation to notices given as mentioned in Grounds 1 to 5 of that Schedule.

(5A) The court shall not make an order for possession of a dwelling-house let
on an assured periodic tenancy arising under Schedule 10 to the Local Government and Housing Act 1989 on any of the following grounds, that is to say,—

(a)   Grounds 1, 2 and 5 in Part I of Schedule 2 to this Act;

(b)   Ground 16 in Part II of that Schedule; and

(c)   if the assured periodic tenancy arose on the termination of a former 1954
      Act tenancy, within the meaning of the said Schedule 10, Ground 6 in
      Part I of Schedule 2 to this Act.

(6) The court shall not make an order for possession of a dwelling-house to take
effect at a time when it is let on an assured fixed term tenancy unless—

(a)   the ground for possession is Ground 2 or Ground 8 in Part I of Schedule 2
      to this Act or any of the grounds in Part II of that Schedule, other than
      Ground 9 or Ground 16; and

(b)   the terms of the tenancy make provision for it to be brought to an end on
      the ground in question (whether that provision takes the form of a
      provision for re-entry, for forfeiture, for determination by notice or
      otherwise).

(7) Subject to the preceding provisions of this section, the court may make an
order for possession of a dwelling-house on grounds relating to a fixed term

---

[32] See pp. 231–249.　　　　　　[33] See pp. 249–258.

tenancy which has come to an end; and where an order is made in such circumstances, any statutory periodic tenancy which has arisen on the ending of the fixed term tenancy shall end (without any notice and regardless of the period) on the day on which the order takes effect.

Note

It can be seen that, whereas in principle all 16 of the grounds are available in relation to periodic assured tenancies (whether contractual or statutory), as regards fixed-term tenancies only those specified in section 7(6) can be relied upon during the fixed term. Furthermore, section 7(6)(b) requires that the terms of the tenancy should "make provision for it to be brought to an end on the ground in question." This phrase is not without its ambiguities. A typical forfeiture clause would provide:

It is hereby mutually agreed between the parties as follows—

> if the rent hereby made payable or any part thereof shall be unpaid for 21 days after becoming payable (whether formally demanded or not) or if any of the foregoing covenants on the tenant's part shall not be performed and observed by the tenant the landlord may at any time thereafter re-enter the premises and resume possession of the premises and the furniture and thereupon this tenancy shall determine.

Although the clause does not expressly refer to any of the grounds contained in Schedule 2, it seems likely that the landlord would be able to rely on Ground 10 (non-payment of rent) and Ground 12 (breach of covenant) during the fixed term. On the other hand, the other grounds which fall within section 7(6) would not appear to be covered by a standard forfeiture clause, and therefore would only be available during the fixed term if expressly incorporated.

The effect of section 7(3) and section 7(4) is to divide the 16 grounds for possession into two categories: the mandatory grounds (Grounds 1 to 8) in relation to which the court "shall make an order for possession"; and the discretionary grounds (Grounds 9 to 16) where the court "may make an order for possession if it considers it reasonable to do so."

As regards the discretionary grounds "reasonableness" is an overriding requirement which must be considered independently of the specific ground for possession on which the landlord seeks to rely. In *Cumming* v. *Danson*[34] Lord Greene M.R. said:

In considering reasonableness ... it is, in my opinion, perfectly clear that the duty of the judge is to take into account all the relevant circumstances as they exist at the date of the hearing. That he must do in what I venture to call a broad, common-sense way as a man of the world, and to come to his conclusion,

---

[34] [1942] All E.R. 653 at 655.

giving such weight as he thinks right to the various factors in the situation. Some factors may have little or no weight, others may be decisive.

It is impossible to draw clear principles from the decided cases. The following list, however, gives some examples of the factors which the courts have regarded as relevant:

— the conduct of the parties, including such matters as a suggestion by the landlord's agent that there would be no objection to a breach of covenant[35];
— the fact that the tenant had occupied the premises for 35 years, and that the landlord's interest was purely financial[36];
— the fact that the tenant had been informed that the letting would be for a short time only.[37]

Certain other factors have been regarded by the courts as irrelevant, for example:

— that the tenant is standing on his legal rights in breach of a "gentleman's agreement"[38];
— that the landlord has only recently purchased the reversion.[39]

Essentially, the discretion conferred by section 7(4) is in the hands of the trial judge. A decision of the judge at first instance will not be set aside on appeal simply because the Court of Appeal might have come to a different conclusion. The Court of Appeal will, however, interfere if the trial judge proceeded on grounds which were wholly unreasonable, or if it is satisfied that the decision is wholly wrong.

Mandatory Grounds

Ground 1

Not later than the beginning of the tenancy the landlord gave notice in writing to the tenant that possession might be recovered on this ground or the court is of the opinion that it is just and equitable to dispense with the requirement of notice and (in either case)—

(a) at some time before the beginning of the tenancy, the landlord who is seeking possession or, in the case of joint landlords seeking possession, at least one of them occupied the dwelling-house as his only or principal home; or

(b) the landlord who is seeking possession or, in the case of joint landlords seeking possession, at least one of them requires the dwelling-house as his or his spouse's only or principal home and neither the landlord (or, in the case of joint landlords, any one of them) nor any other person

---

[35] *Upjohn* v. *Macfarlane* [1922] 2 Ch. 256.
[36] *Battlespring Ltd.* v. *Gates* (1983) 11 H.L.R. 6. See pp. 219–221.
[37] *Gladyric Ltd.* v. *Collinson* (1983) 11 H.L.R. 12.
[38] *Sopwith* v. *Stutchbury* (1983) 17 H.L.R. 50.
[39] *Briddon* v. *George* [1946] 1 All E.R. 609.

who, as landlord, derived title under the landlord who gave the notice mentioned above acquired the reversion on the tenancy for money or money's worth.

Ground 2 is discussed at pp. 328–329.

Ground 3

The tenancy is a fixed term tenancy for a term not exceeding eight months and—

(a) not later than the beginning of the tenancy the landlord gave notice in writing to the tenant that possession might be recovered on this ground; and

(b) at some time within the period of 12 months ending with the beginning of the tenancy, the dwelling-house was occupied under a right to occupy it for a holiday.

Ground 4

The tenancy is a fixed term tenancy for a term not exceeding 12 months and—

(a) not later than the beginning of the tenancy the landlord gave notice in writing to the tenant that possession might be recovered on this ground; and

(b) at some time within the period of 12 months ending with the beginning of the tenancy, the dwelling-house was let on a tenancy falling within paragraph 8 of Schedule 1 to this Act.

Ground 5

The dwelling-house is held for the purpose of being available for occupation by a minister of religion as a residence from which to perform the duties of his office and—

(a) not later than the beginning of the tenancy the landlord gave notice in writing to the tenant that possession might be recovered on this ground; and

(b) the court is satisfied that the dwelling-house is required for occupation by a minister of religion as such a residence.

Ground 6

The landlord who is seeking possession or, if that landlord is a registered housing association or charitable housing trust, a superior landlord intends to demolish or reconstruct the whole or a substantial part of the dwelling-house or to carry out substantial works on the dwelling-house or any part thereof or any building of which it forms part and the following conditions are fulfilled—

(a) the intended work cannot reasonably be carried out without the tenant giving up possession of the dwelling-house because—

    (i) the tenant is not willing to agree to such a variation of the terms of the tenancy as would give such access and other facilities as would permit the intended work to be carried out, or

    (ii) the nature of the intended work is such that no such variation is practicable, or,

(iii)   the tenant is not willing to accept an assured tenancy of such part only of the dwelling-house (in this sub-paragraph referred to as "the reduced part") as would leave in the possession of his landlord so much of the dwelling-house as would be reasonable to enable the intended work to be carried out and, where appropriate, as would give such access and other facilities over the reduced part as would permit the intended work to be carried out, or

(iv)   the nature of the intended work is such that such a tenancy is not practicable; and

(b)   either the landlord seeking possession acquired his interest in the dwelling-house before the grant of the tenancy or that interest was in existence at the time of that grant and neither that landlord (or, in the case of joint landlords, any of them) nor any other person who, alone or jointly with others, has acquired that interest since that time acquired it for money or money's worth; and

(c)   the assured tenancy on which the dwelling-house is let did not come into being by virtue of any provision of Schedule 1 to the Rent Act 1977, as amended by Part I of Schedule 4 to this Act or, as the case may be, section 4 of the Rent (Agriculture) Act 1976, as amended by Part II of that Schedule.

For the purposes of this ground, if, immediately before the grant of the tenancy, the tenant to whom it was granted or, if it was granted to joint tenants, any of them was the tenant or one of the joint tenants of the dwelling-house concerned under an earlier assured tenancy or, as the case may be, under a tenancy to which Schedule 10 to the Local Government and Housing Act 1989 applied, any reference in paragraph (b) above to the grant of the tenancy is a reference to the grant of that earlier assured tenancy or, as the case may be, to the grant of the tenancy to which the said Schedule 10 applied.

For the purposes of this ground, "registered housing association" has the same meaning as in the Housing Associations Act 1985 and "charitable housing trust" means a housing trust, within the meaning of that Act, which is a charity, within the meaning of the Charities Act 1960.

For the purposes of this ground, every acquisition under Part IV of this Act shall be taken to be an acquisition for money or money's worth; and in any case where—

(i)   the tenancy (in this paragraph referred to as "the current tenancy") was granted to a person (along or jointly with others) who, immediately before it was granted, was a tenant under a tenancy of a different dwelling-house (in this paragraph referred to as "the earlier tenancy"), and

(ii)   the landlord under the current tenancy is the person who, immediately before that tenancy was granted, was the landlord under the earlier tenancy, and

(iii)   the condition in paragraph (b) above could not have been fulfilled with respect to the earlier tenancy by virtue of an acquisition under Part IV of this Act (including one taken to be such an acquisition by virtue of the previous operation of this paragraph), the acquisition of the landlord's interest under the current tenancy shall be taken to have been under that Part and the landlord shall be taken to have acquired that interest after the grant of the current tenancy.

Ground 7 is discussed at pp. 302–305.

Ground 8

Both at the date of the service of the notice under section 8 of this Act relating to the proceedings for possession and at the date of the hearing—

  (a)   if rent is payable weekly or fortnightly, at least 13 weeks' rent is unpaid;

  (b)   if rent is payable monthly, at least three months' rent is unpaid;

  (c)   if rent is payable quarterly, at least one quarter's rent is more than three months in arrears; and

  (d)   if rent is payable yearly, at least three months' rent is more than three months in arrears;

and for the purpose of this ground "rent" means rent lawfully due from the tenant.

Notes

(i)   A number of these grounds for possession are modelled on "cases" under the Rent Act 1977; Ground 1 corresponds to Case 11; Ground 3 to Case 13; Ground 4 to Case 14; and Ground 5 to Case 15. Having said that, it is important to note that there are differences between the Rent Act "cases" and these 1988 Act grounds which should not be overlooked.[40]

(ii)   Ground 6 has no counterpart in the Rent Act scheme, but is designed to serve a similar purpose to Ground 10 of the secure tenancy regime[41] and—perhaps more importantly—section 30(1)(f) of the Landlord and Tenant Act 1954 which allows a landlord of business premises to oppose the grant of a new tenancy (under section 24(1)) on the ground that "the landlord intends to demolish or reconstruct the premises comprised in the building or a substantial part of those premises or to carry out substantial work of construction on the building or part thereof and that he could not reasonably do so without obtaining possession of the building."

To be able to rely on Ground 6 a number of conditions must be satisfied. First, assuming that the approach adopted in relation to business tenancies is followed in the context of Ground 6, the landlord must show more than a hope, but a firm and settled

[40] For the various grounds for possession under the Rent Act 1977 see pp. 231–249.
[41] Housing Act 1985, Sched. 2. See p. 253.

intention.[42] In the words of Asquith L.J. in *Cunliffe* v. *Goodman*:

An 'intention' ... connotes a state of affairs which the party 'intending' ... does more than merely contemplate: it connotes a state of affairs which, on the contrary, he decides, so far as in him lies, to bring about, and which, in point of possibility, he has a reasonable prospect of being able to bring about, by his own act of volition.[43]

Secondly, the landlord will not be able to recover possession unless the intended work cannot be reasonably carried out without the tenant giving up possession. Thirdly, the landlord must not have acquired the reversion after the assured tenancy was created. Finally, Ground 6 does not apply to a tenancy which was a protected or statutory tenancy under the Rent Act and which becomes an assured tenancy on succession by a member of the former tenant's family.[44]

If the landlord does recover possession under Ground 6 he will be liable to "pay to the tenant a sum equal to the reasonable expenses likely to be incurred by the tenant in removing from the dwelling-house."[45]

(iii) There is no counterpart to Ground 8 in the other schemes of statutory protection. Under the Rent Act 1977 and the Housing Act 1985 non-payment of rent is always a discretionary ground.

(iv) In relation to Grounds 1 to 5 the landlord must—as a general rule—serve a notice in writing on the tenant "not later than the beginning of the tenancy" informing the tenant that possession might be recovered on the ground in question. (There is no prescribed form.)[46]

The phrase "not later than the beginning of the tenancy" is defined in paragraph 11 of Part IV of Schedule 2 to the 1988 Act as "not later than the day on which the tenancy is entered into." Accordingly, it seems that a landlord may rely on Grounds 1 to 5 even where he serves the relevant notice on the tenant after the tenancy agreement has been concluded (as long as the notice is given on the same day).

(v) In relation to Grounds 1 and 2 the landlord may recover possession, notwithstanding the fact that no notice has been served, if the court is of the opinion that it is "just and equitable to dispense with the requirements of notice."

Some guidance as to how the courts might exercise the discretion conferred by Ground 1 can be gleaned from the cases decided under the Rent Act 1977 in relation to Case 11.

---

[42] *Fisher* v. *Taylor Furnishing Stores Ltd.* [1956] 2 Q.B. 78.
[43] [1950] 2 K.B. 237 at 253. See also *Cappoci* v. *Goble* (1987) 284 E.G. 230.
[44] For a discussion of the succession provisions, see pp. 305–313.
[45] Housing Act 1988, s.11(1).
[46] *Ibid.* Sched. 2, Part IV.

In *Fernandes* v. *Parvardin*[47] the tenants had been informed orally that the landlady might require possession of the premises for her own occupation or for occupation by a member of her family. The judge at first instance held that it was just and equitable to dispense with the requirement of a written notice. In the Court of Appeal Donaldson L.J. said that "the court is wholly concerned to see what injustice or inequity flows from the failure to comply precisely with the terms of the Case."[48] Stephenson L.J., on the other hand, thought that in deciding whether it was just and equitable to dispense with the requirement of written notice the judge is entitled "to take into account all the circumstances— anything which might make it unjust or inequitable ... "[49]

The latter approach found favour with the Court of Appeal in *Bradshaw* v. *Baldwin-Wiseman*,[50] where the landlord was seeking to recover possession under Case 11 even though the tenant had not been given notice, either orally or in writing, that Case 11 might be relied upon. Griffiths L.J. (with whom Browne-Wilkinson L.J. and Sir George Waller agreed) said:

I prefer the approach of Stephenson L.J. The words 'just and equitable' are of very wide import, and I can see nothing in the context which justifies giving them any restrictive meaning. I would regard the use of these words as directing the court to look at all the circumstances of the case. Those would embrace the circumstances affecting the landlord, or his successors in title, and the circumstances of the tenant, and of course the circumstances in which the failure to give written notice arose. It is only if, having considered all those circumstances, the court considers that it would be just and equitable to give possession that it should do so, because it must be borne in mind that, by failing to give the written notice, the tenant may well have been led into a wholly false position.[51]

The divergence between the two approaches is, however, more apparent than real, since in *Bradshaw* v. *Baldwin-Wiseman* Griffiths L.J. went on to say that "where it is apparent that there never was any intention to create what I might call a 'Case 11 tenancy,' it cannot be just and equitable to dispense with written notice."[52]

Discretionary Grounds

Ground 9

Suitable alternative accommodation is available for the tenant or will be available for him when the order for possession takes effect.

---

[47] (1982) 5 H.L.R. 33.
[48] At 39. Sir David Cairns agreed with this view.
[49] At 38.
[50] (1985) 49 P. & C.R. 382.
[51] At 388.
[52] *Ibid.* See also *Minay* v. *Sentongo* (1982) 45 P. & C.R. 190; *Davies* v. *Peterson* (1988) 21 H.L.R. 63.

Part III of Schedule 2 to the 1988 Act defines what is meant by suitable alternative accommodation:

1. For the purposes of Ground 9 above, a certificate of the local housing authority for the district in which the dwelling-house in question is situated, certifying that the authority will provide suitable alternative accommodation for the tenant by a date specified in the certificate, shall be conclusive evidence that suitable alternative accommodation will be available for him by that date.

2. Where no such certificate as is mentioned in paragraph 1 above is produced to the court, accommodation shall be deemed to be suitable for the purposes of Ground 9 above if it consists of either—

(a) premises which are to be let as a separate dwelling such that they will then be let on an assured tenancy, other than—

   (i) a tenancy in respect of which notice is given not later than the beginning of the tenancy that possession might be recovered on any of Grounds 1 to 5 above, or
   (ii) an assured shorthold tenancy, within the meaning of Chapter II of Part I of this Act, or

(b) premises to be let as a separate dwelling on terms which will, in the opinion of the court, afford to the tenant security of tenure reasonably equivalent to the security afforded by Chapter I of Part I of this Act in the case of an assured tenancy of a kind mentioned in sub-paragraph (a) above,

and, in the opinion of the court, the accommodation fulfils the relevant conditions as defined in paragraph 3 below.

3.—(1) For the purposes of paragraph 2 above, the relevant conditions are that the accommodation is reasonably suitable to the needs of the tenant and his family as regards proximity to place of work, and either—

(a) similar as regards rental and extent to the accommodation afforded by dwelling-houses provided in the neighbourhood by any local housing authority for persons whose needs as regards extent are, in the opinion of the court, similar to those of the tenant and of his family; or

(b) reasonably suitable to the means of the tenant and to the needs of the tenant and his family as regards extent and character; and

that if any furniture was provided for use under the assured tenancy in question, furniture is provided for use in the accommodation which is either similar to that so provided or is reasonably suitable to the needs of the tenant and his family.

(2) For the purposes of sub-paragraph (1)(a) above, a certificate of a local housing authority stating—

(a) the extent of the accommodation afforded by dwelling-houses provided by the authority to meet the needs of tenants with families of such number as may be specified in the certificate, and

(b)   the amount of the rent charged by the authority for dwelling-houses affording accommodation of that extent,

shall be conclusive evidence of the facts so stated.

4. Accommodation shall not be deemed to be suitable to the needs of the tenant and his family if the result of their occupation of the accommodation would be that it would be an overcrowded dwelling-house for the purposes of Part X of the Housing Act 1985.

5. Any document purporting to be a certificate of a local housing authority named therein issued for the purposes of this Part of this Schedule and to be signed by the proper officer of that authority shall be received in evidence and, unless the contrary is shown, shall be deemed to be such a certificate without further proof.

6. In this Part of this Schedule "local housing authority" and "district," in relation to such an authority, have the same meaning as in the Housing Act 1985.

Ground 9 is based on section 98(1)(a) of the Rent Act 1977 (as supplemented by Part IV of Schedule 15). The principles established by the courts in the context of tenancies falling within the Rent Act regime will be equally applicable to cases involving assured tenancies.

Two points should be stressed by way of introduction to the materials. First, alternative accommodation is not unsuitable merely by virtue of the fact that it is inferior to the tenant's existing accommodation; indeed, accommodation may be regarded as suitable even where it consists of only part of the premises let to the tenant.

Secondly, the suitability of accommodation is decided by reference to objective criteria, and personal factors are excluded from the equation. However, it must always be remembered that where the landlord seeks to recover possession under one of the discretionary grounds the court must be satisfied that it is reasonable to make the order.

Mykolyshyn v. *Noah* [1970] 1 W.L.R. 1271

Widgery L.J. cited *Thompson* v. *Rolls*[53] and *Parmee* v. *Mitchell*[54] and said (at 1275—1278):

Now since those cases there have been a number of cases in this court, to which we have been referred, in which it is quite clear that the proposition had become accepted as being too clear for argument that to offer a part of the existing demised premises could properly be regarded as an offer of "alternative" accommodation, for this purpose. One gets first of all (if I may cite a selection of the cases) *Wright* v. *Walford* [1955] 1 Q.B. 363, where precisely the same kind of point as that with which we are now concerned was

---

[53] [1926] 2 K.B. 426.
[54] [1950] 2 K.B. 199.

raised, and I refer to it particularly for the view which Lord Evershed M.R. had reached on the point at that time. He says, at p. 380:

> "I have said that the idea that the latter"—that is to say that such an offer could amount to alternative accommodation—"is, or was, regarded by Parliament as being alternative accommodation seems to me to be one of the most surprising results of the legislation; but I think that that somewhat remarkable result being now accepted, the anomaly has in consequence been created."

Lord Evershed M.R., five years after his judgment in *Parmee* v. *Mitchell* [1950] 2 K.B. 199, is there, in my opinion, clearly recognising that an offer of part of the premises presently let can be an offer of "alternative" accommodation for this purpose.

Similar assumption was made in *McIntyre* v. *Hardcastle* [1948] 2 K.B. 82 and yet again in *Scrace* v. *Windust* [1955] 1 W.L.R. 475. In passing, it is of interest that in *Scrace* v. *Windust* the premises which the landlord sought to remove from the letting by this particular device were premises which were actually occupied by the tenant and not premises which he had sublet. ...

Accordingly, I would reject Mr. Baker's first submission and would accept that the judge was right in saying that this accommodation was "alternative" for the purposes of the Act, and then move on to the second question, which is whether it was "suitable" alternative accommodation.

That is a matter which depends on the facts of every case, in the light of the relevant legislation. In the Rent Act, 1968, Schedule 3, Part IV, one has a code defining "suitable alternative accommodation." I need not trouble with paragraphs 1 and 2, which in the first instance concern a certificate from the housing authority, which is not relevant in this case, and, in the second, require that the alternative accommodation shall carry a security of tenure equivalent to that provided by the Act, a point which does not arise in this case. I go to paragraph 3 of Part IV of Schedule 3, which prvides as follows:

> "(1) For the purposes of paragraph 2 above, the relevant conditions are that the accommodation is reasonably suitable to the needs of the tenant and his family as regards proximity to place of work, and either ... (b) reasonably suitable to the means of the tenant and to the needs of the tenant and his family as regards extent and character."

The question therefore is whether the three rooms offered to Mrs. Noah, on the facts of this case, satisfy the criteria laid down in that Part of the Schedule. Mr. Baker's criticism of the judge's finding that the accommodation is "suitable" is that the judge misdirected himself by holding that the accommodation would be suitable if it sufficed for the furniture which the tenant actually used even though it was too small to hold additional articles which were not in actual use and were now stored, for convenience, in the sitting-room.

Mr. Baker referred us to *McIntyre* v. *Hardcastle* [1948] 2 K.B. 82, where this court held that it was wrong to reject alternative accommodation merely on the ground that it would not accommodate all the tenant's furniture, without first considering how much of that furniture the tenant reasonably required. Mr. Baker submits that in the instant case the judge has really gone to the other extreme and treated the presence of the tenant's furniture in the sitting-room as being a wholly irrelevant consideration.

I have considered this submission with care overnight and have come to the conclusion that for my part I cannot accept it. In deciding whether the accommodation offered was reasonably suitable to the tenant's needs, the judge had to consider, amongst other things, whether it would take her furniture, so far as that furniture was required to enable her to live in reasonable comfort. He would, I think, have been right to conclude that the premises were not rendered unsuitable merely because there was no accommodation for additional furniture for which the tenant had no foreseeable need. This is in effect what the judge has done, because he has adopted the defendant's own conduct as the best test of what furniture she really required and has come to the conclusion that the furniture in the sitting-room is surplus to those requirements and, therefore, the alternative offered is not unsuitable merely because it cannot provide a storage place for that furniture.

Accordingly, as it seems to me, and reminding myself that we are concerned only with points of law, I can find nothing wrong in the judge's direction of himself upon the issue whether the accommodation was "suitable."

Redspring Ltd. v. *Francis* [1973] 1 W.L.R. 134

Buckley L.J. said (at 136–138):

The tenant, Mrs. Francis, who is the appellant in this court, had lived for, I think, some 30 years in premises at 47 Lisburne Road, London N.W.3, which was a small flat in a converted house, in connection with which she had a share only of a bathroom with another tenant who had accommodation in the same house, and while she enjoyed the use of the garden she had no legal right in that respect.

The landlord company, Redspring Ltd., served a notice to quit and offered as alternative accommodation premises in Fleet Road, London N.W.3, which is a busy traffic thoroughfare not far distant from Lisburne Road. The accommodation offered was again a flat in a converted house, rooms on the top floor, somewhat larger in size than the rooms which the tenant had occupied, and still occupies, in Lisburne Road, which included a bathroom of which she would have had exclusive possession. But the house had no garden. Not only is Fleet Road a busy traffic thoroughfare, but immediately next door to no. 108, in which the accommodation was offered to the tenant, there is a fried fish shop; there is a hospital in the neighbourhood, a cinema and a public house close by, and it is an area where at all hours of the day and night there are people coming and going and where there is a lot of traffic. The fried fish shop emits smells of a kind which one would expect to be emitted from an establishment of that sort. Lisburne Road, on the other hand, is a quiet residential road, as I gather, and at the back of the house there is the garden which the tenant is pemitted to use. At the back of 108 Fleet Road there is a yard or open space, previously occupied by a tram shed, but which the local authority are proposing to use as a transport depot, where presumably there would be large motor vehicles coming and going from time to time. It is conceded on the part of the tenant that the physical accommodation offered at 108 Fleet Road is more spacious and better in respect of the bathroom than the accommodation enjoyed by the tenant in Lisburne Road. But it is said that because of the environment in which it stands it does not satisfy her needs. ...

The contention of the tenant has been that in considering the character of alternative accommodation not only the physical characteristics of the premises containing the accommodation fall to be considered, but also such matters as neighbourhood, noise, smell and other considerations of a kind which one can perhaps best describe as environmental considerations; and we have been referred to certain authorities bearing on that aspect of the matter, with none of which do I think it necessary to deal in any detail in this judgment because it is conceded on the part of the landlords that environmental questions are matters relevant to the character of the proposed alternative accommodation. That concession was, in my judgment, properly made. For if a tenant who occupies accommodation in a residential area is offered other accommodation which may be physically as good as or better than the accommodation which he is required to vacate, but is situated in an area which is offensive as the result of some industrial activity in the neighbourhood, which perhaps creates offensive smells or noises, or which is extremely noisy as a result of a great deal of traffic passing by, or in some other respect is clearly much less well endowed with amenities than the accommodation which the tenant is required to vacate, then it seems to me that it would be most unreal to say that the alternative accommodation is such as to satisfy the needs of the tenant with regard to its character. What he needs is somewhere where he can live in reasonably comfortable conditions suitable to the style of life which he leads, and environmental matters must inevitably affect the suitability of offered accommodation to provide him with the sort of conditions in which it is reasonable that he should live.

The Court of Appeal held that the alternative accommodation here was not suitable. Orr and Sachs L.JJ. agreed.

Siddiqui v. *Rashid* [1980] 1 W.L.R. 1018

Stephenson L.J. said (at 1019–1023):

This is an appeal from an order for possession of a flat in London, a first floor rear room at 148 Liverpool Road, London N.1, which the judge made against the defendant, Mr. Rashid, at the suit of Mr. Siddiqui and Mr. Rehman, who are the trustees of the United Kingdom Islamic Mission. They wanted to sell the property in which this room is, in order to buy a larger property for their charitable work and they were able to offer the tenant alternative accommodation in another room in a house not in London but in Luton, at 128 Oak Road.
. . .

   The Act does not say that the alternative accommodation must be reasonably suitable to the needs of the tenant as regards location or, of course, as regards environment, and for my part I would regard the judge as right in this case in confining "character" to the "character of the property." I find nothing in the judgment of this court in *Redspring Ltd.* v. *Francis* to indicate that that is wrong, or to extend the meaning of "character" beyond character of the property. The character of the property was directly affected by the environmental matters which were the subject of Mrs. Francis's objection to her move. I have read them from Buckley L.J.'s judgment; noise and smell were matters which would directly affect the tenant in the enjoyment of her property, so they could well be said to relate to the character of the property. I cannot think that Parliament intended to include such matters as the society of friends, or cultural interest, in using the language that it did in the particular word "character." Nor can I accept that Buckley L.J. had any such considerations in mind when he referred, in the passages which the judge quoted from his judgment [1973] 1 W.L.R. 138, to the needs of the tenant to have "somewhere where [the tenant] can live in reasonably comfortable conditions suitable to the style of life which he leads . . . ," and referred to the accommodation providing him with the sort of conditions in which it is reasonable that he should live. To extend the character of the property to cover the two matters on which the defendant relies, namely his friends in London and his mosque and cultural centre would, in my judgment, be unwarranted. The defendant said he did not want to leave London or to live in Luton, although he worked there, but it is clear that his preference for London and objection to Luton was based on those two considerations.

The issue of suitable alternative accommodation was also considered in *Yewbright Properties* v. *Stone*[55]; *Gladyric Ltd.* v. *Collinson*[56]; and *Hill* v. *Rochard*.[57]

Battespring Ltd. v. *Gates* (1983) 11 H.L.R. 6

Watkins L.J. said (at 8–11):

This is an appeal against a judgment of His Honour Judge Babington given on July 29, 1982 at Wandsworth County Court. He had before him an application for possession of a first-floor maisonette at 25 Edgeley Road, London S.W.4. That maisonette is and was occupied by the defendant, an elderly lady, Mrs. Doris Gates.

The judge came to the conclusion that it would not be reasonable in all the circumstances for the order which the plaintiff sought to be made. He therefore dismissed the application for possession.

The plaintiffs appear to be a property company; they purchased these premises in late 1981. The object of doing so was, upon obtaining vacant possession of the whole of the premises, to renovate them and sell them at a profit.

The premises comprise two flats—one occupied by the defendant, the other on the ground floor which, at the relevant time, was vacant.

The evidence which the plaintiffs placed before the judge came from two of their servants—namely their estates manager and property negotiator. They informed him that the defendant had been offered alternative accommodation by the plaintiffs. This accommodation was at premises in the same road, namely 82 Edgeley Road. Those premises are also divided into flats. The flat which was offered to the defendant is similar in many respects to her maisonette. The rent at which she would be able to occupy that accommodation would be slightly less than the rent which she pays at the present time.

The plaintiffs say that the flat at no. 82 will have been considerably renovated by the time the defendant came to occupy it.

We are told the judge was informed that her reasonable costs of moving from one end of the road to the other would have been met by the plaintiffs. Furthermore, that no. 82 is at a more pleasant end of this road than is no. 25. The plaintiffs therefore consider that they have offered the defendant what might be called a modern flat, in a more comfortable and congenial area, and at a lesser rent.

The defendant's reaction to the plaintiffs' offer, as first presented by her solicitors, appears to have been that she considered the flat at 82 Edgeley Road to be wholly unsuitable for her purpose. Her later reaction—and one which was presented to the judge in the course of the hearing—was that it would be wholly unreasonable of anyone to expect her to leave her present home. She had occupied it for 35 years; she had brought up her family there. Her husband died seven years ago. Her children have now grown up and have left home. She is alone. She lives with the assistance of supplementary benefits, but the flat has

[55] (1980) 124 S.J. 311.
[56] (1983) 267 E.G. 761.
[57] [1983] 1 W.L.R. 478.

very tender memories for her and she would be extremely loath to leave there even though the alternative accommodation is not very far away from where she now lives, and it might well be said that, when renovated, that alternative accommodation might be more comfortable than the flat which she now occupies.

There really is nothing more to be said about the facts than that. The judge had to apply his mind, according to well-known principles, to the question of whether or no it would be reasonable, in the circumstances, for him to make the order sought by the plaintiffs.

What should his approach have been? It was thus expressed in *Cresswell* v. *Hodgson* [1951] 2 K.B. 92 in the judgment of Somervell L.J. at p. 95, with reference to earlier but similar legislation:

> "I think that, when Parliament gave this overriding discretion to the county court judge and said "You must consider whether it is reasonable to make an order," it gave him a very wide discretion, which it is most undesirable to seek to limit or interfere with. I think the words of the section themselves indicate that the county court judge must look at the effect of the order on each party to it. I do not see how it is possible to consider whether it is reasonable to make an order unless you consider its effect on landlord and tenant, firstly, if you make it, and secondly, if you do not. I do not think we should say anything which restricts the circumstances which the county court judge should take into consideration. I think he is entitled to take into consideration that this is a case where the landlord is making a pecuniary gain. That might in other cases be a fact in the landlord's favour, and it might be thought reasonable that he should be given the chance of making pecuniary gain."

Watkins L.J. quoted from the judgment of Lord Greene M.R. in *Cumming* v. *Danson* (see pp. 207–208) and continued:

The learned and experienced county court judge in the present case seems to me to have had that guidance well in mind in coming to the conlusion which he did. He expressed his reasons for arriving at his decision finally in this lucid and brief way:

> "I have decided not to make the order and I base my decision on the fact that here is a tenant who has occupied the accommodation for a very long time and a landlord who has only bought the property less than one year ago, and bought it, on the evidence, with the intention of obtaining vacant possession and reselling it. Subject to any authorities which might have been pointed out to me. I feel that that would be an unreasonable order to make."

He had earlier referred to the personal situation and feelings of the defendant, for whom he obviously felt a great deal of sympathy.

I ask myself whether it is possible to say that the judge misdirected himself in the exercise of his discretion. In reviewing the exercise of a judge's discretion in this context, it is well to bear in mind what was said by Singleton L.J. in the *Cresswell* case at p. 96:

> "When there has been an appeal to this court on that question of reasonableness it has been said time and time again that it is really a question of fact, and that unless the appellant can show that the judge has misdirected himself in some measure, this court cannot interfere, for the decision on that question is for the county court judge. It is for him to consider whether he thinks it reasonable to make an order."

Mr. Acton Davis submits that the judge in this case did not exercise his discretion properly; in the first place he took into account the fact that the plaintiffs were new landlords, whose only object was to make a quick profit upon the property in which the defendant now lives. That, he says, was wholly irrelevant and should not have been allowed to have influenced the judge's mind at all. If allowed to influence it, it was a factor to be used in favour of the plaintiffs, rather than against them.

Secondly, he contends that this really was a decision founded almost exclusively upon a sympathetic consideration of the defendant's objection to moving from a place which she had occupied for a very long time—the prospect of going to another and superior place notwithstanding.

Lastly he maintained that to make reference, as the judge did, to the fact that this was a recent acquisition by the plaintiffs of the relevant property, was yet another instance of his taking into account factors which should not have been allowed to influence him.

I regard the decision of the judge as the product of the exercise of a discretion which I cannot possibly fault. What in fact he did was, on the one hand, to consider the position of the plaintiffs, and properly to find that they were landlords who were simply interested in the property for the purpose of gain. There is, as he said, nothing wrong in that motive whatsoever, but that was precisely their position. It was quite unlike the situation of other landlords who seek orders for possession on the basis that they have either nowhere to live, or that the dwelling which they have at the moment is overcrowded.

Balanced against that was the personal position of this elderly defendant, which was, among other things, that she had occupied these premises for 35 years. It seems always to have been her home—all her memories are still there. I do not consider that a factor of that kind should not be allowed to influence the judge in coming to a conclusion as to whether or no it would be reasonable to turn her out—even though alternative and suitable alternative accommodation (as he found) was available to her.

For these reasons I would dismiss this appeal.

May L.J. agreed.

See also *Yoland Ltd.* v. *Reddington.*[58]

Notes

(i) If the landlord recovers possession under Ground 9, section 11(1) of the Housing Act 1988 provides that "the landlord shall pay to the tenant a sum equal to the reasonable expenses likely to be incurred by the tenant in removing from the dwelling-house."

(ii) It was originally envisaged that the provision of suitable alternative accommodation would be a mandatory rather than a discretionary ground for possession. It was only at the House of Commons Report stage that the Bill was amended.

Ground 10

Some rent lawfully due from the tenant—

(a) is unpaid on the date on which the proceedings for possession are begun; and

---

[58] (1982) 263 E.G. 1573.

(b) except where subsection (1)(b) of section 8 of this Act applies, was in arrears at the date of the service of the notice under that section relating to those proceedings.

Note

Breach of the obligation to pay rent is always a potential ground for eviction.[59] The landlord will still be able to rely on Ground 10 even if the tenant pays the arrears of rent into court after proceedings have been initiated. Nevertheless, the clearing of arrears before the hearing will affect the question as to whether it is reasonable to make the order. Normally, if there are no arrears at the date of the hearing it will not be reasonable for the court to make an order for possession, unless there has been a long history of default.[60]

Ground 11

Whether or not any rent is in arrears on the date on which proceedings for possession are begun, the tenant has persistently delayed paying rent which has become lawfully due.

Notes

(i) At first sight Ground 11 appears to demonstrate an obsessive desire to protect the financial interests of the landlord, given that Schedule 2 contains two other grounds for possession founded on the tenant's failure to pay rent (Grounds 8 and 10). However, Ground 8 is not available unless there are arrears at the date of the hearing, and for Ground 10 to apply there must be arrears when proceedings for possession are begun. In the absence of Ground 11, the landlord would have no recourse against a tenant who persistently withholds rent, waits for the landlord to give notice of his intention to start legal proceedings,[61] and pays off the arrears before the commencement of proceedings.

(ii) There is no counterpart to Ground 11 in either the Rent Act 1977 or the Housing Act 1985. Interestingly, under the Bill as originally drafted, this ground for possession was to be mandatory rather than discretionary.

Ground 12

Any obligation of the tenancy (other than one related to the payment of rent) has been broken or not performed.

Note

This ground applies where there has been a breach of one of the terms of the tenancy, but not where the tenant is in breach of some personal obligation. The obligation may be express, or implied.

---

[59] See Rent Act 1977, Sched. 15, Case 1; Housing Act 1985, Sched. 2, Ground 1.
[60] *Dellenty* v. *Pellow* [1951] 2 K.B. 858; *Hayman* v. *Rowlands* [1957] 1 W.L.R. 317.
[61] Under Housing Act 1988, s.8 (pp. 227–228).

Ground 13

The condition of the dwelling-house or any of the common parts has deteriorated owing to acts of waste by, or the neglect or default of, the tenant or any other person residing in the dwelling-house and, in the case of an act of waste by, or the neglect or default of, a person lodging with the tenant or a sub-tenant of his, the tenant has not taken such steps as he ought reasonably to have taken for the removal of the lodger or sub-tenant.

For the purposes of this ground, "common parts" means any part of a building comprising the dwelling-house and any other premises which the tenant is entitled under the terms of the tenancy to use in common with the occupiers of other dwelling-houses in which the landlord has an estate or interest.

Notes

(i)   Although this ground is derived from the Rent Acts, it is broader than Case 3[62] since it extends not only to the deterioration of the dwelling-house, but also to the deterioration of the common parts.

(ii)   It seems unlikely that there will be many cases where Ground 13 will arise independently of Ground 12 (breach of any obligation of the tenancy). In *Holloway* v. *Povey*[63] (which was decided on the basis of Case 3 under the Rent Act 1977) the court indicated that an order for possession could be made against a statutory tenant who failed to prevent the garden from becoming overgrown.

Ground 14

The tenant or any other person residing in the dwelling-house has been guilty of conduct which is a nuisance or annoyance to adjoining occupiers, or has been convicted of using the dwelling-house or allowing the dwelling-house to be used for immoral or illegal purposes.

Notes

(i)   Ground 14, which is in substance the same as Case 2 in the Rent Act regime, involves two different aspects: nuisance or annoyance to adjoining occupiers; and conviction for certain criminal offences.

(ii)   It used to be thought that "adjoining" meant "contiguous," and in *Trustees of Marques of Northampton Estate* v. *Bond*[64] it was held that occupants of a second floor flat were not "adjoining occupiers" to the ground floor flat beneath them. In *Cobstone Investments Ltd.* v. *Maxim*,[65] however, the Court of Appeal took the view that "adjoining" means "neighbouring."

(iii)   Where premises are used for immoral purposes (for example, prostitution) this is likely to constitute a nuisance or annoyance for adjoining occupiers, and therefore the landlord will be able to rely on

---

[62] Rent Act 1977, Sched. 15.
[63] (1984) 15 H.L.R. 104.
[64] (1949) 155 E.G. 412.
[65] [1985] Q.B. 140.

Ground 14, notwithstanding the fact that the tenant has not been convicted of a criminal offence. Although in the past the courts have ordered possession on the basis of the tenant's extra-marital cohabitation,[66] it seems extremely unlikely that nowadays the courts would regard cohabitation as giving rise to nuisance or annoyance within the scope of Ground 14.[67]

Abrahams v. *Wilson* [1971] 2 Q.B. 88

Edmund Davies L.J. said (at 90—93):

The plaintiff sought possession on several grounds, only two of which need now be referred to. The first was that the defendant and a Mr. Cleghorn, who under a separate tenancy occupied a room in that house, had each been convicted of using the rooms the subject of the tenancy, or allowing them to be used, for immoral or illegal purposes, namely, the smoking of cannabis resin. By way of particulars of that allegation, it was pleaded that on May 9, 1969, the tenant and Cleghorn were each convicted at Guildhall Quarter Sessions for being in possession of 66 grains of cannabis resin without being duly authorised. That each of those defendants was so convicted was admitted in the defence. ...

What is more difficult, however, is the claim that the tenant has been convicted (in the words of Case 2) of "using the dwelling-house or allowing the dwelling-house to be used for immoral or illegal purposes." Now the evidence in relation to this matter is, in my view, extremely unsatisfactory. The certificate of conviction itself simply recites that the tenant was on March 10, 1970, "in possession of a drug, namely 66 grains of cannabis resin, without being duly authorised." The certificate itself makes no reference to 10 Chamberlayne Road as being connected in any way with the charge preferred. But it has emerged— in, I repeat, an unsatisfactory way—that those premises did play some part in relation to the prosecution case which found favour with the jury. It seems that a police witness testified that he had found under a cupboard in one of the rooms let to the tenant 66 grains of cannabis resin. As I understand, Mrs. Wilson did not challenge that this quantity of cannabis resin was found in one of her rooms, but she vehemently denied having any knowledge of its existence or of being a party to its being placed there. Nevertheless the jury convicted her. Mr. Pryor has, if I may say so, been extremely helpful to the landlady's case by conceding as much as that. But I think that, in cases (such as the present) where the user of the premises is the focal point of the claim to possession, there should be evidence called as to what actually transpired in the court of criminal trial, so that the civil judge may know with precision the basis of the conviction.

But, having said that the certificate of conviction itself makes no reference to any particular premises, it emerges from a series of cases that this fact does not prevent the circumstances which led to the conviction from being adduced in evidence. The matter was dealt with at length by this court in *S. Schneiders & Sons Ltd.* v. *Abrahams* [1925] 1 K.B. 301, which was a case where a tenant had been convicted under the Larceny Act of receiving at the demised premises certain property, well knowing it to have been stolen. The place where the act of receiving occurs is in general of no materiality in law; but there it was held

---

[66] *e.g. Benton* v. *Chapman* (1953) 161 E.G. 181.
[67] See, generally, *Heglibiston Establishments* v. *Heyman* (1978) 36 P. & C.R. 351.

that the tenant, having made use of the premises in order to commit that crime, must be regarded as having been convicted of "using" the premises for an illegal purpose within the meaning of the statutory provision then applicable, namely, section 4 of the Rent and Mortgage Interest Restrictions Act 1923. But there must be some link between the criminal conviction and the premises which are the subject-matter of the proceedings for possession; and the test applied by Bankes L.J. is one which I would respectfully adopt for the purposes of the present case. Bankes L.J. said, at p. 306:

> "I reject the argument that the section includes only offences in which user of the premises is an essential element. But I think it is necessary to show that the tenant has taken advantage of his tenancy of the premises and of the opportunity they afford for committing the offence. In this view the tenant who uses the demised premises as a coiner's den, or as a deposit for stolen goods, and is convicted of counterfeiting coin or receiving goods, would be 'convicted of using the premises for an ... illegal purpose' within the meaning of section 4."

Scrutton L.J. applied this test, at p. 309:

> "Were the words meant to have their strict meaning or were they meant to cover all cases where a tenant is convicted of a crime and had used the premises to facilitate the commission of it?"

He later said, at p. 310:

> "Giving the case the best consideration I can, I come to the conclusion that the conviction need not be for using the premises for one or another immoral or illegal purpose, and that it is enough if there is a conviction of a crime which has been committed on the premises and for the purpose of committing which the premises have been used; but that it is not enough that the tenant has been convicted of a crime with which the premises have nothing to do beyond merely being the scene of its commission."

Applying that test to the present case, I for my part would put it in this way: In proper and clear circumstances—which must be established, of course, by the landlord—a conviction of using premises for an illegal purpose, within the meaning of Case 2, can be established by proof that in the demised premises a quantity of cannabis resin was found. One must, however, look at the circumstances very carefully before an isolated finding on a single occasion is held to constitute proof of such user. The evidence produced in the civil proceedings was very unsatisfactory regarding what transpired at the criminal trial and I am not prepared to hold that user was established. But, even if it were, my conclusion in relation to Case 2 must ultimately turn upon the overriding requirement, imposed by section 10 of the Act, that no order for possession may be made by the court (even though the circumstances are such as to bring the matter clearly within any other of the Cases set out in Part I of Schedule 3) "unless the court considers it reasonable to make the order."

While a trenchant attack has been made upon the conduct of the county court judge and about the way in which he treated counsel and witnesses—an attack which, if it *is* to be made, should be presented in a wholly different manner from that in which it has been to-day—for my part I do not think that the judge failed to take into consideration those matters which were relevant to determining whether the over-all requirement of "reasonableness" had been established. He was, notwithstanding that this was a Case 8 matter, entitled to consider the purposes for which the landlord was seeking to obtain possession; he was entitled to have regard to the past behaviour of the tenant as presented

by the landlady; and he was, as I think, entitled to have regard to the proof that
the tenant had been convicted of the possession of cannabis. I think that he did
bear those matters in mind. He also made reference to the evidence that the
tenant had on occasion been under the influence of drink. It is complained that
the judge ignored the position of the daughter, who, if she went to live in these
premises, might be cheek-by-jowl with those who certainly on one occasion had
been convicted of the unlawful possession of cannabis; and there was also the
binding over in 1969 of the tenant, to which he expressly made reference. But at
the end he said:

> "I cannot conceive that any judge who has one day's experience of
> rehousing poorer classes would hold that it would be right to throw out the
> lady. Unable to work, daughter aged 15 not yet working, a former
> professional dancer who lives on the State."

Then he referred to the fact that the deputy chairman who had tried the
criminal case at quarter sessions had disposed of it by making a conditional
order for 12 months against Mrs. Wilson, and continued:

> "This court thinks that the chairman of quarter sessions, having considered
> the evidence, could not have been more lenient. The suggestion now is that
> the additional very severe penalty of eviction should be imposed;"

and he expresses incredulity that "any court in the kingdom" would make an
order for possession in such circumstances. Having considered all those matters,
he came to the conclusion that the reasonableness of making an order had not
been made out. Who is to say that he was wrong? There were competing
considerations; but he clearly bore them all in mind. It might be that I
personally would have weighed those considerations in a different manner and
possibly arrived at a different conclusion: but, even so, that would not be
enough for this appeal to succeed. It must further be shown that the judge was
disentitled to conclude that reasonableness had not been established. I do not
think his error in that regard has been demonstrated, and accordingly for my
part I would dismiss this appeal.

Widgery L.J. said (at 94):

Applying Scrutton L.J.'s test, the position in regard to the finding of
dangerous drugs on the demised premises I think is simply this: If the drugs are
on the demised premises merely because the defendant is there and has them in
his or her immediate custody, such as a pocket or a handbag, then I would say
without hesitation that that does not involve a "using" of the premises in
connection with the offence. On the other hand, if the premises are employed as
a storage place or hiding place for dangerous drugs, a conviction for possession
of such drugs, when the conviction is illuminated by further evidence to show
the manner in which the drugs themselves were located, would I think be
sufficient to satisfy the section and come within Case 2. One must not forget
that at the present time landlords may incur heavy penalties if their premises are
used for the smoking of cannabis, and one must not lightly deprive a landlord of
an opportunity of obtaining possession against a tenant who runs the landlord
into that kind of risk.

Ground 15

The condition of any furniture provided for use under the tenancy has, in the
opinion of the court, deteriorated owing to ill-treatment by the tenant or any

other person residing in the dwelling-house and, in the case of ill-treatment by a person lodging with the tenant or by a sub-tenant of his, the tenant has not taken such steps as he ought reasonably to have taken for the removal of the lodger or sub-tenant.

Note

Ground 15 is based on Case 4 under the Rent Act 1977.

Ground 16

The dwelling-house was let to the tenant in consequence of his employment by the landlord seeking possession or a previous landlord under the tenancy and the tenant has ceased to be in that employment.

Notes

(i)   Under the Rent Act 1977 a landlord can seek to recover possession against a former employee under Case 8 if the premises are "reasonably required ... for occupation as a residence for some person engaged in [the landlord's] whole-time employment." Ground 16 is rather broader in scope than Case 8, since all that is required is that the tenancy was granted to the tenant in consequence of his employment,[68] and that the tenant has ceased to be in that employment.

(ii)   It should be remembered that a service occupier (that is, an employee who occupies his employer's premises to perform his duties as an employee) may be a licensee rather than a tenant.[69] Although the Housing Act 1988 will not apply to possession proceedings brought against a service occupier the requirements of the Protection from Eviction Act 1977 must be complied with.[70]

(2) Procedural Aspects

Before an action for possession can be commenced against an assured tenant there must be served on the tenant a notice of intended proceedings. Section 8 of the 1988 Act provides:

(1) The court shall not entertain proceedings for possession of a dwelling-house let on an assured tenancy unless—

(a)   the landlord or, in the case of joint landlords, at least one of them has served on the tenant a notice in accordance with this section and the proceedings are begun within the time limits stated in the notice in accordance with subsections (3) and (4) below; or

---

[68] See *Fuggle* v. *Gadsden* [1948] 2 K.B. 236.
[69] See the discussion of Lord Templeman in *Street* v. *Mountford* [1985] A.C. 809 (pp. 53–54); *Royal Philanthropic Society* v. *County* (1985) 18 H.L.R. 83.
[70] See pp. 258–262.

(b) the court considers it just and equitable to dispense with the requirement of such a notice.

(2) The court shall not make an order for possession on any of the grounds in Schedule 2 to this Act unless that ground and particulars of it are specified in the notice under this section; but the grounds specified in such a notice may be altered or added to with the leave of the court.

(3) A notice under this section is one in the prescribed form informing the tenant that—

(a) the landlord intends to begin proceedings for possession of the dwelling-house on one or more of the grounds specified in the notice; and

(b) those proceedings will not begin earlier than a date specified in the notice which, without prejudice to any additional limitation under subsection (4) below, shall not be earlier than the expiry of the period of two weeks from the date of service of the notice; and

(c) those proceedings will not begin later than twelve months from the date of service of the notice.

(4) If a notice under this section specifies, in accordance with subsection (3)(a) above, any of the Grounds 1, 2, 5 to 7, 9 and 16 in Schedule 2 to this Act (whether with or without other grounds), the date specified in the notice as mentioned in subsection (3)(b) above shall not be earlier than—

(a) two months from the date of service of the notice; and

(b) if the tenancy is a periodic tenancy, the earliest date on which, apart from section 5(1) above, the tenancy could be brought to an end by a notice to quit given by the landlord on the same date as the date of service of the notice under this section.

(5) The court may not exercise the power conferred by subsection (1)(b) above if the landlord seeks to recover possession on Ground 8 in Schedule 2 to this Act.

(6) Where a notice under this section—

(a) is served at a time when the dwelling-house is let on a fixed term tenancy, or

(b) is served after a fixed term tenancy has come to an end but relates (in whole or in part) to events occurring during that tenancy,

the notice shall have effect notwithstanding that the tenant becomes or has become tenant under a statutory periodic tenancy arising on the coming to an end of the fixed term tenancy.

Notes

(i) Notice should be in prescribed form,[71] although the court has a discretion to dispense with the notice requirement where it is just and

---

[71] Housing Act 1988, s.8(3); Assured Tenancies and Agricultural Occupancies (Forms) Regulations 1988, S.I. 1988 No. 2203 (Form 3).

equitable to do so.[72] There is, however, no dispensing power where the landlord is seeking to rely on Ground 8 (serious rent arrears).[73]

(ii) The period of notice is to be determined by reference to subsections (3) and (4). For Grounds 3, 4, 8, and 10 to 15 the minimum period is two weeks.[74] For the other grounds (1, 2, 5 to 7, 9 and 16) the relevant period is the longer of two months and the (notional) notice to quit period at common law.[75]

For example, if a landlord wishes to recover possession from a monthly periodic assured tenant under Ground 9 (suitable alternative accommodation), he must give the tenant at least two months' notice of intended proceedings.[76] If the periodic tenancy was quarterly rather than monthly the landlord would need to give one quarter's notice.[77]

(iii) Section 9 confers discretion on the court to adjourn proceedings[78] and to stay or suspend execution of any order for possession or to postpone the date of possession.[79]

Where the court exercises its discretion under subsections (1) and (2), the court must impose conditions as to the payment of rent by the tenant (including any arrears) unless to do so would cause exceptional hardship to the tenant.[80]

It should be stressed that there is no such discretion if the landlord can establish one of the mandatory grounds for possession.[81]

(3) Compensation

Under section 102 of the Rent Act 1977 compensation may be recovered by a former protected or statutory tenant if the landlord obtains an order for possession "by misrepresentation or concealment of material facts," but only where the landlord recovers possession under Case 8 or Case 9.

In contrast, section 12 of the Housing Act 1988 provides:

Where a landlord obtains an order for possession of a dwelling-house let on an assured tenancy on one or more of the grounds in Schedule 2 to this Act and it is subsequently made to appear to the court that the order was obtained by misrepresentation or concealment of material facts, the court may order the landlord to pay to the former tenant such sum as appears sufficient as

---

[72] s.8(1)(b).
[73] s.8(5).
[74] s.8(3).
[75] s.8(4). Although this subsection preserves the notional notice to quit period it should be remembered that any notice to quit served by the landlord on the tenant will, by virtue of section 5(1), be of no effect.
[76] s.8(4)(a).
[77] s.8(4)(b). If the tenancy was yearly, the landlord would have to give half a year's notice.
[78] s.9(1).
[79] s.9(2).
[80] s.9(3).
[81] s.9(6).

compensation for damage or loss sustained by that tenant as a result of the order.

(B) RECOVERING POSSESSION FROM AN ASSURED SHORTHOLD TENANT

The rules relating to assured tenancies apply equally to assured shorthold tenancies. In addition to the grounds of possession available under section 7 and Schedule 2, section 21 provides that—in relation to assured shorthold tenancies—the landlord has a right to recover possession after the expiry of the fixed term (the "shorthold ground"):

(1) Without prejudice to any right of the landlord under an assured shorthold tenancy to recover possession of the dwelling-house let on the tenancy in accordance with Chapter I above, on or after the coming to an end of an assured shorthold tenancy which was a fixed term tenancy, a court shall make an order for possession of the dwelling-house if it is satisfied—

    (a)   that the assured shorthold tenancy has come to an end and no further assured tenancy (whether shorthold or not) is for the time being in existence, other than an assured shorthold periodic tenancy (whether statutory or not); and

    (b)   the landlord or, in the case of joint landlords, at least one of them has given to the tenant not less than two months' notice stating that he requires possession of the dwelling-house.

(2) A notice under paragraph (b) of subsection (1) above may be given before or on the day on which the tenancy comes to an end; and that subsection shall have effect notwithstanding that on the coming to an end of the fixed term tenancy a statutory periodic tenancy arises.

(3) Where a court makes an order for possession of a dwelling-house by virtue of subsection (1) above, any statutory periodic tenancy which has arisen on the coming to an end of the assured shorthold tenancy shall end (without further notice and regardless of the period) on the day on which the order takes effect.

(4) Without prejudice to any such right as is referred to in subsection (1) above, a court shall make an order for possession of a dwelling-house let on an assured shorthold tenancy which is a periodic tenancy if the court is satisfied—

    (a)   that the landlord or, in the case of joint landlords, at least one of them has given to the tenant a notice stating that, after a date specified in the notice, being the last day of a period of the tenancy and not earlier than two months after the date the notice was given, possession of the dwelling-house is required by virtue of this section; and

    (b)   that the date specified in the notice under paragraph (a) above is not earlier than the earliest day on which, apart from section 5(1) above, the tenancy could be brought to an end by a notice to quit given by the landlord on the same date as the notice under paragraph (a) above.

Notes

(i)   If the landlord relies on the grounds for possession in Schedule 2, he should serve a notice of intended proceedings on the tenant in prescribed form.[82] There is, however, no prescribed form for the shorthold ground; the landlord is merely required to give the tenant notice. Strangely, section 21 does not expressly state that such notice should be in writing, although this may be inferred from the terms of the section.

(ii)   If the landlord wants to recover possession at the end of the fixed term he need give only two months' notice.[83] So, where the landlord grants an assured shorthold tenancy for a fixed term of six months, he may serve the notice required by section 21(1)(b) after four months.

(iii)   When the fixed term has come to an end and the landlord allows the tenant to remain in possession, a statutory periodic assured shorthold tenancy arises (the period being determined by reference to the payment of rent). Whereas in relation to protected shorthold tenancies (governed by the Rent Act 1977 and the Housing Act 1980) the landlord can only recover possession under the shorthold ground at the end of the fixed term or on the successive anniversaries of the expiry of the fixed term,[84] as regards an assured shorthold tenancy the landlord may seek to recover possession at any time once the fixed term has come to an end. The notice requirement for a periodic assured shorthold tenancy is the longer of two months and the (notional) notice to quit period.[85]

So, if an assured shorthold tenant pays rent quarterly during the fixed term, after the fixed term has come to an end the notice period is one quarter[86] rather than two months. If the tenant pays rent weekly or monthly the notice period is two months.[87]

(iv)   In relation to the shorthold ground the court has no power under section 9 to adjourn proceedings, suspend an order for possession, or postpone the date of possession.[88]

IV   SECURITY OF TENURE UNDER THE RENT ACT 1977

The fundamental division of regulated tenancies into protected and statutory tenancies has already been discussed: the fact that the landlord validly terminates a protected tenancy (for example, by serving a notice to quit on a periodic tenant) does not entitle the landlord to

---

[82] s.8(3).
[83] s.21(1)(b).
[84] See pp. 244–245.
[85] s.21(4).
[86] s.21(4)(b).
[87] s.21(4)(a).
[88] s.9(6)(b).

possession.[89] To recover possession against a regulated tenant the landlord must satisfy the terms of the Rent Act 1977 (as amended).

(A) RECOVERING POSSESSION FROM A PROTECTED OR STATUTORY TENANT

Many of the issues which arise under the Rent Act 1977 have been discussed in the context of the assured tenancy regime.[90]

The basic framework of the Rent Act regime is set out in section 98 of the 1977 Act:

(1) Subject to this Part of this Act, a court shall not make an order for possession of a dwelling-house which is for the time being let on a protected tenancy or subject to a statutory tenancy unless the court considers it reasonable to make such an order and either—

(a) the court is satisfied that suitable alternative accommodation is available for the tenant or will be available for him when the order in question takes effect, or

(b) the circumstances are as specified in any of the Cases in Part I of Schedule 15 to this Act.

(2) If, apart from subsection (1) above, the landlord would be entitled to recover possession of a dwelling-house which is for the time being let on or subject to a regulated tenancy, the court shall make an order for possession if the circumstances of the case are as specified in any of the Cases in Part II of Schedule 15.

(3) Part III of Schedule 15 shall have effect in relation to Case 9 in that Schedule and for determining the relevant date for the purposes of the Cases in Part II of that Schedule.

(4) Part IV of Schedule 15 shall have effect for determining whether, for the purposes of subsection (1)(a) above, suitable alternative accommodation is or will be available for a tenant.

(5) Part V of Schedule 15 shall have effect for the purpose of setting out conditions which are relevant to Cases 11 and 12 of that Schedule.

The court has discretion to adjourn proceedings[91] and to suspend execution of an order for possession or to postpone the date of possession.[92] This discretion is excluded if the landlord establishes one of the mandatory grounds for possession, (*i.e.* the Cases in Part II of Schedule 15).[93]

Section 101 provides:

At any time when a dwelling-house is overcrowded within the meaning of Part X of the Housing Act 1985 in such circumstances as to render the occupier

---

[89] See pp. 155–167.
[90] See pp. 204–231.
[91] Rent Act 1977, s.100(1).
[92] s.100(2).
[93] s.100(5).

guilty of an offence, nothing in this Part of this Act shall prevent the immediate landlord of the occupier from obtaining possession of the dwelling-house.

(1) Suitable Alternative Accommodation

The meaning of suitable alternative accommodation is to be found in Part IV of Schedule 15 to the 1977 Act. The essence of these provisions has been re-enacted as Part III to Schedule 2 to the Housing Act 1988.[94]

(2) Part I of Schedule 15: Other Discretionary Grounds

Case 1

Where any rent lawfully due from the tenant has not been paid, or any obligation of the protected or statutory tenancy which arises under this Act, or—

(a) in the case of a protected tenancy, any other obligation of the tenancy, in so far as is consistent with the provisions of Part VII of this Act, or

(b) in the case of a statutory tenancy, any other obligation of the previous protected tenancy which is applicable to the statutory tenancy,

has been broken or not performed.

Case 2

Where the tenant or any person residing or lodging with him or any sub-tenant of his has been guilty of conduct which is a nuisance or annoyance to adjoining occupiers, or has been convicted of using the dwelling-house or allowing the dwelling-house to be used for immoral or illegal purposes.

Case 3

Where the condition of the dwelling-house has, in the opinion of the court, deteriorated owing to acts of waste by, or the neglect or default of, the tenant or any person residing or lodging with him or any sub-tenant of his and, in the case of any act of waste by, or the neglect or default of, a person lodging with the tenant or a sub-tenant of his, where the court is satisfied that the tenant has not, before the making of the order in question, taken such steps as he ought reasonably to have taken for the removal of the lodger or sub-tenant, as the case may be.

Case 4

Where the condition of any furniture provided for use under the tenancy has, in the opinion of the court, deteriorated owing to ill-treatment by the tenant or any person residing or lodging with him or any sub-tenant of his and, in the case of any ill-treatment by a person lodging with the tenant or a sub-tenant of his, where the court is satisfied that the tenant has not, before the making of the

[94] See pp. 214–215.

order in question, taken such steps as he ought reasonably to have taken for the removal of the lodger or sub-tenant, as the case may be.

Case 5

Where the tenant has given notice to quit and, in consequence of that notice, the landlord has contracted to sell or let the dwelling-house or has taken any other steps as the result of which he would, in the opinion of the court, be seriously prejudiced if he could not obtain possession.

Notes

(i)   Under the Rent Act 1977 if a protected tenant gives the landlord notice to quit, when the notice expires the tenant nevertheless becomes a statutory tenant if he continues to occupy the dwelling-house as a residence.[95] Case 5 gives the landlord—on satisfying certain conditions— the opportunity to apply to the court for an order for possession if the tenant attempts to change his mind after serving a notice to quit. It is perhaps surprising that Case 5 is not a mandatory ground for possession.

(ii)   There is no counterpart to Case 5 in the Housing Act 1988. If a periodic assured tenant gives notice to quit to the landlord the assured tenancy comes to an end on the expiry of the notice, and the former assured tenant no longer has a right to remain in possession. Accordingly, the landlord has a right to recover possession independently of the Housing Act 1988.

Case 6 is discussed at pp. 291–292.
Case 7 was repealed by the Housing Act 1980.

Case 8

Where the dwelling-house is reasonably required by the landlord for occupation as a residence for some person engaged in his whole-time employment, or in the whole-time employment of some tenant from him or with whom, conditional on housing being provided, a contract for such employment has been entered into, and the tenant was in the employment of the landlord or a former landlord, and the dwelling-house was let to him in consequence of that employment and he has ceased to be in that employment.

Case 9

Where the dwelling-house is reasonably required by the landlord for occupation as a residence for—

(a)   himself, or

(b)   any son or daughter of his over 18 years of age, or

(c)   his father or mother, or

(d)   if the dwelling-house is let on or subject to a regulated tenancy, the father or mother of his wife or husband,

---

[95] Rent Act 1977, s.2(1)(a).

and the landlord did not become landlord by purchasing the dwelling-house or any interest therein after—

    (i)   7th November 1956, in the case of a tenancy which was then a controlled tenancy;

    (ii)   8th March 1973, in the case of a tenancy which became a regulated tenancy by virtue of section 14 of the Counter-Inflation Act 1973;

    (iii)   24th May 1974, in the case of a regulated furnished tenancy; or

    (iv)   23rd March 1965, in the case of any other tenancy.

Notes

(i)   Part III of Schedule 15 provides:

1. A court shall not make an order for possession of a dwelling-house by reason only that the circumstances of the case fall within Case 9 in Part I of this Schedule if the court is satisfied that, having regard to all the circumstances of the case, including the question whether other accommodation is available for the landlord or the tenant, greater hardship would be caused by granting the order than by refusing to grant it.

(ii)   To rely on Case 9 the landlord must show, first, that he was not a purchaser of the premises within the meaning of the Act, secondly, that he reasonably requires the premises as a residence for himself or a member of his family and, thirdly, that it is reasonable to make an order for possession. Even if these conditions are satisfied the court will not make an order for possession if the tenant can establish that greater hardship will result from granting the order for possession than from refusing to do so. The issue of greater hardship is essentially a matter for the trial judge and the Court of Appeal will interfere only if the appellant can "show that the county court misdirected himself on a question of law or that he based his judgment on some finding of fact of which there was no evidence."[96]

(iii)   Case 9 requires the court to adjudicate on the competing claims of the landlord and the tenant to occupy residential premises. In situations where the claims of the landlord and tenant are finely balanced the courts have tended to make an order for possession.[96a]

Thomas v. *Fryer* [1970] 1 W.L.R. 845

Lord Donovan (sitting in the Court of Appeal) said (at 845–853):

This appeal arises out of a contest for the possession of a dwelling-house. The house is No. 47 Queen's Road, London, N.11. Mrs. Alice Fryer, a widow aged 60 or 61, has lived in the house with members of her family for over 30 years. She has a controlled tenancy.

---

[96] Somervell L.J. in *Smith* v. *Penny* [1947] K.B. 230 at 233. See *Hodges* v. *Blee* (1988) 20 H.L.R. 32.
[96a] See, however, *Baker* v. *MacIver* (1990) 22 H.L.R. 328.

Possession of the house is now sought by the plaintiff, Miss Thomas. She does so pursuant to Case [9]. ...

Miss Thomas became the landlord of the house in the following circumstances. It was owned by her mother, who died on June 26, 1961. In her will she disposed of the house by a residuary gift in these words: "The residue of my estate I give and bequeath in equal shares unto my four children Barbara, Owen, Geoffrey and Mildred if living at my death." Mildred is the Miss Thomas to whom I have already referred. All four children survived their mother. All four were named as executors. The eldest child alone, however—that is, Owen Thomas—proved the will, and he did so on October 5, 1961. Besides the house, the testatrix left some £4,500 in stocks and shares. After making specific bequests of certain chattels, and leaving some pecuniary legacies to others, she disposed of the residue in the terms I have already quoted. The residuary gift therefore comprised the house and such of the investments as were not required to meet the legacies. ...

Miss Thomas had made an unsuccessful attempt to get possession of the house in 1968. The county court judge who tried that case decided no more than that greater hardship would be caused by granting the order than by refusing it. He decided no other question.

The present proceedings represent a second attempt by Miss Thomas to get possession of the premises. The case was heard by Judge Moylan, sitting at Edmonton County Court, and on June 5, 1969, he made an order for possession in Miss Thomas's favour but postponing its operation for nine months.

Counsel on behalf of the tenant in the county court took a preliminary objection which the judge disposed of first. It was that the circumstances in which Miss Thomas acquired the house involved the consequence that she could not discharge the onus which was upon her of proving that she had become landlord otherwise than by purchasing the house or an interest therein after November 7, 1956. Accordingly, she could not bring herself within the aforesaid Case [9] and her application for possession must therefore fail.

The judge rejected this contention. His broad reason was this. Here was a family arrangement between beneficiaries under the will by which Miss Thomas was allowed to have the house as part of the residue, while at the same time making compensatory payments to her fellow residuary legatees in order to achieve equality of benefit. Such a family arrangement was not, he decided, equivalent to becoming a "landlord by purchasing the dwelling-house or any interest therein" within the meaning of Case [9].

In this appeal from that decision Mr. Oliver, in a strenuous argument, insists that it is wrong. A family arrangement and a purchase are not, he says, mutually exclusive terms. So much may be conceded. The motive for a transaction does not determine its legal character. Again, no one would dispute that. Mr. Oliver then goes on to say, in effect:

> "Here is the house. Miss Thomas was left by will an undivided fourth share in it. She wanted, however, the whole. Her fellow residuary legatees let her have it. She agreed to pay compensatory payments to them and indeed paid them £750. That was equivalent to the three-quarters interest which they had in it. What is that" (he asks) "except the purchase of an interest in the dwelling-house?"

Despite the attraction of the argument, I find myself after due consideration unable to accept it. One has to decide what is meant by "purchasing the dwelling-house" in the context of the Rent Act, [1977], and particularly in the context of Case [9]. This particular provision has a history going back at least to the Rent and Mortgage Interest Restrictions (Amendment) Act, 1933, the Rent Act, 1968, being a consolidating measure.

In *Baker* v. *Lewis* [1947] 1 K.B. 186, Morton L.J. said, at p. 191:

> "I am well aware that the word 'purchaser' and the words 'by purchase' have in certain contexts a technical meaning which is well known to all lawyers, but I am not aware of any case in which the words 'by purchasing the dwelling-house' have been given any technical meaning. For my part I feel no doubt that they simply refer to a transaction of purchase or buying."

That, of course, by itself does no more than rule out the technical meaning of "purchase" in the law of property.

In *Littlechild* v. *Holt* [1950] 1 K.B. 1, 7, Denning L.J. said:

> "The intention of the legislature was that people should not be able to buy houses over the heads of the tenants and then turn them out without giving them alternative accommodation. ... The acquisition of the reversion, whether it be a freehold or a leasehold, for money or money's worth, and whether payable in a lump sum or by instalments, is plainly a 'purchase.' But the acquisition of it under a will is not a purchase: *Baker* v. *Lewis* [1947] K.B. 186. ... "

There are certain cases under the Stamp Act, 1891, where family arrangements involving the transfer of assets to a beneficiary for a consideration have been held to be "conveyances on sale": see, for example, *Jopling* v. *Inland Revenue Commissioners* [1940] 2 K.B. 282 and *The Marquess of Bristol* v. *Inland Revenue Commissioners* [1901] 2 K.B. 336. There are other stamp duty cases dealing with such family arrangements where the opposite conclusion has been reached: see the cases cited in *Sergeant on Stamp Duties*, 5th ed. (1968), pp. 119–120. In those circumstances I do not myself get much help from the cases under the Stamp Act.

One returns, I think, to what the county court judge said was the root question: "Would the ordinary and reasonable person call this transaction a purchase and sale of the house?" I think he would not. He would call it a domestic arrangement between members of a family for the division of their mother's estate in a manner which did justice to all of them. Miss Thomas, if asked how she got the house, would, I think, instinctively reply: "I got it as my share under my mother's will, although I had to get my brothers and sister to agree, and I made adjusting payments so as to achieve fairness."

I think that is the true view, and that the county court judge was therefore entitled to rule as he did on the preliminary point. ...

The tenant then contended that greater hardship would be caused by granting than by refusing the order. On this point the judge went with great care into the relevant circumstances of both parties and decided against the contention. This is a finding of fact which would ordinarily be unappealable. But it has been argued that it is vitiated because the judge took into account in favour of Miss Thomas evidence, which he should have ignored, given on her behalf by Dr. William Gooddy, a well-known neurologist. He says that Miss Thomas's failure to obtain possession of the house in the proceedings which she brought in 1968 had worried and depressed her ever since: that in consequence she has not been able to keep up with her teaching work, despite her high qualifications. He gave an instance of her failure to complete the marking of certain Cambridge University examination papers; and eventually expressed his opinion thus:

> "I am quite sure that her preoccupation with the situation which I have outlined is having an adverse effect on her health. I do not say that the situation is necessarily entirely responsible for her present state of health; but in a person of her age and background, who might anyway suffer from

severe depression, her housing problem is damaging her to a serious degree medically. For these reasons, I am quite sure that Miss Thomas is undergoing great hardship on medical grounds. Her general health will, in my opinion, deteriorate quite rapidly, if she is unable to obtain possession of her property. I feel it most important for the future welfare of this conscientious and valuable teacher that, if her case is reconsidered in a county court, this medical point should be considered when assessing the degrees of hardship likely to be experienced by the contending parties."

It is now said by Mr. Oliver that if this sort of evidence is to be admitted where is the line to be drawn? Is it to be contended, for example, that a bad loser will suffer hardship whereas a good loser will not? Is a party to be allowed to say: "If I lose this case all sorts of things may happen to my state of mind which will cause me hardship?"

I recognise the danger that evidence may be given on these lines which could be without real weight, or even be spurious: but the trial judge will normally, I think, be able to recognise truth as distinct from falsehood or exaggeration.

In the present case, where it is proved that the health of one of the parties is already suffering, and that her health is likely to deteriorate rapidly if possession is refused, I can see no reason whatever why the judge should not take this evidence into account, even though such deterioration has its origin in mental suffering.

In my opinion, therefore, this appeal fails and should be dismissed.

Manaton v. *Edwards* (1985) 18 H.L.R. 116

Croom-Johnson L.J. said (at 118–122):

This is an appeal from the Penzance County Court against the refusal of the learned recorder to make an order for possession of a terraced house called 5 Treneglos Terrace, Newlyn. The order was made on May 21, 1985. The plaintiff is the landlord, and the tenant, Mr. Edwards, has been there for about nine years. By leave, Sandra Barnes was added as a defendant because she has been living there with Mr. Edwards for a number of years. The decision turned purely on the question of greater hardship under Schedule 15, Case 9, of the Rent Act 1977.

The house is a three-bedroomed house, and was let to the tenant at a rent of £13.50 a week in 1976. The plaintiff had purchased it in 1974. Miss Barnes joined Mr. Edwards in 1979. They have been living together and now have a six-month-old daughter.

The plaintiff is a ship's cook. At the time of the hearing he had been at sea, while so employed, for about 75 per cent. of the time. He said that when he first let to Mr. Edwards there was mention that he would need the house for his own possession at some time. Mr. Edwards certainly heard him say that, but did not commit himself. For a long time, when the plaintiff was not at sea, he could live with his elderly parents, who were aged 72 and 62 at the date of the hearing. They had a boxroom which he could use. He began possession proceedings in 1981, but failed because he had no grounds.

By 1985 the circumstances had changed. The plaintiff's ship had been the S.S. "Uganda" and had been scrapped. The plaintiff was made redundant, and he was under contract to the Shipping Federation but was at the time of the hearing unemployed. In November 1983 he married a Russian lady. At the time of the hearing in 1985 she was about to come to the United Kingdom from

Odessa and was due to arrive on May 30, very shortly after the county court hearing. The plaintiff's case was that he wanted to claim his house; he wanted a permanent home where he could set himself up with his wife, and they would want to start a family; he could not afford to take any other house, and at that time he was living by himself in a caravan. The letting for the caravan was due to expire on June 16, 1985, and he did not expect that there would be a renewal of that licence because the holiday season was about to begin and he expected that the owner of the caravan would want a more remunerative summer let for holidaymakers. That was the plaintiff's position at the time of the hearing.

His position has changed since then, and it is right that I should briefly touch upon it. His wife did arrive very soon after the county court hearing when the order for possession was refused. They were together for a short time. The plaintiff then got another job which took him away to sea, which finished, as it turns out, yesterday. His wife, finding herself in the caravan in a strange country was very unhappy. The caravan had been kept on after June 26 on the basis of a bare licence, for which they are paying £25 a week to the caravan owner. Finding herself there with no proper home, her husband away at sea, the plaintiff's wife got herself a job in London in a hotel on what is accepted to be a temporary basis. At present she is abroad again on holiday, but that is accepted as being only temporary. So the present position is that the plaintiff is still where he was at the date of the hearing. Having finished at sea, he is now on a month's leave, after which he will be unemployed and he will be in receipt of £15 a week as a retainer from the Shipping Federation providing he is prepared to offer himself for further employment. The wife, when he is here, can go back to the caravan with him. When he is not here, she would not want to go back to the caravan, one assumes, by herself. The situation is extremely uncertain, and the inference could perhaps fairly be drawn that, in so far as there has been a change of circumstances for the plaintiff since the hearing at the county court, it has been for the worse because, as a result of no order having been made, his family life has become disrupted. That is the position of the plaintiff.

The defendant at the hearing before the recorder at Penzance conceded that the plaintiff's claim was a reasonable one, he reasonably required the house for his own occupation, but claimed that, if an order were made, there would be greater hardship to him than there would be to the plaintiff if no order were made. The onus of proving the greater hardship is, of course, on the defendant.

The defendant is a welder. His net take home pay, we have been told, is £81 a week. Miss Barnes has some unemployment benefit and possibly some child allowance for the six-month-old daughter. The evidence originally stated that her own income, in addition to that of Mr. Edwards, was £100 a week, which would have given the family a joint income of £181 a week, but we have been told that that was a misunderstanding and in fact their joint income is £100 a week.

The defendants say that their parents, who do have each a spare room, cannot rehouse them or their children. They have another child that they have to accommodate from time to time, who is a daughter aged 15 of Mr. Edwards by a previous marriage who comes at weekends for staying access. They said that they could not find anywhere else to live.

What they did was to go to the Penwith District Council, and they produced a letter to show what the council held out to them as being open to them if an order were made. It is a letter dated May 10, 1985, which was written by the Chief Housing and Technical Officer to the defendants' solicitors, and it is really a very bare statement of the legal position. It says:

"Should a court order for possession be granted against Mr. Edwards, it would be open to him to apply to the council under the provisions of

[Part III of the Housing Act 1985]. In cases where families are homeless through no fault of their own, then the council accept liability for rehousing although the actual area within the Penwith district would depend upon suitable vacancies.

If the case goes against Mr. Edwards, it would be helpful if you could forward me a copy of the court order, together with the particulars of claim."

Therefore it has to be conceded that, if a court order were made against the defendants, they would be homeless for the purposes of [Part III of the Housing Act 1985]. In addition to that, in accordance with section [59] (1) of that Act, they would be adjudged to have a priority need for accommodation because of the existence of the little girl, Natalie, their six-month-old daughter.

When the learned recorder gave his judgment he set out all the facts as they then existed and came to the question where he had to discuss the issue of whether the defendants had succeeded in proving greater hardship. What he said was this, after reciting the family circumstances:

"He produces from Penwith District Council a letter dated May 20, 1985 which whilst conveying the concept that they would be treated as homeless, it gives no indication of the property that they would be given or when they would be re-housed. There is no guarantee of the nature or of the area or of the accommodation to be provided and it is not for the court to assume other than that something of a bed and breakfast accommodation would be made available in the first place. The court has to decide on the facts at this moment which includes the Statement of Penwith District Council but that is not very helpful in carrying the case further."

Then, after dealing with the burden of proof, he said:

"I have every sympathy with the landlord but one cannot turn a blind eye to greater hardship. He has not made out that it would cause any great hardship on his part if I refuse his application. Mr. Edwards does make out the greater hardship and therefore exercising all matters within the Act reluctantly this claim must be refused."

This is a familiar situation where the plaintiff had prudently made provision for himself, he wants his house, and it is conceded that he needs it. It has also been said that the defendants have been good tenants of the house for the period that they have been there.

When one comes to consider the issue of greater hardship, this court cannot merely upset the decision of the county court judge or recorder simply because it might have come to a different conclusion itself. That has been long established and laid down very clearly in *King* v. *Taylor* [1955] 1 Q.B. 150, which also says that it is relevant to take into account changes in circumstances which have taken place since the hearing. But the point is taken in the present case that the learned recorder misdirected himself when he came to his conclusion that the defendant had proved the greater hardship.

The position under [Part III of the Housing Act 1985] is that the council, first of all, has to be satisfied that the defendants are homeless. If the court made the order, they could not fail to be satisfied of that. They would then be satisfied that there was a priority need for the defendants to have accommodation. With the existence of the little daughter, they could not fail to be satisfied of that. They then have to apply the tests which are laid down in [sections 65–67]; and under section [65(2)], in various circumstances, it is the council's duty to secure that accommodation becomes available for their occupation. Some initial hardship is obviously caused in a way every time a possession order is made against a sitting tenant, but it has to be more than merely that. The landlord has to begin by satisfying the court that he has a reasonable need for the house. That has been conceded as having happened here. The learned recorder, when he came to consider this, seems to have approached it on the basis that the defendants have nowhere else to go. He said: " ... it is not for the court to assume other than that something of a bed and breakfast accommodation would be made available in the first place." That is not something which figured in the only evidence which was adduced independently by the defendants, which was the letter from the Penwith District Council. It may be that, assuming an order were made against the defendants, they would have to begin with bed and breakfast accommodation, but it was certainly for the defendants to provide evidence that the accommodation, which it was the legal obligation for the Penwith District Council to provide for them, would be something which would be unsatisfactory and something which would cause greater hardship to them; and that seems not to have been provided at all.

In coming to the conclusion in the way he did, the learned recorder seems to have done two things. First of all, when he said, "It is not for the court to assume other than that something of a bed and breakfast accommodation would be made available in the first place," he does not seem to have been applying the burden of proof which has to be placed upon the defendant. If anything, he seems to have been putting it the wrong way round. In the second place, the recorder should not have been dealing with the matter on a purely temporary basis. The immediate effect of an order for possession always is to dispossess a tenant and to cause him some initial hardship of a sort. What the recorder should have been looking at is the longer term effect of the order to see whether it had been proved that the accommodation which the council is legally bound to provide would be something which would be unsuitable and would cause hardship, or greater hardship, to the defendants. That he does not seem to have considered at all.

Having approached the case in the way he did, what he has done is to misdirect himself as to the way in which the burden of proof should be discharged by the defendant in circumstances such as these. There is unquestioned hardship to the plaintiff, who is wanting to get back into his own house in the circumstances which he outlined to the court and which still, apparently exist today. But there does not seem to have been any proper evidence given to justify the finding by the learned recorder that there would be greater hardship caused to the defendants if he made the order against them. Accordingly, in my view, he misdirected himself as to the issue which he had to decide. In those circumstances, the defendants not having really proved hardship of any kind, let alone greater hardship, the order for possession should have been made, as it was conceded, as it had to be, that the landlord properly required the house for his own occupation.

I would accordingly allow this appeal and order that the plaintiff should have possession of the house on the basis that the defendant has not discharged his burden of proof and that the learned recorder has misdirected himself in the conclusion to which he came.

Parker L.J. agreed.

(iv) In *Rowe* v. *Truelove*[97] the Court of Appeal held that a landlord who sought to regain possession of a flat so that he could sell it and thereby get out of financial difficulties could not do so.

[97] (1976) 241 E.G. 535.

(v)   In *Cumming* v. *Danson*[98] Lord Greene M.R. remarked that it was not just hardship to the tenant that was to be considered, but also to all those who were living with the tenant.

(vi)   Under section 102 of the Rent Act 1977 a former protected or statutory tenant may recover compensation if the landlord obtains an order for possession under Case 8 or Case 9 "by misrepresentation or concealment of material facts."[99]

Case 10

Where the court is satisfied that the rent charged by the tenant—

(a)   for any sublet part of the dwelling-house which is a dwelling-house let on a protected tenancy or subject to a statutory tenancy is or was in excess of the maximum rent for the time being recoverable for that part, having regard to ... Part III of this Act, or

(b)   for any sublet part of the dwelling-house which is subject to a restricted contract is or was in excess of the maximum (if any) which it is lawful for the lessor, within the meaning of Part V of this Act to require to receive having regard to the provisions of that Part.[1]

(3) Part II of Schedule 15: Mandatory Grounds

Part II of Schedule 15 sets out the mandatory grounds on which a court must order possession. Note that if the landlord establishes one of these grounds the court has no discretion to adjourn proceedings or to postpone the date for possession.[1a] Furthermore, the landlord may be able to use a "special speedy procedure"[2] when seeking possession on one of the mandatory grounds.[3]

Case 11

Where a person (in this Case referred to as "the owner-occupier") who let the dwelling-house on a regulated tenancy had, at any time before the letting, occupied it as his residence and—

(a)   not later than the relevant date the landlord gave notice in writing to the tenant that possession might be recovered under this Case, and

(b)   the dwelling-house has not, since—

(i)   22nd March 1973, in the case of a tenancy which became a regulated tenancy by virtue of section 14 of the Counter-Inflation Act 1973;

(ii)   14th August 1974, in the case of a regulated furnished tenancy; or

(iii) 8th December 1965, in the case of any other tenancy,

been let by the owner-occupier on a protected tenancy with respect to which the condition mentioned in paragraph (a) above was not satisfied, and

---

[98] [1942] 2 All E.R. 653.   [99] Compare with Housing Act 1988, s.12 (pp. 229–230).
[1] See also, Rent Act 1977, s.139 (p. 293).   [1a] Housing Act 1980, s. 89(1).
[2] Megarry, *The Rent Acts* (11th ed., 1988), Vol. 1, p. 461.
[3] The Rent Act (County Court Proceedings for Possession) Rules 1981 (S.I. 1981 No. 139).

(c)   the court is of the opinion that of the conditions set out in Part V of this Schedule one of those in paragraphs (a) and (c) to (f) is satisfied.

If the court is of the opinion that, notwithstanding that the condition in paragraph (a) or (b) above is not complied with, it is just and equitable to make an order for possession of the dwelling-house, the court may dispense with the requirements of either or both of those paragraphs, as the case may require.

The giving of a notice before 14th August 1974 under section 79 of the Rent Act 1968 shall be treated, in the case of a regulated furnished tenancy, as compliance with paragraph (a) of this Case.

Where the dwelling-house has been let by the owner-occupier on a protected tenancy (in this paragraph referred to as "the earlier tenancy") granted on or after 16th November 1984 but not later than the end of the period of two months beginning with the commencement of the Rent (Amendment) Act 1985 and either—

   (i)   the earlier tenancy was granted for a term certain (whether or not to be followed by a further term or to continue thereafter from year to year or some other period) and was during that term a protected shorthold tenancy as defined in section 52 of the Housing Act 1982, or

  (ii)   the conditions mentioned in paragraphs (a) to (c) of Case 20 were satisfied with respect to the dwelling-house and the earlier tenancy,

then for the purposes of paragraph (b) above the condition in paragraph (a) above is to be treated as having been satisfied with respect to the earlier tenancy.

Case 12

Where the landlord (in this Case referred to as "the owner") intends to occupy the dwelling-house as his residence at such time as he might retire from regular employment and has let it on a regulated tenancy before he has so retired and—

(a)   not later than the relevant date the landlord gave notice in writing to the tenant that possession might be recovered under this Case; and

(b)   the dwelling-house has not, since 14th August 1974, been let by the owner on a protected tenancy with respect to which the condition mentioned in paragraph (a) above was not satisfied; and

(c)   the court is of the opinion that of the conditions set out in Part V of this Schedule one of those in paragraphs (b) to (e) is satisfied.

If the court is of the opinion that, notwithstanding that the condition in paragraph (a) or (b) above is not complied with, it is just and equitable to make an order for possession of the dwelling-house, the court may dispense with the requirements of either or both of those paragraphs, as the case may require.

Case 13

Where the dwelling-house is let under a tenancy for a term of years certain not exceeding eight months and—

(a)   not later than the relevant date the landlord gave notice in writing to the tenant that possession might be recovered under this Case; and

(b)   the dwelling-house was, at some time within the period of 12 months ending on the relevant date, occupied under a right to occupy it for a holiday.

For the purposes of this Case a tenancy shall be treated as being for a term of years certain notwithstanding that it is liable to determination by re-entry or on the happening of any event other than the giving of notice by the landlord to determine the term.

Case 14

Where the dwelling-house is let under a tenancy for a term of years certain not exceeding 12 months and—

(a) not later than the relevant date the landlord gave notice in writing to the tenant that possession might be recovered under this Case; and

(b) at some time within the period of 12 months ending on the relevant date, the dwelling-house was subject to such a tenancy as is referred to in section 8(1) of this Act.[3a]

For the purposes of this Case a tenancy shall be treated as being for a term of years certain notwithstanding that it is liable to determination by re-entry or on the happening of any event other than the giving of notice by the landlord to determine the term.

Case 15 deals with accommodation which is "held for the purpose of being available for occupation by a minister of religion as a residence."[4] Cases 16–18 deal with various types of agricultural tenancies.

Case 19

Where the dwelling-house was let under a protected shorthold tenancy (or is treated under section 55 of the Housing Act 1980 as having been so let) and—

(a) there either has been no grant of a further tenancy of the dwelling-house since the end of the protected shorthold tenancy or, if there was such a grant, it was to a person who immediately before the grant was in possession of the dwelling-house as a protected or statutory tenant; and

(b) the proceedings for possession were commenced after appropriate notice by the landlord to the tenant and not later than three months after the expiry of the notice.

A notice is appropriate for this Case if—

(i) it is in writing and states that proceedings for possession under this Case may be brought after its expiry; and

(ii) it expires not earlier than three months after it is served nor, if, when it is served, the tenancy is a periodic tenancy, before that periodic tenancy could be brought to an end by a notice to quit served by the landlord on the same day;

(iii) it is served—

(a) in the period of three months immediately preceding the date on which the protected shorthold tenancy comes to an end; or

---

[3a] See p. 157.
[4] Housing Act 1988, Sched. 2, Ground 5 (p. 209).

    (b)   if that date has passed, in the period of three months immediately preceding any anniversary of that date; and

(iv)   in a case where a previous notice has been served by the landlord on the tenant in respect of the dwelling-house, and that notice was an appropriate notice, it is served not earlier than three months after the expiry of the previous notice.

Section 55(2) of the Housing Act 1980 provides:

If, in proceedings for possession under Case 19 set out above, the court is of the opinion that, notwithstanding, that the condition of paragraph (b) or (c) of section 52(1) above is not satisfied, it is just and equitable to make an order for possession, it may treat the tenancy under which the dwelling-house was let as a protected shorthold tenancy.

Case 20

Where the dwelling-house was let by a person (in this Case referred to as "the owner") at any time after the commencement of section 67 of the Housing Act 1980 and—

(a)   at the time when the owner acquired the dwelling-house he was a member of the regular armed forces of the Crown;

(b)   at the relevant date the owner was a member of the regular armed forces of the Crown;

(c)   not later than the relevant date the owner gave notice in writing to the tenant that possession might be recovered under this Case;

(d)   the dwelling-house has not, since the commencement of section 67 of the Act of 1980 been let by the owner on a protected tenancy with respect to which the condition mentioned in paragraph (c) above was not satisfied; and

(e)   the court is of the opinion that—

    (i)   the dwelling-house is required as a residence for the owner; or
    (ii) of the conditions set out in Part V of this Schedule one of those in paragraphs (c) to (f) is satisfied.

If the court is of the opinion that, notwithstanding that the condition in paragraph (c) or (d) above is not complied with, it is just and equitable to make an order for possession of the dwelling-house, the court may dispense with the requirements of either or both of these paragraphs, as the case may require.

For the purposes of this Case "regular armed forces of the Crown" has the same meaning as in section 1 of the House of Commons Disqualification Act 1975.

Part V of Schedule 15 provides:

2. The conditions referred to in paragraph (c) in each of Cases 11 and 12 and in paragraph (e)(ii) of Case 20 are that—

(a)   the dwelling-house is required as a residence for the owner or any member of his family who resided with the owner when he last occupied the dwelling-house as a residence;

(b)   the owner has retired from regular employment and requires the dwelling-house as a residence;

(c)   the owner has died and the dwelling-house is required as a residence for a member of his family who was residing with him at the time of his death;

(d)   the owner has died and the dwelling-house is required by a successor in title as his residence or for the purpose of disposing of it with vacant possession;

(e)   the dwelling-house is subject to a mortgage, made by deed and granted before the tenancy, and the mortgagee—

    (i)   is entitled to exercise a power of sale conferred on him by the mortgage or by section 101 of the Law of Property Act 1925; and
    (ii)   requires the dwelling-house for the purpose of disposing of it with vacant possession in exercise of that power; and

(f)   the dwelling-house is not reasonably suitable to the needs of the owner, having regard to his place of work, and he requires it for the purpose of disposing of it with vacant possession and of using the proceeds of that disposal in acquiring, as his residence, a dwelling-house which is more suitable to those needs.

Notes

(i)   For the purposes of Case 11, whether a landlord is to be regarded as having occupied a dwelling-house as his residence prior to the letting is a question of fact and degree.[5]

(ii)   Case 11 is similar to the second limb of Ground 1 under the Housing Act 1988. Case 11 is, however, broader in two respects. First, the landlord may rely on Case 11 where occupation is required "for the owner or any member of his family who resided with the owner,"[6] whereas under Ground 1 of Schedule 2 to the 1988 Act accommodation may be recovered only for the landlord or the landlord's spouse. Secondly, under Case 11 the landlord has to show only that the dwelling-house is required as a residence,[7] whereas possession can be recovered under sub-paragraph (b) of Ground 1 only if the premises are required as the only or principal home of the landlord or the landlord's spouse.[8]

The courts have considered the meaning of "required." In *Kennealy* v. *Dunne*[9] the landlords had a residence in Hayling Island, and access to their daughter's flat in London. They sought possession of a flat that had been let under Case 11. For the tenants it was argued that the word "required" must mean "reasonably required."

Stephenson L.J., having analysed Case 11 and compared it with Case 9, said:

---

[5] See *Ibie* v. *Trubshaw* (1990) 22 H.L.R. 191.
[6] Rent Act 1977, Sched. 15, Part V, para. 2(a).
[7] See *Naish* v. *Curzon* (1985) 51 P. & C.R. 229; *Mistry* v. *Isidore* (1990) 22 H.L.R. 281.
[8] See pp. 208–209.
[9] [1977] 1 Q.B. 837.

That leads me to the inescapable conclusion that "required" in Case [11] does not mean "reasonably" required: it means no more than bona fide wanted and genuinely intended to be occupied as a residence at once, or at any rate within a reasonable time, but so wanted and intended whether reasonably or unreasonably, even from the landlord's point of view.

There is force in [counsel for the landlords'] submission that the purpose of Case [11] is that a landlord who is living in his own house should be free to take up a post in another part of the country or abroad and let his home to a tenant, secure in the knowledge that when the job is finished and he wants to return home he can, on giving the proper notice, come back and resume life in his own home, without being confronted with all the difficulties which a landlord who seeks possession under Case [9] has to overcome. If that is the purpose of Case [11], it explains the apparently deliberate omission of the qualifying adverb "reasonably."

I agree with the way the matter is put in *Megarry, The Rent Acts*, 10th ed., (1967), vol. 1, pp. 309–310. Dealing with "Unrestricted Grounds for Possession" and "Required," the author says:

"In each case the word "required" is used, without being prefixed by "reasonably." The dwelling-house must be "required" as a residence for the owner-occupier, or for occupation by a minister of religion, or for occupation by an agricultural employee. Though "required" is ambiguous, the absence of any qualifying adverb removes most of the difficulty. It appears that all that the landlord need establish is that he genuinely (and not merely colourably) seeks possession in order to use the dwelling-house for the stated purpose; and if he does this it seems to be immaterial that other and more reasonable courses of action are open to him. In short, the issue is merely whether the requirement is genuine, not whether it is reasonable; and sometimes the genuine may be far from reasonable."

For these reasons, the judge, was in my opinion wrong in saying that "requires" means more than "wants" and more than bona fide "intention," and in saying that there was "something objective as well." There is nothing more objective about this provision than that it must be a genuine requirement and there must be a present intention; and, if the landlord proves that, he is entitled to possession under Case [11].[10]

Although the landlord is required to give notice in writing to the tenant that possession might be recovered under Case 11, the court may dispense with the requirement if it is just and equitable to make an order for possession.[11]

(iii)   Case 19 was introduced by section 55 of the Housing Act 1980. The notice procedure for the termination of a protected shorthold tenancy is extremely complicated and presents a variety of traps for the unwary. If the landlord who wishes to recover possession under Case 19 fails to comply with the time limits imposed by these provisions he will have to wait another year.

---

[10] At 849–850.
[11] See the cases discussed at pp. 212–213. For the problems posed by joint landlords see *Tilling* v. *Whiteman* [1980] A.C. 1.

In view of the fact that protected shorthold tenancies are by definition granted for a limited period, and that from January 15, 1989 no new protected shorthold tenancies can be granted, it is likely that before too long this type of tenure will become very nearly extinct.[12]

Under section 53 of the Housing Act 1980 a specific right is given to tenants to terminate their shorthold tenancies prematurely: on one month's notice if the term is for two years or less; on three months' notice if the term is for more than two years. Shorthold tenants are entitled to exercise this right without penalty or other disability. It should be noted that the assured shorthold tenant has no equivalent right under the regime introduced by the Housing Act 1988.

(B) RESTRICTED CONTRACTS

Restricted contracts used to be referable to rent tribunals which had power to postpone any notice to quit. In 1980 this jurisdiction was abolished except for contracts entered into before the coming into force of section 69 of the Housing Act 1980. The courts are given a special jurisdiction to decide cases under section 106A of the Rent Act 1977 (introduced by section 69(2) of the Housing Act 1980):

106A.—(1)This section applies to any dwelling-house which is the subject of a restricted contract entered into after the commencement of section 69 of the Housing Act 1980.

(2) On the making of an order for possession of such a dwelling-house, or at any time before the execution of such an order, the court may—

(a) stay or suspend execution of the order, or

(b) postpone the date of possession,

for such period or periods as, subject to subsection (3) below, the court thinks fit.

(3) Where a court makes an order for possession of such a dwelling-house, the giving up of possession shall not be postponed (whether by the order or any variation, suspension or stay of execution) to a date later than 3 months after the making of the order.

(4) On any such stay, suspension or postponement as is referred to in subsection (2) above, the court shall, unless it considers that to do so would cause exceptional hardship to the lessee or would otherwise be unreasonable, impose conditions with regard to payment by the lessee of arrears of rent (if any) and rent or payments in respect of occupation after termination of the tenancy (mesne profits) and may impose such other conditions as it thinks fit.

---

[12] Of course, if the landlord takes no action to terminate the protected shorthold at the end of the fixed term the tenant may hold over as a statutory tenant. However, where there is succession to a tenancy to which Case 19 applies, the successor becomes an assured shorthold tenant (Housing Act 1988, s.39(7)).

(5) Subsection (6) below applies in any case where—

(a)   proceedings are brought for possession of such a dwelling-house;

(b)   the lessee's spouse or former spouse, having rights of occupation under the Matrimonial Homes Act 1967, is then in occupation of the dwelling-house; and

(c)   the restricted contract is terminated as a result of those proceedings.

(6) In any case to which this subsection applies, the spouse or former spouse shall, so long as he or she remains in occupation, have the same rights in relation to, or in connection with, any such stay, suspension or postponement as is referred to in subsection (2) above, as he or she would have if those rights of occupation were not affected by the termination of the restricted contract.

V   SECURITY OF TENURE UNDER THE HOUSING ACT 1985

The security of tenure provisions in Part IV of the Housing Act 1985 are broadly similar to the private sector regimes contained in the Rent Act 1977 and the Housing Act 1988. There are, however, a number of significant differences: in particular, some of the grounds for possession, which are set out in Schedule 2 to the 1985 Act, have no counterpart in the legislation governing the private sector, and reflect the fact that local authorities, unlike private individuals and companies, have duties as regards the provision of housing.

It will be immediately apparent that it was the conceptual structure of the Housing Act 1985 rather than the Rent Act 1977 which provided the inspiration for the assured tenancy regime introduced by the Housing Act 1988.

82.—(1) A secure tenancy which is either—

(a)   a weekly or other periodic tenancy, or

(b)   a tenancy for a term certain but subject to termination by the landlord,

cannot be brought to an end by the landlord except by obtaining an order of the court for the possession of the dwelling-house or an order under subsection (3).

(2) Where the landlord obtains an order for the possession of the dwelling-house, the tenancy ends on the date on which the tenant is to give up possession in pursuance of the order.

(3) Where a secure tenancy is a tenancy for a term certain but with a provision for re-entry or forfeiture, the court shall not order possession of the dwelling-house in pursuance of that provision, but in a case where the court would have made such an order it shall instead make an order terminating the tenancy on a date specified in the order and section 86 (periodic tenancy arising on termination of fixed term) shall apply.

(4) Section 146 of the Law of Property Act 1925 (restriction on and relief against forfeiture), except subsection (4) (vesting in under-lessee), and any other enactment or rule of law relating to forfeiture, shall apply in relation to proceedings for an order under subsection (3) of this section as if they were proceedings to enforce a right of re-entry or forfeiture.

86.—(1) Where a secure tenancy ("the first tenancy") is a tenancy for a term certain and comes to an end—

(a)   by effluxion of time, or

(b)   by an order of the court under section 82(3) (termination in pursuance of provision for re-entry or forfeiture),

a periodic tenancy of the same dwelling-house arises by virtue of this section, unless the tenant is granted another secure tenancy of the same dwelling-house (whether a tenancy for a term certain or a periodic tenancy) to begin on the coming to an end of the first tenancy.

(2) Where a periodic tenancy arises by virtue of this section—

(a)   the periods of the tenancy are the same as those for which rent was last payable under the first tenancy, and

(b)   the parties and the terms of the tenancy are the same as those of the first tenancy at the end of it;

except that the terms are confined to those which are compatible with a periodic tenancy and do not include any provision for re-entry or forfeiture.

83.—(1) The court shall not entertain—

(a)   proceedings for the possession of a dwelling-house let under a secure tenancy, or

(b)   proceedings for the termination of a secure tenancy,

unless the landlord has served on the tenant a notice complying with the provisions of this section.

(2) The notice shall—

(a)   be in a form prescribed by regulations made by the Secretary of State,

(b)   specify the ground on which the court will be asked to make an order for the possession of the dwelling-house or for the termination of the tenancy, and

(c)   give particulars of that ground.

(3) Where the tenancy is a periodic tenancy the notice—

(a)   shall also specify a date after which proceedings for the possession of the dwelling-house may be begun, and

(b)   ceases to be in force twelve months after the date so specified;

and the date so specified must not be earlier than the date on which the tenancy could, apart from this Part, be brought to an end by notice to quit given by the landlord on the same date as the notice under this section.

(4) Where the tenancy is a periodic tenancy, the court shall not entertain any such proceedings unless they are begun after the date specified in the notice and at a time when the notice is still in force.

(5) Where a notice under this section is served with respect to a secure tenancy for a term certain, it has effect also with respect to any periodic tenancy arising on the termination of that tenancy by virtue of section 86; and subsections (3) and (4) of this section do not apply to the notice.

(6) Regulations under this section shall be made by statutory instrument and may make different provision with respect to different cases or descriptions of case, including different provision for different areas.

The notice required by section 83(2) should be in the form specified by the Secure Tenancies (Notices) Regulations 1987.[13] The courts have no power to dispense with the requirement of notice. The notice should include a full explanation of why the landlord is relying on the particular ground (or grounds) specified in the notice.[14]

84.—(1) The court shall not make an order for the possession of a dwelling-house let under a secure tenancy except on one or more of the grounds set out in Schedule 2.

(2) The court shall not make an order for possession—

(a) on the grounds set out in Part I of that Schedule (grounds 1 to 8), unless it considers it reasonable to make the order,

(b) on the grounds set out in Part II of that Schedule (grounds 9 to 11), unless it is satisfied that suitable accommodation will be available for the tenant when the order takes effect,

(c) on the grounds set out in Part III of that Schedule (grounds 12 to 16), unless it both considers it reasonable to make the order and is satisfied that suitable accommodation will be available for the tenant when the ordertakes effect;

and Part IV of that Schedule has effect for determining whether suitable accommodation will be available for a tenant.

(3) The court shall not make such an order on any of those grounds unless the ground is specified in the notice in pursuance of which proceedings for possession are begun; but the grounds so specified may be altered or added to with the leave of the court.

The distinctive feature of the public sector regime is that there is no direct equivalent of the mandatory grounds for possession which are such an integral part of the security of tenure provisions in the private sector. To recover possession of accommodation occupied by a secure tenant the landlord must establish: (i) that it is reasonable to make the order (Grounds 1 to 8); or (ii) that suitable alternative accommodation will be available (Grounds 9 to 11); or (iii) both that it is reasonable to make the order and that suitable alternative accommodation will be available (Grounds 12 to 16). Accordingly, the Housing Act 1985 provides more complete protection for the tenant than either the Rent Act 1977 or the Housing Act 1988.

The grounds for possession are to be found in Schedule 2 to the 1985 Act:

---

[13] S.I. 1987 No. 755.
[14] See *Torridge District Council* v. *Jones* (1985) 18 H.L.R. 107.

PART I

GROUNDS ON WHICH COURT MAY ORDER POSSESSION
IF IT CONSIDERS IT REASONABLE

Ground 1

Rent lawfully due from the tenant has not been paid or an obligation of the tenancy has been broken or not performed.

Ground 2

The tenant or a person residing in the dwelling-house has been guilty of conduct which is a nuisance or annoyance to neighbours, or has been convicted of using the dwelling-house or allowing it to be used for immoral or illegal purposes.

Ground 3

The condition of the dwelling-house or of any of the common parts has deteriorated owing to acts of waste by, or the neglect or default of, the tenant or a person residing in the dwelling-house and, in the case of an act of waste by, or the neglect or default of, a person lodging with the tenant or a sub-tenant of his, the tenant has not taken such steps as he ought reasonably to have taken for the removal of the lodger or sub-tenant.

Ground 4

The condition of furniture provided by the landlord for use under the tenancy, or for use in the common parts, has deteriorated owing to ill-treatment by the tenant or a person residing in the dwelling-house and, in the case of ill-treatment by a person lodging with the tenant or a sub-tenant of his, the tenant has not taken such steps as he ought reasonably to have taken for the removal of the lodger or sub-tenant.

Ground 5

The tenant is the person, or one of the persons, to whom the tenancy was granted and the landlord was induced to grant the tenancy by a false statement made knowingly or recklessly by the tenant.

Ground 6 is discussed at p. 300.

Ground 7

The dwelling-house forms part of, or is within the curtilage of, a building which, or so much of it as is held by the landlord, is held mainly for purposes other than housing purposes and consists mainly of accommodation other than housing accommodation, and—

(a) the dwelling-house was let to the tenant or a predecessor in title of his in consequence of the tenant or predecessor being in the employment of the landlord, or of—
a local authority,
a new town corporation,

a housing action trust,
an urban development corporation,
the Development Board for Rural Wales, or
the governors of an aided school,
and

(b) the tenant or a person residing in the dwelling-house has been guilty of conduct such that, having regard to the purpose for which the building is used, it would not be right for him to continue in occupation of the dwelling-house.

Ground 8

The dwelling-house was made available for occupation by the tenant (or a predecessor in title of his) while works were carried out on the dwelling-house which he previously occupied as his only or principal home and—

(a) the tenant (or predecessor) was a secure tenant of the other dwelling-house at the time when he ceased to occupy it as his home,

(b) the tenant (or predecessor) accepted the tenancy of the dwelling-house of which possession is sought on the understanding that he would give up occupation when, on completion of the works, the other dwelling-house was again available for occupation by him under a secure tenancy, and

(c) the works have been completed and the other dwelling-house is so available.

PART II

GROUNDS ON WHICH THE COURT MAY ORDER POSSESSION IF SUITABLE ALTERNATIVE ACCOMMODATION IS AVAILABLE

Ground 9

The dwelling-house is overcrowded within the meaning of Part X, in such circumstances as to render the occupier guilty of an offence.

Ground 10

The landlord intends, within a reasonable time of obtaining possession of the dwelling-house—

(a) to demolish or reconstruct the building or part of the building comprising the dwelling-house, or

(b) to carry out work on that building or on land let together with, and thus treated as part of, the dwelling-house,

and cannot reasonably do so without obtaining possession of the dwelling-house.

Ground 10A

The dwelling-house is in an area which is the subject of a redevelopment scheme approved by the Secretary of State or the Corporation in accordance with Part

V of this Schedule and the landlord intends within a reasonable time of obtaining possession to dispose of the dwelling-house in accordance with the scheme.

or

Part of the dwelling-house is in such an area and the landlord intends within a reasonable time of obtaining possession to dispose of that part in accordance with the scheme and for that purpose reasonably requires possession of the dwelling-house.

Ground 11

The landlord is a charity and the tenant's continued occupation of the dwelling-house would conflict with the objects of the charity.

PART III

GROUNDS ON WHICH THE COURT MAY ORDER POSSESSION IF IT CONSIDERS IT REASONABLE AND SUITABLE ALTERNATIVE ACCOMMODATION IS AVAILABLE

Ground 12

The dwelling-house forms part of, or is within the curtilage of, a building which, or so much of it as is held by the landlord, is held mainly for purposes other than housing purposes and consists mainly of accommodation other than housing accommodation, or is situated in a cemetery, and—

(a) the dwelling-house was let to the tenant or a predecessor in title of his in consequence of the tenant or predecessor being in the employment of the landlord or of—
a local authority,
a new town corporation,
a housing action trust,
an urban development corporation,
the Development Board for Rural Wales, or
the governors of an aided school,
and that employment has ceased, and

(b) the landlord reasonably requires the dwelling-house for occupation as a residence for some person either engaged in the employment of the landlord, or of such a body, or with whom a contract for such employment has been entered into conditional on housing being provided.

Ground 13

The dwelling-house has features which are substantially different from those of ordinary dwelling-houses and which are designed to make it suitable for occupation by a physically disabled person who requires accommodation of a kind provided by the dwelling-house and—

(a) there is no longer such a person residing in the dwelling-house, and

(b)   the landlord requires it for occupation (whether alone or with members of his family) by such a person.

Ground 14

The landlord is a housing association or housing trust which lets dwelling-houses only for occupation (whether alone or with others) by persons whose circumstances (other than merely financial circumstances) make it especially difficult for them to satisfy their need for housing, and—

(a)   either there is no longer such a person residing in the dwelling-house or the tenant has received from a local housing authority an offer of accommodation in premises which are to be let as a separate dwelling under a secure tenancy, and

(b)   the landlord requires the dwelling-house for occupation (whether alone or with members of his family) by such a person.

Ground 15

The dwelling-house is one of a group of dwelling-houses which it is the practice of the landlord to let for occupation by persons with special needs and—

(a)   a social service or special facility is provided in close proximity to the group of dwelling-houses in order to assist persons with those special needs,

(b)   there is no longer a person with those special needs residing in the dwelling-house, and

(c)   the landlord requires the dwelling-house for occupation (whether alone or with members of his family) by a person who has those special needs.

Ground 16 is discussed at p. 316.

Notes

(i)   Although there are some differences in detail, a number of these grounds for possession were derived from Schedule 15 to the Rent Act 1977 (and have subsequently been inserted into or adapted for the assured tenancy regime) and have been discussed above.

Grounds 1 to 4 are based on Cases 1 to 4 under the Rent Act 1977, and they correspond to Grounds 10 and 12, and 13 to 15 in Schedule 2 to the Housing Act 1988. It may be noted that some local authorities make use of Ground 2 in cases of racial harassment.

(ii)   Ground 10 bears some similarity to Ground 6 under the Housing Act 1988. However, there are two significant differences: first, under Ground 10 suitable alternative accommodation must be available, whereas Ground 6 is a mandatory ground for possession; secondly, Ground 10 is drafted rather more clearly than Ground 6 (which both prevents a landlord who purchases the reversion from relying on Ground 6, and seeks to protect tenants of premises which were let on a protected tenancy).

To rely on Ground 10 the landlord must show a settled and clearly defined intention.[15]

(iii)   Grounds 11, 13, 14 and 15 reflect particular concerns of public and quasi-public bodies and have no counterparts in the Rent Act 1977 nor the Housing Act 1988.

(iv)   The factors to be taken into account when determining the suitability of alternative accommodation are set out in Part IV of Schedule 2 (as amended by section 140 of the Housing Act 1988 and Schedule 17):

1. For the purposes of section 84(2)(b) and (c) (cases in which court is not to make an order for possession unless satisfied that suitable accommodation will be available) accommodation is suitable if it consists of premises—

(a)   which are to be let as a separate dwelling under a secure tenancy, or

(b)   which are to be let as a separate dwelling under a protected tenancy, not being a tenancy under which the landlord might recover possession under one of the Cases in Part II of Schedule 15 to the Rent Act 1977 (cases where court must order possession), or

(c)   which are to be let as a separate dwelling under an assured tenancy which is neither an assured shorthold tenancy, within the meaning of Part I of the Housing Act 1988, nor a tenancy under which the landlord might recover possession under any of Grounds 1 to 5 in Schedule 2 to that Act,

and, in the opinion of the court, the accommodation is reasonably suitable to the needs of the tenant and his family.

2. In determining whether the accommodaton is reasonably suitable to the needs of the tenant and his family, regard shall be had to—

(a)   the nature of the accommodation which it is the practice of the landlord to allocate to persons with similar needs;

(b)   the distance of the accommodation available from the place of work or education of the tenant and of any members of his family;

(c)   its distance from the home of any member of the tenant's family if proximity to it is essential to that member's or the tenant's well-being;

(d)   the needs (as regards extent of accommodation) and means of the tenant and his family;

(e)   the terms on which the accommodation is available and the terms of the secure tenancy;

(f)   if furniture was provided by the landlord for use under the secure tenancy, whether furniture is to be provided for use in the other accommodation, and if so the nature of the furniture to be provided.

3. Where possession of a dwelling-house is sought on ground 9 (overcrowding such as to render occupier guilty of offence), other accommodation may be reasonably suitable to the needs of the tenant and his family notwithstanding

[15] See *Wansbeck District Council* v. *Marley* (1988) 20 H.L.R. 247.

that the permitted number of persons for that accommodation, as defined in section 326(3) (overcrowding: the space standard), is less than the number of persons living in the dwelling-house of which possession is sought.

4.—(1) A certificate of the appropriate local housing authority that they will provide suitable accommodation for the tenant by a date specified in the certificate is conclusive evidence that suitable accommodation will be available for him by that date.

(2) The appropriate local housing authority is the authority for the district in which the dwelling-house of which possession is sought is situated.

(3) This paragraph does not apply where the landlord is a local housing authority.

Section 85 corresponds to section 9 of the Housing Act 1988 and section 100 of the Rent Act 1977:

(1) Where proceedings are brought for possession of a dwelling-house let under a secure tenancy on any of the grounds set out in Part I or Part III of Schedule 2 (grounds 1 to 8 and 12 to 16: cases in which the court must be satisfied that it is reasonable to make a possession order), the court may adjourn the proceedings for such period or periods as it thinks fit.

(2) On the making of an order for possession of such a dwelling-house on any of those grounds, or at any time before the execution of the order, the court may—

(a)   stay or suspend the execution of the order, or

(b)   postpone the date of possession,

for such period or periods as the court thinks fit.

(3) On such an adjournment, stay, suspension or postponement the court—

(a)   shall impose conditions with respect to the payment by the tenant of arrears of rent (if any) and rent or payments in respect of occupation after the termination of the tenancy (mesne profits), unless it considers that to do so would cause exceptional hardship to the tenant or would otherwise be unreasonable, and

(b)   may impose such other conditions as it thinks fit.

(4) If the conditions are complied with, the court may, if it thinks fit, discharge or rescind the order for possession.

(5) Where proceedings are brought for possession of a dwelling-house which is let under a secure tenancy and—

(a)   the tenant's spouse or former spouse, having rights of occupation under the Matrimonial Homes Act 1983, is then in occupation of the dwelling-house, and

(b)   the tenancy is terminated as a result of those proceedings,

the spouse or former spouse shall, so long as he or she remains in occupation, have the same rights in relation to, or in connection with, any adjournment, stay, suspension or postponement in pursuance of this section as he or she would have if those rights of occupation were not affected by the termination of the tenancy.

VI PROHIBITION OF EVICTION WITHOUT DUE PROCESS OF LAW: TENANCIES AND LICENCES NOT STATUTORILY PROTECTED

The methods whereby a landlord may lawfully recover possession of premises occupied by a statutorily protected tenant have already been outlined. However, it must be remembered that not all residential occupiers are statutorily protected: many tenants and licensees fall outside the schemes of statutory protection contained in the Rent Act 1977, the Housing Act 1985 and the Housing Act 1988. As regards this category of residential occupier the Protection from Eviction Act 1977 (as amended) provides:

3.—(1) Where any premises have been let as a dwelling under a tenancy which is neither a statutorily protected tenancy nor an excluded tenancy and—

(a) the tenancy (in this section referred to as the former tenancy) has come to an end, but

(b) the occupier continues to reside in the premises or part of them,

it shall not be lawful for the owner to enforce against the occupier, otherwise than by proceedings in the court, his right to recover possession of the premises.

(2) In this section 'the occupier', in relation to any premises, means any person lawfully residing in the premises or part of them at the termination of the former tenancy.

(2A) Subsections (1) and (2) above apply in relation to any restricted contract (within the meaning of the Rent Act 1977) which—

(a) creates a licence; and

(b) is entered into after the commencement of section 69 of the Housing Act 1980;

as they apply in relation to a restricted contract which creates a tenancy.

(2B) Subsections (1) and (2) above apply in relation to any premises occupied as a dwelling under a licence, other than an excluded licence, as they apply in relation to premises let as a dwelling under a tenancy, and in those subsections the expressions 'let' and 'tenancy' shall be construed accordingly.

(2C) References in the preceding provisions of this section and section 4(2A) below to an excluded tenancy do not apply to—

(a) a tenancy entered into before the date on which the Housing Act 1988 came into force, or

(b) a tenancy entered into on or after that date but pursuant to a contract made before that date,

but, subject to that, 'excluded tenancy' and 'excluded licence' shall be construed in accordance with section 3A below.

(3) This section shall, with the necessary modifications, apply where the owner's right to recover possession arises on the death of the tenant under a statutory tenancy within the meaning of the Rent Act 1977 or the Rent (Agriculture) Act 1976.

3A.—(1) Any reference in this Act to an excluded tenancy or an excluded licence is a reference to a tenancy or licence which is excluded by virtue of any of the following provisions of this section.

(2) A tenancy or licence is excluded if—

  (a) under its terms the occupier shares any accommodation with the landlord or licensor; and

  (b) immediately before the tenancy or licence was granted and also at the time it comes to an end, the landlord or licensor occupied as his only or principal home premises of which the whole or part of the shared accommodation formed part.

(3) A tenancy or licence is also excluded if—

  (a) under its terms the occupier shares any accommodation with a member of the family of the landlord or licensor;

  (b) immediately before the tenancy or licence was granted and also at the time it comes to an end, the member of the family of the landlord or licensor occupied as his only or principal home premises of which the whole or part of the shared accommodation formed part; and

  (c) immediately before the tenancy or licence was granted and also at the time it comes to an end, the landlord or licensor occupied as his only or principal home premises in the same building as the shared accommodation and that building is not a purpose-built block of flats.

(4) For the purposes of subsections (2) and (3) above, an occupier shares accommodation with another person if he has the use of it in common with that person (whether or not also in common with others) and any reference in those subsections to shared accommodation shall be construed accordingly, and if, in relation to any tenancy or licence, there is at any time more than one person who is the landlord or licensor, any reference in those subsections to the landlord or licensor shall be construed as a reference to any one of those persons.

(5) In subsections (2) to (4) above—

  (a) 'accommodation' includes neither an area used for storage nor a staircase, passage, corridor or other means of access;

  (b) 'occupier' means, in relation to a tenancy, the tenant and, in relation to a licence, the licensee; and

  (c) 'purpose-built block of flats' has the same meaning as in Part III of Schedule 1 to the Housing Act 1988;[15a]

and section 113 of the Housing Act 1985 shall apply to determine whether a person is for the purposes of subsection (3) above a member of another's family as it applies for the purposes of Part IV of that Act.[15b]

[15a] See p. 150.
[15b] See p. 315.

(6) A tenancy or licence is excluded if it was granted as a temporary expedient to a person who entered the premises in question or any other premises as a trespasser (whether or not, before the beginning of that tenancy or licence, another tenancy or licence to occupy the premises or any other premises had been granted to him).

(7) A tenancy or licence is excluded if—

(a)　it confers on the tenant or licensee the right to occupy the premises for a holiday only; or

(b)　it is granted otherwise than for money or money's worth.

(8) A licence is excluded if it confers rights of occupation in a hostel, within the meaning of the Housing Act 1985, which is provided by—

(a)　the council of a county, district or London Borough, the Common Council of the City of London, the Council of the Isles of Scilly, the Inner London Education Authority, a joint authority within the meaning of the Local Government Act 1985 or a residuary body within the meaning of that Act;

(b)　a development corporation within the meaning of the New Towns Act 1981;

(c)　the Commission for the New Towns;

(d)　an urban development corporation established by an order under section 135 of the Local Government, Planning and Land Act 1980;

(e)　a housing action trust established under Part III of the Housing Act 1988;

(f)　the Development Board for Rural Wales;

(g)　the Housing Corporation or Housing for Wales;

(h)　a housing trust which is a charity or a registered housing association, within the meaning of the Housing Associations Act 1985; or

(i)　any other person who is, or who belongs to a class of person which is specified in an order made by the Secretary of State.

(9) The power to make an order under subsection (8)(i) above shall be exercisable by statutory instrument which shall be subject to annulment in pursuance of a resolution of either House of Parliament.

Notes

(i)　As originally drafted, section 3 of the Protection from Eviction Act 1977 applied only to tenants and a very limited class of licensees (namely, service occupiers, who by virtue of section 8(2) were deemed to be tenants if they had exclusive possession of the premises which they occupied).

In 1980 section 3 was extended to another category of licences—those licences which were restricted contracts entered into after the entry into force of section 69 of the Housing Act 1980.[16]

---

[16] subs. (2A).

The amendments introduced by sections 30 to 33 of the Housing Act 1988 have brought about more significant changes in two respects. First, section 3 applies equally to tenancies and licences.[17] Secondly, the Housing Act 1988 has introduced the category of 'excluded tenancies' (which by virtue of section 3(2B) also includes licences) which fall outside all statutory protection.[18]

It should be noted that the amendments effected by the Housing Act 1988 apply only to tenancies and licences entered into on or after January 15, 1989 (the commencement date of the relevant provisions of the Housing Act 1988).[19]

(ii) "Statutorily protected tenancies" are excluded from the scope of section 3 because they fall within their own particular schemes of protection. Section 8(1) of the Protection from Eviction Act 1977 provides:

In this Act 'statutorily protected tenancy' means—

(a) a protected tenancy within the meaning of the Rent Act 1977 or a tenancy to which Part I of the Landlord and Tenant Act 1954 applies;

(b) a protected occupancy or statutory tenancy as defined in the Rent (Agriculture) Act 1976;

(c) a tenancy to which Part II of the Landlord and Tenant Act 1954 applies;

(d) a tenancy of an agricultural holding within the meaning of the Agricultural Holdings Act 1986;

(e) an assured tenancy or assured agricultural occupancy under Part I of the Housing Act 1988.

(f) a tenancy to which Schedule 10 to the Local Government and Housing Act 1989 applies.[20]

(iii) Under section 3(2) the occupier must be lawfully on the premises. The tenant, members of his household, lodgers and guests will all be regarded as lawfully occupying the premises. However, in *Bolton Building Society* v. *Cobb*[21] the Court of Appeal held that a tenant of a mortgagor is a lawful occupier but only if the tenancy is granted before the mortgage is entered into, or the mortgagor's right to grant tenancies[22] is not excluded by the mortgage deed. If, as is usual, the mortgage contains a provision which prohibits the mortgagor from granting tenancies, any occupier who goes into possession on the basis of a tenancy granted after the mortgage is executed will not be a lawful occupier for the purposes of section 3. By analogy it can be argued that

---

[17] s.3(2B).
[18] s.3A.
[19] s.3(2C).
[20] Paragraph (e) was added by Housing Act 1988, s.33(1); paragraph (f) was added by Local Government and Housing Act 1989, s.194(1) and Sched. 11, para. 54.
[21] [1966] 1 W.L.R. 1.
[22] Law of Property Act 1925, s.99.

where the tenant sublets the premises in breach of the terms of the lease the subtenant is not a lawful occupier.[23]

(iv)   Breach of section 3 is a tort, and therefore may give rise to civil liability.[24]

(v)   Even though the landlord is not legally required to go through the courts in order to recover possession of premises occupied by an excluded tenant or licensee, a number of risks are avoided if a court order is obtained. A landlord who tries to evict an excluded tenant without a court order may nevertheless commit a criminal offence[25] or may perform acts which render him liable for damages in tort.[26]

VII   UNLAWFUL EVICTION, HARASSMENT AND QUIET ENJOYMENT

It has been seen that as a result of various statutory provisions the situations in which a landlord may lawfully recover possession of residential premises are strictly limited. If a landlord unlawfully evicts a residential occupier, or engages in actions which are designed to encourage residential occupiers to leave their homes, the law provides the occupier with a variety of remedies.

Both civil and criminal liability are discussed in the pages which follow. It should be stressed that a single set of facts may both constitute a crime and give rise to civil liability. For example, if a landlord evicts a protected tenant without a court order, the landlord runs the risk of being prosecuted for unlawful eviction under section 1 of the Protection from Eviction Act 1977, and of being sued for damages by the displaced tenant.

(A) CRIMINAL LAW

Section 1 of the Protection from Eviction Act 1977 (as amended by section 29 of the Housing Act 1988) provides:

> (1) In this section 'residential occupier,' in relation to any premises, means a person occupying the premises as a residence, whether under a contract or by virtue of any enactment or rule of law giving him the right to remain in occupation or restricting the right of any other person to recover possession of the premises.

---

[23] For a discussion of problems posed by the tenant subletting and by the landlord mortgaging the premises see Chapter 5.
[24] *Warder* v. *Cooper* [1970] Ch. 495 (pp. 268–270).
[25] *e.g.* under Criminal Law Act 1977, s.6. See pp. 33–34.
[26] See pp. 268–277.

(2) If any person unlawfully deprives the residential occupier of any premises of his occupation of the premises or any part thereof, or attempts to do so, he shall be guilty of an offence unless he proves that he believed, and had reasonable cause to believe, that the residential occupier had ceased to reside in the premises.

(3) If any person with intent to cause the residential occupier of any premises—

(a) to give up the occupation of the premises or any part thereof, or

(b) to refrain from exercising any right or pursuing any remedy in respect of the premises or part thereof;

does acts likely to interfere with the peace or comfort of the residential occupier or members of his household, or persistently withdraws or withholds services reasonably required for the occupation of the premises as a residence he shall be guilty of an offence.

(3A) Subject to subsection (3B) below, the landlord of a residential occupier or an agent of the landlord shall be guilty of an offence if—

(a) he does acts likely to interfere with the peace or comfort of the residential occupier or members of his household, or

(b) he persistently withdraws or withholds services reasonably required for the occupation of the premises in question as a residence.

and (in either case) he knows, or has reasonable cause to believe, that the conduct is likely to cause the residential occupier to give up the occupation of the whole or part of the premises or to refrain from exercising any right or pursuing any remedy in respect of the whole or part of the premises.

(3B) A person shall not be guilty of an offence under subsection (3A) above if he proves that he had reasonable grounds for doing the acts or withdrawing or withholding the services in question.

(3C) In subsection (3A) above 'landlord', in relation to a residential occupier of any premises, means the person who, but for—

(a) the residential occupier's right to remain in occupation of the premises, or

(b) a restriction on the person's right to recover possession of the premises,

would be entitled to occupation of the premises and any superior landlord under whom that person derives title.

(4) A person guilty of an offence under this section shall be liable—

(a) on summary conviction, to a fine not exceeding the prescribed sum or to imprisonment for a term not exceeding six months or to both;

(b) on conviction on indictment, to a fine or to imprisonment for a term not exceeding two years or to both.

(5) Nothing in this section shall be taken to prejudice any liability or remedy to which a person guilty of an offence thereunder may be subject in civil proceedings.

(6) Where an offence under this section committed by a body corporate is proved to have been committed with the consent or connivance of, or to be

attributable to any neglect on the part of, any director, manager or secretary or other similar officer of the body corporate or any person who was purporting to act in any such capacity, he as well as the body corporate shall be guilty of that offence and shall be liable to be proceeded against and punished accordingly.

Notes

(i)   Subsections (3A) to (3C) were introduced by section 29 of the Housing Act 1988 and apply only to acts committed on or after January 15, 1989.

(ii)   The concept of 'residential occupier' is wide enough to include tenants and licensees (other than excluded tenants and licensees), including former tenants and licensees. For example, a former licensee will continue to be a residential occupier within section 1(1) even if the licence has been properly determined since section 3 of the Protection from Eviction Act 1977 is an "enactment ... restricting the right of any other person to recover possession of the premises."

   In certain circumstances a trespasser or an excluded tenant may be a residential occupier because section 6 of the Criminal Law Act 1977 restricts the rights of owners to recover possession of their premises.[27]

   A deserted spouse of a tenant or licensee is a 'residential occupier' within the meaning of section 1(1). By virtue of section 1 of the Matrimonial Homes Act 1983 a spouse has a statutory right of occupation in respect of the matrimonial home.[28]

(iii)   The offences contained in section 1 can be committed in relation to 'premises,' which is a wider term than 'dwelling.'[29] It has been held to include a caravan, which, although not attached to the ground, had been static for 10 years and could easily be towed away.[30] One room has also been regarded as sufficient to constitute premises.[31]

(iv)   The courts have had some difficulty in determining the precise relationship between the offences of eviction and harassment created by subsections (2) and (3). For example, if a landlord excludes the tenant from the premises for only a relatively short period of time (say, a few hours or overnight), should the landlord be charged with unlawful eviction under subsection (2), or harassment under subsection (3)?

   In *R.* v. *Yuthiwattana*[32] Kerr L.J. said:

Mr. Stephenson referred us to a decision of this court which is a long way from the present case but which was concerned with the concept of eviction:

---

[27] See pp. 33–34.
[28] For further discussion see pp. 318–323.
[29] Rent Act 1977, s.1; Housing Act 1988, s.79; Housing Act 1988, s.1.
[30] *Norton* v. *Knowles* [1969] 1 Q.B. 572.
[31] *Thurrock U.D.C.* v. *Shina* (1972) 23 P. & C.R. 205.
[32] (1984) 80 Cr.App.R. 55 at 63.

Commissioners of Crown Lands v. *Page* [1960] 2 Q.B. 274. I need not refer to the facts of that case, but at page 279 Lord Evershed M.R. said that the short point raised in the action and the appeal was whether the exercise by the Minister of certain rights of requisition operated as an eviction of the lessee, as that term is properly understood. At page 284, having referred to some of the authorities, he said that to constitute an eviction it "must be of a permanent character"; and that is in substance what Mr. Stephenson submits.

In our view "permanency" goes too far. For instance, if the owner of the premises unlawfully tells the occupier that he must leave the premises for some period, it may be months or weeks, and then excludes him from the premises, or does anything else with the result that the occupier effectively has to leave the premises and find other accommodation, then it would in our view be open to a jury to convict the owner under subsection (2) on the ground that he had unlawfully deprived the occupier of his occupation. On the other hand, cases which are more properly described as "locking out" or not admitting the occupier on one or even more isolated occasions so that in effect he continues to be allowed to occupy the premises but then is unable to enter, seem to us to fall appropriately under subsection (3)(a) or (b), which deal with acts of harassment.

Commenting on this passage in *Costelloe* v. *Camden L.B.C.*[33] Glidewell L.J. said:

It is clear ... that if a residential occupier is excluded from premises, apparently permanently, in circumstances in which he thinks he has been permanently excluded and it appears to be the intention of the landlord to exclude him or her permanently, but for whatever reason, whether because the landlord changes his mind or is obliged to do so, the occupier is later readmitted, such a case could nevertheless come within subsection (2) of section 1 of the Protection from Eviction Act 1977 even though the absence was only for a short time.[34]

(v) The offences attract a maximum fine at level 5 on the standard scale on summary conviction[35] and/or imprisonment. However, average penalties imposed under section 1(4) tend to be derisory. Although there are some isolated occasions where severe sentences have been imposed[36] it is relatively rare for defendants to be imprisoned.

It should also be noted that the number of prosecutions has been very low (some 100 a year for the years 1983–1988[37]). The police consider that responsibility for bringing prosecutions lies with local authorities (which have the power to institute proceedings for offences of harassment and unlawful eviction[38]), and they do not normally intervene unless physical violence is involved. Accordingly, much of the enforcement of the Protection from Eviction Act 1977 is undertaken by

[33] [1986] Crim.L.R. 249.
[34] See also *R.* v. *Phekoo* [1981] 1 W.L.R. 1117; *R.* v. *Ahmad* (1986) 18 H.L.R. 416; *Schon* v. *Camden L.B.C.* (1986) 18 H.L.R. 341 (cases concerning the offence of harassment under subsection (3)).
[35] Currently, £2,000. See p. 33, n. 21. There is no statutory maximum where conviction is on indictment.
[36] In *R.* v. *Bokhari* (1974) 59 Cr.App.R. 303 the defendant was sentenced to two year's imprisonment (in addition to being required to pay £1,600 compensation and £400 costs).
[37] See D.O.E. circular 3/89, para. 7 (issued jointly by the Department of the Environment and the Welsh Office on January 20, 1990).
[38] Protection from Eviction Act 1977, s.6.

local authority tenancy relations officers who tend to prefer to conciliate between parties rather than initiate prosecutions.

In its report[39] the Francis Committee stated:

In England and Wales before the passing of the Protection from Eviction Act 1964 and the Rent Act 1965, police responsibilities in disputes between landlord and tenant were confined to preventing breaches of the peace. In investigating allegations of offences under Part III of the 1965 Act the police are faced with some difficulties. These difficulties are broadly as follows:

(a) Eviction—A residential occupier is protected but not a trespasser or a person with no valid right to remain in occupation. A constable on the spot is in obvious difficulty in distinguishing between these categories or dealing with a situation in which the intricacies of sub-tenancy agreements are involved.

(b) Harassment—Allegations that there may have been acts calculated to interfere with the peace and comfort of a residential occupier, or a persistent withdrawal of services take time to investigate and a constable is in no position to take immediate action.

The police have no power to arrest for offences under the Rent Act. Even if the legal situation between the parties were to be clearly established a constable cannot take any person into custody; he can only make a report on the case.

The police, therefore, act as follows when complaints are made to them (apart from any action that might be necessary to prevent or deal with a breach of the peace):

(a) if called to the scene of a dispute between landlord and tenant, or if there are allegations of unlawful eviction or harassment, the police make such investigations as are possible on the spot;

(b) where it appears from these investigations that there may have been, or may be, a breach of the Act the investigating officer warns the landlord about the provisions of Part III and about the possibility of prosecution;

(c) whether or not such a warning is issued, a full report of the incident is sent to the local authority;

(d) in appropriate cases, the police inform the complainant in writing that the complaint has been passed to the local authority.

The forms of activity that come under this head were discussed by the National Citizens' Advice Bureaux Council, who noted the following problems[40]:

Harassment
Except in cases of actual or threatened violence or cutting off essential supplies it is extremely difficult to prove harassment in the sense that it is behaviour deliberately designed to cause the tenant to give up his tenancy. Bureaux receive many complaints about so-called harassment but say that in some cases the behaviour referred to may be the result of people's differing standards. Some bureaux say that it is sometimes no more than the irritation caused by people having to live in multi-occupation of accommodation not originally designed for that purpose. The stories of the two parties to the event are often so different that it would be difficult to determine who is more to blame—landlord or tenant. Noise is frequently mentioned as harassment and

---

[39] *Report of the Committee on the Rent Acts* (1971) Cmd. 4609, pp. 105–106.
[40] *Ibid.* pp. 108–109.

this may vary from noisy parties to noisy children but except in the most blatant cases (as in an example quoted of a landlord who, when his tenants appealed to the rent tribunal and were given six months security of tenure, used abusive language and stamped on the floor of his bedroom to keep them awake at night) it is very difficult to judge whether this is deliberate harassment. Apparently valid examples of harassment quoted by one bureau include:

> tenant bolted out (temporarily)
> essential services being turned off
> landlord assaulting tenant with knives
> landlord taking up floor boards every weekend on pretext of doing electric wiring
> taking slates off the roof to let the rain in
> throwing petrol bombs through the letter box.

Harassment is not however confined to acts by the landlord against the tenant. There are some quite horrifying stories reported of tenants harassing landlords particularly if they are elderly or women on their own. As this is not an offence against the Rent Act the only remedy for the landlord is to seek possession through the county courts and it is in these situations that fear of court procedures and their slowness as well as the need for special provisions for people letting rooms in their own home is emphasized.

Illegal eviction
There is some evidence that this does take place. Several bureaux state that it is more likely to happen in connection with furnished accommodation than unfurnished because it is easier to pack up the belongings of a tenant of furnished accommodation and to lock him out.

Although it is clear that in some cases the action is a deliberate flouting of the law, there is a good deal of experience that ignorance of the requirements of the law is the root cause. Bureaux say that ignorance is particularly acute amongst small landlords. There are particular areas of difficulty where the landlords and tenants are immigrants unaccustomed to the law of this country. Many an immigrant buys a house with a sitting tenant and is genuinely surprised when he finds he cannot evict him.

(vi) Although it was thought for a number of years that section 1 created a new tort of unlawful eviction,[41] in *McCall* v. *Abelesz*[42] the Court of Appeal held that this was not so.[43] However, a new basis on which damages may be recovered for unlawful eviction has recently been introduced by the Housing Act 1988.[44]

(vii) There is no requirement that an act of harassment should be an actionable civil wrong in order for it to constitute a criminal offence under section 1(3) of the Protection of Eviction Act 1977.[45]

(viii) In very severe cases of harassment the local authority may consider drastic measures to protect the welfare of the tenants. The

[41] See *Mafo* v. *Adams* [1970] 1 Q.B. 548.
[42] [1976] Q.B. 585.
[43] Compare the interpretation of s.3 of the 1977 Act in *Warder* v. *Cooper* [1970] Ch. 495 (pp. 268–270).
[44] See pp. 271–274.
[45] *R.* v. *Burke* [1990] 2 W.L.R. 1313.

Secretary of State for the Environment has issued the following guidance:

Following the judgment in the case of *R.* v. *Secretary of State for the Environment ex p. Royal London Borough of Kensington and Chelsea* (1987) it may be possible for authorities to resort to compulsory purchase under Part II [of the Housing Act 1985] where a property is not sub-standard, under-occupied or vacant, but where harassment or other grave conduct of the landlord has been such that proper housing accommodation could not be said to exist when the authority resolved to make the compulsory acquisition order. ... If an authority contemplates making a compulsory purchase order on the basis of harassment, it should consult the Department ... first, to ensure as far as possible that no legal difficulties would arise in relation to the order.[45a]

(B) CIVIL LAW

Often the primary objective of civil proceedings in this area is to obtain an injunction from the court ordering the landlord to allow the plaintiff back into the premises, or to stop landlords engaging in acts of harassment. However, a tenant or other residential occupier may also seek damages, and in certain cases damages will be substantial.

There are a number of different heads of civil liability on which a displaced or harassed residential occupier may seek to rely. It should be stressed that while a plaintiff may be entitled to damages under a number of different heads, he can only recover damages for any particular loss once.

(1) Breach of Statutory Duty

Warder v. *Cooper* [1970] Ch. 495

Stamp J. said (at 498–501):

The defendant company has a garage and filling station business on the Bath Road at Beenham, in Berkshire. The property, which includes a bungalow, is let on a lease to the defendant company and the lease contains an unqualified covenant against under-letting. The bungalow was erected so that it might be used to house a garage employee. The garage is rather isolated and it is difficult to get employees unless accommodation can be offered. The first defendant, Mr. Cooper, has authority to grant, on behalf of the defendant company, a licence to occupy the bungalow to persons employed in the garage business, but he says that neither he nor the defendant company has any permission from the landlord to create a tenancy in respect of the bungalow.

Towards the end of September, 1969, the first defendant, who is the managing director and the majority shareholder of the defendant company, acting on behalf of the defendant company, engaged the first plaintiff as foreman. It is the first defendant's evidence that he told the first plaintiff that the bungalow would be available for the first plaintiff while he was working for the first defendant. The first defendant was desperate for a foreman and took on the first plaintiff without a reference.

The terms of the employment are recorded in a document dated October 15, 1969, which reads as follows:

[45a] D.O.E. circular 3/89, para. 27.

"Terms of Employment. Hours. Monday to Friday, 8 a.m. to 5.30 p.m. Lunch hour 1 p.m. to 2 p.m. Saturdays, 8 a.m. to 1 p.m. Wages. £25 per week, overtime above the hours stated 12/6 per hour. Bungalow. Rent free, whilst employed. Holidays. Two weeks' paid holiday a year wth the normal bank holidays. Notice. Two weeks' notice to be served either way."

In the meantime, the first plaintiff had commenced his duties and had moved himself and his wife and his family and his furniture into the bungalow. Shortly before November 19, the first defendant gave the first plaintiff oral notice to terminate employment on Friday, December 5. On November 19, the defendant company gave the first plaintiff a written notice, which, for the purposes of this motion, I must take to have been in these terms:

"Dear Sir, With reference to our conversation of last week wherein it was promised that you would get notice to quit we herein give you this notice. After a month's trial we have decided that you are unsatisfactory. As per our agreement you have two weeks' notice to date from November 21, 1969. We also remind you that the bungalow is to be vacant on December 5, 1969."

December 5, the day on which the notice expired, was a Friday. On that day, the first plaintiff and his family left the bungalow and remained away until the following Monday evening. The first defendant asserts that he had grounds, which he specifies, for thinking that the plaintiff had left permanently. But his goods and furniture were still there.

At some time prior to the evening of Monday, December 8, the first defendant changed the locks on the bungalow and moved some of the plaintiffs' furniture into the garage. When, on December 8, in the evening, the first plaintiff returned to the bungalow, he could not get in. He asks for an injunction designed to secure access to the bungalow.

The first plaintiff puts forward three grounds upon which he claims such an injunction. First, he urges that he became, and is, a statutory tenant of the bungalow and that, therefore, no valid notice to quit has been served. Given the premise, no doubt the conclusion follows. The plaintiff has not, however, in my judgment, made out a prima facie case that his occupation was occupation as a tenant. The fact that no rent was specified to be payable, that the landlord could not, without breaking his covenant in the lease under which he held the bungalow, sub-let the bungalow, and the fact that the employment was liable to be determined on two weeks' notice, suggests though it may turn out otherwise at the trial, that the occupation was under a licence rather than as a tenant. ...

However, the first plaintiff was deemed to be a tenant for the purposes of the legislation.

The defendants invite me to find, for the purposes of this motion, that before the lock on the bungalow was changed the first plaintiff had ceased to reside in the premises, so that subsection (1)(b) is not satisfied. But the first plaintiff was unquestionably resident at the bungalow on December 5. He did not remove his furniture, and on the facts at present before the court, again it may turn out otherwise at the trial, I can only find that the first plaintiff has made out a prima facie case of residence at the time of his exclusion. The fact that the lock was changed suggests that the landlord did not think that residence had ceased.

Upon the facts before me, I, therefore, find that, in locking the first plaintiff out, the defendants were in breach of section [3](1) of the [Protection from Eviction Act 1977]. Ought I, then, to grant the injunction sought? The defendants, pointing to the fact that section [3] does not confer any rights on the first plaintiff—not even a right to remain in occupation—urges that an injunction ought not to be granted. Much reliance was placed by the first plaintiff upon the recent decision of the Court of Appeal in *Luganda* v. *Service Hotels Ltd.* [1969] 2 Ch. 209. The plaintiff in that case, who was, as the court held, entitled to six months' security of tenure under the Act, was locked out of his residence by the landlord an obtained an injunction against the landlord to give him access. But, as Mr. Ferris pointed out, the distinction between that case and this is that in that case the statute conferred a right to six months' security of tenure,[46] whereas there is nothing like that conferred by section [3]. And, indeed, Edmund Davies L.J., in holding the plaintiff entitled to the injunction which he sought, pointed to this right to remain in the premises for six months and distinguished the case from *Thompson* v. *Park* [1944] K.B. 408, where the Court of Appeal held that where a licence to use certain premises had been wrongfully revoked the licensee could be restrained from entering on or using the premises and must content himself with a claim for damages for breach of contract. In *Thompson* v. *Park*, the expelled party, having no interest in the land, was, after revocation of the licence, a trespasser, whereas in the *Luganda* case he was not: so tested, the present case falls within *Thompson* v. *Park* and outside *Luganda* v. *Service Hotels Ltd.* But I distinguish *Thompson* v. *Park* from the present case upon another ground. There, what the owner of the land was assumed to have done was to have broken the terms of the licence under which the defendant claimed to use it—a mere breach of contract—whereas here, what the owners have done is to have infringed the terms of a statute and so committed a tort. For although section [3] conferred upon the first plaintiff no proprietary interest in the bungalow, the breach of its terms by the defendants was, in my judgment, a tort. The first plaintiff was clearly one of the class of persons the section was intended to protect, the injury—the evidence is that the first plaintiff is homeless—is of the kind the section is intended to prevent, and it is the breach of the statutory duty which is causing the damage to the first plaintiff.

However much sympathy I may feel for a defendant who has taken on a servant whom he finds unsatisfactory and cannot really recover the accommodation required for another employee who is to replace him, I feel bound to grant the injunction sought. The intention of Parliament that possession of premises occupied by a person in the position of the first plaintiff may not be obtained except by proceedings in the court is clear from section [3]. The first plaintiff is entitled to the benefit of the section. If the court were to refuse the injunction leaving the first plaintiff to a remedy in damages for the tort, it would be allowing just the mischief the section was designed to prevent. If the matter had come before the court on a threat by the defendants to lock out the first plaintiff, I entertain no doubt that an injunction would have been granted. And to quote Lord Denning M.R. in the *Luganda* case [1969] 2 Ch. 209, 220: "They should not be in a better position by wrongfully locking him out."

It has already been noted that in *McCall* v. *Abelesz*[47] it was held that civil liability could not be founded on breach of section 1 of the 1977 Act. However, sections 27 and 28 of the Housing Act 1988 have brought about an important change in the law by providing that in certain circumstances civil liability may be based on the commission of acts which would constitute an offence under section 1 of the Protection from Eviction Act 1977. It should be noted that civil liability under

---

[46] This right to protection from the rent tribunal has since been abolished.
[47] [1976] Q.B. 585.

section 27(3) does not depend on a conviction having been obtained, although if criminal liability has been established, the conviction can be used as evidence in subsequent civil proceedings.[48]

27.—(1) This section applies if, at any time after 9th June 1988, a landlord (in this section referred to as "the landlord in default") or any person acting on behalf of the landlord in default unlawfully deprives the residential occupier of any premises of his occupation of the whole or part of the premises.

(2) This section also applies if, at any time after 9th June 1988, a landlord (in this section referred to as "the landlord in default") or any person acting on behalf of the landlord in default—

(a)   attempts unlawfully to deprive the residential occupier of any premises of his occupation of the whole or part of the premises, or

(b)   knowing or having reasonable cause to believe that the conduct is likely to cause the residential occupier of any premises—

(i)   to give up his occupation of the premises or any part thereof, or

(ii)   to refrain from exercising any right or pursuing any remedy in respect of the premises or any part thereof,

does acts likely to interfere with the peace or comfort of the residential occupier or members of his household, or persistently withdraws or withholds services reasonably required for the occupation of the premises as a residence,

and, as a result, the residential occupier gives up his occupation of the premises as a residence.

(3) Subject to the following provisions of this section, where this section applies, the landlord in default shall, by virtue of this section, be liable to pay to the former residential occupier, in respect of his loss of the right to occupy the premises in question as his residence, damages assessed on the basis set out in section 28 below.

(4) Any liability arising by virtue of subsection (3) above—

(a)   shall be in the nature of a liability in tort; and

(b)   subject to subsection (5) below, shall be in addition to any liability arising apart from this section (whether in tort, contract or otherwise).

(5) Nothing in this section affects the right of a residential occupier to enforce any liability which arises apart from this section in respect of his loss of the right to occupy premises as his residence; but damages shall not be awarded both in respect of such a liability and in respect of a liability arising by virtue of this section on account of the same loss.

(6) No liability shall arise by virtue of subsection (3) above if—

(a)   before the date on which proceedings to enforce the liability are finally disposed of, the former residential occupier is reinstated in the premises

---

[48] Civil Evidence Act 1968, s.11.

in question in such circumstances that he becomes again the residential occupier of them; or

(b) at the request of the former residential occupier, a court makes an order (whether in the nature of an injunction or otherwise) as a result of which he is reinstated as mentioned in paragraph (a) above;

and, for the purposes of paragraph (a) above, proceedings to enforce a liability are finally disposed of on the earliest date by which the proceedings (including any proceedings on or in consequence of an appeal) have been determined and any time for appealing or further appealing has expired, except that if any appeal is abandoned, the proceedings shall be taken to be disposed of on the date of the abandonment.

(7) If, in proceedings to enforce a liability, arising by virtue of subsection (3) above, it appears to the court—

(a) that, prior to the event which gave rise to the liability, the conduct of the former residential occupier or any person living with him in the premises concerned was such that it is reasonable to mitigate the damages for which the landlord in default would otherwise be liable, or

(b) that, before the proceedings were begun, the landlord in default offered to reinstate the former residential occupier in the premises in question and either it was unreasonable of the former residential occupier to refuse that offer or, if he had obtained alternative accommodation before the offer was made, it would have been unreasonable of him to refuse that offer if he had not obtained that accommodation,

the court may reduce the amount of damages which would otherwise be payable to such amount as it thinks appropriate.

(8) In proceedings to enforce a liability arising by virtue of subsection (3) above, it shall be a defence for the defendant to prove that he believed, and had reasonable cause to believe—

(a) that the residential occupier had ceased to reside in the premises in question at the time when he was deprived of occupation as mentioned in subsection (1) above or, as the case may be, when the attempt was made or the acts were done as a result of which he gave up his occupation of those premises; or

(b) that, where the liability would otherwise arise by virtue only of the doing of acts or the withdrawal or withholding of services, he had reasonable grounds for doing the acts or withdrawing or withholding the services in question.

28.—(1) The basis for the assessment of damages referred to in section 27(3) above, is the difference in value, determined as at the time immediately before the residential occupier ceased to occupy the premises in question as his residence, between—

(a) the value of the interest of the landlord in default determined on the assumption that the residential occupier continues to have the same right to occupy the premises as before that time; and

(b)   the value of that interest determined on the assumption that the residential occupier has ceased to have that right.

(2) In relation to any premises, any reference in this section to the interest of the landlord in default is a reference to his interest in the building in which the premises in question are comprised (whether or not that building contains any other premises) together with its curtilage.

(3) For the purposes of the valuations referred to in subsection (1) above, it shall be assumed—

(a)   that the landlord in default is selling his interest on the open market to a willing buyer;

(b)   that neither the residential occupier nor any member of his family wishes to buy; and

(c)   that it is unlawful to carry out any substantial development of any of the land in which the landlord's interest subsists or to demolish the whole or part of any building on that land.

Notes

(i)   Liability under section 27(3) can be based on acts after June 9, 1988, although the commencement date for these provisions was January 15, 1989.

(ii)   There is no liability unless the tenant has given up occupation. Similarly, if the former occupier is reinstated no liability under section 27 arises.[49] Therefore, in cases of harassment which do not lead to eviction the occupier will have to rely on the general civil law.

(iii)   Section 27 applies to acts committed by the landlord or any person acting on behalf of the landlord.[50] In contrast, the criminal offences established by section 1(2) and (3) of the Protection from Eviction Act 1977 may be committed by "anyone"; the offence established by section 1(3A) applies to "the landlord. ... or an agent of the landlord."[51]

(iv)   The basic principle in computing damages under section 28 is that the former occupier is entitled to the difference between the value of the premises with the occupier in occupation, and the value of those premises on the assumption that the occupier no longer has a right of occupation.[52]

Where the former occupier was a tenant with full security of tenure either under the Rent Act 1977 or the Housing Act 1988 damages under section 27 should be substantial. In *Murray* v. *Lloyd*[53] an action for damages was brought against a solicitor who had negligently caused the plaintiff to lose his statutory tenancy. The premises with vacant

---

[49] s.27(6).
[50] s.27(2).
[51] See p. 263.
[52] s.28(1).
[53] [1989] 1 W.L.R. 1060.

possession were valued at £460,000, and the reduction in value of the premises as a result of a statutory tenancy was reckoned to be 25 per cent. The court awarded the plaintiff damages of £115,000.

However, if the occupation of the former occupier was in any event precarious (which will be the case where the former occupier was a licensee or an assured shorthold tenant) damages will be much lower.

It should also be noted that damages may be reduced if either the plaintiff unreasonably refuses to accept the landlord's offer to reinstate him in the premises,[54] or more generally if the plaintiff has acted unreasonably prior to the unlawful eviction.[55]

(2) Breach of the Landlord's Covenant for Quiet Enjoyment

A landlord is under an obligation not to disturb the tenant's possession either legally or physically. If the tenancy does not contain an express covenant, the law will imply a covenant for quiet enjoyment, which imposes on the landlord an obligation to allow the tenant to use the premises peacefully and to exercise all his rights as a tenant.

The landlord will be in breach of this obligation if he does acts which physically interfere with the tenant's use and occupation of the premises: for example, if he threatens the tenant with physical violence[56]; if he removes the tenant's belongings from the premises while the tenant is out and changes the locks[57]; if he cuts off the services (gas, water, electricity) to the premises occupied by the tenant[58]; if he removes the doors and windows of the premises[59]; if he erects scaffolding in such a way that the tenant's access is obstructed.[60]

Where an occupier is a licensee there can be no implied covenant of quiet enjoyment (covenants being a characteristic of a lease and not a licence). However, the courts may imply terms into a contractual licence if the contract is silent on certain important questions. For example, where the licensor acts in such a way that the licensee is effectively prevented from using the premises as envisaged when the parties entered into the licence agreement the licensee should be able to establish that the licensor is in breach of his implied contractual obligations.[61]

(3) Liability in Tort

In addition to contractual liability, a landlord may be liable under general tort principles (in addition to liability for breach of statutory

---

[54] s.27(7)(b).
[55] s.27(7)(a).
[56] *McMillan* v. *Singh* (1985) 17 H.L.R. 120.
[57] *Drane* v. *Evangelou* [1978] 1 W.L.R. 455.
[58] *Perera* v. *Vandivar* [1953] 1 W.L.R. 672.
[59] *Lavender* v. *Betts* [1942] 2 All E.R. 72.
[60] *Owen* v. *Gadd* [1956] 2 Q.B. 99.
[61] *Smith* v. *Nottinghamshire C.C.*, *The Times*, November 13, 1981.

duty). Where premises are occupied by a tenant (but not a licensee) a person who enters the premises without authority under the lease or without the permission of the tenant commits the tort of trespass to land; a tort is also committed by anyone who threatens or perpetrates physical violence against the occupier (trespass to the person), or who intentionally damages the occupier's property (trespass to goods); a person may also be liable to an occupier for the tort of nuisance if he performs acts which interfere with the occupier's reasonable enjoyment of the land (many acts of harassment—such as cutting off services, or playing loud music late at night—will amount to the tort of nuisance).

(4) Remedies

In many cases an injunction will be the most significant remedy available to the occupier. The court may grant an injunction requiring the landlord to allow the tenant back into occupation (an order in this form will prevent the tenant from recovering damages under the Housing Act 1988).[62] In cases of harassment an injunction can be made ordering the landlord to stop further harassment.

Although an injunction is a civil remedy, the dividing line between civil and criminal proceedings may become rather blurred. A person who fails to comply with the terms of an injunction commits a contempt of court, and in *Jennison* v. *Baker*[63]—a case where a landlady flagrantly broke an injunction not to commit a breach of her implied covenant of quiet enjoyment—the Court of Appeal confirmed that county court judges have the power to commit to prison for contempt of court.

A further example of the intermingling of civil and criminal issues arises in the context of damages. Of course, the plaintiff may recover quantifiable out-of-pocket expenses by way of special damages. So, if as a result of unlawful eviction a tenant is forced to stay in a hotel for a short period pending reinstatement, these costs (if reasonable) can be recovered. As noted above, if the occupier is permanently evicted then damages under the Housing Act 1988 may be available. Under the head of general damages the occupier may recover for more intangible losses, such as distress, pain and suffering and inconvenience. In addition, exemplary damages may be available in serious cases of unlawful eviction, but only in relation to actions in tort.

Drane v. *Evangelou* [1978] 1 W.L.R. 455

Lord Denning M.R. said (at 457–459):

Mr. George Evangelou, the defendant, is the owner of a leasehold house 172a, Bowes Road, New Southgate, London. He let a maisonette in it to a

---

[62] s.27(6)(b).
[63] [1972] 2 Q.B. 52.

young man, Mr. Anthony Malcolm Drane, the plaintiff, who lived there with a woman, Ann Watts—not his wife—but who lived with him as if she was his wife. The maisonette was let to them furnished at a rent of £25 a week inclusive of rates from August 31, 1974.

On July 11, 1975, the tenant, Mr. Drane, applied to the rent officer for a revision of the rent. This annoyed the landlord, Mr. Evangelou, greatly. So on July 21, 1975, the landlord gave Mr. Drane notice to quit. That was not effective because the tenant was protected by statute from eviction. On October 8, 1975, the rent officer fixed the rent and adjudged it be £16 a week inclusive. Note the date—October 8, 1975.

Six days later on October 14, 1975, the landlord behaved atrociously. He waited until the young couple were out—when Mr. Drane had taken Ann Watts to college in the morning—and then got three men to invade the maisonette. The judge described what Mr. Drane found on his return:

"When he came back a little later, I think at 9.30, there he found that a large Greek Cypriot was barring the entrance: all his belongings had been put outside in the back yard; the lock had been hammered in of the door; the door was bolted on the inside, about four to five people were inside his premises and two women among them ... some of their belongings were broken and books were damaged."

Mr. Drane called the police. They told Mrs. Evangelou—that is the landlord's wife—that she was committing an offence and that it would be reported to the Town Hall. Nevertheless she did not let the tenants back into their maisonette. They had to go and stay with friends. They stored some of their belongings in their friend's garage, and slept on the living room floor of their friend's house.

Mr. Drane went to the county court and asked for an injunction so that he and Ann Watts could be restored to their premises. The judge on October 31, 1975, granted an injunction against the landlord. But the landlord did not obey it. He had moved his wife's father and mother into the maisonette. The landlord or his in-laws appealed to this court. This court heard the appeal and rejected it: see *Drane* v. *Evangelou*, November 27, 1975, Court of Appeal (Civil Division) Transcript No. 508 of 1975, Lawton L.J., giving the judgment of the court, said:

"I am surprised that this appeal has been made to this court. The defendant's behaviour was reprehensible ... it is right and just that the plaintiff should be put back where he is entitled to be ... this court should take every step it can to see that landlords who behave like the defendant in this case has behaved should get no benefit whatsoever from what they have done."

So the appeal was dismissed on November 27, 1975. Still the landlord did not go out. Mr. Drane had to apply again for an injunction to the county court on December 19, 1975. The landlord and his in-laws were ordered to leave by 6 p.m. on Sunday, December 21. They gave Mr. Drane a key, but it did not fit. So he could not get in. On December 23 Mr. Drane applied to commit them for contempt. That at least brought results. The in-laws left. It was only then, on December 23, that the in-laws and the defendant went out. The plaintiff had been kept out for ten weeks. Mr. Drane eventually moved in on January 1. He found everything dirty and damaged: and went on with his action for damages. He was awarded exemplary damages in the sum of £1,000.

Now there is an appeal to this court. ...

Mr. Cousins, for the defendant, submitted that it was not open to the judge to award exemplary damages. He has taken us through Lord Devlin's judgment in *Rookes* v. *Barnard* [1964] A.C. 1129, referring us especially to the passages from 1226–1230. He said that the general principle nowadays is that in a civil action damages are awarded by way of compensation for damage actually done or for any aggravation by way of injured feelings of the plaintiff; but the court cannot in the ordinary way award punitive damages over and above that which is compensation: because punishment is the prerogative of the criminal courts and should have no place in the civil courts.

That exclusion of exemplary damages has not found favour in the other common law countries, such as Canada, Australia, New Zealand and the United States of America. But since *Broome* v. *Cassell & Co. Ltd.* [1972] A.C. 1027 it must be accepted in England. Lord Devlin in *Rookes* v. *Barnard* [1964] A.C. 1129, 1226, acknowledged that there are some categories of tort in which exemplary damages may still be awarded. This case seems to me to come within the second category. Lord Devlin said, at p. 1227:

> "This category is not confined to moneymaking in the strict sense. It extends to cases in which the defendant is seeking to gain at the expense of the plaintiff some object—perhaps some property which he covets—which either he could not obtain at all or not obtain except at a price greater than he wants to put down. Exemplary damages can properly be awarded whenever it is necessary to teach a wrongdoer that tort does not pay."

To my mind this category includes cases of unlawful eviction of a tenant. The landlord seeks to gain possession at the expense of the tenant—so as to keep or get a rent higher than that awarded by the rent tribunal—or to get possession from a tenant who is protected by the Rent Acts. So he resorts to harassing tactics. Such conduct can be punished now by the criminal law. But it can also be punished by the civil law by an award of exemplary damages. In the recent case of *McCall* v. *Abelesz* [1976] Q.B. 585 it was held that the provisions of the Rent Act 1965 against harassment only created a criminal offence: but I said, at p. 594:

> "I see no need to give any new civil remedy for harassment. As I understand it, the law already gives a perfectly good civil action for damages."

So in a case of this kind damages can be awarded not only by way of compensation but also by way of exemplary damages.

Generally speaking, damages for unlawful eviction have been relatively low (although there are signs that county courts are increasingly making awards in excess of £1,000[64]) and it is against this background that the new head of liability in the Housing Act 1988 was introduced. However, as a result of the limitations which are imposed on the cause of action under section 27 of the Housing Act 1988 (in particular, that liability depends on the occupier having been evicted and not reinstated) the general civil law principles will continue to play an important role in cases of harassment and eviction.

---

[64] For a series of examples indicating the level of damages awarded in eviction and harassment cases see Sylvester & Hunter (eds.), *Arden & Partington on Quiet Enjoyment* (3rd ed., 1990) pp. 31–44. A case decided by Birmingham County Court on July 6, 1989 (*Nawaz* v. *Shafak*) which is cited at page 43 provides a modern illustration of the courts' approach: "P returned home from visiting his pregnant wife in hospital to find all his belongings in the street and the landlord, D, with various members of his family outside. P was too frightened to seek an injunction and spent six months in a hostel with his wife, new-born child and two other sons; he was awarded £4,000 exemplary damages, general damages for distress and inconvenience of £850 and special damages (cost of removal) of £150."

VIII FURTHER READING

Schemes of protection

All the main textbooks on the law of landlord and tenant include sections discussing security of tenure under the various statutory schemes. In addition to the works cited below, the guides to the Housing Act 1988 listed on pages 184–185 contain chapters dealing with security of tenure as it applies to assured tenancies:

J. E. Martin, *Residential Security* (1989, Sweet & Maxwell), Chapter 7 (regulated tenancies), Chapter 14 (assured tenancies); A. Arden, *Manual of Housing Law* (4th ed., 1989, Sweet & Maxwell) paras. 3.37–3.68 (Rent Act tenancies), paras. 4.19–4.35 (secure tenancies), paras. 5.25–5.40 (assured tenancies), paras. 8.01–8.57 (quiet enjoyment), D.C. Hoath, *Public Housing Law* (1989, Sweet & Maxwell) Chapters 7 and 8 (secure tenancies).

For a discussion of some of the implications of security of tenure see C. Hand, The statutory tenancy: an unrecognised proprietary interest? [1980] Conv. 351; J. Hill, Security of tenure: competing interests [1987] J.S.W.L. 77.

There is an interesting comparative analysis of security of tenure regimes in England, France and Germany in T. Honoré, *The Quest for Security: Employees, Tenants, Wives* (1982, Stevens). The author summarises his thesis in the following terms: "A policy which can loosely be described as aiming at security of tenure can have one of three objectives: it can try to protect those who are at risk during a housing shortage until such time as the market again operates normally. It can aim to protect the economically weak. Lastly it can try to provide those who cannot afford to buy their own homes with a substitute for home ownership. ... [W]hile French law has so far aimed mainly at satisfying the first interest, German law has sought a compromise; and in England the third interest has come to predominate."[65]

Unlawful eviction, harassment and quiet enjoyment

For a comprehensive, but relatively brief guide to both the criminal and civil law aspects see S. Carrott & C. Hunter (eds.), *Arden and Partington on Quiet Enjoyment* (3rd ed., 1990, L.A.G.). See also A. Arden, *Manual of Housing Law* (4th ed., 1989, Sweet & Maxwell), paras. 8.01–8.57; J. E. Martin, *Residential Security* (1989, Sweet & Maxwell), Chapter 3.

For a general review of the criminal law in this area see A. Ashworth, Protecting the home through the criminal law [1978–79] J.S.W.L. 76. More specific aspects are taken up by J. Hill, Section 1 of the Protection

[65] p. 37.

from Eviction Act 1977: the meaning of "occupation" [1987] Conv. 265; M. Wasik, The intention to harass [1981] Conv. 377.

A detailed study of the impact of the criminal law has been conducted by D. Nelken, *The Limits of the Legal Process: A Study of Landlords, Law and Crime* (1983, Academic Press). In the words of the author: "This study of the criminal behaviour of private landlords deals with the practices which were turned into crimes by the 1965 Rent Act as a result of the Rachman scandal. It describes the kinds of landlord who are typically prosecuted for the offences of harassment and illegal eviction of those occupying privately rented accommodation, discusses the way the legislative provisions came to be enacted and examines the manner in which the law is enforced. In addition, however, it also discusses the practices of other landlords whose conduct remains immune from criminal sanctions and discusses why such immunity is retained despite recurrent moral panics concerning their behaviour."[66]

It appears that there has been an increase in harassment and illegal eviction since the introduction of the Housing Act 1988. See L. Burrows & N. Hunter, *Forced Out!* (1990, Shelter).

Casenotes

Finally, there are a few short notes discussing cases referred to in this chapter: R. G. Lee, [1980] Conv. 443 (*Siddiqui* v. *Rashid*); T. J. Lyons, "Adjoining occupiers" under the Rent Acts [1985] Conv. 168 (*Cobstone Investments* v. *Maxim*); P. F. Smith [1983] Conv. 320 (*Hill* v. *Rochard*); D. Morgan, (1979) 41 Conv. 223 (*Drane* v. *Evangelou*).

---

[66] p. vii.

CHAPTER 5

SECURITY OF TENURE II: PROBLEMS ARISING FROM ASSIGNMENT AND SUB-LETTING, SUCCESSION, RELATIONSHIP BREAKDOWN, AND MORTGAGE OR SALE OF THE REVERSION

The previous chapter contains an outline of security of tenure provisions as they apply to a tenant who is in a direct contractual relationship with the landlord. In this chapter we consider a number of more specific issues which have implications for security of tenure. All the problems which are discussed in this chapter arise from the involvement of third parties.

I ASSIGNMENT AND SUB-LETTING

The distinction between assignment and sub-letting has already been noted.[1] To be legal (as opposed to equitable) an assignment of a tenancy must be by deed[2] even where the original tenancy was created orally. If the assignment is not effected by deed, it may be enforced on the equitable principles which apply in relation to informal leases.[3]

(A) LAWFUL AND UNLAWFUL ASSIGNMENT AND SUB-LETTING AT COMMON LAW

(1) The Terms of the Tenancy

The extent to which a common law tenant may lawfully assign or sub-let depends upon the terms of the tenancy. There are three possibilities:

(i) If the tenancy agreement makes no mention of the issue, the tenant has an unrestricted right to assign or sub-let. *A fortiori* the tenant will have such a right where there is no written tenancy agreement.

---

[1] See pp. 25–26.
[2] Law of Property Act 1925, s.52.
[3] See pp. 93–95.

However, it will be seen that in relation to regulated, secure and assured tenancies the common law position has been significantly modified by statute.

(ii) It is common for a lease to contain a "qualified" covenant imposing restrictions on the right to assign or sub-let. If a tenancy contains a qualified covenant it is unlawful for the tenant to assign or sub-let without the landlord's consent. It is provided, however, by section 19(1) of the Landlord and Tenant Act 1927 that any qualified covenant against assignment or sub-letting is subject to the proviso that "consent is not to be unreasonably withheld." The precise meaning of this phrase has been the subject of considerable litigation.

In *International Drilling Fluids Ltd.* v. *Louisville Investments (Uxbridge) Ltd.*,[4] the Court of Appeal reviewed many of the earlier cases. Balcombe L.J. said:

From the authorities I deduce the following propositions of law.

(1) The purpose of a covenant against assignment without the consent of the landlord, such consent not to be unreasonably withheld, is to protect the lessor from having his premises used or occupied in an undesirable way, or by an undesirable tenant or assignee: *per* A. L. Smith L.J. in *Bates* v. *Donaldson* [1896] 2 Q.B. 241, 247, approved by all the members of the Court of Appeal in *Houlder Brothers & Co. Ltd.* v. *Gibbs* [1925] Ch. 575.

(2) As a corollary to the first proposition, a landlord is not entitled to refuse his consent to an assignment on grounds which have nothing whatever to do with the relationship of the landlord and tenant in regard to the subject matter of the lease: see *Houlder Brothers & Co. Ltd.* v. *Gibbs*, a decision which (despite some criticism) is binding on this court: *Bickel* v. *Duke of Westminster* [1977] Q.B. 517. A recent example of a case where the landlord's consent was unreasonably withheld because the refusal was designed to achieve a collateral purpose unconnected with the terms of the lease is *Bromley Park Garden Estates Ltd.* v. *Moss* [1982] 1 W.L.R. 1019.

(3) The onus of proving that consent has been unreasonably withheld is on the tenant: see *Shanly* v. *Ward* (1913) 29 T.L.R. 714 and *Pimms Ltd.* v. *Tallow Chandlers Company* [1964] 2 Q.B. 547, 564.

(4) It is not necessary for the landlord to prove that the conclusions which led him to refuse consent were justified, if they were conclusions which might be reached by a reasonable man in the circumstances: *Pimms Ltd.* v. *Tallow Chandlers Company* [1964] 2 Q.B. 547, 564.

(5) It may be reasonable for the landlord to refuse his consent to an assignment on the ground of the purpose for which the proposed assignee intends to use the premises, even though that purpose is not forbidden by the lease: see *Bates* v. *Donaldson* [1896] 2 Q.B. 241, 244.

(6) There is a divergence of authority on the question, in considering whether the landlord's refusal of consent is reasonable, whether it is permissible to have regard to the consequences to the tenant if consent to the proposed assignment is withheld. In an early case at first instance, *Sheppard* v. *Hongkong and*

Shanghai Banking Corporation (1872) 20 W.R. 459, 460, Malins V.-C. said that by withholding their consent the lessors threw a very heavy burden on the lessees and they therefore ought to show good grounds for refusing it. In *Houlder Brothers & Co. Ltd* v. *Gibbs* [1925] Ch. 575, 584, Warrington L.J. said:

> "An act must be regarded as reasonable or unreasonable in reference to the circumstances under which it is committed, and when the question arises on the construction of a contract the outstanding circumstances to be considered are the nature of the contract to be construed, and the relations between the parties resulting from it."

In a recent decision of this court, *Leeward Securities Ltd.* v. *Lilyheath Properties Ltd.* (1983) 271 E.G. 279 concerning a sub-letting which would attract the protection of the Rent Act, both Oliver L.J. and O'Connor L.J. made it clear in their judgments that they could envisage circumstances in which it might be unreasonable to refuse consent to an underletting, if the result would be that there was no way in which the tenant (the sub-landlord) could reasonably exploit the premises except by creating a tenancy to which the Rent Act protection would apply, and which inevitably would affect the value of the landlord's reversion. O'Connor L.J. said, at p. 283:

> "It must not be thought that, because the introduction of a Rent Act tenant inevitably has an adverse effect upon the value of the reversion, that that is a sufficient ground for the landlords to say that they can withhold consent and that the court will hold that that is reasonable."

To the opposite effect are the dicta, obiter but nevertheless weighty, of Viscount Dunedin and Lord Phillimore in *Viscount Tredegar* v. *Harwood* [1929] A.C. 72, 78, 82. There are numerous other dicta to the effect that a landlord need consider only his own interests: see, *e.g.*, *West Layton Ltd.* v. *Ford* [1979] Q.B. 593, 605, and *Bromley Park Garden Estates Ltd.* v. *Moss* [1982] 1 W.L.R. 1019, 1027. Those dicta must be qualified, since a landlord's interests, collateral to the purposes of the lease, are in any event ineligible for consideration: see proposition (2) above. But in my judgment a proper reconciliation of those two streams of authority can be achieved by saying that while a landlord need usually only consider his own relevant interests, there may be cases where there is such a disproportion between the benefit to the landlord and the detriment to the tenant if the landlord withholds his consent to an assignment that it is unreasonable for the landlord to refuse consent.

(7) Subject to the propositions set out above, it is in each case a question of fact, depending upon all the circumstances, whether the landlord's consent to an assignment is being unreasonably withheld: see *Bickel* v. *Duke of Westminster* [1977] Q.B. 517, 524, and *West Layton Ltd.* v. *Ford* [1979] Q.B. 593, 604, 606–607.[5]

It is normally regarded as reasonable for a landlord to refuse consent to assignment or sub-letting where a tenant who does not have statutory protection proposes to assign or sub-let to someone who would acquire such protection.[6] This is not, however, an immutable rule.

Deverall v. *Wyndham*[7] concerned a tenancy of premises which were converted into three dwelling units. The lease clearly contemplated

---

[5] At 519–521.
[6] *Bickel* v. *Duke of Westminster* [1977] Q.B. 517; *West Layton Ltd.* v. *Ford* [1979] Q.B. 593.
[7] (1989) 58 P. & C.R. 12.

multiple occupation of the premises. The tenant, who was not a protected tenant under the Rent Acts, proposed to sub-let parts of the premises. The landlord refused to give consent to the sub-letting on the ground that there was a risk that the sub-tenants would become statutory tenants at the end of the term.

Paul Baker Q.C. (sitting as a deputy judge in the High Court) said:

As I have said at the outset, the landlord's case is a very simple and persuasive one. It is the loss to the landlord of £600,000 in the premium that they can expect to get if they are left with statutory tenants at the end of the lease. And it is said, having regard to that both as a figure in itself and as a proportion of the premium which can be obtained (which was about a third of the whole premium), it cannot be said to be unreasonable in withholding consent in order to preserve that valuable right to them.

On the other side it is said, first of all, that there is not a certain loss here. It is not like a case where the losses are inevitable. Indeed, as I would find having listened to the evidence, the probability is that if and when the plaintiff goes the others will go with him, having regard to their close ties: one is the son of the plaintiff and his wife, the others are their very old friends who have decided to make their homes together.

Secondly, the mere fact of loss from being saddled at the end of the lease with statutory tenants is not enough of itself to justify refusal. Otherwise, of course, a landlord could always resist underletting where there was a likelihood or a certainty of statutory tenants at the end of the lease.

Thirdly (and this I regard as of considerable importance), the lease expressly contemplated and required multiple occupation of this house. Thus, as it seems to me, to refuse consent is to deprive the tenant of an important part of the benefit of the lease; not only the loss of income from the property which he can legitimately expect to get from his lease, but also the companionship of the underlessees.

Then I observe that a statutory tenant is not irremovable; that the defendants have a substantial estate and so possibly the provision of alternative accommodation may be easier for them than for others.

Fourthly, this is not a case where the statutes or other outside circumstances have moved against the landlord giving rise to unexpected burdens such as the Leasehold Reform Act. All the changes that have taken place since the lease was granted have been in the landlords' favour or have been under their control. For example, when the lease was granted underlettings which were unfurnished would immediately attract protection; now the proposed underleases are initially unprotected.

What has changed is the property boom which gives an enhanced value. Of course I agree one must look at the circumstances now, but it is not a case where the landlords' interest has been depreciated from what they originally expected. That was so in the case of the butcher's shop, for example. But the situation here is that the landlords may not be able fully to take advantage of the property boom.

Lastly I notice that the landlords have changed their policy. The tenant is simply seeking to follow the original policy on which the lease was granted, and he does not require the whole house for his own occupation.

It seems to me those arguments outweigh the very persuasive arguments of the landlords. ...[8]

---

[8] At 23–24.

By statute it is provided that it is unlawful for a landlord or any other person to discriminate against a person on grounds of race or sex by withholding the relevant consent to assign or sub-let.[9]

In *Greene* v. *Church Commissioners*[10] the lease of a flat contained a qualified covenant against assignment subject to a proviso that the tenant "shall first by notice in writing to the lessor ... offer to surrender [the premises] ... without consideration." Lord Denning M.R. suggested, *obiter*, that such a clause might be void as being contrary to section 19. However, in *Adler* v. *Upper Grosvenor Street Investment Ltd.*[11] Hilbery J. had upheld such a proviso, and in the more recent case of *Bocardo SA* v. *S & M Hotels Ltd.*[12] the Court of Appeal held that a proviso requiring the tenant to offer to surrender the lease before seeking the landlord's consent to assignment or sub-lettng is valid, and effectively enables the landlord to avoid the impact of section 19.

The operation of section 19 has been criticised. It was proposed by the Law Commission that "a landlord should be under a duty not to withhold his consent unreasonably and to inform the tenant of his decision within a reasonable time."[13] The Law Commission's report led to the Landlord and Tenant Act 1988[13a]:

1.—(1) This section applies in any case where—

    (a) a tenancy includes a covenant on the part of the tenant not to enter into one or more of the following transactions, that is—

        (i)   assigning,

        (ii) underletting,

        (iii) charging, or

        (iv) parting with the possession of,

        the premises comprised in the tenancy or any part of the premises without the consent of the landlord or some other person, but

    (b) the covenant is subject to the qualification that the consent is not to be unreasonably withheld (whether or not it is also subject to any other qualification).

(2) In this section and section 2 of this Act—

    (a) references to a proposed transaction are to any assignment, underletting, charging or parting with possession to which the covenant relates, and

---

[9] Race Relations Act 1976, s.24; Sex Discrimination Act 1975. s.31. These provisions do not apply in the case of small premises (defined in, respectively, ss.22(2) and 32(2)). These provisions apply to tenancies created before and after the passing of the Acts.

[10] [1974] Ch. 467.

[11] [1957] 1 W.L.R. 227.

[12] [1980] 1 W.L.R. 17.

[13] *Leasehold Conveyancing* (1985) Law Com. No. 161, para. 1.2.

[13a] These provisions were considered in *Midland Bank plc* v. *Chart Enterprises Inc.* [1990] 44 E.G. 68.

(b) references to the person who may consent to such a transaction are to the person who under the covenant may consent to the tenant entering into the proposed transaction.

(3) Where there is served on the person who may consent to a proposed transaction a written application by the tenant for consent to the transaction, he owes a duty to the tenant within a reasonable time—

(a) to give consent, except in a case where it is reasonable not give consent,

(b) to serve on the tenant written notice of his decision whether or not to give consent specifying in addition—

    (i) if the consent is given subject to conditions, the conditions

    (ii) if the consent is withheld, the reasons for withholding it.

(4) Giving consent subject to any condition that is not a reasonable condition does not satisfy the duty under subsection (3)(a) above.

(5) For the purposes of this Act it is reasonable for a person not to give consent to a proposed transaction only in a case where, if he withheld consent and the tenant completed the transaction, the tenant would be in breach of a covenant.

(6) It is for the person who owed any duty under subsection (3) above—

(a) if he gave consent and the question arises whether he gave it within a reasonable time, to show that he did,

(b) if he gave consent subject to any condition and the question arises whether the condition was a reasonable condition, to show that it was,

(c) if he did not give consent and the question arises whether it was reasonable for him not do so, to show that it was reasonable,

and, if the question arises whether he served notice under that subsection within a reasonable time, to show that he did.

2.—(1) If, in a case where section 1 of this Act applies, any person receives a written application by the tenant for consent to a proposed transaction and that person—

(a) is a person who may consent to the transaction or (though not such a person) is the landlord, and

(b) believes that another person, other than a person who he believes has received the application or a copy of it, is a person who may consent to the transaction,

he owes a duty to the tenant (whether or not he owes him any duty under section 1 of this Act) to take such steps as are reasonable to secure the receipt within a reasonable time by the other person of a copy of the application.

(2) The reference in section 1 (3) of this Act to the service of an application on a person who may consent to a proposed transaction includes a reference to

the receipt by him of an application or a copy of an application (whether it is for his consent or that of another).

3.—(1) This section applies in any case where—

    (a)   a tenancy includes a covenant on the part of the tenant not without the approval of the landlord to consent to the sub-tenant—

        (i)   assigning,
        (ii) under-letting,
        (iii) charging, or
        (iv) parting with the possession of,

        the premises comprised in the sub-tenancy or any part of the premises, but

    (b)   the covenant is subject to the qualification that the approval is not to be unreasonably withheld (whether or not it is also subject to any other qualification).

(2) Where there is served on the landlord a written application by the tenant for approval or a copy of a written application to the tenant by the sub-tenant for consent to a transaction to which the covenant relates the landlord owes a duty to the sub-tenant within a reasonable time—

    (a)   to give approval, except in a case where it is reasonable not to give approval,

    (b)   to serve on the tenant and the sub-tenant written notice of his decision whether or not to give approval specifying in addition—

        (i)   if approval is given subject to conditions, the conditions,
        (ii) if approval is withheld, the reasons for withholding it.

(3) Giving approval subject to any condition that is not a reasonable condition does not satisfy the duty under subsection (2)(a) above.

(4) For the purposes of this section it is reasonable for the landlord not to give approval only in a case where, if he withheld approval and the tenant gave his consent, the tenant would be in breach of covenant.

(5) It is for a landlord who owed any duty under subsection (2) above—

    (a)   if he gave approval and the question arises whether he gave it within a reasonable time, to show that he did,

    (b)   if he gave approval subject to any condition and the question arises whether the condition was a reasonable condition, to show that it was,

    (c)   if he did not give approval and the question arises whether it was reasonable for him not to do so, to show that it was reasonable,

and, if the question arises whether he served notice under that subsection within a reasonable time, to show that he did.

4. A claim that a person has broken any duty under this Act may be made the subject of civil proceedings in like manner as any other claim in tort for breach of statutory duty.

By virtue of section 5(3) the Landlord and Tenant Act 1988 does not apply to secure tenancies, but compare section 94 of the Housing Act 1985.[14]

(iii) A third possibility is that the lease contains an absolute covenant against assignment or sub-letting. In this class of case the tenant may assign or sub-let if the landlord gives his consent either expressly, or impliedly (for example by accepting rent from the assignee[15]). But, where the lease contains an absolute covenant the landlord can legitimately refuse to consent to assignment or sub-letting for any reason.

In 1950 the Uthwatt-Jenkins Committee recommended that absolute covenants should be deemed to be qualified covenants and therefore governed by section 19 of the Landlord and Tenant Act 1927.[16] Although the issue was subsequently examined by the Law Commission,[17] no legislative proposals have been forthcoming.

(2) The Position of Assignees

One consequence of lawful assignment of a tenancy to a new tenant is that the assignee steps into the shoes of the assignor. Therefore, even though the assignee was not party to the original tenancy, the doctrine of privity of estate ensures that those covenants which "touch and concern the land"[18] are directly enforceable by or against the assignee. The assignor remains liable for any breach of covenant by the assignee, but in any assignment for value a covenant of indemnity by the assignee is implied by section 77(1) of the Law of Property Act 1925. Furthermore, where the lease has been assigned more than once the original tenant has a right of indemnity at common law against the assignee in possession.[19]

Where assignment is in breach of covenant the tenancy nevertheless becomes vested in the assignee. However, unless the landlord waives the breach of covenant (for example, by accepting rent from the assignee) the landlord may seek to exercise any right to re-entry contained in the tenancy (thereby bringing the tenancy to an end), and to recover damages from the assignor.

---

[14] See p. 296.
[15] *Hyde* v. *Pimley* [1952] 2 Q.B. 506.
[16] *Committee on Leasehold, Final Report* (Cmnd. 7982) (1950).
[17] Working Paper No. 25 (1970).
[18] See pp. 26–28.
[19] *Moule* v. *Garrett* (1872) L.R. 7 Ex. 101.

(3) The Position of Sub-tenants

In contrast to the principles which apply to cases of assignment, the covenants in the tenancy cannot be directly enforced by the landlord against the sub-tenant for there is no privity of estate.[20]

Since a sub-tenancy must be for a term which is shorter than that of the tenancy, the sub-tenancy should expire some time before the termination of the tenancy. It is possible for problems to arise, however, where the tenancy is brought to an end prematurely.

Where the tenant surrenders his tenancy, the landlord is bound by any sub-tenancy created by the tenant for so long as the tenant would have been bound had the tenancy not been surrendered.[21] It is arguable that this principle applies to any method used by the original lessee to terminate his tenancy (for example, by issuing a notice to quit), so that the sub-tenant effectively becomes the direct tenant of the original landlord (albeit on the terms of the sub-tenancy). Moreover, it seems that this principle applies in cases where the sub-letting has been in breach of covenant. So, if the tenant surrenders his lease to the landlord, the landlord is nevertheless bound by the sub-tenancy.[22]

If a landlord forfeits the tenancy, any sub-tenant (whether lawful or not) may seek relief from forfeiture under section 146(4) of the Law of Property Act 1925. The court's power to grant relief is, however, discretionary and will depend on the circumstances of the case. The court may make an order whereby the sub-tenant becomes the direct tenant of the landlord, although the sub-tenant is in no case "entitled to require a lease to be granted to him for any longer term that he had under his original sub-lease."[23] It should be noted that the court may be prepared to grant relief to a sub-tenant in cases where the sub-letting was in breach of covenant.[24]

(B) ASSIGNEES AND SUB-TENANTS UNDER THE HOUSING ACT 1988

In relation to a fixed-term assured tenancy the common law principles outlined above apply. As regards periodic assured tenancies section 15 of the Housing Act 1988 provides:

(1) Subject to subsection (3) below, it shall be an implied term of every assured tenancy which is a periodic tenancy that except with the consent of the landlord, the tenant shall not—

    (a)   assign the tenancy (in whole or in part); or

---

[20] By virtue of the doctrine of *Tulk* v. *Moxhay* (1834>) 2 My. & K. 517 the landlord may be able to enforce restrictive covenants in the lease directly against a sub-tenant notwithstanding the absence of privity of estate.

[21] *David* v. *Sabin* [1893] 1 Ch. 523. For the problems surrounding the surrender of statutory tenancies and the effect on sub-tenants see pp. 292–295.

[22] *Parker* v. *Jones* [1910] 2 K.B. 32.

[23] Law of Property Act 1925, s.146(4).

[24] *Factors (Sundries) Ltd.* v. *Miller* [1952] 2 All E.R. 630.

(b)   sub-let or part with possession of the whole or any part of the dwelling-house let on the tenancy.

(2) Section 19 of the Landlord and Tenant Act 1927 (consent to assign not be unreasonably withheld etc.) shall not apply to a term which is implied into an assured tenancy by subsection (1) above.

(3) In the case of a periodic tenancy which is not a statutory periodic tenancy or an assured tenancy arising under Schedule 10 to the Local Government and Housing Act 1989 subsection (1) does not apply if—

(a)   there is a provision (whether contained in the tenancy or not) under which the tenant is prohibited (whether absolutely or conditionally) from assigning or sub-letting or parting with possession or is permitted (whether absolutely or conditionally) to assign, sub-let or part with possession; or

(b)   a premium is required to be paid on the grant or renewal of the tenancy.

(4) In subsection (3)(b) above "premium" includes—

(a)   any fine or other like sum;

(b)   any other pecuniary consideration in addition to rent; and

(c)   any sum paid by way of deposit, other than one which does not exceed one-sixth of the annual rent payable under the tenancy immediately after the grant or renewal in question.

It should be stressed that where section 15(1) applies the landlord may refuse consent for any reason, and the Landlord and Tenant Act 1988 is effectively excluded. The landlord is, however, subject to the race relations and sex discrimination legislation.[25]

Where there is assignment or sub-letting by an assured tenant in breach of covenant, the landlord may seek to recover possession under Ground 12.[26] This is, of course a discretionary ground. In cases involving unlawful sub-letting it seems likely that that landlord may rely on Ground 12 as a basis on which to recover possession from both the tenant and the sub-tenant.[27]

As regards lawful sub-letting section 18 of the 1988 Housing Act provides:

(1) If at any time—

(a)   a dwelling-house is for the time being lawfully let on an assured tenancy, and

(b)   the landlord under the assured tenancy is himself a tenant under a superior tenancy; and

(c)   the superior tenancy comes to an end,

then, subject to subsection (2) below, the assured tenancy shall continue in existence as a tenancy held of the person whose interest would, apart from the continuance of the assured tenancy, entitle him to actual possession of the dwelling-house at that time.

(2) Subsection (1) above does not apply to an assured tenancy if the interest which, by virtue of that subsection, would become that of the landlord, is such

---

[25] See p. 284, n. 9.   [26] See p. 222.   [27] *Leith Properties* v. *Byrne* [1983] Q.B. 433.

that, by virtue of Schedule 1 to this Act, the tenancy could not be an assured tenancy.

(3) Where, by virtue of any provision of this Part of this Act, an assured tenancy which is a periodic tenancy (including a statutory periodic tenancy) continues beyond the beginning of a reversionary tenancy which was granted (whether before, on or after the commencement of this Act) so as to begin on or after—

    (a)   the date on which the previous contractual assured tenancy came to an end, or

    (b)   a date on which, apart from any provision of this Part, the periodic tenancy could have been brought to an end by the landlord by notice to quit,

the reversionary tenancy shall have effect as if it had been granted subject to the periodic tenancy.

(4) The reference is subsection (3) above to the previous contractual assured tenancy applies only where the periodic tenancy referred to in that subsection is a statutory periodic tenancy and is a reference to the fixed-term tenancy which immediately preceded the statutory periodic tenancy.

Notes

(i)   If an assured tenant lawfully sub-lets the whole of the premises the tenancy ceases to be assured, since the tenant no longer "occupies the dwelling-house as his only or principal home."[28] However, a sub-tenant may have assured status notwithstanding the fact that the tenant is not an assured tenant. The status of the sub-tenant has to be determined by reference to section 1 of the 1988 Act.

(ii)   If the sub-tenant is assured, when the tenancy comes to an end, as a general rule, the sub-tenant retains his assured status and holds directly from the landlord. The effect of section 18 is that the tenant merely drops out of the picture. There is, however, an important exception.

(iii)   Section 18 will not protect an assured sub-tenant where the landlord is a body which by virtue of Schedule 1 cannot let on assured tenancies (for example, a local authority).

(iv)   The effect of these rules can be illustrated by simple factual examples:

L (an individual) lets premises to T (a company) which lawfully sub-lets the premises to ST (an individual). If ST's sub-tenancy falls within the definition set out in section 1 and Schedule 1 ST has assured status notwithstanding the fact that T cannot be an assured tenant. When T's interest comes to an end, T drops out of the the picture and ST retains his assured status as against L.

---

[28] Housing Act 1988, s.1(1)(b).

If L is a local authority, ST is an assured tenant as against T, but once T's interest has come to an end, ST is no longer protected by the legislation.

(C) ASSIGNEES AND SUB-TENANTS UNDER THE RENT ACT 1977

The security of tenure provisions of the Rent Act 1977 in relation to sub-tenants are notoriously complex. The position regarding assignment is more straightforward.

(1) Assignment and Sub-letting the Whole of the Dwelling-house without the Landlord's Consent

If a protected tenant assigns the tenancy to a third party or sub-lets the whole of the premises without the landlord's consent the landlord may seek to recover possession of the premises under Case 6:

Case 6

Where without the consent of the landlord, the tenant has, at any time after—

(a) . . .

(b) 22nd March 1973, in the case of a tenancy which became a regulated tenancy by virtue of section 14 of the Counter-Inflation Act 1973;

(bb) the commencement of section 73 of the Housing Act 1980, in the case of a tenancy which became a regulated tenancy by virtue of that section;

(c) 14th August 1974, in the case of a regulated furnished tenancy; or

(d) 8th December 1965, in the case of any other tenancy,

assigned or sub-let the whole of the dwelling-house or sub-let part of the dwelling-house, the remainder being already sub-let.

Case 6 is available regardless of the terms of the tenancy, even if the assignment or sub-letting is lawful.[29] In cases concerning assignment an order from the court under Case 6 entitles the landlord to possession against the assignee. Case 6 is, of course, a discretionary ground for possession, and therefore the court must be satisfied that it is reasonable to make the order.

Case 6 does not apply to cases involving assignment of a statutory tenancy. Where a statutory tenant purports to assign his rights to a third party the statutory tenancy comes to an end (since the statutory tenant ceases to occupy the premises "as his residence"[30]) and the purported assignment is a nullity.[31] Accordingly, the landlord is entitled to recover possession of the premises (without having to rely on any of the grounds

[29] *Leith Properties Ltd.* v. *Byrne* [1983] Q.B. 433.
[30] Rent Act 1977, s.2(1)(a).
[31] See, *e.g. Atyeo* v. *Fardoe* (1978) 37 P. & C.R. 494.

for possession contained in Schedule 15), even if the statutory tenant who has purported to assign the tenancy has regained possession before the landlord commences proceedings.[32]

It is, however, provided that a statutory tenancy may be transferred by an agreement in writing between the outgoing tenant and the incoming tenant as long as the landlord is a party to the transaction.[33]

There are problems surrounding the sub-letting of the whole of the dwelling-house by a statutory tenant. Although the effect of such a sub-letting is to bring the statutory tenancy to an end, it seems that the sub-letting is not a legal nullity, and if the sub-letting is lawful the sub-tenant may be protected.[34]

Finally, it should be noted that Case 6 has no application where the tenant sub-lets part of the premises—even if he does so without the landlord's consent. Having said that, it is important to note that if the tenant sub-lets in breach of covenant the landlord may seek to recover possession under Case 1.

(2) Position of Sub-tenants

The most important provision regulating the position of sub-tenants is section 137 of the Rent Act 1977:

(1) If a court makes an order for possession of a dwelling-house from—

(a)　a protected or statutory tenant, or

(b)　a protected occupier or statutory tenant as defined in the Rent (Agriculture) Act 1976,

and the order is made by virtue of section 98(1) or 99(2) of this Act or, as the case may be, under Part I of Schedule 4 to that Act, nothing in the order shall affect the right of any sub-tenant to whom the dwelling-house or any part of it has been lawfully sub-let before the commencement of the proceedings to retain possession by virtue of this Part of this Act, nor shall the order operate to give a right to possession against any such sub-tenant.

(2) Where a statutorily protected tenancy of a dwelling-house is determined, either as a result of an order for possession or for any other reason, any sub-tenant to whom the dwelling-house or any part of it has been lawfully sub-let shall, subject to this Act, be deemed to become the tenant of the landlord on the same terms as if the tenant's statutorily protected tenancy had continued.

(3) Where a dwelling-house—

(a)　forms part of premises which have been let as a whole on a superior tenancy but do not constitute a dwelling-house let on a statutorily protected tenancy; and

(b)　is itself subject to a protected or statutory tenancy,

---

[32] *Finkle* v. *Strzelczyk* [1961] 1 W.L.R. 1201.
[33] See Rent Act 1977, Sched. 1, para. 13.
[34] *Trustees of Henry Smith's Charity* v. *Willson* [1983] Q.B. 316.

then, from the coming to an end of the superior tenancy, this Act shall apply in relation to the dwelling-house as if, in the lieu of the superior tenancy, there had been separate tenancies of the dwelling-house and of the remainder of the premises, for the like purposes as under the superior tenancy, and at rents equal to the just proportion of the rent under the superior tenancy.

In this subsection "premises" includes, if the sub-tenancy in question is a protected or statutory tenancy to which section 99 of this Act applies, an agricultural holding within the meaning of the Agricultural Holdings Act 1986.[35]

Section 138 provides that if the sub-tenancy was furnished and the sub-tenant becomes the tenant of the landlord by the operation of section 137 the landlord is not to be landed with obligations to provide furniture or services if certain conditions are met.

Section 139 imposes an obligation on the tenant to give notice to the landlord of any sub-letting within 14 days. A tenant who fails to comply with this formality without reasonable excuse is liable under subsection (3) to a small fine—not exceeding level 2 on the standard scale.[36]

It is important to note that the rights conferred on the sub-tenant by section 137 are in addition to those which exist at common law.[37] To understand the operation of section 137 and its interrelationship with the grounds for possession contained in Schedule 15 a number of different factual situations should be distinguished.

(a) A Sub-tenant of a Regulated Tenant

If the sub-letting is unlawful the sub-tenant has no rights against the landlord under section 137.[38] So, if the tenant sub-lets part of the premises in breach of covenant the landlord may seek to recover possession against the tenant on the basis of Case 1. (Where the tenant sub-lets the whole of the dwelling-house in breach of covenant the landlord may also rely on Case 6.) There is no obstacle to the landlord recovering possession from the sub-tenant, and it seems that the unlawful sub-letting is even outside the scope of section 3 of the Protection from Eviction Act 1977.[39]

If the sub-letting is lawful the sub-tenant falls within the scope of section 137(1) and (2), as long as the sub-tenancy is itself a protected or statutory tenancy.[40] From the wording of section 137(1) and (2) it would appear that the sub-tenant enjoys security of tenure against the landlord after the tenancy comes to an end. However, the actual effect of section 137(1) and (2) is severely limited.

---

[35] This final paragraph of subsection (3) was added to reverse the decision reached by the House of Lords in *Maunsell* v. *Olins* [1975] A.C. 373.

[36] See p. 33, n. 21.

[37] See p. 280–288.

[38] A sub-letting in breach of covenant may become lawful by waiver (p. 190). See *Maley* v. *Fearn* [1946] 2 All E.R. 583; *Oak Property Co. Ltd.* v. *Chapman* [1947] 1 K.B. 886.

[39] Martin, *Security of Tenure under the Rent Acts* (1986), p. 122.

[40] *Stanley* v. *Compton* [1951] 1 All E.R. 859.

In *Leith Properties Ltd.* v. *Byrne*[41] it was held that, notwithstanding the lawfulness of the sub-letting, where the tenant sub-lets the whole of the dwelling-house the landlord may rely on Case 6 with a view to recovering possession from the tenant and the sub-tenant. Although it is not entirely clear how the reasoning in this case applies to other grounds for possession, it has been suggested that wherever the landlord recovers possession against the tenant on Cases 1, 2, 5 and 8 these grounds for possession should also be available against the sub-tenant.[42] As Martin notes: "If these views are correct, there is hardly a ground which will not be available against the sub-tenant as well as the tenant."[43]

Arguably, the sub-tenant is in a better position as against the landlord if the tenancy comes to an end otherwise than by the landlord recovering possession under one of the grounds contained in Schedule 15 to the 1977 Act (for example, where the statutory tenant ceases to occupy the dwelling-house as his residence). In such a case, the sub-tenant becomes a tenant of the landlord by virtue of section 137(2) and therefore it would seem that the landlord will have to establish a ground for possession against the sub-tenant directly.[44]

(b) A Sub-tenant of a Tenant Who is Not a Regulated Tenant

Section 137(3) applies where the tenant lawfully sub-lets parts of the promises to a sub-tenant who—as against the tenant—is within the scope of Rent Act protection. The effect of section 137(3) is to give the sub-tenant statutory protection *vis-à-vis* the landlord when the tenancy comes to an end. (If the sub-letting is unlawful the sub-tenant has no rights against the landlord under section 137.)

Section 137(3) has been narrowly interpreted. In *Maunsell* v *Olins*[45] the House of Lords held that for the purposes of this subsection "premises" means premises regarded as dwelling-houses for the purposes of the Rent Acts.[46] In the case of *Pittalis* v *Grant* [47] the scope of section 137(3) was subjected to further consideration by the Court of Appeal. The landlord granted a tenancy of a shop with a flat above. (This tenancy was governed by Part II of the Landlord and Tenant Act 1954.) The tenant sub-let the flat for three years, and when the sub-lease expired the sub-tenant stayed on as a statutory tenant. The tenancy was subsequently surrendered, and the question facing the court was whether the sub-tenant was protected by section 137(3). It was held that the sub-tenancy was not within the scope of this provision. Nourse

---

[41] [1983] Q.B. 433.
[42] *Lord Hylton* v. *Heal* [1921] 2 K.B. 438.
[43] *Security of Tenure under the Rent Acts* (1986), p. 127.
[44] *Idem.*
[45] [1975] A.C. 373.
[46] Even though the effect of this decision was reversed by amending legislation, the principle formulated by the House of Lords still applies in those cases which are not within the scope of the amendment.
[47] [1989] Q.B. 605.

L.J., having noted that the tenancy was a business tenancy, said that "[i]t necessarily follows that the property, whatever its actual state may have been, was not to be treated as a dwelling-house for the purposes of the Act of 1977 and for that reason was not 'premises' within the contemplation of section 137(3)."[48]

This conclusion has been convincingly criticised from a number of angles[49]: section 137(3) cannot be inapplicable because the tenancy was not regulated, since subsection (3) is designed expressly to cover situations where the tenancy does not fall within the scope of Rent Act protection; the suggestion that section 137(3) does not apply because the tenancy was governed by the 1954 Act is doubtful in the light of Lord Wilberforce's speech in *Maunsell* v *Olins*; the implication that premises which are partly used for business purposes cannot be dwelling-houses for the purposes of the Rent Acts is not supported by authority.[50]

From this brief discussion it can be seen that section 137 is riddled with difficulties. In marked contrast, the equivalent provisions of the Housing Act 1988 are relatively simple. In view of the fact that no new Rent Act tenancies can be created on or after January 15, 1989, and that existing Rent Act tenancies are being phased out,[51] the complexities of section 137 will soon become of limited importance in practice.

Bibliographical note

For an authoritative and clear account of the law relating to sub-tenants under the Rent Act see J. E. Martin, *Residential Security* (1989, Sweet & Maxwell), Chapter 10. Also worthy of note are: J. Martin, The statutory subtenancy: a right against all the world (1977) 41 Conv. 96; J. Martin [1983] Conv. 248 (a discussion of *Trustees of Henry Smith's Charity* v. *Willson*); and C. P. Rogers, Shopping residential subtenants [1990] Conv. 204 (which analyses *Pittalis* v. *Grant*).

(3) Protected Shorthold Tenancies

It is expressly provided by section 54(1) of the Housing Act 1980 that section 137 does not apply to shorthold tenancies, so that whenever the landlord becomes entitled to possession against the tenant, he automatically becomes entitled to possession against any sub-tenant.

(D) ASSIGNEES AND SUB-TENANTS UNDER THE HOUSING ACT 1985

The Housing Act 1985 contains a number of provisions dealing with assignment and sub-letting.

---

[48] At 610.
[49] Martin, Living over the shop; no protection for subtenants (1989) 139 New L.J. 1260.
[50] See, for example, *Ellen* v. *Goldstein* (1920) 123 L.T. 644; *Cohen* v. *Benjamin* (1922) 39 T.L.R. 10; *Hyman* v. *Steward* [1925] 2 K.B. 702.
[51] See pp. 312–313.

(1) Lodgers and Sub-tenants

A secure tenant has an absolute right to take in lodgers, and a qualified right to sub-let. Section 93 of the Housing Act 1985 provides:

(1) It is a term of every secure tenancy that the tenant—

(a) may allow any persons to reside as lodgers in the dwelling-house, but

(b) will not, without the written consent of the landlord, sub-let or part with possession of part of the dwelling-house.

(2) If the tenant under a secure tenancy parts with the possession of the dwelling-house or sub-lets the whole of it (or sub-lets first part of it and then the remainder), the tenancy ceases to be a secure tenancy and cannot subsequently become a secure tenancy.

Notes

(i)   The distinction between a lodger (who is a licensee) and a tenant was discussed by Lord Templeman in *Street* v. *Mountford*.[52]

(ii)   Consent to sub-letting is governed by section 94, which provides:

(1) This section applies to the consent required by virtue of section 93(1)(b) (landlord's consent to sub-letting of part of dwelling-house).

(2) Consent shall not be unreasonably withheld (and if unreasonably withheld shall be treated as given), and if a question arises whether the withholding of consent was unreasonable it is for the landlord to show that it was not.

(3) In determining that question the following matters, if shown by the landlord, are among those to be taken into account—

(a) that the consent would lead to overcrowding of the dwelling-house within the meaning of Part X (overcrowding);

(b) that the landlord proposes to carry out works on the dwelling-house, or on the building of which it forms part, and that the proposed works will affect the accommodation likely to be used by the sub-tenant who would reside in the dwelling-house as a result of the consent.

(4) Consent may be validly given notwithstanding that it follows, instead of preceding, the action requiring it.

(5) Consent cannot be given subject to a condition (and if purporting to be given subject to a condition shall be treated as given unconditionally).

(6) Where the tenant has applied in writing for consent, then—

(a) if the landlord refuses to give consent, it shall give the tenant a written statement of the reasons why consent was refused, and

(b) if the landlord neither gives nor refuses to give consent within a reasonable time, consent shall be taken to have been withheld.

This section may be contrasted with the Landlord and Tenant Act 1988 according to which failure by the landlord to comply with the statutory

---

[52] [1985] A.C. 809. See pp. 50–61.

provisions may give rise to liability in tort for breach of statutory duty.[53]
It should, however, be noted that section 94 and the 1988 Act have
broadly similar objectives, in the sense that they aim to reduce delays in
cases where a tenant is required to seek the landlord's consent before
entering a transaction with a third party.

(iii) A sub-tenant may have assured status (under the Housing Act
1988) as against the tenant, but when the tenancy comes to an end the
sub-tenant will have no security under the Housing Act 1988 (or the
1985 Act) *vis-à-vis* the landlord.[54]

(iv) Where the tenant sub-lets the whole of the premises the tenancy
ceases to be secure.[55]

(2) Assignment

As a general principle a secure tenancy cannot be assigned. Section 91
of the Housing Act 1985 states:

(1) A secure tenancy which is—

(a) a periodic tenancy, or

(b) a tenancy for a term certain granted on or after 5th November 1982,

is not capable of being assigned except in the cases mentioned in subsection (3).

(2) If a secure tenancy for a term certain granted before 5th November 1982 is
assigned, then, except in the cases mentioned in subsection (3), it ceases to be a
secure tenancy and cannot subsequently become a secure tenancy.

(3) The exceptions are—

(a) an assignment in accordance with section 92 (assignment by way of
exchange);

(b) an assignment in pursuance of an order made under section 24 of the
Matrimonial Causes Act 1973 (property adjustment orders in connection
with matrimonial proceedings);

(c) an assignment to a person who would be qualified to succeed the tenant
if the tenant died immediately before the assignment.

Notes

(i) A purported assignment of a secure tenancy does not transfer any
rights to the intended assignee. However, if having purported to assign
the tenancy to a third party, the tenant gives up possession of the
dwelling-house, the tenancy ceases to be secure, and can be determined
by the landlord according to common law principles.

---

[53] See pp. 284–287.
[54] See pp. 288–291.
[55] Housing Act 1985, s.93(2).

(ii) Assignment by way of exchange is regulated by section 92 and Schedule 3 to the 1985 Act:

(1) It is a term of every secure tenancy that the tenant may, with the written consent of the landlord, assign the tenancy to another secure tenant who satisfies the condition in subsection (2) or to an assured tenant who satisfies the conditions in subsection (2A).

(2) The condition is that the other secure tenant has the written consent of his landlord to an assignment of his tenancy either to the first-mentioned tenant or to another secure tenant who satisfies the condition in this subsection.

(2A) The conditions to be satisfied with respect to an assured tenant are—

(a) that the landlord under his assured tenancy is either the Housing Corporation, Housing for Wales, a registered housing association or a housing trust which is a charity; and

(b) that he intends to assign his assured tenancy to the secure tenant referred to in subsection (1) or to another secure tenant who satisfies the condition in subsection (2).

(3) The consent required by virtue of this section shall not be withheld except on one or more of the grounds set out in Schedule 3, and if withheld otherwise than on those grounds shall be treated as given.

(4) The landlord may not rely on any of the grounds set out in Schedule 3 unless he has, within 42 days of the tenant's application for the consent, served on the tenant a notice specifying the ground and giving particulars of it.

(5) Where rent lawfully due from the tenant has not been paid or an obligation of the tenant has been broken or not performed, the consent required by virtue of this section may be given subject to a condition requiring the tenant to pay the outstanding rent, remedy the breach or perform the obligation.

(6) Except as provided by subsection (5), a consent required by virtue of this section cannot be given subject to a condition, and a condition imposed otherwise than as so provided shall be disregarded.

SCHEDULE 3

GROUNDS FOR WITHHOLDING CONSENT TO ASSIGNMENT BY WAY OF EXCHANGE

Ground 1

The tenant or the proposed assignee is obliged to give up possession of the dwelling-house of which he is the secure tenant in pursuance of an order of the court, or will be so obliged at a date specified in such an order.

Ground 2

Proceedings have begun for possession of the dwelling-house of which the tenant or the proposed assignee is the secure tenant on one or more of grounds 1 to 6 in Part I of Schedule 3 (grounds on which possession may be ordered despite absence of suitable alternative accommodation), or there has been served on the tenant or the proposed assignee a notice under section 83 (notice of proceedings for possession) which specifies one or more of those ground rules and is still in force.

Ground 3

The accommodation afforded by the dwelling-house is substantially more extensive than is reasonably required by the proposed assignee.

Ground 4

The extent of the accommodation afforded by the dwelling-house is not reasonably suitable to the needs of the proposed assignee and his family.

Ground 5

The dwelling-house—

(a) forms part of or is within the curtilage of a building which, or so much of it as is held by the landlord, is held mainly for purposes other than housing purposes and consists mainly of accommodation other than housing accommodation, or is situated in a cemetery, and

(b) was let to the tenant or a predecessor in title of his in consequence of the tenant or predecessor being in the employment of—

the landlord,
a local authority,
a new town corporation,
a housing action trust,
the Development Board for Rural Wales,
an urban development corporation, or
the governors of an aided school.

Ground 6

The landlord is a charity and the proposed assignee's occupation of the dwelling-house would conflict with the objects of the charity.

Ground 7

The dwelling-house has features which are substantially different from those of ordinary dwelling-houses and which are designed to make it suitable for occupation by a physically disabled person who requires accommodation of the kind provided by the dwelling-house and if the assignment were made there would no longer be such a person residing in the dwelling-house.

Ground 8

The landlord is a housing association or housing trust which lets dwelling-houses only for occupation (alone or with others) by persons whose circumstances (other than merely financial circumstances) make it especially difficult for them to satisfy their need for housing and if the assignment were made there would no longer be such a person residing in the dwelling-house.

Ground 9

The dwelling-house is one of a group of dwelling-houses which it is the practice of the landlord to let for occupation by persons with special needs and social service or special facility is provided in close proximity to the group of dwelling-houses in order to assist persons with those special needs and if the assignment were made there would no longer be a person with those special needs residing in the dwelling-house.

Ground 10

The dwelling-house is the subject of a management agreement under which the manager is a housing association of which at least half the members are tenants of dwelling-houses subject to the agreement, at least half the tenants of the dwelling-houses are members of the association and the proposed assignee is not, and is not willing to become a member of the association.

It should be noted that a secure tenant who tries to derive financial advantage from the right to exchange runs the risk of being evicted under Ground 6 (of Schedule 2):

Ground 6

The tenancy was assigned to the tenant, or to a predecessor in title of his who is a member of his family and is residing in the dwelling-house, by an assignment made by virtue of section 92 (assignments by way of exchange) and a premium was paid either in connection with that assignment or the assignment which the tenant or predecessor himself made by virtue of that section.

In this paragraph "premium" means any fine or other like sum and any other pecuniary consideration in addition to rent.

The court may make an order for possession under Ground 6 if it considers it reasonable to do so[56]; there is no requirement that suitable alternative accommodation should be available.

(iii) The transfer of tenancies on relationship breakdown, and succession to secure tenancies are discussed in subsequent sections.[57]

(3) Assignment or Sub-letting where the Tenant Condition is not Satisfied

Section 95 provides:

(1) This section applies to a tenancy which is not a secure tenancy but would be if the tenant condition referred to in section 81 (occupation by the tenant) were satisfied.

---

[56] Housing Act 1985, s.84(2)(a).
[57] See pp. 317–325 and 313–317.

(2) Sections 91 and 93(2) (restrictions on assignment or sub-letting of whole dwelling-house) apply to such a tenancy as they apply to a secure tenancy, except that—

(a) section 91(3)(b) and (c) (assignments expected from restrictions) do not apply to such a tenancy for a term certain granted before 5th November 1982, and

(b) references to the tenancy ceasing to be secure shall be disregarded, without prejudice to the application of the remainder of the provisions in which those references occur.

The effect of these provisions is to ensure that the restrictions on assignment and sub-letting imposed by section 91 and section 93(2) apply notwithstanding the fact that the tenant does not satisfy section 81 (the tenant condition). One instance where this section would be of practical significance is the following:

L (a local authority) lets residential accommodation to T (an individual) for a fixed term; the lease contains no covenant against assignment. Before the end of the contractual term T ceases to occupy the premises as his only or principal home, thereby ceasing to be a secure tenant. T, however, remains a contractual tenant, and at common law may lawfully assign the tenancy. In the absence of section 95, T could assign the tenancy to A, who would be a secure tenant if he occupied the premises as his only or principal home.

II SUCCESSION

Although legislation in both the private and public sectors has made some provision for members of the tenant's family to remain in occupation of the dwelling-house after the tenant's death, the various statutory schemes are very different in scope. The most liberal regime was that contained in the Rent Act 1977 (as originally enacted) which permitted two successions either by the tenant's spouse or members of the tenant's family. At the other end of the spectrum, the Housing Act 1988 provides for only one succession and no one other than the tenant's spouse[58] is entitled to succeed. The Housing Act 1985 occupies an intermediate position, allowing for one succession by either the tenant's spouse or a member of the tenant's family.

Through the provision of long-term security of tenure, the Rent Acts may be seen as an attempt "to provide those who cannot afford to buy their own homes with a substitute for home ownership, a right to remain in occupation for a least one lifetime and often more."[59] It is, of course, very difficult to assess the extent to which the decline of the private rented sector results from the provision of long-term security of tenure as opposed to rent control. Nevertheless, succession to Rent Act

---

[58] As defined by Housing Act 1988, s.17(4).
[59] Honoré, *The Quest for Security: Employees, Tenants, Wives* (1982), p. 37.

tenancies has proved to be one of the more controversial features of the law regulating the private rented sector of the housing market. The Housing Act 1988 clearly involves a policy decision to limit the temporal scope of security of tenure for new lettings in the private sector.

Succession to regulated tenancies has recently taken on additional significance since it is through the succession provisions of the Rent Act 1977 (as amended by the Housing Act 1988) that existing regulated tenancies are to be phased out. These succession provisions are extremely complicated and no more than an outline will be attempted.

(A) GENERAL PRINCIPLES

A tenancy is an estate in land which, on the death of the tenant, passes under general principles to the person who is entitled under the tenant's will (if any) or on intestacy. Subject to any provisions in the lease to the contrary, the person who becomes entitled to the tenancy on the tenant's death enjoys the same rights as the deceased.

In cases of joint tenancy, the rule of survivorship applies. So, for example, where a husband and wife are joint tenants, on the death of one of them the survivor becomes absolutely entitled to the tenancy. The operation of the rule of survivorship does not involve the transfer of the tenancy to the survivor under the rules relating to wills or intestacy; rather the deceased simply drops out of the picture.

It should be noted that, because of the special rules which apply to cases involving assured, regulated and secure tenancies, these general principles are of limited application in the context of residential tenancies. Having said that, it should not be thought that they are redundant.

(B) SUCCESSION TO ASSURED TENANCIES

The Housing Act 1988 (unlike the Rent Act 1977 and the Housing Act 1985) makes no special provision for succession to fixed-term tenancies. Accordingly, where a fixed-term assured tenant dies the remainder of the term will pass to whoever is entitled under the tenant's will or on intestacy.

As regards periodic assured tenancies (whether contractual or statutory) succession rights are expressly limited. Ground 7 (of Schedule 2 to the Housing Act 1988) provides a mandatory ground for possession on the death of a periodic assured tenant:

Ground 7

The tenancy is a periodic tenancy (including a statutory periodic tenancy) which has devolved under the will or intestacy of the former tenant and the proceedings for the recovery of possession are begun not later than 12 months after the death of the former tenant or, if the court so directs, after the date on which, in the opinion of the court, the landlord or, in the case of joint landlords, any one of them became aware of the former tenant's death.

For the purposes of this ground, the acceptance by the landlord of rent from a new tenant after the death of the former tenant shall not be regarded as creating a new periodic tenancy, unless the landlord agrees in writing to a change (as compared with the tenancy before the death) in the amount of the rent, the period of the tenancy, the premises which are let or any other term of the tenancy.

The only exception to the general rule contained in Ground 7 is to be found in section 17:

(1) In any case where—

(a) the sole tenant under an assured periodic tenancy dies, and

(b) immediately before the death, the tenant's spouse was occupying the dwelling-house as his or her only or principal home, and

(c) the tenant was not himself a successor, as defined in subsection (2) or subsection (3) below,

then, on the death, the tenancy vests by virtue of this section in the spouse (and, accordingly, does not devolve under the tenant's will or intestacy).

(2) For the purposes of this section, a tenant is a successor in relation to a tenancy if—

(a) the tenancy became vested in him either by virtue of this section or under the will or intestacy of a previous tenant; or

(b) at some time before the tenant's death the tenancy was a joint tenancy held by himself and one or more other persons and, prior to his death, he became the sole tenant by survivorship; or

(c) he became entitled to the tenancy as mentioned in section 39(5) below.

(3) For the purposes of this section, a tenant is also a successor in relation to a tenancy (in this subsection referred to as "the new tenancy") which was granted to him (alone or jointly with others) if—

(a) at some time before the grant of the new tenancy, he was, by virtue of subsection (2) above, a successor in relation to an earlier tenancy of the same or substantially the same dwelling-house as is let under the new tenancy; and

(b) at all times since he became such a successor he has been a tenant (alone or jointly with others) of the dwelling-house which is let under the new tenancy or of a dwelling-house which is substantially the same as that dwelling-house.

(4) For the purposes of this section, a person who was living with the tenant as his or her wife or husband shall be treated as the tenant's spouse.

(5) If, on the death of the tenant, there is, by virtue of subsection (4) above, more than one person who fulfils the condition in subsection (1)(b)

above, such one of them as may be decided by agreement or, in default of agreement, by the county court shall be treated as the tenant's spouse for the purposes of this section.

Notes

(i)   Ground 7 builds on the general law: a periodic assured tenancy passes under the tenant's will or intestacy, but the landlord is given a mandatory ground for possession against the successor. Section 17 has the effect of bypassing Ground 7 altogether by providing that, if certain conditions are satisfied, there is a statutory transfer of the tenancy to the spouse (and the tenancy does not devolve under the tenant's will or intestacy).

(ii)   When deciding cases involving succession to Rent Act tenancies the courts have had considerable difficulty in coming to terms with the reality of extra-marital cohabitation. The particular question which has to be addressed is whether a co-habitant is to be regarded as a member of the tenant's "family."[60] Section 17(4) avoids many of these difficulties by extending succession rights to "a person who was living with the tenant as his or her wife or husband."

Nevertheless, the precise scope of section 17(4) is not without its difficulties. Does it include homosexual couples? In view of the courts' interpretation of similar legislative provisions, the answer would appear to be "No."[61] What is the legal position of an unmarried couple who continue to occupy the same dwelling-house, but who live totally separate lives? On a literal interpretation, it can be argued that in these circumstances the couple are not "living together" as husband and wife. However, in *Adeoso* v. *Adeoso*[62] it was held that a couple living in a flat with only two rooms were to be regarded as living together as husband and wife, notwithstanding the fact that for months they had not spoken to each other (communicating by written notes), and that they slept in different rooms.

(iii)   For the purposes of the succession rules a surviving joint tenant is to be regarded as a successor.[63]

(iv)   Because only one succession is permitted under section 17 there are situations where a surviving spouse will not be entitled to succeed. Consider, for example, the following facts: H and W1 are joint tenants of a dwelling-house under a periodic assured tenancy; W dies; H marries W2; H dies. The landlord is able to rely on Ground 7 to recover possession against W2.

[60] See pp. 306–307.

[61] *Harrogate B.C.* v. *Simpson* [1986] 2 F.L.R. 91, which centred on the similar, though not identical formula in section 113(1)(a) of the Housing Act 1985 ("he and that person live together as husband and wife"). See p. 315.

[62] [1980] 1 W.L.R. 1535 (a case decided under the Domestic Violence and Matrimonial Proceedings Act 1976).

[63] s.17(2)(b).

(v) It is possible that more than one person may be entitled under section 17, in which case section 17(5) applies. This provision will be most relevant in cases concerning polygamous marriages. However, because of section 17(4) the same problem could theoretically arise where a married tenant is living with another person since both the legal spouse and the co-habitee will be regarded as a "spouse" for the purposes of section 17(1). It should be stressed that this problem will arise in only the most exceptional cases, since to qualify under section 17 a successor must be occcupying the dwelling-house as his only or principal home at the time of the tenant's death.

(C)   SUCCESSION UNDER THE RENT ACT 1977

The succession provisions applicable to Rent Act tenancies are complicated, and their complexity has been exacerbated by amendments introduced by the Housing Act 1988.

(1) The Basic Outline

Section 2 of the Rent Act 1977 provides:

(1) Subject to this Part of this Act—

. . .

(b)   Part I of Schedule I to this Act shall have effect for determining what person (if any) is the statutory tenant of a dwelling-house at any time after the death of a person who, immediately before his death, was either a protected tenant of the dwelling-house or a statutory tenant of it by virtue of paragraph (a) above....[64]

(5) A person who becomes a statutory tenant of a dwelling-house as mentioned in subsection (1)(b) above, is, in this Act referred to as a statutory tenant by succession.

The effect of section 2 is that on the death of a regulated tenant the successor becomes a statutory tenant. (This is so even in the case of the death of a protected tenant before the expiry of the contractual term, with the result that the contractual tenancy is suspended during the subsistence of the statutory tenancy by succession.)

As regards deaths which occurred before January 15, 1989 (the date of the entry into force of the Housing Act 1988) the basic scheme of the legislation was to allow two successions on the death of a protected or statutory tenant. On the death of the original tenant either the tenant's spouse or, if the tenant had no spouse, a "member of the original tenant's family" could become the statutory tenant by succession: a spouse was entitled to succeed if he was "residing in the dwelling-house immediately before the death of the original tenant"; a member of the family was only entitled if he had been "residing with" the tenant "at

---

[64] For a discussion of Rent Act 1977, s.2(1)(a) see pp. 162–167.

the time of and for the period of six months immediately before his death."[65] In the case of succession by a member of the tenant's family, if more than one person was qualified then the successor would be "such one of them as may be decided by agreement," or in default of agreement by the county court."[66] It should, of course, be noted that a statutory tenant by succession is protected by the Rent Act 1977 "if and so long as he or she occupies the dwelling-house as his or her residence."[66a]

On the death of a statutory tenant by succession (the first successor), another succession was possible as long as the appropriate conditions were satisfied.[67] So, the first successor's spouse or a member of his family might also become a statutory tenant by succession (the second successor). On the death of the second successor, the statutory tenancy came to an end, and the landlord was entitled to recover possession.

Various problems were raised by this basic scheme. First, the courts struggled to define what was meant by "member of the ... tenant's family." The term "spouse" was treated by the courts as referring only to legally married couples, and therefore succession by unmarried partners had to be dealt with under the rubric of "member of the tenant's family." In *Dyson Holdings Ltd.* v. *Fox*[68] the Court of Appeal had to decide whether a woman who had lived with the tenant for many years was a member of his family. They had lived together as man and wife, and she had taken the man's name. Lord Denning M.R., having referred to *Gammans* v. *Elkins*[69] and *Hawes* v. *Evenden*[70] said:

If both of those cases were rightly decided, it seems to me that an unmarried woman (who has lived with a man as his wife for many years) is a 'member of the tenant's family' if she has children by him: but she is not a member of his family if she has no children. ... That seems to me a ridiculous distinction. So ridiculous, indeed, that it should be rejected by this court: and that we should hold that a couple who live together as man and wife for 20 years are members of the same family, whether they have children or not.[71]

When a similar issue arose in *Helby* v. *Rafferty*[72] Stamp L.J. stated:

I conclude that *Dyson Holdings Ltd.* v. *Fox* established two propositions: first, that, notwithstanding *Gammans* v. *Elkins*, a relationship between an unmarried man and an unmarried woman living together over a long period can constitute the family relationship which is necessary in order to satisfy the section, and second, that on the facts in *Dyson Holdings Ltd.* v. *Fox* such a relationship was

---

[65] Rent Act 1977, Sched. 1, paras. 2 and 3.
[66] para. 3.
[66a] Rent Act 1977, s.2(1)(a).
[67] paras. 5–7.
[68] [1976] Q.B. 503.
[69] [1950] 2 K.B. 328.
[70] [1953] 1 W.L.R. 1169.
[71] At 509.
[72] [1979] 1 W.L.R. 13.

established. One has to ask: has the union such a degree of apparent permanence and stability that the ordinary man would say that the parties were, in the words of Bridge L.J., 'members of a single family'?[73]

Although the couple had lived together for five years, they were held not to be members of the same family. The Court of Appeal drew the following contrasts with the situation in *Dyson Holdings Ltd.* v. *Fox*: the woman had not taken the man's name; they had not presented themselves to the outside world as a married couple; and the woman had "wanted to keep her freedom ... to withdraw from the relationship with the minimum of disruption and without legal or other formalities."[74]

However, in *Watson* v. *Lucas*[75] it was held that a man might succeed to his co-habitant's tenancy even though he was legally married to another woman. More striking is *Chios Property Investment Co. Ltd.* v. *Lopez*[76] where a woman was held to be a member of the tenant's family notwithstanding the fact that she had cohabited with the tenant for only two years, she had retained her maiden name and she had not had children. It should be noted, however, that Sir George Waller indicated that "this was a most exceptional case, and it should not be regarded as a precedent entitling courts to draw a similar inference from a similar short period of time, unless there are wholly exceptional surrounding circumstances."[77]

The problem posed by cohabiting couples has now been largely resolved, since as from January 15, 1989 "a person who was living with the tenant as his or her wife or husband shall be treated as the spouse of the original tenant."[78]

There are, however, still difficulties in the context of other relationships.[79]

Sefton Holdings v. *Cairns* (1988) 20 H.L.R. 124

Lloyd L.J. said (at 125–128):

This is an appeal from a decision of Her Honour Judge Downey sitting in the Liverpool County Court on August 11, 1987. It concerns a house at No. 49 Cherry Avenue, Liverpool. The question is whether the defendant, Miss Florence Cairns, is entitled to protection under the Rent Acts, that is to say, whether she is a statutory tenant under section 2 of the Rent Act 1977. The answer depends on the meaning to be given to the word "family" in paragraph 7 of Part I of Schedule 1 of that Act.

---

[73] At 18. Citations omitted.
[74] Stamp L.J. at 22, citing the judgment of the county court judge.
[75] [1980] 1 W.L.R. 1493.
[76] (1988) 20 H.L.R. 120.
[77] At 122–123.
[78] Rent Act 1977, Sched. 1, para. 2(2) (inserted by Housing Act 1988, s.39 and Sched. 4, para. 2).
[79] See, *e.g., Ross* v. *Collins* [1964] 1 W.L.R. 425; *Carega Properties* v. *Sharratt* [1979] 1 W.L.R. 928.

The facts are that the plaintiffs, Sefton Holdings Ltd., are the landlords of the premises in question. They let it to a Mr. Richard Gamble some time between 1939 and 1941 when the house was built. Mr. Gamble died in 1965. His daughter, Ada, then succeeded to the tenancy. Miss Ada Gamble died in 1986. The defendant came to live with Mr. and Mrs. Gamble and their daughter Ada in 1941. She was then 23 and single. Both her parents had died. Her boyfriend had just been killed in the war. Miss Ada Gamble asked her parents if they would take the defendant in, which they did. They treated her as their own daughter. She called then "Mom and Pop." She has lived in the same house ever since. She is now some 70 years of age.

On June 6, 1986, shortly after Miss Ada Gamble died, the plaintiffs served on the defendant a notice to quit. The defendant claims that she is entitled to remain on in the house as a statutory tenant under paragraph 7 of Part I of the first schedule, which provides as follows:

"Where paragraph 6 above does not apply but a person who was a member of the first successor's family was residing with him at the time of and for the period of six months immediately before his death then, after his death, that person or if there is more than one such person such one of them as may be decided by agreement, or in default of agreement by the county court, shall be the statutory tenant if and so long as he occupies the dwelling-house as his residence."

Miss Ada Gamble was the first successor within the meaning of that paragraph. So what we have to decide in this case is whether the defendant is a member of her family who was residing with her at the time of, and for the period of six months immediately before, her death. The defendant was clearly residing with Miss Ada Gamble at the time of Miss Ada Gamble's death. But was she a member of Miss Ada Gamble's family? That is the question. The county court judge has decided that she was, and there is now an appeal to this court.

No court could help feeling sympathy for an elderly lady of 70 who is in danger of being turned out of the house in which she has lived for nearly 50 years. But it goes without saying that we have to put sympathy on one side and apply the law to the best of our ability. It has been held over and over again that, in deciding whether a person is a member of another person's family, we must give the word "family" its ordinary everyday meaning. We cannot extend that meaning in order to cover what might might appear to be a hard case; we must not let affection press upon judgment.

If the judge has given the word too wide a meaning, then she has erred in law and we are obliged in this court to correct her, however much we might like to agree.

We have been referred to a number of cases as to what is meant by saying that a person is a member of another person's family. The cases go back at least 60 years. Not all the cases are, at first sight at any rate, easy to reconcile. That may be because, as has been suggested, the meaning of the word "family" has broadened over the years. But we do not have to go into that question now.

The most useful passage from among the decided cases is to be found in the judgment of Russell L.J. in the case of *Ross* v. *Collins* [1964] 1 W.L.R. 425, 432. In that case Russell L.J. said this:

"Granted that 'family' is not limited to cases of a strict legal familial nexus, I cannot agree that it extends to a case such as this. It still requires, it seems to me, at least a broadly recognisable *de facto* familial nexus. This may be capable of being found and recognised as such by the ordinary man—where the link would be strictly familial had there been a marriage, or where the link is through adoption of a minor, *de jure* or *de facto*, or where the link is 'step-,' or where the link is 'in-law' or by marriage. But two strangers cannot, it seems to me, ever establish artificially for the purpose of this section a familial nexus by acting as brothers or as sisters, even if they call each other such and consider their relationship to be tantamount to that. Nor, in my view, can an adult man and woman who establish a platonic relationship establish a familial nexus by acting as a devoted brother and sister or father and daughter would act, even if they address each other as such and even if they refer to each other as such and regard their association as tantamount to such. Nor in my view, would they indeed be recognised as familial links by the ordinary man."

That passage was expressly approved and adopted by Lord Diplock giving the leading speech in the House of Lords in *Carega Properties S.A.* v *Sharratt* [1979] 1 W.L.R. 928.

It seems to me that the facts of the present case are covered by the principle stated by Russell L.J. I have no doubt that the defendant and Miss Ada Gamble did regard each other as sisters and may well have called each other such. There is evidence, to which I have already referred, that the defendant called Mr. and Mrs. Gamble "Mom and Pop." But the fact remains that when the defendant was taken in nearly 50 years ago she was taken in, to use the language of Russell L.J., as a stranger; and however long she may have lived with the family and however kindly they may have treated her, and however close their friendship may have become, the defendant did not, and in my judgment could not, have become a member of Ada's family. As Miss Goodman put it in the course of the argument, length of residence cannot transform a resident into a member of the family.

Miss Pearce, in seeking to support the judge's judgment, argued that the defendant at any rate became a member of Mr. and Mrs. Gamble's family by adoption. If she had, then she would have been within the protection of the Act. For it has been held by this court in the case of *Brock* v. *Wollams* [1949] 2 K.B. 388, that *de facto* adoption is good enough to make a child a member of the family in question.

But there are two difficulties with that argument. In the first place, the section requires us to ask whether the defendant was a member of Miss Ada Gamble's family, not the family of her parents. Even if we could surmount that difficulty, there is a second difficulty. There is no case which has been drawn to our attention in which the courts have held that the protection of the Rent Acts covers the adoption of an *adult* (if such a concept is possible). It will be noted that in the passage I have read from Russell L.J.'s judgment he refers to the adoption of a minor; and Lord Diplock (at p. 929) refers to "adoption (*de jure* or *de facto*) during minority."

Miss Pearce sought to distinguish *Ross* v. *Collins* and *Carega Properties* v. *Sharratt* from the present case. She submits that in those cases a young person went to live with an older person and gradually took over the running of the house; here, by contrast, a young person, an orphan, was taken in by family as a whole. It was not a case, says Miss Pearce, of one adult taking in another. The relationship therefore had, so she submits, the necessary quality to make it a familial relationship. Mr. and Mrs. Gamble should be treated as being *in loci parentis*.

I would, as I have said already, like to accept Miss Pearce's distinction if I could find a way of doing so. I agree that there are factual differences between the cases. There always are. But our approach should be the same as that laid down by Russell L.J. and adopted by Lord Diplock. No case has gone as far as Miss Pearce would like us to go in the present case. The defendant was 23 when she came to live with Mr. and Mrs. Gamble and their daughter. It cannot be said that she was brought up as an adopted child of the family. It may be that things were different in 1941 from what they are now. But, if I ask myself the question whether the defendant became a member of Mr. and Mrs. Gamble's family (if that be the right question) by adoption, whether *de facto* or *de jure*, I am in all honesty compelled to answer that question "No."

Various attempts have been made by the courts from time to time to define the word "family," by identifying various categories within which a person would be a member of another person's family. But Lord Diplock did not embark on that task in *Carega Properties* v. *Sharratt*, and I do not propose to embark on that task myself. All I would say is that, in approaching this case, I have found it useful to bear two matters in mind. First, there is the distinction drawn by Viscount Dilhorne in *Carega Properties* v. *Sharratt* between being a member of the family and being a member of the household. Secondly, there is the distinction between *being* a member of the family and living *as* a member of the family. There is no doubt that the defendant lived as a member of the family, and that may be why the judge decided this case in her favour. But the question we have to ask ourselves is not whether she lived as a member of the family, but whether she was a member of the family. I am clear that she was not, and that the man in the street would take the same view.

We should in this court be slow to reverse a county court judge on a matter of this kind. But, for the reasons which I have attempted to give, I for my part feel compelled to allow this appeal.

Sir Roualeyn Cumming-Bruce agreed.

Secondly, in the context of succession by a member of the tenant's family, the courts have not interpreted the phrase "residing with" in an entirely consistent manner. Although in the handful of cases in which the phrase "residing with" has been considered the courts have repeatedly stated that the words should be interpreted by reference to their ordinary meaning,[80] it has been accepted that "residing with" means something more than "living at."[81] The fact that two people may reside at the same house does not inexorably lead to the conclusion that each is residing with the other.

The courts have employed two slightly different tests in deciding whether a potential successor was residing with the tenant. In some cases, the court has asked whether the dwelling-house had become the potential successor's home. In *Collier* v. *Stoneman*,[82] for example, the flat which was being claimed by the plaintiff consisted of two rooms and a kitchen. The front room had been occupied by the plaintiff's grandmother as her bedroom; the other was occupied by the plaintiff and her husband. The kitchen was the only shared room. Although it was clear that the plaintiff and the tenant led very separate lives, Sellers

---

[80] See, *e.g.* Evershed M.R. in *Edmunds* v. *Jones* [1957] 1 W.L.R. 1118n. at 1120.
[81] See Sachs L.J. in *Foreman* v. *Beagley* [1969] 1 W.L.R. 1387 at 1393.
[82] [1957] 1 W.L.R. 1108.

L.J. took the view that it was "difficult to see how ... the plaintiff and her husband, making their home there could be said not to be residing with the grandmother up to the date of her death."[83] Similarly in *Morgan* v. *Murch*[84] the Court of Appeal upheld the claim of the tenant's son who had lived in his mother's house for seven months prior to her death. What Winn L.J. regarded as important was the fact that "this man had been living with his mother for more than six months before she died, in the sense that he was making his home there."[85]

On the other hand, the courts have on occasion considered the relevant question as being whether the potential successor had become part of the tenant's household.[86] In *Foreman* v. *Beagley*[87] all three members of the Court of Appeal indicated that the phrase "residing with" connotes an element of community: according to Russell L.J. the claimant "must be able to point to his situation as being a member of the tenant's household"[88]; Sachs L.J. thought that "the words 'residing with' import some measure of factual community of family living and companionship"[89]; Fenton Atkinson L.J. decided that the defendant had not been residing with his mother since "[t]here was never a household or domestic establishment ... of which they were both members."[90]

In *Swanbrae Ltd.* v. *Elliot*,[91] the most recent authority in this area, both tests were referred to, and in a key passage Swinton Thomas J. who gave the leading judgment of the Court of Appeal, suggested that the two tests should be combined:

In my view the person claming the statutory tenancy must show that he or she has made a home at the premises which they are claiming and has become in the true sense a part of the household.[92]

Finally, a member of the tenant's family must reside with the tenant for the relevant period in the particular premises.[93] One commentator has noted:

On a literal reading of the statute, residing with the tenant on other premises would suffice, as where the requisite period of residence with the tenant occurred while the tenant was temporarily living in other premises, or if part of it had occurred before the tenant occupied the premises in question. But such an interpretation ill-accords with the objects of the legislation or with the

---

[83] At 1118.
[84] [1970] 1 W.L.R. 778.
[85] At 782.
[86] See, *e.g.*, *Edmunds* v. *Jones* [1957] 1 W.L.R. 1118n.
[87] [1969] 1 W.L.R. 1387.
[88] At 1391.
[89] At 1392.
[90] At 1393.
[91] (1987) 19 H.L.R. 86.
[92] At 95. See also *Hedgedale Ltd.* v. *Hards, The Times*, January 11, 1991.
[93] This was decided in *South Northamptonshire C.C.* v. *Power* [1987] 1 W.L.R. 1433 in the context of public sector tenancies, but the reasoning applies equally to cases falling under the Rent Acts. See p. 315.

authorities, and it has now been laid down that nothing satisfies the statute except residence in the premises in question."[94]

(2) The Effect of the Housing Act 1988 on Succession to Rent Act Tenancies

The Rent Act scheme has been modified in a number of ways in relation to deaths which occur on or after January 15, 1989. Although the term "spouse" has been extended to cover those living together as husband and wife, in general terms succession rights under the Rent Act 1977 have been significantly curtailed. The effects of the amendments introduced by section 39 and Part I of Schedule 4 to the Housing Act 1988 are as follows:

(a) Where the Deceased was the Original Tenant

Where a tenancy was granted before January 15, 1989 and the tenant dies on or after January 15, 1989, the tenant's spouse (which includes "a person who was living with the tenant as his or her wife or husband"[95]) is entitled to succeed to a statutory tenancy. If there is no spouse who is entitled, a member of the tenant's family may succeed. There are, however, two points to note. First, the residence requirement is now two years rather than six months. (There is a transitional period of 18 months following the entry into force of the Housing Act 1988. During this period, a member of the tenant's family will be able to succeed if he resided with the tenant for the six months prior to January 15, 1989 and continuously thereafter until the tenant's death.) Secondly, the member of the tenant's family succeeds to an assured periodic tenancy governed by the Housing Act 1988, rather than a statutory tenancy under the Rent Act 1977.

(b) Where the Deceased was the First Statutory Tenant by Succession

There are essentially two situations where there can be succession following the death of the first successor: either where the original tenant died before January 15, 1989, and the tenant's spouse or a member of his family succeeded to a statutory tenancy; or where the original tenant died on or after January 15, 1989 and the tenant's spouse succeeded to a statutory tenancy. (Where the original tenant dies after January 15, 1989 and a member of his family succeeds to an assured tenancy the tenancy passes under the first successor's will or intestacy, but the landlord has a mandatory ground for possession under Ground 7 of Schedule 2.)

---

[94] Megarry, *The Rent Acts* (11th ed., 1988), p. 276. Citations omitted.
[95] Rent Act 1977, Sched. 1, para. 2(2).

Where the first successor is a statutory tenant, on the first successor's death there may be a second succession if (a) the second successor was a member of the original tenant's family and the family of the first successor, and (b) the second successor resided with the first successor during the two years immediately prior to the first successor's death. If the second successor satisfies these requirements, then he succeeds to an assured periodic tenancy.

The effect of these amendments to the Rent Act succession provisions is to accelerate the process of phasing out Rent Act tenancies.

(D) SUCCESSION TO SECURE TENANCIES

The succession provisions of the Housing Act 1985 are set out in sections 87 to 90.

87. A person is qualified to succeed the tenant under a secure tenancy if he occupies the dwelling-house as his only or principal home at the time of the tenant's death and either—

(a) he is the tenant's spouse, or

(b) he is another member of the tenant's family and has resided with the tenant throughout the period of 12 months ending with the tenant's death;

unless, in either case, the tenant was himself a successor, as defined in section 88.

88.—(1) The tenant is himself a successor if—

(a) the tenancy vested in him by virtue of section 89 (succession to a periodic tenancy), or

(b) he was a joint tenant and has become the sole tenant, or

(c) the tenancy arose by virtue of section 86 (periodic tenancy arising on ending of term certain) and the first tenancy there mentioned was granted to another person or jointly to him and another person, or

(d) he became the tenant on the tenancy being assigned to him (but subject to subsections (2) and (3)), or

(e) he became the tenant on the tenancy being vested in him on the death of the previous tenant.

(2) A tenant to whom the tenancy was assigned in pursuance of an order under section 24 of the Matrimonial Causes Act 1973 (property adjustment orders in connection with matrimonial proceedings) is a successor only if the other party to the marriage was a successor.

(3) A tenant to whom the tenancy was assigned by virtue of section 92 (assignments by way of exchange) is a successor only if he was a successor in relation to the tenancy which he himself assigned by virtue of that section.

(4) Where within six months of the coming to an end of a secure tenancy which is a periodic tenancy ("the former tenancy") the tenant becomes a tenant under another secure tenancy which is a periodic tenancy, and—

(a) the tenant was a successor in relation to the former tenancy, and

(b) under the other tenancy either the dwelling-house or the landlord, or both, are the same as under the former tenancy,

the tenant is also a successor in relation to the other tenancy unless the agreement creating that tenancy otherwise provides.

89.—(1) This section applies where a secure tenant dies and the tenancy is a periodic tenancy.

(2) Where there is a person qualified to succeed the tenant, the tenancy vests by virtue of this section in that person, or if there is more than one such person is the one to be preferred in accordance with the following rules—

(a) the tenant's spouse is to be preferred to another member of the tenant's family;

(b) of two or more other members of the tenant's family such of them is to be preferred as may be agreed between them or as may, where there is no such agreement, be selected by the landlord.

(3) Where there is no person qualified to succeed the tenant and the tenancy is vested or otherwise disposed of in the course of the administration of the tenant's estate, the tenancy ceases to be a secure tenancy unless the vesting or other disposal is in pursuance of an order made under section 24 of the Matrimonial Causes Act 1973 (property adjustment orders in connection with matrimonial proceedings).

(4) A tenancy which ceases to be a secure tenancy by virtue of this section cannot subsequently become a secure tenancy.

90.—(1) This section applies where a secure tenant dies and the tenancy is a tenancy for a term certain.

(2) The tenancy remains a secure tenancy until—

(a) it is vested or otherwise disposed of in the course of the administration of the tenant's estate, as mentioned in subsection (3), or

(b) it is known that when it is so vested or disposed of it will not be a secure tenancy.

(3) The tenancy ceases to be a secure tenancy on being vested or otherwise disposed of in the course of administration of the tenant's estate, unless—

(a) the vesting or other disposal is in pursuance of an order made under section 24 of the Matrimonial Causes Act 1973 (property adjustment orders in connection with matrimonial proceedings), or

(b) the vesting or other disposal is to a person qualified to succeed the tenant.

(4) A tenancy which ceases to be a secure tenancy by virtue of this section cannot subsequently become a secure tenancy.

Notes

(i) Section 113 defines what is meant by a member of the tenant's family:

(1) A person is a member of another's family within the meaning of this Part if—

- (a) he is the spouse of that person, or he and that person live together as husband and wife, or

- (b) he is that person's parent, grandparent, child, grandchild, brother, sister, uncle, aunt, nephew or niece.

(2) For the purpose of subsection (1)(b)—

- (a) a relationship by marriage shall be treated as a relationship by blood,

- (b) a relationship of the half-blood shall be treated as a relationship of the whole blood,

- (c) the stepchild of a person shall be treated as his child, and

- (d) an illegitimate child shall be treated as the legitimate child of his mother and reputed father.

It was held in *Harrogate B.C.* v. *Simpson*[96] that a lesbian couple were not living together as husband and wife so as to allow the survivor to succeed to a secure tenancy.

(ii) A member of the tenant's family who claims to be entitled to succeed to a secure tenancy on the basis of 12 months' residence with the tenant must show residence at the premises in question for the 12 months prior to the tenant's death. In *South Northamptonshire C.C.* v. *Power*[97] the defendant had lived with Mrs. Tulloch during the three years prior to her death. In May 1985 Mrs. Tulloch sold her house and became a secure tenant of council accommodation. Mrs. Tulloch died in October of the same year. Although the defendant had lived with the tenant for more than 12 months the Court of Appeal held that he was not entitled to succeed to the tenancy, since the defendant had only resided with the tenant in the council flat for the five months prior to her death. (It seems, however, that if Mrs. Tulloch had been a council tenant for more than 12 months, then the result might have been different.[98])

[96] [1986] 2 F.L.R. 91.
[97] [1987] 1 W.L.R. 1433. See also *Waltham Forest L.B.C.* v. *Thomas*, *The Times*, February 18, 1991.
[98] See the judgment of Woolf L.J. at 1441.

Of course, the cases decided under the Rent Acts on the meaning of "residing with" are also relevant in the context of the Housing Act 1985.[99]

(iii)   The local authority will in certain circumstances have a ground for possession against the successor. Schedule 2 to the Housing Act 1985 includes the following ground for possession:

Ground 16

The accommodation afforded by the dwelling-house is more extensive than is reasonably required by the tenant and—

- (*a*)   the tenancy vested in the tenant by virtue of section 89 (succession to periodic tenancy), the tenant being qualified to succeed by virtue of section 87(*b*) (members of family other than spouse), and

- (*b*)   notice of the proceedings for possession was served under section 83 more than six months but less than 12 months after the date of the previous tenant's death.

The matters to be taken into account by the court in determining whether it is reasonable to make an order on this ground include—

- (*a*)   the age of the tenant,

- (*b*)   the period during which the tenant has occupied the dwelling-house as his only or principle home, and

- (*c*)   any financial or other support given by the tenant to the previous tenant.

To recover possession under this ground the landlord must provide suitable alternative accommodation, and the court must be satisfied that it is reasonable to make the order.

Bibliographical note

There is a considerable body of literature dealing with the general area of succession to statutorily protected tenancies, as well as comments on individual cases.

The items listed below are of some interest:

J. E. Martin, *Residential Security* (1989, Sweet & Maxwell) Chapter 8 (succession to statutory tenancies)

D. C. Bradley, Meaning of "family": changing morality and changing justice (1976) 39 M.L.R. 222 (*Dyson Holdings Ltd.* v. *Fox*)

M. A. Jones, [1988] J.S.W.L. 203 (*Sefton Holdings* v. *Cairns*)

M. A. Jones, [1988] J.S.W.L. 263 (*South Northamptonshire C.C.* v. *Power*)

J. Hill, Succession to a statutory tenancy [1987] Conv. 349 (*Swanbrae Ltd.* v. *Eliot*)

---

[99] See pp. 310–312.

C. H. Sherrin, (1980) 43 M.L.R. 77 (*Helby* v. *Rafferty*)
A. Sydenham, [1981] Conv. 78 (*Watson* v. *Lucas*)
P. Tennant, Cohabitation and the Rent Act [1980] C.L.J. 31 (*Carega Properties* v. *Sherrat*)

III RELATIONSHIP BREAKDOWN

There is a substantial body of law relating to relationship breakdown which is beyond the scope of this book. In this section all that is attempted is an outline of the most important issues which directly concern the landlord/tenant relationship.

(A) INTRODUCTION

It is important to distinguish two different factual situations: first, where a joint tenancy of premises is granted to a couple; secondly, where a tenancy is granted to one person, but the premises are jointly occupied as a matrimonial or quasi-matrimonial home.

Where the lease has been formally granted, it will normally be easy to decide whether or not a joint tenancy has been created. In informal situations, however, it may be difficult to determine whether there is a joint tenancy or a tenancy granted to an individual. According to a leading commentator:

Such cases sometimes have to be resolved on relatively slender evidence; and an important part is often played by any rent book which exists.[1]

In cases involving a joint tenancy, the joint tenants are equally entitled to the protection of the law. So, if one of the joint tenants abandons the property, the landlord is not entitled to recover possession against the joint tenant who remains in possession except according to the terms of the applicable statutory scheme.[2] It should be noted, however, that the joint tenants are, as a general rule, jointly and severally liable for the full rent.

There is, however, a potential problem on relationship breakdown if one of the joint tenants gives the landlord notice to quit. It has been held that a periodic tenancy may be determined by a notice to quit given by only one of a number of joint tenants (although a surrender offered by only one joint tenant is ineffective).[3] In *Opoku-Forfieh* v. *Haringey L.B.C.*,[4] for example, a husband and wife were joint secure

---

[1] Megarry, *The Rent Acts* (11th ed., 1988), p. 80.
[2] In relation to the Housing Act 1988, a joint tenancy retains its assured status as long as one of the joint tenants occupies the dwelling-house as his only or principal home (s.1(1)(b)). The same position applies in the secure tenancy regime (Housing Act 1985, s.81). Although there is no express provision under the Rent Act 1977, it has been decided that if one or two joint tenants ceases to live in the dwelling-house during the contractual term, the other, on holding over, will become the statutory tenant; similarly, where there are joint statutory tenants, if one of them ceases to reside in the premises, the other becomes the sole statutory tenant (*Lloyd* v. *Sadler* [1978] Q.B. 774).
[3] *Greenwich L.B.C.* v. *McGrady* (1982) 46 P. & C.R. 223; *Hammersmith & Fulham L.B.C.* v. *Monk*; *Barnet L.B.C.* v. *Smith*, The Times, November 5, 1990.   [4] Unreported.

tenants of council premises. The wife, having signed and delivered to the local authority a notice purporting to determine the joint tenancy, moved out of the premises. The local authority successfully argued that the wife's notice was effective to bring the secure tenancy to an end, and therefore the husband's claim to exercise the right to buy failed.

Statutory protection under the Rent Act 1977, the Housing Act 1985 or the Housing Act 1988 is conferred on the tenant. Accordingly, in cases where the tenancy is not jointly vested in the parties, the tenant's spouse or a cohabitant has no security of tenure under the statutory scheme which applies to the tenancy. Furthermore, at common law, a cohabitant or spouse living with a tenant does not have rights of occupation which are enforceable against third parties.[5] However, as will be seen, there has been statutory intervention in the context of the matrimonial home. In other situations the general law continues to apply.

(B) MARRIED COUPLES

Under the Matrimonial Homes Act 1983 a spouse who is not a sole or joint tenant enjoys considerable security of tenure. Section 1 of the 1983 Act provides:

(1) Where one spouse is entitled to occupy a dwelling-house by virtue of a beneficial estate or interest or contract or by virtue of any enactment giving him or her the right to remain in occupation, and the other spouse is not so entitled, then, subject to the provisions of this Act, the spouse not so entitled shall have the following rights (in this Act referred to as "rights of occupation")—

(a) if in occupation, a right not to be evicted or excluded from the dwelling-house or any part thereof by the other spouse except with the leave of the court given by an order under this section;

(b) if not in occupation, a right with the leave of the court so given to enter into and occupy the dwelling-house.

(2) So long as one spouse has rights of occupation, either of the spouses may apply to the court for an order—

(a) declaring, enforcing, restricting or terminating those rights, or

(b) prohibiting, suspending or restricting the exercise by either spouse of the right to occupy the dwelling-house, or

(c) requiring either spouse to permit the exercise by the other of that right.
. . . . . .

(5) Where a spouse is entitled under this section to occupy a dwelling-house or any part thereof, any payment or tender made or other thing done by that spouse in or towards satisfaction of any liability of the other spouse in respect of rent, rates, mortgage payments or other outgoings affecting the dwelling-house shall, whether or not it is made or done in pursuance of an order under this section, be as good as if made or done by the other spouse.

[5] *National Provincial Bank* v. *Ainsworth* [1965] A.C. 1175.

(6) A spouse's occupation by virtue of this section shall, for the purposes of the Rent (Agriculture) Act 1976, and of the Rent Act 1977 (other than Part V and sections 103 to 106), be treated as possession by the other spouse and for the purposes of Part IV of the Housing Act 1985 and Part I of the Housing Act 1988 (secure tenancies) be treated as occupation by the other spouse. . . .

(10) This Act shall not apply to a dwelling-house which has at no time been a matrimonial home of the spouses in question; and a spouse's rights of occupation shall continue only so long as the marriage subsists and the other spouse is entitled as mentioned in subsection (1) above to occupy the dwelling-house, except where provision is made by section 2 of this Act for those rights to be a charge on an estate or interest in the dwelling-house.

By virtue of these provisions a non-tenant spouse who has been deserted by the tenant will generally have the same security of tenure as the tenant. Occupation by the non-tenant spouse is equivalent to occupation by the tenant,[6] and the landlord is required to accept any rent tendered by the non-tenant.

It should be stressed that the protection provided by section 1 is limited by the two qualifications in subsection (10). First, the non-tenant spouse is only protected as regards the matrimonial home. This means not only that the non-tenant must be married to the tenant but also that they must have lived together in the premises in question.

Hall v. *King* (1987) 19 H.L.R. 440

Sir John Donaldson M.R. said (at 441–444):

In August 1984 Mr. Hall let his cottage at Harefield, Middlesex, to Mr. King for a period of 364 days. One year later he began proceedings to resume possession, only to find that he was destined to join the long line of landlords who, however unwillingly, have contributed to the legal learning concerning the Rent Acts.

The Facts

Mr. and Mrs. King had married in 1971 and had a son who, in August 1984, was aged 11. Some six years before Mrs. King had developed schizophrenia, which had adversely affected her behaviour and had led to the breakdown of the marriage. The son had been made a ward of court in 1982 and care and control given to Mr. King. At about the same time Mr. King started living with a Miss Driver in Clapham. Mrs. King was living in Wales. At some stage between 1982 and 1984, Mrs. King's health appeared to improve and Mr. King found accommodation for her in Battersea, allowing their son to live with her, but there was no question of the Kings resuming married life. This arrangement did not work out, because Mrs. King preferred more rural surroundings, and it was with a view to meeting this wish that Mr. King sought other accommodation for her and found it at Harefield.

---

[6] See *Griffiths* v. *Renfree* (1989) 21 H.L.R. 338.

When Mrs. King moved to Harefield, she took their son with her. For the first six or seven weeks Mr. King slept at the Harefield cottage for four or five nights each week, arriving late at night and leaving early in the morning. However, his home continued to be Miss Driver's house in Clapham. The purpose of the overnight visits to Harefield, as found by the learned judge, was not to attempt to effect a reconciliation and still less to resume married life with Mrs. King. It was to assist in getting their son used to living with his mother. This process came to an abrupt end after seven weeks when Powys County Council, who had a supervisory role under the wardship order, objected to Mr. King having allowed the son to live with his mother. Thereafter Mrs. King lived alone at the Harefield cottage.

The proceedings

Mr. Hall's claim for possession was made against both Mr. and Mrs. King and was heard by Mr. Assistant Recorder Schaffer in the Uxbridge County Court on December 8, 1986. The learned judge made orders for possession against both defendants and Mr. King has accepted that decision. Mrs. King has, however, appealed, claiming that she is entitled to security of tenure under the Rent Act 1977.

The issues

Mr. King's tenancy of the Harefield cottage was a protected tenancy under the Rent Act 1977 and, accordingly, upon its termination he would become and remain a statutory tenant "if and so long as he occupies the dwelling-house as his residence" (section 2(1)(a)). Quite plainly upon the termination of the tenancy in July 1985 the Harefield cottage was not in fact occupied by Mr. King as his residence or at all. Mr. Walter, for Mrs. King, has therefore sought to make good a claim for what might be described as "a deemed residential occupancy." He does so in reliance alternatively upon the Matrimonial Homes Act 1983, and upon case law.

The Matrimonial Homes Act 1983

Section 1(6) of the Act provides that a spouse's occupation of a dwelling-house by virtue of the section shall, for the purposes of the Rent Act 1977, be treated as possession by the other spouse. I need not explore this subsection further, because its effect is dependent upon section 1(10) which provides that "This Act shall not apply to a dwelling-house which has at no time been a matrimonial home of the spouses in question" and it is clear beyond argument that the Harefield cottage was never the matrimonial home of Mr. and Mrs. King. It was the home of Mrs. King, which had been provided for her by Mr. King.

Case law

One might have thought that the phrase "if and so long as he occupies the dwelling-house as his residence" bore a quite intelligible meaning and that, in any event, it would fall to be construed in the light of any judicial decision on its meaning in the context of previous Rent Acts. However section 2(3) has been included to inform us that the phrase is to be construed "as it was immediately before the commencement of this Act (that is to say in accordance with section 3(2) of the Rent Act 1968)." All agog for enlightenment, we turned to that subsection only to learn that the phrase was to be construed

"as requiring the fulfilment of the same, and only the same, qualifications (whether as to residence or otherwise) as had to be fulfilled before the commencement of this Act to entitle a tenant, within the meaning of the Increase of Rent and Mortgage Interest (Restrictions) Act 1920, to retain possession, by virtue of that Act and not by virtue of a tenancy, of a dwelling-house to which that Act applied."

Bearing in mind the well known complexity of the five statutes constituting the Rent and Mortgage Interest (Restrictions) Acts 1920 to 1939 in force at the time of the passing of the 1968 Act, not to mention the mass of case law, I do not find this helpful and, in terms of informing ordinary citizens of their rights and obligations, which must be one of the principle purposes of any statute of this nature, quite useless.

Fortunately, unlike ordinary citizens, we have had the assistance both of Mr. Walter and of Mr. Aldous (appearing for Mr. Hall), who have taken us through the authorities on the rights of deserted wives. From these it is clear that a wife's right to occupy the matrimonial home is of a very special nature, depending upon her status as a wife and not upon any leave or licence of her husband (*National Provincial Bank Ltd.* v. *Ainsworth* [1965] A.C. 1175). This accords with common sense and experience. Whoever heard of a husband expressly or impliedly saying to his wife, "Do come and stay with me in the matrimonial home, dear." By contrast the right of a parent, parent in law or other dependent relative to occupy a matrimonial home can only rest upon leave or licence, in the absence of having a legal or equitable interest in the land. Attempts were made to elevate this status based right into an overriding interest in property, but failed. The adverse social consequences of that failure, when the wife was living in a house which was or had been the matrimonial home, were remedied by the Matrimonial Homes Acts 1967 and 1983. Similar attempts in relation to the position of wife where the husband was the statutory tenant of the matrimonial home were more successful and it is to that line of authority that I therefore turn.

It stretches from *Brown* v. *Draper* [1944] K.B. 309, *Robson* v. *Headland* (1948) 64 T.L.R. 596 and *Old Gate Estates* v. *Alexander* [1950] 1 K.B. 311 to *Penn* v. *Dunn* [1970] 2 Q.B. 686. In the latter case it was explained by Salmon L.J. in the following terms at page 691:

"Clearly, the Rent Act 1968, and the statutes it replaced did not by themselves directly confer any protection upon anyone other than the tenant. The common law, however, applied the Rent Act so that they indirectly afforded considerable protection to a tenant's wife if she was in occupation of the matrimonial home. Her 'occupation' has been treated as the husband's so as to give her the benefit against the landlord of the tenant's statutory protection: see *National Provincial Bank Ltd.* v. *Hastings Car Mart Ltd.* [1965] A.C. 1175, 1252. This was achieved on the following basis: a husband owes his wife a duty to provide her with a home: therefore he cannot turn her out of the house she occupies unless he provides her with another; accordingly, a wife occupies the house on behalf of her husband and her occupation is deemed to be his occupation. The husband is still notionally in occupation of the house, even though he had left his wife and had no intention of returning to it and, indeed, was anxious for the landlord to resume possession. The husband as the statutory tenant cannot contract out of his rights under the Rent Acts. It follows that no order for possession could be made against him or his wife save on the grounds specified in the Rent Acts: see, for example, *Old Gate Estates Ltd.* v. *Alexander* [1950] 1 K.B. 311."

However the one factor which is common to all these cases is that the wife was in occupation of what was or, before the husband moved out, had been the matrimonial home. Her occupation was deemed to be that of the husband, because of her status as a wife *and* the fact that it was the matrimonial home.

She no doubt had a right to be maintained by the husband, but no case suggests that she had a right to occupy premises which he was occupying, unless it was the matrimonial home. This again makes sense. Take this case. Throughout the currency of the contractual tenancy Mr. King was occupying the house of Miss Driver and it would have been astonishing if that had given Mrs. King a right to move in. Take another scenario. Mr. King might well have taken a lease of the cottage at Harefield to accommodate himself and Miss Driver. Again it would have been astonishing, and is not the law, that Mrs. King should have had a right to move in too.

So what is Mr. King's position in relation to that cottage? Mr. King took the tenancy not in order to provide a matrimonial home for his wife and himself. He took it to provide a home for her and invited her to live in it *without him*. This is very different from a wife exercising a status based right to live with her husband. It involves either expressly or impliedly the granting of a licence by the husband. It is in fact indistinguishable from the situation which exists where a son provides a separate home for his widowed mother. That being so, it is impossible to hold that when the contractual tenancy terminated, Mrs. King was occupying the cottage "on behalf of her husband," to use the words of Salmon L.J., so as to enable him to claim the protection of the Rent Acts and thus legitimise her occupation. She was simply the licensee of an absentee tenant. It follows that her occupation was unprotected and Mr. Hall was entitled to an order against her for possession.

I would dismiss the appeal.

Lloyd and Balcombe L.JJ. agreed.

Secondly, the protection provided by section 1 is limited to the duration of the marriage. However, on the break up of a marriage the courts have a broad discretion to adjust the property rights of the husband and wife.[7] Furthermore, on a decree of divorce, nullity or judicial separation or at any time thereafter the court has the power to order a transfer of a tenancy from one spouse to the other. This is provided for by Schedule 1 to the Matrimonial Homes Act 1983.

1.—(1) Where one spouse is entitled, either in his or her own right or jointly with the other spouse, to occupy a dwelling-house by virtue of—

    (a)   a protected tenancy or statutory tenancy within the meaning of the Rent Act 1977, or

    (b)   a statutory tenancy within the meaning of the Rent (Agriculture) Act 1976, or

    (c)   a secure tenancy within the meaning of section 79 of the Housing Act 1985, or

    (d)   an assured tenancy or assured agricultural occupancy within the meaning of Part I of the Housing Act 1988,

then, on granting a decree of divorce, a decree of nullity of marriage or a decree of judicial separation, or at any time thereafter (whether, in the case of a decree of divorce or nullity of marriage, before or after the decree is made absolute), the court by which the decree is granted may make an order under Part II below.

---

[7] Matrimonial Causes Act 1973, s.24.

2.—(1) Where a spouse is entitled to occupy the dwelling-house by virtue of a protected tenancy within the meaning of the Rent Act 1977, or a secure tenancy within the meaning of the Housing Act 1985 or an assured tenancy or assured agricultural occupancy within the meaning of the Housing Act 1988, the court may by order direct that, as from such date as may be specified in the order, there shall, by virtue of the order and without further assurance, be transferred to, and vested in, the other spouse—

    (a) the estate or interest which the spouse so entitled had in the dwelling-house immediately before that date by virtue of the lease or agreement creating the tenancy and any assignment of that lease or agreement, with all rights, privileges and appurtenances attaching to that estate or interest but subject to all covenants, obligations, liabilities and incumbrances to which it is subject; and

    (b) where the spouse so entitled is an assignee of such lease or agreement, the liability of that spouse under any covenant of indemnity by the assignee expressed or implied in the assignment of the lease or agreement to that spouse.

(2) Where an order is made under this paragraph, any liability or obligation to which the spouse so entitled is subject under any covenant having reference to the dwelling-house in the lease or agreement, being a liability or obligation falling due to be discharged or performed on or after the date so specified, shall not be enforceable against that spouse.

3.—(1) Where the spouse is entitled to occupy the dwelling-house by virtue of a statutory tenancy within the meaning of the Rent Act 1977, the court may by order direct that, as from such date as may be specified in the order, that spouse shall cease to be entitled to occupy the dwelling-house and that the other spouse shall be deemed to be the tenant or, as the case may be, the sole tenant under that statutory tenancy.

In practical terms it is often important that the court should order a transfer of the tenancy in the context of the divorce proceedings before the decree absolute, since problems may arise if the marriage comes to an end before the tenancy is transferred. Consider the following example:

H, who is an assured tenant, leaves the matrimonial home to live with another woman. W remains in occupation of the former matrimonial home.[8] In due course H and W are divorced: the court makes a decree absolute, but the assured tenancy is not transferred to W. On the parties' divorce the tenancy ceases to be assured (because H, the tenant, no longer occupies the premises as his only or principal home[9]), and therefore the court cannot subsequently transfer the tenancy to the wife under the powers conferred by the Matrimonial Homes Act 1983. Of course, if W had left the matrimonial home and H had remained in occupation, even after the divorce the tenancy would continue to be assured, and therefore the court would retain its power under the 1983 Act to transfer the tenancy to W.

---

[8] And is therefore protected by Matrimonial Homes Act 1983, s.1(5) and (6).
[9] Housing Act 1988 s.1(1)(b).

(C) UNMARRIED COUPLES

The provisions described above have no application to unmarried couples. Although a cohabitant may in certain circumstances succeed to a statutorily protected tenancy, there is no provision for the court to transfer a tenancy on the break up of an extra-marital relationship.

Equally, a cohabitant who is deserted by the tenant has no security of tenure.

Notes

(i) For further discussion see A. Arden, *Manual of Housing Law* (4th ed., 1989, Sweet & Maxwell) Chapter 9.

(ii) It is very important to note that as a result of relationship breakdown one of the parties may find themselves homeless (for example, a woman might leave the matrimonial home as a result of domestic violence). The duties of local authorities to rehouse people who are homeless are disscussed in Chapter 9.

(D) DOMESTIC VIOLENCE

The Domestic Violence and Matrimonial Proceedings Act 1976, which came into force on June 6, 1977, gives the courts power to protect victims of domestic violence. Section 1 provides:

(1) Without prejudice to the jurisdiction of the High Court, on an application by a party to a marriage a county court shall have jurisdiction to grant an injunction containing one or more of the following provisions, namely—

  (a) a provision restraining the other party to the marriage from molesting the applicant;

  (b) a provision restraining the other party from molesting a child living with the applicant;

  (c) a provision excluding the other party from the matrimonial home or a part of the matrimonial home or from a specified area in which the matrimonial home is included;

  (d) a provision requiring the other party to permit the applicant to enter and remain in the matrimonial home or a part of the matrimonial home;

whether or not any other relief is sought in the proceedings.

(2) Subsection (1) above shall apply to a man and a woman who are living with each other in the same household as husband and wife as it applies to the parties to a marriage and any reference to the matrimonial home shall be construed accordingly.

Notes

(i)   Unlike the Matrimonial Homes Act 1983 the 1976 Act applies to cohabiting couples (as long as they satisfy the formula in subsection (2)).[9a]

(ii)   Although the Act cannot operate to alter the proprietary rights of the parties, the victim of domestic violence may seek an injunction under section 1, regardless of whether the person being excluded is the tenant (or even the freehold owner) of the premises in question.

IV   TENANTS OF MORTGAGORS

According to the Law of Property Act 1925 a mortgagor has the right to grant tenancies in relation to premises which are subject to a mortgage, unless that right is expressly excluded by the terms of the mortgage.[10] Most mortgage deeds, however, contain a prohibition against the creation of tenancies. Such prohibitions may be made absolute or conditional on the consent of the mortgagee. If a tenancy is granted in contravention of the terms of the mortgage, the tenancy does not usually bind the mortgagee. Accordingly, the tenant has no security of tenure if the mortgagee decides to recover possession of the premises as a preliminary to realising the security by exercising the power of sale. The mortgagee does not have to rely on the statutory scheme of protection which would be applicable if the landlord were seeking possession. So, where premises are occupied by statutory tenants in breach of the terms of the mortgage, the mortgagee who wishes to recover possession does not have to establish any of the grounds for possession set out in the Rent Act 1977.[11] Equally, tenants cannot seek relief under the Administration of Justice Act 1970 (which gives the courts a discretion to postpone making possession orders against mortgagees in default.)

There is, however, an exceptional case in which the Court of Appeal was prepared to exercise its equitable jurisdiction in favour of residential tenants.

Quennell v. *Maltby* [1979] 1 W.L.R. 318

Lord Denning M.R. (with whom Bridge and Templeman L.JJ. agreed) said (at 320–323):

[9a] See *Adeoso* v. *Adeoso* [1980] 1 W.L.R. 1535. (This case is discussed briefly at p. 304).
[10] s.99.
[11] See, *e.g.*, *Britannia Building Society* v. *Earl* [1990] 1 W.L.R. 422.

Mr. Quennell is a gentleman who lives in Cheyne Row in London. But he is the owner of a large house in Lewes. It is No. 6 Wallands Crescent, Lewes, with about nine bedrooms. He has an agent in Lewes who looks after it for him. The house is very suitable for students. In 1973 the agent let it to some students of the University of Sussex. Two of them became the tenants. They were Mr. Maltby and Mr. Jack. They were let into possession for a term of one year at a rent of £90 a month, expiring on December 31, 1974. They had other students there with them, about nine students in the house.

Whilst Mr. Maltby and Mr. Jack were tenants Mr. Quennell borrowed money from Barclays Bank Ltd. and mortgaged this house to secure the loan. It was only for the sum of £2,500. He executed a legal charge on August 13, 1974, in favour of Barclays Bank to cover any moneys which might from time to time be owing to the bank. In that legal charge there was this clause 4 which is in common form:

"During the continuance of this security no statutory or other power of granting or agreeing to grant or of accepting or agreeing to accept surrenders of leases or tenancies of the mortgaged property or any part thereof shall be capable of being exercised by the mortgagor without the previous consent in writing of the bank." ...

That meant that thereafter from August 13, 1974, so long as this legal charge subsisted to the bank, Mr. Quennell could not let the premises or accept surrenders without the consent in writing of the bank.

The tenancy of Mr. Maltby and Mr. Jack came to an end at the end of December 1974. The house was then relet to two other students, a Mr. Quilter and a Mr. Lyeth, again for a year. It was not relet to Mr. Maltby because it was thought he was going to the United States. As it happened Mr. Maltby did not go to the United States. In fact he stayed on living in the house. So did several other students.

At all events, the important thing to note is that the bank did not give its consent to this letting to Mr. Quilter and Mr. Lyeth. No one asked the bank for its consent. No one realised it was necessary. No one interfered and nothing happened. That year 1975 passed. Then on March 19, 1976, there was a fresh letting. This was between Mr. Quennell as landlord and Mr. Maltby and a Mr. Lupton, the first and second defendants, as tenants. That tenancy lasted until December 1, 1976. Again no one asked the bank for consent. No one realised it was necessary. And from December 1976 onwards the tenants remained as statutory tenants, paying the rent to the agents.

The position then arose that Mr. Quennell wanted to get possession of the house. If he could get vacant posession, he could sell it at a high price. It might be worth £30,000 to £40,000 with vacant possession. Mr. Quennell started proceedings for nuisance and annoyance, but he dropped them. Then he went to lawyers for advice. After consulting them, in October 1977, Mr. Quennell went to the bank and told them about the tenants in the house. The bank had not heard before about the various changes in the tenancies. Even when they were told the bank made it clear that they had no intention of taking any proceedings to enter the property or to turn the tenants out or anything of that kind. The bank were not concerned to get possession.

Then Mr. Quennell's lawyers in London advised him that there was a good way in which possession could be achieved. This is what it was: Mr. Quennell's wife, Mrs. Quennell, paid off the bank. She paid the £2,500 which was owing to the bank and took a transfer of the charge. The bank transferred it to her by a transfer dated January 17, 1978.

Then Mrs. Quennell brought proceedings against the tenants, Mr. Maltby and Mr. Lupton, seeking possession. She said that she stood in the shoes of the bank: and, seeing that the tenancy was granted without the consent of the bank, it was void. So she could recover possession. The judge accepted this submission. He held that the wife, Mrs. Quennell, was entitled to possession of the premises and could turn Mr. Maltby and all the other students out of the house.

Now it has been held that, when the bank holds a charge and there is a clause in it whereby there are to be no tenancies granted or surrendered except with the consent of the bank in writing, then in those circumstances, if the mortgagor does thereafter grant tenancies without the consent of the bank, then those tenancies are not binding on the bank, and the tenants are not entitled to the protection of the Rent Acts. That was decided in *Dudley and District Benefit Building Society* v. *Emerson* [1949] Ch. 707. Mrs. Quennell relies on that case. She says that, as transferee of the legal charge, she stands in the shoes of the bank and can obtain possession.

The judge accepted that submission. His decision, if right, opens the way to widespread evasion of the Rent Acts. If the owner of a house wishes to obtain vacant possession, all he has to do is charge it to the bank for a small sum. Then grant a new tenancy without telling the bank. Then get his wife to pay off the bank and take a transfer. Then get the wife to sue for possession.

That indeed was what happened here. In October 1977, when Mr. Quennell went to the bank, he told them about the tenancies. They said that they did not intend to take proceedings. So he got Mrs. Quennell to do it. In evidence, she said:

"I paid £2,500. This was for my husband. I took the charge to make the debt to his bank less onerous. I was aware he wanted to obtain possession of the house to sell it, I merely paid off the charge. These proceedings have been brought to get possession to sell."

So the objective is plain. It was not to enforce the security or to obtain repayment or anything of that kind. It was in order to get possession of the house and to overcome the protection of the Rent Acts.

Is that permissible? It seems to me that this is one of those cases where equity steps in to mitigate the rigour of the law. Long years ago it did the same when it invented the equity of redemption. As is said in *Snell's Principles of Equity*, 27th ed. (1973), p. 376:

"The courts of equity left the legal effect of the transaction unaltered but declared it to be unreasonable and against conscience that the mortgagee should retain as owner for his own benefit what was intended as a mere security."

So here in modern times equity can step in so as to prevent a mortgagee, or a transferee from him, from getting possession of a house contrary to the justice of the case. A mortgagee will be restrained from getting possession except when it is sought bona fide and reasonably for the purpose of enforcing the security and then only subject to such conditions as the court thinks fit to impose. When the bank itself or a building society lends the money, then it may well be right to allow the mortgagee to obtain possession when the borrower is in default. But so long as the interest is paid and there is nothing outstanding, equity has ample power to restrain any unjust use of the right to possession.

It is plain that in this transaction Mr. and Mrs. Quennell had an ulterior motive. It was not done to enforce the security or due payment of the principal or interest. It was done for the purpose of getting possession of the house in order to resell it at a profit. It was done so as to avoid the protection which the Rent Acts afford to tenants in their occupation. If Mr. Quennell himself had sought to evict the tenants, he would not be allowed to do so. He could not say the tenancies were void. He would be estopped from saying so. They certainly would be protected against him. Are they protected against his wife now that she is the transferee of the charge? In my opinion they are protected. For this simple reason, she is not seeking possession for the purpose of enforcing the loan or the interest or anything of that kind. She is doing it simply for an ulterior purpose of getting possession of the house, contrary to the intention of Parliament as expressed in the Rent Acts.

On that simple ground it seems to me that this action fails and it should be dismissed. The legal right to possession is not to be enforced when it is sought for an ulterior motive. I would on this account allow the appeal and dismiss the action for possession.

It appears that the doctrine of waiver does not apply in these cases, so that the mortgage company is not bound by a tenancy even if it continues to accept mortgage repayments from the landlord after becoming aware of the unlawful letting.[12] However, where the tenancy was granted before the mortgage, it is binding on the mortgagee.[13] If the mortgagee obtains possession against the mortgagor, the tenant becomes the tenant of the mortgagee.

The general rule that the mortgagee is bound by tenancies granted before the creation of the mortgage is subject to an exception which was revealed in *Walthamstow Building Society* v. *Davies*.[14] The landlord let his house to tenants in breach of the terms of his mortgage. Subsequently, the mortgage was discharged and replaced by another mortgage granted to the same mortgagee and on very similar terms. When the mortgagee sought to recover possession, the tenants argued that they were lawful occupiers because the tenancy was granted before the second mortgage. The Court of Appeal rejected this argument on the basis that the reality of the transaction was a variation of the terms of the mortgage, notwithstanding the fact that the mechanism used to achieve this end was to discharge the original mortgage and create a new one. There was, therefore, no point of time when the tenants were in lawful occupation of the premises as against the mortgagee.

Even where premises are mortgaged, the mortgagee may choose to consent to the creation of a tenancy by the mortgagor, in which case the tenant is a lawful occupier and the mortgagee is bound by the tenancy. However, the mortgagee will be unwilling to give consent unless appropriate steps are taken to ensure that the mortgagee's security is protected. In relation to assured tenancies the most obvious way in

---

[12] *Bolton Building Society* v. *Cobb* [1966] 1 W.L.R. 1; *Dudley and District Building Society* v. *Emerson* [1949] Ch. 707.
[13] *Mornington Permanent Building Society* v. *Kenway* [1953] Ch. 553.
[14] (1990) 22 H.L.R. 60.

which the mortgagee can protect his interest is by requiring service of a notice on the tenant prior to the grant of the tenancy. Ground 2 provides:

The dwelling-house is subject to a mortgage granted before the beginning of the tenancy and—

(a) the mortgagee is entitled to exercise a power of sale conferred on him by the mortgage or by section 101 of the Law of Property Act 1925; and

(b) the mortgagee requires possession of the dwelling-house for the purpose of disposing of it with vacant possession in exercise of that power; and

(c) either notice was given as mentioned in Ground 1 above[14a] or the court is satisfied that it is just and equitable to dispense with the requirement of notice;

and for the purposes of this ground "mortgage" includes a charge and "mortgagee" shall be construed accordingly.

The effect of a Ground 2 notice is to make available to the landlord a mandatory ground for possession in cases where the mortgagee intends to realise his security by exercising the power of sale.

As a final point it should be noted that where the tenant is evicted as a result of the mortgagee taking possession, the tenant will normally have the right to sue the landlord for breach of the covenant for quiet enjoyment. There would, of course, be no breach of covenant by the landlord if he lawfully recovered possession of premises let on an assured tenancy under Ground 2.

Note

For further discussion of some of the problems posed by mortgages in this context see R. A. Pearce, Keeping a mortgagee out of possession [1979] C.L.J. 257; P. Smith, Statutory tenants and mortgagees (1977) 41 Conv. 197.

V LANDLORD AND TENANT ACT 1987

Some aspects of the Landlord and Tenant Act 1987 are discussed elsewhere in this book.[15] In the context of third parties, the relevant provisions are to be found in Part I of the Act.

A. Jessup and S. Burrage, Landlord and Tenant Act 1987[16]

In Part I, the Act gives tenants the right of first refusal to purchase the landlord's interest, when s/he considers selling it. In practice, the right applies in

---

[14a] See pp. 208–209.

[15] See pp. 101–103 (landlords' duties to provide tenants with information) and pp. 385–388 (remedies for the landlord's breach of his covenant to repair).

[16] (1988) Legal Action, November p. 14 at pp. 15–17.

limited circumstances, involves complex procedures, and can be evaded by a landlord if tenants are not organised.

Has the tenant got the right?

In order to determine whether the case is one to which the Act applies, the adviser must check that:

    (*a*)   the premises are covered;
    (*b*)   the landlord is within the definition;
    (*c*)   the tenants qualify; and
    (*d*)   the sale is a "relevant disposal."

Only if all these are satisfied can the tenant exercise the right of first refusal.

(a) Premises (s.1)

Blocks of flats or houses converted into two or more flats, in which more than half of the flats are held by qualifying tenants, count as premises on which the right can be exercised. The first question is: what is a "flat"? While s.60 gives some guidance, the definition there is not adequate.

The meaning of "flat" in the Act

The word is defined in s.60 as: "a separate set of premises, whether or not on the same floor, which—(a) forms part of a building, (b) is divided horizontally from some other part of that building, and (c) is constructed or adapted for use for the purposes of a dwelling...." The archetype would be the self-contained, purpose-built flat in a block, containing at least one living room, a kitchen and bathroom all on the same floor. Clearly, something not purpose-built but adapted as a flat satisfies, so, for instance, converted warehouses made into shops with flats above are covered.

Can one room be a "flat" for the Act? The words "a set of" seem to suggest that more than one is needed. Although mathematics recognises sets with only one member, in ordinary language a set connotes more than one thing gathered together; so a set of premises would be more than one room. However, it remains to be seen how the courts interpret the words and it is not yet clear whether bedsitting rooms with shared bathrooms and WC are included in the Act.

(b) Landlord (s.2)

The landlord must be the immediate landlord. The right cannot be exercised against the superior landlord, unless the immediate landlord has a tenancy of less than seven years, or one terminable within seven years at the discretion of the superior landlord also. In this case the right is exercisable against the superior landlord. If the superior landlord has an interest of less than seven years, then the right is exercisable against his or her superior landlord, and so on.

In addition, the landlord must not be "exempt." The following are exempt:

- local authorities;
- the Inner London Education Authority;
- the Commission for New Towns and new town development corporations;
- urban development corporations;
- the Development Board for Rural Wales;
- charitable housing trusts;
- registered housing associations; and
- resident landlords.

There is a new definition of resident landlord (s.58(2)) for these purposes. The landlord of the whole or part of a building will be resident if the premises are not a purpose-built block of flats and the landlord occupies a flat on the premises as his or her only principal home, and has done so for at least 12 months. This is quite different from the Rent Act definition; any Rent Act resident landlord will be Landlord and Tenant Act resident, but not vice versa.

(c) Qualifying tenants (s.3)

Contractual tenants, protected tenants, new style (Housing Act 1988) assured tenants, statutory tenants and long leaseholders qualify under the Act. The following are excluded:
- Housing Act 1980 assured tenants;
- protected shorthold tenants;
- Landlord and Tenant Act 1954 Part II business tenants;
- service tenants;
- any tenant whose tenancy includes any common parts or more than one flat;
- any tenant who holds tenancies of more than half of the flats in the block—this allows someone to qualify even though s/he holds tenancies of more than one flat, provided they do not make up more than half the building; and
- a tenant of an exempt or resident landlord:

Advisers should note that the expression "qualifying tenant" means something different in Part III of the Act. Where the Act refers to "tenancy" it means any tenancy, including a long lease unless otherwise stated.

(d) Relevant disposals (s.4)

The typical case of disposal is the sale of a freehold. However, there are many other kinds of interest in property which may be exchanged. The Act excludes certain sorts of disposal from the tenant's right of first refusal. These include:
- grant of a single tenancy (including long leases);
- disposal under a mortgage (usually sale of a mortgagor's interest to a building society);
- sale when the landlord is insolvent;
- disposal under matrimonial law;
- compulsory purchase;
- gifts to the landlord's family or charity;
- disposal between old and new trustees where the property interest is on trust;
- surrender of a tenancy under any covenant;
- disposal to the Crown; and
- disposal to an associated company.

Also excluded by implication are disposals of an interest in something else, particularly shares in a company which holds the building as its asset; although thought to be less attractive to the property market at the moment, this may become a more popular form of evasion for landlords; tenants must be alert to detect sham sales of shares. Tenants will also need to be wary of the creation of sham mortgages to evade the right of first refusal. The scheme works in this way: A is the current landlord and B a prospective purchaser; A mortgages the block to B; B pays A a capital sum secured against the mortgage; A defaults on the mortgage; B gets possession. This kind of operation can sometimes be challenged in the courts.

The procedure

If the tenant has the right of first refusal, then the landlord is under an obligation to offer him or her the chance to exercise it. The tenant may then accept the landlord's terms of sale or else make a counter offer, and the procedure laid down in the Act provides exacting time limits for this process. The procedure can be bypassed by prospective purchasers in certain circumstances.

(a) The offer notice (s.5)

A landlord intending to make a relevant disposal must first serve notices on at least 90 per cent. of the qualifying tenants, or all but one if there are less than 10. These notices confer the right of first refusal. The notice must state the principal terms of the disposal, which property is to be disposed of, and the price demanded, state that the notice constitutes an offer to sell to the qualifying tenants, provided that the requisite majority agree to the terms, and give a period in which they may respond. This period must be at least two months from the date of service of the notice, and at least two months after the end of the reply period in which the qualifying tenants can nominate the person(s) who will buy; where not all the tenants receive the notice on the same day, the notices all expire on the last day of the latest notice.

(b) The acceptance notice (s.6)

If the qualifying tenants want to accept the landlord's offer, then at least 50 per cent. of them, including those who did not receive notices, must vote to do so; 50 per cent. of those actually voting will not be sufficient unless all qualifying tenants vote; joint tenants have only one vote, since there is only one vote per flat.

Having got the requisite majority, the tenants then serve on the landlord a notice in writing, giving the names and addresses of all the qualifying tenants on whose behalf it is served, accepting the offer. Following this, the landlord may not sell for three months from the date of service of the notice to anyone but the person(s) nominated by the tenants.

If the tenants do not serve such a notice, then the landlord can proceed to sell to a person of his or her own choice, but within 12 months of the expiry of the offer notice the terms of such a sale cannot be more favourable to the purchaser than were offered to the tenants.

(c) Counter offer notice (s.7)

If the tenants do not accept the landlord's terms, they can make a counter offer, stating their preferred terms, and the name and address of the person on whom the landlord must serve his or her notice in reply, and that it has the support of the requisite majority of the qualifying tenants. The landlord then serves either an acceptance or a rejection notice. If the landlord makes a new offer (s.8), it is treated in the same way as the first offer, with the same time periods; if the landlord accepts the counter offer, then the tenants have two months in which to nominate their purchaser. If they cannot agree, the landlord is free to sell but, in the first 12 months, only on terms no more favourable to the purchaser than were offered to the tenants; thereafter a new offer notice is required.

(d) Prospective purchasers (s.18)

Tenants need to be aware that the Act provides a special procedure by which prospective purchasers can serve a notice first.

A prospective purchaser may serve on 80 per cent. of the tenants who need not be qualifying tenants, a notice indicating her or his interest in buying the property, informing them of the proposed terms of the purchase including the price, and inviting the tenants to serve notices on the prospective purchaser stating whether or not an offer has been made to them under the procedure above, and whether they know of any other reason why they (the tenants) are not entitled to the right of first refusal, and if there is no such reason, whether they wish to buy. The notice must also caution the tenants that it could lead to the loss of their right to first refusal.

Only if more than 50 per cent. of the tenants actually served with this notice reply within 28 days saying that they are entitled to the right of first refusal and wish to exercise it, is the right preserved. Otherwise, the sale to the prospective purchaser can go ahead without the procedure outlined above.

(e) Forcing sale where the right has been ignored (s.12)

If neither the landlord nor the prospective purchaser has served the notices under these procedures, and a relevant disposal has taken place, the tenants can apply by originating application to the county court to compel, by injunction, the new owner to sell to them or their nominee on the same terms as those on which the disposal took place. To find out whether there has been such a disposal, the new right to information[17] ... is relevant.

(f) Withdrawing from a sale (s.9)

All offer, counter offer and acceptance notices under the Act are subject to contract. This means that tenants can withdraw from a sale despite having served a notice on the landlord saying that they accept an offer. However, withdrawing later than certain time periods will result in tenants being liable for the costs incurred by their landlords in processing the sale. Taking the time periods on each notice stage together, tenants can delay a sale by a landlord for up to five months, or, where a prospective purchaser serves a notice, four months, without incurring costs. They have two months from service of the offer to serve their acceptance or rejection; if they accept, they have a further two months to make their nomination; from one month after the end of the nomination period, tenants will incur costs if they withdraw. There is, of course, no binding contract until exchange of contracts, as in any other conveyance. The landlord can also withdraw from the sale; in practice, this is likely to happen only if the property has ceased to be covered by the Act, unless s/he wishes to sell to someone else on terms no more favourable to the prospective purchaser than were offered to the tenants. The most likely reason why a property would

[17] See pp. 101–103.

cease to be covered would be if so many flats become vacant that 50 per cent. of the property was no longer let to qualifying tenants.

Advising tenants

Tenants will need support and a variety of types of advice in using the procedure. Tenants will not always be interested in purchase; they may be engaged in some other activity for which it is important to delay or deter a sale by the landlord; and tenants' advisers should be aware of this. Those interested in purchasing may need help with:

- raising finance from mortgage sources;
- getting valuations;
- forming a company;
- contacting housing associations with capital available to buy;
- deciding on management after purchase;
- deciding whether or not to change tenancy agreements once they have bought; and
- accounting procedures.

Practitioners should be ready to co-ordinate with different sorts of advisers, and those with little experience of conveyancing will probably have to become more familiar with that area of work.

Note

Part I of the 1987 Act has begun to produce a steady stream of reported litigation.[18] For further analysis see M. E. Percival, The Landlord and Tenant Act 1987 (1988) 51 M.L.R. 97; C. P. Rogers, Residential flats—a new deal? The Landlord and Tenant Act 1987 [1988] Conv. 122.

---

[18] *Cousins* v. *Metropolitan Guarantee Ltd.* [1990] 1 E.G.L.R. 223; *Wilkins* v. *Horrowitz* [1990] 29 E.G. 57; *Bhatti* v. *Berkley Court Investments Ltd.* (1991) 23 H.L.R. 6; *139 Finborough Road Management Ltd.* v. *Maasoor* [1990] 32 E.G. 55; *Sullivan* v. *Safeland Investments Ltd.* [1990] 33 E.G. 52; *Tyson* v. *Carlisle Estates Ltd.* [1990] 36 E.G. 127; *Englefield Court Tenants* v. *Skeels* [1990] 37 E.G. 91; *30 Upperton Gardens Management Ltd.* v. *Alcano* [1990] 45 E.G. 121 & 46 E.G. 131; *Venus* v. *Khan* [1990] 47 E.G. 71.

CHAPTER 6

REPAIRS AND IMPROVEMENTS

Introduction: Data on Housing Conditions

The state of Britain's housing leaves much to be desired. The 1986 English Housing Condition Survey classified dwellings "in poor condition" into three categories: unfit, lacking basic amenities and in poor repair. For the purposes of the report:

— an unfit dwelling is one which is unsuitable for human habitation as defined by section 604 of the Housing Act 1985[1];

— basic amenities are those listed in section 508 of the Housing Act 1985: a kitchen sink, a bath or shower in a bathroom, a wash hand basin, hot and cold water provided to each of these and an indoor WC; and

— a dwelling is taken to be in a poor state of repair "where urgent repairs to the external fabric of the property are estimated to cost more than £1,000."[2]

A certain number of dwellings fall within two or more categories. The results are summarised below:

Condition	Thousand dwellings	Percentage
Lacking basic amenities	463	2.5
Unfit	909	4.8
In poor repair	2,430	12.9
Satisfactory dwellings	15,971	84.8
All dwellings	18,839	100

It is worth noting that privately rented accommodation lacks proportionately more of the standard amenities than other types of housing:

---

[1] See pp. 408–409.
[2] *English House Condition Survey 1986* (1988) para. 5.1.

Dwellings lacking basic amenities by tenure

thousands/%dwellings

	Owner Occupied	Private Rented	Local Authority/ New Town	Housing Associa- tion	Vacant	All Dwellings
Dwellings Lacking 1 or	144(31.1)	102(22.0)	72(15.5)	5(1.1)	140(30.3)	463(100)
More Amenity	(1.2)	(8.2)	(1.6)	(1.1)	(17.2)	(2.5)

These figures suggest that in certain respects there have been improvements in the state of England's housing during the last 10 years: for example, there are fewer houses today lacking amenities than was the case in 1976.[3] Nevertheless, the repairs problem continues to be a very serious one.

According to the 1986 survey 13 per cent. of owner-occupied dwellings are in poor condition; 42 per cent. of privately rented housing; 11 per cent. of dwellings rented from local authorities; and only seven per cent. of dwellings rented from housing associations.[4]

In general terms there is a correlation between the condition of housing and its age:

Dwellings in poor condition by tenure and construction date

thousands/%dwellings in poor condition

	Owner Occupied	Private Rented	Local Authority/ New Town	Housing Associa- tion	Vacant	All Dwellings
Pre-1900	773(31.3)	313(48.3)	38(32.4)	16(10.1)	198(57.5)	1,338(36.2)
1901–1918	237(26.4)	114(43.6)	10(19.9)	1(12.1)	45(53.2)	407(31.3)
1919–1944	344(12.9)	60(32.3)	169(17.6)	8(16.6)	45(35.2)	626(15.8)
Post-1944	162 (2.8)	36(18.3)	258 (7.7)	6 (2.3)	35(13.7)	497 (5.0)
All Dwell- ings	1,516(12.8)	523(42.0)	475(10.6)	31 (6.6)	323(39.8)	2,868(15.2)

These figures indicate that the private rented sector is proportionately in the poorest condition. However, local authorities own over half the dwellings in poor condition built after 1944.

It is extremely difficult to assess how much it would cost to undertake the repairs which are currently necessary, although clearly the cost

---

[3] See Table 7.1 in Partington, *Landlord and Tenant* (2nd ed., 1980), p. 328.
[4] *English House Condition Survey 1986* (1988), para. 5.6.

would run into billions. The 1986 English Housing Condition Survey gives some indication of the extent of the problem:

Estimated cost of repair by construction date and tenure

mean cost £

	Pre-1919	1919–1944	1945–1964	Post-1964	All Ages
Owner Occupied	1,920	940	480	170	900
Private Rented	2,570	1,720	880	300	2,030
Local Authority/New Town	1,600	970	730	300	670
Housing Association	940	830	780	110	480
Vacant	2,970	1,550	770	410	1,980
All Dwellings	2,090	1,010	600	210	950

To the lawyer these figures may be particularly shocking since, as this chapter reveals, there is a great amount of law relating to housing conditions. None of it, notably in the landlord-tenant sector, has worked particularly well. For example, most leases contain repairing covenants; yet they are not effective in securing decent housing conditions.

Public health legislation has a long history: the first major public health Act was passed in 1848. But, in so far as this area of law relates to housing conditions, it has always been concerned with patching up emergencies rather than enforcing long-term solutions. Although under various Housing Acts local authorities have been given powers to deal with housing conditions, they have not proved effective. More recently, grants towards improvements in housing conditions have been introduced, but frequently they have not been taken up by those for whom they were designed, and their use seems to be declining. The law on improvement grants has been completely recast by Part VIII of the Local Government and Housing Act 1989. It is too early to tell whether this reform will bring about a significant change in practice.

In recent years, considerable energy has been spent on attempts to utilise the law. Law centres, housing aid centres, specialist advice agencies (such as Shelter) have all gone to great lengths to take cases before the courts. While in individual cases a ruling favourable to tenants may be obtained, as the figures show, the general problem of poor housing conditions remains.

There are many possible reasons for the apparent ineffectiveness in the use of the law. Partly it may be said to derive from the law itself, much of which gives discretionary powers to local authorities rather than imposing duties on them. Also, the judges have on occasion interpreted the rules so that their scope has been limited. More generally, the economic climate has not been encouraging. Public expenditure restraints have contributed to a fall in the numbers of improvement grants being made, prevented local authorities from acting as positively as they might in enforcing the law, and discouraged local authorities from maintaining the stock of public sector housing. Private sector landlords have complained that low rent levels (fixed under the Rent Acts) have made improvements and repairs financially impossible. One of the aims of the Housing Act 1988 is to overcome this problem by the deregulation of rents of new lettings in the private sector.

It must also be remembered that the problem is a dynamic one, not one that can be resolved once and for all. As standards and expectations about the quality of life change, so attitudes as to what are, or are not, adequate housing conditions will also change.

Finally, although this chapter concentrates on an analysis of the relevant substantive law, the problems of enforcement should constantly be borne in mind.

I COVENANTS TO REPAIR

(A) THE MEANING OF REPAIR

The meaning which the law attaches to "repair" is clearly of prime importance since defects, however extensive they may be, which are not within the legal definition of repair fall outside the scope of repairing covenants (whether express or implied). Repair is said not to be the same as improvement, nor renewal. In numerous cases the courts have tried to distinguish these various concepts.

Denning L.J. in *Morcom* v. *Campbell-Johnson*[5] described the difference between repairs and improvement as follows:

[I]f the work which is done is the provision of something new for the benefit of the occupier, that is, properly speaking, an improvement; but if it is only the replacement of something already there, which has become dilapidated or worn out, then, albeit that it is the replacement by its modern equivalent, it comes within the category of repairs and not improvements.

Buckley L.J. in *Lurcott* v. *Wakely and Wheeler*[6] said:

Repair is restoration by renewal or replacement of subsidiary parts of a whole. Renewal, as distinguished from repair, is reconstruction of the entirety, meaning by the entirety not necessarily the whole but substantially the whole.

Notwithstanding extensive litigation in this area, the courts have continued to struggle with the problems of fixing the boundaries of repairing covenants.

---

[5] [1956] 1 Q.B. 106 at 115.
[6] [1911] 1 K.B. 905 at 924.

Quick v. *Taff-Ely B.C.* [1986] Q.B. 809

The case involved a council house which suffered from severe damp as a result of condensation. It was agreed between the parties that by virtue of section 32 of the Housing Act 1961[7] the landlord was under an obligation "to keep in repair the structure and exterior of the dwelling-house." The tenant argued that the condensation—which had caused damage to his furniture, etc.—was a result of the exterior being in a bad state of repair, and claimed damages. The landlord resisted the claim on the basis that the defect complained of was not disrepair within the meaning of the covenant. At first instance, the judge found for the tenant and awarded damages. The local authority appealed.
Dillon L.J. said (at 814–819):

To understand the problem about condensation, it is necessary to say a bit more about the house. It is a quite small terraced house though, because of levels, the terrace is stepped. On the ground floor the front door leads into a hall, with stairs up to the first floor. To the left of the hall is the kitchen and at the back of the hall and kitchen, across the full width of the house, is the living room. There is a W.C. to the right of the front door. Upstairs there are three bedrooms and a bathroom. Most importantly, all the windows in the house are single-glazed with metal frames set in wooden window surrounds, and the lintels above the windows have no insulation material facing them; the lintels are, in fact, of concrete, though thought at the trial to have been metal, but nothing turns on any difference between metal and concrete. The house was fitted with central heating by a warm air ducted system. The plaintiff lived in the house with his wife and four daughters. It is his misfortune that for the last five years he has been unemployed.

There is no doubt at all that there has for years been very severe condensation in the house, which has rendered the living conditions of the plaintiff and his family appalling. The house was redecorated by the council shortly before the plaintiff became tenant, but the effects of condensation became soon apparent. There is uncontradicted evidence that the plaintiff complained again and again to the council's officials about the condition of the house, but all his complaints were ignored and in the end he started this action.

The detailed evidence about the condensation and its causes was given by the plaintiff's architect, Mr. Pryce Thomas of Pontypridd. He wrote two reports, of January 24, 1983 and December 22, 1983, which were in evidence, and he also gave oral evidence at the trial which confirmed his reports. The council called no evidence and the judge found Mr. Pryce Thomas to be an impressive and fair-minded expert witness whose evidence he accepted.

The evidence shows that there was severe condensation on the walls, windows and metal surfaces in all rooms of the house. Water had frequently to be wiped off the walls; paper peeled off the walls and ceilings, woodwork rotted, particularly inside and behind the fitted cupboards in the kitchen. Fungus or mould growth appeared in places and particularly in the two back bedrooms there was a persistent and offensive smell of damp. Among the places where there was mould growth were the wooden sills and surrounds of the windows in the bedrooms, and some of these have become rotten. Additionally, in the

[7] Now Landlord and Tenant Act 1985, s.11. See pp. 361–363.

bedrooms condensation caused the nails used for fixing the ceiling plasterboard to sweat and, though it is not mentioned in the judge's judgment, there was some perishing of the plaster due to excessive moisture.

The condensation came about from the warm air of the environment in the rooms reaching the cold surfaces of the building. The moisture of the condensation was then absorbed by the atmosphere, and transferred to bedding, clothes and other fabrics which became mildewed and rotten. There was evidence that carpets and curtains had been ruined—but such damage in the living room and hall could well be attributable to the water penetration. There was evidence which the judge accepted that a three-piece suite in the living room was ruined by damp so that it smelt and rotted and had to be thrown out. The evidence of the plaintiff and his wife was that, because of the appearance and smell, they hardly used the living room, took visitors to the kitchen and sent the children up to their parents' bedroom to watch television. I would conclude that, by modern standards, the house was in winter, when, of course, the condensation was worst, virtually unfit for human habitation.

Mr. Pryce Thomas said that the condensation was caused by: (a) cold bridging from the window lintels because there was no insulating material; (b) sweating from the single-glazed metal windows (and a wooden infill panel under the living room window); and (c) inadequate heating both in respect of the system and by the occupier not maintaining a high enough thermostat setting. He added that the problem was aggravated by the plaintiff's gas cooker and washing machine, presumably because these, when in use, would be sources of heat.

He said in his second report of December 1983 that, to "alleviate" the problems the property was experiencing, the existing metal windows should be replaced by windows with frames of warm material, such as timber or UPVC window frames, and the lintels over the windows should have insulation material facings. He added that, in his opinion, a new radiator system to all rooms, designed to give the proper standards to the various rooms, was necessary in place of the existing warm air system, which he regarded as "doubtful in being able to maintain normal accepted heating standards."

He made it clear, however, in the course of his evidence that the house was built in accordance with the regulations in force and standards accepted at the time it was built. He said that, when these houses were built, no-one realised the problems of cold bridging nor the inadequacy of central heating systems such as that which was installed in the house. Condensation had become more and more of a problem in recent years. ...

The judge delivered a careful reserved judgment in which he reviewed many of the more recent authorities on repairing covenants, starting with *Pembery* v. *Lamdin* [1940] 2 All E.R. 434. His ultimate reasoning seems to me to be on the following lines *viz.*: (1) recent authorities such as *Ravenseft Properties Ltd.* v. *Davstone (Holdings) Ltd.* [1980] Q.B. 12 and *Elmcroft Developments Ltd.* v. *Tankersley-Sawyer* (1984) 270 E.G. 140 show that works of repair under a repairing covenant, whether by a landlord or a tenant, may require the remedying of an inherent defect in a building; (2) the authorities also show that it is a question of degree whether works which remedy an inherent defect in a building may not be so extensive as to amount to an improvement or renewal of the whole which is beyond the concept of repair; (3) in the present case the replacement of windows and the provision of insulation for the lintels does not amount to such an improvement or renewal of the whole; (4) therefore, the replacement of the windows and provision of the insulation to alleviate an inherent defect is a repair which the council is bound to carry out under the repairing covenant.

But, with every respect to the judge, this reasoning begs the important question. It assumes that any work to eradicate an inherent defect in a building must be a work of repair, which the relevant party is bound to carry out if, as a matter of degree, it does not amount to a renewal or improvement of the building. In effect, it assumes the broad proposition urged on us by Mr. Blom-Cooper for the plaintiff that anything defective or inherently inefficient for living in or ineffective to provide the conditions of ordinary habitation is in disrepair. But that does not follow from the decisions in *Ravenseft's* case [1980] Q.B. 12 and *Elmcroft's* case, 270 E.G. 140 that works of repair *may* require the remedying of an inherent defect.

Mr. Blom-Cooper's proposition has very far-reaching implications indeed. The covenant implied under section 32 of the Act of 1961 is an ordinary repairing covenant. It does not only apply to local authorities as landlords, and this court has held in *Wainwright* v. *Leeds City Council* (1984) 270 E.G. 1289 that the fact that a landlord is a local authority, which is discharging a social purpose in providing housing for people who cannot afford it, does not make the burden of the covenant greater on that landlord than it would be on any other landlord. The construction of the covenant must be the same whether it is implied as a local authority's covenant in a tenancy of a council house or is expressly included as a tenant's or landlord's covenant in a private lease which is outside section 32. A tenant under such a lease who had entered into such a repairing covenant would, no doubt, realise, if he suffered from problems of condensation in his house, that he could not compel the landlord to do anything about those problems. But I apprehend that the tenant would be startled to be told—as must follow from Judge Francis's decision—that the landlord has the right to compel him, the tenant, to put in new windows. If the reasoning is valid, where is the process to stop? The evidence of Mr. Pryce Thomas was that changing the windows and insulating the lintels would "alleviate" the problems, not that it would cure them. If there was evidence that double glazing would further alleviate the problems, would a landlord, or tenant, under a repairing covenant be obliged to put in double glazing? Mr. Pryce Thomas said that a radiator system of heating to all rooms in the place of the warm air system was "necessary"; if the judge's reasoning was correct, it would seem that, if the point had been properly pleaded early enough, the plaintiff might have compelled the council to put in a radiator system of heating.

In my judgment, the key factor in the present case is that disrepair is related to the physical condition of whatever has to be repaired, and not to questions of lack of amenity or inefficiency. I find helpful the observation of Atkin L.J. in *Anstruther-Gough-Calthorpe* v. *McOscar* [1924] 1 K.B. 716, 734 that repair "connotes the idea of making good damage so as to leave the subject so far as possible as though it had not been damaged." Where decorative repair is in question one must look for damage to the decorations but where, as here, the obligation is merely to keep the structure and exterior of the house in repair, the covenant will only come into operation where there has been damage to the structure and exterior which requires to be made good.

If there is such damage caused by an unsuspected inherent defect, then it may be necessary to cure the defect, and thus to some extent improve without wholly renewing the property as the only practicable way of making good the damage to the subject matter of the repairing covenant. That, as I read the case, was the basis of the decision in *Ravenseft* [1980] Q.B. 12. There there was an inherent defect when the building, a relatively new one, was built in that no expansion joints had been included because it had not been realised that the different coefficients of expansion of the stone of the cladding and the concrete of the structure made it necessary to include such joints. There was, however, also physical damage to the subject matter of the covenant in that, because of the differing coefficients of expansion, the stones of the cladding had become bowed, detached from the structure, loose and in danger of falling. Forbes J. in a very valuable judgment rejected the argument that no liability arose under a repairing covenant if it could be shown that the disrepair was due to an inherent defect in the building. He allowed in the damages under the repairing covenant the cost of putting in expansion joints, and in that respect improving the building, because, as he put it, at p. 22, on the evidence "In no realistic sense ... could it be said that there was any other possible way of reinstating this cladding than by providing the expansion joints which were, in fact, provided."

The *Elmcroft* case, 270 E.G. 140, was very similar. There was physical damage from rising damp in the walls of a flat in a fashionable area of London. That was due to an inherent defect in that when the flat had been built in late Victorian times as a high-class residential flat, the slate damp-proof course had been put in too low and was therefore ineffective. The remedial work necessary to eradicate the rising damp was, on the evidence, the installation of a horizontal damp-proof course by silicone injection and formation of vertical barriers by silicone injection. This was held to be within the landlord's repairing covenant. It was necessary in order to repair the walls and, although it involved improvement over the previous ineffective slate damp-proof course, it was held that, as a matter of degree, having regard to the nature and locality of the property, this did not involve giving the tenant a different thing from that which was demised. The decision of this court in *Smedley* v. *Chumley & Hawke Ltd.* (1982) 44 P. & C.R. 50 is to the same effect; the damage to a recently constructed restaurant built on a concrete raft on piles over a river could only be cured by putting in further piles so that the structure of the walls and roof of the restaurant were stable and safe upon foundations made structurally stable.

The only other of the many cases cited to us which I would mention is *Pembery* v. *Lamdin* [1940] 2 All E.R. 434. There the property demised was a ground floor shop and basement, built 100 years or more before the demise. The landlord was liable to repair the external part of the premises and there was physical damage to the walls of the basement in that they were permeated with damp because there had never been any damp-proof course. The works required by the tenant to waterproof the basement were very extensive, involving cleaning and asphalting the existing walls, building internal brick walls and laying a concrete floor. This would have involved improvement to such an extent as to give the tenant a different thing from what had been demised and it was therefore outside the repairing covenant. But Slesser L.J. appears to recognise, at p. 438, that repointing of the existing basement walls where the mortar had partly perished would have been within the repairing covenant.

In the present case the liability of the council was to keep the structure and exterior of the house in repair—not the decorations. Though there is ample evidence of damage to the decorations and to bedding, clothing and other fabrics, evidence of damage to the subject matter of the covenant, the structure and exterior of the house, is far to seek. Though the condensation comes about from the effect of the warm atmosphere in the rooms on the cold surfaces of the walls and windows, there is no evidence at all of physical damage to the walls— as opposed to the decorations—or the windows.

Lawton L.J. agreed and said (at 821–823):

As a matter of the ordinary usage of English that which requires repair is in a condition worse than it was at some earlier time. This usage of English is, in my judgment, the explanation for the many decisions on the extent of a landlord's or tenant's obligation under covenants to keep houses in repair. Broadly stated, they come to this: a tenant must take the house as he finds it; neither a landlord nor a tenant is bound to provide the other with a better house than there was to start with; but, because almost all repair work requires some degree of renewal, problems of degree arise as to whether after the repair there is a house which is different from that which was let. I do not find it necessary to review the cases which were decided before 1980.

During the last 20 years the way in which houses and other buildings have been constructed has produced new problems. Traditional materials may not have been used: new methods of construction may have been employed. The materials may fail; the methods may prove to have been unsatisfactory, causing damage; the building may have got into a worse condition than it was when the lease was granted. In such cases there is need for repair. The landlord or the tenant may be under an obligation to put right what has gone wrong; and, in putting right what has gone wrong, it may be necessary to abandon the use of the defective materials or to use a different and better method of construction.

When something like this happens, does the landlord or the tenant have a better building? In one sense he does: he gets a building without the design defect which caused the damage; but the repair could only have been done in a sensible way by getting rid of the design defect. Forbes J. had to consider this problem in *Ravenseft Properties Ltd.* v. *Davstone (Holdings) Ltd.* [1980] Q.B. 12. In that case the repair work could not be done satisfactorily without getting rid of a design fault. He adjudged that doing so did not amount to such a change in the character of the building as to take the works out of the ambit of the covenant to repair: see pp. 21–22. This court in *Smedley* v. *Chumley & Hawke Ltd.*, 44 P. & C.R. 50, approached the problem in the same way. The *Ravenseft* case [1980] Q.B. 12 does not seem to have been cited. It was, however, cited to this court in *Elmcroft Developments Ltd.* v. *Tankersley-Sawyer*, 270 E.G. 140 and clearly approved. It was not cited to this court in *Wainwright* v. *Leeds City Council*, 270 E.G. 1289. In the latter case counsel for the tenant seems to have based his unsuccessful submissions on social rather than legal grounds. I am satisfied that the approach of Forbes J. in the *Ravenseft* case [1980] Q.B. 12 was right.

It follows that, on the evidence in this case, the trial judge should first have identified the parts of the exterior and structure of the house which were out of repair and then have gone on to decide whether, in order to remedy the defects, it was reasonably necessary to replace the concrete lintels over the windows, which caused "cold bridging," and the single glazed metal windows, both of which were among the causes, probably the major causes, of excessive condensation in the house. An argument along the following lines was put before this court: the evidence established that some of the wooden frames into which the single glazed metal windows were inserted had rotted and that nearby plaster had crumbled away. Mr. Hague, for the purposes of this case, accepted that the plaster was part of the structure. Repairing the wooden frames and the plaster could only be done sensibly if the single glazed metal windows and the lintels were replaced by ones of better design. The council should have appreciated that this was so. A submission of this kind would have required the trial judge to make findings of the same kind as Forbes J. made in *Ravenseft Properties Ltd.* v. *Davstone (Holdings) Ltd.* [1980] Q.B. 12. He made none, almost certainly because he was not asked to do so. He referred to Forbes J.'s judgment in these terms:

"He held that want of repair due to an inherent defect could fall within the ambit of a repairing covenant, and that it was a question of degree whether work could properly be described as repair or whether it so changed the character of the building as to involve giving back to the landlord a different building from that demised."

He seems to have overlooked the important fact in the *Ravenseft* case that the cladding around the building was in disrepair and could only be repaired in a sensible way if the design fault were put right.

In my judgment, there must be disrepair before any question arises as to whether it would be reasonable to remedy a design fault when doing the repair. In this case, as the trial judge found, there was no evidence that the single glazed metal windows were in any different state at the date of the trial from what they had been in when the plaintiff first became a tenant. The same could have been said of the lintels. The judge misdirected himself in finding that these windows required repair.

Neill L.J. delivered a brief concurring judgment.

Note

(i) It would be difficult to exaggerate the practical significance of this decision. Dillon L.J. noted that "the case is of an importance to the local authority which is far beyond the award of damages because, as the judge surmised, his decision as to the effect of the repairing covenant in relation to this house will affect very many other houses on this and other council estates. We are told by counsel for the local authority that the total cost in respect of the local authority's other houses of similarly replacing metal-framed windows with timber or UPVC framed windows and of facing the lintels with insulation material has been estimated as in the region of £9 m."[8]

(ii) In *McDougall* v. *Easington D.C.*[9] the Court of Appeal had to consider whether certain building works undertaken by the local authority constituted repairs or improvements. Mustill L.J. said:

[I]n my opinion three different tests may be discerned, which may be applied separately or concurrently as the circumstances of the individual case may demand, but all to be approached in the light of the nature and age of the premises, their condition when the tenant went into occupation, and the other express terms of the tenancy:

(i)   Whether the alterations went to the whole or substantially the whole of the structure or only to a subsidiary part;
(ii) Whether the effect of the alterations was to produce a building of a wholly different character than that which had been let;
(iii) What was the cost of the works in relation to the previous value of the building, and what was their effect on the value and lifespan of the building.

Whichever of these tests one chooses to apply, and whether they are taken separately or together, the answer in the present case seems to me the same. When the work was complete, the house not only looked different; it was different. The changes were not simply cosmetic. The roofs, elevations and fenestration were of different configurations and material. With the exception of

---

[8] [1986] Q.B. 809 at 816.
[9] (1989) 21 H.L.R. 310.

the basic concrete boxes, no feature of the house was left untouched in the course of the work. The outcome was a house with a substantially longer life, and worth nearly twice as much as before. Acknowledging that repairs, properly so called, inevitably involve an element of renewal and improvement, I still think it clear that the learned Recorder was right to hold that these could not be described as repairs. They gave the building a new life in a different form.[10]

Mustill L.J. did not give any guidance on how the courts should decide a case where the application of the three tests would not produce the same result.[11]

(B) EXPRESS COVENANTS

When a dispute arises between a landlord and tenant as to the condition of a house, or indeed any other type of property that has been let, the first question will be: what are the terms of the lease or tenancy agreement? At common law, the division of repairing obligations was often a matter of negotiation or conveyancing practice:

The landlord may by covenant undertake to do the repairs or some of them and it is not uncommon in short leases for the landlord to agree to be liable for external repairs. It is important to observe that except in so far as he expressly covenants to do so, he is generally speaking under no implied obligation to repair nor in general does he warrant that the premises are fit for occupation for any particular purpose. If therefore the lease is silent as to repairs the tenant must take the premises as he finds them ... [12]

On the other hand:

... in the case of a lease for say the typical building lease period of 99 years, containing, as is almost invariably the case, the usual "full" repairing covenants, the aggregate liability over the whole period may amount to a formidable total ...

Put very shortly, the full repairing covenants normally entered into by the tenant under a typical long lease are:—

(i)   To keep the premises in good repair both internally and externally.

(ii) To do certain specific works of repair at stated intervals—*e.g.* to paint inside once every seven and outside once every three years.

(iii) To permit the landlord from time to time during the term to enter and view the state of repair; and to make good defects on notice.

---

[10] At 316.
[11] See also *Murray* v. *Birmingham C.C.* (1988) 20 H.L.R. 39; *Post Office* v. *Aquarius Properties* (1987) 54 P. & C.R. 61; *Stent* v. *Monmouth D.C.* (1987) 19 H.L.R. 269.
[12] Uthwatt-Jenkins, *Committee on Leasehold, Final Report* (1950) Cmd. 7952, para. 228.

(iv) To deliver up the premises in good repair at the expiration or sooner determination of the term.

Unless loss or damage by fire is excepted from the repairing covenants, the tenant under full repairing covenants such as these will be liable to reinstate the premises at his own cost. In leases of this type there is commonly a covenant by the tenant to insure the premises against loss or damage by fire, and to apply the moneys received under such insurance in reinstating the premises and sometimes also to make good out of his own pocket any deficiency in such insurance moneys as compared with the amount required to reinstate the premises.[13]

Interpretation of repairing covenants has been the subject of much litigation. Given the expense frequently involved this is not surprising. The courts have developed a number of basic principles in their attempt to determine liability in these cases:

(a) When a tenant has covenanted to repair and keep in repair premises at all times during the lease, it is implied that he must put them into repair when the tenancy begins; otherwise they cannot be kept or left in repair according to the covenant.[14] The same principle applies to a landlord's covenant to repair.[15]

(b) The word repair is frequently qualified by an adjective such as "good," or "tenantable" or "habitable." In *Proudfoot* v. *Hart*[16] Lopes L.J. said, in a case concerning a lease for three years, that this amounted to "such repair as, having regard to the age, character and locality of the house, would make it reasonably fit for a reasonably minded tenant of the class who would be likely to take it."[17] The standard for Belgravia would be different from that for Spitalfields.

However, in *Anstruther-Gough-Calthorpe* v. *McOscar*[18] premises were let on a 95-year lease. Originally the houses were in the country; at the time of the dispute the district had become built up. It was argued that, since the tenants were now prepared to take only short-term lettings, the proper standard of repair was that which they would require now. The Court of Appeal rejected this, saying that the premises had to be put into a reasonable state of repair to suit the type of tenant who would originally have taken the lease.[19]

(c) An exception for fair wear and tear is also frequently found in repairing covenants. This is another formula which has caused difficulty. In *Regis Property Co. Ltd.* v. *Dudley*[20] the House of Lords approved

---

[13] *Ibid.* paras. 216–217.
[14] *Proudfoot* v. *Hart* (1890) 25 Q.B.D. 42.
[15] *Saner* v. *Bilton* (1878) 7 Ch.D. 815.
[16] (1890) 25 Q.B.D. 42.
[17] At 55.
[18] [1924] 1 K.B. 716.
[19] See also *Jaquin* v. *Holland* [1960] 1 W.L.R. 258.
[20] [1959] A.C. 370.

the following statement of principle from the judgment of Talbot J. in
Haskell v. *Marlow*:

The meaning is that the tenant ... is bound to keep the house in good repair
and condition, but is not liable for what is due to reasonable wear and tear. ...
If any want of repair is alleged and proved in fact, it lies on the tenant to show
that it comes within the exception. Reasonable wear and tear means the
reasonable use of the house by the tenant and the ordinary operation of natural
forces. The exception of want of repair due to wear and tear must be construed
as limited to what is directly due to wear and tear, reasonable conduct on the
part of the tenant being assumed. It does not mean that if there is a defect
originally proceeding from reasonable wear and tear the tenant is released from
his obligation to keep in good repair and condition everything which it may be
possible to trace ultimately to that defect. He is bound to do such repairs as may
be required to prevent the consequences flowing originally from wear and tear
from producing others which wear and tear would not directly produce.[21]

(C) COVENANTS IMPLIED BY THE COMMON LAW AFFECTING
LANDLORDS

(1) Furnished Dwellings

Notwithstanding the general freedom of the parties to agree terms,
the common law implies an obligation on landlords to let furnished
dwellings in a habitable condition. To comply with this obligation the
landlord may have to carry out certain repairs before premises are let.

Smith v. *Marrable* (1843) 11 M. & W. 5[22]

At the trial before Lord Abinger, C.B., ... , it appeared that the action was
brought to recover a balance of five weeks' rent of a furnished house at
Brighton, which had been taken by the defendant of the plaintiff under the
following agreement:—

Brighton, September 14, 1842.
Mr John Smith, of 24, St. James's-street, agrees to let, and Sir Thomas
Marrable agrees to take, the house No. 5, Brunswick-place, at the rent of eight
guineas per week, for five or six weeks at the option of the said Sir Thomas
Marrable.

THOMAS MARRABLE.
JOHN SMITH.
The rent to commence on the 15th September.   T.M.
                                                      J.S.

Under this agreement, the defendant and his family entered into possession of
the house on Friday the 16th of September. On the following day, Lady
Marrable having complained to the plaintiff that the house was infested with
bugs, he sent a person in to take means for getting rid of them, which however

---

[21] [1928] K.B. 45 at 58–59. See also *Warren* v. *Keen* [1954] 1 Q.B. 15 (pp. 356–358).
[22] See also *Bird* v. *Lord Greville* (1884) Cab & El. 317; *Wilson* v. *Finch Hatton* (1877) 2 Ex.D. 336;
Collins v. *Hopkins* [1923] 2 K.B. 617.

did not prove successful; and on the 19th Lady Marrable wrote the following note to the wife of the plaintiff:—

"5, Brunswick Place, Sept. 19, 1842.

Lady Marrable informs Mrs Smith, that it is her determination to leave the house in Brunswick Place as soon as she can take another, paying a week's rent, as all the bedrooms occupied but one are so infested with bugs that it is impossible to remain."

On the following Thursday, the 22nd, the defendant accordingly sent the key of the house, together with the amount of a week's rent, to the plaintiff, and removed with his family to another residence. Evidence was given to shew that the house was in fact greatly infested by bugs. The Lord Chief Baron, in summing up, stated to the jury, that in point of law every house must be taken to be let upon the implied condition that there was nothing about it so noxious as to render it uninhabitable; and that if they believed that the defendant left the plaintiff's house on account of the nuisance occasioned by these vermin being so intolerable as to render it impossible that he could live in it with any reasonable comfort, they ought to find a verdict for the defendant. The jury having found for the defendant,

Hayward now moved for a new trial, on the ground of misdirection ...

Parke, B: This case involves the question whether, in point of law, a person who lets a house must be taken to let it under the implied condition that it is in a state fit for decent and comfortable habitation, and whether he is at liberty to throw it up, when he makes the discovery that it is not so. The case of *Edwards* v. *Etherington* (Ry. & M. 268; S.C., 7 D. & R. 117) appears to me to be an authority very nearly in point. There the defendant, who held a house as tenant from year to year, quitted without notice, on the ground that the walls were in so dilapidated a state that it had become unsafe to reside in it; and Lord Tenterden, at Nisi Prius, held these facts to be an answer to an action by the landlord for use and occupation: telling the jury, that although slight circumstances would not suffice, such serious reasons might exist as would justify a tenant's quitting at any time, and that it was for them to say whether, in the case before them, such serious reasons existed as would exempt the defendant from the plaintiff's demand, on the ground of his having had no beneficial use and occupation of the premises. The jury found for the defendant, and the Court of King's Bench was afterwards moved for a new trial on the ground of misdirection, but they refused to disturb the verdict. There is also another case of *Collins* v. *Barrow* (1 M. & Rob. 112), in which Bayley, B., held that a tenant was justified in quitting without notice premises which were noxious and unwholesome for want of proper sewerage. These authorities appear to me fully to warrant the position, that if the demised premises are incumbered with a nuisance of so serious a nature that no person can reasonably be expected to live in them, the tenant is at liberty to throw them up. This is not the case of a contract on the part of the landlord that the premises were free from this nuisance; it rather rests in an implied condition of law, that he undertakes to let them in a habitable state ...

Note

The decision in *Smith* v. *Marrable* might have provided the starting-point for the development of a coherent body of law which would guarantee the environmental quality of rented housing. However, in a number of subsequent cases the courts restricted the potential scope of the landlord's obligation: the landlord's obligation does not extend to situations where the premises are habitable when let, and only become unfit for human habitation at some later point during the tenancy[23]; the rule in *Smith* v. *Marrable* relates only to unfitness for human habitation, and not to disrepair generally[24]; the obligation has been held not to apply to unfurnished lettings[25]; and the tenant cannot require the landlord to make the premises fit for human habitation, his only remedy is to repudiate the tenancy and claim damages.

(2) General

More generally, the courts have from time to time been prepared to imply covenants into a letting agreement. An important attempt to formulate criteria to govern the circumstances in which it is proper to imply such terms was made by the House of Lords.

Liverpool City Council v. *Irwin* [1977] A.C. 239

Lord Wilberforce said (at 251–257):

Haigh Heights, Liverpool, is one of several recently erected tower blocks in the district of Everton. It has some 70 dwelling units in it. It was erected 10 years ago following a slum clearance programme at considerable cost, and was then, no doubt, thought to mark an advance in housing standards. Unfortunately, it has since turned out that effective slum clearance depends upon more than expenditure upon steel and concrete. There are human factors involved too, and it is these which seem to have failed. The defendants moved in to one of the units in this building in July 1966; this was a maisonette of two floors, corresponding to the ninth and tenth floors of the block. Access to it was provided by a staircase and by two electrically operated lifts. Another facility provided was an internal chute into which tenants in the block could discharge rubbish or garbage for collection at the ground level.

There has been a consistent history of trouble in this block, due in part to vandalism, in part to non-co-operation by tenants, in part, it is said, to neglect by the corporation. The defendants, with other tenants, stopped payment of rent so that in May 1973 the corporation had to start proceedings for possession. The defendants put in a counterclaim for damages and for an injunction, alleging that the corporation was in breach of its implied covenant for quiet enjoyment, that it was in breach of the statutory covenant implied by section 32 of the Housing Act 1961 and that it was in breach of an obligation implied by law to keep the "common parts" in repair. . . .

I consider first the tenants' claim in so far as it is based on contract. The first step must be to ascertain what the contract is. This may look elementary, even naive, but it seems to me to be the essential step and to involve, from the start, an approach different from, if simpler than, that taken by the members of the Court of Appeal. We look first at documentary material. As is common with council lettings there is no formal demise, or lease or tenancy agreement. There

---

[23] *Hart* v. *Windsor* (1844) 12 M. & W. 68.
[24] *Maclean* v. *Currie* (1884) Cab. & El. 361.
[25] *Hart* v. *Windsor* (1844) 12 M. & W. 68.

is a document headed "Liverpool Corporation, Liverpool City Housing Dept." and described as "Conditions of Tenancy." This contains a list of obligations upon the tenant—he shall do this, he shall not do that, or he shall not do that without the corporation's consent. This is an amalgam of obligations added to from time to time, no doubt, to meet complaints, emerging situations, or problems as they appear to the council's officers. In particular there have been added special provisions relating to multi-storey flats which are supposed to make the conditions suitable to such dwellings. We may note under "Further special notes" some obligations not to obstruct staircases and passages, and not to permit children under 10 to operate any lifts. I mention these as a recognition of the existence and relevance of these facilities. At the end there is a form for signature by the tenant stating that he accepts the tenancy. On the landlords' side there is nothing, no signature, no demise, no covenant: the contract takes effect as soon as the tenants sign the form and are let into possession.

We have then a contract which is partly, but not wholly, stated in writing. In order to complete it, in particular to give it a bilateral character, it is necessary to take account of the actions of the parties and the circumstances. As actions of the parties, we must note the granting of possession by the landlords and reservation by them of the "common parts"—stairs, lifts, chutes, etc. As circumstances we must include the nature of the premises, *viz.*, a maisonette for family use on the ninth floor of a high block, one which is occupied by a large number of other tenants, all using the common parts and dependent upon them, none of them having any expressed obligation to maintain or repair them.

To say that the construction of a complete contract out of these elements involves a process of "implication" may be correct; it would be so if implication means the supplying of what is not expressed. But there are varieties of implications which the courts think fit to make and they do not necessarily involve the same process. Where there is, on the face of it, a complete, bilateral contract, the courts are sometimes willing to add terms to it, as implied terms: this is very common in mercantile contracts where there is an established usage: in that case the courts are spelling out what both parties know and would, if asked, unhesitatingly agree to be part of the bargain. In other cases, where there is an apparently complete bargain, the courts are willing to add a term on the ground that without it the contract will not work—this is the case, if not of *The Moorcock* (1889) 14 P.D. 64 itself on its facts, at least of the doctrine of *The Moorcock* as usually applied. This is, as was pointed out by the majority in the Court of Appeal, a strict test—though the degree of strictness seems to vary with the current legal trend—and I think that they were right not to accept it as applicable here. There is a third variety of implication, that which I think Lord Denning M.R. favours, or at least did favour in this case, and that is the implication of reasonable terms. But though I agree with many of his instances, which in fact fall under one or other of the preceding heads, I cannot go so far as to endorse his principle; indeed, it seems to me, with respect, to extend a long, and undesirable, way beyond sound authority.

The present case, in my opinion, represents a fourth category, or I would rather say a fourth shade on a continuous spectrum. The court here is simply concerned to establish what the contract is, the parties not having themselves fully stated the terms. In this sense the court is searching for what must be implied.

What then should this contract be held to be? There must first be implied a letting, that is, a grant of the right of exclusive possession to the tenants. With this there must, I would suppose, be implied a covenant for quiet enjoyment, as a necessary incident of the letting. The difficulty begins when we consider the common parts. We start with the fact that the demise is useless unless access is obtained by the staircase; we can add that, having regard to the height of the block, and the family nature of the dwellings, the demise would be useless without a lift service; we can continue that, there being rubbish chutes built into the structures and no other means of disposing of light rubbish, there must be a right to use the chutes. The question to be answered—and it is the only question in this case—is what is to be the legal relationship between landlord and tenant as regards these matters.

There can be no doubt that there must be implied (i) an easement for the tenants and their licensees to use the stairs, (ii) a right in the nature of an easement to use the lifts, (iii) an easement to use the rubbish chutes.

But are these easements to be accompanied by any obligation upon the landlord, and what obligation? There seem to be two alternatives. The first, for which the council contends, is for an easement coupled with no legal obligation, except such as may arise under the Occupiers' Liability Act 1957 as regards the safety of those using the facilities, and possibly such other liability as might exist under the ordinary law of tort. The alternative is for easements coupled with some obligation on the part of the landlords as regards the maintenance of the subject of them, so that they are available for use.

My Lords, in order to be able to choose between these, it is necessary to define what test is to be applied, and I do not find this difficult. In my opinion such obligation should be read into the contract as the nature of the contract itself implicitly requires, no more, no less: a test, in other words, of necessity. The relationship accepted by the corporation is that of landlord and tenant: the tenant accepts obligations accordingly, in relation inter alia to the stairs, the lifts and the chutes. All these are not just facilities, or conveniences provided at discretion: they are essentials of the tenancy without which life in the dwellings, as a tenant, is not possible. To leave the landlord free of contractual obligation as regards these matters, and subject only to administrative or political pressure, is, in my opinion, inconsistent totally with the nature of this relationship. The subject matter of the case (high rise blocks) and the relationship created by the tenancy demand, of their nature, some contractual obligation on the landlord.

Lord Wilberforce then discussed *Lister* v. *Romford Ice & Cold Storage Co. Ltd.*[26]; *Miller* v. *Hancock*[27]; *De Meza* v. *Ve-Ri-Best Manufacturing Co. Ltd.*[28]; *Penn* v. *Gatenex Co. Ltd.*[29] and continued:

I accept, of course, the argument that a mere grant of an easement does not carry with it any obligation on the part of the servient owner to maintain the subject matter. The dominant owner must spend the necessary money, for example in repairing a drive leading to his house. And the same principle may apply when a landlord lets an upper floor with access by a staircase: responsibility for maintenance may well rest on the tenant. But there is a difference between that case and the case where there is an essential means of access, retained in the landlord's occupation, to units in a building of multi-occupation, for unless the obligation to maintain is, in a defined manner, placed upon the tenants, individually or collectively, the nature of the contract, and the circumstances, require that it be placed on the landlord.

It remains to define the standard. My Lords, if, as I think, the test of the existence of the term is necessity the standard must surely not exceed what is necessary having regard to the circumstances. To imply an absolute obligation to

[26] [1957] A.C. 555.
[27] [1893] 2 Q.B. 177.
[27] (1952) 160 E.G. 364.
[29] [1958] 2 Q.B. 210.

repair would go beyond what is a necessary legal incident and would indeed be unreasonable. An obligation to take reasonable care to keep in reasonable repair and usability is what fits the requirements of the case. Such a definition involves—and I think rightly—recognition that the tenants themselves have their responsibilities. What it is reasonable to expect of a landlord has a clear relation to what a reasonable set of tenants should do for themselves .... .

I would hold therefore that the landlords' obligation is as I have described. And in agreement, I believe, with your Lordships I would hold that it has not been shown in this case that there was any breach of that obligation. On the main point therefore I would hold that the appeal fails.

Lords Cross of Chelsea, Salmon, Edmund Davies and Fraser of Tullybelton delivered similar speeches.

Note

The Housing Act 1988 has amended section 11 of the Landlord and Tenant Act 1985 so that landlords are in certain circumstances subject to an implied statutory obligation to maintain the common parts of buildings in multiple occupation[30] (although only in relation to tenancies entered into on or after January 15, 1989[31]).

Although in *Liverpool City Council* v. *Irwin* terms were implied on the basis of necessity, in a number of recent cases the courts have implied into tenancy agreements terms imposing repairing obligations on landlords on the basis of business efficacy.[32]

Barrett v. *Lounova (1982) Ltd.* [1989] 2 W.L.R. 137

Kerr L.J. said (at 139–145):

The case concerns an end of terrace house in the East End of London in the Borough of Hackney, 70, Lansdowne Drive, London E.8, which has been occupied under the Rent Acts since 1941. The outside of the premises is in a bad state of repair and dilapidated; probably no work has been done to it for decades.

The issue is whether the landlord is bound to repair the outside. The tenancy contained a covenant that the tenant should keep the inside in good repair and it gives the landlord access for any reasonable purpose. But there is no express obligation on anyone to keep the outside in repair. The recorder held that a term was to be implied, correlative to the tenant's obligation, to the effect that the landlord would keep the outside in a reasonable state of repair.

The landlords relied strongly on a well known passage in *Woodfall's Law of Landlord and Tenant*, 28th ed. (1987) vol. 1, p. 618, para. 1–1465, in the following terms:

---

[30] Landlord and Tenant Act 1985, s.11(1A) (inserted by Housing Act 1988, s.116(1)).
[31] Housing Act 1988, s.116(3).
[32] See *Duke of Westminster* v. *Guild* [1985] 1 Q.B. 688; *Gordon* v. *Selico Co. Ltd.* (1986) 18 H.L.R. 219.

"In general, there is no implied covenant by the lessor of an unfurnished house or flat, or of land, that it is or shall be reasonably fit for habitation, occupation or cultivation, or for any other purposes for which it is let. No covenant is implied that the lessor will do any repairs whatever ... "

The first authority cited was the old case *Hart* v. *Windsor* (1843) 12 M. & W. 68. There was a full tenant's repairing covenant of a house, but he declined to pay the rent because the house was bug-infested to such an extent that he said it was unfit for human habitation. That plea was rejected. Parke B., giving the judgment of the court, said, at pp. 87–88:

"We are all of opinion ... that there is no contract, still less a condition, implied by law on the demise of real property only, that it is fit for the purpose for which it is let. The principles of the common law do not warrant such a position; and though, in the case of a dwelling house taken for habitation, there is no apparent injustice in inferring a contract of this nature, the same rule must apply to land taken for other purposes—for building upon, or for cultivation; and there would be no limit to the inconvenience which would ensue. It is much better to leave the parties in every case to protect their interests themselves, by proper stipulations, and if they really mean a lease to be void by reason of any unfitness in the subject for the purpose intended, they should express that meaning."

Secondly, there is an even stronger passage in a dictum of Bankes L.J. in *Cockburn* v. *Smith* [1924] 2 K.B. 119, a decision of this court. The owner of a block of flats had let one of the top flats but had kept the roof of the building and the guttering in his own possession and control. The guttering became defective, water escaped and wetted the tenant's outside wall and so caused damage to the inside. Not surprisingly, it was held that since the landlord had retained control of the guttering he was under a duty to take reasonable care to remedy any defects in it of which he had notice and which were a source of damage. Those facts, of course, do not apply here, but in an *obiter dictum* Bankes L.J. said, at p. 128:

"I want to make it plain at the outset that this is not a letting of the whole house where, without an express covenant or a statutory obligation to repair, the landlords would clearly be under no liability to repair any part of the demised premises whether the required repairs were structural or internal and whether they had or had not notice of the want of repair."

That statement was not only *obiter*, but if it purported to lay down any general rule that no repairing covenant could arise by implication then, with all respect, it clearly went too far, as shown by later cases.

Finally in this context the landlord relied on the decision of Goddard J. in *Wilchick* v. *Marks and Silverstone* [1934] 2 K.B. 56. But implication derived from the true construction of the terms of the letting was not raised in argument in that case. It was also not dealt with by the judge since no relevant implication could have been derived from the terms of that particular instrument.

I turn now to the more recent cases. They show that there is no rule of law against the implication of any repairing covenant against landlords and that the ordinary principles of construction concerning implied terms apply to leases in that context as they apply generally in the law of contract. That is illustrated, but in a very different context, by the decision of the House of Lords in *Liverpool City Council* v. *Irwin* [1977] A.C. 239. I need not refer to that case, but I should mention two other cases, both decisions of this court, which show that implication of a landlord's repairing covenant is a permissible approach if the terms of the agreement and circumstances justify it.

The first is *Sleafer* v. *Lambeth Borough Council* [1960] 1 Q.B. 43. That was an extraordinary case, in which the tenant found that he was unable to open his front door due to a minor defect which caused it to jam. So he pulled hard on the only external handle, the letter box knocker. That came off, and he fell backwards against an iron balustrade and suffered injury to his back. He sued the landlord for allowing the door to get into that state. Perhaps not surprisingly, it was held that in relation to a minor defect of that kind no question of any obligation on the landlord could arise. It is also to be noted that the lease provided, by clause 2, that the tenant was to reside in the dwelling—that is to say, in the same way as here, that it was not to be used for any business purposes; and by clause 9 the tenant was not to do, or allow to be done, any decorative or other work without the landlord's consent in writing. In rejecting the tenant's claim against the landlord, Morris L.J., who gave the first judgment, quoted the passages in *Hart* v. *Windsor*, 12 M. & W. 68, and *Cockburn* v. *Smith* [1924] 2 K.B. 119 which I have already set out. But I do not think that he said anything about the possibility of implying a term dealing with repairs. However, that was dealt with by Ormerod L.J., in a passage which I must read, at p. 60:

"When this matter was argued before the judge it was contended by counsel for the defendants that in no circumstances could a condition be implied that the landlords should be under an obligation to repair. The judge dealt with that in this way: 'Although I cannot follow Mr. Lowe in saying that the mere fact that the landlord has reserved the right to do repairs means that there is imposed on him an obligation, I cannot agree with Mr. Rawlinson when he says to me that the absence of some express term in the tenancy, whether oral or in writing, means that there can never arise a contractual duty on the landlord to do the repairs—in other words, that such term can never be implied. I am not sure that that is right; I am not prepared to say that circumstances may not arise in which a court could find itself impelled to imply such terms in a tenancy agreement. Without having, of course, to decide that question, as at present advised, I should certainly agree with the judge. A tenancy agreement, like any other agreement, must be read as a whole, and it may very well be that in construing the agreement it is possible to imply an obligation on the landlord to do repairs. But the question which the judge had to decide and which this court has to decide was whether in this particular agreement such an obligation could be implied."

That is equally the issue which arises on the present appeal. Willmer L.J. said, at p. 63:

"I think there is much to be said for the view that clause 2 of the agreement, which requires the tenant to reside in the dwelling house, does by implication require the landlords to do such repairs as may make it possible for the tenant to carry out that obligation. At least it seems to me that that is a possible view."

Then he said that even if that view be right, in his judgment the obligation would not extend to cover the type of repairs which fell to be considered in that case, which was no more than easing the bottom of the jammed door. He said in that regard:

"Wherever the line is drawn, even assuming that Mr. Beney is right in saying that some obligation on the part of the council to execute repairs must be implied, that line must be drawn, I should have thought, well short of including the responsibility for such a trivial repair as the unsticking of this door."

Finally, there is a recent decision of this court in *Duke of Westminster* v. *Guild* [1985] Q.B. 688, in which the judgment was delivered by Slade L.J. At pp. 696–697 he referred to *Barnes* v. *City of London Real Property Co.* [1918] 2 Ch. 18 in which an obligation on landlords had been implied to do certain work, in the first case the cleaning of the common parts of the premises and in the second painting the premises. These obligations were implied from terms imposed on the tenants to pay for the cost of a cleaner in the first case, and for the cost of the necessary paint in the second. The position in those cases was of course far stronger than here. Before quoting the general proposition from *Woodfall's Law of Landlord and Tenant*, which I have already set out, Slade L.J. said at p. 697:

"We do not question the correctness of these two decisions on their particular facts, or doubt that in some instances it will be proper for the court to imply an obligation against a landlord, on whom an obligation is not in terms imposed by the relevant lease, to match a correlative obligation thereby expressly imposed on the other party. Nevertheless we think that only rather limited assistance is to be derived from these earlier cases where obligations have been implied."

and then he referred to the proposition preceded by the words "In general" from *Woodfall's Law of Landlord and Tenant*, which I have read.

So it follows that a repairing obligation upon the landlord can clearly arise as a matter of implication. But that leaves the question already mentioned, which I find difficult and on the borderline, whether the terms and circumstances of this particular lease enable such an implication to be made. As to that, although I have not found this an easy case, I agree with the conclusion of the recorder. In my view the clue lies in what Slade L.J. referred to as a "correlative obligation," in this case one which is correlative to the express covenant by the tenant to keep the inside and fixtures in good repair, order and condition.

The considerations which lead me to that conclusion are the following. It is obvious, as shown by this case itself, that sooner or later the covenant imposed on the tenant in respect of the inside can no longer be complied with unless the outside has been kept in repair. Moreover, it is also clear that the covenant imposed on the tenant was intended to be enforceable throughout the tenancy. For instance, it could not possibly be contended that it would cease to be enforceable if the outside fell into disrepair. In my view it is therefore necessary, as a matter of business efficacy to make this agreement workable, that an obligation to keep the outside in repair must be imposed on someone. For myself, I would reject the persuasive submission of Mr. Pryor on behalf of the landlord, that both parties may have thought that in practice the landlord—or possibly the tenant—would do the necessary repairs, so that no problem would arise. In my view that is not a businesslike construction of a tenancy agreement.

Accordingly, on the basis that an obligation to keep the outside in a proper state of repair must be imposed on someone, three answers are possible.

First, that the tenant is obliged to keep the outside in repair as well as the inside, at any rate to such extent as may be necessary to enable him to perform his covenant. I would reject that as being unbusinesslike and unrealistic. In the case of a tenancy of this nature, which was to become a monthly tenancy after one year, the rent being paid weekly, it is clearly unrealistic to conclude that this could have been the common intention. In that context it is to be noted that in *Warren* v. *Keen* [1954] 1 Q.B. 15, this court held that a weekly tenant was under no implied obligation to do any repairs to the structure of the premises due to wear and tear or lapse of time or otherwise, and that it was doubtful whether he was even obliged to ensure that the premises remained wind and watertight. Any construction which casts upon the tenant the obligation to keep the outside in proper repair must in my view be rejected for these reasons; and also because there is an express tenant's covenant relating to the inside, so that it would be wrong, as a matter of elementary construction, to imply a covenant relating to the outside as well.

The second solution would be the implication of a joint obligation on both parties to keep the outside in good repair. I reject that as being obviously unworkable and I do not think that Mr.Pryor really suggested the contrary.

That leaves one with the third solution, an implied obligation on the landlord. In my view this is the only solution which makes business sense. The recorder reached the same conclusion by following much the same route, and I agree with him.

Accordingly I would dismiss this appeal.

Notes

(i) In this case the landlord was not under an implied statutory obligation to repair the exterior of the premises because the tenancy agreement pre-dated the introduction of what is now section 11 of the Landlord and Tenant Act 1985.

(ii) Any covenant implied by the common law may be excluded by an express provision to the contrary. This is not true of repairing covenants implied by section 11 of the Landlord and Tenant Act 1985.[33]

(D) COVENANTS IMPLIED BY THE COMMON LAW AFFECTING TENANTS

Warren v. *Keen* [1954] 1 Q.B. 15

Premises which were subject to the control of the Rent Restrictions Acts had been let by the plaintiff landlord to the tenant on a weekly tenancy. Various repairs had been carried out at times by the landlord. When she was served by the Heston and Isleworth local authority with a notice to remedy certain defects, which rendered the premises unfit for habitation by reason of their not being wind and water tight, she carried out the necessary repairs and in the present

[33] Landlord and Tenant Act 1985, s.12.

action claimed to recover from the tenant the cost of those repairs which amounted to £23 5s. By the particulars of claim the landlord contended that it was an implied term of the tenancy that the defendant would use the premises in a tenantlike manner, would keep them wind and water tight, and would make fair and tenantable repairs thereto. The tenant denied liability for repairs.

The county court judge, according to his written notes, held that there was an implied covenant that the tenant would keep the premises in a good and tenantable condition and do such repairs as were necessary to that end. He therefore gave judgment for the landlord.

The tenant appealed.

Somervell L.J. said (at 17–19):

The particulars of disrepair are important: '(*a*) First floor front room (Large). Walls—plaster damp—stained below window opening. (*b*) First floor front room (Small). Walls—plaster damp—stained and perished below window opening. (*c*). External. Front wall—rendering cracked and broken in parts. Front floor window opening—sills not weatherproof, joints and pointwork decayed. (*d*) Leak in hot water boiler.' ...

The case for the landlord before us was put as it appears in the particulars of claim. It was alleged that a tenant from year to year was under an obligation not only to use and cultivate the land or premises in a husbandlike or tenantlike manner but also to keep the buildings wind and water tight. That obligation will be found stated in the judgment of Swinfen Eady L.J. in *Wedd* v. *Porter* ([1916] 2 K.B. 91, 100) and in various other cases and in textbooks. On the other hand the researches of counsel have failed to discover any case which throws light on the scope of that obligation, in other words, any case where a tenant has been held liable for failure to keep wind and water tight where the damage would not be covered by the obligation not to commit voluntary waste or the obligation to use the premises and land in a tenantlike manner ...

The argument is first that that obligation to keep wind and water tight applies to a weekly tenant as well as a tenant from year to year, and then, assuming that it does, the next submission is that the matters set out in the particulars of claim come within the covenant to keep the buildings wind and water tight. I think that submission fails at both stages. If there is a minor, but so far indefinite, obligation on a tenant from year to year to do certain minor repairs necessary to keep premises wind and water tight—and I will assume without deciding it that there is some such limited obligation—then I see no ground in principle for applying that to a tenancy from week to week. It is quite true that under the Rent Restriction Acts many tenants from week to week are enabled to remain in premises year after year, and the landlord may find great difficulty in fulfilling the conditions which have to be fulfilled under those Acts if he is to get possession. But that does not to my mind affect the question of what are the implications of a weekly tenancy. It seems to me that it would be absurd to suggest that a weekly tenant was under an obligation to repair. It is difficult to think of repairs which would not in themselves cost more than the weekly rent in many cases and yet it is suggested that he is impliedly liable to expend that money although his right to the premises may be terminated in a week's time.

In the second place, I am myself quite clear that matters particularised in the particulars of claim would not fall within the words "wind and water tight." It seems to me clear that the damage here was due to decay of walls, and there is no suggestion that that was due to any other cause than fair wear and tear. There is no suggestion that the tenant started knocking the walls about or anything of that sort, but in the course of time they had become cracked and presumably required re-pointing, because water was seeping in through the cracks which had appeared. The same would appear to have applied to the wood of the window sills. That may have been due not only to age but also to the positive failure to have the external woodwork re-painted every three years, or whatever is the normal time. Those would be both matters which in my opinion could not on any construction come under this formula of keeping the building wind and water tight, having regard to the principles which are to be found in the cases with regard to the implied liability of a tenant from year to year. Therefore, for these reasons, I think this appeal succeeds and the claim made by the landlord fails.

Denning L.J. said (at 20–21):

Apart from express contract, a tenant owes no duty to the landlord to keep the premises in repair. The only duty of the tenant is to use the premises in a husbandlike, or what is the same thing, a tenantlike manner. ... But what does "to use the premises in a tenantlike manner" mean? It can, I think, best be shown by some illustrations. The tenant must take proper care of the place. He must, if he is going away for the winter, turn off the water and empty the boiler. He must clean the chimneys, when necessary, and also the windows. He must mend the electric light when it fuses. He must unstop the sink when it is blocked by his waste. In short, he must do the little jobs about the place which a reasonable tenant would do. In addition, he must, of course, not damage the house, wilfully or negligently; and he must see that his family and guests do not damage it: and if they do, he must repair it. But apart from such things, if the house falls into disrepair through fair wear and tear or lapse of time, of for any reason not caused by him, then the tenant is not liable to repair it.

The landlord sought to put upon the tenant a higher obligation. She said that the duty of the tenant was to keep the premises wind and water tight and to make fair and tenantable repairs thereto. ... I do not think that is a correct statement of the obligation ...

After analysing the obligation, he concluded:

It was suggested by Mr. Willis that an action lies against a weekly tenant for permissive waste. I do not think that that is so. It has been held not to lie against a tenant at will, see the *Countess of Shrewsbury's* case ((1600) 5 Co. Rep. 13b) and in my opinion it does not lie against a weekly tenant. In my judgment, the only obligation on a weekly tenant is to use the premises in a tenantlike manner. That does not cover the dampness and other defects alleged in the particulars of claim. The appeal should be allowed accordingly.

Romer L.J. agreed.

Note

The cases concerning implied covenants at common law reveal the problems which the courts have had in deciding when covenants should be implied. In 1975 the Law Commission proposed that the law relating to implied covenants should be codified.[34] In the draft Landlord and

---

[34] *Obligations of Landlords and Tenants* (1975).

Tenant (Implied Covenants) Bill implied covenants are classified as "overriding" (which cannot be excluded by the parties) or "variable" (that is, variable by the parties). These proposals have not been implemented.

(E) COVENANTS IMPLIED BY STATUTE

The dreadful housing conditions found in many urban areas in the nineteenth century, and the consequent social unrest that began to manifest itself, led to a number of official responses. In addition to the legal powers given to local authorities to take direct action on housing conditions,[35] tenants were given by statute opportunities for taking legal action directly against their landlord. For example, section 12 of the Housing of the Working Classes Act 1885 gave the tenant the power to recover damages for the landlord's "neglect or default in sanitary matters." After subsequent amendment it emerged as sections 14 and 15 of the Housing, Town Planning, etc. Act 1909. Reynolds notes: "the intention of the Government introducing the provisions was that it was more than a mere technical addition to landlord-tenant law and had a valuable role to play in the fight against the slum."[36]

Two statutory provisions are currently in force.

(1) Landlord and Tenant Act 1985, s.8

(1) In a contract to which this section applies for the letting of a house for human habitation there is implied, notwithstanding any stipulation to the contrary—

(a) a condition that the house is fit for human habitation at the commencement of the tenancy, and

(b) an undertaking that the house will be kept by the landlord fit for human habitation during the tenancy.

(2) The landlord, or a person authorised by him in writing, may at reasonable times of the day, on giving 24 hours' notice in writing to the tenant or occupier, enter premises to which this section applies for the purpose of viewing their state and condition.

(3) This section applies to a contract if—

(a) the rent does not exceed the figure applicable in accordance with subsection (4), and

(b) the letting is not on such terms as to the tenant's responsibility as are mentioned in subsection (5).

(4) The rent limit for the application of this section is shown by the following Table, by reference to the date of making of the contract and the situation of the premises:

---

[35] See now pp. 408–424.
[36] Statutory covenants of fitness and repair: social legislation and the judges (1974) 37 M.L.R. 377, 380.

TABLE

Date of making of contract	Rent limit
Before 31st July 1923.	In London: £40. Elsewhere: £26 or £16.
On or after 31st July 1923 and before 6th July 1957.	In London: £40. Elsewhere: £26.
On or after 6th July 1957.	In London: £80. Elsewhere: £52.

(5) This section does not apply where a house is let for a term of three years or more (the lease not being determinable at the option of either party before the expiration of three years) upon terms that the tenant puts the premises into a condition reasonably fit for human habitation.

(6) In this section "house" includes—

(a) a part of a house, and
(b) any yard, garden, outhouses and appurtenances belonging to the house or usually enjoyed with it.

This provision (which was formerly section 6 of the Housing Act 1957) was discussed by the Court of Appeal in *Quick* v. *Taff Ely B.C.*.[37] Dillon L.J. noted:

There is in section 6 of the Housing Act 1957 a provision that, in any contract for the letting of a house for human habitation at an annual rent not exceeding £80 in the case of a house in London and £52 in the case of a house elsewhere, there is to be implied a condition that the house is at the commencement of the tenancy, and an undertaking that the house will be kept by the landlord during the tenancy, fit for human habitation. That section has legislative antecedents, albeit at lower rent levels, in the Housing Act 1936, and before that in the Housing Act 1925 and before that in the Housing, Town Planning, Etc. Act 1909. It was amended by the London Government Act 1963 as a result of the creation of the Greater London Council, but without altering the rent levels. It seems that the section as so amended has remained on the statute book ever since, but—for whatever reason—the rent levels have never been increased. Therefore, in view of inflation, the section must now have remarkably little application. It is not available to the plaintiff in the present case because his rent is too high, even though he is an unemployed tenant of a small council house.[38]

Lawton L.J. commented in a similar vein:

When I read the papers in this case I was surprised to find that the plaintiff had not based his claim on an allegation that at all material times the house let to him by the council had not been fit for human habitation. The uncontradicted

---

[37] [1986] Q.B. 809.
[38] At 816–817.

evidence, accepted by the trial judge, showed that furniture, furnishings and clothes had rotted because of damp and the sitting room could not be used because of the smell of damp. I was even more surprised to be told by counsel that the provisions of the Housing Act 1957, as amended by the London Government Act 1963, did not apply to the plaintiff's house. By section 6 of the Act of 1957, on the letting of a house at a specified low rent, a covenant is implied that the landlord will keep it in a condition fit for human habitation. For most of the time the plaintiff was in occupation of the house let to him by the council it is arguable that it was not fit for human habitation. Unfortunately, the figures which were fixed as being low rents have not been changed for over 20 years. In 1965 a low rent outside central Greater London was one not exceeding £52 per annum. The present day equivalent of that figure, when inflation is taken into account, is over £312. The plaintiff's rent of £6.75 per week in 1976 was well above the statutory figure. This case would seem to indicate that a new definition of a low rent is needed.[39]

(2) Landlord and Tenant Act 1985, ss.11 to 13 (as amended by Housing Act 1988, s.116)

Section 11 of the Landlord and Tenant Act 1985 replaced section 32 of the Housing Act 1961. Its aim is to stop landlords from imposing unreasonable repairing obligations on tenants: "The right policy is not only to relieve short term tenants of unreasonable obligations, but, in the case of short term tenancies, to put definite obligations on the landlord."[40]

11.—(1) In a lease to which this section applies (as to which, see sections 13 and 14) there is implied a covenant by the lessor—

(a) to keep in repair the structure and exterior of the dwelling-house (including drains, gutters and external pipes),

(b) to keep in repair and proper working order the installations in the dwelling-house for the supply of water, gas and electricity and for sanitation (including basins, sinks, baths and sanitary conveniences, but not other fixtures, fittings and appliances for making use of the supply of water, gas or electricity), and

(c) to keep in repair and proper working order the installations in the dwelling-house for space heating and heating water.

(1A) If a lease to which this section applies is a lease of a dwelling-house which forms part only of a building, then, subject to subsection (1B), the covenant implied by subsection (1) shall have effect as if—

(a) the reference in paragraph (a) of that subsection to the dwelling-house included a reference to any part of the building in which the lessor has an estate or interest; and

(b) any reference in paragraphs (b) and (c) of that subsection to an installation in the dwelling-house included a reference to an installation

---

[39] At 821.
[40] Brooke, H.C.Deb., 1961, Vol. 637 cols. 974–975.

which, directly or indirectly, serves the dwelling-house and which either—

(i)   forms part of any part of a building in which the lessor has an estate or interest; or

(ii)   is owned by the lessor or under his control.

(1B) Nothing in subsection (1A) shall be construed as requiring the lessor to carry out any works or repairs unless the disrepair (or failure to maintain in working order) is such as to affect the lessee's enjoyment of the dwelling-house or of any common parts, as defined in section 60(1) of the Landlord and Tenant Act 1987, which the lessee, as such, is entitled to use.

(2) The covenant implied by subsection (1) ("the lessor's repairing covenant") shall not be construed as requiring the lessor—

(a)   to carry out works or repairs for which the lessee is liable by virtue of his duty to use the premises in a tenantlike manner, or would be so liable but for an express covenant on his part,

(b)   to rebuild or reinstate the premises in the case of destruction or damage by fire, or by tempest, flood or other inevitable accident, or

(c)   to keep in repair or maintain anything which the lessee is entitled to remove from the dwelling-house.

(3) In determining the standard of repair required by the lessor's repairing covenant, regard shall be had to the age, character and prospective life of the dwelling-house and the locality in which it is situated.

(3A) In any case where—

(a)   the lessor's repairing covenant has effect as mentioned in subsection (1A), and

(b)   in order to comply with the covenant the lessor needs to carry out works or repairs otherwise than in, or to an installation in, the dwelling-house, and

(c)   the lessor does not have a sufficient right in the part of the building or the installation concerned to enable him to carry out the required works or repairs,

then, in any proceedings relating to a failure to comply with the lessor's repairing covenant, so far as it requires the lessor to carry out the works or repairs in question, it shall be a defence for the lessor to prove that he used all reasonable endeavours to obtain, but was unable to obtain, such rights as would be adequate to enable him to carry out the works or repairs.

(4) A covenant by the lessee for the repair of the premises is of no effect so far as it relates to the matters mentioned in subsection (1)(a) to (c), except so far as it imposes on the lessee any of the requirements mentioned in subsection (2)(a) or (c).

(5) The reference in subsection (4) to a covenant by the lessee for the repair of the premises includes a covenant—

(a)   to put in repair or deliver up in repair,

(b)   to paint, point or render,

(c)   to pay money in lieu of repairs by the lessee, or

(d)   to pay money on account of repairs by the lessor.

(6) In a lease in which the lessor's repairing covenant is implied there is also implied a covenant by the lessee that the lessor, or any person authorised by him in writing, may at reasonable times of the day and on giving 24 hours' notice in writing to the occupier, enter the premises comprised in the lease for the purpose of viewing their condition and state of repair.

12.—(1) A covenant or agreement, whether contained in a lease to which section 11 applies or in an agreement collateral to such a lease, is void in so far as it purports—

(a)   to exclude or limit the obligations of the lessor or the immunities of the lessee under that section, or

(b)   to authorise any forfeiture or impose on the lessee any penalty, disability or obligation in the event of his enforcing or relying upon those obligations or immunities,

unless the inclusion of the provision was authorised by the county court.

(2) The county court may, by order made with the consent of the parties, authorise the inclusion in a lease, or in an agreement collateral to a lease, of provisions excluding or modifying in relation to the lease, the provisions of section 11 with respect to the repairing obligation of the parties if it appears to the court that it is reasonable to do so, having regard to all the circumstances of the case, including the other terms and conditions of the lease.

13.—(1) Section 11 (repairing obligations) applies to a lease of a dwelling-house granted on or after 24th October 1961 for a term of less than seven years.

(2) In determining whether a lease is one to which section 11 applies—

(a)   any part of the term which falls before the grant shall be left out of account and the lease shall be treated as a lease for a term commencing with the grant,

(b)   a lease which is determinable at the option of the lessor before the expiration of seven years from the commencement of the term shall be treated as a lease for a term of less than seven years, and

(c)   a lease (other than a lease to which paragraph (b) applies) shall not be treated as a lease for a term of less than seven years if it confers on the lessee an option for renewal for a term which, together with the original term, amounts to seven years or more.

Notes

(i) The obligations contained in section 11(1) apply to tenancies granted on or after October 24, 1961.[41]

---

[41] Landlord and Tenant Act 1985, s.13(1).

(ii)   Subsections (1A) (1B) and (3A) apply only to tenancies granted on or after January 15, 1989.[42]

(iii)   Tenancies granted before October 24, 1961 are outside the scope of these provisions altogether, although there may be implied obligations in contract or tort.[43]

A number of difficulties have arisen from section 11 of the 1985 Act and its predecessors:

(a) Parties

Since it is, in essence, a contractual remedy, only parties to the contract can sue. Therefore, a tenant's wife[44] and daughter[45] have both been held to fall outside the scope of the legislation.[46] Third parties may, however, be able to rely on section 4 of the Defective Premises Act 1972.[47]

(b) Extent of the Covenant

Although most cases are clear-cut, some difficult cases have arisen. The following materials illustrate the way in which the courts have attempted to determine the meaning of the phrase "structure and exterior."[48]

Brown v. *Liverpool Corporation* [1969] 3 All E.R. 1345

Danckwerts L.J. said (at 1341):

The matter concerns the front access to the dwelling. There are, apparently, no steps down from the dwelling, as is usual in cases of houses of this type, which is a terraced house; instead there are about three flagstones, some 7 feet, and then there are four steps up, very shallow steps only about 1½ inches each. The trouble arose in this case because one of the steps was broken and, therefore formed a danger for persons using the access to the house. The plaintiff in fact had a fall as a result of that and suffered injury.

The question is, simply, whether, for the purposes of section 32 of the Housing Act 1961, the steps and the short bit of flagstones leading down to the entrance of the house are within the terms "the structure and exterior of the dwelling-house (including drains, gutters and external pipes)."

---

[42] Housing Act 1988, s.116(4).
[43] See *Liverpool City Council* v. *Irwin* [1977] A.C. 239 and *Barrett* v. *Lounova (1982) Ltd.* [1989] 2 W.L.R. 137 (pp. 349–356) and Defective Premises Act 1972, s.4 (pp. 391–394).
[44] *Middleton* v. *Hall* (1913) 108 L.T. 804.
[45] *Ryall* v. *Kidwell* [1914] K.B. 135.
[46] Though these cases were decided on the basis of earlier legislation, it is generally assumed that the same interpretation would be adopted in relation to the Landlord and Tenant Act 1985.
[47] See pp. 392–394.
[48] See also *Smith* v. *Bradford Metropolitan Council* (1983) 4 H.L.R. 86; *Douglas-Scott* v. *Scorgie* [1984] 1 W.L.R. 716.

It is clear to me that this is not part of the structure of the dwelling-house. I think I have a very fair idea of what is meant by the structure of a dwelling-house, and this is not part, of course, of the structure. On the other hand it seems to me equally clear that the 7 feet of flagstones and the steps up do form part of the exterior of the dwelling-house. They are attached in that manner to the house for the purpose of access to this dwelling-house, and they are part of the dwelling-house which is necessary for the purpose of anybody who wishes to live in the dwelling-house enjoying that privilege. If they have no means of access of some sort they could not get there, and these are simply the means of access. The steps are an outside structure, and therefore, it seems to me they are plainly part of the building, and, therefore, the covenant implied by section 32 of the Act of 1961 fits and applies to the obligations of the landlords in this case.

Hopwood v. *Cannock Chase D.C.* [1975] 1 W.L.R. 373

Cairns L.J. said (at 374–378):

It was an action for damages for personal injuries which the plaintiff suffered when she fell in the back yard of the house and injured her knee.

The house is a terraced house; it is some 16 feet in width and at the back of it there is a little yard consisting first of a concrete area adjoining the house for the full width of the house and probably about five feet going out from the back of the house; then there is a row of nine paving slabs, again across the full width of the house; then next to them, on the other side, another concrete area, a rather narrower one, perhaps between two and three feet wide. Still further away from the house is a garden.

At the time the plaintiff had come from the back door of the house and she had walked diagonally across the first concrete area; she was intending to go and have a chat with her neighbour at the next house. But when she came to one edge of the paving slabs—it is not clear whether it was the first edge that she came to or the second edge going up on to the other piece of concrete—at one of those two places she tripped and fell; and it was common ground that there was a difference in height between the concrete and the paving slab of an inch and a half, the paving slab being lower than the concrete. It was found by the learned judge that the defendants, by their servants, well knew of this condition.

The judge had however to consider whether there was any obligation on the defendants to keep this part of the premises in repair. He held that there was no such obligation, and he gave judgment for the defendants, though he assessed the damages in case there should be a successful appeal ...

The plaintiff's case depended on whether there was an obligation on the defendants to repair this part of the premises, it being acknowledged that they were out of repair and it being found that they knew they were out of repair ...

Cairns L.J. then discussed *Brown* v. *Liverpool Corporation* and continued:

One matter on which all three members of the court founded their judgments was that in that case the path and steps formed an essential part of the means of access to the house, in that it was the only way in. In this case that certainly was not so; the ordinary means of access to the house was from the front of the house and to my mind it is very doubtful whether this yard could be regarded as a means of access to the house at all. It is true that there was a way out from one side of the yard, apparently into an alley or lane, this house being at the end of the terrace of houses; and there was also a way through from the yard into the corresponding yard of the adjoining house. But that is very far from saying, as could be said in *Brown's* case [1969] 3 All E.R. 1345, that it was necessary to the house as the means of access to it.

Sachs L.J. in *Brown's* case went no further than to say that there were materials on which it was open to the county court judge to reach the conclusion that he did. Here, the county court judge has reached the opposite conclusion; he did I think approach it as a question of degree and of fact, and it appears to me that the facts were such as entitled him to reach that conclusion. I should be prepared to go still further and say that, treating it as Danckwerts L.J. and Salmon L.J. did, as a matter of law and construction of the section, in my view the section cannot be extended beyond what was held in *Brown's* case to include a yard of this kind.

For these reasons I would dismiss this appeal.

Stephenson L.J. and Brightman J. agreed.

Campden Hill Towers Ltd. v. *Gardner* [1977] Q.B. 823

Clause 2 of the lease stated that what was let was:

All that flat ... numbered 20 and being on the third floor of the said Gate Hill Court ... (but so that this demise shall not include any part of the outside walls or roof thereof) together with the Landlord's fixtures and fittings installed therein and together also with the right and privileges specified in the First Schedule hereto ...

The question arose as to what was within the scope of what is now section 11(1)(a). Megaw L.J. said (at 834):

Anything which, in the ordinary use of words, would be regarded as part of the structure, or of the exterior, of the particular "dwelling-house," regarded as a separate part of the building, would be within the scope of paragraph (a). Thus, the exclusion by the words of clause 2 of the underlease of "any part of the outside walls" would not have the effect of taking outside the operation of paragraph (a) that which, in the ordinary use of language, would be regarded as the exterior wall of the flat—an essential integral part of the flat, as a dwelling-house; that part of the outside wall of the block of flats which constitutes a wall of the flat. The paragraph applies to the outside wall or walls of the flat; the outside of inner party walls of the flat; the outer sides or horizontal division between flat 20 and flats above and below; the structural framework and beams directly supporting floor, ceilings and walls of the flat.

On the scope of section 11(1)(b) Megaw L.J. said (at 835):

The lessors contend that the words "in the dwelling-house" have the effect of limiting the application of the paragraph to "installations" of the prescribed types which are physically within the dwelling-house. Thus, to take an example debated in argument, if there is in the flat a hot-water radiator, the paragraph puts on the lessors the obligation to keep the radiator "in repair and proper working order." But it does not impose any obligation on the lessors in respect of, nor preclude them from making charges in respect of, repairs to anything outside the flat, for example a boiler in the basement which heats the water which is supplied to all the radiators in all the flats in the building.

The lessees contend that, despite the words of the paragraph "installations *in* the dwelling-house," the paragraph applies to anything outside the flat, the proper functioning of which is required in order to enable the installation within the flat to function as it is intended to do. If it were not for the words "proper working order" in paragraph (b), it would, we think, be difficult to find any support for the lessees' contention. But the inclusion of those words does provide some possible support. It would, however, produce very odd results if that were so. First, there is nothing in section [11] which requires a lessor to provide such installations. Any such obligation would have to be derived from either non-statutory terms of the lease itself, which would be a matter of contractual negotiation, or from some other statute. Secondly, if "proper working order" did include, for example, the necessity of a supply of hot water to a radiator, or water to a cistern there would be imposed by statute an absolute obligation, with no qualifications, which in some respects would be quite outside the lessors' control. For example, the central heating boiler in the basement may be operated by gas. The gas supply is cut off by the gas board for some reason outside the control of the lessors; or the water supply is cut off, or limited to certain times of the day, by the water authority. The hot water radiator, or the water cistern, while in perfectly good repair and perfectly good "working order," cannot perform their function. If the covenant has the meaning suggested by the lessees, the lessors are liable for breach of the implied covenant.

In our judgment, the meaning of paragraph (b) is as is contended for by the lessors. The installations in the physical confines of the flat must be kept in repair and capable, so far as their own structural and mechanical condition is concerned, of working properly. But no more than that. The lessors may be under additional obligations but if so they do not arise from this statute.

Notes

(i)   For lettings which take place on or after January 15, 1989, section 11(1A) applies, so that installations which are not physically within the confines of the premises occupied by the tenant are nevertheless within the scope of the landlord's repairing obligations.

(ii)   The House of Lords also had some terse comments to make on the nature of liability under what is now section 11 of the 1985 Act in *Liverpool City Council* v. *Irwin*.[49] Lord Salmon said:

It remains to consider whether the council were in breach of their obligations under section [11(1)(b)] of the [Landlord and Tenant Act 1985] which admittedly applies to the tenancy in question. ... The judge found that every time a water closet was used the water overflowed and was apt to flood the floor and escape on to the landing where it lay without any means of draining away. Whether the ball-cock as fitted caused this tiresome fault or whether it was due to the design of the sanitary convenience is not clear—nor in my view does it

---

[49] [1977] A.C. 239.

matter. Some tenants tried using pails to catch the overflow.⁺Others attempted
to bend the ball-cock down which stopped the overflow but did not allow
sufficient water to flush the water closet efficiently. For my part I do not
understand how on any acceptable construction of the section it can be held that
in the circumstances I have recited the council complied with their statutory
obligation to keep the sanitary conveniences in proper working order. I can well
understand that sanitary conveniences may be in proper working order even if
they are too small or there are too few of them, but how they can be said to be
in proper working order if every time they are used they may swamp the floor
passes my comprehension.

My Lords, I would accordingly allow the appeal in relation to that part of the
counterclaim based on the council's breach of the [Landlord and Tenant Act
1985] and reduce the damages awarded from £10 to £5.[50]

(c) Notice

It is a long established principle of the common law that for a
landlord to be liable under a covenant to do repairs the tenant must first
give notice of want of repair.[51] The question has arisen as to whether
this principle should apply to covenants implied by statute. This issue
has come before the courts on a number of occasions.

McCarrick v. *Liverpool Corporation* [1947] A.C. 219

Lord Simmons said (at 227–230):

My Lords, this appeal ... is brought to test the correctness of an earlier
decision of the Court of Appeal in *Morgan* v. *Liverpool Corporation* ([1927] 2
K.B. 131). The relevant facts are few and not in dispute in this House. The
appellant was at all material times the tenant of the respondent corporation of a
dwelling-house, No. 6, Brown Street, in the city of Liverpool. This house, which
was subject to the provisions of the Housing Act, 1936, was by reason of the
defective condition of two stone steps leading from the kitchen to the back-
kitchen not "reasonably fit for human habitation." In consequence of this defect
the appellant's wife fell and fractured her leg. The appellant suffered special
damage assessed at £70. The question is whether this damage is recoverable in
law from the respondents. They have so far successfully contended and contend
before your Lordships that it is not recoverable, alleging that no notice of the
defect was given to them and that notice is a condition precedent to their
liability. It has been found as a fact, and your Lordships will not disturb that
finding, that no notice was given. The question of law remains whether notice is
a condition precedent to liability. So it was held in *Morgan's* case which must
now be reviewed ...

The first question for consideration is what is the effect of a statutory
provision that "in any contract for letting ... there shall, notwithstanding any
stipulation to the contrary, be implied a condition ... " In *Ryall* v. *Kidwell &
Son* ([1914] 3 K.B. 135) ... it was held that the effect of the enactment was to
import a new term into the contract of tenancy and no more. I think that this
was manifestly right and respectfully adopt the language used by Lush J. (143):

---

[50] At 263–264.
[51] *Makin* v. *Watkinson* (1870) L.R. 6 Ex. 25.

"But the character and quality of the obligation which is imported by the statute are none the less contractual, although the contract is derived from and owes its existence to the statute." To the same effect is the observation of Atkin L.J. in *Morgan's* case ([1927] 2 K.B. 131, 149): "The clause in the Housing Act is imposed as a contractual term and as such it appears to be only available to the tenant because it is a term of the tenancy." ...

The rival contentions can now be stated. By the appellant it is said that the promise by the landlord thus imported into the contract is an absolute one, by the respondents that the obligation is not absolute but that it is a condition of liability that notice of the material defect shall be given to them. My Lords, I find it impossible to approach a question of this kind as if similar questions had not for generations been the subject of decisions in the courts of this country and conveyancing practice had not grown up on the faith of them. On a long line of authority beginning with *Makin* v. *Watkinson* ((1870) L.R. 6 Ex. 25) it is clear that on a covenant by a lessor to keep demised premises in repair he cannot be sued for non-repair unless he has received notice of want of repair. In the case cited it appears that the lease did not reserve to the lessor the right to enter and inspect the demised premises and counsel for the appellant has urged that this makes all the difference and that the right of entry given by the imported term distinguishes the present from other cases. I think that this is not a valid distinction. In *London & South Western Ry. Co.* v. *Flower* ((1875) 1 C.P.D. 77, 84), the principle was applied though, as Brett J. said: "I will assume also that by implication they had a right to go upon the railway for the purpose of examining the condition of the bridge and ascertaining whether or not it needed repair." So also in *Hugall* v. *M'Lean* ((1884) 53 L.T. 94) (a case which was, I think, misunderstood in *Fisher* v. *Walter* ([1926] 2 K.B. 315), itself a decision which is, I think, inconsistent with higher authority and cannot stand). So also in *Torrens* v. *Walker* ([1906] 2 Ch. 166, 172), where Warrington J., after referring to *Hugall* v. *M'Lean*, of which case he says: "There, as here, the lease contained a covenant by the lessee to repair the inside of the premises, and to allow the lessor to enter and view the state of repair," applied the same principle. I will refer finally to *Morgan's* case again. Atkin L.J. closely examines the principle. I will cite only two short passages, he says ([1927] 2 K.B. 131, 150): "The result is, to my mind, that in all cases of that kind, speaking generally, it is a condition of the liability of the landlord that he should receive notice of the repairs," and later: "I think the power of access that is given, extensive though it may be, does not take the case away from the principle from which the courts have inferred the condition that the liability is not to arise except on notice." The judgment that I have cited of Lord Atkin is the more valuable because it was given after the judgment of this House in *Murphy* v. *Hurley* ([1922] 1 A.C. 369), on which the appellant relies. There, the question being whether notice was a condition precedent to the liability of a landlord to keep in repair a sea-wall erected by him for the common protection of a number of holdings, it was held that it was not. The salient fact was that the sea-wall, so far from being in the exclusive occupation of any tenant was, as Lord Buckmaster said (373), "intended to be within the control of the landlord." It is, I think, true that in the speeches of Lord Buckmaster and of the other noble and learned Lords who heard the case there are observations which suggest that the principle has no application where the landlord has means of access and therefore means of knowing of the defect, but the ratio decidendi of the case is that the sea-wall was not in the exclusive occupation of any tenant, a fact always held sufficient to exclude the principle, see, *e.g.*, *Melles & Co.* v. *Holme* ([1918] 2 K.B. 100). In none of the speeches is there any suggestion that the cases in which, though there was a right to enter and therefore means of knowledge, yet the principle was applied, were wrongly decided. It is on this footing that the

Court of Appeal decided *Morgan's* case and in my opinion they were right. I conclude, then, that the provision imported by statute into the contractual tenancy must be construed in the same way as any other term of the tenancy and, so construed, does not impose any obligation on the landlord unless and until he has notice of the defect which renders the dwelling not "reasonably fit for human habitation." That is the only question which your Lordships have to decide and I do not think it desirable or necessary to consider what may constitute such notice . . .

The principle that the landlord's liability depends on his having notice of the defect was applied in *O'Brien* v. *Robinson*.[52] In this case the O'Briens were injured when their bedroom ceiling fell on them. It was found that this was a result of a latent defect, so that the tenant could not have given notice of it to the landlord even if they had wanted to. The House of Lords held unanimously that the fact that no notice was given to the landlord was fatal to the O'Briens' claim. The rule requiring notice had to apply in circumstances where no notice could be given. Lord Diplock did concede: "An examination of the reasoning in the judgments in the cases on this subject during the last one hundred years suggests that the law might easily have developed on different lines from those which it in fact followed. But, for my part, I am not persuaded that this development was clearly wrong or leads to results which are clearly unjust."[53]

In *McGreal* v. *Wake*,[54] however, the Court of Appeal was more critical. Sir John Donaldson M.R. said on behalf of the whole court:

It is, as we think, unfortunate that the House of Lords felt impelled in *O'Brien* v. *Robinson* [1973] A.C. 912 to hold that liability under this covenant only arises when the landlord learns, or perhaps is put on inquiry, that there is a need for such repairs, because such a construction penalises the conscientious landlord and rewards the absentee.[55]

Two further points should be noted:

First, what is important is the fact that the landlord has notice of disrepair; the source of the notice and its form are irrelevant. So, in *Hall* v. *Howard*[56] the tenant sought to exercise the right to buy, and in the course of the negotiations a surveyor's report was given to the landlord outlining certain disrepairs. The sale fell through, the landlord brought an action for arrears of rent, and the tenant counterclaimed for disrepair. It was held that the landlord was liable for the disrepair since the report constituted sufficient notice.[57]

Secondly, once notice of disrepair has been given, the obligation of the landlord is to carry out the necessary repairs within a reasonable

---

[52] [1973] A.C. 912.
[53] At 930.
[54] (1984) 13 H.L.R. 107.
[55] At 109.
[56] (1988) 20 H.L.R. 566.
[57] See also *Dinefwr B.C.* v. *Jones* (1987) 19 H.L.R. 445.

time. The landlord is not in breach until a reasonable time has elapsed.[58] The onus of proof is on the tenant to show unreasonable delay by the landlord.[59]

(d) Standard of Repair: Landlord and Tenant Act 1985, s.11(3)

Section 11(3) of the 1985 Act was formerly section 32(3) of the Housing Act 1961.

Newham L.B.C. v. *Patel* (1978) 13 H.L.R. 77

A house in a redevelopment area in Newham had been let by the local authority to Mr. Patel. It was acknowledged that the house was unfit for human habitation.[60] Mr. Patel sought damages for alleged breaches of the landlord's covenant to repair.
Templeman L.J. said (at 83–84):

In my judgment there was ample evidence on which the learned judge could take the view that, having regard to the state of the house which I have outlined and the evidence which he had heard, the prospective life of the dwelling house affected the duty of the council under [section 11], and that they were not bound to carry out repairs which would be wholly useless.

In my judgment, also, the judge was quite right when he took into account the low rent charged for 35, Prince of Wales Road and came to the conclusion that the defendant had not suffered damage. ... Mr. Patel cannot have both the benefit of a low rent and an award of damages for the same reason—that is why the rent was so low.

The council were, as I have said, heavily criticised in this case but they were bound to be criticised. If they had spent money on a house which, having regard to the fact that it is due to be redeveloped and the state in which it was, meant that money was wasted in doing those repairs they would be criticised. If they left the house vacant they would be bound to be criticised in the present state of the housing demand. Now, because they let it to Mr. Patel at a very low rent, they are being criticised again.

In any event, those are matters which do not affect the legal problem with which we are faced here. As I have said, it seems to me that, having regard to the damages which were pleaded, the learned judge was quite right in coming to the conclusion that damages had not been set out. In the result, the appeal must be dismissed.

Ormrod L.J. agreed and added a few comments of his own (at 84–85):

It is conceded that the council is subject to [section 11 of the Landlord and Tenant Act 1985], but in construing that Act the court must have regard to the circumstances of the case and the general social conditions to which it is sought to be applied.

---

[58] *Calabar Properties Ltd.* v. *Stitcher* [1984] 1 W.L.R. 287.
[59] *Morris* v. *Liverpool City Council* (1987) 20 H.L.R. 498.
[60] See pp. 408–409.

The position in this case is to my mind perfectly clear. If Mr. Sedley's argument on this appeal is right, it will have the effect of greatly increasing the number of unfit houses which are standing empty and, correspondingly, of increasing the number of homeless persons in the stress areas of the cities of this country. It may be, of course, that that is a necessary consequence of the legislation which has to be accepted, although it is difficult to imagine that Parliament thought they were going to produce such a result. It is however a matter which the court is bound to bear in mind when it comes to construing the section. ... When one looks at [section 11], one observes first that in general the extent of the obligation placed on the landlord is not very onerous. But where the property is thoroughly run down as in this case, and in the view of everybody concerned is virtually incapable of being repaired and rendered fit within the meaning of the terms of the housing legislation it could be extremely onerous. (It is perhaps a rather emotive way of putting it to describe it as "unfit for human habitation" when what is referred to, of course, is a technical definition of that phrase.) When, however, one looks at [section 11] in detail one finds that in it there is a subsection (3), plainly put in by Parliament to avoid the sort of absurdity that Mr. Sedley's argument leads to in this case. It is perfectly true, as Mr. Sedley pointed out, that the terms of subsection (3) are almost, but significantly not entirely, in line with the common law decisions relating to the construction of covenants for repair. In subsection (3) the crucially important addition is the phrase "prospective life of the dwelling-house." In my judgment that is an exceedingly important qualification. If the prospective life of the dwelling-house, as in this case, is short, then it is perfectly proper, sensible and reasonable to adjust the landlord's obligations accordingly and not to seek to impose a construction on the statute, which can be described as pedantic. ...

On the question of damages, it would be totally absurd to accept Mr. Sedley's submission that the fact that the tenant had been let into possession in the first place at a very low rent, (on the evidence about a third of the rent which would have been expected for such a house in reasonable condition) should be disregarded in assessing damages had there been a breach of the statutory obligation to repair. If Mr. Sedley's submission is right, local authorities have three alternatives when faced with a property like this. One is to spend a great deal of money on it and devote resources to it which would be plainly wasteful. One is to leave it empty. And one is to let it to the Mr. Patels of this world and pay them damages from the moment they enter. One only has to state the argument in that form to see how absurd it is.

Orr L.J. agreed with both judgments.

Section 11(3) was considered by the Court of Appeal in *McClean* v. *Liverpool C.C..*[61] The local authority had argued that because the property in question had a limited life, no breach of section 11 had been committed. However, as Nourse L.J. noted:

Because it has a limited life, that does not mean that if put into a proper state of repair, it will not have some form of life, albeit only for a matter of a few years.[62]

The case was, therefore, distinguishable from *Newham L.B.C.* v. *Patel.*

[61] (1988) 20 H.L.R. 25.
[62] At 31.

(e) Access for Repairs

Both the Rent Act 1977 and the Housing Act 1988 provide landlords with a right of access to carry out repairs of dwelling-houses let on protected, statutory and assured tenancies. Section 16 of the Housing Act 1988 provides:

It shall be an implied term of every assured tenancy that the tenant shall afford to the landlord access to the dwelling-house let on the tenancy and all reasonable facilities for executing therein any repairs which the landlord is entitled to execute.

Equivalent provisions in the Rent Act 1977 apply to dwelling-houses occupied by protected tenants[63] and statutory tenants.[64]

II REMEDIES FOR BREACH OF COVENANT

(A) TENANTS' REMEDIES AGAINST THE LANDLORD

(1) Damages

A tenant may have an action for damages against the landlord who is in breach of the covenant to repair, but only after he has given the landlord notice of disrepair.[65] The measure of damages is the difference in value to the tenant between the premises as they are and as they would be if repaired in accordance with the covenant.[66]

Calabar Properties Ltd. v. *Stitcher* [1984] 1 W.L.R. 287

The measure of damages was discussed by the Court of Appeal in this case in which the tenant was claiming, *inter alia*, damages for disrepair in relation to the cost of alternative accommodation while the premises were uninhabitable, the cost of redecoration, and compensation for discomfort.[67]
Griffiths L.J. said (at 297–299):

The object of awarding damages against a landlord for breach of his covenant to repair is not to punish the landlord but, so far as money can, to restore the tenant to the position he would have been in had there been no breach. This object will not be achieved by applying one set of rules to all cases regardless of

[63] s.148.
[64] s.3(2).
[65] See pp. 368–371.
[66] *Hewitt* v. *Rowlands* (1924) 131 L.T. 757.
[67] See also *McGreal* v. *Wake* (1984) 13 H.L.R. 107.

the particular circumstances of the case. The facts of each case must be looked at carefully to see what damage the tenant has suffered and how he may be fairly compensated by a monetary award.

In this case on the findings of the judge the plaintiff landlords, after notice of the defect, neglected their obligation to repair for such a length of time that the flat eventually became uninhabitable. It was also clear that unless ordered to do so by an order of the court, the plaintiffs had no intention of carrying out the repairs. In these circumstances the defendant had two options that were reasonably open to her: either of selling the flat and moving elsewhere, or alternatively of moving into temporary accommodation and bringing an action against the plaintiffs to force them to carry out the repairs, and then returning to the flat after the repairs were done. If the defendant had chosen the first option then the measure of damages would indeed have been the difference in the price she received for the flat in its damaged condition and that which it would have fetched in the open market if the plaintiffs had observed their repairing covenant. If however the defendant did not wish to sell the flat but to continue to live in it after the plaintiffs had carried out the necessary structural repairs it was wholly artificial to award her damages on the basis of loss in market value, because once the plaintiffs had carried out the repairs and any consequential redecoration of the interior was completed there would be no loss in market value. The defendant should be awarded the cost to which she was put in taking alternative accommodation, the cost of redecorating, and some award for all the unpleasantness of living in the flat as it deteriorated until it became uninhabitable. These three heads of damage will, so far as money can, compensate the defendant for the plaintiffs' breach.

But it was said that the court cannot award the cost of the alternative accommodation because of the decision of the Court of Queen's Bench in *Green* v. *Eales*, 2 Q.B. 225, and in particular the passage in the judgment of Lord Denman C.J. in which he said, at p. 238:

"We are of opinion that the defendant was not bound to find the plaintiff another residence whilst the repairs went on, any more than he would have been bound to do so if the premises had been consumed by fire."

But I take that passage to do no more than draw attention to the fact that a landlord is not in breach of his covenant to repair until he has been given notice of the want of repair and a reasonable time has elapsed in which the repair could have been carried out. If in this case the plaintiffs had sent workmen round to carry out the repairs promptly on receiving notice of the defect and the defendant for her own convenience had decided to move to a hotel whilst the repairs were carried out, she could not have claimed the cost of the hotel because the plaintiffs would not have been in breach of the repairing covenant. That Lord Denman C.J. meant no more than this is I think apparent from his observation that the tenant might have had a claim on the basis that the time he had to be in alternative accommodation had been lengthened by the delay in carrying out repairs. For these reasons I do not regard *Green* v. *Eales* as an authority for the proposition that there can be no claim for the costs of alternative accommodation, but if it did purport so to decide, it was in my view wrongly decided.

If the defendant in this case had claimed for the cost of alternative accommodation it would in principle have been an allowable head of damage. It would naturally have been closely investigated in the evidence; was the defendant's true reason for leaving the flat that she and her husband found the conditions intolerable, or were there other reasons for going to live in the Isle of

Man; was the cost of the alternative accommodation reasonable?—and so forth. However, the claim was not made and I agree that it is now too late to put it forward.

The judge awarded the defendant part of the costs of the internal decorations which she had had to carry out as a result of the plaintiffs' breach of covenant. In my view he should have awarded the whole of the costs of the repairs. However, he deducted one-third of the cost of repairs as a betterment element because he was attempting the unreal exercise of putting a price on the diminution in value of the flat in circumstances when there was no need to do so.

The judge was however invited to assess damages in this way by the defendant's counsel because it was thought that the decision of the Court of Appeal in *Hewitt* v. *Rowlands*, 93 L.J.K.B. 1080, left no other approach to the assessment. That was a case in which a statutory tenant claimed damages against his landlord for breach of the landlord's duty to repair. The sums involved were very small and in giving directions to the registrar as to the basis on which damages should be assessed Bankes L.J. said, at p. 1082:

"Prima facie the measure of damage for breach of the obligation to repair *is the difference in value to the tenant* during that period between the house in the condition in which it now is and the house in the condition in which it would be if the landlord on receipt of the notice had fulfilled his obligation to repair." (My emphasis.)

Whatever Bankes L.J. meant by "the difference in value to the tenant," the one thing he cannot have meant in the circumstances of that case was the diminution in the market value of the tenancy, for it was a statutory tenancy which the tenant could not sell, and thus it had no market value. In my view the difference in value to the tenant must vary according to the circumstances of the case. If the tenant is in occupation during the period of breach he is entitled to be compensated for the discomfort and inconvenience occasioned by the breach and I suspect that that is what Bankes L.J. had in mind when he used the phrase "the difference in value to the tenant" in *Hewitt* v. *Rowlands*, 93 L.J.K.B. 1080, 1082, for which the judge in this case awarded £3,000. If the tenant has rented the property to let it and the landlord is aware of this, then "the difference in value to the tenant" may be measured by his loss of rent if he cannot let it because of the landlord's breach. If the tenant is driven out of occupation by the breach and forced to sell the property then "the difference in value to the tenant" may be measured by the difference between the selling price and the price he would have obtained if the landlord had observed his repairing covenant. But each case depends upon its own circumstances and *Hewitt* v. *Rowlands* should not be regarded as an authority for the proposition that it is in every case necessary to obtain valuation evidence.

In my view there was no need for any valuation evidence in this case. I repeat that damages in a case such as this should include the cost of the redecoration, a sum to compensate for the discomfort, loss of enjoyment and health involved in living in the damp and deteriorating flat and any reasonable sum spent on providing alternative accommodation after the flat became uninhabitable.

The modern trend is to award substantial damages for distress, discomfort and inconvenience. In *Choidi* v. *De Marney*,[68] for example, the tenant was awarded damages for distress and inconvenience totalling

---

[68] (1989) 21 H.L.R. 6.

£5,460 (assessed on the basis of £30 per week for 182 weeks) even though the weekly rent was only £8.

In *Davies* v. *Peterson*[69] the landlord sought to recover possession of accommodation occupied by the tenant and claimed arrears of rent. The tenant counterclaimed for damages for disrepair, including a sum for discomfort, anxiety and inconvenience. Under this head the trial judge had awarded the tenant the sum of £250. In the Court of Appeal, Russell L.J. thought that this figure did not amount to adequate compensation:

> Mr. Parker, on behalf of the landlord in this case, submits that the evidence discloses, if anything, a very short period of time during which the tenant must have suffered. I do not agree. Again—and I repeat—there is in the judgment an absence of a specific finding as to the period during which this tenant was a victim of the consequences of disrepair. One cannot be specific about it. I do not accept, on an overall view of the evidence, that it was limited to a matter of three or four months. My own view, looking at the evidence as a whole, is that it must have extended over a period of at least 12 months, for which this landlord was responsible. In 1988 the sum of £250 must in my judgment be regarded, when awarded by way of compensation for inconvenience, anxiety and discomfort, as little more than nominal. I do not regard this as a case in which nominal damages in respect of this part of the award were appropriate.
>
> Accordingly, though conscious of the fact that this court will not interfere with an award of damages unless it is satisfied that such an award is wholly out of keeping with established authority, for my part I would increase the award made by the judge under this heading from the sum of £250 to the sum of £1,000.[70]

Kerr L.J. agreed.

It is a general principle relating to the recovery of damages that the plaintiff is under a duty to mitigate his loss. This principle was applied in *Minchburn* v. *Peck*.[71] According to the terms of the lease the landlord was under an obligation to "maintain repair and redecorate and renew the main structure and foundations the boundary walls fences and areas of the Building and the roof and external parts and other retained parts of the Building ... " The tenant claimed damages resulting from disrepair, and was awarded £1050 (including £800 general damages) by the trial judge. The landlord appealed, and the Court of Appeal reduced the award of general damages to £700 on the basis that the tenant's losses would have been less extensive if he had "badgered" the landlord at an earlier date.

(2) Specific Performance

Although it has been held that a tenant's repairing obligation cannot be enforced by an order of specific performance,[72] in *Jeune* v. *Queens*

[69] (1989) 21 H.L.R. 63.
[70] At 70.
[71] (1988) 20 H.L.R. 392.
[72] *Hill* v. *Barclay* (1810) 16 Ves. 402.

Cross Properties[73] Pennycuick V.-C. held that the court had jurisdiction to grant specific performance in cases involving a breach of the landlord's repairing obligations where there is "a plain breach of a covenant to repair and there is no doubt at all what is required to be done to remedy the breach."[74]

This jurisdiction has been given statutory confirmation, at least in the housing sphere, by section 17 of the Landlord and Tenant Act 1985[75]:

(1) In proceedings in which a tenant of a dwelling alleges a breach on the part of his landlord of a repairing covenant relating to any part of the premises in which the dwelling is comprised, the court may order specific performance of the covenant whether or not the breach relates to a part of the premises let to the tenant and notwithstanding any equitable rule restricting the scope of the remedy, whether on the basis of a lack of mutuality or otherwise.

(2) In this section—

(a)   "tenant" includes a statutory tenant,

(b)   in relation to a statutory tenant the reference to the premises let to him is to the premises of which he is a statutory tenant,

(c)   "landlord," in relation to a tenant, includes any person against whom the tenant has a right to enforce a repairing covenant, and

(d)   "repairing covenant" means a covenant to repair, maintain, renew, construct or replace any property.

In *Francis* v. *Cowcliffe Ltd.*[76] the defendant landlords decided to install new lifts in a block of flats. However, they lacked adequate finance to complete the task. The plaintiff, a 70 year old widow living on the third floor, sought an order of specific performance. Judge Rubin (sitting as a deputy judge in the High Court) said that this was a case in which the defendants had brought the hardship on themselves. The defendants had chosen to purchase and embark upon an expensive scheme for development of the property without any adequate finance:

[F]or these reasons I propose to make the order for specific performance which the plaintiff seeks. It is said that this will inevitably result in the defendants being wound up. Even if this were so, that does not seem to me to be any reason why the plaintiff should not have her order. In any event I am far from satisfied that the guarantors of the mortgage loan and others interested in the defendants will not provide the necessary money to do the requisite works and stave off the creditors of the defendants.[77]

[73] [1974] Ch. 97.
[74] At 101.
[75] This provision was formerly Housing Act 1974, s.125. See *Gordon* v. *Selico Co. Ltd.* (1986) 18 H.L.R. 219.
[76] (1977) 33 P. & C.R. 368.
[77] At 375.

(3) Using Rent to Pay for Repairs

Goff J. said in *Lee-Parker* v. *Izzet*[78] (a complex case relating to a contract for the sale of land):

> However, the third and fourth defendants further claim a lien for the cost of the repairs or alternatively for the value of any permanent improvement effected thereby, and they also claim a set off against rent in their capacity as tenants.
>
> First, they say that in so far as the first defendant was, as landlord, liable to do the repairs by the express or implied terms of the tenancy agreement, including the covenants imported by section 32(1) of the Housing Act 1961, they, having done them themselves, are entitled to treat the expenditure as a payment of rent, for which reliance is placed on *Taylor* v. *Beal* (1591) Cro.Eliz. 222. . . .
>
> I do not think this is bound up with technical rules of set off. It is an ancient common law right. I therefore declare that so far as the repairs are within the express or implied covenants of the landlord, the third and fourth defendants are entitled to recoup themselves out of future rents and defend any action for payment thereof. It does not follow however that the full amount expended by the third and fourth defendants on such repairs can properly be treated as payment of rent. It is a question of fact in every case whether and to what extent the expenditure was proper.
>
> For the sake of avoiding misunderstanding I must add that of course the *Taylor* v. *Beal* right can only be exercised when and so far as the landlord is in breach and any necessary notice must have been given to him.
>
> In so far as the repairs fall outside the landlord's covenants there can in my judgment be no set off against the plaintiffs.

Some doubts were expressed as to the correctness of this proposition. However, subsequent cases have confirmed the principle.[79] In *British Anzani (Felixstowe)* v. *International Marine Management*[80] Forbes J. said:

> On a consideration of these cases it seems to me that *Taylor* v. *Beal*, Cro.Eliz. 222, is authority for the proposition that there are at least two sets of circumstances in which at common law there can be a set off against rent, one where the tenant expends money on repairs to the demised premises which the landlord has covenanted to carry out, but in breach has failed to do so (at any rate where the breach significantly affects the use of the premises), and the other where the tenant has paid money at the request of the landlord in respect of some obligation of the landlord connected with the land demised. To this proposition there must be added two riders. First, that as the landlord's obligation to repair premises demised does not arise until the tenant has notified him of want of repair, such notification must have been given before the set off can arise; and secondly that the set off must be for a sum which is not to be regarded as unliquidated damages, that is, it is a sum certain which has actually been paid and in addition its quantum has either been acknowledged by the landlord or in some other way can no longer be disputed by him, as for instance, if it is the subject of an award on a submission to arbitration. The latest expression of opinion about this matter is in *Lee-Parker* v. *Izzet* [1971] 1

---

[78] [1971] 1 W.L.R. 1688 at 1692–1693.
[79] *Asco Developments Ltd.* v. *Gordon* (1978) 248 E.G. 683.
[80] [1980] Q.B. 137 at 147–148.

W.L.R. 1688. ... I do not think that there is any difference between the principle as seen by Goff J. and that which I have set out above save for this. Goff J. took the view that it was money properly expended which could form a subject of this right. My view is that the right was slightly more restricted, namely, that it could only be exercised when the sum was certain and its amount could not really be disputed by the landlord. This restriction which I think should be made arises from a consideration of the judgment of Lord Kenyon C.J. in *Weigall* v. *Waters*, 6 Term. 488, which was not quoted to Goff J. In that case the tenant had in fact paid £30 but Lord Kenyon C.J. still regarded the cross-claim as one for uncertain damages. It seems the quantum of the sum must have been either unchallenged or unchallengeable before it could be regarded as deductible.

It has been suggested that a tenant who proposes to withhold rent to pay for repairs should be careful not to allow the landlord any opportunity of recovering possession on grounds of non-payment of rent:

Before exercising the right to use rent to pay for repairs in default, tenants should follow carefully certain preliminary steps:

(a) inform the landlord of the intention to take this form of action if repairs are not carried out;
(b) allow a further reasonable period for the landlord to comply with the repairing obligations;
(c) obtain three estimates for the costs of carrying out the remedial works and submit copies to the landlord with a "final warning";
(d) engage the contractor at the lowest tender and have the work carried out;
(e) submit a copy of the contractor's invoice to the landlord and request reimbursement;
(f) if no money is forthcoming, recoup the costs by deduction from future rent.[81]

There are limitations to the common law right to recoup from rent. In particular, the tenant may only claim for the cost of the repairs, and not for damage resulting from disrepair. There is, however, an equitable right of set-off against rent as regards this type of damage.

(4) Equitable Set-off

There is no general right for the tenant to withhold rent on the ground that the landlord is in breach of his obligations under the lease (whether express or implied).

The legitimacy (or otherwise) of tenants participating in a rent strike was discussed in *Camden Nominees* v. *Forcey*.[82] The case concerned a block of flats which was let to a number of tenants holding on monthly tenancies under a standard form of agreement. The tenants agreed to pay rent one month in advance, and the landlords agreed to provide central heating, constant hot water, a lift, cleaning and lighting of the staircase and passages, porterage and other services. In the autumn of

---

[81] Luba, *Repairs: Tenant's Rights* (2nd ed., 1991), p. 50. [82] [1940] Ch. 352.

1939 certain of the tenants complained that the landlords were not carrying out their obligations under the tenancy agreements.

Miss Forcey, the defendant, decided not to pay her rent. Simonds J. said of this action: "It is clear ... that it is no answer to a claim for rent for the tenant to say that the landlord has not performed his obligation to clean the staircase or furnish hot water."[83]

The tenants held a number of meetings, and a tenants' association was formed. In consequence, some tenants withheld their rents for some months, and others threatened to do so unless certain grievances were remedied. The landlord sought an injunction to restrain the defendant "from doing any acts or making any statements or taking any steps calculated or intended to cause or induce the plaintiff's tenants. ... , or any of them, to commit breaches of their tenancy agreements by non-payment of rent or otherwise."[84]

The issue which arose for determination by the court was set out by Simonds J. in the following terms:

The law as I understand it is that if A without justification knowingly interferes with a contract between B and C he commits an actionable wrong. It is on the words "without justification" that the difficulty arises, and it was to consider them that I reserved judgment in a case otherwise very clear.[85]

Simonds J. said:

In the present case, if I rightly understand their learned counsel, the defendants have pleaded that they are justified in their otherwise actionable wrong on two grounds; the first, that they and those whom they would persuade to break their contracts have a common interest in making the landlords perform their obligations; and the second, that there is such a state of affairs here existing, on the one side tenants who are weak and on the other landlords who are strong and take advantage of their strength, that it is justifiable for the defendants to use a weapon which would otherwise be wrongful.

In my judgment, there is no validity in either of these contentions. The defendants owed no duty to their fellow tenants; they sought their co-operation for their own ends, though no doubt a successful campaign would have been for the benefit of all alike. The end which they sought, namely, the performance by the landlords of their obligations, was one which could be reached by process of law. If the landlords broke their contract the law gave the defendants their remedy by way of damages, or in a proper case by way of specific performance. There is neither reason nor authority for the suggestion that in such circumstances a common interest can justify the interference with contractual rights. If A, B, C, and D meet together and agree that in order to persuade or coerce X to a certain course they will each break their contracts with him, that would, I apprehend, be an actionable conspiracy. It would be a strange thing if A, calling together B, C, and D, and urging them to break their contracts could justify that act on the ground of common interest. This contention must, in my judgment, fail.

[83] At 356.
[84] Simonds J. at 354–355.
[85] At 355.

The second contention was one which appeared to be directed less to my reason than to my emotions. The case was put as something analogous to *Brimelow* v. *Casson* ([1924] 1 Ch. 302), in which any step that put an end to an intolerable position might be regarded as justifiable. *Brimelow* v. *Casson* stands alone, and has been the subject of a good deal of controversy. In a comparable case it would be my duty to follow it, though I would humbly suggest that on the facts stated in the judgment that case might have been simply disposed of by the application of the maxim Ex turpi causa non oritur actio. But, however that may be, there is no real analogy between the two cases. It is a dangerous proposition that inequality in wealth or position justifies a course otherwise actionable, and that tenants may against their landlord adopt measures of self-help because in their judgment the law does not afford them adequate remedy for his default.

I would only add, in deference to the argument addressed to me, which I think was intended to be founded on *Brimelow* v. *Casson*, that neither that case nor any other case supports the view that those who assume the duty of advising the withholding of rent or any other breach of contract can justify their action by protesting that they are performing a public service. Advice which is intended to have persuasive effects is not distinguishable from inducement, and there is no reason to suppose that the giving of such advice is justifiable except by those persons in whom the law recognises a moral duty to give it.

In the result I hold that the defendants without justification interfered with the plaintiff's contractual rights and it is clear that at the date of the issue of the writ they intended to continue to do so. I must therefore grant an injunction as asked.[86]

There is, however, a general principle of equitable set-off, which was defined by Parker J. in *The Teno*[87] in the following terms:

[W]here the cross-claim not only arises out of the same contract as the claim but is so directly connected with it that it would be manifestly unjust to allow the claimant to recover without taking into account the cross claim there is a right of set-off in equity of an unliquidated claim.

In *British Anzani (Felixstowe)* v. *International Marine Management*[88] it was held that an unliquidated claim in damages could be set-off against accrued arrears of rent, notwithstanding the argument—put forward on behalf of the landlord—that "rent is something special, that it is invested with something almost in the nature of an aura."
Forbes J. said:

Now originally Mr. Harman argued that the principle of equitable set off did not apply where what was sought to be set off was an unliquidated demand, but *Bankes* v. *Jarvis* [1903] 1 K.B. 549 is a distinct authority for the proposition that unliquidated damages may be set off against a claim for debt. There is this passage in the judgment of Channell J., at p. 553:

" . . . the Judicature Act, and more especially the rules, distinctly put an unliquidated claim on the same footing as a liquidated claim for the purpose

---

[86] At 365–366.
[87] [1977] 2 Lloyd's Rep. 289 at 297.
[88] [1980] Q.B. 137.

of set off; and consequently the defendant's claim against the plaintiff's son, which, if liquidated, could have been pleaded before the Judicature Act as a set off to the plaintiff's claim, can now, although unliquidated, be relied on as a defence to the extent of the claim."

This proposition is recognised in the sentence from the judgment of Parker J. in *The Teno* [1977] 2 Lloyd's Rep. 289, 297. But Mr. Harman, driven from that point, still argues that at any rate the sum must not be so vague as to be unquantifiable at the time of the claim. He cited no authority for this proposition and I can find no warrant for it in any broad legal principle. It is of the nature of unliquidated damages that they may remain unquantified until an award is made. A set off of unliquidated damages is a defence to so much of the claim as is represented by the eventual amount of the award made. If the defendant in some way limits his damages to a sum less than that claimed, then it is obvious that there is no defence to the balance over and above the sum so limited and, no doubt, summary judgment could be obtained for this balance. But where the damages claimed to be set off are at large and it is claimed bona fide, as is here admitted, that they over-top the claim, then even though not precisely quantified, it seems to me that the set off amounts to a complete defence to the whole claim.[89]

The issue of set-off will normally arise in proceedings by the landlord for possession on the basis of non-payment of rent. If the tenant's damages exceed the amount of the arrears, the tenant will have a complete defence against the landlord.[90] Where the arrears exceed the tenant's damages the court may allow the set-off but make an order for possession.[91]

(5) The Secure Tenant's "Right to Repair"

Section 96 of the Housing Act 1985 provides:

(1) The Secretary of State may by regulations make a scheme for entitling secure tenants, subject to and in accordance with the provisions of the scheme—

(a) to carry out to the dwelling-houses of which they are secure tenants repairs which their landlords are obliged by repairing covenants to carry out, and

(b) after carrying out the repairs, to recover from their landlords such sums as may be determined by or under the scheme.

(2) The regulations may make such procedural, incidental, supplementary and transitional provision as may appear to the Secretary of State to be necessary or expedient, and may in particular—

(a) provide for questions arising under the scheme to be referred to and determined by the county court;

---

[89] At 145–146.
[90] See *Melville* v. *Grapelodge Developments* (1978) 39 P. & C.R. 179.
[91] See *Davies* v. *Peterson* (1989) 21 H.L.R. 63.

(b)   provide that where a secure tenant makes application under the scheme his landlord's obligation under the repairing covenants shall cease to apply for such period and to such extent as may be determined by or under the scheme.

(3) The regulations may make different provision with respect to different cases or descriptions of case, including different provision for different areas.

(4) Regulations under this section shall be made by statutory instrument which shall be subject to annulment in pursuance of a resolution of either House of Parliament.

(5) In this section "repairing covenant," in relation to a dwelling-house, means a covenant, whether express or implied, obliging the landlord to keep in repair the dwelling-house or any part of the dwelling-house.

This section has been implemented by the Secure Tenancies (Right to Repair Scheme) Regulations 1985.[92] The statutory procedure is terribly complicated, and there seems no reason why a secure tenant should not rely on the more straightforward principle of common law set-off as explained in *Lee-Parker* v. *Izzet.*

This section does not apply to a secure tenancy from a co-operative housing association.[93]

The Housing Act 1985 also gives secure tenants a right to carry out improvements with the consent of the landlord.[94] Although any such improvements will be at the tenant's expense, after the end of the tenancy the landlord may "make to the tenant. ... such payment in respect of the improvement as the landlord considers to be appropriate."[95] The Act also restricts the extent to which the landlord can increase the rent on account of improvements for which the tenant has paid.[96]

(6) Receivers

Where a landlord fails to comply with his repairing obligations, the High Court has jurisdiction (under section 37(1) of the Supreme Court Act 1981) to appoint a receiver to take over management of the property, the receipt of rent, and the undertaking of repairs. The section provides that a receiving order may be made "in all cases in which it appears to the court to be just and convenient to do so."

A clear case where it would be "just and convenient" to appoint a receiver arose in *Hart* v. *Emelkirk Ltd.*[97] where the property in question required urgent repairs. There are, however, problems with this remedy.

---

[92] S.I. 1985 No. 1493.
[93] Housing Act 1985, s.109.
[94] ss.97–99. Again, this right is not enjoyed by tenants of co-operative housing associations (s.109).
[95] s.100(1).
[96] s.101.
[97] [1983] 1 W.L.R. 1298.

Evans v. *Clayhope Properties Ltd.* [1988] 1 W.L.R. 358

Nourse L.J. said (at 360–363):

This appeal raises a short point of principle as to the court's power, before the rights of the parties have been determined at trial, to order one of them to meet a deficit in the sums coming into the hands of a court appointed receiver and manager for payment of his expenditure or remuneration. Vinelott J. [1987] 1 W.L.R. 225, relying on the decision of Warrington J. in *Boehm* v. *Goodall* [1911] 1 Ch. 155, has held that there is no such power and the question must now be determined by this court.

In *Hart* v. *Emelkirk Ltd.* [1983] 1 W.L.R. 1289 Goulding J. held that the court has power to make an interlocutory order appointing a receiver and manager in a case where (1) a block of flats is held on leases at low rents containing covenants by the landlord to repair, with provisions for the tenants to bear the cost of the repairs by way of service charge, and (2) the landlord, for want of repair, allows the property to deteriorate. That decision, although novel at the time, was an application of the court's jurisdiction to appoint a manager in order to preserve property which is affected by the action. The dispute does not centre, as it usually does, on the ownership of the property, but on the liability to preserve it. In that respect the decision ought no doubt to be regarded as an extension of those which had preceded it, although one which is clearly beneficial in the conditions of many modern residential developments.

The order for the appointment of the receiver and manager in the present case was modelled on the order made in *Hart* v. *Emelkirk Ltd.*, but, as Vinelott J. pointed out, there is one very significant difference between the two cases. In *Hart* v. *Emelkirk Ltd.* the service charge provisions enabled the landlord, and thus the receiver and manager, to recover from the tenants estimated contributions towards the cost of the repairs in advance of their being carried out. In the present case the cost of the repairs and of the attendant expenses is not recoverable from the tenants unless and until it has been incurred in pursuance of the landlord's obligations. Accordingly, the only sums which have come into the hands of the receiver and manager are the rents, negligible in amount, which are wholly insufficient to fund his remuneration and expenses to date, let alone the cost of the necessary repairs. Unless this appeal succeeds, so that the landlord can be ordered to pay what has to be paid, the appointment of the receiver and manager will have been of no practical value. ...

Boehm v. *Goodall* [1911] 1 Ch. 155 was a case of a partnership action in which the court had made, by consent, a final order for dissolution, together with orders for the usual inquiry and accounts, an order for sale of the business as a going concern, and also an order for the appointment of an individual as receiver and manager of the business until sale. Upon completion of the receiver and manager's duties there was a certified balance owing to him on his account, but no assets of the partnership available for its payment. The receiver and manager issued a summons in the action asking that the partners (other than one who had become bankrupt) might be ordered to pay to him the balance thus owing.

The principal argument advanced in support of the claim was that, since the order for his appointment had been made by consent, the receiver and manager must be taken to have undertaken the management of the partnership business and to have made expenditure and incurred liabilities at the request of the partners and under an implied promise on their part to repay him. His position was said to be analogous to that of a trustee, who was not confined to his indemnity out of the trust estate, but was entitled to be indemnified by the beneficiaries personally. In rejecting that argument, Warrington J. referred to authority, in particular to passages from the judgments of Cairns L.J. in *Gardner* v. *London Chatham and Dover Railway Co.* (1867) L.R. 2 Ch.App. 201, 211–212 and Lord Esher M.R. in *Burt, Boulton & Hayward* v. *Bull* [1895] 1 Q.B. 276, 279–280. (He might also have referred to the subsequent observation of Lord Esher M.R. to the same effect in *In re Flowers & Co.* [1897] 1 Q.B. 14, 15). What Cairns L.J. said, L.R. 2 Ch.App. 201, 211–212, was:

> "When the court appoints a manager of a business or undertaking, it in effect assumes the management into its own hands; for the manager is the servant or officer of the court, and upon any question arising as to the character or details of the management, it is the court that must direct and decide. The circumstance that in this particular case the persons appointed were previously the managers employed by the company is immaterial. When appointed by the court they are responsible to the court, and no orders of the company, or of the directors, can interfere with this responsibility."

Warrington J. in *Boehm* v. *Goodall* [1911] 1 Ch. 155 said that he could not come to the conclusion that the principles of the cases with reference to trustees applied to the case of a receiver and manager appointed by the court without running counter to the decisions in all the cases relating to those acting in the latter capacity. He continued, at p. 161:

> "Such a receiver and manager is not the agent of the parties, he is not a trustee for them, and they cannot control him. He may, as far as they are concerned, incur expenses or liabilities without their having a say in the matter. I think it is of the utmost importance that receivers and managers in this position should know that they must look for their indemnity to the assets which are under the control of the court. The court itself cannot indemnify receivers, but it can, and will, do so out of the assets, so far as they extend, for expenses properly incurred; but it cannot go further. It would be an extreme hardship in most cases to parties to an action if they were to be held personally liable for expenses incurred by receivers and managers over which they have no control."

He then went on to say that it made no difference that the order there was made by consent and also to reject an alternative argument based on subrogation.

Boehm v. *Goodall* was a decision based on statements of principle of high authority. In my judgment it was correctly decided and it applies to this case.

It should also be noted that the courts refused to appoint a receiver where the landlord was a local authority.[98]

To overcome some of the difficulties surrounding the appointment of a receiver the general jurisdiction of section 37(1) has given way to the provisions of Part II of the Landlord and Tenant Act 1987 (although the courts continue to have jurisdiction under section 37(1) if the 1987 Act does not apply).

The Landlord and Tenant Act 1987 provides:

---

[98] *Parker* v. *Camden L.B.C.* [1986] Ch. 162.

21.—(1) The tenant of a flat contained in any premises to which this Part applies may, subject to the following provisions of this Part, apply to the court for an order under section 24 appointing a manager to act in relation to those premises.

(2) Subject to subsection (3), this Part applies to premises consisting of the whole or part of a building if the building or part contains two or more flats.

(3) This Part does not apply to any such premises at a time when—

(a)   the interest of the landlord in the premises is held by an exempt landlord or a resident landlord, or

(b)   the premises are included within the functional land of any charity....

(6) An application to the court for it to exercise in relation to any premises any jurisdiction existing apart from this Act to appoint a receiver or manager shall not be made by a tenant (in his capacity as such) in any circumstances in which an application could be made by him for an order under section 24 appointing a manager to act in relation to those premises.

22.—(1) Before an application for an order under section 24 is made in respect of any premises to which this Part applies by a tenant of a flat contained in those premises, a notice under this section must (subject to subsection (3)) be served on the landlord by the tenant.

(2) A notice under this section must—

(a)   specify the tenant's name, the address of his flat and an address in England and Wales (which may be the address of his flat) at which the landlord may serve notices, including notices in proceedings, on him in connection with this Part;

(b)   state that the tenant intends to make an application for an order under section 24 to be made by the court in respect of such premises to which this Part applies as are specified in the notice, but (if paragraph (d) is applicable) that he will not do so if the landlord complies with the requirement specified in pursuance of that paragraph;

(c)   specify the grounds on which the court would be asked to make such an order and the matters that would be relied on by the tenant for the purpose of establishing those grounds;

(d)   where those matters are capable of being remedied by the landlord, require the landlord, within such reasonable period as is specified in the notice, to take such steps for the purpose of remedying them as are so specified; and

(e)   contain such information (if any) as the Secretary of State may by regulations prescribe.

(3) The court may (whether on the hearing of an application for an order under section 24 or not) by order dispense with the requirement to serve a notice under this section in a case where it is satisfied that it would not be reasonably practicable to serve such a notice on the landlord, but the court may, when doing so, direct that such other notices are served, or such other steps are taken, as it thinks fit.

(4) In a case where—

(a)   a notice under this section has been served on the landlord, and

(b) his interest in the premises specified in pursuance of subsection (2)(b) is subject to a mortgage,

the landlord shall, as soon as is reasonably practicable after receiving the notice, serve on the mortgagee a copy of the notice.

23.—(1) No application for an order under section 24 shall be made to the court unless—

(a) in a case where a notice has been served under section 22, either—

  (i) the period specified in pursuance of paragraph (d) of subsection (2) of that section has expired without the landlord having taken the steps that he was required to take in pursuance of that provision, or

  (ii) that paragraph was not applicable in the circumstances of the case; or

(b) in a case where the requirement to serve such a notice has been dispensed with by an order under subsection (3) of that section, either—

  (i) any notices required to be served, and any other steps required to be taken, by virtue of the order have been served or (as the case may be) taken, or

  (ii) no direction was given by the court when making the order.

24.—(1) The court may, on an application for an order under this section, by order (whether interlocutory or final) appoint a manager to carry out in relation to any premises to which this Part applies—

(a) such functions in connection with the management of the premises, or

(b) such functions of a receiver,

or both, as the court thinks fit.

(2) The court may only make an order under this section in the following circumstances, namely—

(a) where the court is satisfied—

  (i) that the landlord either is in breach of any obligation owed by him to the tenant under his tenancy and relating to the management of the premises in question or any part of them or (in the case of an obligation dependent on notice) would be in breach of any such obligation but for the fact that it has not been reasonably practicable for the tenant to give him the appropriate notice, and

  (ii) that the circumstances by virtue of which he is (or would be) in breach of any such obligation are likely to continue, and

  (iii) that it is just and convenient to make the order in all the circumstances of the case; or

(b) where the court is satisfied that other circumstances exist which make it just and convenient for the order to be made.

Note

For the purposes of section 21(3)(a) an "exempt landlord" is defined by section 58(1) as including local authorities and certain housing associations; "resident landlord" is defined by section 58(2). The Act has no application to tenancies from the Crown.[99]

(7) Compulsory Purchase of the Landlord's Interest

In extreme cases the court may make an "acquisition order" under the Landlord and Tenant Act 1987 whereby the tenants acquire the landlord's interest by way of compulsory purchase.[1] There are, however, various conditions which must be satisfied, and in order to apply for an acquisition order the tenants must be holding under long leases (*i.e.* leases for a term exceeding 21 years[2]).

(B) LANDLORD'S REMEDIES AGAINST THE TENANT

In cases where the tenant is in breach of his repairing obligations, at common law, the landlord has a number of options. First, if the lease so provides the landlord may enter and repair at the tenant's expense, though he will not be granted a mandatory injunction or specific performance. Secondly, the landlord may sue the tenant for damages resulting from the breach. Thirdly, the landlord may seek to terminate the tenancy. In relation to a periodic tenancy, the landlord may end the tenancy by notice to quit.[3] In relation to a fixed-term tenancy the landlord may, if the lease contains a right of re-entry, seek to forfeit the lease.[4]

The landlord's position is, however, modified in a number of respects:

(1) Law of Property Act 1925, s.146

Section 146(1) of the Law of Property Act 1925 imposes a general limitation on the ability of landlords to forfeit leases. Section 146(2) contains a power for the court to provide relief for a tenant against whom an action for forfeiture is brought.[5]

(2) Leasehold Property (Repairs) Act 1938 (as amended by the Landlord and Tenant Act 1954)

1.—(1) Where a lessor serves on a lessee under sub-section (1) of section 146 of the Law of Property Act, 1925, a notice that relates to a breach of a covenant or agreement to keep or put in repair during the currency of the lease all or any of the property comprised in the lease, and at the date of the service of the notice three years or more of the term of the lease remain unexpired, the lessee may within 28 days from that date serve on the lessor a counter-notice to the effect that he claims the benefit of this Act.

[99] s.56.
[1] ss.25–29.
[2] s.59(3).
[3] See pp. 199–201.
[4] See pp. 189–198.
[5] See p. 191.

(2) A right to damages for a breach of such a covenant as aforesaid shall not be enforceable by action commenced at any time at which three years or more of the term of the lease remain unexpired unless the lessor has served on the lessee not less than one month before the commencement of the action such a notice as is specified in subsection (1) of section 146 of the Law of Property Act, 1925, and where a notice is served under this subsection, the lessee may, within 28 days from the date of the service thereof, serve on the lessor a counter-notice to the effect that he claims the benefit of this Act.

(3) Where a counter-notice is served by a lessee under this section, then, notwithstanding anything in any enactment or rule of law, no proceedings, by action or otherwise, shall be taken by the lessor for the enforcement of any right of re-entry or forfeiture under any proviso or stipulation in the lease for breach of the covenant or agreement in question, or for damages for breach thereof, otherwise than with the leave of the court.

(4) A notice served under subsection (1) of section 146 of the Law of Property Act, 1925, in the circumstances specified in subsection (1) of this section, and a notice served under subsection (2) of this section shall not be valid unless it contains a statement, in characters not less conspicuous than those used in any other part of the notice, to the effect that the lessee is entitled under this Act to serve on the lessor a counter-notice claiming the benefit of this Act, and a statement in the like characters specifying the time within which, and the manner in which, under this Act a counter-notice may be served and specifying the name and address for service of the lessor.

(5) Leave for the purposes of this section shall not be given unless the lessor proves—

(a) that the immediate remedying of the breach in question is requisite for preventing substantial diminution in the value of his reversion, or that the value thereof has been substantially diminished by the breach;

(b) that the immediate remedying of the breach is required for giving effect in relation to the premises to the purposes of any enactment, or of any byelaw or other provision having effect under an enactment, or for giving effect to any order of a court or requirement of any authority under any enactment or any such byelaw or other provision as aforesaid;

(c) in a case in which the lessee is not in occupation of the whole of the premises as respects which the covenant or agreement is proposed to be enforced, that the immediate remedying of the breach is required in the interests of the occupier of those premises or of part thereof;

(d) that the breach can be immediately remedied at an expense that is relatively small in comparison with the much greater expense that would probably be occasioned by postponement of the necessary work; or

(e) special circumstances which in the opinion of the court, render it just and equitable that leave should be given.

(6) The court may, in granting or in refusing leave for the purposes of this section, impose such terms and conditions on the lessor or on the lessee as it may think fit.

Section 1(4) was discussed in *Middlegate Ltd.* v. *Messimiris*[6] by Lord Denning M.R., who said: "We should construe 'not less conspicuous' so

---

[6] [1973] 1 W.L.R. 168.

as to mean 'equally readable' or 'equally sufficient' to tell the tenant of his right to give a counter-notice."[7] Section 1(5) was discussed in *Sidnell* v. *Wilson*.[8] There is no recent reported case which concerns the application of the 1938 Act in the context of residential premises.[9]

(3) Law of Property Act 1925, s.147

(1) After a notice is served on a lessee relating to the internal decorative repairs to a house or other building, he may apply to the court for relief, and if, having regard to all the circumstances of the case (including in particular the length of the lessee's term or interest remaining unexpired), the court is satisfied that the notice is unreasonable, it may, by order, wholly or partially relieve the lessee from liability for such repairs.

(2) This section does not apply:—

  (i)   where the liability arises under an express covenant or agreement to put the property in a decorative state of repair and the covenant or agreement has never been performed;

  (ii) to any matter necessary or proper—
     (a) for putting or keeping the property in a sanitary condition, or
     (b) for the maintenance or preservation of the structure;

  (iii) to any statutory liability to keep a house in all respects reasonably fit for human habitation;

  (iv) to any covenant or stipulation to yield up the house or other building in a specified state of repair at the end of the term.

(3) In this section "lease" includes an underlease and an agreement for a lease, and "lessee" has a corresponding meaning and includes any person liable to effect the repairs.

(4) This section applies whether the notice is served before or after the commencement of this Act, and has effect notwithstanding any stipulation to the contrary.

(5) The county court has jurisdiction under this section where the net annual value for rating of the house or other building does not exceed the county court limit.

(4) Measure of Damages

Section 18(1) of the Landlord and Tenant Act 1927 limits the damages which the landlord can recover:

Damages for a breach of a covenant or agreement to keep or put premises in repair during the currency of a lease, whether such covenant or agreement is expressed or implied, and whether general or specific, shall in no case exceed the amount (if any) by which the value of the reversion (whether immediate or not) in the premises is diminished owing to the breach of such covenant or agreement as aforesaid; and in particular no damage shall be recovered for a breach of any such covenant or agreement to leave or put premises in repair at the termination of a lease, if it is shown that the premises, in whatever state of

---

[7] At 172.
[8] [1966] 2 Q.B. 67.
[9] *Associated British Ports* v. *C. H. Bailey* [1990] 2 W.L.R. 812 involved commercial premises.

repair they might be, would at or shortly after the termination of the tenancy have been or be pulled down, or such structural alterations made therein as would render valueless the repairs covered by the covenant or agreement ...

The purpose of section 18(1) is to prevent the landlord from making a profit out of repairing covenants by recovering damages representing the cost of repairs which, if done, would add nothing to the value of the property. To recover damages the landlord must prove a diminution of the value of the reversion resulting from the failure to repair to an extent at least equal to the damages claimed.[10]

Note

Many residential tenancies fall within the scope of statutory schemes of protection.[11] In relation to regulated tenancies under the Rent Act 1977, secure tenancies governed by the Housing Act 1985 and assured tenancies under the Housing Act 1988, the landlord may seek to recover possession on the basis of the tenant's failure to carry out repairing obligations imposed by the terms of the lease. The landlord must, however, comply with the relevant statutory provisions, and must obtain an order for possession from the court. In any event, the landlord does not have a right to possession, since the tenant's breach of covenant gives rise only to a discretionary ground for possession.[12]

(C) LIABILITY IN TORT

Some of the problems relating to bringing actions in contract, in particular the principle that only parties to the contract can sue for breaches of it, can be avoided if there is liability in tort.

(1) Negligence

In *Cavalier* v. *Pope*[13] (a case which pre-dated *Donoghue* v. *Stevenson*[14]) the House of Lords held that a landlord is not liable for damage caused — whether to a person or to property — by defects in unfurnished premises at the time of the letting. The Court of Appeal decided in *McNerny* v. *Lambeth L.B.C.*[15] that it was still bound by this decision. Accordingly, there is no duty of care to ensure that unfurnished premises are reasonably safe at the time of the letting.[16]

---

[10] See, *e.g. Hibernian Property* v. *Liverpool Corporation* [1973] 1 W.L.R. 751.
[11] See Chapter 3.
[12] Case 1 (Rent Act 1977, Sched. 15); Ground 1 (Housing Act 1985, Sched. 2); and Ground 12 (Housing Act 1988, Sched. 2).
[13] [1906] A.C. 428.
[14] [1932] A.C. 562.
[15] (1988) 21 H.L.R. 188.
[16] This decision is entirely consistent with the approach taken recently by the House of Lords in *Murphy* v. *Brentwood D.C.* [1990] 3 W.L.R. 414 and *Caparo* v. *Dickman* [1990] 2 W.L.R. 358.

(2) Defective Premises Act 1972

In the early 1970s the Law Commission recommended an extension of the law of tort "to provide that where the landlord has an obligation or right to repair ... he should in the discharge or execution of that obligation be under a general duty of care to see that injury or damage is not suffered by those who are likely to be affected by any failure to discharge that obligation or exercise that right with reasonable diligence."[17] The Law Commission's recommendations were implemented by the Defective Premises Act 1972.

4.—(1) Where premises are let under a tenancy which puts on the landlord an obligation to the tenant for the maintenance or repair of the premises, the landlord owes to all persons who might reasonably be expected to be affected by defects in the state of the premises a duty to take such care as is reasonable in all the circumstances to see that they are reasonably safe from personal injury or from damage to their property caused by a relevant defect.

(2) The said duty is owed if the landlord knows (whether as the result of being notified by the tenant or otherwise) or if he ought in all the circumstances to have known of the relevant defect.

(3) In this section "relevant defect" means a defect in the state of the premises existing at or after the material time and arising from, or continuing because of, an act or omission by the landlord which constitutes or would if he had had notice of the defect, have constituted a failure by him to carry out his obligation to the tenant for the maintenance or repair of the premises; and for the purposes of the foregoing provision "the material time" means—

   (a)   where the tenancy commenced before this Act, the commencement of this Act; and

   (b)   in all other cases, the earliest of the following times, that is to say—

      (i)   the time when the tenancy commences;
      (ii)   the time when the tenancy agreement is entered into;
      (iii) the time when possession is taken of the premises in contemplation of the letting.

(4) Where premises are let under a tenancy which expressly or impliedly gives the landlord the right to enter the premises to carry out any description of maintenance or repair of the premises, then, as from the time when he first is, or by notice or otherwise can put himself, in a position to exercise the right and so long as he is or can put himself in that position, he shall be treated for the purposes of subsections (1) to (3) above (but for no other purpose) as if he were under an obligation to the tenant for that description of maintenance or repair of the premises; but the landlord shall not owe the tenant any duty by virtue of this subsection in respect of any defect in the state of the premises arising from, or continuing because of, a failure to carry out an obligation expressly imposed on the tenant by the tenancy.

(5) For the purposes of this section obligations imposed or rights given by any enactment in virtue of a tenancy shall be treated as imposed or given by the tenancy.

---

[17] *Civil Liability of Vendors and Lessors for Defective Premises* (1970–71) Law Com. No. 40, para. 69.

(6) This section applies to a right of occupation given by contract or any enactment and not amounting to a tenancy as if the right were a tenancy, and "tenancy" and cognate expressions shall be construed accordingly.

Notes

(i) Although section 4 was enacted primarily to bring third parties within the protective ambit of repairing obligations, tenants may sue the landlord either on the basis of the landlord's liability under the covenant or under section 4.[18]

(ii) Under section 4 "the statutory protection for those in occupation of defective premises is geared to the landlord's obligation to repair the premises. It goes no wider than the repair covenant."[19] Accordingly, if there is no disrepair, section 4 cannot be relied upon.[20]

(iii) However, section 4 is formulated differently from section 11 of the Landlord and Tenant Act 1985, and as a result the landlord's potential liability under the 1972 Act is more extensive than under section 11 of the 1985 Act. There are three aspects to this:

First, the obligation under section 4(1) arises not only where the landlord is under an express or implied covenant to repair, but also where he has a right to repair.[21]

Secondly, whereas the repairing obligation imposed by section 11 of the 1985 Act extends to the "structure and exterior of the dwelling-house,"[22] the 1972 Act refers to the "premises."[23] In *Smith* v. *Bradford Metropolitan Council*[24] Stephenson L.J. said (in the context of a claim for damages by a tenant who had been injured when he fell from a raised patio which was in a dangerous condition):

'Premises' seem to me to be a wide word. In this Act I would regard it as meaning the premises let—the letting—the subject of the tenancy—all of it; the whole letting, land and buildings; and it would need clear language to restrict the premises let to the plaintiff so as to exclude what was obviously part of them, namely, the patio.[25]

Thirdly, in relation to section 11 the courts have imposed notice requirements such that the landlord is liable only where he has actual knowledge of the defect.[26] Section 4(2), on the other hand, states that the landlord owes a duty where "he ought in all the circumstances to have known of the relevant defect."

[18] See *Smith* v. *Bradford Metropolitan Council* (1982) 4 H.L.R. 86.
[19] Dillon L.J. in *McNerny* v. *Lambeth L.B.C.* (1989) 21 H.L.R. 188 at 193.
[20] For the meaning of repair see pp. 338–345.
[21] s.4(4).
[22] s.11(1)(a).
[23] s.4(1).
[24] (1982) 4 H.L.R. 86.
[25] At 93.
[26] See pp. 368–371.

The potential importance of this distinction was revealed in *Clarke* v. *Taff Ely B.C.*[27] The plaintiff went to visit her sister, who was the tenant of a house owned by the defendant local authority, with a view to helping her to re-decorate. In order to wash the ceiling the plaintiff stood on a table, the leg of the table went through the floorboards, and the plaintiff was thrown to the ground and injured. One of the questions facing the court was whether the defendant ought to have known of the defective floorboards.

Expert evidence indicated not only that with knowledge of the age of the house, the type of construction, and the presence of damp it was foreseeable that rot would occur, but also that if rot did occur the floors would be likely to give way without notice. Wood J. held that the local authority were liable on the basis that they should have undertaken a programme of inspection of their housing stock in which case the dangerous condition of the floors would have been revealed.

(iv) Normally, where the plaintiff relies on section 4 of the Defective Premises Act 1972 the appropriate remedy will be damages. Nevertheless, in *Barrett* v. *Lounova* (1982) *Ltd.*[28] Kerr L.J. indicated that in appropriate circumstances a plaintiff claiming under the 1972 Act would be entitled to a mandatory injunction to compel the landlord to undertake repair work.

(v) Although section 4 has shifted much of the liability for damages suffered by third parties onto landlords, tenants may still be liable for damage caused by defects for which they are responsible and which fall outside the landlord's repairing obligations. Tenants are only liable for breaches of the "common duty of care" imposed by the Occupiers' Liability Act 1957 and of the duty to persons other than visitors which arises under the Occupiers' Liability Act 1984.

III   PUBLIC HEALTH LEGISLATION AND HOUSING ACTS

Introduction

The foregoing sections have described the basic common law principles relating to repairs, as amended in the case of many residential tenancies by legislation. However, in practice, many legal proceedings relating to housing conditions are taken under the Environmental Protection Act 1990 (formerly the Public Health Act 1936), the Housing Act 1985 or the Local Government and Housing Act 1989. These provisions, which have a long history, are derived from the first

[27] (1980) 10 H.L.R. 44.
[28] [1989] 2 W.L.R. 137 at 146.

legislative attempts to regulate the operation of the private sector of the housing market.[29]

It cannot be said that the law is entirely satisfactory. There is a considerable overlap between the powers contained in the Environmental Protection Act 1990, on the one hand, and the Housing Act 1985 and the Local Government and Housing Act 1989, on the other, and it may be difficult to know under which head to proceed.

From a practical point of view the Environmental Protection Act 1990 can result in swift action since it prescribes relatively simple procedures. However, Part III of the Environmental Protection Act 1990 is not aimed at the repair of residential premises as such; rather its objective is the elimination of housing conditions which amount to a "statutory nuisance." Accordingly, action taken under the Environmental Protection Act 1990 may not result in any long-term improvement of defective housing.

Conversely, the Housing Act 1985 and the Local Government and Housing Act 1989 may result in permanent improvement, but the procedures involved are much slower. It is also worth noting that, as regards premises which are unfit for human habitation, the local housing authority may decide that the most satisfactory course of action is to order the demolition of the premises rather than their improvement. In such cases, residential occupiers will generally be entitled to be rehoused.

(A) PART III OF THE ENVIRONMENTAL PROTECTION ACT 1990

Part III of the 1990 Act (which came into force on January 1, 1991) replaces Part III of the Public Health Act 1936. It provides a basis for attacking the effects of unsatisfactory housing conditions. In certain instances a tenant will be able to rely on the support of the local authority, but, even where the premises in question are owned by the local authority or where the local authority declines to intervene, an individual occupier may institute proceedings under the Act.

In the materials which follow reference is made to the relevant cases decided under the Public Health Act 1936.

(1) Definition of "Statutory Nuisance"

The key to the operation of Part III of the Environmental Protection Act 1990, is the concept of a "statutory nuisance," which is defined by section 79(1) of the 1990 Act (replacing section 92 of the Public Health Act 1936):

---

[29] There are, for example, provisions of the Housing Act 1985 which can be traced back to the Artizans' and Labourers' Dwellings Act 1868.

Subject to subsections (2) to (6) below, the following matters constitute "statutory nuisances" for the purposes of this Part, that is to say—

(a) any premises in such a state as to be prejudicial to health or a nuisance;
...

(e) any accumulation or deposit which is prejudicial to health or a nuisance;
...

and it shall be the duty of every local authority to cause its area to be inspected from time to time to detect any statutory nuisances which ought to be dealt with under section 80 below and, where a complaint of a statutory nuisance is made to it by a person living within its area, to take such steps as are reasonably practicable to investigate the complaint.

Section 343 states that "prejudicial to health" means "injurious, or likely to cause injury, to health."

Coventry City Council v. *Cartwright* [1975] 1 W.L.R. 845

Lord Widgery C.J. said (at 848–849):

The facts on which the justices made an abatement order against the local authority were these. There is a piece of vacant land where the houses in Arthur Street formerly stood. Arthur Street was demolished about three or four years ago and re-development has not yet taken place. The justices found that the local authority had allowed indiscriminate tipping to take place on the site since demolition, the local authority having taken no action to prevent tipping by either erecting fences or trenching or displaying official notice boards stating that the tipping of material and trespassing was prohibited. They found that the material deposited could encourage rodent infestation, this having been visible on the site in close proximity. They found that the items deposited consisted of large quantities of building materials, such as brick ends, tarmacadam, old reinforcements, earth, scrap iron, broken glass and household refuse.

The local authority had periodically removed the household refuse, but had taken no action to remove the other materials dumped to which I have referred.

The question which they put to us however is restricted. The question is whether inert matter, such as builder's rubble, without any putrescible matter attached to it is within the ambit of section [79(1) of the Environmental Protection Act 1990].

The justices concluded that the case had been made out that there was a statutory nuisance under section [79](1), and they put it on two clear bases.

The first was that in their opinion the tipping of materials such as are referred to in this case are dangerous to health and limb and constituted a particular hazard, especially where children were concerned who had easy access to the site. In other words, they find a threat to health from these facts on the footing that people who went on to the site, and particularly if children went on to the site, might hurt themselves by reason of the physical properties present—broken glass, old tin cans and whatever it may be ...

For my part, I think that that is taking too wide a view of the section. The words are obviously very wide, and one should hesitate, in construing the section in proceedings such as the present, to lay down boundaries which may in another case prove to be unsuitable. But I think that the underlying conception of the section is that that which it struck at is an accumulation of something which produces a threat to health in the sense of a threat of disease, vermin or the like.

Ashworth J. agreed, but noted (at 851):

For my part I regard this case as somewhere near the borderline, and if there had been more evidence, for example, about the effect of the refuse and whether that had set up infestation of rats, it may be that the justices would have been justified in reaching the conclusion they did, but on the material now before this court I agree with Lord Widgery C.J. that there is not enough to justify the order which they made. I would allow the appeal.

Michael Davies L.J. agreed.

National Coal Board v. *Thorne* [1976] 1 W.L.R. 543

Watkins J. said (at 545–548):

The National Coal Board, the "board," own premises known as 38, Roman Road, in the village of Banwen in South Wales. That village, for local government purposes, lies within the jurisdiction of the Neath Borough Council, the local authority. The local authority have the duty under section [79 of the Environmental Protection Act 1990] to inspect from time to time property within their area for the detection of matters requiring to be dealt with under the provisions of Part III of the Act as statutory nuisances.

At some time or other an officer of the local authority inspected 38, Roman Road, Banwen, and found the place to be in a state of disrepair in that there were two defective windows, there was no stop end for a rain water gutter, and there was a defective skirting board. Those were matters reported to the local authority. They determined that a nuisance was present in the premises and, using the power which they have under section [80] of the Act, they served upon the board a notice to abate the nuisance, a notice which one supposes set out in terms the precise things which the board had to do in order to bring about an effective abatement. The board did nothing to abate the so-called nuisance so an information was laid before the local justices. A hearing followed, the result of which was that on April 4, 1975, the justices found that an abatement notice had been served on the board on January 9, 1975, by recorded delivery and the requirements of the abatement notice had not been complied with by the board. So they decided that, having regard to those findings and the state of the law as they understood it to be, they had no alternative but to issue a nuisance order. The effect of issuing a nuisance order is to compel the person upon whom it is served to comply with its terms under penalty. The penalty is laid down in the Act; it amounts to the maximum sum of £50.

Before however, the board could be expected to carry out the terms of the nuisance order, they appealed. The appeal comes to this court by way of case stated.

The justices had addressed to them argument affecting the meaning to be attached to the word "nuisance" as it appears in section [79](1) of the Act. Nothing was said at that hearing suggestive of the fact that there had been any injury or anticipated injury to the health of persons residing either in the premises or in any premises adjoining them. The information itself was laid simply upon the basis that there was a nuisance present at the material time at the premises.

The short point, therefore, arising in this appeal is what is the meaning to be attached to the word "nuisance." *Betts* v. *Penge Urban District Council* [1942] 2 K.B. 154 has been referred to. What happened in that case was that the landlord of a flat, of which the rent was in arrears, made no application for possession but removed the front door and some of the window sashes thereby interfering with the personal comfort of the occupier. It was held that there was a distinction between public and private nuisance which was material to the question whether a statutory nuisance under section [79](1) of the [Environmental Protection Act 1990] existed on the premises, and that it was sufficient in order to sustain a conviction of the appellant for permitting a statutory nuisance on the premises to prove that by his act or default they were in such a state as to interfere with the personal comfort of the occupiers, without necessarily being injurious to health. If the law is accurately stated in that case, then the justices in the present case, it seems to me, cannot be criticised for issuing a nuisance order, since I see no basis for assuming that they came to conclusions of fact which were not properly founded upon the evidence which came before them, and upon their findings of fact they were entitled, assuming the law is correctly stated in *Betts'* case, to proceed to make the nuisance order.

In his very able argument Mr. Roch appearing for the board says that the word "nuisance" cannot have and should not be understood to have the meaning attached to it by *Betts'* case, and that the word "nuisance" as used in section [79](1) must be understood to equate with the same word as that is understood at common law in relation to nuisances, public or private. A public nuisance at common law has been expressed to be an act or omission which materially affects the material comfort and quality of life of a class of Her Majesty's subjects. A private nuisance has often been defined in this way: private nuisances, at least in the vast majority of cases, are interferences for a substantial length of time by owners or occupiers of property with the use or enjoyment of neighbouring property. The distinction which immediately springs to mind therefore between a private nuisance at common law and a nuisance of the kind as found by the justices in the present case is that the justices, feeling compelled to follow the decision in *Betts'* case, found that a nuisance could exist in a dwelling-house in relation to the occupier of it, whereas that notion is obviously alien to the concept of a common law private nuisance.

When the justices reached their conclusion in April 1975 *Salford City Council* v. *McNally* [1975] 3 W.L.R. 87 had not been decided. Accordingly, they had not the advantage of knowing what I now propose to quote from the speeches made in that case. Lord Wilberforce said, at p. 91:

> "In dealing with each Act it is better to use its own terminology. A similar confusion occurs in some of the cases through the use of the words 'personal comfort.' These words are appropriate enough in the context of what is a 'nuisance' for the purposes of the Public Health Act (see as to this the clear judgment of Stephen J. in *Bishop Auckland Local Board* v. *Bishop Auckland Iron and Steel Co. Ltd.* (1882) 10 Q.B.D. 138), but they are quite inappropriate in relation to the other limb 'prejudicial to health.' Health is not the same as comfort and interference with the latter does not bring a case within the 'health' limb of the Public Health Act. In my opinion *Betts* v. *Penge Urban District Council* [1942] 2 K.B. 154 is guilty of this confusion and was wrongly decided. It was simply a case of what is now called 'harassment,' and not, in my view, under the Act at all. I express no opinion upon *Coventry City Council* v. *Cartwright* [1975] 1 W.L.R. 845, which was reported after argument had been closed in the present case."

Lord Simon of Glaisdale expressly agreed with Lord Wilberforce. Lord Edmund-Davies, at p. 95, said of *Betts'* case:

> "Be that as it may, no. 20 Johnson Street being at the material time undoubtedly a 'statutory nuisance,' *i.e.* injurious to the health of the occupier,

this House is not presently called upon to determine the correctness of the decision in *Betts* v. *Penge Urban District Council* [1942] 2 K.B. 154 that, in order to sustain a conviction for permitting a statutory nuisance, it is sufficient to prove that premises were in such a state as to interfere with the *personal comfort* of the occupiers, without being injurious to their health, though for my part I think it desirable to make clear that I respectfully think it was wrongly decided."

Lord Cross of Chelsea and Lord Fraser of Tullybelton agreed with Lord Edmund-Davies.

Mr. Fletcher, in common with Mr. Roch, submits that the effect of these speeches is such as to cause this court to pronounce that in its opinion *Betts'* case was in fact wrongly decided and does not represent the true law upon the crucial matter of the meaning of the word "nuisance" in section [79](1) of the [Environmental Protection Act 1990]. I welcome the opportunity of saying that what Lord Wilberforce said in the *Salford* case leads me to the conclusion that *Betts* unquestionably does not express the proper law upon this question. Speaking for myself, I would adopt the words of Lord Wilberforce so as to state that a nuisance cannot arise if what has taken place affects only the person or persons occupying the premises where the nuisance is said to have taken place. A nuisance coming within the meaning of the [Environmental Protection Act 1990] must be either a private or a public nuisance as understood by common law.

For that reason, it seems to me that the proper course is to direct that the order of the justices should be quashed.

Lord Widgery C.J. and Kilner Brown J. agreed.

Notes

As a result of the courts' interpretation of "nuisance" for the purposes of what is now section 79(1)(a) a state of affairs which is a source of discomfort and inconvenience only to the occupier of the premises in question cannot be a statutory nuisance unless the premises are prejudicial to health.

Parliament attempted to mitigate the effect of the interpretation adopted in *National Coal Board* v. *Thorne* through section 190(1)(b) of the Housing Act 1985.[30] It should, however, be stressed that section 190 of the 1985 Act is limited in two ways: (i) it has no application to premises controlled by the local authority; (ii) if the local authority fails to take action under section 190, an aggrieved occupier's only remedy is judicial review. By contrast, action can be taken by an individual under the Environmental Protection Act 1990, and such action may be taken in relation to local authority housing.

Notwithstanding the courts' narrow interpretation of "nuisance" the Environmental Protection Act 1990 can be used as a means of tackling many types of bad housing conditions (for example, premises which are not properly insulated against noise[31]).

---

[30] See p. 412.
[31] *Southwark L.B.C.* v. *Ince* (1989) 21 H.L.R. 504.

It has been seen that tenants have experienced great difficulty in obtaining effective remedies under the common law for damp resulting from condensation, notably because it is difficult to establish that the landlord is in breach of his obligations under the lease.[32] Under the Environmental Protection Act 1990, however, it is perfectly possible to prove the existence of a statutory nuisance even though there has been no breach by the landlord of his obligations to repair.[33] Accordingly, dampness, if prejudicial to health may constitute a statutory nuisance.[33a]

For action under the Environmental Protection Act 1990 to be successful it is important to define the premises which suffer the nuisance. This was revealed in *Birmingham D.C.* v. *McMahon.*[34] This case involved a large block of flats (Beale House) which was owned by the local authority. Beale House suffered from excessive condensation, and the tenants took proceedings under what is now Part III of the Environmental Protection Act 1990. It was alleged that Beale House was prejudicial to health or a nuisance. The Divisional Court decided that as regards each tenant, it was his own dwelling—rather than the block as a whole—which constituted the "premises" which were prejudicial to health.

There is, of course a policy aspect to the result achieved in this case. Kennedy J. said:

> Generally speaking it is for the housing authority to decide when to embark on major works such as refurbishment of a large block of flats. If such work is not done, and if as a result the flat of an individual tenant gets into such a state that it is a statutory nuisance, and if he cannot otherwise obtain redress, then it is certainly open to him to bring that nuisance to the attention of the Court, and to obtain a nuisance order. The effect of this action on the finances of the local authority is likely to be negligible. But the making of an order in relation to the entire block could heavily strain a local authority's finances and disrupt its housing department's programme for years to come. I do not say that such an order can never be made. It is possible to envisage in a block of flats a prejudice to health which is not confined to any one constituent unit in the block, and which can only be related to the entire block. In that event, providing the evidence of nuisance is sufficiently compelling, the Court might well be driven to making a comprehensive order of the kind sought here, but that is not this case.[35]

(2) Action by the Local Authority: Environmental Protection Act 1990, ss. 80–81

80.—(1) Where a local authority is satisfied that a statutory nuisance exists, or is likely to occur or recur, in the area of the authority, the local authority shall serve a notice ("an abatement notice") imposing all or any of the following requirements—

---

[32] *Quick* v. *Taff Ely B.C.* [1986] Q.B. 809 (pp. 339–344).
[33] *Birmingham City D.C.* v. *Kelly* [1986] 2 E.G.L.R. 239.
[33a] *Dover D.C.* v. *Farrar* (1982) 2 H.L.R. 32; *G.L.C.* v. *Tower Hamlets L.B.C.* (1984) 15 H.L.R. 54.
[34] (1987) 19 H.L.R. 452.   [35] At 456–457.

(a) requiring the abatement of the nuisance or prohibiting or restricting its occurrence or recurrence;

(b) requiring the execution of such works, and the taking of such other steps, as may be necessary for any of those purposes,

and the notice shall specify the time or times within which the requirements of the notice are to be complied with.

(2) The abatement notice shall be served—

(a) except in a case falling within paragraph (b) or (c) below, on the person responsible for the nuisance;

(b) where the nuisance arises from any defect of a structural character, on the owner of the premises;

(c) where the person responsible for the nuisance cannot be found or the nuisance has not yet occurred, on the owner or occupier of the premises.

(3) The person served with the notice may appeal against the notice to a magistrates' court within the period of 21 days beginning with the date on which he was served with the notice.

(4) If a person on whom an abatement notice is served, without reasonable excuse, contravenes or fails to comply with any requirement or prohibition imposed by the notice, he shall be guilty of an offence.

(5) Except in a case falling within subsection (6) below, a person who commits an offence under subsection (4) above shall be liable on summary conviction to a fine not exceeding level 5 on the standard scale together with a further fine of an amount equal to one-tenth of that level for each day on which the offence continues after the conviction.[36]

(6) A person who commits an offence under subsection (4) above on industrial, trade or business premises shall be liable on summary conviction to a fine not exceeding £20,000.

(7) Subject to subsection (8) below, in any proceedings for an offence under subsection (4) above in respect of a statutory nuisance it shall be a defence to prove that the best practicable means were used to prevent, or to counteract the effects of, the nuisance.

(8) The defence under subsection (7) above is not available—

(a) in the case of a nuisance falling within paragraph (a) [or] (e) ... of section 79(1) above except where the nuisance arises on industrial, trade or business premises; ...

81.—(1) Where more than one person is responsible for a statutory nuisance section 80 above shall apply to each of those persons whether or not what any one of them is responsible for would by itself amount to a nuisance.

(2) Where a statutory nuisance which exists or has occurred within the area of a local authority, or which has affected any part of that area, appears to the local authority to be wholly or partly caused by some act or default committed or taking place outside the area, the local authority may act under section 80 above as if the act or default were wholly within that area, except that any

---

[36] See p. 33 n. 21.

any appeal shall be heard by a magistrates' court having jurisdiction where the act or default is alleged to have taken place.

(3) Where an abatement notice has not been complied with the local authority may, whether or not they take proceedings for an offence under section 80(4) above, abate the nuisance and do whatever may be necessary in execution of the notice.

(4) Any expenses reasonably incurred by a local authority in abating, or preventing the recurrence of, a statutory nuisance under subsection "(3) above may be recovered by them from the person by whose act or default the nuisance was caused and, if that person is the owner of the premises from any person who is for the time being the owner thereof; and the court may apportion the expenses between persons by whose acts or defaults the nuisance is caused in such manner as the court consider fair and reasonable.

(5) If a local authority is of opinion that proceedings for an offence under section 80(4) above would afford an inadequate remedy in the case of any statutory nuisance, they may, subject to subsection (6) below, take proceedings in the High Court for the purpose of securing the abatement, prohibition or restriction of the nuisance, and the proceedings shall be maintainable notwithstanding the local authority have suffered no damage from the nuisance.

Notes

(i)   As a general rule an abatement notice under section 80 must be served on "the person responsible for the nuisance." Accordingly, a landlord may defend proceedings taken under the 1990 Act on the basis that the tenant is responsible for the statutory nuisance. For example, in *Dover D.C.* v. *Farrar*[37] (a case involving residential premises which suffered from severe damp) the court was required to consider not only the way the premises had been constructed, but also the way in which they had been used by the tenants.
Ormerod L.J. said:

[T]he construction of the houses, and the method of heating supplied by the appellant Council, were perfectly proper and perfectly adequate and would have maintained these houses in a state in which there was no question of their being prejudicial to health, provided that the system supplied was used by the tenant. The only reason it was not used by the tenant, a reason one can very well understand, is that they found it too expensive. So putting it in its simplest terms, the cause of this so called statutory nuisance was the unwillingness of the tenants themselves to spend the amount of money that was required to provide themselves with adequate heating with the system provided in the first place by the appellant Council.[38]

(ii)   Where residential premises are found to be prejudicial to health, the statutory nuisance is not abated merely by the landlord obtaining vacant possession.[39] It is only possible to comply with a section 80 notice by taking some remedial action. Furthermore, the phrase "prejudicial to health" is defined by section 79(7) as meaning "injurious,

---

[37] (1980) 2 H.L.R. 32.   [38] At 38.   [39] *Lambeth L.B.C.* v. *Stubbs* (1980) 78 L.G.R. 650.

or likely to cause injury to health." By removing tenants from premises which are found to be prejudicial to health the landlord reduces the likelihood of injury, but he does not put an end to the nuisance.

(iii) The defence of "best practicable means" in subsection (7) must be read in conjunction with the definition in section 79(9):

In this Part "best practicable means" is to be interpreted by reference to the following provisions—

(a) "practicable" means reasonably practicable having regard among other things to local conditions and circumstances, to the current state of technical knowledge and to the financial implications;

(b) the means to be employed include the design, installation, maintenance and manner and periods of operation of plant and machinery, and the design, construction and maintenance of buildings and structures;

(c) the test is to apply only so far as compatible with any duty imposed by law;

(d) the test is to apply only so far as compatible with safety and safe working conditions, and with the exigencies of any emergency or unforeseeable circumstances;

and, in circumstances where a code of practice under section 71 of the Control of Pollution Act 1974 (noise minimisation) is applicable, regard shall also be had to guidance given in it.

(iv) There is a special nine-day procedure under section 76 of the Building Act 1984, which may be employed where premises are in a very defective state:

(1) If it appears to a local authority that—

(a) any premises are in such a state (in this section referred to as a "defective state") as to be prejudicial to health or a nuisance, and

(b) unreasonable delay in remedying the defective state would be occasioned by following the procedure prescribed by section 80 of the Environmental Protection Act 1990,

the local authority may serve on the person on whom it would have been appropriate to serve an abatement notice under the said section 80 (if the local authority had proceeded under that section) a notice stating that the local authority intend to remedy the defective state and specifying the defects that they intend to remedy.

(2) Subject to subsection (3) below, the local authority may, after the expiration of nine days after service of a notice under subsection (1) above, execute such works as may be necessary to remedy the defective state, and recover the expenses reasonably incurred in so doing from the person on whom the notice was served.

(3) If, within seven days after service of a notice under subsection (1) above, the person on whom the notice was served serves a counter-notice that he intends to remedy the defects specified in the first-mentioned notice, the local authority shall take no action in pursuance of the first-mentioned notice unless the person who served the counter-notice—

(a)   fails within what seems to the local authority a reasonable time to begin to execute works to remedy the said defects, or

(b)   having begun to execute such works fails to make such progress towards their completion as seems to the local authority reasonable.

(4) In proceedings to recover expenses under subsection (2) above, the court—

(a)   shall inquire whether the local authority were justified in concluding that the premises were in a defective state, or that unreasonable delay in remedying the defective state would have been occasioned by following the procedure prescribed by section 80 of the Environmental Protection Act 1990, and

(b)   if the defendant proves that he served a counter-notice under subsection (3) above, shall inquire whether the defendant failed to begin the works to remedy the defects within a reasonable time, or failed to make reasonable progress towards their completion,

and if the court determines that—

(i)   the local authority were not justified in either of the conclusions mentioned in paragraph (a) of this subsection, or
(ii) there was no failure under paragraph (b) of this subsection,

the local authority shall not recover the expenses or any part of them.

(5) Subject to subsection (4) above, in proceedings to recover expenses under subsection (2) above, the court may—

(a)   inquire whether the said expenses ought to be borne wholly or in part by some person other than the defendant in the proceedings, and

(b)   make such order concerning the expenses or their apportionment as appears to the court to be just,

but the court shall not order the expenses or any part of them to be borne by a person other than the defendant in the proceedings unless the court is satisfied that that other person has had due notice of the proceedings and an opportunity of being heard.

(6) A local authority shall not serve a notice under subsection (1) above, or proceed with the execution of works in accordance with a notice so served, if the execution of the works would, to their knowledge, be in contravention of a building preservation order under section 29 of the Town and Country Planning Act 1947.

(7) The power conferred on a local authority by subsection (1) above may be exercised notwithstanding that the local authority might instead have proceeded under Part VI of the Housing Act 1985 (repair notices).

(3) Action by Individuals: Environmental Protection Act 1990, s. 82

(1) A magistrates' court may act under this section on a complaint made by any person on the ground that he is aggrieved by the existence of a statutory nuisance.

(2) If the magistrates' court is satisfied that the alleged nuisance exists, or that although abated it is likely to recur on the same premises, the court shall make an order for either or both of the following purposes—

(a)   requiring the defendant to abate the nuisance, within a time specified in the order, and to execute any works necessary for that purpose;

(b)   prohibiting a recurrence of the nuisance, and requiring the defendant, within a time specified in the order, to execute any works necessary to prevent the recurrence;

and may also impose on the defendant a fine not exceeding level 5 on the standard scale.

(3) If the magistrates' court is satisfied that the alleged nuisance exists and is such as, in the opinion of the court, to render premises unfit for human habitation, an order under subsection (2) above may prohibit the use of the premises for human habitation until the premises are, to the satisfaction of the court, rendered fit for that purpose.

(4) Proceedings for an order under subsection (2) above shall be brought—

(a)   except in a case falling within paragraph (b) or (c) below, against the person responsible for the nuisance;

(b)   where the nuisance arises from any defect of a structural character, against the owner of the premises;

(c)   where the person responsible for the nuisance cannot be found, against the owner or occupier of the premises.

(5) Where more than one person is responsible for a statutory nuisance, subsections (1) to (4) above shall apply to each of those persons whether or not what any one of them is responsible for would by itself amount to nuisance.

(6) Before instituting proceedings for an order under subsection (2) above against any person, the person aggrieved by the nuisance shall give to that person such notice in writing of his intention to bring the proceedings as is applicable to proceedings in respect of a nuisance of that description and the notice shall specify the matter complained of.

(7) The notice of the bringing of proceedings in respect of a statutory nuisance required by subsection (6) above which is applicable is—

(a)   in the case of a nuisance falling within paragraph (g) of section 79(1) above, not less than three days' notice; and

(b)   in the case of a nuisance of any other description, not less than 21 days' notice;

but the Secretary of State may, by order, provide that this subsection shall have effect as if such period as is specified in the order were the minimum period of notice applicable to any description of statutory nuisance specified in the order.

(8) A person who, without reasonable excuse, contravenes any requirement or prohibition imposed by an order under subsection (2) above shall be guilty of an offence and liable on summary conviction to a fine not exceeding level 5 on the standard scale together with a further fine of an amount equal to one-tenth of that level for each day on which the offence continues after the conviction.

(9) Subject to subsection (10) below, in any proceedings for an offence under subsection (8) above in respect of a statutory nuisance it shall be a defence to prove that the best practicable means were used to prevent, or to counteract the effects of, the nuisance.

(10) The defence under subsection (9) above is not available—

(a)   in the case of a nuisance falling within paragraph (a) [or] (e) of section 79(10) above except where the nuisance arises on industrial, trade or business premises; . . .

(11) If a person is convicted of an offence under subsection (8) above, a magistrates' court may, after giving the local authority in whose area the nuisance has occurred an opportunity of being heard, direct the authority to do anything which the person was required to do by the order to which the conviction relates.

(12) Where on the hearing of proceedings for an order under subsection (2) above it is proved that the alleged nuisance existed at the date of the making of the complaint, then, whether or not at the date of the hearing it still exists or is likely to recur, the court shall order the defendant (or defendants in such proportions as appears fair and reasonable) to pay to the person bringing the proceedings such amount as the court considers reasonably sufficient to compensate him for any expenses properly incurred by him in the proceedings.

(13) If it appears to the magistrates' court that neither the person responsible for the nuisance nor the owner or occupier of the premises can be found the court may, after giving the local authority in whose area the nuisance has occurred an opportunity of being heard, direct the authority to do anything which the court would have ordered that person to do.

Notes

Section 82 deals with the implications of the House of Lords' decision in *Sandwell M.B.C.* v. *Bujok.*[40] In the context of section 99 of the Public Health Act 1936, it was held that proceedings could be brought by an individual even where no notice had previously been served on the landlord; furthermore, a successful litigant was held not to be entitled to mandatory costs.

Subsection (7) imposes notice requirements for proceedings brought under section 82, and subsection (12) gives a right to mandatory costs if the nuisance is proved.

Proceedings under this section are criminal proceedings, and therefore the burden of proof is "beyond reasonable doubt" rather than "on the balance of probabilities."[41]

(4) Effect of Environmental Protection Act 1990

If proceedings under the 1990 Act are successful the magistrates' court will make an order against the landlord or the local authority requiring action to be taken to put an end to the statutory nuisance. The magistrates' court has a wide discretion as to the precise form which the order should take. The court may make an order which will require substantial works of renovation, such as the installation of central heating, rewiring, insulation, the renewal of defective windows. However, the level of repair required by the order may be very limited, especially if the premises in question are soon to be demolished.

[40] [1990] 1 W.L.R. 1350.
[41] *R.* v. *Newham East Justices ex p. Hunt* [1976] 1 W.L.R. 420.

In *Nottingham City District Council* v. *Newton*[42] Lord Widgery C.J. said (in the context of the Public Health Act 1936):

> In my view the position of the justices as a matter of law was this: once they were satisfied that the house constituted a statutory nuisance they were bound to make a nuisance order ... but they have within the framework of the section a considerable tolerance as regards the precise terms which the nuisance order shall take. It must be directed, of course, to the abatement of the nuisance, that is the purpose of the order, but the section makes it clear that the justices have a discretion as to whether to require the owner to do the whole of that work referred to in the abatement notice as opposed to only part of it. Further the section expressly gives a discretion in regard to the time within which the work has to be done, and in my judgment would certainly enable the justices to divide the work into phases or programmes requiring some to be done quickly and others to be done at a later time. If there is real danger to the health of the occupier of the house, the justices of course ... can impose a prohibition on the house being lived in until the work is done, a prohibition which might have been unpopular with the tenant, but nevertheless it was urged by her counsel as one of the factors which might be taken into account.
>
> In deciding within that wide ambit of detailed discretion just what the terms of the nuisance order should be, I have no doubt it is the duty of the justices, as common sense dictates, to look at the whole circumstances of the case and to try and make an order which is in its terms sensible and just having regard to the entire prevailing situation. They were wrong in my judgment in closing their eyes to the Housing Act proceedings and the imminence of demolition, and had they had regard to those factors as well as all the other relevant factors, it may be that they would have provided for the nuisance to be abated by perhaps March 1974 so that if the demolition proceedings had taken effect meanwhile, the danger of money being spent on the house abortively in view of the subsequent demolition would be avoided.

This flexible approach was endorsed by Lord Wilberforce in *Salford City Council* v. *McNally*[43]:

> In making the order the magistrate should take into account the circumstances in which the property is being occupied including, of course, the likely duration of the occupation. The shorter the period before probable demolition, the more severe must be the injury to health or, as the case may be, the nuisance, to justify action by way of abatement. This aspect of the matter was well explained by the Divisional Court in *Nottingham City District Council* v. *Newton* [1974] 1 W.L.R. 923, the keynote of which is the need in making abatement notices, to use discretion and common sense.

More recently, in *Southwark L.B.C.* v. *Ince*,[44] the Court of Appeal reiterated the point that the magistrates should use discretion and common sense in framing the abatement notice. In particular, the magistrates should take care to ensure that they do not place unreasonable obligations upon local authorities.

---

[42] [1974] 1 W.L.R. 923 at 929–930.
[43] [1976] A.C. 379 at 389–390.
[44] (1989) 21 H.L.R. 504.

(B)   THE HOUSING ACT 1985 (AS AMENDED) AND THE LOCAL GOVERN-
MENT AND HOUSING ACT 1989

(1) General Duty of Local Housing Authorities: Housing Act 1985, s. 605

(1) The local housing authority shall at least once in each year consider the housing conditions in their district with a view to determining what action to take in performance of their functions under:

(a)   Part VI (repair notices);

(b)   Part IX (slum clearance);

(c)   Part XI (houses in multiple occupation);

(d)   Part VII of the Local Government and Housing Act 1989 (renewal areas); and

(e)   Part VIII of that Act (grants towards cost of improvements and repairs, etc.).

(2) For the purposes of carrying out their duty under subsection (1), the authority and their officers shall comply with any directions the Secretary of State may give and shall keep such records and supply him with such information as he may specify.

(2) Definition of "Unfit for Human Habitation": Housing Act 1985, s. 604

(1) Subject to subsection (2) below, a dwelling-house is fit for human habitation for the purposes of this Act unless, in the opinion of the local housing authority, it fails to meet one or more of the requirements in paragraphs (a) to (i) below and, by reason of that failure, is not reasonably suitable for occupation,—

(a)   it is structurally stable;

(b)   it is free from serious disrepair;

(c)   it is free from dampness prejudicial to the health of the occupants (if any);

(d)   it has adequate provision for lighting, heating and ventilation;

(e)   it has an adequate piped supply of wholesome water;

(f)   there are satisfactory facilities in the dwelling-house for the preparation and cooking of food, including a sink with a satisfactory supply of hot and cold water;

(g)   it has a suitably located water-closet for the exclusive use of the occupants (if any);

(h)   it has, for the exclusive use of the occupants (if any), a suitably located fixed bath or shower and wash-hand basin each of which is provided with a satisfactory supply of hot and cold water; and

(i)   it has an effective system from the draining of foul, waste and surface water;

and any reference to a dwelling-house being unfit for human habitation shall be construed accordingly.

(2) Whether or not a dwelling-house which is a flat satisfies the requirements in subsection (1), it is unfit for human habitation for the purposes of this Act if, in the opinion of the local housing authority, the building or a part of the building outside the flat fails to meet one or more of the requirements in paragraphs (a) to (e) below and, by reason of that failure, the flat is not reasonably suitable for occupation,—

(a)   the building or part is structurally stable;

(b)   it is free from serious disrepair;

(c)   it is free from dampness;

(d)   it has adequate provision for ventilation; and

(e)   it has an effective system for the draining of foul, waste and surface water.

(3) Subsection (1) applies in relation to a house in multiple occupation with the substitution of a reference to the house for any reference to a dwelling-house.

(4) Subsection (2) applies in relation to a flat in multiple occupation with the substitution for any reference to a dwelling-house which is a flat of a reference to the flat in multiple occupation.

(5) The Secretary of State may by order amend the provisions of subsection (1) or subsection (2) in such manner and to such extent as he considers appropriate; and any such order—

(a)   may contain such transitional and supplementary provisions as the Secretary of State considers expedient; and

(b)   shall be made by statutory instrument which shall be subject to annulment in pursuance of a resolution of either House of Parliament.

The concept of unfitness is the cornerstone of local authority action under the Housing Act 1985. Nevertheless, the definition, although less open-textured than used to be the case,[45] is still somewhat vague and leaves great room for interpretation and ad hoc decision-taking. Attempts to define the standard in more detail have not really been successful[46] and there has been little helpful judicial interpretation. In *Summers* v. *Salford Corporation*,[47] a broken sash-cord which jammed open a bedroom window was held by the House of Lords to be sufficient to render the house unfit for human habitation. Lord Atkin noted that "disrepair to a single room would not be sufficient [to render the house unfit] unless the effect was to render the whole house not reasonably fit for human habitation" (as was the case in the litigation in question). Cases will tend to be decided on their individual facts.

---

[45] See Housing Act 1957, s.4 (as amended) in Partington, *Landlord and Tenant* (2nd ed., 1980), p. 389.
[46] See, *e.g.* M.L.G.H. Circular 69/67.
[47] [1943] A.C. 283.

(3) Duties and Powers

Under the Housing Act 1985 as originally drafted (and its predecessors) if the local authority were satisfied that a house was unfit for human habitation they were under a duty to take some form of action under the Act.[48] This was the case even if alternative action under the Public Health Act 1936 was being taken. If the local authority failed to act, an aggrieved person could seek judicial review with a view to obtaining an order of mandamus.

As a consequence of the amendments introduced by the Local Government and Housing Act 1989, the structure of the provisions relating to unfit housing has changed. Where the local authority are satisfied that housing is unfit for human habitation, there are a number of possible courses of action which they can take under the Housing Act 1985: serving a repair notice under section 189; making a closing order under section 264; making a demolition order under section 265[49]; or declaring the area in which the dwelling-house, house in multiple occupation or building is situated to be a clearance area in accordance with section 289. In deciding which is the most satisfactory of these possible courses of action "the local housing authority shall have regard to such guidance as may from time to time be given by the Secretary of State."[50] Once the local authority are satisfied, in accordance with section 604A, that taking action under a particular provision is the most satisfactory course of action then the local authority shall, (*i.e.* are under a duty to) take that particular course of action.

But, what is the position if the local authority are satisfied that taking no action under the Housing Act 1985 is the most satisfactory course of action? As a general principle, such a failure to act may be challenged by way of judicial review on the basis of *Wednesbury*[51] unreasonableness, and where premises which are unfit for human habitation are used for residential purposes it is prima facie unreasonable if the local authority allow residential occupation to continue but take no steps to ensure that the premises are rendered fit.

However, it must be remembered that local authorities are empowered to take action in relation to statutory nuisances under the Environmental Protection Act 1990. Since the powers conferred by the Environmental Protection Act 1990 overlap with those contained in the

---

[48] *Salford City Council* v. *McNally* [1976] A.C. 379; *R.* v. *Kerrier D.C. ex p. Guppy's (Bridport) Ltd.* (1977) 32 P. & C.R. 411; *Holmes* v. *Ministry of Housing and Local Government* (1960) 12 P. & C.R. 72.

[49] A demolition order may not be made in respect of a flat.

[50] Housing Act 1985, s.604A(1). Subsection (2) sets out the Secretary of State's powers to issue guidance to local authorities: "he may, in particular, give guidance in respect of financial and social considerations to be taken into account by authorities." Subsection (3) requires that the Secretary of State shall lay a draft of the proposed guidance before each House of Parliament for a period of 40 days beginning with the day on which the draft is laid. Extensive guidance has been provided by the Secretary of State in D.O.E. circular 6/90 (issued on March 20, 1990). This document is well in excess of 100 pages.

[51] *Associated Provincial Picture Houses Ltd.* v. *Wednesbury Corporation* [1948] 1 K.B. 223.

Housing Act 1985, in certain circumstances a local authority may be quite justified in being satisfied that the most satisfactory course is to take no action under the Housing Act 1985, notwithstanding the fact that the premises in question are unfit for human habitation.[52]

Legislation also confers on local authorities a range of powers which may be exercised in relation to housing which is unsatisfactory, although not unfit for human habitation. The following courses of action are available: as regards premises which are in a state of disrepair, a local authority may serve a repair notice under section 190; with respect to houses in multiple occupation they may require works to be carried out under section 352; if the living conditions in an area within their district are unsatisfactory they may declare that area to be a renewal area under section 89 of the Local Government and Housing Act 1989; they may also with the approval of the Secretary of State prepare group repair schemes and they may make available grants for the costs of repairs and improvements under Part VIII of the Local Government and Housing Act 1989.

(4) Repairs: Housing Unfit for Human Habitation and Housing in a State of Disrepair: Housing Act 1985, ss. 189–190

189.—(1) Subject to subsection (1A) where the local authority are satisfied that a dwelling-house or house in multiple occupation is unfit for human habitation, they shall serve a repair notice on the person having control of the dwelling-house or house in multiple occupation, if they are satisfied, in accordance with section 604A, that serving a notice under this subsection is the most satisfactory course of action.

(1A) Where the local housing authority are satisfied that either a dwelling-house which is a flat or a flat in multiple occupation is unfit for human habitation by virtue of section 604(2), they shall serve a repair notice on the person having control of the part of the building in question if they are satisfied, in accordance with section 604A, that serving a notice under this subsection is the most satisfactory course of action.

(1B) In the case of a house in multiple occupation, a repair notice may be served on the person managing the house instead of on the person having control; and where a notice is so served, then, subject to section 191, the person managing the house shall be regarded as the person having control of it for the purposes of the provisions of this Part following that section.

(2) A repair notice under this section shall—

(a) require the person on whom it is served to execute the works specified in the notice (which may be works of repair or improvement or both) and to begin those works not later than such reasonable date, being not earlier than the twenty-eighth day after the notice is served, as specified in the notice and to complete those works within such reasonable time as is so specified, and

---

[52] For the position before the entry into force of the amendments made by the Local Government and Housing Act 1989 see *R.* v. *Kerrier D.C. ex p. Guppy's (Bridport) Ltd.* (1977) 32 P. & C.R. 411.

   (b)   state that in the opinion of the authority the works specified in the notice will render the dwelling-house or, as the case may be, house in multiple occupation, fit for human habitation.

(3) The authority, in addition to serving the notice

   (a)   on the person having control of the dwelling-house or part of the building concerned or

   (b)   on the person having control of or, as the case may be, on the person managing the house in multiple occupation which is concerned,

shall serve a copy of the notice on any other person having an interest in the dwelling-house or part of the building or house concerned, whether as a freeholder, mortgagee, or lessee.

(4) The notice becomes operative, if no appeal is brought, on the expiration of 21 days from the date of the service of the notice and is final and conclusive as to matters which could have been raised on an appeal.

(5) A repair notice under this section which has become operative is a local land charge.

(6) This section has effect subject to the provisions of section 190A.

190.—(1) Subject to subsection (1B) where the local housing authority—

   (a)   are satisfied that a dwelling-house is in such a state of disrepair that, although not unfit for human habitation, substantial repairs are necessary to bring it up to a reasonable standard, having regard to its age, character and locality, or

   (b)   are satisfied, whether on a representation made by an occupying tenant or otherwise, that a dwelling-house is in such a state of disrepair that, although not unfit for human habitation, the condition of a part of the building outside the flat is such as to interfere materially with the personal comfort of the occupying tenant,

they may serve a repair notice on the person having control of the dwelling-house.

(1A) Subject to subsection (1B) where a local housing authority—

   (a)   are satisfied that a building containing a flat is in such a state of disrepair that, although the flat is not unfit for human habitation, substantial repairs are necessary to a part of the building outside the flat to bring the flat up to a reasonable standard, having regard to its age, character and locality, or

   (b)   are satisfied, whether on a representation made by an occupying tenant or otherwise, that a building containing a flat is in such a state of disrepair that, although the flat is not unfit for human habitation, the condition of a part of the building outside the flat is such as to interfere materially with the personal comfort of the occupying tenant,

they may serve a repair notice on the person having control of part of the building concerned.

(1B) The authority may not serve a notice under subsection (1) or subsection (1A) unless—

   (a)   there is an occupying tenant of the dwelling-house or flat concerned; or

(b) the dwelling-house or flat concerned falls within a renewal area within the meaning of Part VII of the Local Government and Housing Act 1989.

(1C) In the case of a house in multiple occupation, a notice under subsection (1) or subsection (1A) may be served on the person managing the house instead of on the person having control of it; and where a notice is so served, then, subject to section 191, the person managing the house shall be regarded as the person having control of it for the purposes of the provisions of this Part following that section.

(2) A repair notice under this section shall require the person on whom it is served to execute the works specified in the notice, not being works of internal decorative repair, and—

(a) to begin those works not later than the twenty-eighth day after the notice is served, as is specified in the notice; and

(b) to complete those works within such reasonable time as is so specified.

(3) The authority, in addition to serving the notice

(a) on the person having control of the dwelling-house or part of the building concerned or

(b) on the person having control of or, as the case may be, on the person managing the house in multiple occupation which is concerned,

shall serve a copy of the notice on any other person interested in the dwelling-house or part of the building or house concerned, whether as freeholder, mortgagee or lessee.

(4) The notice becomes operative, if no appeal is brought, on the expiry of 21 days from the date of service of the notice and is final and conclusive as to matters which could have been raised on appeal.

(5) A repair notice under this section which has become operative is a local land charge.

Notes

(i) Section 189(1), as originally drafted, provided that the local housing authority should be under a duty to issue a repair notice in relation to a house which was unfit for human habitation unless they were satisfied that the house was "not capable of being rendered fit at reasonable expense."[53]

Although local authorities are no longer expressly required by section 189 to consider whether the premises can be made fit for human habitation at reasonable expense, they must have regard to guidance given by the Secretary of State under section 604A.[54] Such guidance includes the financial considerations which the local authority must take into account.

---

[53] The issue of "reasonable expense" (defined by Housing Act 1985, s.206) gave plenty of scope for litigation. See A. Arden, *Housing Act 1985* (1986), pp. 68–249—68–251. Section 206 is now repealed: Local Government and Housing Act, Sched. 9, Part I, para. 11.
[54] D.O.E. circular 6/90.

(ii) "Person having control" is defined by section 207(1):

"person having control," subject to sections 189(1B), 190(1B), 190(1C) and 191—

>   (a) in relation to a dwelling-house or a house in multiple occupation means the person who receives the rack-rent of the premises (that is to say, a rent which is not less than 2/3rds of the full net annual value of the premises), whether on his own account or as agent or trustee for another person, or who would so receive it if the premises were let at such rack-rent and

>   (b) in relation to a part of a building to which relates a repair notice served under subsection (1A) of section 189 or section 190, means a person who is an owner in relation to that part of the building (or the building as a whole) and who, in the opinion of the authority by whom the notice is served, ought to execute the works specified in the notice.

This extended definition is designed to deal with some of the problems of interpretation to which the definition as originally drafted gave rise.[55]

(iii) Where the "person having control" of premises is the local authority itself, section 189 is not applicable.[56]

(iv) Subsection (6) states that the local authority's duties under section 189 are subject to section 190A. According to this section, if the local authority, having decided that repair is the most satisfactory course of action, determine that "the premises concerned form part of a building which would be a qualifying building in relation to a group repair scheme" and that "within the period of 12 months beginning at that time, they expect to prepare a group repair scheme in respect of the qualifying building" then the local authority may serve a repair notice "with respect only to those works which, in their opinion, will not be carried out to the premises concerned in pursuance of the relevant scheme."

A "group repair scheme" is governed by Part VIII of the Local Government and Housing Act 1989.[57]

(v) Section 191 makes provision for appeals to be brought against repair notices (made either under section 189 or section 190):

>   (1) A person aggrieved by a repair notice may within 21 days after the date of service of the notice, appeal to the county court.

>   (1A) Without prejudice to the generality of subsection (1), it shall be a ground of appeal that some person other than the appellant, being a person who is an owner in relation to the dwelling-house or part of the building concerned,

---

[55] See *Pollway Nominees* v. *Croydon L.B.C.* [1987] 1 A.C. 79; *White* v. *Barnet L.B.C.* [1989] 3 W.L.R. 131.

[56] *R.* v. *Cardiff C.C. ex p. Cross* (1981) 1 H.L.R. 54.

[57] See p. 424.

ought to execute the works or pay the whole or part of the cost of executing them.

(1B) Without prejudice to the generality of subsection (1), it shall be a ground of appeal, in the case of a repair notice under section 189, that making a closing order under section 264 or a demolition order under section 265 is the most satisfactory course of action; and, where the grounds on which the appeal is brought are or include that specified in this subsection, the court, on the hearing of the appeal, shall have regard to any guidance given to the local housing authority under section 604A.

(2) On appeal the court may make such order either confirming, quashing or varying the notice as it thinks fit.

Where an appeal is based on the ground specified in subsection (1A)—that some person other than the appellant ought to execute the works in question—the county court may vary the notice so as to require the other person to carry out the works or contribute to the cost.[58] In exercising its powers under subsection (3A) the court must take into account, as between the appellant and the other person, certain factors listed in subsection (3B):

(a) their relative interests in the dwelling-house or part of the building concerned (considering both the nature of the interests and the rights and obligations arising under or by virtue of them);

(b) their relative responsibility for the state of the dwelling-house or building which gives rise to the need for the execution of the works; and

(c) the relative degree of benefit to be derived from the execution of the works.

(vi) If the repair notice is not complied with the local housing authority may themselves do the work required to be done in the notice.[59] Where the local authority have decided to enforce the repair notice by doing the work themselves, they "shall give notice in writing of their intention to do so to the person having control of the premises and, if they think fit, to any owner of the premises."[60] On having completed the works, the local housing authority may recover the expenses they have incurred under section 193 "from the person having control of the dwelling-house or part of the building to which the notice relates."[61]

It is a criminal offence under section 198 intentionally to obstruct an officer of the local housing authority who is authorised to enter premises. It is also an offence under section 198A for a person having control of premises to which a repair notice relates intentionally to fail to comply with the notice.

[58] s.191(3A).
[59] s.193.
[60] s.194.
[61] s.193(3) and Sched. 10, para. 2.

(vii)   When the person on whom the repair notice has been served fails to comply with the notice, the local authority may, rather than resorting to the enforcement provisions contained in section 193 to 198A of the Housing Act 1985, seek to come to an agreement whereby the local authority carries out the repairs at the expense of the person having control of the premises.[62]

(viii)   Part VIII of the Local Government and Housing Act 1989 governs the award of grants for the repair and improvement of residential premises. "Renovation grants"[63] are generally available in respect of premises which are unfit for human habitation, if completion of the relevant works will cause the dwelling to be fit for human habitation, and the local authority are satisfied that completion of the works is the most satisfactory course of action.[64] Furthermore, it is expressly provided that where works have been carried out to tenanted premises pursuant to a repair notice served under section 189 or under section 190, or to a notice served under section 352 (requiring works to render a house in multiple occupation fit for the number of occupants) the local authority shall approve the landlord's application for a grant.[65]

(5) Closing Orders and Demolition Orders: Housing Act 1985, ss. 264 *et seq.*

If the local authority decides not to require premises which are unfit for human habitation to be made fit by serving a repair notice under section 189, they are normally required to take steps to prevent the premises being occupied. As alternatives to serving a repair notice, the local authority may make a closing order under section 264 (which, although preventing the premises from being used for residential purposes, may allow the owner of the premises to use them for other purposes), make a demolition order under section 265, or declare the area in question to be a clearance area under section 289—in which case the premises will in due course be demolished.

It is provided, however, that the local authority may, instead of closing or demolishing the premises, purchase the property in question for temporary accommodation "if it appears to them that the dwelling-house (not being a flat), a house in multiple occupation (not being a flat in multiple occupation) or the whole of a building is or can be rendered capable of providing accommodation of a standard which is adequate for the time being."[66]

---

[62] s.191A.

[63] Grants "relating to the improvement or repair of a dwelling or to the provision of dwellings by the conversion of a house or other building": Local Government and Housing Act 1989, s.101(2)(a).

[64] s.112.

[65] s.113.

[66] Housing Act 1985, s.300(1). A housing authority cannot use property acquired under section 300 as temporary accommodation indefinitely: *R.* v. *City of Birmingham Corporation ex p. Sale* (1983) 9 H.L.R. 33. Nor can the local authority use section 300 as a means of increasing their stock of permanent housing: *Victoria Square Property Co.* v. *Southwark L.B.C.* [1978] 1 W.L.R. 463.

If an order is made under section 264 or 265 the premises must be vacated, and tenants cannot rely on the security of tenure provisions contained in the Rent Acts or Part I of the Housing Act 1988.[67] If the local authority exercise their powers under the clearance area provisions, private sector tenants will lose their security of tenure under the Rent Acts or Part I of the Housing Act 1988 when the local authority compulsorily purchase the property in question.[68] Tenants who are displaced through the exercise by the local authority of the powers contained in Part IX of the Housing Act 1985 are entitled to be rehoused and to be compensated.[69]

264.—(1) Where the local housing authority are satisfied that a dwelling-house or house in multiple occupation is unfit for human habitation and that, in accordance with section 604A, taking action under this subsection is the most satisfactory course of action, they shall make a closing order with respect to the dwelling-house or house in multiple occupation.

(2) Where the local housing authority are satisfied that, in a building containing one or more flats, some or all of the flats are unfit for human habitation and that, in accordance with section 604A, taking action under this subsection is the most satisfactory course of action, they shall make a closing order with respect to the whole or part of the building.

(3) In deciding for the purposes of subsection (2)—

(a)   whether to make a closing order with respect to the whole or part of the building; or

(b)   in respect of which part of the building to make a closing order;

the authority shall have regard to such guidance as may from time to time be given by the Secretary of State under section 604A.[70]

(4) This section has effect subject to section 300(1) (power to purchase for temporary housing use houses liable to be demolished or closed).

265.—(1) Where the local housing authority are satisfied that—

(a)   a dwelling-house which is not a flat, or

(b)   a house in multiple occupation which is not a flat in multiple occupation,

is unfit for human habitation and that, in accordance with section 604A, taking action under this subsection is the most satisfactory course of action, they shall make a demolition order with respect to the dwelling-house or house concerned.

(2) Where the local housing authority are satisfied that, in a building containing one or more flats, some or all of the flats are unfit for human habitation and that, in accordance with section 604A, taking action under this subsection is the most satisfactory course of action, they shall make a demolition order with respect to the building.

[67] s.270(1) (demolition orders) and s.276 (closing orders).
[68] s.290(1) (see p. 420). Former protected and assured tenants do not become secure tenants in these circumstances: Housing Act 1985, s.79(2)(a) and Sched. 1, para. 3.
[69] Land Compensation Act 1973, s.29. See *R.* v. *East Hertfordshire D.C. ex p. Smith* (1991) 23 H.L.R. 26.
[70] D.O.E. circular 6/90.

(3) This section has effect subject to sections 300(1) (power to purchase for temporary housing use houses liable to be demolished or closed) and 304(1) (listed buildings and buildings protected by notice pending listing).

267.—(1) A demolition order is an order requiring that the premises—

(a) be vacated within a specified period (of at least 28 days) from the date on which the order becomes operative, and

(b) be demolished within six weeks after the end of that period or, if it is not vacated before the end of that period, after the date on which it is vacated or, in either case, within such longer period as in the circumstances the local housing authority consider it reasonable to specify.

(2) A closing order is an order prohibiting the use of the premises to which it relates for any purpose not approved by the local housing authority.

(3) The approval of the local housing authority shall not be unreasonably withheld, and a person aggrieved by the withholding of such approval by the authority may, within 21 days of the refusal, appeal to the county court.

269.—(1) A person aggrieved by a demolition or closing order may, within 21 days after the date of the service of the order, appeal to the county court.

(2) No appeal lies at the instance of a person who is in occupation of the premises or part of the premises under a lease or agreement with an unexpired term of three years or less.

(2A) Without prejudice to the generality of subsection (1), it shall be a ground of appeal—

(a) in the case of a closing order, that serving a repair notice under section 189 or making a demolition order under section 265 is the most satisfactory course of action; and

(b) in the case of a demolition order, that serving a repair notice under section 189 or making a closing order under section 264 is the most satisfactory course of action;

and, where the grounds on which an appeal is brought are or include that specified in paragraph (a) or paragraph (b), the court, on hearing the appeal, shall have regard to any guidance given to the local housing authority under section 604A.

(3) On an appeal the court may make such an order either confirming or quashing or varying the order as it thinks fit.

When the local authority have made a demolition or closing order it becomes operative at the end of the period of 21 days from the date of service (unless an appeal under section 268 has been raised).[71]

Once a demolition order has become operative the local authority must serve a notice on the occupier requiring the occupier to quit the premises.[72] If the occupier fails to comply with the notice the local

[71] s.268(2).
[72] s.270(1).

authority can obtain possession by a county court action, and recover any expenses so incurred.[73] It is a criminal offence (punishable by a fine) to occupy premises in relation to which a demolition order has become operative.[74]

271.—(1) When a demolition order has become operative, the owner of the premises to which it applies shall demolish the premises within the time limited by the order, and if the premises are not demolished within that time the local housing authority shall enter and demolish them and sell the materials.

Where the local authority are required to act under section 271(1), they may recover their expenses from the owner of the premises.[75] Section 271(1) is also subject to sections 273, 274 and 275 under which the local authority:

(i) may take steps to destroy or remove vermin prior to demolition[76];

(ii) allow the owner the opportunity of reconstructing the premises[77]; or

(iii) on the submission of the owner or any other person who has an interest in the premises determine the demolition order and make a closing order, so that the premises may be used for purposes other than for human habitation.[78]

Once a closing order has become operative it is a criminal offence for a person to use the premises in contravention of the order.[79] If, after a closing order has been made, the premises in question are rendered fit for human habitation, the local authority must determine the closing order, and if the local authority refuse to determine the order in these circumstances, any person aggrieved (other than a person who is in occupation of the premises, or a relevant part of the premises, under a lease or an agreement of which the unexpired term is three years or less) may appeal against the refusal to the county court.[80] Finally, a local housing authority may generally revoke a closing order and make a demolition order instead, although there is no such power where it is a flat which is subject to the closing order.[81]

(6) Clearance Areas

Whereas demolition orders and closing orders are designed to deal with the problems posed by individual dwellings, houses or buildings which are unfit for human habitation, the more extensive powers

[73] s.270(2)–(4).
[74] s.270(5).
[75] s.272.
[76] s.273.
[77] s.274.
[78] s.275.
[79] s.277.
[80] s.288.
[81] s.279.

conferred on local authorities by sections 289 to 298 by the Housing Act 1985 are aimed at the problems of extensive areas of unfit or dangerous housing.

Section 289 of the Housing Act 1985 provides:

(1) A clearance area is an area which is to be cleared of all buildings in accordance with the following provisions of this Part.

(2) Subject to subsections (2B) to (2F), (4) and (5B), the local housing authority shall declare an area to be a clearance area if they are satisfied—

(a) that the buildings in the area which are dwelling-houses or houses in multiple occupation or contain one or more flats (in this section referred to as "residential buildings") are unfit for human habitation or are by reason of their bad arrangement, or the narrowness or bad arrangement of the streets, dangerous or injurious to the health of the inhabitants of the area, and

(b) that the other buildings, if any, in the area are for a like reason dangerous or injurious to the health of the inhabitants of the area,

and in accordance with section 604A the most satisfactory course of action is the demolition of all the buildings in the area.

The Act includes detailed provisions which set out the procedures to be followed and the precise powers and duties of the local authority. It is worth noting, however, section 289(4) which provides that, before passing a resolution declaring a clearance area, the authority shall satisfy themselves:

(a) that, in so far as suitable accommodation does not already exist for the persons who will be displaced by the clearance of the area, the authority can provide, or secure the provision of, such accommodation in advance of the displacements which will from time to time become necessary as the demolition of the buildings in the area, or in different parts of it, proceeds, and

(b) that the resources of the authority are sufficient for the purposes of carrying the resolution into effect.

Although the detailed provisions of the law relating to clearance areas is complex, the basic idea is very simple. Section 290(1) provides:

So soon as may be after the local housing authority have declared an area to be a clearance area, they shall proceed to secure the clearance of the area (subject to and in accordance with the provisions of this Part) by purchasing the land comprised in the area and themselves undertaking, or otherwise securing, the demolition of the buildings on the land.

(7) Further Powers in Relation to Houses in Multiple Occupation

Part XI of the Housing Act 1985 confers on local housing authorities various powers in relation to houses in multiple occupation. Section 352 provides:

(1) Subject to section 365 the local housing authority may serve a notice under this section where in the opinion of the authority, a house in multiple

occupation fails to meet one or more of the requirements in paragraphs (a) to (e) of subsection (1A) and, having regard to the number of individuals or households or both for the time being accommodated on the premises, by reason of that failure the premises are not reasonably suitable for occupation by those individuals or households.

(1A) The requirements in respect of a house in multiple occupation referred to in subsection (1) are the following, that is to say,—

(a) there are satisfactory facilities for the storage, preparation and cooking of food including an adequate number of sinks with a satisfactory supply of hot and cold water;

(b) it has an adequate number of suitably located water-closets for the exclusive use of the occupants;

(c) it has, for the exclusive use of the occupants, an adequate number of suitably located fixed baths or showers and wash-hand basins each of which is provided with a satisfactory supply of hot and cold water;

(d) subject to section 365, there are adequate means of escape from fire; and

(e) there are adequate other fire precautions.

(2) Subject to subsection (2A) the notice shall specify the works which in the opinion of the authority are required for rendering the house reasonably suitable—

(a) for accommodation by the individuals or households for the time being accommodated there, and

(b) for a smaller number of individuals or households and the number of individuals or households, or both, which, in the opinion of the authority, the house could reasonably accommodate if the works were carried out,

but the notice shall not specify any works to any premises outside the house.

Notes

(i) The term "house in multiple occupation" is defined by section 345(1) as "a house which is occupied by persons who do not form a single household." Subsection (2) provides:

For the purposes of this section "house," in the expression "house in multiple occupation," includes any part of a building which—

(a) apart from this section would be regarded as a house; and

(b) was originally constructed or subsequently adapted for occupation by a single household;

and any reference in this Part to a flat in multiple occupation is a reference to a part of a building which, whether by virtue of this subsection or without regard to it, constitutes a house in multiple occupation.

(ii) The appeals procedure is set out in section 353.[82]

---

[82] See also *Nolan* v. *Leeds C.C.*, *The Times*, November 5, 1990.

(iii)   If the notice under section 352 is not complied with the local housing authority may themselves do the work required to be done by the notice.[83]

(iv)   If the local authority exercise their powers under section 375(1), they may recover their expenses in accordance with Schedule 10.[84]

(v)   A person who wilfully fails to comply with a notice under section 352 commits an offence and is liable to a fine.[85]

(8) Renewal Areas

Part VII of the Local Government and Housing Act 1989 replaces Part VIII of the Housing Act 1985. Under section 89 of the 1989 Act a local authority may declare a particular area of housing to be a renewal area. In deciding whether to declare a renewal area the local authority must have regard to the guidance of the Secretary of State,[86] and a number of conditions specified by the Secretary of State must be satisfied.[87] The most important powers of local authorities in relation to renewal areas are set out in section 93:

(1) Where a local housing authority have declared an area to be a renewal area, the authority may exercise the powers conferred by this section.

(2) For the purpose of securing or assisting in securing all or any of the objectives mentioned in subsection (3) below, the authority may acquire by agreement, or be authorised by the Secretary of State to acquire compulsorily, any land in the area on which there are premises consisting of or including housing accommodation or which forms part of the curtilage of any such premises; and the authority may provide housing accommodation on land acquired under this subsection.

(3) The objectives referred to in subsection (2) above are—

(a)   the improvement or repair of the premises, either by the authority or by a person to whom they propose to dispose of the premises;

(b)   the proper and effective management and use of the housing accommodation, either by the authority or by a person to whom they propose to dispose of the premises comprising the accommodation; and

(c)   the well-being of the persons for the time being residing in the area.

(4) For the purpose of effecting or assisting the improvement of the amenities in the area, the authority may acquire by agreement, or be authorised by the Secretary of State to acquire compulsorily, any land in the area (including land which the authority propose to dispose of to another person who intends to effect or assist the improvement of those amenities).

[83] s.375.
[84] s.375(4).
[85] s.376.
[86] s.89(4).
[87] s.90.

(5) The authority may—

(a) carry out works (including works of demolition) on land owned by the authority in the area (whether or not that land was acquired under subsection (2) or subsection (4) above); and

(b) assist in the carrying out of works on any land in the area not owned by the authority, either by providing grants, loans or guarantees or by incurring expenditure for the benefit of the person assisted or by executing the works themselves or by providing materials for the carrying out of the works;

but assistance may not be given under paragraph (b) above in respect of works for which assistance is being or as been provided under Part VIII of this Act.

These powers are in addition to the powers which local authorities have by virtue of other statutory provisions.[88]

(9) Grants Towards the Cost of Improvement and Repairs

It has already been noted that where a local authority has served a repair notice under section 189 or section 190 or a notice under section 352 the landlord may apply for and is entitled to a grant from the local authority. Part VIII of the Local Government and Housing Act 1989 (which replaces the grant system contained in Part XV of the Housing Act 1985) introduces a new regime. The principal categories of grant under the 1989 Act are:

(i) renovation grants: grants relating to the improvement or repair of a dwelling or to the provision of dwellings by the conversion of a house or other building;

(ii) common parts grants: grants relating to the improvement or repair of the common parts of a building;

(iii) disabled facilities grants: grants for the provision of facilities for a disabled person in a dwelling or in the common parts of a building containing one or more flats;

(iv) H.M.O. grants: grants for the improvement or repair of a house in multiple occupation or for the provision of a house in multiple occupation by the conversion of a house or other building.[89]

Although the details of Part VIII of the 1989 Act are complex the following points should be noted:

(i) The Act lays down conditions which must be satisfied, and procedures which must be followed as regards applications for grant aid.[90]

---

[88] s.93(8).
[89] s.101.
[90] ss.103–106.

(ii)   As far as the local authority's decision-making is concerned there are three different categories of application. First, there are some applications which the local authority must approve. For example, the local authority must approve an application for a renovation grant if the dwelling in question is not fit for human habitation, the relevant works will cause the dwelling to be rendered fit, and they are satisfied that completion of the works is the most satisfactory course of action.[91] Similarly, the local authority must approve a landlord's application for a grant where works are necessary to comply with notices served under sections 198, 190 and 352.[92] Secondly, there are some applications which the local authority may not approve. For example, the local authority may not approve an application for a grant if the relevant works have been commenced before the application is approved.[93] Finally, there are applications which the local authority have a discretion whether or not to approve.

(iii)   Sections 127 to 130 set out the rules applicable to "group repair schemes." Section 127(1) provides:

In accordance with a scheme under this section prepared by a local authority and approved by the Secretary of State, the authority may, with the consent of the persons participating in the scheme, enter into agreements to secure the carrying out of such external works to qualifying buildings to which the scheme relates as will ensure that, on completion of the works, the exterior of those buildings will be in reasonable repair; and in this Part such a scheme is referred to as a "group repair scheme."

The essence of such a scheme is that the owner of any qualifying building[94] within the group repair scheme is eligible to participate in the scheme as an assisted participant. That is to say, the owner will be liable to pay only a proportion of the costs of repair (not exceeding 25 per cent. if the building is in a renewal area or 50 per cent. in any other case).[95]

IV   FURTHER READING

Introduction

Two very obvious points emerge from the materials in this chapter: first, that the law on housing conditions is both very complex and confused; secondly, that the law has failed to provide a solution to the problem of bad housing.

---

[91] s.112.
[92] s.113.
[93] s.108(1). This is subject to the exceptions in subsections (2) and (3).
[94] s.128.
[95] s.129.

There have been frequent calls for a complete overhaul of the law in this area. See, for example, D. J. Hughes, Housing repairs—a suitable case for reform [1984] J.S.W.L. 137. Hughes discusses the failure of the common law to produce an adequate response to the issues involved, criticises the chaotic state of the public law provisions, and argues in favour of a codification of the law. Of course, it must be recognised that housing conditions can be improved only if more financial resources are made available—either through the private sector or from public funds. Although such resources may seem difficult to justify in the current economic climate, it can be argued that "[t]he *social cost* of ignoring the need for an integrated and improved code on housing conditions is too great."[96]

(A) GENERAL

A useful guide to the law relating to the problems posed by disrepair—from the tenant's point of view—is to be found in J. Luba, *Repairs: Tenant's Remedies* (2nd ed., 1991, Legal Action Group). This work does not deal only with covenants to repair, but also the public law aspects of the law (notably, the Housing Act 1985 (as amended)). The book clearly illustrates the point made by the author that "our repairs law is a messy, overlapping conglomeration of rules, rights, powers and duties derived from a host of statutes, cases and regulations."[97]

An overview of the enormous body of law in this area is given by A. Arden, *Manual of Housing Law* (4th ed., 1989, Sweet & Maxwell), Chapters 11 to 13; D. J. Hughes, *Public Sector Housing Law* (2nd ed., 1987, Butterworths), Chapters 7 to 10. (Note, however, that those sections dealing with the Housing Act 1985 and the Public Health Act 1936 are already out of date as a result of the amendments contained in the Local Government and Housing Act 1989 and the Environmental Protection Act 1990.)

(B) SPECIFIC ASPECTS

(1) The Scope of Covenants to Repair

The decision of the Court of Appeal in the case of *Quick* v. *Taff-Ely B.C.* on the meaning of the repair endorses the approach taken by Forbes J. in *Ravenseft Properties Ltd.* v. *Davstone (Holdings) Ltd.*[98] This latter case is helpfully discussed by P. F. Smith, Repairs, renewal and improvement (1979) 43 Conv. 429. The same author also examines

---

[96] Hughes, Housing repairs—a suitable case for reform [1984] J.S.W.L. 137 at 161.
[97] p. vii.
[98] [1980] Q.B. 12.

the implications of *Barrett* v. *Lounova (1982) Ltd.*: A fallen idol? [1988]
Conv. 448.

It is widely acknowledged that the impact of what is now section 11 of
the Landlord and Tenant Act 1985 has been less than it might have
been—one of the reasons being the way in which the courts have
interpreted it. It has been argued that the courts have effectively
frustrated the social policy and purpose of the statutory covenants by
restrictive interpretation of the provisions: J. I. Reynolds, Statutory
covenants of fitness and repair: social legislation and the judged (1974)
37 M.L.R. 377. (But see, also, the reply by M. J. Robinson, "Social
legislation" and the judges: a note by way of rejoinder (1976) 39
M.L.R. 43.)

(2) Tenants' Remedies for Breach of the Landlord's Covenant

One of the potentially most attractive ways for a tenant to enforce the
landlord's repairing covenants is through the exercise of the right of set-
off. The implications of Goff J.'s judgment in *Lee-Parker* v. *Izzett* and
subsequent case law are discussed by P. M. Rank, Repairs in lieu of
rent (1976) 40 Conv. 196; A. Waite, Repairs and deduction from rent
[1981] Conv. 199; A. Waite, Disrepair and set-off of damages against
rent: the implications of *British Anzani* [1984] Conv. 373.

For a brief discussion of *Evans* v. *Clayhope Properties Ltd.* (and the
ways in which the Landlord and Tenant Act 1987 attempts to deal with
the problems which that case exposed) see C. P. Rogers, Flat out in
London SW7 and SW9—continuing problems for long leaseholders
[1988] Conv. 363.

(3) Defective Premises Act 1972

An analysis of the 1972 Act is given by J. R. Spencer, The Defective
Premises Act 1972: defective law and defective law reform [1974] C.L.J.
307 & [1975] C.L.J. 48. Section 4 is discussed at [1975] C.L.J. 62–78.
Spencer concludes that section 4 "is open to the criticism that it further
complicates an area of law which is far too complicated already."[99]

(4) Public Health Act 1936 and Environmental Protection Act 1990

There is an interesting discussion of *Coventry C.C.* v. *Cartwright*,
Salford C.C. v. *McNally* and *National Coal Board* v. *Thorne* in two
articles by D. J. Hughes, Public health legislation and the improvement
of housing conditions in England and Wales and in Northern Ireland
(1976) 27 N.I.L.Q. 1 and What is a nuisance?—the Public Health Act
1936 revisited (1976) 27 N.I.L.Q. 131.

---

[99] At 78.

The case of *Birmingham D.C.* v. *McMahon* has been commented upon by D. C. Hoath, Dampness in high-rise blocks: the criminal implications [1988] Conv. 377 and by N. Wikeley [1988] J.S.W.L. 134.

(5) Housing Act 1985

For a brief description of the way in which local authorities exercise their statutory powers see J. N. Hawke & G. A. Taylor, The compulsory repair of individual, physically substandard housing: the law in practice [1984] J.S.W.L. 129. A fuller discussion of local authority practice is provided by T. Hadden, *Compulsory Repair and Improvement: A Study of the Operation of the Housing Acts 1957 to 1974* (1978, Centre for Socio-Legal Studies). This work had as its objective an assessment of the adequacy of the then current framework for the rehabilitation of bad housing. Although the statutory structure has changed, many of the practical and administrative problems which the author identified have not. The study showed that problems included the complexity of the procedures, the existence of overlapping procedures, procedural delays, non-compliance by those on whom notices were served and the unwillingness of local authorities to carry out works in default. Not surprisingly, Hadden argued for a radical reformulation of the legislation.

Chapter 7

RENT AND OTHER TERMS

The bulk of this chapter concentrates on the private law relating to rent and the public law regulating, or otherwise affecting, rent levels; the remedies available to landlords if tenants fail to pay their rent are noted; and certain other measures of tenant protection are discussed at the end of the chapter.

I RENT: COMMON LAW PRINCIPLES

(A) INTRODUCTION

For a whole variety of factors, a completely free market in housing has not worked. There has, historically, been an inexorable tendency for demand for housing to outstrip supply, particularly since the days of the industrial revolution and the resulting concentration of households around centres of major economic activity.

For those in employment, some assistance can be given through the mechanism of the salary paid by the employer for the employee's services. There has been some recognition of this at a general level in the concept of a "London weighting allowance"—an additional element of salary paid to many employees working in the London area. In the case of many individual firms or companies, high wages are negotiated for key groups of skilled employees which has the effect of improving the ability of those employees to participate in the housing market (and, indeed, increase the cost of housing in those areas more generally). But, for the low-paid, the elderly, the sick and disabled, the wage mechanism is not an effective method for providing assistance with housing costs. Instead, it has come to be accepted that the state has a part to play in terms of controlling levels of rents and assisting with the ability of residential occupiers of accommodation to pay for their accommodation.

Nevertheless, the policy measures that have been adopted since 1915 have been characterised by a lack both of coherence and of consistency. There has been a complex series of measures designed in particular to subsidise housing costs. Some of these have been indirect, for example, limiting the levels of rents chargeable by landlords; others have been direct, such as the provision of subsidised housing, or, more recently, means-tested rent rebates and allowances. (Of course it is not just the poor, nor just tenants, who have been subsidised. All owner-occupiers benefit from the tax rule that the sale of one's principal residence is exempt from capital gains tax; and for those buying on mortgage, interest payments may be set off against income tax. Indeed, it is widely argued that the present system of housing finance is extremely regressive, benefitting the better-off rather than the poor.)

In the following sections, we consider statutory limits to rent levels; subsidies for housing costs; and subsidies for rent costs (housing benefits). First, however, we look at the common law rules relating to rent.

(B)   THE LEGAL OBLIGATION TO PAY RENT

At common law, no rent has to be reserved for a valid lease to be created. Whether or not rent is payable depends essentially on the intention of the parties, interpreted where necessary by the courts. However, the existence of a rent clause is often extremely helpful in determining whether a lease exists. (For tenancies within the Housing Acts and Rent Acts, rent must be paid.[1])

If, as is usually the case, rent is reserved then it must be a profit. But it need not be a money payment: "it may as well be in delivery of hens, capons, roses, spurs, bowes, shafts, horses, haws, pepper, cummin, wheat or other profit. ... "[2]

Further, it must be certain, or capable of being reduced to certainty. In *Greater London Council* v. *Connelly*,[3] a council tenant (representing 2½ per cent. of all G.L.C. tenants who had been on rent strike) challenged a condition on his rent card which stated that the rent and other sums shown on the rent card "are liable to be increased or decreased on notice being given." Notice of increase had been given; but it did not comply with section 12(3) of the Prices and Incomes Act 1968, which stated that notices of increase of rent must tell the tenant of his right to terminate the tenancy. The tenants argued first that this section provided a procedure for all rent increases. The Court of Appeal disagreed. It was also argued that the notices issued by G.L.C. were to be regarded as invalid since the formulation of the rent was not sufficiently certain to meet the common law criteria. Not surprisingly,

---

[1] See above, p. 137.
[2] Coke, *A Commentarie upon Littleton*, (1670) p. 142a.
[3] [1970] 2 Q.B. 100.

however, it was decided that the rent clause *was* certain. Lord Denning M.R. said: "The courts are always loath to hold a condition bad for uncertainty. They will give it a reasonable interpretation whenever possible. It is possible here ... "[4]

Where there is a formally documented lease or tenancy, the tenant's covenant to pay rent will invariably be one of the terms.[5] Even where there is no such term, the courts will protect the right of the landlord by implying an obligation to pay rent. The full extent of this obligation was discussed in *Youngmin* v. *Heath*[6] by Lord Denning M.R.:

Mr. Youngmin, the plaintiff, is the owner of a house—no. 31 Hartham Road, London, N.7. Some years ago his predecessor let two rooms furnished to Miss Reni at £3 a week. She shared the bath and w.c. with other tenants. Mr. Youngmin bought the house. Her tenancy continued. She paid rent to Mr. Youngmin regularly until October 3, 1970. Then she was taken ill and died on October 29, 1970. She had made no will and died intestate. Mr. Youngmin did not take possession of the two rooms. He left them as they were. His furniture remained there. Her clothing remained there. The rooms were left unoccupied. Miss Reni had no relatives living in his country. Her only relation was a sister who lived in Russia. This sister instructed the lawyer, a Mr. Heath, in London to take out administration of Miss Reni's estate. He took it out as attorney for the sister. The letters of administration were granted on May 24, 1972. The administrator claimed the clothing of Miss Reni. He also terminated the tenancy of the two rooms. On September 26, 1972 he gave to Mr. Youngmin a notice to terminate the tenancy on October 28, 1972.

Now Mr. Youngmin claims the rent of £3 a week from the last time it was paid by Miss Reni on October 3, 1970, up to the time of the expiry of the notice to quit on October 28, 1972. He claims the rent from Mr. Heath, the defendant, as the attorney administrator of the estate of Miss Reni. Mr. Youngmin admits that there are the clothes in the rooms and that Mr. Heath can take them. But the question is whether he is entitled to sue Mr. Heath for the rent. Mr. Heath says that the liability for rent ceased when Miss Reni died, and that he, as administrator, is not liable thereafter because he never entered into possession ... When there is an ordinary letting of premises furnished or unfurnished at a weekly rent the tenancy does not determine on the tenant's death. It is an implied term that the obligation to pay rent continues *during the currency of the tenancy.* This is a contractual obligation which binds the tenant and his personal representative to pay rent so long as the tenancy continues—that is, until it is determined by proper notice to terminate it. If the tenant dies and the executor does not take possession, the personal representative must fulfil the obligation to pay the rent, but only to the extent of the assets in his hands ... The administrator is liable for the rent to the extent of the deceased's assets until the tenancy is properly determined by notice to quit.

Stamp and Roskill L.JJ. agreed.

---

[4] At 108. (See, too, *Brown* v. *Gould* [1972] Ch. 53, where an option to review a tenancy in 21 years' time at a rent "to be fixed having regard to the market value of the premises at the time of exercising the option taking into account to the advantage of the tenant any increased value of such premises attributable to structural improvements made by the tenant during the ... present lease" was held to be valid by Megarry J.)

[5] See above, pp. 83, 104.

[6] [1974] 1 W.L.R. 135.

Legal recognition of the importance of the landlord's right to rent is also indicated in the wide range of remedies which are available to the landlord for breach of the covenant. Distress for rent, the recovery of rent by ordinary action for debt, compensation for use and occupation and, as a last resort, the right to forfeit the lease or tenancy and eviction from the premises are discussed elsewhere.[7]

II STATUTORY REGULATION OF RENT LEVELS

When governments seek to set limits to the amounts landlords can charge by way of rent, the economic effect is to provide a subsidy to the tenant, the cost of which is borne by the landlord. For the landlord may thus no longer be able to achieve levels of rent which would otherwise be obtainable in the market place. Although this mechanism may be a way of preventing profiteering in times of emergencies (as appeared to be the case when rent control was first introduced in 1915) and may therefore be a plausible short-term policy option, the long-term consequence of the adoption of such a policy is likely to be that private landlords will seek to disinvest the capital they have invested in housing and seek to reinvest it in other forms of investment from which a higher return can be obtained. Although, as already noted, it would be quite wrong to attribute all the decline in the private rented sector of the housing market to the introduction of rent control,[8] there is little doubt that it has been a contributory factor. Indeed a primary objective of the Housing Act 1988 has been to attempt to reverse this trend by substantially relaxing controls on rent levels in the hope that, by offering landlords a higher return on capital, they will be tempted back into the market.

Since 1915, there have been three main statutory regimes for regulating rents: rent control, rent regulation and the new regime for assured tenancies.

(A) RENT CONTROL

The first method of restricting rent levels was rent control introduced in 1915 by the Increase of Rent and Mortgage Interest (War Restrictions) Act 1915. Although the details of the scheme changed over time with great frequency, the basic principle was that houses within relevant rateable value limits had their rents controlled according to strict formulae and increases were only permitted in exceptional circumstances. This scheme is now defunct.[9]

---

[7] At pp. 482–483.
[8] See, *e.g. Housing Policy* (1977) Technical Vol. 1, Chapter 1.
[9] For an outline see, Partington, *Landlord and Tenant* (1975) pp. 177–178.

(B) ASSURED TENANCIES AND ASSURED SHORTHOLD TENANCIES

The Housing Act 1988 was, as already noted, intended to "free" rent levels so that market rents can be charged.

(1) Assured Tenancies

The position in relation to *assured tenancies* is that there is no direct control over rent levels on the initial letting of an assured tenancy.[10]

The Housing Act 1988 provides for a limited form of regulation of rents, when they come to be reviewed. Thus, section 13 states:

(1) This section applies to—

(a) a statutory periodic tenancy other than one which, by virtue of paragraph 11 or paragraph 12 in Part 1 of Schedule 1 to this Act, cannot for the time being be an assured tenancy; and

(b) any other periodic tenancy which is an assured tenancy, other than one in relation to which there is a provision, for the time being binding on the tenant, under which the rent for a particular period of the tenancy will or may be greater than the rent for an earlier period.

(2) For the purpose of securing an increase in the rent under a tenancy to which this section applies, the landlord may serve on the tenant a notice in the prescribed form proposing a new rent to take effect at the beginning of a new period of the tenancy specified in the notice, being a period beginning not earlier than—

(a) the minimum period after the date of the service of the notice; and

(b) except in the case of a statutory periodic tenancy, the first anniversary of the date on which the first period of the tenancy began; and

(c) if the rent under the tenancy has previously been increased by virtue of a notice under this subsection or a determination under section 14 below, the first anniversary of the date on which the increased rent took effect.

(3) The minimum period referred to in subsection (2) above is—

(a) in the case of a yearly tenancy, six months;

(b) in the case of a tenancy where the period is less than a month, one month; and

(c) in any other case, a period equal to the period of the tenancy.

(4) Where a notice is served under subsection (2) above, a new rent specified in the notice shall take effect as mentioned in the notice unless, before the beginning of the new period specified in the notice,—

(a) the tenant by an application in the prescribed form refers the notice to a rent assessment committee; or

---

[10] For the possibility of some form of "indirect" control, associated with the revised housing benefit scheme, see pp. 463–477.

(b)   the landlord and the tenant agree on a variation of the rent which is different from that proposed in the notice or agree that the rent should not be varied.

(5) Nothing in this section (or in section 14 below) affects the right of the landlord and the tenant under an assured tenancy to vary by agreement any term of the tenancy (including a term relating to rent).

Notes

(i)   The statutory periodic tenancies excluded under section 13(1)(a) are Crown tenancies and local authority tenancies.[11]

(ii)   Section 13(1)(b) provides, in effect, that if a periodic tenancy contains its own terms for varying rent levels, they shall prevail over the statutory scheme.

(iii)   By virtue of subsection (5) even if there is no rent review mechanism in the lease, the landlord and tenant may, by agreement, vary any term, including the rent.

(iv)   The provisions only apply to periodic tenancies (whether statutory or otherwise): fixed-term tenancies must contain their own rent review clauses if the rent is to be varied.

(v)   The notice prescribed in section 13(2) is to be found in the Assured Tenancies and Agricultural Occupancies (Forms) Regulations.[12]

(vi)   Where a Form 5 notice is issued, the rent proposed therein will become the new rent unless reference is made, under section 13(4) to a rent assessment committee.[13] In such a case, the powers of the committee are determined by section 14 of the Housing Act 1988 which states:

(1) Where, under subsection (4)(a) of section 13 above, a tenant refers to a rent assessment committee a notice under subsection (2) of that section, the committee shall determine the rent at which, subject to subsections (2) and (4) below, the committee consider that the dwelling-house concerned might reasonably be expected to be let in the open market by a willing landlord under an assured tenancy—

(a)   which is a periodic tenancy having the same periods as those of the tenancy to which the notice relates;

(b)   which begins at the beginning of the new period specified in the notice;

(c)   the terms of which (other than relating to the amount of the rent) are the same as those of the tenancy to which the notice relates;

[11] See p. 151.
[12] S.I. 1988 No. 2203 (Form 5).
[13] Using S.I. 1988 No. 2203 (Form 6).

(d) in respect of which the same notices, if any, have been given under any of Grounds 1 to 5 of Schedule 2 to this Act[14] as have been given (or have effect as if given) in relation to the tenancy to which the notice relates.

(2) In making a determination under this section, there shall be disregarded—

(a) any effect on the rent attributable to the granting of a tenancy to a sitting tenant;

(b) any increase in the value of the dwelling-house attributable to a relevant improvement carried out by a person who at the time it was carried out was the tenant, if the improvement—

(i) was carried out otherwise than in pursuance of an obligation to his immediate landlord, or

(ii) was carried out pursuant to an obligation to his immediate landlord being an obligation which did not relate to the specific improvement concerned but arose by reference to consent given to the carrying out of that improvement; and

(c) any reduction in the value of the dwelling-house attributable to a failure by the tenant to comply with any terms of the tenancy.

(3) For the purposes of subsection (2)(b) above, in relation to a notice which is referred by a tenant as mentioned in subsection (1) above, an improvement is a relevant improvement if either it was carried out during the tenancy to which the notice relates or the following conditions are satisfied, namely—

(a) that it was carried out not more than 21 years before the date of service of the notice; and

(b) that, at all times during the period beginning when the improvement was carried out and ending on the date of service of the notice, the dwelling-house has been let under an assured tenancy; and

(c) that, on the coming to an end of an assured tenancy at any time during that period, the tenant (or, in the case of joint tenants, at least one of them) did not quit.

(4) In this section "rent" does not include any service charge, within the meaning of section 18 of the Landlord and Tenant Act 1985, but, subject to that, includes any sum payable by the tenant to the landlord on account of the use of furniture or for any of the matters referred to in subsection (1)(a) of that section, whether or not those sums are separate from the sums payable for the occupation of the dwelling-house concerned or are payable under separate agreements.

(5) Where any rates in respect of the dwelling-house concerned are borne by the landlord or a superior landlord, the rent assessment committee shall make their determination under this section as if the rates were not so borne.

(6) In any case where—

(a) a rent assessment committee have before them at the same time the reference of a notice under section 6(2) above relating to a tenancy (in this subsection referred to as "the section 6 reference") and the

---

[14] See pp. 208–209.

reference of a notice under section 13(2) above relating to the same tenancy (in this subsection referred to as "the section 13 reference"), and

(b)   the date specified in the notice under section 6(2) above is not later than the first day of the new period specified in the notice under section 13(2) above, and

(c)   the committee propose to hear the two references together,

the committee shall make a determination in relation to the section 6 reference before making their determination in relation to the section 13 reference and, accordingly, in such a case the reference in subsection (1)(c) above to the terms of the tenancy to which the notice relates shall be construed as a reference to those terms as varied by virtue of the determination made in relation to the section 6 reference.

(7) Where a notice under section 13(2) above has been referred to a rent assessment committee, then, unless the landlord and the tenant otherwise agree, the rent determined by the committee (subject, in a case where subsection (5) above applies, to the addition of the appropriate amount in respect of rates) shall be the rent under the tenancy with effect from the beginning of the new period specified in the notice or, if it appears to the rent assessment committee that that would cause undue hardship to the tenant, with effect from such later date (not being later than the date the rent is determined) as the committee may direct.

(8) Nothing in this section requires a rent assessment committee to continue with their determination of a rent for a dwelling-house if the landlord and tenant give notice in writing that they no longer require such a determination or if the tenancy has come to an end.

Given the relative ease with which these provisions may be contracted out of either initially, under section 13(1)(b), or upon reference to the rent assessment committee, under section 14(8) it must be anticipated that these provisions will not be much used.

Section 6 of the Housing Act 1988 is set out below, page 499.

(2) Assured Shorthold Tenancies

In relation to assured shorthold tenancies, there is one limited opportunity for referring an initially agreed rent to a Rent Assessment Committee. Section 22 provides:

(1) Subject to section 23 and subsection (2) below, the tenant under an assured shorthold tenancy in respect of which a notice was served as mentioned in section 20(2) above may make an application in the prescribed form to a rent assessment committee for a determination of the rent which, in the committee's opinion, the landlord might reasonably be expected to obtain under the assured shorthold tenancy.

(2) No application may be made under this section if

(a)   the rent payable under the tenancy is a rent previously determined under this section; or

(b)   the tenancy is an assured shorthold tenancy falling within subsection (4) of section 20 above (and, accordingly, is one in respect of which notice need not have been served as mentioned in subsection (2) of that section).

(3) Where an application is made to a rent assessment committee under subsection (1) above with respect to the rent under an assured shorthold tenancy, the committee shall not make such a determination as is referred to in that subsection unless they consider—

(a)   that there is a sufficient number of similar dwelling-houses in the locality let on assured tenancies (whether shorthold or not); and

(b)   that the rent payable under the assured shorthold tenancy in question is significantly higher than the rent which the landlord might reasonably be expected to be able to obtain under the tenancy, having regard to the level of rents payable under the tenancies referred to in paragraph (a) above.

(4) Where, on application under this section, a rent assessment committee make a determination of a rent for an assured shorthold tenancy—

(a)   the determination shall have effect from such date as the committee may direct, not being earlier than the date of the application;

(b)   if, at any time on or after the determination takes effect, the rent which, apart from this paragraph, would be payable under the tenancy exceeds the rent so determined, the excess shall be irrecoverable from the tenant; and

(c)   no notice may be served under section 13(2) above with respect of a tenancy of the dwelling-house in question until after the first anniversary of the date on which the determination takes effect.

(5) Subsections (4), (5) and (8) of section 14 above apply in relation to a determination of rent under this section as they apply in relation to a determination under that section and, accordingly, where subsection (5) of that section applies, any reference in subsection (4)(b) above to rent is a reference to rent exclusive of the amount attributable to rates.

Notes

(i)   The effect of section 22(2)(a) is that only *one* reference may be made under this section.

(ii)   The prescribed form is to be found in the Assured Tenancies and Agricultural Occupancies (Forms) Regulations 1988,[15] Form 8.

(iii)   The rent assessment committee has *no* jurisdiction unless the condition in section 22(3)(a) is satisfied—proof of which could well be difficult.

---

[15] S.I. 1988 No. 2203.

(iv) The basic principle is still one of *market rent*; it is only rent "significantly higher" than that which may be cut back.[16]

(v) Section 23 (referred to in section 22(1)) states:

23.—(1) If the Secretary of State by order made by statutory instrument so provides, section 22 above shall not apply in such cases or to tenancies of dwelling-houses in such areas or in such other circumstances as may be specified in the order.

(2) An order under this section may contain such transitional, incidental and supplementary provisions as appear to the Secretary of State to be desirable.

(3) No order shall be made under this section unless a draft of the order has been laid before, and approved by a resolution of, each House of Parliament.

This power has not, to date, been exercised.

(3) Housing Association Tenancies

As noted above,[17] tenancies granted by housing associations on or after January 15, 1989 fall into the category of assured tenancies. Since most housing associations were created to provide low-cost housing, it might be thought that they would not be seeking to achieve "market rents" in the same way that private landlords might. For this reason, representatives of the housing association movement lobbied hard, during the passage of the Housing Act 1988 through Parliament, that there should be a separate regime for housing association rents. This argument was rejected by the Government.

The position in relation to tenancies granted since January 15, 1989 is that rents will be determined in the same way as other private sector tenancies. Nevertheless, the Housing Corporation has produced a "Tenants' Guarantee." This is guidance on the management by housing associations of housing accommodation let on assured tenancies, issued under section 36A of the Housing Associations Act 1985, (supplied by section 49 of the Housing Act 1988) and approved by the Secretary of State for the Environment. In relation to rent levels, the Guidance states:

D Principles upon which Rent (and other Charges) for Assured Tenancies are to be determined

D1 For tenants of registered housing associations whose tenancy commenced before January 15, 1989 rents will continue to be registered Fair Rents. That will also apply to such tenants who, after that date, are granted the tenancy of other accommodation belonging to the same

---

[16] s.22(3)(b).
[17] p. 90.

housing association; or exchange tenancies by mutual agreement with another secure tenant. This Guidance applies to other new tenancies, which are assured tenancies.

D2   Where housing association accommodation has been provided with the help of public subsidy, (including accommodation originally provided by public bodies and subsequently transferred to housing associations, for example by a local authority, a New Town or a Housing Action Trust), it is intended to be accessible to people on low incomes, whether or not they are in paid employment or in receipt of housing benefit. Associations are therefore expected to set and maintain their rents at levels which are within the reach of those in low paid employment. This will usually entail setting rents below market level. Associations should not discriminate in their rent setting between those who are eligible for housing benefits and others.

D3   In addition associations are expected to take account of the need to cover the costs (after subsidy) of loan charges and of management and maintenance, including the requirement to make prudent provision for future repairs; and, in setting the rent for each dwelling, its size, amenities, location and condition.

D4   Associations should inform their tenants of their right to refer any proposed increases, other than those within the terms set out in the tenancy agreement, to the Rent Assessment Committee which will fix a market rent for the accommodation, above which the association should not increase the rent for 12 months.

D5   Where associations require tenants to pay variable service charges they should provide those tenants with written information explaining their rights under the Landlord and Tenant Act 1985.

The extent to which particular housing associations will be able to follow this advice will clearly depend on the financial state of the particular housing association, and the level of subsidy it receives by way of housing association grant.

(C) REGULATION OF RENTS OF PROTECTED TENANCIES

(1) Definition of "Fair Rent"

The system of rent regulation, which applies to *protected tenancies* under the Rent Act 1977, was introduced in 1965, when the Rent Act of that year created the concept of the "fair rent."[18] The statutory definition of "fair rent" is now to be found in section 70 of the Rent Act 1977 (as amended by the Housing Act 1980, and the Housing and Planning Act 1986):

70.—(1) In determining, for the purposes of this Part of this Act, what rent is or would be a fair rent under a regulated tenancy of a dwelling-house, regard shall be had to all the circumstances (other than personal circumstances) and in particular to—

(a)   the age, character, locality and state of repair of the dwelling-house,

[18] See Crossman, *The Diaries of a Cabinet Minister* (1975), vol. I pp. 77–78.

(b) if any furniture is provided for use under the tenancy, the quantity, quality and condition of the furniture; and

(c) any premium, or sum in the nature of a premium, which has been or may be lawfully required or received on the grant, renewal, continuance or assignment of the tenancy.

(2) For the purposes of the determination it shall be assumed that the number of persons seeking to become tenants of similar dwelling-houses in the locality on the terms (other than those relating to rent) of the regulated tenancy is not substantially greater than the number of such dwelling-houses in the locality which are available for letting on such terms.

(3) There shall be disregarded—

(a) any disrepair or other defect attributable to a failure by the tenant under the regulated tenancy or any predecessor in title of his to comply with any terms thereof;

(b) any improvement carried out, otherwise than in pursuance of the terms of the tenancy, by the tenant under the regulated tenancy or any predecessor in title of his;

(c) [...]

(d) [...]

(e) if any furniture is provided for use under the regulated tenancy, any improvement to the furniture by the tenant under the regulated tenancy or any predecessor in title of his or, as the case may be, any deterioration in the condition of the furniture due to any ill-treatment by the tenant, any person residing or lodging with him, or any sub-tenant of his.

(4) In this section "improvement" includes the replacement of any fixture or fitting.

(4A) In this section "premium" has the same meaning as in Part IX of this Act, and "sum in the nature of a premium" means—

(a) any such loan as is mentioned in section 119 or 120 of this Act,

(b) any such excess over the reasonable price of furniture as is mentioned in Section 123 of this Act, and

(c) any such advance payment of rent as is mentioned in section 126 of this Act.

Notes

(i) Despite the breadth of the phrase, "all the circumstances," Lord Widgery L.J. has said that this must refer only to *relevant* circumstances[19] and that "one must have regard to the sort of factors which tend to push rents up or down in the market."[20] Personal circumstances (such as the age, sex, race, wealth) of a tenant or landlord are, by definition, excluded.

---

[19] See *Palmer* v. *Peabody Trust* [1975] Q.B. 604 at 608.
[20] *Metropolitan Property Holdings* v. *Finegold* [1975] 1 W.L.R. 349 at 351.

(ii) Particular circumstances which may be relevant (in addition to those mentioned in section 70(1)(a)), are the *terms* of any lease or tenancy agreement; and the quality and quantity of *services* provided by the landlord. The exact impact of these on the assessment of a fair rent will depend on the distribution of any benefit and burden as between landlord and tenant. The courts have been less clear on the extent to which *inflation*, and especially future inflation, should be taken into account.[21]

(iii)   In assessing fair rents, the report of the Francis Committee on the operation of the Rent Acts[22] looked in detail at the operation of section 70. It noted that the process of determining a fair rent usually involved three elements:

—   looking at comparables;
—   looking at recently registered market rents in respect of which there was no scarcity;
—   calculating what would be a reasonable rent on the basis of various conventional criteria.

In the absence of any absurd result, the courts have tended to leave this to the experience of the rent officers. Thus in *Mason* v. *Skilling*[23] (an appeal from Scotland) Lord Reid said:

In my view, this section leaves it open to the rent officer or committee to adopt any method or methods of ascertaining a fair rent provided that they do not use any method which is unlawful or unreasonable. The most obvious and direct method is to have regard to registered rents of comparable houses in the area. In the initial stages this method may not be available but as the number of comparable registered rents increases the more likely it will be that it will lead to a correct result. Of course it must be open to either party to show that those comparable rents have been determined on a wrong basis but until that is shown it must be assumed that rents already determined have been rightly ascertained.
    In the present case the committee did consider comparable rents and it is not said that they acted wrongly in this respect. Criticism is limited to the manner in which they dealt with the capital value of the house.
    The committee were quite entitled and may well have been well advised to use other methods in addition to considering comparable rents. In particular they were entitled to have regard to the capital value. A fair rent should be fair to the landlord as well as fair to the tenant and it can be regarded as fair to the landlord that he should receive a fair return on his capital. We are not concerned in this case with the percentage which in present circumstances can be regarded as a fair return.
    It is notorious that in existing circumstances the price which a house will fetch in the market is much higher if the buyer can get possession immediately, than if there is a sitting tenant with a statutory right to remain in possession. Admittedly the committee had regard to the capital value with vacant possession

---

[21] *Metropolitan Properties Co. (F.G.C.)* v. *Lannon* [1968] 1 W.L.R. 815 at 838 (Widgery J.); on appeal
    [1969] 1 Q.B. 577; *cf. Metropolitan Property Holdings* v. *Laufer* (1975) 29 P. & C.R. 172.
[22] (1971) Cmnd 4609.
[23] [1974] 1 W.L.R. 1437, at 1439

but the respondent argues that the only relevant capital value is the price which the appellants could get for the house today; as the respondent is a sitting tenant that would be much lower than if the appellants could give vacant possession. Their argument was accepted by the Second Division ...

It is quite true that the fact that there is a sitting tenant is a "circumstance" but in my opinion it is excluded by the Act. Section [70] (1) directs that regard shall be had to "all the circumstances (other than personal circumstances)." In my view the tenant's right to remain in possession is a personal circumstance. A right to possess a house (or anything else) appears to me to pertain to the person who has the right, whether the right is statutory or contractual. The house itself remains the same whoever is entitled to possess it. Moreover, under the Act the tenant's right to possess lasts so long, but only so long, as he complies with certain obligations. I am confirmed in this view by the fact that all the circumstances specified at the end of the subsection relate entirely to the house itself.

If this were not so it would lead to strange results. Suppose two identical adjacent houses one of which is vacant and the other occupied by a tenant with a regulated tenancy. If the respondent's argument is right then the fair rents would be different. No reasons have been suggested why two such houses should have different fair rents. Moreover, the Act appears to aim at uniformity but if the respondent is right there would be no uniformity and it would be difficult to find comparable cases. Of two similar houses one might be occupied by a tenant in the prime of life who has a wife and family who could succeed him in the event of his death. Then the selling price of the house would be low; it would be improbable that the purchaser could obtain vacant possession for a very long time to come. But the other house might be occupied by an aged, infirm tenant with no wife or family, or a tenant who was likely soon to leave. Then the selling price would be higher because the purchaser was likely to be able to get vacant possession quite soon. I find it impossible to believe that the statute contemplates different fair rents in these two cases ...

Lord Morris of Borth-y-Gest commented:

[It] would not be appropriate to restrict a committee in its consideration of any relevant evidence that might be put before them provided it is evidence which, when considered in the light of the statutory directions, may be of help in assessing a figure of fair rent.[24]

Lord Kilbrandon implied that courts should not be too anxious to interfere:

The fixing of a fair rent calls for a skilled estimate of a hypothetical figure, namely, the rent which a landlord could demand and a tenant would be prepared to pay if the market were roughly in a state of equilibrium ... [We] have here a valuation problem rather than a legal question of law ... [25]

Lords Diplock and Cross of Chelsea agreed.

The emphasis on registered comparables was given further support in *Western Heritable Investment Co. Ltd.* v. *Husband*[26]; and *London Rent Assessment Committee* v. *St. George's Court Ltd.*[27]

---

[24] At p. 1442.   [25] At p. 1443.   [26] [1983] 2 A.C. 849.
[27] (1984) 16 H.L.R. 15. For criticisms of the use of comparables as "economic incest," see Pennance, *Verdict on Rent Control* (1972), p. xv.

(iv)   The Francis Committee did also note, however, that evidence of scarcity was only rarely submitted by either landlords or tenants to rent officers and rent assessment committees. This seems odd since the object of section 70(2) was to try to ensure that tenants paid a rent that was fair, given the quality and location of the accommodation, but excluding that element of the rent that might be attributable to scarcity of accommodation pushing the price up. Instead, those whose task it was to fix fair rents had to rely on their own knowledge of the locality to determine the amount of the contracted rent that should be attributable to scarcity.

In *Crofton Investment Trust* v. *Greater London Rent Assessment Committee*[27a] Lord Parker C.J., commenting on a complaint that the rent assessment committee had no actual evidence of scarcity put before it, said:

I am quite satisfied that this committee, that is to say, a committee of this kind under a procedure which is clearly to be intended to be informal and not to be carried through with the precision of a court of justice, is fully entitled to act, as it has been said, on their own impression and on their own knowledge. It is idle in my view to think of gentlemen manning this committee and sitting maybe day after day without acquiring experience and knowledge of conditions in the locality, and to say that they should shut their eyes to what they know of their own knowledge, and act only on such evidence as may or may not be put before them, seems to me to reduce the matter to absurdity.

In *Metropolitan Properties Co. (F.G.C.) Ltd.* v. *Lannon*[27b] the Court of Appeal upheld Lord Parker's basic principle, though Lord Denning did remark that if a committee is given evidence on a particular point, their freedom to act on their own knowledge "does not mean that they should throw over the evidence altogether. At any rate, they should not throw over the evidence without saying why. That is what troubles me most about their written decision. They threw over the figure of the rent officer (himself an expert), the figures of the experts on each side, and the figure of the tenant himself. They fixed a much lower figure— without a word to say why they did it."

Anglo-Italian Properties v. *London Rent Panel* [1969] 1 W.L.R. 731

Lord Parker C.J. said (at 732–733):

The flat is an old-fashioned house in a terrace which was acquired by the landlords, the appellants, in 1962 and converted into four flats, and this basement flat has the added attraction of a garden. The landlords let it to a Miss

[27a] [1967] 2 Q.B. 955, at 967.
[27b] [1969] 1 Q.B. 577 at 597.

Cassidy, who applied then to the rent officer to determine and register the fair rent; the rent she was being charged was £600 per annum exclusive. The rent officer went into the matter, and in due course determined a fair rent of £335; whereupon the landlords objected and the matter was referred to the rent assessment committee.

The committee's reasons for determining the fair rent at £400 are contained succinctly in one paragraph of their decision and reasons, that is:

"We accepted Mr. Tuckerman's valuation [for the landlords] of the purchase price in 1962 plus the cost of conversion, namely, £13,863; we considered that a fair yield would be 10 per cent. of this capital and that a fair apportionment of this capital cost to the subject flat would be one-quarter. Thus we reached the figure of, say, £348 per annum as a basis for assessment of a fair rent for that flat. We did not dissent from the landlords' estimate of the average annual cost of repairs, namely, £250, and apportioning this to the subject flat in the same proportion as for the capital, we arrived at a total of £410."

The committee then went on:

"But at the time of the purchase and conversion of the property, a developer would have obtained higher rents than those obtainable since the coming into effect of the Act of 1965, which excluded 'scarcity value' from the assessment of fair rents. We put the 'scarcity value' of the subject property at about 10 per cent. We therefore considered that a fair rent for the flat under reference would be £369 subject to some addition in respect of the tenant having the use and benefit of the landlords' furniture and effects. We did not agree the landlords' valuation of these items; we thought that a fair annual charge for them would be £31. Accordingly, we concluded that a fair rent within the meaning and for the purposes of section 46 of the 1968 Act would be £400 per annum."

That is, adding the £31 to the figure of £369.

The point which is taken by Mr. Wellings in this appeal is a very short one; the landlords do not quarrel with the calculation that the committee have done to arrive at £410 per annum. What he does say is that on this method of calculation there really is no room for any deduction in respect of scarcity value; accordingly he says that the true rent on this method of calculation would be the £410 plus the £31 for the use of the landlords' effects, in other words, £441.

I confess that for my part I can see no answer to Mr. Wellings' contention. As I understand the calculation, a rent of £348 is first arrived at as a fair rent as at 1962 being 10 per cent of the capital cost in 1962. That being so, I cannot see that there is any room for deducting anything for scarcity. Of course, the committee might have said: "true that capital cost in 1962 represents, let us say, £18,000—because there is evidence of that—in 1968," and then it would be right to deduct something for scarcity value, as compared with the position in 1962. Looking at it in that way, I can see no room for any deduction for scarcity value.

Having said that, however, I would for myself, and I do not claim to be an expert, voice the view that this is a quite novel method of valuation which the landlords put forward and the committee adopted. It is certainly one that I have never seen before. It is not arrived at on comparables, it is not based on square footage, it is certainly not based on the contractors' theory. But it is based on original cost, taking a percentage thereof as the fair rent. It may be, because there is no fixed yardstick by which a fair rent is to be arrived at, that this is a permissible method and that a just conclusion can thereby be arrived at. I only mention this because in my experience this method is a novel one. Bearing all these matters in mind I think that the proper course here is to allow this appeal, and send the case back to the committee with the opinion of this court. That would enable them to adhere, if they desire, to this method of calculation, but not eliminate scarcity value or to take into consideration any other method of calculation they desire.

Tormes Property Co. Ltd. v. *Landau* [1971] 1 Q.B. 261

Lord Parker C.J. said (at 264–266):

The appellants in this case are a property company of which Mr. Rambridge is director and main shareholder. The company in 1963 purchased premises known as 24, Belitha Villas, N.1, and in 1967 Mr. Rambridge acquired control of the company. In 1967 and 1968 improvements were effected and the premises were converted into flats ... By October 1969 the appellants were desirous of letting flat no. 3 in these premises and on October 6, 1969, they made an application, as they were entitled to do, under section 45 of the Rent Act, 1968, asking for a certificate of fair rent in the sum of £565 on the basis of a seven-year lease, the tenant doing internal repairs and the appellants the rest. The only services to be supplied were those of lighting and cleaning the common parts of the premises at a charge of £8 per annum.

The matter was considered on November 1, 1969, by the rent officer, who, after going into the matter in great detail by reference to a number of alleged "comparables," arrived at a figure of £330 per annum as the fair rent. The appellants were not satisfied with that. They appealed, as they were entitled to do, to a rent assessment committee, who heard the appeal on February 17, 1970, and certified £360 per annum, to include the £8 for heating and cleaning, as the fair rent on the terms suggested. The appellants now appeal to this court on what has to be a point of law.

I do not propose to go through the matter in great detail, but what the appellants did at the hearing through Mr. Rambridge was to put forward a valuation on the basis of a reasonable return to the landlords. It has been said many times that the "contractor's theory" based on building costs can do no more than set a ceiling when one is considering old premises. Equally, an adaptation of the contractor's theory to cover historic costs is something which may lead to very odd results according to the time when the costs were incurred, and, indeed, it may well be that a fair rent will show a landlord a loss on historic costs. What the appellants did was to prefer yet another adaptation, as it were, of the contractor's theory by starting with an estimate of replacement costs, allowing what was thought to be a reasonable interest on that cost and then adding management expenses, to use a general term, and something in respect of equipment provided ...

In my judgment, the committee were perfectly entitled to do what they did. Without criticising the yardstick put forward by the landlords, it seems to me that the committee were perfectly entitled to reject it and to apply another, and, for my part, I cannot believe that, when one is approaching residential premises for which there are any number of comparables, as is the case here, much weight can properly be given to any version of the contractor's theory. As I have said, the true contractor's theory can only produce a ceiling. The adaptation based on historic costs may produce false results, and the present suggested adaptation based on replacement cost is an attempt to achieve indirectly something which can be achieved directly from market-rent comparables or in the fair rents of comparables which have been fixed. I myself think that there are great dangers in approaching the matter in the way in which the landlords approached it in the present case where, as here, undoubtedly there are comparable market rents and comparable fair rents. Accordingly, I do not think that the committee can be criticised for just saying that they were not going to go into this method of approach advanced by the landlords ...

Could it be argued that permitting rent officers or rent assessment committees to use their own expertise, without revealing their thinking to the parties, amounts to a breach of the rules of natural justice?

(v) The word "locality" appears in both section 70 subsections (1) and (2). The interaction of these subsections has been considered by the courts.

Metropolitan Property Holdings v. *Finegold* [1975] 1 W.L.R. 349

Lord Widgery C.J. said (at 350–353):

This is an appeal affecting a large number of flats belonging to the appellants in a block known as South Lodge in St. John's Wood. [There] was recently built in St. John's Wood a substantial school restricted in its entry to the children of American families in London. The result of that school being built has undoubtedly rendered this part of St. John's Wood far more attractive to American families than it might otherwise have been because of the facility for the education of their children which this school provides. Although there is no specific finding to this effect on the part of the committee, it is a reasonable inference, I think, from the material which has been put before us that the presence of this school has almost certainly put up the market rental values of flats and houses in the neighbourhood. And it may be, although again there is no specific finding to this effect, that this has produced locally an element of scarcity in the sense that more Americans want to come and live in St. John's Wood and have the facility of having their children educated at that school than the accommodation vacant and to let in St. John's Wood would permit. I think it only right to approach the problem on the footing that both those assumptions are good, namely, that the school in its own immediate surroundings has produced an increase in the number of Americans and, secondly, it may well have produced an element of scarcity, or accentuated an element of scarcity which previously existed ...

[Looking] for the moment only at sub-section (1), any amenity (as the word has been used frequently in this argument), any advantage which the premises inherently have, either in their construction, their nature, their scale, their situation, their proximity to a school, a zoo or a theatre, whatever it may be, all those factors which would tend in the market to increase the rental, are factors to be taken into account by the committee in fixing the fair rent. To what extent they are taken into account is, of course, the duty of the committee to decide, but that these are matters which are eligible for consideration is beyond doubt. At this point, as I have already said, the presence of the American school would, on the face of it, tend to put up the fair rent because it would be an amenity making the premises more attractive.

Then one comes to section [70] (2) ... This is the provision which is intended to eliminate what is popularly called "scarcity value" from the fair rent fixed by the committee, and it is a provision which has given rise to a great deal of difficulty in practice ... It seems to me that what Parliament is saying is this: if the house has inherent amenities and advantages, by all means let them be reflected in the rent under section [70] (1); but if the market rent would be influenced simply by the fact that in the locality there is a shortage, and in the locality rents are being forced up beyond the market figure, then that element of market rent must not be included when the fair rent is being considered. Parliament, I am sure, is not seeking to deprive the landlord of a proper return on the inherent value and quality of his investment in the house, but Parliament is undoubtedly seeking to deprive a landlord of a wholly unmeritorious increase in rent which has come about simply because there is a scarcity of houses in the district and thus an excess of demand over supply.

The committee have come to the conclusion and expressed it in more than one way that the presence of the American school has created a local scarcity of premises. When I say "local," I deliberately do not attempt at this stage to define it further. But what was in the committee's mind undoubtedly was that the attraction of the school has produced a local scarcity of houses, and that there is consequently in the premises now under review all the elements contained in section [70] (2) of a scarcity which ought to be eliminated when the fair rent is assessed ... I do not think that Parliament was concerned with this kind of local scarcity when section [70] was passed. If one looked for the unearned, unmeritorious increase in rent which might accrue to landlords if section [70] (2) had never been passed, one must, I think, take a very much wider sweep than the sort of area to which the committee seems to have applied its mind in this case. Of course if you look at half a dozen streets round the American school, you may well find a scarcity. As you go out to a greater radius round the school, then the effect of the school is less and less. But, as I emphasised, we are not looking at the effect of the school as such; we are looking for scarcity in the locality which results from an excess of demand over supply.

It seems to me, with all deference to the committee, that they have somewhat lost sight of the fact that the sort of scarcity we are concerned with is a broad, overall, general scarcity affecting a really substantial area, and they wrongly focussed their attention on the extremely limited area which would not, I think, qualify as a "locality" for the purposes of section [70] (2) of the [1977] Act.

Mais and Croom-Johnson JJ. agreed. The case was referred back to the Committee.[28]

---

[28] *Cf. Palmer* v. *Peabody Trust* [1975] Q.B. 604, in which Lord Widgery C.J. emphasised that, in the normal case, it was for the rent assessment committee to determine the extent of a "locality."

(2) Getting a Fair Rent Registered

(i) The Rent Officer

The country has been divided into registration areas[29]; rent officers have been appointed to each area.[30] They have the responsibility for maintaining a register of fair rents for each area; this is a public document, available for inspection.[31] Applications for the registration of a fair rent may be made in prescribed form by the landlord, or the tenant, or both together.[32] Areas may be amalgamated[33] by the Secretary of State approving a scheme to this effect. Applications may either be for first-time registration; or for re-registration as specified in section 67(3) and (4), and as amended by section 60(1) of the Housing Act 1980.

(3) Subject to subsection (4) below, where a rent for a dwelling-house has been registered under this Part of this Act, no application by the tenant alone or by the landlord alone for the registration of a different rent for that dwelling-house shall be entertained before the expiry of two years from the relevant date (as defined in subsection (5) below) except on the ground that, since that date, there has been such a change in—

(a) the conditions of the dwelling-house (including the making of any improvement therein);

(b) the terms of the tenancy;

(c) the quantity, quality or condition of any furniture provided for use under the tenancy (deterioration by fair wear and tear excluded), or

(d) any other circumstances taken into consideration when the rent was registered or confirmed,

as to make the registered rent no longer a fair rent.

(4) Notwithstanding anything in subsection (3) above, an application such as is mentioned in that subsection which is made by the landlord alone and is so made within the last three months of the period of two years referred to in that subsection may be entertained notwithstanding that that period has not expired.

The "relevant date" is usually the date of registration of the last registered rent by the rent officer.[34].

---

[29] Rent Act 1977 s.62.
[30] s.63.
[31] s.66.
[32] s.67.
[33] s.64A.
[34] s.67(5) and (5A), as amended by Housing Act 1980, s.61(5).

Notes

(i)   Where there are joint tenants or landlords, an application in the name of one of them will suffice if clearly made on behalf of all.[35]

(ii)   The applications must be in prescribed form; model forms for applications and other matters are prescribed in the Rent Regulation (Forms, etc.) Regulations 1980.[36] Attempts have been made to make these forms more comprehensible to the general public; it is worth studying them and asking whether this objective has been satisfied. One question that has to be completed by the applicant relates to the proposed rent for the property; failure to complete this renders the application invalid.[37]

(iii)   Once a valid application has been submitted the rent officer takes the following steps[38]:

— he may and usually does request further information;
— he notifies the other party;
— if there are no representations from either party, he makes such inquiries as he thinks necessary and registers as a fair rent the rent mentioned in the application;
— if he disagrees with the rent mentioned, or if there are representations, he must hold a "consultation."

In *R.* v. *Brighton Rent Officers ex p. Elliott*[39] Lord Widgery C.J. said:

... [T]he rent officer, having received an application to fix a fair rent of the relevant properties, sent out a notice under paragraph 4(2) of Part I of Schedule [11] calling the parties for a consultation. He made it clear that in his determination of a fair rent in this case he would be guided by other comparable rents which had already been determined or approved by the rent assessment committee ...
This produced a complaint from the present applicant on this basis: that it was unfair for him to be required to attend the consultation mentioned in paragraph 4(2) of Schedule [11] without first being told what comparable properties the rent officer had in mind to rely on. His argument ... is that the consultation was the one and only opportunity which the landlord would have of seeking to influence the mind of the rent officer and that he could only effectively seek to influence the mind of the rent officer if he knew what was in the rent officer's mind, and particularly what comparable properties the rent officer was minded to rely on. The crunch, if one may use the word, comes at this point: that the rent officer is saying: "No, I am not going to disclose in advance what

---

[35] *R.* v. *Rent Officer for London Borough of Camden, ex p. Felix* (1989) 21 H.L.R. 34.
[36] S.I. 1980 No. 1697.
[37] *Chapman* v. *Earl* [1968] 1 W.L.R. 1315; *cf. R.* v. *London Rent Assessment Panel, ex p. Braq Investments* [1969] 1 W.L.R. 970 where it was held that this requirement was satisfied if words are used from which the rent can be calculated with certainty. See s.67(2)(a) (as amended). Similarly payments for services must be stated (ibid. s.67(2)(b)).
[38] Rent Act 1977, Sched. 11, paras. 1–6 now subject to further detailed amendment, Housing Act 1980, Sched. 6.
[39] (1975) 29 P. & C.R. 456 at 459–460.

comparable properties I may find of value and influence" and the applicant, through Mr. Galpin, is saying: "You are denying me natural justice if you do not give me this information before the consultation takes place so that I can consider it and, if necessary, comment on it." That is the short point.

The conception of a consultation is in my experience novel and I cannot think of another instance in which this kind of step is included in this kind of procedure. In many other instances, such as that of the valuation officer rating, no such step is provided by the legislation and the officer makes his determination and leaves the dissatisfied party to appeal.

Here, the step of consultation is brought in, and I think that it may have a number of purposes. One surely possible purpose is that it provides an opportunity for the parties to sit round the table with the rent officer and have an opportunity for a settlement of the matter by agreement. True, the rent officer's authority does not extend to requiring a settlement, but one can see that a potentially hard-fought case might in the course of the consultation lose much of its sting if the consultation was operated skilfully by the rent officer.

In any case, however, I think that a function, and a very important function, of the consultation must be to enable the rent officer to approach the problem of decision with the knowledge that he has heard what the parties want to say about this particular instant case. I do not take the view that the rent officer is expected to decide the matter in the course of the consultation, still less that he comes to the consultation with any sort of preconceived idea of what the rent ought to be. I think that an important function, as I have said, of the consultation is to enable the rent officer to pick up the atmosphere of the matter, make contact with the parties, listen to their observations and thus, one hopes, come to a conclusion which reflects what the parties have to say. I feel quite confident that there is no kind of obligation on the rent officer to determine what comparable properties he will rely on before he comes to the consultation. Indeed, I would have thought that it would be entirely wrong for him to do so because in this type of case, once the comparables are settled, the answer very often is only a matter of mathematics and if the rent officer came to the consultation with a firm decision in his mind to rely on certain particular comparables I think that he would be wrong.

It seems to me that the principal suggestion that he must disclose his comparables at or before the consultation is totally misconceived and quite inconsistent with the whole purpose of those provisions.

— the rent officer registers a fair rent, at the same time informing the parties of their right to lodge an objection which will be referred to a rent assessment committee. Such objection should be made within 28 days though the period is extendable.[40]

(iv) The courts have been called upon to consider applications for re-registering on the ground of change of circumstances within the two year period.

London Housing and Commercial Properties Ltd. v. *Cowan*
[1977] Q.B. 148

Lord Widgery C.J. said (at 151–153):

On January 16, 1973 application had been made to the rent officer to fix a fair rent in respect of this flat. He had fixed a rent of £295 per annum, which

---

[40] Rent Act 1977, Sched. 11, para. 6.

included £28 for services. The effective date for that determination ... was February 28, 1973.

Shortly afterwards, the landlords took out a somewhat unreliable gas boiler from the flat and substituted a modern electric boiler. It cost them £220 to do it, and, having done it, they approached the rent officer with a view of getting an increase in rent on account of this improvement ...

It seems to me, and I have no doubt about this, that the proper approach to section [67](3) is to ask whether there have been changes in the condition of the house or in the other factors specifically referred to in the section, and, if there have been, to ask the second question, which is whether as a result of those changes the registered rent is no longer a fair rent. In other words, there must be changes of a statutory kind before any question of review arises at all. It must be shown that those changes have given rise to a situation in which the rent is no longer a fair rent. Then the door is open for the normal procedure to be followed and for an application to be made to the rent officer ...

Given the circumstances to which I have already referred, there is jurisdiction for the rent officer to come in and reassess a fair rent for the house or flat, and two alternative obligations have been canvassed in argument in that situation. On the one hand, it is said that when he comes to assess the new fair rent he must not increase the existing registered rent except to the extent that an increase is warranted by the conditions which gave rise to the review. In other words, it is said that the rent officer coming in within the three year period, or as it has been put in argument in mid-term, to assess a new rent must confine any increases in rental to those which follow from the alteration in the condition of the house which itself gave rise to his right to come in mid-term.

For my part, I am quite satisified that that is not the right answer. It seems to me perfectly clear that when the rent officer comes in to make an assessment of the fair rent he does so under section [70] ... and under no limitation beyond the limitations contained in that section. I think it would have a very strange result if that were not so. It would mean that a further application in regard to the increase of the rent might be postponed for a new period of three [now two] years, and furthermore that might be done on a basis which resulted in only the smallest adjustments in the rent itself ...

[Counsel for the tenant] pleads that this attitude will be unfair to a tenant in conditions of inflation. He says, and he is absolutely right about this, that if an assessment is made mid-term it means that the tenant has to face a higher rent somewhat earlier in time than would otherwise be the case.

This is perfectly true, but again it must be remembered that, in my view, that all that is happening when a reassessment in mid-term is made is that the tenant in question is having his rent brought up to a fair rent somewhat earlier than he would otherwise have done. The three year limitation generally applied is not in my view intended to give the tenant a right to live on less that a fair rent for the better part of three years; its purpose is to supply an administrative limit within which in normal circumstances an application for a rent review cannot be made. But if under section [67](3) a review in mid-term is permissible, then although it does in fact mean that the tenant is out of pocket to some degree compared with what would otherwise happen, it does not to my mind produce the kind of injustice which would make me wonder whether my construction of the section was the right one.

The interaction of section 67(3) and section 44(1) was considered more recently by the Court of Appeal:

Rakhit v. *Carty* [1990] 2 Q.B. 315

Russell L.J. said (at 322–327):

No. 24 Burnham Court, Brent Street, London N.W.4, is a third-floor flat. On September 30, 1986 the plaintiff, Mr. Sunil Rakhit (the landlord), granted a lease of the flat to four tenants for a period of one year at a rent of £433.33 per calendar month. At the time of the letting the flat had been substantially furnished by the landlord. On December 10, 1986 the plaintiff, Mrs. Carty (the tenant), joined the other tenants in occupation of the flat and on October 1, 1987 she entered into a tenancy agreement with the landlord for a term of 364 days from October 1, 1987 at the rent of £450 per month. Unknown to any of the parties to these tenancy agreements a rent officer had, much earlier, determined a fair rent for the flat effective from November 19, 1973 of £550 per annum, that rent being registered in the rent register for the London borough of Barnet on March 12, 1974. At that date the flat was unfurnished and was so recorded in the rent register. The landlord had no interest in the premises at that time.

The tenant's came to an end by effluxion of time, but she remained in occupation as a statutory tenant entitled to the protection of the Rent Act 1977. However, within a matter of days, on October 9, 1988, the landlord commenced proceedings in the Willesden County Court seeking possession of the flat ...

At the end of the hearing, possession was granted. However another important issue was raised.

I turn to those submissions of counsel that occupied the court for most of this hearing. The landlord claimed arrears of rent and the judge awarded him £2,710.58 together with mesne profits of £380 per month until possession. The arrears were based on the rent payable under the tenancy agreement of October 1, 1987 up to December 8, 1988 when, on an application lodged by the tenant, the rent officer had determined and registered a fair rent of £380 per month. The entry in the register on December 9, 1988 recorded the flat as furnished.

The submission made to the judge and repeated before this court can be shortly stated. Counsel for the tenant contends that the rent registration on March 12, 1974 limited the rent payable by the tenant under the agreement dated October 1, 1987 and that, far from there being arrears of rental, the tenant had overpaid £3,069.82 from October 1, 1987 to the date of the hearing. There was a counterclaim in respect of overpaid rent.

The judge rejected this submission, regarding himself as bound by *Kent* v. *Millmead Properties Ltd.* (1982) 44 P. & C.R. 353 and *Cheniston Investments Ltd.* v. *Waddock* [1988] 2 E.G.L.R. 136. The landlord's claim for arrears and mesne profits was therefore upheld, and the tenant's counterclaim dismissed.

It is now convenient to look at the relevant statutory provisions which bear on this appeal. The starting point is section 44(1) of the Rent Act 1977, which provides:

"Where a rent for a dwelling-house is registered under Part IV of this Act, the rent recoverable for any contractual period of a regulated tenancy of the dwelling-house shall be limited to the rent so registered."

Part IV of the Act contains detailed provisions relating to the registration of rents under regulated tenancies. Section 67 deals with the machinery for making an application for the registration of a rent. Section 70 is concerned with the circumstances to which regard must be paid by the rent officer in fixing a fair rent under a regulated tenancy. Both the application for registration and the assessment must deal with details of any furniture provided for use under the tenancy. ...

Russell L.J. set out the terms of section 66(1) and (2) and section 72(1) and (5) (as amended) and referred to section 73. He continued . . .

However, in the context of this appeal, section 67(3) (as amended by section 60(1) of the 1980 Act) is of greater importance. [See above p. 447]

Subsection (4) enables a landlord alone to make an application within the last three months of the period referred to in sub-section (3), and sub-section (5), for the purposes of this appeal, defines the relevant date as the date when the registration took effect, *i.e.* when entered in the register.

In my judgment, the scheme of Pts III and IV of the 1977 Acts is plain. Once a fair rent is registered, it remains the recoverable rent for the dwelling-house in respect of which the rent is payable until either the demised premises undergo such a change in their structure as to render them no longer the dwelling-house referred to in section 44 or there is a cancellation of the registration under section 73 or there is a new registration consequent on a fresh application pursuant to section 67(3) or section 68(4). This last subsection (which has since been repealed) is in similar terms to section 67(3) and deals with applications by a local authority.

Section 67(3) deals specifically with a change in the terms of the tenancy or in the quantity of any furniture provided as preconditions without which no application for registration of a different rent "for that dwelling-house shall be entertained." In other words, provided the dwelling-house remains as the same demised property, the provision of furniture as a term of the tenancy does not affect the recoverable rent until the registered rent is increased and that rent is registered. So much, to my mind, is clear from the terms of section 44(1), which does not refer to any change in the terms of the tenancy of the dwelling-house, but expressly provides that the rent recoverable "for any contractual period of a regulated tenancy of the dwelling-house shall be limited to the rent so registered."

The authority which led the judge to the conclusion at which he arrived in relation to rent and mesne profits was, as earlier indicated, *Kent* v. *Millmead Properties Ltd.* (1982) 44 P. & C.R. 353. I take the facts from the headnote. In all material respects they cannot be distinguished from the facts in the instant case. In 1974 a registration of a fair rent of a flat was determined as £5 a week. The register kept under the Rent Act showed that the tenancy was a weekly tenancy and that it was an unfurnished tenancy. In May 1977 the flat became vacant and was fully furnished, extensively redecorated and improved by the defendant landlords. It was let in August 1978 to the plaintiff tenants at a weekly rent of £28.50. In June 1980 a fair rent of £17.50 per week for the premises and £5 for furniture was registered. The tenants discovered that there was a registered rent of £5 per week for the premises. They withheld the excess rent. They brought proceedings in the county court claiming the excess rent paid by them. The landlords counterclaimed for arrears of rent on the ground that, as in March 1974, before the commencement of the Rent Act 1974, the premises were unfurnished, the rent then registered did not apply to the premises relet furnished and improved. The county court judge gave judgment for the landlords. The tenants appealed. Giving the leading judgment, Ormrod L.J. said (at 357):

> "One should start from this position that, anybody looking at the rent register in order to discover what the registered rent of these premises was, would see immediately that the registered rent of some £260 per annum was the rent registered in respect of an unfurnished tenancy and so it could not possibly be said that anyone inspecting the register, who was intending to take a furnished tenancy of this flat, could be misled in any way. Going back to the 1977 Act which, as I have said is the operative Act for our purposes, I

think section 44(1) must be read in the light of section 66(2) and that the reference to a 'rent of a dwelling-house registered under Part IV of this Act' means the rent for a dwelling-house registered under Part IV of this Act as set out in the register, that is for the premises, and for the type of tenancy described in the register for which the rent was fixed and not otherwise, so that, if there is a material change either in the specification of the dwelling-house, by either adding or subtracting a room or rooms, or a material change in the particulars with regard to the tenancy, then the rent registered in respect of a different tenancy, different in the sense of different in character and incidence, is not the registered rent for the purposes of section 44(1) and so does not operate to enable the tenants in this case to enjoy for the price of £5 a week the tenancy of a furnished flat for which, in 1980, the fair rent was considered to be £22.50."

Kent v. *Millmead Properties Ltd.* was followed in *Cheniston Investments* v. *Waddock* [1988] 2 E.G.L.R. 136 with obvious reluctance (see, in particular, the judgments of Lloyd and Ralph Gibson L.JJ. (at 141)). However, it was not argued in *Cheniston's* case that the *Kent* decision was per incuriam.

Counsel for the tenant has now submitted to this court that the *Kent* decision was indeed per incuriam, in that she submits that the judgment of Ormrod L.J., with which Dunn L.J. and Sir Sebag Shaw agreed, made no reference to section 67(3), that if the Court of Appeal had been referred to that subsection and had had regard to its terms the decision would plainly have been different and that, consequently, this court should not follow *Kent's* case. I have already expressed my own views as to the proper construction of section 44(1) and the impact of section 67(3).

In *Rickards* v. *Rickards* [1989] 3 W.L.R. 748 at 755 Lord Donaldson M.R. said:

"The importance of the rule of stare decisis in relation to the Court of Appeal's own decision can hardly be overstated. We now sometimes sit in eight divisions and, in the absence of such a rule, the law would quickly become wholly uncertain. However, the rule is not without exceptions, albeit very limited. These exceptions were considered in *Young* v. *Bristol Aeroplane Co. Ltd.* [1944] K.B. 718, *Morelle Ltd.* v. *Wakeling* [1955] 2 Q.B. 379 and, more recently, in *Williams* v. *Fawcett* [1986] Q.B. 604 at 615–616, where relevant extracts from the two earlier decisions are set out. These decisions show that this court is justified in refusing to follow one of its own previous decisions not only where that decision is given in ignorance or forgetfulness of some inconsistent statutory provision or some authority binding on it, but also, in rare and exceptional cases, if it is satisfied that the decision involved a manifest slip or error. In previous cases the judges of this court have always refrained from defining this exceptional category and I have no intention of departing from that approach save to echo the words of Lord Greene M.R. (in *Young's* case [1944] 1 K.B. 718 at 729) and Evershed M.R. (in *Morelle's* case [1955] 2 Q.B. 379 at 406) and to say that they will be of the rarest occurrence."

In my judgment, the effect of allowing this appeal will produce no injustice to the landlord, for the 1977 Act provided him and his advisers with ample opportunity to protect his interests by the simple process of inspecting the public register of rents before letting the flat to the tenant. A fresh application for registration of a fair rent could then have been made enabling that fair rent to be recoverable from the commencement of the tenant's tenancy.

For my part, I am satisfied that this court erred in *Kent* v. *Millmead Properties Ltd.* and that, following the observations of Lord Donaldson M.R. in *Rickard's* case, this court is justified in declining to follow *Kent* v. *Millmead Properties Ltd.*

Accordingly, I would allow the tenant's appeal and hold that the landlord's monetary claim should be dismissed and that judgment should be entered in favour of the tenant on the counterclaim.

Sir Roualeyn Cumming-Bruce and Lord Donaldson of Lymington M.R. agreed.

(ii) The Rent Assessment Committee

Rent assessment committees (RACs) follow broadly similar procedures in order to get what information they need, though they have to seek it on prescribed forms. Failure to provide such information is a criminal offence.[41] Further details are contained in regulations.[42] Thus they may decide cases by oral hearings or, if the parties agree, by written representations. The procedure of the RACs is relatively formal but less so than the court's. Majority decisions are permitted. A feature of their procedure is the visiting of the property for which a fair rent is to be determined. They have no legal power to enter premises, but tenants have not been known to refuse entry. Representation is allowed but legal aid cannot be obtained. In *Daejan Properties* v. *Chambers*[43] it was observed that the RAC was not entitled to reject a landlord's evidence, simply on the ground that they could not gain access to the dwelling in question.

RACs have power to confirm or vary the rent officer's decision.[44] If they decide to vary, their task is to determine the fair rent at the time they find the property.[45] Given the delays inherent in such proceedings this almost invariably means they raise the level decided by the rent officer. The decisions of RACs are now effective from the date of registration.[46]

The extent of the need for RACs to give reasons was discussed in *Metropolitan Property Holdings Ltd.* v. *Laufer*[47] where Lord Widgery C.J. remarked:

> So there is an obligation to state reasons, and it is necessary to say that this is a provision applicable to a wide range of tribunals, not merely the rent assessment committee, and it is, I think, obvious that the character of the reasons given, the nature of the reasons, the extent of the reasons, must in some measure be governed by the nature of the problem which the particular tribunal has been set to resolve ...
>
> [If], as so often happens in the typical simple case, the landlord's experts say that the rent should be X and the tenant's experts say that the rent should be X minus Y, if the committee thinks that neither figure is the right one not only can it choose a figure in between the two extremes but it should do so.
>
> Now, what reasons should the committee give in that situation? The answer is that in the simple typical case to which I have referred there are no reasons which the committee can give, save that it was not satisfied with either of the alternatives put forward in evidence and on its own expert knowledge preferred

---

[41] Rent Act 1977, Sched. 11, para. 7(2).
[42] S.I. 1971 No. 1065 as amended by S.I. 1980 No. 1699.
[43] (1985) 277 E.G. 308.
[44] Rent Act 1977, Sched. 11, para. 9.
[45] And see *Western Heritable Investment Co. Ltd.* (1978) S.L.T. 233.
[46] Rent Act 1977, s.72(4) as amended by Housing Act 1980, s.61(1).
[47] (1975) 29 P. & C.R. 172 at 176–177.

another figure. If that is all that the decision was, a simple matter of valuation opinion and nothing else, that is all that the decision involves, and if the decision is based simply on the committee's own views, having regard to the evidence put before them, then there are no reasons which the committee can give save to say that they think that their figure is right. Great complication and trouble would ensue if it were sought to make committees give reasons in such a situation beyond the simple and single reason to which I have referred.

So, when one bears those considerations in mind and goes back to the notice of motion, it seems to me quite clear that the first three grounds of complaint, overlapping as they do, cannot be sustained. The committee did not fail to give reasons which deal with the substantial case made by the appellants because the substantial case made by the appellants was that Mr. Burrow's opinion of a certain rent being a fair one was correct. If the committee make it clear, as they have done, that they did not accept his rental figure, then they would be giving the only reason for that purpose, to deal with the substantial case made by the appellants.

The landlords also complain in their notice of motion that the committee overthrew highly qualified expert and other evidence. Perhaps they did. I hope that I have already made it clear that, if they took the view that that was necessary in order to give the right answer, they acted fully within their discretion.

In *Guppys (Bridport) Ltd.* v. *Sandoe*[48] Lord Widgery C.J. was again called upon to adjudicate:

True to form, the tenant here based his claim principally, as the rent officer had done, on the proposition that other registered rents which were of comparable properties showed a rent equivalent or equal to that for which the tenant contended.

The landlord, on the other hand, as is the modern trend in these cases, sought to justify a higher figure by a variety of different approaches, some of which involved capital value and some, as I understand it, which did not. The landlords' case as summarised, and no doubt very briefly summarised, by the committee is a criticism of the reliance by the tenant on comparable rents.

Having discussed *Mason* v. *Skilling*[49] and *Tormes Property Co. Ltd.* v. *Landau*,[50] he continued:

It is therefore indisputable, in my view, on those authorities that if the committee are faced with a landlord's case based on capital value, and a fair return thereon, and the tenant's case is based on the other registered comparable rents, it is open to the committee, if they think it right in accordance with their judicial function, to choose the method of registered comparable rents. If they do choose that, then ... they can do it without criticising the landlord's approach on the basis of a capital value and a fair return on capital value.

Under the Tribunals and Inquiries Act [1971] reasons are required to be given [section 12(1)], and Mr. Pryor says that if the committee do not explain in some detail and by means of analysis why they are not prepared to accept the landlord's figures then they fail to give the proper reasons. In doing so he recognises, I think that he is putting up a submission ... which, in my view, is not to be found in the authorities at all.

[48] (1975) 30 P. & C.R. 69 at 70–75.
[49] [1974] 1 W.L.R. 1437, see p. 440.
[50] [1971] 1 Q.B. 261, see p. 444.

There are plenty of judicial officers, not the least that of a High Court judge, where reasons undoubtedly have to be given for every decision, but that does not mean that if the judge has two conflicting opinions put before him in evidence he has to explain why he chooses one in preference to the other. Such explanations are not possible. They are matters of judgment, impression and sometimes even instinct, and it is quite impossible to give detailed reasons to explain how the system of decision has worked, and so with a rent assessment committee. If they have decided, having carefully weighed the evidence, that they must reject one approach and adopt another, then all they need to do is to say than in the exercise of their discretion and relying on their skill and judgment they prefer the method which in fact they do prefer. If they say that, it cannot be said against them that their decision is invalidated by the fact that no further or more detailed explanation of why they prefer method A and reject method B is given.[51]

In *Guppy's Properties Ltd.* v. *Knott* (*No.* 3)[52] the position was summarised as follows:

(1) the reasons must be intelligible;
(2) although they do not have to deal with every point raised, they must deal with the substantial points showing what matters were taken into consideration and what view was reached on them;
(3) where the committee (having conformed with rule (2)) decide to rely on their own knowledge and experience they are not required to further explain how their figure is determined ...

Does this approach of the Divisional Court represent robust common sense? Or is it a somewhat feeble stance in which they have failed to exercise the control one should expect from the Divisional Court? Interestingly, the approach of the English court is markedly different from its Scottish equivalent where the Court of Session has not hesitated to quash decisions on the ground that inadequate reasons were given.[53]

(3) Effect of Getting a Fair Rent Registered

Once a rent has been registered it becomes the "contractual rent limit"[54] and is effective from the date of registration.[55] If the fair rent is lower than the originally agreed contractual rent, the registered fair rent becomes the "contracual rent limit"[56] which is effective from the date of registration by the rent officer[57]; any excess is irrecoverable from the tenant.[58]

---

[51] Consider, too, *Mountview Court Properties Ltd.* v. *Devlin* (1970) 21 P. & C.R. 689; *cf. Guppys Properties Ltd.* v. *Knott* (1980) 124 S.J. 81.
[52] (1981) 258 E.G. 1083.
[53] See *Albyn Properties* v. *Knox* (1977) S.L.T. 41.
[54] Rent Act 1977, s.44(1).
[55] s.72, as amended by Housing Act 1980, s.61.
[56] s.44(1).
[57] s.72.
[58] s.44(2).

If the registered fair rent is higher than the originally agreed contractual rent, this higher fair rent cannot be changed until the original contract has been brought to an end. This may be done by issuing a statutory notice of increase[59] which, if it shows a date which is *after* the date on which a valid notice to quit would operate to bring the contractual tenancy to an end, is deemed to have the effect of a notice to quit[60] and thus to terminate the (contractual) protected tenancy, and bring a statutory tenancy into existence. In such a case the higher fair rent is effective from that date. Thus, in the case of a weekly tenancy, the notice of increase cannot come into effect until at least 28 days have elapsed.[61]

If an existing tenancy has already become a statutory tenancy (for example because the term of a lease has expired, or a valid notice to quit has been issued and expired, or a notice of increase of rent to similar effect has been issued and expired) then, where a fair rent is registered which is lower than the existing rent, that fair rent is the rent limit and any excess is irrecoverable.[62] If the registered fair rent is higher than the existing rent, then the rent may be increased if a statutory notice of increase is served. Such a notice can, in these circumstances, be valid from up to four weeks before the date of service of the notice, or from the date of registration, whichever is the later.[63]

It is essential that any notice of increase be in the statutorily prescribed form[64] or in any form substantially to the same effect.[65] Apart from details relating to the levels of rent which have been determined by the rent officer, such forms also contain information about, for example, rent allowances.[66] They are thus another example of a procedure designed to get information about legal rights over to tenants. The effectiveness of these procedures has not been adequately investigated. However the Francis Committee did state:

It is not an offence for the landlord of a regulated tenancy to charge more than the registered rent. The position under the present law is that (i) the landlord cannot recover by legal proceedings such part of the rent as is in excess of the registered rent, and (ii) the tenant can recover the excess payments within a period of two years after payment. By contrast, it is an offence for the landlord of a furnished tenancy to charge more than the registered rent. This distinction is, on the face of it, quite illogical. The rule with regard to excess payments under a regulated tenancy was presumably adopted by analogy to the rule governing excess rents for controlled premises. It has not been an offence to charge more than the recoverable rent for controlled premises. There was,

---

[59] s.49.
[60] s.49(4).
[61] For notices to quit, see pp. 199–201.
[62] s.45(2)(b).
[63] ss.45(3) and 72; and see *Avenue Properties (St. John's Wood) Ltd.* v. *Aisinzon* [1977] Q.B. 628.
[64] See now S.I. 1980 No. 1697, Sched. 1, Forms 1 and 2.
[65] Rent Act 1977, s.61(1).
[66] See pp. 463–477.

however, a good reason for this, in that it might be difficult to ascertain the precise amount of the controlled rent. This, however, is not the case with a registered rent.

The 1970 Tenants' Survey has unearthed the disquieting fact that a substantial proportion of regulated tenants appear to be paying rents in excess of registered rents.[67]

Once a rent has been registered it continues to apply to the property, no matter who the tenant is. Registrations may, in defined circumstances, be cancelled.[68]

Bibliographical note

Despite the protections relating to rents theoretically afforded to tenants by the Rent Acts, there is considerable evidence that the legislation did not work as suggested in Parliament that it would. In addition to the *Report of the Committee on the Working of the Rent Acts* (1971, HMSO),[69] see also B. Paley *Attitudes to Letting* (1978, HMSO) and J. Doling and M. Davies, *Public Control of Privately Rented Housing* (1984, Gower).

(4) Restricted Contracts

Rents of restricted contracts can, in theory, still be referred to rent assessment committees (sitting, for these purposes, as rent tribunals) to set, not "fair" but "reasonable" rents.[70] But, since under section 36(2) of the Housing Act 1988, any variation in rent (other than one decided by a rent tribunal) has the effect of ending the original restricted contract,[71] and since tenants who do refer cases to the rent tribunal have no effective security of tenure (and thus little protection if they do so refer), it is unlikely, in practice, that many cases will now arise under this part of the Rent Act. For this reason, the issue will not be discussed further here.[72]

(5) Housing Association Tenancies: Rent Limits

Under Part VI of the Rent Act 1977, rent officers were able to determine and register fair rents of dwellings let by housing associations, housing trusts and the Housing Corporation. In practice, a substantial part of the rent officer's work related to these categories of dwellings.

---

[67] Report of the Committee on the Rent Acts (1971), p. 117.
[68] Rent Act 1977, s.73, as amended by Housing Act 1980, s.62.
[69] Cmnd. 4609.
[70] See Part V, Rent Act, 1977.
[71] See pp. 173–174.
[72] See Partington *Landlord & Tenant* (2nd ed., 1980), pp. 292–301.

Registration of rents of housing association tenancies granted prior to January 15, 1989[73] was substantially on the same basis as that for private sector, regulated tenancies.[74] Once set, the registered rent became the rent limit which the tenant has to pay.[75] Where as a result of the registration of a fair rent, or a revised fair rent, the rent limit was increased, there are special provisions relating to notices of increase of rent,[76] which are rather different from these which apply to regulated tenancies.[77] Sums paid in excess of the rent limit are recoverable.[78]

These provisions do not apply to housing association tenancies granted on or after January 15, 1989.[79]

III   PUBLIC SECTOR RENT LEVELS

Rent levels for council housing were traditionally determined under very broadly formulated statutory provisions.

Section 24 of the Housing Act 1985, (which was the most recent consolidation of the relevant provisions) stated, apparently simply:

(1) A local housing authority may make such reasonable charges as they may determine for the tenancy or occupation of their houses.

(2) The authority shall from time to time review rents and make such charges, either of rents generally or of particular rents, as circumstances may require.

These broad discretionary powers have on a number of occasions, been challenged in court, but save for one bizarre exception,[80] no case has succeeded in overturning a local authority's determination of what was reasonable.

Hemsted v. *Lees and Norwich City Council* (1986) 18 H.L.R. 424

McCowan J. said (at 427–430):

[The applicant, a ratepayer] contends that the Council's approach to fixing the rents to be charged in respect of the Housing Stock in respect of the financial year 1982–83 was contrary to law. He says that the approach of the Council to the fixing of rents in respect of the Housing Stock for that year was not to consider, as it should have done, the open market rental value of the Housing Stock, but to treat rent as the balancing item in the Housing Revenue Account once all other items of income and expenditure had been brought into account. In particular, he submits the Council decided upon a rate fund contribution in respect of the social expenditure item prior to considering the level at which

---

[73] As defined in Rent Act 1977, s.86.
[74] s.87.
[75] s.88.
[76] s.93.
[77] p. 457.
[78] s.94.
[79] See p. 90.
[80] *Backhouse* v. *Lambeth L.B.C.* (1972) 116 S.J. 802.

rents should be fixed. Since the Council managed the Housing Revenue Account in such a way as to make rental income the balancing item the effect of a rate fund contribution was, he submits, to reduce the amount of rental income and thus to subsidise the general body of tenants at the expense of general body of ratepayers to the extent of whatever rate fund contribution was agreed.

I have been referred by the parties to various cases ... *Belcher and Others* v. *Reading Corporation* [1950] 1 Ch. 380 is a decision of Mr. Justice Romer on reasonable charges by a local authority for the tenancy of council houses. On page 391 he says:

> "The corporation's tenants are not the only people whose interests they have to consider, for they have to bear the general body of ratepayers in mind as well. It seems to me that in solving the economic problems with which local authorities are confronted today, and which arise mainly from the greatly increased cost of materials and labour, they are placed in a position of not inconsiderable difficulty. It is, of course, clear that they have to consider the welfare of their tenants and to remember that those tenants are people of small, sometimes of very small, means. On the other hand they have also to be mindful of the interests of the ratepayers as a whole; the majority of whom, in Reading, as I was informed, are people of comparable means with the tenants of the council houses. It is their duty, so far as possible, to maintain a balance between these two sections of the local community, having due regard, of course, to any specific requirements of the Housing Acts. If the council house rents were much below those prevailing in comparable private estates in the locality, then *prima facie* a local authority might be suspected of unduly favouring the tenants; while, if they were much in excess of such other rents, the presumption would be the other way round. I have already indicated that in my opinion the past policy of the corporation, as established by the evidence, is not deserving of the criticism that has been levelled against it; and does not *per se* support any suggestion of unreasonableness on their part or any failure to take into account any consideration which they ought to have taken into account for the purpose of maintaining the balance to which I have referred."

Next, I look at the case of *Luby* v. *Newcastle-under-Lyme Corporation* [1964] 2 Q.B. 64. This was a decision of Diplock L.J., as he then was, sitting as an additional judge of the Queen's Bench Division, on the choice of a rent structure for its tenants by a local authority. I need only look at some words of Diplock L.J. at page 72 where he said:

> "The court's control over the exercise by a local authority of a discretion conferred upon it by Parliament is limited to ensuring that the local authority has acted within the powers conferred. It is not for the court to substitute its own view of what is a desirable policy in relation to the subject matter of the discretion so conferred. It is only if it is exercised in a manner which no reasonable man could consider justifiable that the court is entitled to interfere. In determining the rent structure to be applied to houses provided by a local authority the local authority is applying what is, in effect, a social policy upon which reasonable men may hold different views. Since any deficit in the housing revenue account has to be made good from the general rate fund, the choice of rent structure involves weighing the interests of the tenants as a whole and of individual impoverished tenants against those of the general body of ratepayers. Since the passing of the National Assistance Act, 1948, and the making of the National Assistance (Determination of Need) Regulations, 1948, which provide that the matters to be taken into consideration in assessing the relief to be granted to applicants shall include the net

rent payable or such a part thereof as is reasonable in the circumstances, there is also involved a choice as to whether the individual impoverished tenant should be assisted at the expense of the general body of ratepayers by a reduction in the rent or at the expense of the general body of taxpayers by way of National Assistance.

"The evidence shows that the defendant corporation has directed its mind to this problem and to the desirability or otherwise of applying a differential rent scheme. It has determined that the burden of assisting individual tenants who cannot afford to pay the rents which the corporation has fixed as appropriate for the type of house which they occupy ought to fall upon the general body of taxpayers and not upon the general body of ratepayers in their district. It is in my view quite impossible for this court to say that this choice, which is one of social policy, is one which no reasonable man could have made, and is therefore *ultra vires*, any more that it could be said that the opposite choice would have been *ultra vires*. The policy which the defendant corporation has adopted was, I think, within the descretion conferred upon them by section 111(1) of the Housing Act, 1957,[81] that subsection being the statutory provision which confers the general power to determine the rent structure."

Finally, I look at the case of *Evans* v. *Collins and Another* [1965] 1 Q.B. 580, which was a Divisional Court decision, on a similar subject to that in the last case to which I referred. On page 591, Widgery J., as he then was, quoted the passage from Romer J.'s judgment in *Belcher and Others* v. *Reading Corporation*, to which I have already referred. He then continued:

"That statement of principle, as it seems to me, although laid down in a case decided under the Act of 1936, is not dependent upon the statutory duty of considering other rentals which that Act imposed. As I see it, the judge is stating a proposition of general application which has to be borne in mind by those examining the activities of a local authority in the conduct of its housing revenue account. Before I leave that case I think it pertinent to point out that the decision was given in 1949 at a time when, as is well known, the Rent Restriction Act, 1939, was in full effect and was of very wide application throughout the country. It seems to me that in 1949 it may well have been that rents prevailing in private estates would not be significantly different from the rents which a council would be required to charge if they desired to recoup the entire cost of providing the houses in question. The rent which a council would be required to charge on that basis is conveniently referred to as the economic rent, and I inclined to think that if Romer J. had been expressing his opinion at the present day he might have been minded to use the phrase 'economic rent' in that sense rather than rents prevailing in comparable estates. I say that because in a period of inflation and complete relaxation of rent control the rents of private premises far outstrip the economic rent which a local authority might be minded to charge, it would, in my view, be unreal to suggest that the local authority is under any duty to charge market rents to its tenants.

"I can see no reason why a local authority should ever be under a duty to make a profit out of its tenants, and it seems to me that the proper basis of comparison at the present time is between rents charged by the authority and economic rents as I have sought to define them. Applying the dictum of Romer J. in this way one would consider whether the difference between the

[81] Now Housing Act 1985, s.24(1).

rents charged and the economic rent was so great as to indicate that the local authority were not holding the scales fairly between the two branches of the community to whom they owe a duty."

Mr. Carnwath, who has appeared for the District Auditor, submits that three principles emerge from these authorities: first, that the council has a wide discretion in the fixing of reasonable rents; secondly, that it is entitled to approach it as a matter of social policy; and, thirdly, that it is neither obliged to relate its rents to market rents nor to seek to make a profit. I accept his argument that those principles do indeed emerge from the authorities. ...

Notes

A number of important issues are involved in this, and other cases.

(i)   What, if any, relationship should local authority rents have to rents charged in the private sector? In 1972, the Housing Finance Act made an attempt to bring local authority and private sector rents more in line by providing that the former should be brought within the "fair rent" scheme. This was abandoned when the Labour Government came to power in 1974.

The issue has been revived in a new guise with the passing of section 162 of the Local Government and Housing Act 1989, which adds the following subsections to section 24 of the Housing Act 1985:

(3) In exercising their functions under this section, a local housing authority shall have regard in particular to the principle that the rents of houses of any class or description should bear broadly the same proportion to private sector rents as the rents of houses of any other class or description.

(4) In subsection (3) "private sector rents," in relation to houses of any class or description, means the rents which would be recoverable if they were let on assured tenancies within the meaning of the Housing Act 1988 by a person other than the authority.

These new provisions may make challenges of the kind raised in *Hemsted* easier to sustain. There is, of course, considerable ambiguity in the concept of "private sector rents" since as noted above, housing association rents are still likely to be determined on grounds different from those determined by private landlords.[82]

(ii)   A second issue in *Hemsted* is the more general issue of the extent to which local authorities were entitled to subsidise local authority rent levels by making contributions to Housing Revenue Accounts from the general rates. As a result of new rules relating to Housing Revenue Accounts, enacted by the Local Government and Housing Act 1989,[83] the list of items which may appear as credits in the Housing Revenue Account has been so defined as, in effect, to outlaw transfers from the

[82] See p. 437.
[83] ss.74–76 and Sched. 4.

general rates (or now revenue derived from the community charge). As a result of this "ring-fencing," no longer will local authorities be able to make the kinds of general contributions that were in issue in the case of *Hemsted*.

(iii)   Section 24 of the Housing Act 1985 (even as amended) cannot, in fact, be understood in isolation from broader questions of housing finance and the level of subsidy being provided by the central government. Put simply, the lower the central provision, the higher the rent levels that have to be charged by local authorities if the Housing Revenue Account is to be kept in balance. (See further, p. 477) Under section 76 of the Local Government and Housing Act 1989, local housing authorities are placed under a statutory duty to prevent debit balances arising in the Housing Revenue Account.

IV   HOUSING BENEFITS

Rent control has the effect of depressing rent levels, but the costs of this are borne by the landlord. The argument that such costs should more appropriately be borne by the State has gained increasing recognition with the introduction of rent rebates and allowances— housing benefits designed to assist the poorly paid and unemployed with their housing costs.

The "modern" system of housing benefits began with the enactment of the Housing Finance Act 1972; it has undergone major changes in the 1980's as governments have increasingly sought to "target" assistance with the cost of housing on individuals, through housing benefit, rather than more generally through the provision of subsidies for the provision of housing.

Legislative authority for the present scheme of housing benefits is to be found in section 20 of the Social Security Act 1986:

(7) A person is entitled to housing benefit if—

(a)   he is liable to make payments in respect of a dwelling in Great Britain which he occupies as his home and also if, in respect of a particular day falling after 31st March, 1989 but before 1st April, 1990, the condition specified in subsection (7A) below is satisfied;

(b)   there is an appropriate maximum housing benefit in his case; and

(c)   either—

   (i)   he has no income or his income does not exceed the applicable amount; or

   (ii)   his income exceeds that amount, but only by so much that there is an amount remaining if the deduction for which section 21(5) below provides is made.

(7A) The condition to which subsection (7)(a) above refers is that—

(a)   in respect of the day the person concerned is shown in a community charges register as being liable to pay the personal community charge and is not there shown as undertaking a full time course of education or nursing education on the day; or

(b) the day consists of or falls within a contribution period in respect of which the person concerned is liable to pay a collective community charge contribution under section 11(11) of the 1987 Act.

(8) In subsection (7) above "payments in respect of a dwelling" means such payments as may be prescribed, but the power to prescribe payments does not include power to prescribe mortgage payments or, in relation to Scotland, payments under heritable securities.

Section 21(5) states:

Where a person is entitled to housing benefit ... , the amount shall be what remains after the deduction from the appropriate maximum housing benefit of prescribed percentages of the excess of his income over the applicable amount.

Notes

(i) The effect of section 20(8) is to exclude repayments of mortgage capital from the housing benefit scheme.

(ii) As is common these days, the bulk of the details of the housing benefit scheme are to be found in regulations made under the authority of the Act of 1986. The principal regulations relating to housing benefit are the Housing Benefit (General) Regulations 1987[84] and the Housing Benefit (Subsidy) Order 1991.[85] Also relevant is the Rent Officers (Additional Functions) Order 1989.[86]

(iii) Technically, "housing benefit" is a generic title covering four separate benefits: rent *rebates* (payable to tenants of local authorities); rent *allowances* (payable to other tenants); rate rebates (now no longer operative with the abolition of domestic rates); and community charge rebates.[87] We shall discuss only the first two benefits.

Although very complex in detail, the broad outline of the rent rebate and rent allowance schemes is relatively straightforward. After four preliminary definition regulations, the General Regulations consist of 12 further parts (over 100 regulations). The following points may be noted.

(A) DEFINITION OF "OCCUPIES"

Regulations 5–7 set out in detail rules relating to when a person is deemed to be treated as occupying (or not occupying) a dwelling as his

---

[84] S.I. 1987 No. 1972 (as amended).
[85] S.I. 1991 No. 441.
[86] S.I. 1989 No. 590.
[87] Social Security Act 1986, s.28(1) (as amended).

home. For example, housing benefit may normally be claimed in respect of one dwelling only; there is an important exception in regulation 5(5) which reads:

(5) Where a person is liable to make payments in respect of two (but not more than two) dwellings, he shall be treated as occupying both dwellings as his home only—

   (a) where he has left and remains absent from the former dwelling occupied as his home through fear of violence in that dwelling or by a former member of his family and it is reasonable that housing benefit should be paid in respect of both his former dwelling and his present dwelling occupied as the home; or

   (b) in the case of a married or unmarried couple or a member of a polygamous marriage, where he or one partner is a student or is on a training course and it is unavoidable that the partners should occupy two separate dwellings and reasonable that housing benefit should be paid in respect of both dwellings; or

   (c) in the case where, because of the number of persons referred to in paragraph (1), they have been housed by a housing authority in two separate dwellings; or

   (d) in the case where a person has moved into a new dwelling occupied as the home, except where paragraph (4) applies, for a period not exceeding four benefit weeks if his liability to make payments in respect of two dwellings is unavoidable.

There are also rules about how someone who has recently moved but has been unable to dispose of their original dwelling is to be treated.[88] Temporary absences from home are dealt with in regulation 5(8):

(8) A person shall be treated as occupying a dwelling as his home while he is temporarily absent therefrom for a period not exceeding 52 weeks only if—

   (a) he intends to return to occupy the dwelling as his home; and

   (b) the part of the dwelling normally occupied by him has not been let or, as the case may be, sub-let; and

   (c) the period of absence is unlikely to exceed 52 weeks or, in exceptional circumstances (for example where the person is in hospital or otherwise has no control over the length of his absence), is unlikely substantially to exceed that period.[89]

Special rules relating to the liability to make payments are set out in regulations 6 and 7.

---

[88] Reg. 5(6).
[89] For a case under an earlier version of these rules, see *R. v. H.B. Review Board, ex p. Robinson, The Independent*, March 5, 1988.

(B) DEFINITION OF "RENT"

Payments must be in respect of a dwelling.[90] For these purposes, "rent" is very broadly defined in regulation 10:

10.—(1) Subject to the following provisions of this regulation, the payments in respect of which housing benefit is payable in the form of a rent rebate or allowance are the following periodical payments which a person is liable to make in respect of the dwelling which he occupies as his home—

    (a)   payments of, or by way of, rent;

    (b)   payments in respect of a licence or permission to occupy the dwelling;

    (c)   payments by way of mesne profits or, in Scotland, violent profits;

    (d)   payments in respect of, or in consequence of, use and occupation of the dwelling;

    (e)   payments of, or by way of, service charges payment of which is a condition on which the right to occupy the dwelling depends;

    (f)   mooring charges payable for a houseboat;

    (g)   where the home is a caravan or a mobile home, payments in respect of the site on which it stands;

    (h)   any contribution payable by a person resident in an almshouse provided by a housing association which is either a charity of which particulars are entered in the register of charities established under section 4 of the Charities Act 1960 (register of charities) or an exempt charity within the meaning of that Act, which is a contribution towards the cost of maintaining that association's almshouses and essential services in them;

    (i)   payments under a rental purchase agreement, that is to say an agreement for the purchase of a dwelling which is a building or part of one under which the whole or part of the purchase price is to be paid in more than one instalment and the completion of the purchase is deferred until the whole or a specified part of the purchase price has been paid; and

    (j)   where, in Scotland, the dwelling is situated on or pertains to a croft within the meaning of section 3(1) of the Crofters (Scotland) Act 1955, the payment in respect of the croft land.

(2) A rent rebate or, as the case may be, a rent allowance shall not be payable in respect of the following periodical payments—

    (a)   payments under a long tenancy except a shared ownership tenancy granted by a housing association or a housing authority;

    (b)   payments under a co-ownership scheme;

---

[90] Reg. 8.

(c) payments by an owner;

(d) payments under a hire purchase, credit sale or conditional sale agreement except to the extent the conditional sale agreement is in respect of land; and

(e) payments by a Crown tenant. ...

Note that these rules make it clear that a much wider range of payments than "rent" in the common law sense is eligible for assistance under the housing benefit scheme.

(C) ELIGIBLE RENT

Having defined the "rent," rebates and allowances are calculated by reference to the "eligible" rent.[91] These rules deal with a number of matters: such as apportionment of rent, where liability to pay is divided; and what service charges may or may not be included in the rent.

The most important issue relates to the limits beyond which a rent will not be eligible. Formally, there is no upper limit beyond which rent levels are eligible. This could, however, cause major problems; landlords might be tempted to fill substantial buildings with large numbers of poor people, charge what they will and receive 100 per cent. of the sums charged via housing benefit. This would be as distorting of the free market as rent regulation.

The housing benefit scheme therefore includes a number of devices designed to control this potential problem: regulation 11 places restrictions on "unreasonable payments"; regulation 12 places restrictions on rent increases; and regulation 12A creates a duty to refer claims relating to rent allowances to rent officers.

11.—(1) Where a rent is registered in respect of a dwelling under Part IV or V of the Rent Act 1977 and the rent recoverable from a claimant is limited to the rent so registered, his eligible rent determined in accordance with regulation 10 (rent) shall not exceed the rent so registered.

(1A) Where a rent has been determined by a rent assessment committee in respect of a dwelling under Part I of the Housing Act 1988 the claimant's eligible rent determined in accordance with regulation 10 shall not exceed the rent determined by the committee during the period of 12 months beginning with the first day on which the determination had effect.

(2) Subject to paragraphs (3) to (4), where the appropriate authority considers—

(a) whether by reference to a determination made by a rent officer in exercise of a function conferred on him by an order under section 121 of the Housing Act 1988, or otherwise, that a claimant occupies a

---

[91] Defined in reg. 10(3)–(6), regs. 11 and 12, and Sched. 1.

dwelling larger than is reasonably required by him and others who also occupy that dwelling (including any non-dependents of his and any person paying rent to him) having regard in particular to suitable alternative accommodation occupied by a household of the same size; or . . .

(c)   whether by reference to a determination made by a rent officer in exercise of a function conferred on him by an order under section 121 of the Housing Act 1988 or otherwise that the rent payable for his dwelling is unreasonably high by comparison with the rent payable in respect of suitable alternative accommodation elsewhere, the authority may treat the claimant's eligible rent as reduced by such amount as it considers appropriate having regard in particular to the cost of suitable alternative accomodation elsewhere and the claimant's maximum housing benefit shall be calculated by reference to the eligible rent as so reduced.

(3) If any person to whom paragraph (7) applies—

(a)   is aged 60 or over; or

(b)   is incapable of work for the purposes of one or more of the provisions of the Social Security Act, or Part I of the Social Security and Housing Benefit Act 1982 or Part II of the Act; or

(c)   is a member of the same household as a child or young person for whom he or his partner is responsible,

no deduction shall be made under paragraph (2) unless suitable cheaper alternative accommodation is available and the authority considers that, taking into account the relevant factors, it is reasonable to expect the claimant to move from his present accommodation.

(3A) No deduction shall be made under paragraph (2) for a period of 12 months from the date of death of any person to whom paragraph (7) applied or, had a claim been made, would have applied, if the dwelling which the claimant occupies is the same as that occupied by him at that date except where the deduction began before the death occurred.

(3B) For the purposes of paragraph (3A), a claimant shall be treated as occupying the dwelling if paragraph (8) of regulation 5 (circumstances in which a person is to be treated as occupying a dwelling) is satisfied and for that purpose sub-paragraph (b) of that paragraph shall be treated as if it were omitted.

(4) Without prejudice to the operation of paragraph (3), but subject to paragraph (5), where the appropriate authority is satisfied that a person to whom paragraph (7) applies was able to meet the financial commitments for his dwelling when they were entered into, no deduction shall be made under paragraph (2) during the first 13 benefit weeks of the claimant's benefit period.

(5) Paragraph (4) shall not apply where a claimant was previously entitled to benefit in respect of a benefit period which fell wholly or partly less than 52 weeks before the commencement of his current benefit period.

(6) For the purposes of this regulation—

(a)   in deciding what is suitable alternative accommodation, the appropriate authority shall take account of the nature of the alternative accommodation and the facilities provided having regard to the age and state of health of all the persons to whom paragraph (7) applies and, in particular, where a claimant's present dwelling is occupied with security of tenure, accommodation shall not be treated as suitable alternative accommodation unless that accommodation will be occupied on terms which will afford security of tenure reasonably equivalent to that presently enjoyed by the claimant; and

(b) the relevant factors in paragraph (3) are the effects of a move to alternative accommodation on—

    (i) the claimant's prospects of retaining his employment; and

    (ii) the education of any child or young person referred to in paragraph (3)(c) if such a move were to result in a change of school.

(7) This paragraph applies to the following persons—

(a) the claimant;

(b) any member of his family;

(c) if the claimant is a member of a polygamous marriage, any partners of his and any child or young person for whom he or a partner is responsible and who is a member of the same household;

(d) subject to paragraph (8), any relative of the claimant or his partner who occupies the same dwelling as the claimant, whether or not they reside with him.

(8) Paragraph (7)(d) shall only apply to a relative who has no separate right of occupation of the dwelling which would enable him to continue to occupy it even if the claimant ceased his occupation of it.

12.—(1) Subject to paragraph (2), where a claimant's eligible rent is increased during a benefit period, the appropriate authority may, if it considers whether by reference to a determination made by a rent officer in exercise of a function conferred on him by an order under section 121 of the Housing Act 1988 or otherwise either—

(a) that the increase is unreasonably high having regard in particular to the level of increases for suitable alternative accommodation, or

(b) in the case of an increase which takes place less than 12 months after the date of the previous increase, that the increase is unreasonable having regard to the length of time since that previous increase,

treat the eligible rent as reduced either by the full amount of the increase or, if it considers that a lesser increase was reasonable in all the circumstances, by the difference between the full amount of the increase and the increase that is reasonable having regard in particular to the level of increases for suitable alternative accommodation, and the claimant's maximum housing benefit shall be calculated by reference to the eligible rent as so reduced.

(2) No deduction shall be made under this regulation for a period of 12 months from the date of death of any person to whom paragraph (7) of regulation 11 (restrictions on unreasonable payments) applied or, had a claim been made, would have applied, if the dwelling which the claimant occupies is the same as that occupied by him at that date except where the deduction began before his death occurred.

(3) For the purposes of paragraph (2), a claimant shall be treated as occupying the dwelling if paragraph (8) of regulation 5 (circumstances in which a person is to be treated as occupying a dwelling) is satisfied and for that purpose sub-paragraph (b) of that paragraph shall be treated as if it were omitted.

As to reg. 5(8), see p. 465.

12A.—(1) Subject to paragraph (2), an appropriate local authority shall apply to a rent officer for a determination to be made in pursuance of the Housing Act functions where it has received—

(a) a claim on which rent allowance may be awarded; or

(b) a notification of a change relating to a rent allowance.

(2) An application shall not be required under paragraph (1) where a claim or notification relates to either—

(a) a dwelling in a hostel if, during the period of 12 months which ends on the day on which that claim or notification is received by the appropriate local authority—

   (i) a rent officer has already made a determination in the exercise of the Housing Act functions in respect of a dwelling in that hostel which is a similar dwelling to the dwelling to which the claim or notification relates; and

  (ii) that determination or, if there has been more than one such determination, the most recent, was made in respect of a claim for a period beginning on or after 9th October, 1989; and

 (iii) there has been no change relating to a rent allowance that has affected the dwelling in respect of which that determination was made; or

(b) an "excluded tenancy" within the meaning of Schedule 1A (excluded tenancies).

(3) Where an application to a rent officer is required by paragraph (1) it shall be made within three days, or as soon as practicable thereafter, of the appropriate local authority receiving—

(a) a claim on which rent allowance may be awarded; or

(b) a notification of a change relating to a rent allowance.

(4) For the purposes of calculating the period of three days mentioned in paragraph (3), no regard shall be had to any day on which the offices of the appropriate local authority are closed for the purposes of receiving or determining claims. ...

The definition of excluded tenancies in Schedule 1A of the Housing Benefit (General) Regulations has the effect of excluding a significant range of tenancies from the rent officer's jurisdiction, including regulated tenancies, tenancies entered into before January 15, 1989 and tenancies which have recently been the subject of a rent officer's determination.

Also excluded are assured tenancies, assured agricultural occupancies or licences to occupy "where the landlord (or any superior landlord) is a registered housing association unless the local authority stated in the application for determination that the circumstances set out in regulation 11(2)(a) or (c) exist."[92] Thus there is a presumption that rents set by housing associations will be reasonable for housing benefit purposes.

Notes

(i) Where a fair rent is registered,[93] this is the maximum "eligible rent" for housing benefit purposes.

(ii) It is unlikely that many rents of assured tenancies will be determined by the rent assessment committee.[94]

(iii) The power of local authorities to "cap" rents is carefully defined, but is related to new powers that have been given to rent officers, and which are set out in Schedule 1 to the Rent Officers (Additional Functions) Order 1990:

Rent determinations

1.—(1) The rent officer shall determine whether, in his opinion, the rent payable under the tenancy of the dwelling at the relevant[94a] time is significantly higher than the rent which the landlord might reasonably be expected to obtain under the tenancy at that time, having regard to the level of rent under similar tenancies of similar dwellings in the locality (or as similar as regards tenancy, dwelling and locality as is reasonably practicable), but on the assumption that no person who would have been entitled to housing benefit had sought or is seeking the tenancy.

(2) If the rent officer determines under sub-paragraph (1) that the rent is significantly higher, the rent officer shall also determine the rent which the landlord might reasonably be expected to obtain under the tenancy at the time the application for a determination is made, having regard to the same matter and on the same assumption as in sub-paragraph (1).

Size and rent determinations

2.—(1) The rent officer shall determine whether the dwelling exceeds the size criteria for the occupiers.

(2) If the rent officer determines that the dwelling exceeds the size criteria, the rent officer shall also determine the rent which a landlord might reasonably have been expected to obtain, at the relevant[94a] time for a

---

[92] Sched. 1A, para. 3.
[93] Above pp. 438–459.
[94] Above pp. 432–438.
[94a] The relevant time is the time the application for determination is made or, if earlier, the tenancy ends.

tenancy which is similar to the tenancy of the dwelling and on the same terms (other than the term relating to the amount of rent), and of a dwelling which is in the same locality as the dwelling but which—

(a) accords with the size criteria for the occupiers;

(b) is in a reasonable state of repair, and

(c) corresponds in other respects, in the rent officer's opinion, as closely as is reasonably practicable to the dwelling.

(3) When making a determination under paragraph 2(2), the rent officer shall have regard to the same matter and make the same assumption as in paragraph 1(1), except that in judging the similarity of other tenancies and dwellings the comparison shall be with the tenancy of the second dwelling referred to in paragraph 2(2) and the assumption shall be made in relation to that tenancy.

Services determinations

3.—(1) Where the rent officer makes a determination under paragraph 1(2) or 2(2), or (where no determination is to be made under paragraph 1(2)) paragraph (1), and the dwelling is not a hostel (within the meaning of regulation 12A of the Housing Benefit (General) Regulations 1987, he shall also determine whether, in his opinion, any of the rent at the relevant time is fairly attributable to the provision of services which are ineligible to be met by housing benefit and, if so, the amount which in his opinion is so attributable (except where he considers the amount is negligible).

(2) In sub-paragraph (1) "rent," in relation to a determination under paragraph 1(2) or 2(2), means the rent determined under paragraph 1(2) or 2(2) and, in relation to a determination under paragraph 1(1), means the rent payable under the tenancy at the relevant time; and "services" means services performed or facilities (including the use of furniture) provided for, or rights made available to the tenant, but not the provision of meals (including the preparation of meals or provision of unprepared food).

Medical, nursing and other care services

4.—Where the rent includes any of the charges specified in sub-paragraph (d), (e) or (f) of paragraph 1 of Part I of Schedule 1 to the Housing Benefit (General) Regulations 1987, the rent officer, when making a determination, shall assume that—

(a) the items to which the charges relate were not to be provided or made available, and

(b) the rent payable under the tenancy at the relevant time is such amount as is specified in the application as the rent which would have been payable under the tenancy at that time if those items were not to be provided or made available.

Interim and further determinations

5.—If notice of a determination under paragraph 1 or 3 is not given to the local authority within the 5-day period mentioned in paragraph 6(a) solely because the rent officer intends to inspect the dwelling before making such a determination, the rent officer shall make both an interim determination and a further determination.

Notifications

6.—The rent officer shall give notice to the local authority of a determination—

(a) except in the case of a further determination, within the period of five working days beginning with the date on which the rent officer received the application or, where the rent officer requests further information under article 3(2), with the date on which he receives the information, or as soon as practicable after that period.

(b) in the case of a further determination within the period of 20 working days beginning with the date on which notice of the interim determination was given to the local authority, or as soon as practicable after that period.

7.—(1) If the rent officer becomes aware that the tenancy is not one to which article 3(1) applies the rent officer shall give the local authority notice to that effect.

(2) If the rent officer is precluded by article 5(2) from making a determination or a re-determination under paragraph 1 (or that paragraph as applied by Schedule 3), the rent officer shall give the local authority notice of the rent determined by the rent assessment committee.

Notes

(i)   Article 3(1) states:

3.—(1) Where, in connection with housing benefit and rent allowance subsidy, a local authority applies to a rent officer for determinations relating to a tenancy of a dwelling (and is required by regulations made under section 30 (2B) or (2C) of the Social Security Act 1986 to make that application) the rent officer shall (subject to article 5) make the determinations and give notice in accordance with Schedule 1 to this Order.

(ii) Article 5(2) states:

(2) No determination or re-determination shall be made under paragraph 1 of Schedule 1 (or that paragraph as applied by Schedule 3) if the tenancy is an assured tenancy or an assured agricultural occupancy and—

(a) the rent payable under the tenancy on the date the application for the determination (or, as the case may be, re-determination) was received was an amount determined under section 22 of the Housing Act 1988, or

(b) the rent so payable on that date was an amount determined under section 14 of that Act and that rent took effect within the period of 12 months ending with the date the application was received.

(iii)   The "size criteria" are to be found in Schedule 2:

1. One bedroom shall be occupied for each of the following categories of occupiers (and each occupier shall come within only the first category for which he is eligible)—

(a)   a married couple or an unmarried couple (within the meaning of Part II of the Social Security Act 1986),

(b)   a person who is not a child,

(c)   two children of the same sex,

(d)   two children who are less than 10 years old,

(e)   a child.

2. The number of rooms (excluding any allowed as a bedroom under paragraph 1) suitable for living in allowed are—

(a)   if there are less than four occupiers, one,

(b)   if there are more than three and less than seven occupiers, two,

(c)   in any other case, three.

Note that the rent officer can only make a determination where the rent is "significantly" higher,[95] not simply "higher." The local authority also has a right to apply for a redetermination within 10 weeks of being given the notice of determination.[95a]

Notwithstanding the fact that a rent officer's determination has been made, the local authority has a *discretion* ("may"), not a duty to decide whether or not to use it to determine the maximum eligible rent. However, once a rent officer's determination has been made, this will affect the level of housing benefit subsidy paid by central government to the administering local authority.[96] There may therefore be a tendency for local authorities to treat rent officer determinations as binding, although this could be contrary to regulation 11 and contrary to normal principles of administrative law.

There has as yet been no reported case on the new powers of the rent officer, but the impact of regulation 11 and the interaction of that with the housing subsidy rules was discussed briefly in *R.* v. *Brent L.B.C. ex p. Connery.*[97] Schiemann J. noted that regulation 11(2) contained two discretions. In deciding whether a rent was or was not unreasonably high, the authority could not take its financial

---

[95] *Cf.* Housing Act 1988, s.22 (p. 435).
[95a] Housing Benefit (General) Regulations, 1987 (as amended) Reg. 11(2).
[96] Housing Benefit (Subsidy) Order 1991, Art. 8 and Sched. 5.
[97] [1990] 2 All E.R. 353.

position, (*i.e.* the level of housing benefit subsidy) into account; but in deciding whether to reduce the "eligible rent" to that which would be charged for suitable alternative accommodation, the local authority was entitled to take its financial position including its projected subsidy income into account. (It could not, of course, reduce the "eligible rent" to a level *below* that which would be paid for the alternative accommodation.)

Notes

(i) The restrictions on rent increases in regulation 12 are limited to what is "unreasonably high." This rule must be seen in the context of the scheme of the Housing Act 1988 which provides, in effect, that there should be no statutory control over rent increases, unless the tenancy makes no provision for rent increases.[98]

(ii) Until the experience of operating these rules becomes more widespread, the impact of the rent officers' new powers will be unclear. It can however be argued that they do represent an attempt to reintroduce, by the back door, a measure of rent control, apparently abolished by the Housing Act 1988.

(D) DEFINITION OF FAMILY

Regulations 13 to 15 define who are members of a family, for housing benefit purposes. The size of the family crucially affects the means-testing process on which the calculation of housing benefit is determined.

(E) APPLICABLE AMOUNT

Regulations 16 to 18 and Schedule 2 defines the "applicable amount" relevant to each claimant of benefit (plus the members of the family, if any).

(F) THE MEANS-TEST RULES

Regulations 19 to 45, (Part VI of the Regulations) set down the rules for determining the claimant's income and capital. There are rules for disregarding certain categories of income and including other categories of "notional income". If the claimant has capital in excess of £8,000, there is no entitlement to housing benefit; if the claimant

---

[98] See p. 432.

has between £3,000 and £8,000, this sum is converted by a statutory formula into a normal weekly sum. Capital of less that £3,000 is disregarded. All these rules are structured on lines very similar to those applicable to the income support scheme. It is through the mechanism of the means-test that the government seeks to "target" financial assistance to the poorer sections of the community.

(G) STUDENTS

Regulations 46 to 60 prescribe special rules relating to students.

(H) AMOUNT OF HOUSING BENEFIT

Regulation 61 States that the the maximum permitted level of a rent rebate or rent allowance can be 100 per cent. of the "eligible rent." (Hence the importance of determining what the upper limit of "eligible rent" should be.)

If a claimant's "applicable amount" is exactly the same or above his weekly income, then the claimant gets his housing costs met in full.[99]

If the claimant's income exceeds the "applicable amount," the amount of the maximum housing benefit is reduced by 65p for every pound for which the claimant's income is in excess of the "applicable amount."[1]

Further deductions are made for "non-dependents" living in the dwelling, who are, in effect, deemed to be making a contribution to the housing costs.[2] No benefit is payable, where entitlement falls below 50p per week (reg. 64).

(I) OTHER MATTERS

The rest of the regulations deal with further detailed matters including the conversion of sums into weekly amounts; what happens where there is a change of circumstances; how claims are to be made; who is to take decisions in relations to claims; the time and manner of payment, including the circumstances in which payment of rent allowance may be made direct to a landlord[3]; and what happens when there has been an overpayment.

One specific regulation to which attention may be drawn is reg. 69(8) which provides:

---

[99] Social Security Act 1986, s.20(7)(c)(i).
[1] Reg. 62.
[2] Reg. 63.
[3] Reg. 94.

The appropriate authority may, if a claimant's circumstances are exceptional, increase the weekly amount of any housing benefit to be paid in his case, but only where such an increase is in respect of costs which are eligible housing costs.

This discretion is, however, limited in practice by the Housing Benefit (Permitted Totals) Order 1990,[4] article 2 of which substantially limits authorities' freedom of action.

Apart from this specific point, while the rules mentioned do raise some interesting issues, detailed consideration is beyond the scope of this work.[5]

V HOUSING SUBSIDIES

A final mechanism that has been used for keeping rent levels down is the provision of housing subsidies. The details of the law on housing subsidies have changed dramatically over time and it is not possible to give more than an outline of the principal forms of housing subsidy that are currently operative. As will be seen, the actual law gives considerable discretion to the Secretary of State to determine the bases on which subsidies should be provided. A primary feature of the policy of the last decade has been to reduce sharply the subsidies towards the costs associated with the direct provision of housing accommodation and to increase the subsidies payable for housing benefit.

The context within which these subsidies must be seen is the general government objective of reducing levels of public expenditure, combined with the more specific objective of endeavouring to control levels of spending by local authorities.

(A) LOCAL AUTHORITY HOUSING

The law on local authority housing subsidies was last revised by Part VI of the Local Government and Housing Act 1989. Section 79 states that *Housing Revenue Account subsidy* shall be payable each year to housing authorities. This is to be determined under section 80:

(1) The amount of Housing Revenue Account subsidy (if any) payable to a local housing authority for a year shall be calculated in accordance with such formula as the Secretary of State may from time to time determine; and for any year the first such determination shall be made before December 25, immediately preceding that year.

(2) If the amount so calculated is a negative amount, the authority shall for the year carry the equivalent positive amount from their Housing Revenue Account to the credit of some other revenue account of theirs.

---

[4] S.I. 1990, No. 534.
[5] See Findlay, *Housing Benefit and Community Charge Rebate Legislation* (3rd ed., 1990).

(3) In determining a formula for the purposes of this section for any year, the Secretary of State may include variables framed (in whatever way he considers appropriate) by reference to—

  (a)   any amounts which fall to be or were credited or debited to the authority's Housing Revenue Account for that year or any previous year;

  (b)   any amounts which, on such assumptions as the Secretary of State may determine (whether or not borne out or likely to be borne out by events), would fall to be or would have been so credited or debited; and

  (c)   such other matters relating to the authority, or to (or to tenants of) houses and other property which are or have been within the account, as he thinks fit;

and the Secretary of State may make any determination falling to be made for the purposes of a formula on the basis of information received by him on or before such date as he thinks fit.

(4) Without prejudice to the generality of subsection (3) above, a formula may require it to be assumed that the amount for any year of the rental income or housing expenditure of each authority (or each authority in England or in Wales) is to be determined—

  (a)   by taking the amount which the Secretary of State considers (having regard, amongst other thing, to past and expected movements in incomes, costs and prices) should be or should have been the aggregate amount for that year of the rental incomes, or, as the case may be, the housing expenditure of all of the authorities (or all of the authorities in England or Wales) taken together; and

  (b)   by apportioning that amount between them in such manner as the Secretary of State considers appropriate (which may involve, if he thinks fit, inferring the aggregate values of the houses and other property within their respective Housing Revenue Accounts from the average value of any of the houses and other property which they have disposed of);

and in this subsection "rental income" means income falling within item 1 of Part I of Schedule 4 to this Act and "housing expenditure" means expenditure falling within item 1 of Part II of that Schedule or falling to be debited to the authorities' Housing Repairs Accounts.

Notes

(i)   The detail is, in effect, all left to Government discretion.[6]

(ii)   The reference to "rental income" which *should* be achieved by local authorities provides the lever by which the government seeks to "persuade" local authorities to increase rental levels. As has already been noted[7] there is a clear intention to get housing authorities to increase rental levels to bring them nearer to those in the private sector. Failure to do this will result in the provision of inadequate subsidies.

---

[6] *cf.* Housing Act 1985 ss.421, *et seq* which are now superseded by these new provisions.
[7] See p. 462.

The new provisions relating to "ring-fencing,"[8] combined with more general measures to reduce local authority spending, means that the freedom of manoeuvre for local housing authorities has been generally reduced.

Housing benefit subsidy is not strictly a direct housing subsidy, since it does not go to the direct support of housing costs, but rather an indirect subsidy for the costs of housing benefits. It is paid to those local authorities responsible for the administration of housing benefit. Current details of the housing benefit subsidy are found in the Housing Benefit (Subsidy) Order, 1990. Some of the interactions, indeed tensions, between the housing benefit schemes and housing benefit subsidy have already been noted.[9]

Although local authorities are able to claim the bulk of their housing benefit expenditure back from central government, the normal rule is that only 97 per cent. of qualifying expenditure is reimbursed.[10] This figure is reduced where late claims have been admitted,[11] where there are deemed to be disproportionate rent increases as between different categories of tenants,[12] where there are high rents,[13] where rent officers have made a determination (or should have done so)[14] and where there have been overpayments of rebates or allowances.[15] There are also special rules regarding payments for the homeless in board and lodging accommodation.[16]

While these rules are, at least in part, designed to ensure efficiency of administration on the part of local authorities, legal and administrative problems can arise where the rules of the scheme itself are more generous than the subsidy rules provide. Clearly the former rules prevail, but this can burden local authorities financially.

(B) HOUSING ASSOCIATION GRANTS

Housing association subsidies have also altered substantially over the years. The most recent legislative provision concerning housing associations is to be found in the Housing Act 1988. The powers to make grants are now given to the Housing Corporation (or Housing for Wales). Two types of grant are envisaged: housing association grant and revenue deficit grant. Sections 50 and 51 provide:

50.—(1) The Housing Corporation and Housing for Wales may make grants to registered housing associations in respect of expenditure incurred or to be

---

[8] See pp. 462–463.
[9] See p. 475.
[10] See Art. 3.
[11] Art. 4.
[12] Art. 5.
[13] Art. 6.
[14] Art. 7 and Sched. 4.
[15] Art. 11.
[16] Art. 10.

incurred by them in connection with housing activities; and any reference in the following provisions of this section to "the Corporation" shall be construed accordingly.

(2) As respects grants under this section the following, namely—

(a)   the procedure to be followed in relation to applications for grant;

(b)   the circumstances in which grant is or is not to be payable;

(c)   the method for calculating, and any limitations on, the amount of grant; and

(d)   the manner in which, and time or times at which, grant is to be paid,

shall be such as may be specified by the Corporation, acting in accordance with such principles as it may from time to time determine.

(3) In making a grant under this section, the Corporation may provide that the grant is conditional on compliance by the association with such conditions as it may specify.

(4) On such terms as it may, with the appropriate approval, specify, the Corporation may appoint a local housing authority which is willing to do so to act as its agent in connection with the assessment and payment of grant under this section; and, where such an appointment is made, the local housing authority shall act as such an agent in accordance with the terms of their appointment.

(5) In subsection (4) above, "the appropriate approval" means the approval of the Secretary of State given with the consent of the Treasury.

(6) Where—

(a)   a grant under this section is payable to an association, and

(b)   at any time property to which the grant relates become vested in, or is leased for a term of years to, or reverts to, some other registered housing association, or trustees for some other such association,

this section (including this subsection) shall have effect after that time as if the grant, or such proportion of it as is specified or determined under subsection (7) below, were payable to that other association.

(7) The proportion referred to in subsection (6) above is that which, in the circumstances of the particular case—

(a)   the Corporation, acting in accordance with such principles as it may from time to time determine, may specify as being appropriate; or

(b)   the Corporation may determine to be appropriate.

(8) Where one of the associations mentioned in subsection (6) above is registered by the Housing Corporation and another is registered by Housing for Wales, the determination mentioned in subsection (7) above shall be such as shall be agreed between the two Corporations.

51.—(1) The Housing Corporation or, as the case may be, Housing for Wales may make a grant to a registered housing association if—

(a)   in relation to all housing activities of the association,

(b) in relation to housing activities of the association of a particular description, or

(c) in relation to particular housing activities of the association,

the association's expenditure as calculated by the Corporation concerned for any period (including a period which is wholly or partly a future period) exceeds its income as so calculated for that period.

(2) In calculating an association's expenditure or income for the purposes of subsection (1) above, the Housing Corporation or, as the case may be, Housing for Wales—

(a) shall act in accordance with such principles as it may from time to time determine; and

(b) may act on such assumptions (whether or not borne out or likely to be borne out by events) as it may from time to time determine.

(3) Subsections (2) and (3) of section 50 above shall apply for the purposes of this section as they apply for the purposes of that section.

Section 52 gives power to the Corporation to recover grants if the terms on which they are made are not being complied with.

The apparent scope of the Corporation's powers is, however, subject to section 53 which states:

53.—(1) A general determination may either—

(a) make the same provision for all cases; or

(b) make different provision for different cases or descriptions of cases, including different provision for different areas or for different descriptions of housing associations or housing activities;

and for the purposes of this subsection descriptions may be framed by reference to any matters whatever, including in particular, in the case of housing activities, the manner in which they are financed.

(2) The Corporation shall not make a determination under the foregoing provisions of this Part except with the approval of the Secretary of State given, in the case of a general determination, with the consent of the Treasury.

(3) Before making a general determination, the Corporation shall consult such bodies appearing to it to be representative of housing associations as it considers appropriate; and after making such a determination, the Corporation shall publish the determination in such manner as it considers appropriate for bringing the determination to the notice of the associations concerned.

(4) In this section "general determination" means a determination under any provision of sections 50 to 52 above, other than a determination relating solely to a particular case.

Note

Notwithstanding the apparent devolution to the Housing Corporation (and Housing for Wales), the effect of these provisions, especially section 53, is that central government retains control over levels of grant expenditure.

VI REMEDIES OF THE LANDLORD FOR FAILURE TO PAY RENT

Failure by the tenant to pay rent may result in a number of legal (and thus social) consequences.

(A) EVICTION

The ultimate sanction for non-payment of rent is eviction.[17] The landlord may seek possession of the property in addition to the other remedies.

(B) DISTRESS FOR RENT

This is an ancient remedy, and an area of law of great technicality.[18] In essence, it allows the goods of the defaulting tenant to be seized in lieu of payment of rent. Distress is usually levied by a bailiff, who has the protection of a warrant to distrain. Distress can only be levied after sunrise and before sunset. Over the years, various enactments have been passed to ensure that the basic necessities of life are not seized. In particular, distress for rent relating to an assured or a regulated tenancy shall only be levied with leave of the county court.[19]

The law has recently been examined by the Law Commission.[20]

(C) A CIVIL ACTION FOR DAMAGES

Since failure to pay rent will usually amount to a breach of the covenant to pay rent, an ordinary civil action for damages for breach of contract can be brought. Since 1971 there has also existed a special procedure in the county court—the "rent action"—for the recovery of rent arrears while the tenant remains in occupation.[21] Landlords who obtain judgment may also obtain an attachment of earnings order against the tenant. However, this is only effective against tenants who are in employment; it becomes very difficult to enforce against those who change employment.

In principle, a successful claim for rent (or for use and occupation or for mesne profits) must be paid in full; the tenant is not usually allowed to set-off damages for breach of covenant against such a claim.[22]

---

[17] Discussed in Chapter 3.
[18] Woodfall, *Landlord and Tenant* (1978), pp. 317–404.
[19] Housing Act 1988, s.19; Rent Act 1977, s.147. See also Rent (Agriculture) Act 1976, s.8. There are no similar rules relating to secure tenancies.
[20] *Working Paper No. 97. Distress for Rent* (1986).
[21] County Court Rules, Order 24, Part II.
[22] *Hart* v. *Rogers* [1916] 1 K.B. 646; *Old Grovebury Manor Farm* v. *W. Seymour Ltd.* [1979] 1 W.L.R. 263. See, though, pp. 378–382.

(D)   COMPENSATION FOR USE AND OCCUPATION

If no rent is agreed but the circumstances indicate that there was an implicit promise to compensate the landlord for the use of premises by a tenant, the law permits the owner of property to recover damages due on an implied agreement to pay for the use of the landlord's property.[23] This implication is rebutted where the circumstances show that the occupation was to be without compensation.[24]

As the right to compensation is based on the fact that no rent has been agreed, the landlord may recover a "reasonable satisfaction" for the use and occupation.[25]

(E)   MESNE PROFITS

After the tenancy has been finally determined (including any period of statutory protection), but the tenant remains in possession, the landlord may, if he wishes, claim "mesne profits." They are calculated according to the fair value of the premises which may or may not be the same as the rent under the preceding tenancy.[26] Where the Rent Acts apply to property, the measure of damages is usually the registered rent, even though a "fair value" might be higher.[27]

(F)   DAMAGES FOR TRESPASS

Where no tenancy existed, but the landlord discovers trespassers on his property, he may sue for damages. In *Swordheath Properties Ltd.* v. *Tabet*[28] the Court of Appeal held that damages could be claimed, even though the landlord did not prove that he could have let the premises during the period of occupation. The measure of damages, "in the absence of anything special in the particular case, would be the ordinary letting value of the property."[29]

VII   ILLEGAL PREMIUMS

"By the end of the [19th] century, the asking for 'key money' ... was becoming very common in areas where houses were hard to find."[30]

It is clear that it would have been futile for Parliament to try to control rent levels but not prohibit premiums. The three elements of the Rent Acts: control of rent, security of tenure and prohibition of illegal

---

[23] *Smith* v. *Eldridge* (1854) 15 C.B. 236.
[24] *Howard* v. *Shaw* (1841) 8 M. & W. 118.
[25] *Tomlinson* v. *Davy* (1821) 2 Brod. & B. 680.
[26] *Clifton Securities* v. *Huntley* [1948] W.N. 267.
[27] *Rawlance* v. *Croydon Corporation* [1952] 2 Q.B. 803; *Newman* v. *Dorrington Developments* [1975] 1 W.L.R. 1642.
[28] [1979] 1 W.L.R. 285.
[29] Megaw L.J. at 288.   [30] Gauldie, *Cruel Habitations* (1974) p. 159.

premiums, are all inter-related. When rent control legislation was first introduced in 1915, however, asking for premiums, though outlawed, was not made a criminal offence; this development occurred in 1920. The current law on illegal premiums is to be found in the Rent Act 1977, sections 119 to 128 (as amended). The most important sections are discussed below.

The relaxation of rent regulation relating to assured tenancies means that there are no prohibitions or premiums charged in relation to them. Local authorities could, in theory, charge premiums in relation to the granting of secure tenancies; in practice they do not.

(A) PROTECTED TENANCIES

119.—(1) Any person who, as a condition of the grant, renewal or continuance of a protected tenancy, requires, in addition to the rent, the payment of any premium or the making of any loan (whether secured or unsecured) shall be guilty of an offence.

(2) Any person who, in connection with the grant, renewal or continuance of a protected tenancy, receives any premium in addition to the rent shall be guilty of an offence.

(3) A person guilty of an offence under this section shall be liable to a fine not exceeding level 3 on the standard scale.

(4) The court by which a person is convicted of an offence under this section relating to requiring or receiving any premium may order the amount of the premium to be repaid to the person by whom it was paid.

Sections 120 and 121 deal with premiums on the assignment of protected tenancies. In such cases, certain sums may legitimately be passed on by the assignor to the assignee. (There is also special protection contained in section 121 and Schedule 18 in the case of tenancies which became regulated as a result of the Counter Inflation Act 1973.)

(B) RESTRICTED CONTRACTS

122.—(1) This section applies in relation to any premises if—

(a)   under Part V of this Act, a rent is registered for those premises in the register kept in pursuance of section 79 of this Act; and

(b)   in a case where the approval, reduction or increase of the rent by the rent tribunal is limited to rent payable in respect of a particular period, that period has not expired.

(2) Any person who, as a condition of the grant, renewal, continuance or assignment of rights under a restricted contract, requires the payment of any premium shall be guilty of an offence.

(3) Nothing in subsection (2) above shall prevent a person from requiring—

(a)   that there shall be paid so much of any outgoings discharged by a grantor or assignor as is referable to any period after the grant or assignment takes effect; or

(b) that there shall be paid a reasonable amount in respect of goodwill of a business, trade, or profession, where the goodwill is transferred to a grantee or assignee in connection with the grant or assignment or accrues to him in consequence thereof.

(4) A person guilty of an offence under this section shall be liable to a fine not exceeding level 3 on the standard scale.

(5) The court by which a person is convicted of an offence under this section may order the amount of the premium, or so much of it as cannot lawfully be required under this section, to be repaid to the person by whom it was paid.

(C) TREATMENT OF FURNITURE

123.—Where the purchase of any furniture has been required as a condition of the grant, renewal, continuance or assignment—

(a) of a protected tenancy, or

(b) of rights under a restricted contract which relates to premises falling within section 122(1) of this Act, then, if the price exceeds the reasonable price of the furniture, the excess shall be treated, for the purposes of this Part of this Act, as if it were a premium required to be paid as a condition of the grant, renewal, continuance or assignment of the protected tenancy or, as the case may be, the rights under the restricted contract.

One commentator, adapting the judgment of Denning L.J. in *Eales* v. *Dale*,[31] wrote:

"The reasonable price" means the price which in all the relevant circumstances was the reasonable price for the parties to have agreed; and this is a question of fact for the trial judge. It is not the price which would be realised if the articles were removed and sold by auction, but the price which an outgoing tenant who is willing to leave would agree with an incoming tenant who is willing to take them over; and this leaves much latitude. Fitted carpets are worth more in situ than removed, and furniture may be particularly suited to the premises. Where articles have a recognisable market value, this is important but not necessarily conclusive; but a price which exceeds the replacement cost cannot be reasonable. Extraneous elements must be excluded, such as the incoming tenant's desire to obtain a tenancy, or any payments for agent's commission or redecoration. The onus is on the tenant to establish that the price is excessive. This provision is confined to furniture, fittings and other articles; there is no corresponding provision to the effect that only the excess of any payment for other matters, such as repairs shall be treated as a premium.[32]

Enforcement of section 123 may be assisted in theory by a complex procedure laid down in section 124. Among other things this gives power to local authority officials to enter premises and inspect furniture where the price asked is thought to be excessive.

---

[31] [1954] 1 Q.B. 539.
[32] Megarry, *The Rent Acts* (11th ed., 1988) pp. 718–719.

(D) RENT IN ADVANCE

126.—(1) Where a protected tenancy which is a regulated tenancy is granted, continued or renewed, any requirement that rent shall be payable—

(a) before the beginning of the rental period in respect of which it is payable, or

(b) earlier than six months before the end of the rental period in respect of which it is payable (if that period is more than six months).

shall be void, whether the requirement is imposed as a condition of the grant, renewal or continuance of the tenancy or under the terms thereof.

(2) Any requirement avoided by subsection (1) above is, in this section, referred to as a "prohibited requirement."

(3) Rent for any rental period to which a prohibited requirement relates shall be irrecoverable from the tenant.

(4) Any person who purports to impose any prohibited requirements shall be liable to a fine not exceeding level 3 in the standard scale and the court by which he is convicted may order any amount of rent paid in compliance with the prohibited requirement to be repaid to the person by whom it was paid ...

If "irrecoverable" payments have in fact been made, they may be recovered for up to two years after the date of payment[33] either from the landlord or his personal representatives[34] or by deduction from rent.[35] False entries in rent books are also punishable.[36]

(5) DEPOSITS

In section 128(1)(c)[37] of the Rent Act 1977 "premium" is defined as including:

any sum paid by way of a deposit, other than one which does not exceed one-sixth of the annual rent under the tenancy and is reasonable in relation to the potential liability in respect of which it is paid.

(F) RECOVERY OF PREMIUMS

In addition to creating criminal offences, there is a general right given to those who have paid illegal premiums to recover them from those persons to whom they have been paid (section 125).

Notes

(i) As already noted, not all premiums are illegal. Only if the tenancy is within the Rent Act will any accompanying premium be unlawful.

[33] s.126(7).
[34] s.126(5).
[35] s.126(6).
[36] ss.126(8) and (9).
[37] Introduced by Housing Act 1980, s.70.

Thus most long leases with a very low ground rent fall outside these provisions. Special rules apply to long leases that also happen to be Rent Act protected[38] in order that, as far as possible, premiums are not rendered illegal.

(ii) The meaning of "person" in section 119 was discussed by the House of Lords in *Farrell* v. *Alexander*.[39]

Lord Wilberforce said:

> My Lords, the appellants, Mrs. Farrell and her daughter, have brought an action to recover from the respondent, Mrs. Alexander, a sum of money which was paid to her in order to obtain the tenancy of a flat. They claim that this money was a premium which it was illegal for the respondent to require or to receive and that they have the right to recover it ...
>
> The respondent had a protected tenancy of this flat with some four years unexpired from the Church Commissioners. There were negotiations with the appellants with a view to an assignment of it and the appellants were asked for a sum of £4,000 for the fixtures and fittings. Though the actual value of these fixtures and fittings has not been determined, it was certainly less than £4,000 so that the balance was a premium for the proposed assignment ... The transaction proceeded in this way. A formal agreement was drawn up under which the respondent agreed to surrender the lease subject to acceptance of the surrender by the landlords and to the simultaneous grant by them of a new lease to the appellants. On completion the new lessees were to pay to the respondent the sum of £4,000 for fixtures and fittings, and this money was in fact paid ... So the question to be decided is whether it is illegal for a lessee to require or to receive a premium as a condition of surrendering her lease, and in order that a new lease may be granted to the payer of the premium ...
>
> My Lords, I must say that, in relation to the facts which I have stated, these sections are to me, if not transparently clear, at least unambiguous in the legal sense. They refer to "any person," words wide enough to include landlords, tenants, agents or middlemen. They apply to what was done here because the respondent required the premium as a condition of the grant of a protected tenancy (see the words "subject to ... the simultaneous grant" mentioned above). The words "any person" ... are words of wide generality and fit, without any strain whatever, the present facts.

Difficulties arose because two decisions of the Court of Appeal, *Remmington* v. *Larchin*[40] and *Zimmerman* v. *Grossman*[41] had decided that "person" meant "landlord" only. Nonetheless, Lord Wilberforce decided that these decisions should not be followed and held that the sum demanded in the present case was recoverable. Viscount Dilhorne, Lords Simond, Edmund-Davies and Russell of Killowen all delivered concurring judgments. (Much of what their lordships had to say related to the proper method of interpreting consolidating Acts of Parliament, where the words of earlier legislation had not been changed.)

---

[38] See s.127 and Sched. 18, Part II (as amended by Housing Act 1980, s.78 and further amended by Housing Act 1988, s.115).
[39] [1977] A.C. 59, at 70.
[40] [1921] 3 K.B. 404.
[41] [1972] 1 Q.B. 167.

(iii)   Apart from the specific cases relating to furniture, rent in advance and deposits, premium is defined by section 128 of the Rent Act 1977, as amended as:

(a)   any fine or other like sum;

(b)   any other pecuniary consideration in addition to rent ...

The scope for interpretation is obviously extensive though, surprisingly perhaps, the amount of judicial authority is small.[42]

VIII   AGENTS' COMMISSIONS

It is an offence for certain commissions to be demanded from potential tenants. The Accommodation Agencies Act 1953 provides:

1.—(1) Subject to the provisions of this section, any person who, during the continuance in force of this Act,—

(a)   demands or accepts payment of any sum of money in consideration of registering, or undertaking to register, the name or requirements of any person seeking the tenancy of a house;

(b)   demands or accepts payment of any sum of money in consideration of supplying, or undertaking to supply, to any person addresses or other particulars of houses to let; or

(c)   issues any advertisement, list or other document describing any house as being to let without the authority of the owner of the house or his agent,

shall be guilty of an offence.

(2) A person shall not be guilty of an offence under this section by reason of his demanding or accepting payment from the owner of a house of any remuneration payable to him as agent for the said owner.

(3) A person being a solicitor shall not be guilty of an offence under this section by reason of his demanding or accepting payment of any remuneration in respect of business done by him as such.

(4) A person shall not be guilty of an offence under this section by reason of his demanding or accepting any payment in consideration of the display in a shop, or of the publication in a newspaper, of any advertisement or notice, or by reason of the display or publication as aforesaid of an advertisement or notice received for the purpose in the ordinary course of business.

(5) Any person guilty of an offence under this section shall be liable on summary conviction to a fine not exceeding level 5 on the standard scale or to imprisonment for a term not exceeding three months, or to both such fine and imprisonment.

(6) In this section the following expressions have the meanings hereby assigned to them that is to say:—

"house" includes any part of a building which is occupied or intended to be occupied as a dwelling;

---

[42] See Megarry, *The Rents Acts* (11th ed., 1988), pp. 682–688.

"newspaper" includes any periodical or magazine;
"owner," in relation to a house, means the person having power to grant a lease of the house.

Although the level of fine suggests that breach of this provision should be regarded as a serious matter, it appears that the Act is widely ignored (indeed an anonymous solicitor was reported in *The Guardian*, August 12, 1971, as saying it was "one of those laws where nobody can believe what it appears to mean, so everybody ignores it"). It has, however, been subject to some judicial interpretation.

Saunders v. *Soper* [1975] A.C. 239

Viscount Dilhorne said:

My Lords, the appellant ... carries on and has carried on for some 6½ years a highly respectable agency under the name of Wilson's Accommodation Bureau. On January 25, 1973 a Miss Christine Nichols came to see her, wanting accommodation for herself and two friends. The appellant at that time did not know of any likely to suit but agreed to try and find some and asked Miss Nichols to call on her again. Miss Nichols did so on a number of occasions.

The appellant, or someone on her behalf, inspected premises at 27 Dawlish Drive, Southend-on-Sea, and thought they might suit Miss Nichols, and so Miss Nichols was given that address.

On February 17, 1973 Miss Nichols signed an agreement in writing which contained the following paragraph:

"In consideration of the services of Wilson's Accommodation Bureau in finding or introducing accommodation acceptable to me/us, I/We agree to pay to Wilson's Accommodation Bureau a Fee of the equivalent of one week's rent (minimum £5.25) for the accommodation accepted by me/us. No fee is payable to Wilson's Accommodation Bureau unless and until I or We become the tenant(s) of the accommodation found or introduced by Wilson's Accommodation Bureau to me/us."

Miss Nichols, having inspected the premises, entered into an agreement to rent them for £7 a week. She thereupon under the agreement into which she had entered became liable to pay to the appellant £7 and she paid that sum on February 20, 1973.

Later Miss Nichols again came to see the appellant and again told her that she wanted accommodation for three persons. Again, the appellant had no suitable accommodation on her books and Miss Nichols was asked to call again. She did so on a number of occasions and one the last occasion was given an address, 34 Retreat Road, Westcliff-on-Sea. On March 16, 1973 she signed an agreement similar in all respects to that which she had previously made with the appellant. She became tenant of those premises at a weekly rent of £16 a week and so became liable under the agreement to pay the appellant £16. This she did not do and has not done although payment was demanded.

On July 12, 1973 the respondent, a police inspector, preferred two informations against her, the first alleging that she had on February 20, 1973 accepted from Miss Nichols £7 in consideration of supplying her with addresses of houses to let contrary to section 1(1)(b) of the Accommodation Agencies Act 1953; and the second alleging that she had demanded £16 in consideration of supplying Miss Nichols with addresses of houses to let contrary to that subsection of that Act. The appellant was convicted of both offences and her appeal to the Divisional Court was dismissed. She now appeals to this House with the leave of that court.

That she accepted £7 from Miss Nichols and demanded payment of £16 by her is not disputed. The question to be decided is whether by doing so she committed offences against this subsection ...

It is to be noted that the object of the Act is not stated to be the prohibition of the taking of all commissions in dealings with such persons but only of the taking of certain commissions ...

The first matter to consider is what was the mischief at which this Act was aimed. One can only deduce that from its terms. Section 1(1)(a) was clearly directed to preventing persons desirous of accommodation being charged merely for the registration of their names or their requirements. Section 1(1)(b) was, in my view, equally clearly directed to preventing charges being made just for supplying addresses. It is obvious what section 1(1)(c) was intended to prevent.

Commission of any of the three offences created by this section does not in any way depend on the character of the agency. Whether the agency be reputable or bogus, the person who runs it and charges for supplying addresses to persons wanting accommodation, commits an offence against section 1(1)(b).

The object of section 1(2) is not at first sight easy to discern but if it was not there, a person who at the request of the owner, say, of a block of new flats, supplied the addresses of those flats to would-be occupants, would be unable to obtain from the owner or his agent any remuneration for his services.

It was not in this case contended that the agreements signed by Miss Nichols did not correctly and completely state the terms on which the bureau would become entitled to payment from her. The respondent, however, contended that if in the course of carrying out the contract made, the address of premises to let was supplied, then the demand or acceptance of payment, even though no payment was due unless and until acceptable accommodation has been found and rented by the client, was, inter alia, a demand or acceptance of payment for the supplying of the address.

If this be right, it follows that an agent employed by a prospective tenant to find for him, it may be, a large house or whose requirements are of an unusual character, cannot lawfully demand payment for his services from his client when he finds premises which suit his client and of which his client becomes the tenant. Counsel for the respondent in the course of his argument was unable to suggest that in such circumstances there was any mischief in the agent claiming commission which Parliament would want to prevent.

In my opinion, the mischief to which section 1(1)(b) was directed was simply to prevent charges being made for supplying addresses and did not extend beyond that.

So, in my opinion, the question for decision in this appeal is simply, did the appellant accept or demand payment for supplying addresses? If instead of supplying one address on each occasion, she had supplied 100 or 1,000 addresses, under the agreements which she signed Miss Nichols would not have been liable to make any payment. She was not asked to pay nor did she pay for being given addresses. Under the agreements she became liable to pay not for the giving of addresses but for the finding of accommodation acceptable to her and accommodation of which she became the tenant.

On the facts of this case and in view of the terms of the agreements entered into, consideration of the terms of the section leads me to the conclusion that this appeal should be allowed; and as I read Lord Widgery C.J.'s judgment in this case, that would appear to have been his view were it not that he felt himself bound by some previous decisions to which I must now refer.

The first of these was *McInnes* v. *Clarke*. In my opinion, the decision in that case was clearly right and is clearly distinguishable from this case ... The judgments in that case make it clear that the decision was founded on the payment of the deposit. In the present case there was no demand for or acceptance of payment just for supplying addresses.

The next case was *Crouch and Lees* v. *Haridas* ... With the greatest respect, I do not think that it was accurate to say that the fact there was no advance payment made no difference at all or that in each case there would have been no payment if the client was not satisfied. In *McInnes* v. *Clarke* there was a payment, which if the client was dissatisfied he might recover. In *Crouch and Lees* v. *Haridas* no payment of any sum was made or became due unless and until the client became a tenant of the premises of which the address had been supplied to him. In that case the other Lords Justices agreed with Davies L.J. I think that the decision was wrong for it does not appear to me from the facts set out in the report of the case that any payment was either accepted or demanded just for supplying addresses ...

As in my view it was not proved in this case that any payment was demanded or accepted for the supplying of an address and as it was proved that the payments were accepted or demanded not for that but for finding Miss Nichols suitable accommodation and due only on her entering into a tenancy, in my opinion she was wrongly convicted and that this appeal should be allowed ...

IX   SERVICE CHARGES

Many tenants are required by the terms of the lease to pay not only rent, but also service charges to cover the cost of certain expenditure on the building—such as repairs and insurance. These service charges are normally paid to the landlord, or to a managing agent.

Some measure of statutory control over service charges is provided by sections 18 to 30 of the Landlord and Tenant Act 1985 (as amended by the Landlord and Tenant Act 1987). The primary aim of the legislation is to ensure that the money received by the landlord (or his agent) is used for the purposes for which it is collected.

As will be seen, the provisions themselves are rather complex. The basic outline however, is relatively straightforward. Under the Landlord and Tenant Act 1985 service charges are limited to costs which have been reasonably incurred or are likely to be incurred in the provision of services and works; furthermore, recovery is only possible for work which has been carried out to a reasonable standard.[43] Where works cost more than £500 (or more than £25 per dwelling) two estimates must be obtained, one of which should be from a firm not connected with the landlord; recognised tenants' associations must be consulted prior to the carrying out of the work, and tenants are entitled to be given a break-down of the costing.[44] Where costs have been incurred more than 18 months before a demand is made of the tenant the costs cannot be recovered.[45]

[43] s.19.
[44] s.20.
[45] s.20B.

The full text of sections 18 to 20C reads as follows:

18.—(1) In the following provisions of this Act "service charge" means an amount payable by a tenant of a flat as part of or in addition to the rent—

    (a)   which is payable, directly or indirectly, for services, repairs, maintenance or insurance or the landlord's costs of management, and

    (b)   the whole or part of which varies or may vary according to the relevant costs.

(2) The relevant costs are the costs or estimated costs incurred or to be incurred by or on behalf of the landlord, or a superior landlord, in connection with the matters for which the service charge is payable.

(3) For this purpose—

    (a)   "costs" includes overheads, and

    (b)   costs are relevant costs in relation to a service charge whether they are incurred, or to be incurred, in the period for which the service charge is payable or in an earlier or later period.

19.—(1) Relevant costs shall be taken into account in determining the amount of a service charge payable for a period—

    (a)   only to the extent that they are reasonably incurred, and

    (b)   where they are incurred on the provision of services or the carrying out of works, only if the services or works are of a reasonable standard;

and the amount payable shall be limited accordingly.[45a]

(2) Where a service charge is payable before the relevant costs are incurred, no greater amount than is reasonable is so payable, and after the relevant costs have been incurred any necessary adjustment shall be made by repayment, reduction or subsequent charges or otherwise.

(3) An agreement by the tenant of a dwelling (other than an arbitration agreement within the meaning of section 32 of the Arbitration Act 1950) is void in so far as it purports to provide for a determination in a particular manner, or on particular evidence, of any question—

    (a)   whether costs incurred for services, repairs, maintenance, insurance or management were reasonably incurred,

    (b)   whether services or works for which costs incurred are of a reasonable standard, or

    (c)   whether an amount payable before costs are incurred is reasonable.

(4) A county court may make a declaration—

    (a)   that any such costs were or were not reasonably incurred,

    (b)   that any such services or works are or are not of a reasonable standard, or

    (c)   that any such amount is or is not reasonable,

[45a] See *Renton Ltd.* v. *Hudson* [1990] 37 E.G. 86.

notwithstanding that no other relief is sought in the proceedings.

(5) If a person takes any proceedings in the High Court in pursuance of any of the provisions of this Act relating to service charges and he could have taken those proceedings in the county court, he shall not be entitled to recover any costs.

20.—(1) Where relevant costs incurred on the carrying out of any qualifying works exceed the limit specified in subsection (3), the excess shall not be taken into account in determining the amount of a service charge unless the relevant requirements have been either—

(a) complied with, or

(b) dispensed with by the court in accordance with subsection (9);

and the amount payable shall be limited accordingly.

(2) In subsection (1) "qualifying works," in relation to a service charge, means works (whether on a building or on any other premises) to the costs of which the tenant by whom the service charge is payable may be required under the terms of his lease to contribute by the payment of such a charge.

(3) The limit is whichever is the greater of—

(a) £25, or such other amount as may be prescribed by order of the Secretary of State, multiplied by the number of dwellings let to the tenants concerned; or

(b) £500, or such other amount as may be so prescribed.

(4) The relevant requirements in relation to such of the tenants concerned as are not represented by a recognised tenants' association are—

(a) At least two estimates for the works shall be obtained, one of them from a person wholly unconnected with the landlord.

(b) A notice accompanied by a copy of the estimates shall be given to each of those tenants or shall be displayed in one or more places where it is likely to come to the notice of all those tenants.

(c) The notice shall describe the works to be carried out and invite observations on them and on the estimates and shall state the name and the address in the United Kingdom of the person to whom the observations may be sent and the date by which they are to be received.

(d) The date stated in the notice shall not be earlier than one month after the date on which the notice is given or displayed as required by paragraph (b).

(e) The landlord shall have regard to any observations received in pursuance of the notice; and unless the works are urgently required they shall not be begun earlier than the date specified in the notice.

(5) The relevant requirements in relation to such of the tenants concerned as are represented by a recognised tenants' association are—

(a) The landlord shall give to the secretary of the association a notice containing a detailed specification of the works in question and specifying a reasonable period within which the association may propose to the landlord the names of one or more persons from whom estimates for the works should in its view be obtained by the landlord.

(b)   At least two estimates for the works shall be obtained, one of them from a person wholly unconnected with the landlord.

(c)   A copy of each of the estimates shall be given to the secretary of the association.

(d)   A notice shall be given to each of the tenants concerned represented by the association, which shall—

  (i)   describe briefly the works to be carried out,
  (ii)   summarise the estimates,
  (iii) inform the tenant that he has a right to inspect and take copies of a detailed specification of the works to be carried out and of the estimates,
  (iv)   invite observations on those works and on the estimates, and
  (v)   specify the name and the address in the United Kingdom of the person to whom the observations may be sent and the date by which they are to be received.

(e)   The date stated in the notice shall not be earlier than one month after the date on which the notice is given as required by paragraph (d).

(f)   If any tenant to whom the notice is given so requests, the landlord shall afford him reasonable facilities for inspecting a detailed specification of the works to be carried out and the estimates, free of charge, and for taking copies of them on payment of such reasonable charge as the landlord may determine.

(g)   The landlord shall have regard to any observations received in pursuance of the notice and, unless the works are urgently required, they shall not be begun earlier than the date specified in the notice.

(6) Paragraphs (d)(ii) and (iii) and (f) of subsection (5) shall not apply to any estimate of which a copy is enclosed with the notice given in pursuance of paragraph (d).

(7) The requirement imposed on the landlord by subsection (5)(f) to make any facilities available to a person free of charge shall not be construed as precluding the landlord from treating as part of his costs of management any costs incurred by him in connection with making those facilities so available.

(8) In this section "the tenants concerned" means all the landlord's tenants who may be required under the terms of their leases to contribute to the costs of the works in question by the payment of service charges.

(9) In proceedings relating to a service charge the court may, if satisfied that the landlord acted reasonably, dispense with all or any of the relevant requirements.

(10) An order under this section—

(a)   may make different provision with respect to different cases or descriptions of case, including different provision for different areas, and

(b) shall be made by statutory instrument which shall be subject to annulment in pursuance of a resolution of either House of Parliament."

20A.—(1) Where relevant costs are incurred or to be incurred on the carrying out of works in respect of which a grant has been or is to be paid under Part XV of the Housing Act 1985 or Part VIII of the Local Government and Housing Act 1989 (grants for works of improvement, repair or conversion), the amount of the grant shall be deducted from the costs and the amount of the service charge payable shall be reduced accordingly.

(2) In any case where—

(a) relevant costs are incurred or to be incurred on the carrying out of works which are included in the external works specified in a group repair scheme, within the meaning of Part VIII of the Local Government and Housing Act 1989, and

(b) the landlord participated or is participating in that scheme as an assisted participant,

the amount which, in relation to the landlord, is the outstanding balance determined in accordance with subsections (3) and (4) of section 130 of that Act shall be deducted from the costs, and the amount of the service charge payable shall be reduced accordingly.

20B.—(1) If any of the relevant costs taken into account in determining the amount of any service charge were incurred more than 18 months before a demand for payment of the service charge is served on the tenant, then (subject to subsection (2)), the tenant shall not be liable to pay so much of the service charge as reflects the costs so incurred.

(2) Subsection (1) shall not apply, if, within the period of 18 months beginning with the date when the relevant costs in question were incurred, the tenant was notified in writing that those costs had been incurred and that he would subsequently be required under the terms of his lease to contribute to them by the payment of a service charge.

20C.—(1) A tenant may make an application to the appropriate court for an order that all or any of the costs incurred, or to be incurred, by the landlord in connection with any proceedings are not to be regarded as relevant costs to be taken into account in determining the amount of any service charge payable by the tenant or any other person or persons specified in the application; and the court may make such order on the application as it considers just and equitable in the circumstances.

(2) In subsection (1) "the appropriate court" means—

(a) if the application is made in the course of the proceedings in question, the court before which the proceedings are taking place; and

(b) if the application is made after those proceedings are concluded, a county court.

Sections 21 to 23 give tenants the right to request information relating to service charges, and by virtue of section 25 it is an offence for the landlord to fail to comply with the obligations imposed by these provisions. (Section 24 states that the validity of a request under sections 21 to 23 is not affected by assignment of the tenancy.)

Sections 18 to 25 of the Landlord and Tenant Act 1985 do not apply to certain public sector landlords—namely, local authorities, new town corporations and the Development Board for Rural Wales—unless the tenancy in question is a long tenancy (which means, generally speaking, a tenancy for a term exceeding 21 years).[46]

It is also provided by section 42 of the Landlord and Tenant Act 1987 that service charges must be held by the landlord or his agent in a trust fund. This means that the money collected by the levying of service charges can only be used for specific purposes, namely paying for those items of expenditure to which the service charges relate. At the end of his lease the tenant cannot, however, recover a share of the money which has been paid into the fund. The fund continues to be used for the benefit of the tenants who are for the time being occupying the building. If all the leases expire and the building becomes vacant, the landlord is entitled to any money remaining in the trust fund.

It should be noted that the service charge provisions of the Landlord and Tenant Act 1985 apply only to flats. However, under section 45 to 51 of the Housing Act 1985 similar controls on the recovery of service charges are applicable to houses which have been transferred—either individually or collectively—from the public into the private sector.

X RIGHTS OF PUBLIC SECTOR TENANTS

The general obligations of landlords to provide information to their tenants (either by means of a rent book or otherwise) have already been discussed.[47] Certain public sector landlords must also comply with a number of obligations imposed by the Housing Act 1985. Sections 104 to 106 require public sector landlords (other than co-operative housing associations[48]) to publish various pieces of information, and to consult their tenants on matters of housing management:

104.—(1) Every body which lets dwelling-houses under secure tenancies shall from time to time publish information about its secure tenancies, in such form as it considers best suited to explain in simple terms, and so far as it considers it appropriate, the effect of—

    (a)   the express terms of its secure tenancies,

    (b)   the provisions of this Part and Part V (the right to buy), and

    (c)   the provisions of sections 11 to 16 of the Landlord and Tenant Act 1985 (landlord's repairing obligations),

---

[46] Landlord and Tenant Act 1985, s.26.
[47] See pp. 95–103.
[48] Housing Act 1989, s.109.

and shall ensure that so far as is reasonably practicable the information so published is kept up to date.

(2) The landlord under a secure tenancy shall supply the tenant with—

(a)   a copy of the information for secure tenants published by it under subsection (1), and

(b)   a written statement of the terms of the tenancy, so far as they are neither expressed in the lease or written tenancy agreement (if any) nor implied by law;

and the statement required by paragraph (b) shall be supplied on the grant of the tenancy or as soon as practicable afterwards.

105.—(1) A landlord authority shall maintain such arrangements as it considers appropriate to enable those of its secure tenants who are likely to be substantially affected by a matter of housing management to which this section applies—

(a)   to be informed of the authority's proposals in respect of the matter, and

(b)   to make their views known to the authority within a specified period;

and the authority shall, before making any decision on the matter, consider any representations made to it in accordance with those arrangements.

(2) For the purposes of this section, a matter is one of housing management if, in the opinion of the landlord authority, it relates to—

(a)   the management, maintenance, improvement or demolition of dwelling-houses let by the authority under secure tenancies, or

(b)   the provision of services or amenities in connection with such dwelling-houses;

but not so far as it relates to the rent payable under a secure tenancy or to charges for services or facilities provided by the authority.

(3) This section applies to matters of housing management which, in the opinion of the landlord authority, represent—

(a)   a new programme of maintenance, improvement or demolition, or

(b)   a change in the practice or policy of the authority,

and are likely substantially to affect either its secure tenants as a whole or a group of them who form a distinct social group or occupy dwelling-houses which constitute a distinct class (whether by reference to the kind of dwelling-house, or the housing estate or other larger area in which they are situated).

(4) In the case of a landlord authority which is a local housing authority, the reference in subsection (2) to the provision of services or amenities is a reference only to the provision of services or amenities by the authority acting in its capacity as landlord of the dwelling-houses concerned.

(5) A landlord authority shall publish details of the arrangements which it makes under this section, and a copy of the documents published under this subsection shall—

(a)   be made available at the authority's principal office for inspection at all reasonable hours, without charge, by members of the public, and (b)　be given, on payment of a reasonable fee, to any member of the public who asks for one.

(6) A landlord authority which is a registered housing association shall, instead of complying with paragraph (a) of subsection (5), send a copy of any document published under that subsection—

(a)　to the Housing Corporation, and

(b)　to the council of any district or London borough in which there are dwelling-houses let by the association under secure tenancies;

and a council to whom a copy is sent under this subsection shall make it available at its principal office for inspection at all reasonable hours, without charge, by members of the public.

106.—(1) A landlord authority shall publish a summary of its rules—

(a)　for determining priority as between applicants in the allocation of its housing accommodation, and

(b)　governing cases where secure tenants wish to move (whether or not by way of exchange of dwelling-houses) to other dwelling-houses let under secure tenancies by that authority or another body.

(2) A landlord authority shall—

(a)　maintain a set of the rules referred to in subsection (1) and of the rules which it has laid down governing the procedure to be followed in allocating its housing accommodation, and

(b)　make them available at its principal office for inspection at all reasonable hours, without charge, by members of the public.

(3) A landlord authority which is a registered housing association shall, instead of complying with paragraph (b) of subsection (2), send a set of the rules referred to in paragraph (a) of that subsection—

(a)　to the Housing Corporation, and

(b)　to the council of any district or London borough in which there are dwelling-houses let or to be let by the association under secure tenancies;

and a council to whom a set of rules is sent under this subsection shall make it available at its principal office for inspection at all reasonable hours, without charge by members of the public.

(4) A copy of the summary published under subsection (1) shall be given without charge, and a copy of the set of rules maintained under subsection (2) shall be given on payment of a reasonable fee, to any member of the public who asks for one.

(5) At the request of a person who has applied to it for housing accommodation, a landlord authority shall make available to him, at all reasonable times and without charge, details of the particulars which he has given to the authority about himself and his family and which the authority has recorded as being relevant to his application for accommodation.

Note

The impact (or lack of it) of these measures is discussed in A. Kay, C. Legg and J. Foot, *The 1980 Tenants' Rights in Practice* (1983; City University, Housing Research Group).

XI VARIATION OF TERMS

According to ordinary contractual principles, the obligations agreed by the parties may be altered either under the terms of the tenancy agreement itself, or by the mutual consent of the parties. However, both the Housing Act 1985 and the Housing Act 1988 lay down special statutory mechanisms whereby the terms of secure tenancies and certain assured tenancies may be varied.

(A) ASSURED TENANCIES

Section 6 of the Housing Act 1988 provides:

6.—(1) In this section, in relation to a statutory periodic tenancy,—

(a) "the former tenancy" means the fixed term tenancy on the coming to an end of which the statutory periodic tenancy arises; and

(b) "the implied terms" means the terms of the tenancy which have effect by virtue of section 5(3)(e) above, other than terms as to the amount of the rent;

but nothing in the following provisions of this section applies to a statutory periodic tenancy at a time when, by virtue of paragraph 11 or paragraph 12 in Part 1 of Schedule 1 to this Act, it cannot be an assured tenancy.

(2) Not later than the first anniversary of the day on which the former tenancy came to an end, the landlord may serve on the tenant, or the tenant may serve on the landlord, a notice in the prescribed form proposing terms of the statutory periodic tenancy different from the implied terms and, if the landlord or the tenant considers it appropriate, proposing an adjustment of the amount of the rent to take account of the proposed terms.

(3) Where a notice has been served under subsection (2) above,—

(a) within the period of three months beginning on the date on which the notice was served on him, the landlord or the tenant, as the case may be, may, by an application in the prescribed form, refer the notice to a rent assessment committee under subsection (4) below; and

(b) if the notice is not so referred, then, with effect from such date, not falling within the period referred to in paragraph (a) above, as may be specified in the notice, the terms proposed in the notice shall become terms of the tenancy in substitution for any of the implied terms dealing with the same subject matter and the amount of the rent shall be varied in accordance with any adjustment so proposed.

(4) Where a notice under subsection (2) above is referred to a rent assessment committee, the committee shall consider the terms proposed in the notice and

shall determine whether those terms, or some other terms (dealing with the same subject matter as the proposed terms), are such as, in the committee's opinion, might reasonably be expected to be found in an assured periodic tenancy of the dwelling-house concerned, being a tenancy—

(a) which begins on the coming to an end of the former tenancy; and

(b) which is granted by a willing landlord on terms which, except in so far as they relate to the subject matter of the proposed terms, are those of the statutory periodic tenancy at the time of the committee's consideration.

(5) Whether or not a notice under subsection (2) above proposes an adjustment of the amount of the rent under the statutory periodic tenancy, where a rent assessment committee determine any terms under subsection (4) above, they shall, if they consider it appropriate, specify such an adjustment to take account of the terms so determined.

(6) In making a determination under subsection (4) above, or specifying an adjustment of an amount of rent under subsection (5) above, there shall be disregarded any effect on the terms or the amount of the rent attributable to the granting of a tenancy to a sitting tenant.

(7) Where a notice under subsection (2) above is referred to a rent assessment committee, then, unless the landlord and the tenant otherwise agree, with effect from such date as the committee may direct—

(a) the terms determined by the committee shall become terms of the statutory periodic tenancy in substitution for any of the implied terms dealing with the same subject matter; and

(b) the amount of the rent under the statutory periodic tenancy shall be altered to accord with any adjustment specified by the committee;

but for the purposes of paragraph (b) above the committee shall not direct a date earlier than the date specified, in accordance with subsection (3)(b) above, in the notice referred to them.

(8) Nothing in this section requires a rent assessment committee to continue with a determination under subsection (4) above if the landlord and tenant give notice in writing that they no longer require such a determination or if the tenancy has come to an end.

(B)   SECURE TENANCIES

The means whereby the terms of a secure tenancy can be varied are set out in sections 102 and 103 of the Housing Act 1985 (previously, section 40 of the Housing Act 1980):

102.—(1) The terms of a secure tenancy may be varied in the following ways, and not otherwise—

(a) by agreement between the landlord and the tenant

(b) to the extent that the variation relates to rent or to payments in respect of rates or services, by the landlord or the tenant in accordance with a provision in the lease or agreement creating the tenancy, or in an agreement varying it;

(c)   in accordance with section 103 (notice of variation of periodic tenancy).

(2) References in this section and section 103 to variation include addition and deletion; and for the purposes of this section the conversion of a monthly tenancy into a weekly tenancy, or a weekly tenancy into a monthly tenancy, is a variation of a term of the tenancy, but a variation of the premises let under a tenancy is not.

(3) This section and section 103 do not apply to a term of a tenancy which—

(a)   is implied by an enactment, or

(b)   may be varied under section 93 of the Rent Act 1977 (housing association and other tenancies: increase of rent without notice to quit).

(4) This section and section 103 apply in relation to the terms of a periodic tenancy arising by virtue of section 86 (periodic tenancy arising on termination of a fixed term) as they would have applied to the terms of the first tenancy mentioned in that section had that tenancy been a periodic tenancy.

103.—(1) The terms of a secure tenancy which is a periodic tenancy may be varied by the landlord by a notice of variation served on the tenant.

(2) Before serving a notice of variation on the tenant the landlord shall serve on him a preliminary notice—

(a)   informing the tenant of the landlord's intention to serve a notice of variation,

(b)   specifying the proposed variation and its effect, and

(c)   inviting the tenant to comment on the proposed variation within such time, specified in the notice, as the landlord considers reasonable;

and the landlord shall consider any comments by the tenant within the specified time.

(3) Subsection (2) does not apply to a variation of the rent, or of payments in respect of services or facilities provided by the landlord or of payments in respect of rates.

(4) The notice of variation shall specify—

(a)   the variation effected by it, and

(b)   the date on which it takes effect;

and the period between the date on which it is served and the date on which it takes effect must be at least four weeks or the rental period, whichever is the longer.

(5) The notice of variation, when served, shall be accompanied by such information as the landlord considers necessary to inform the tenant of the nature and effect of the variation.

(6) If after the service of a notice of variation the tenant, before the date on which the variation is to take effect, gives a valid notice to quit, the notice of variation shall not take effect unless the tenant, with the written agreement of the landlord, withdraws his notice to quit before that date.

Notes

(i)   These provisions do not apply to situations where the landlord is a co-operative housing association.[49]

(ii)   The variation procedure provided by what is now section 103 of the 1985 Act was considered by the Court of Appeal in *Palmer* v. *Sandwell M.B.C.*[50] The court held that, in order for there to be an effective variation under this section, the formal requirements imposed by subsection (2) must be complied with.

(C)   RENT ACT TENANCIES

The terms of a protected tenancy can be varied only by mutual consent, or by a mechanism expressly provided for by the tenancy agreement itself. Furthermore, the terms of the protected tenancy will carry over into the statutory tenancy which arises when the protected tenancy comes to an end. There is no provision of the Rent Act 1977 equivalent to section 6 of the Housing Act 1988.

Section 3(1) of the Rent Act 1977 provides:

So long as he retains possession, a statutory tenant shall observe and be entitled to the benefit of all the terms of the original contract of tenancy, so far as they are consistent with the provisions of this Act.

[49] Housing Act 1985, s.109.
[50] (1988) 20 H.L.R. 74.

CHAPTER 8

THE PRIVATISATION OF PUBLIC SECTOR HOUSING

Introduction

One of the significant housing trends this century has been a major increase in council housing "from only 10 per cent. of all housing immediately before the War to 24 per cent. today."[1] This increased significance of council housing is to be contrasted with the decline of the private rented sector "from about 90 per cent. of the total stock in 1914 to only 8 per cent. in 1986."[2]

The predominant role of local authority landlords in the provision of rented housing was not, however, consistent with the market-oriented policies of the Conservative Government in the 1980s.

Housing: The Government's Proposals (1987)

1.9 Local authority housing now dominates the rented sector. The growth of municipal housing since the War has certainly been effective in increasing the total housing stock, and in clearing slums. But the system of ownership and management brought with it is often not in the tenant's long term interest. In some areas the system has provided good quality housing and management. But in many big cities local authority housing operations are so large that they inevitably risk becoming distant and bureaucratic. Insensitive design and bad management have alienated tenants and left housing badly maintained. As the quality of the housing and of its environment has declined, so a wide range of social problems has emerged: crime and violence have increased; many people have left for better opportunities elsewhere; local enterprise and employment have disappeared; and whole communities have slipped into a permanent dependence on the welfare system from which it is extremely difficult for people to escape.

1.10 These problems have often been compounded by indiscriminate subsidies from the rates to hold down rents, which have meant that people who do not need subsidy have become accustomed to it alongside those whose needs are real. Not only are resources wasted as a result, but the independence and self-motivation of communities can in the long term be damaged. The Government's

---

[1] *Housing: The Government's Proposals* (1987), para. 1.6.
[2] *Ibid.*

objective is to begin to reverse this process in the worst areas, and to support the independence of local communities where that spirit already exists, by giving more opportunity for tenants to control their own destinies, and by targetting the help that will very often be needed on those who genuinely require it.

1.11 There are other reasons too why it is not healthy for the public sector to dominate provision of rented housing. At the national level, investment in housing has to compete with other public sector spending programmes; and private investment has not been available to supplement limited public sector resources, in order to provide alternative forms of renting on a sufficient scale. At the local level, short term political factors can override efficient and economic management of housing in the long term, leading to unrealistically low rents and wholly inadequate standards of maintenance. Local authority housing allocation methods can all too easily result in inefficiencies and bureaucracy, producing queuing and lack of choice for the tenant. A more pluralist and more market-oriented system will ensure that housing supply can respond more flexibly to demand, will give the tenant greater choice over his housing and will allow greater scope for private investment and more effective use of public sector money.

Legislation introduced during the 1980s was aimed at transforming the role of local authorities in relation to housing. Rather than being the major providers of rented housing, local authorities were to become co-ordinators and facilitators:

The future of local authorities will essentially be a strategic one identifying housing needs and demands, encouraging innovative methods of provision by other bodies to meet such needs, maximising the use of private finance, and encouraging the new interest in the revival of the independent sector. In order to fulfil this strategic role they will have to work closely with housing associations; private landlords; developers; and building societies and other providers of finance.[3]

The symbolic transformation of the role of local authorities in housing matters was achieved by the amendment of section 9 of the Housing Act 1985 by the Local Government and Housing Act 1989. As originally drafted, section 9 of the 1985 Act—one of the key sections of Part II of the Act (entitled "Provision of Housing Accommodation")—read as follows:

(1) A local housing authority may provide housing accommodation—

(a)   by erecting houses, or converting buildings into houses, on land acquired by them for the purposes of this Part, or

(b)   by acquiring houses.

(2) The authority may alter, enlarge, repair or improve a house so erected, converted or acquired.

---

[3] *Ibid.*, para. 5.1.

(3) These powers may equally be exercised in relation to land acquired for the purposes—

(a)   of disposing of houses provided, or to be provided, on the land, or

(b)   of disposing of the land to a person who intends to provide housing accommodation on it.

(4) A local housing authority may not under this Part provide a cottage with a garden of more than one acre.

Section 161 of the Local Government and Housing Act 1989 added the following subsection:

(5) Nothing in this Act shall be taken to require (or to have any time required) a local housing authority itself to acquire or hold any houses or other land for the purposes of this Part.

The policy of reducing the stock of local authority housing has been pursued from a number of angles. First, the Housing Act 1980 introduced the right to buy, whereby certain secure tenants can purchase their homes at a significant discount. The relevant statutory code is now contained in Part V of the Housing Act 1985 (as amended). Secondly, local authorities have the power voluntarily to transfer housing accommodation into the private sector. Thirdly, Part IV of the Housing Act 1988 and section 172 of the Local Government and Housing Act 1989 have introduced mechanisms whereby local authorities and new town corporations may be required to transfer their housing stock to private sector landlords. Fourthly, Part III of the Housing Act 1988 created the housing action trust, a new public body designed to tackle housing problems particularly in inner city areas.

Note

It should, however, be stressed that the sale of council houses did not start in the 1980s. Prior to the introduction of the right to buy in 1980 the voluntary sale of council houses was possible under section 104 of the Housing Act 1957 (now section 32 of the 1985 Act[4]). An analysis of the exercise of this power is to be found in A. Murie, *The Sale of Council Houses*: *A Study in Social Policy* (1975, Centre for Urban and Regional Studies, University of Birmingham).

P. N. Balchin, *Housing Policy*: *an Introduction* (2nd ed., 1989, Routledge) Chapter 9 provides an account of the policy of privatisation of local authority housing both through sales of council houses to individual tenants, and the disposal of council estates to private sector landlords or housing associations.

---

[4] See p. 533.

I THE RIGHT TO BUY

Housing: The Government's Proposals (1987)

2.10 Many tenants of local authorities want to buy their present homes rather than move out to acquire another home in the open market. The right to buy, introduced in 1980, has proved to be one of the most successful reforms undertaken by the present Government. About a million tenants have already bought their homes under the right to buy or by agreement since April 1979.

2.11 The spread of owner-occupation on council estates is also improving the repair and maintenance of the stock, with a recent national survey reporting that nine out of ten buyers had carried out some type of improvement since purchase. As a result estates become more diverse and attractive as places to live.

It should be added, however, that the pattern of sales of public sector dwellings has not been even: for example, there have been many more sales to tenants of houses than to tenants of flats. Furthermore, there is evidence to suggest that it is the better houses on more desirable suburban estates that have in the main been purchased under the right to buy, leaving local authorities with a stock of less desirable housing in less favourable locations.[5]

(A) THE RIGHT TO BUY

Sections 118 to 121 of the Housing Act 1985—as supplemented by Schedules 4 and 5—define the circumstances in which a secure tenant has the right to buy.

118.—(1) A secure tenant has the right to buy, that is to say, the right, in the circumstances and subject to the conditions and exceptions stated in the following provisions of this Part—

(a) if the dwelling-house is a house and the landlord owns the freehold, to acquire the freehold of the dwelling-house;

(b) if the landlord does not own the freehold or if the dwelling-house is a flat (whether or not the landlord owns the freehold), to be granted a lease of the dwelling-house.

(2) Where a secure tenancy is a joint tenancy then, whether or not each of the joint tenants occupies the dwelling-house as his only or principal home, the right to buy belongs jointly to all of them or to such one or more of them as may be agreed between them; but such an arrangement is not valid unless the person or at least one of the persons to whom the right to buy is to belong occupies the dwelling-house as his only or principal home.

---

[5] Hughes, *Public Sector Housing Law* (2nd ed., 1987), p. 49.

119.—(1) The right to buy does not arise unless the period which, in accordance with Schedule 4, is to be taken into account for the purposes of this section is at least two years.

(2) Where the secure tenancy is a joint tenancy the condition in subsection (1) need be satisfied with respect to one only of the joint tenants.

120. The right to buy does not arise in the cases specified in Schedule 5 (exceptions to the right to buy).

121.—(1) The right to buy cannot be exercised if the tenant is obliged to give up possession of the dwelling-house in pursuance of an order of the court or will be so obliged at a date specified in the order.

(2) The right to buy cannot be exercised if the person, or one of the persons, to whom the right to buy belongs—

   (a)   has a bankruptcy petition pending against him,

   (b)   has a receiving order in force against him,

   (c)   is an undischarged bankrupt, or

   (d)   has made a composition or arrangement with his creditors the terms of which remain to be fulfilled.

SCHEDULE 4

QUALIFYING PERIOD FOR RIGHT TO BUY AND DISCOUNT

Introductory

1. The period to be taken into account—

   (a)   for the purposes of section 119 (qualification for right to buy), and

   (b)   for the purposes of section 129 (discount).

is the period qualifying, or the aggregate of the periods qualifying, under the following provisions of this Schedule.

Periods occupying accommodation subject to public sector tenancy

2. A period qualifies under this paragraph if it is a period during which, before the relevant time—

   (a)   the secure tenant, or

   (b)   his spouse (if they are living together at the relevant time), or

   (c)   a deceased spouse of his (if they were living together at the time of the death),

was a public sector tenant or was the spouse of a public sector tenant and occupied as his only or principal home the dwelling-house of which the spouse was such a tenant.

3. For the purposes of paragraph 2 a person who, as a joint tenant under a public sector tenancy, occupied a dwelling-house as his only or principal home shall be treated as having been the public sector tenant under that tenancy.

4.—(1) This paragraph applies where the public sector tenant of a dwelling-house died or otherwise ceased to be a public sector tenant of the dwelling-house, and thereupon a child of his who occupied the dwelling-house as his only or principal home (the "new tenant") became the public sector tenant of the dwelling-house (whether under the same or under another public sector tenancy).

(2) A period during which the new tenant, since reaching the age of 16, occupied as his only or principal home a dwelling-house of which a parent of his was the public sector tenant or one of joint tenants under a public sector tenancy, being either—

(a)   the period at the end of which he became the public sector tenant, or

(b)   an earlier period ending two years or less before the period mentioned in paragraph (a) or before another period within this paragraph,

shall be treated for the purposes of paragraph 2 as a period during which he was a public sector tenant.

(3) For the purposes of this paragraph two persons shall be treated as parent and child if they would be so treated under section 186(2) (members of a person's family: relationships other than those of the whole blood).

Periods occupying forces accommodation

5. A period qualifies under this paragraph if it is a period during which, before the relevant time—

(a)   the secure tenant, and

(b)   his spouse (if they are living together at the relevant time), or

(c)   a deceased spouse of his (if they were living together at the time of the death),

occupied accommodation provided for him as a member of the regular armed forces of the Crown or was the spouse of a person occupying accommodation so provided and also occupied that accommodation.

Periods during which right to buy is preserved

5A. A period qualifies under this paragraph if it is a period during which, before the relevant time—

(a)   the secure tenant, or

(b)   this spouse (if they are living together at the relevant time), or

(c)   a deceased spouse of his (if they were living together at the time of the death),

was a qualifying person for the purposes of the preserved right to buy or was the spouse of such a person and occupied the qualifying dwelling-house as his only or principal home.

Meaning of "public sector tenant"

6.—(1) In this Schedule a "public sector tenant" means a tenant under a public sector tenancy.

(2) For the purposes of this Schedule, a tenancy, other than a long tenancy, under which a dwelling-house was let as a separate dwelling was a public sector tenancy at any time when the conditions described below as the landlord condition and the tenant condition were satisfied.

(3) The provisions of this Schedule apply in relation to a licence to occupy a dwelling-house (whether or not granted for a consideration) as they apply in relation to a tenancy.

(4) Sub-paragraph (3) does not apply to a licence granted as a temporary expedient to a person who entered the dwelling-house or any other land as a trespasser (whether or not, before the grant of that licence, another licence to occupy that or another dwelling-house had been granted to him).

The landlord condition

7.—(1) The landlord condition is, subject to paragraph 7A and any order under paragraph 8, that the interest of the landlord belonged to, or to a predecessor of—

> a local authority,
> a new town corporation,
> a housing action trust,
> the Development Board for Rural Wales,
> an urban development corporation,
> the Housing Corporation,
> a registered housing association which is not a co-operative housing association. . .

7A.—(1) The landlord condition shall be treated as having been satisfied in the case of a dwelling-house comprised in a housing co-operative agreement made—

(a) in England and Wales, by a local housing authority, new town corporation or the Development Board for Rural Wales, or

(b) in Scotland, by an islands or district council,

if the interest of the landlord belonged to the housing co-operative.

(2) In sub-paragraph (1) "housing co-operative agreement" and "housing co-operative"—

(a) as regards England and Wales have the same meaning as in section 27B (agreements with housing co-operatives under superseded provisions), and

(b) as regards Scotland mean an agreement made under section 5 of the Housing Rents and Subsidies (Scotland) Act 1975 and a housing co-operative within the meaning of that section.

8.—(1) The landlord condition shall also be treated as having been satisfied, in such circumstances as may be prescribed for the purposes of this paragraph by order to the Secretary of State, if the interest of the landlord belonged to a person who is so prescribed.

(2) An order under this paragraph—

(a) may make different provision with respect to different cases or descriptions of case, including different provision for different areas, and

(b) shall be made by statutory instrument which shall be subject to annulment in pursuance of a resolution of either House of Parliament.

The tenant condition

9. The tenant condition is that the tenant was an individual and occupied the dwelling-house as his only or principal home; or, where the tenancy was a joint tenancy, that each of the joint tenants was an individual and at least one of them occupied the dwelling-house as his only or principal home.

Application to certain housing association tenancies

10. For the purposes of determining whether at any time a tenant of a housing association was a public sector tenant and his tenancy a public sector tenancy, the association shall be deemed to have been registered at that time, under the Housing Associations Act 1985 or the corresponding Northern Ireland legislation, if it was so registered at any later time.

SCHEDULE 5

EXCEPTIONS TO THE RIGHT TO BUY[6]

Charities

1. The right to buy does not arise if the landlord is a housing trust or a housing association and is a charity.

Certain housing associations

2. The right to buy does not arise if the landlord is a co-operative housing association.

3. The right to buy does not arise if the landlord is a housing association which at no time received a grant under—

any enactment mentioned in paragraph 2 of Schedule 1 to the Housing Associations Act 1985 (grants under enactment superseded by the Housing Act 1974),
section 31 of the Housing Act 1974 (management grants),
section 41 of the Housing Associations Act 1985 (housing association grants),

---

[6] Paragraphs 6 and 8 were repealed by Housing Act 1988, s.123.

section 54 of that Act (revenue deficit grants),
section 55 of that Act (hostel deficit grants),
section 58(2) of that Act (grants by local authorities),
section 50 of the Housing Act 1988 (housing association grants), or
section 51 of that Act (revenue deficit grants).

Landlord with insufficient interest in the property

4. The right to buy does not arise unless the landlord owns the freehold or has an interest sufficient to grant a lease in pursuance of this Part for—

(a)   where the dwelling-house is a house, a term exceeding 21 years, or

(b)   where the dwelling-house is a flat, a term of not less than 50 years,

commencing, in either case, with the date on which the tenant's notice claiming to exercise the right to buy is served.

Dwelling-houses let in connection with employment

5.—(1) The right to buy does not arise if the dwelling-house—

(a)   forms part of, or is within the curtilage of, a building which, or so much of it as is held by the landlord, is held mainly for purposes other than housing purposes and consists mainly of accommodations other than housing accommodation, or is situated in a cemetery, and

(b)   was let to the tenant or a predecessor in title of his in consequence of the tenant or predecessor being in the employment of the landlord or of—
a local authority,
a new town corporation,
the Development Board for Rural Wales,
an urban development corporation, or
the governors of an aided school,

(2) In sub-paragraph (1)(a) "housing purposes" means the purposes for which dwelling-houses are held by local housing authorities under Part II (provision of housing) or purposes corresponding to those purposes.

Certain dwelling-houses for the disabled

7. The right to buy does not arise if the dwelling-house has features which are substantially different from those of ordinary dwelling-houses and are designed to make it suitable for occupation by physically disabled persons, and—

(a)   it is one of a group of dwelling-houses which it is the practice of the landlord to let for occupation by physically disabled persons, and

(b)   a social service or special facilities are provided in close proximity to the group of dwelling-houses wholly or partly for the purpose of assisting those persons.

9.—(1) The right to buy does not arise if—

(a)   the dwelling-house is one of a group of dwelling-houses which it is the practice of the landlord to let for occupation by persons who are suffering or have suffered from a mental disorder, and

(b) a social service or special facilities are provided wholly or partly for the purpose of assisting those persons.

(2) In sub-paragraph (1)(a) "mental disorder" has the same meaning as in the Mental Health Act 1983.

Certain dwelling-houses for persons of pensionable age

10.—(1) The right to buy does not arise if the dwelling-house is one of a group of dwelling-houses—

(a) which are particularly suitable, having regard to their location, size, design, heating systems and other features, for occupation by persons of pensionable age, and

(b) which it is the practice of the landlord to let for occupation by persons of pensionable age, or for occupation by such persons and physically disabled persons,

and special facilities such as are mentioned in sub-paragraph (2) are provided wholly or mainly for the purposes of assisting those persons.

(2) The facilities referred to above are facilities which consist of or include—

(a) the services of a resident warden, or

(b) the services of a non-resident warden, a system for calling him and the use of a common room in close proximity to the group of dwelling-houses.

11.—(1) The right to buy does not arise if the Secretary of State has determined, on the application of the freeholder, that it is not to be capable of being exercised with respect to the dwelling-house.

(2) The Secretary of State shall so determine if, and only if, he is satisfied that the dwelling-house—

(a) is particularly suitable, having regard to its location, size, design, heating system and other features, for occupation by persons of pensionable age, and

(b) was let to the tenant or a predecessor in title of his for occupation by a person of pensionable age (whether the tenant or predecessor or another person).

(3) The Secretary of State shall for the purposes of this paragraph disregard the presence of any feature provided by the tenant or a predecessor in title of his.

(4) An application for a determination under this paragraph shall be made within the period for service of the freeholder's notice under section 124 (notice admitting or denying right to buy).

(5) This paragraph does not apply unless the dwelling-house concerned was first let before 1st January 1990.[7]

---

[7] This version of paragraph 11 of Sched. 5 was supplied by section 164(1) of the Local Government and Housing Act 1989. This amended version does not apply in any case where the tenant served a notice claiming to exercise the right to buy before March 1, 1990: Local Government and Housing Act 1989, s.164(2).

Dwelling-houses held on Crown tenancies

12.—(1) The right to buy does not arise if the dwelling-house is held by the landlord on a tenancy from the Crown, unless—

(a) the landlord is entitled to grant a lease in pursuance of this Part without the concurrence of the appropriate authority, or

(b) the appropriate authority notifies the landlord that as regards any Crown interest affected the authority will give its consent to the granting of such a lease.

(2) In this paragraph "tenancy from the Crown" means a tenancy of land in which there is a Crown interest superior to the tenancy, and "Crown interest" and "appropriate authority" mean respectively—

(a) an interest comprised in the Crown Estate, and the Crown Estate Commissioners or other government department having the management of the land in question;

(b) an interest belonging to Her Majesty in right of the Duchy of Lancaster, and the Chancellor of the Duchy;

(c) an interest belonging to the Duchy of Cornwall, and such person as the Duke of Cornwall or the possessor for the time being of the Duchy appoints;

(d) any other interest belonging to a government department or held on behalf of Her Majesty for the purposes of a government department, and that department.

(3) Section 179(1) (which renders ineffective certain provisions restricting the grant of leases under this Part) shall be disregarded for the purposes of sub-paragraph (1)(a).

Notes

In view of the length of time which it may take between the tenant giving notice of his intention to exercise the right to buy and the completion of the sale, there are potential problems if the tenant's status changes during the course of the procedure. A similar problem arises when at some point after the tenant has served on the landlord notice of his intention to exercise the right to buy the landlord becomes entitled to an order for possession on one of the grounds set out in Schedule 2 to the 1985 Act.

Sutton L.B.C. v. *Swann* (1986) 18 H.L.R. 140

Ackner L.J. said (at 142–145):

This is an appeal from the order of Her Honour Judge Jean Graham-Hall, given on August 6, 1984 at the Croydon County Court, when she granted an order to the plaintiffs, who are the respondents to this appeal, the Mayor and Burgesses of the London Borough of Sutton, for possession of 24 Hinchcliffe Close, Roundshaw, Wallington, Surrey. She also gave judgment for the sum of £2,722.05, being arrears of rent and mesne profits up to and including the date on which she gave judgment, August 6, 1984 and ordered that the mesne profits should continue to be paid from August 7 until possession was given.

The history of this matter can be quite briefly summarised as follows. As far back as September 15, 1969 Mr. Swann, the appellant, became a tenant of 24 Hinchcliffe Close. On March 17, 1982 he gave notice under section 5 of the Housing Act 1980 [now, Housing Act 1985, s.122] claiming to buy the premises.

Under section 1 of that Act [now, Housing Act 1985, s.118], it is provided that "A secure tenant has the right ... (b) if the ... dwelling-house is a flat, to be granted a long lease of the dwelling-house; in the circumstances and subject to conditions and exceptions stated in the following provisions of this Chapter."

That was followed on March 23, 1982 with a notice in reply, served by the respondents, admitting the claim of both Mr. and Mrs. Swann, because she was the joint signatory. In April 1982 Mrs. Swann left and she has dropped out of the picture.

Pursuant to the claim made by Mr. Swann, a valuation was then considered and on July 7, 1982 the respondents wrote a long letter to Mr. and Mrs. Swann, explaining to them at the outset that the council was prepared to offer the sale of the property, that is, the long lease, at the open value of £24,696, without any restriction upon sale, or alternatively to sell the property at the price of £13,583, which represented the open market value less a discount of 45 per cent. But that involved Mr. and Mrs. Swann agreeing not to sell for some five years. They then set out various other conditions. First of all, that it was on a leasehold basis for a term of 125 years; there was an estimated initial service charge; they specified the services to be provided, and they informed Mr. and Mrs. Swann, as they were obliged to, that if they considered the council's valuation to be incorrect, they had a right to a revaluation to be determined by the district valuer, whose decision under the statute was final. They told him about his rights with regard to a mortgage. The letter set out the time limits, and ended by pointing out that " ... the Borough Secretary will be unable to proceed with the preparation of the contract for sale until all the information [which they required as mentioned in the letter] has been received." It also said, "If you require any further information ... please do not hesitate to contact [the assistant who was in charge at the offices of the council]." The offer was expressed to be subject to contract, which was an unnecessary observation, but one put in out of an abundance of caution, because, since it set out various options in the letter, it was incapable of being accepted, in view of the other matters that had first to be clarified.

In my judgment there is nothing which can be criticised about that letter. Section 16 of the Act recognises that there must be many matters relating to the exercise of the option, because it provides in section 16(1) [now Housing Act, 1985, s.138(1)] that,

"Where a secure tenant has claimed to exercise the right to buy and that right had been established, the landlord shall be bound, subject to the following provisions of the section, to make to the tenant ... [it then refers to the grant of the 125 year lease] as soon as all matters relating to the grant and to the amount to be left outstanding or advanced on the security of the dwelling-house, have been agreed or determined."

So the Act clearly contemplates that there is not an obligation upon the local authority to grant the lease, in this case of 125 years, merely by simply replying. "We will agree to make such a grant, the notice under section 5 having been served."

What happened thereafter? The learned judge had evidence from the council that they received no reply to their letter. The acceptance slip, which was to be used, was not received by them. Mr. Swann gave evidence to the effect that he had replied and that he had accepted the offer, though he did not specify which. The learned judge, having considered the evidence on each side, concluded that on the balance of probabilities, Mr. Swann did not sent any acceptance slip, neither did he deal in any letter with the matters raised by the respondents in the letter which I have quoted. In those circumstances it must follow that, although Mr. Swann had made his claim to buy under section 5 of the Act, following the respondents' acceptance of that claim, he did not take the matter any further. In the result, after a reasonable length of time, the council's offer would, in my judgment, lapse, and that is what happened in this case, having regard to what subsequently followed.

In August 1982, which was not long after Mrs. Swann left home, Mr. Swann began an association with a Miss Montgomery. In the early part of 1983 he began negotiations for the purchase on mortgage of 4 Clarice Way, Wallington. There was an agreement for sale entered into on February 14 and the transfer on March 23, 1983.

The learned judge had another dispute to resolve and that was whether or not those premises became the only, or principal, home of Mr. Swann. She said this in her judgment:

" . . . I find that by April 1, 1983 Mr. Swann occupied the dwelling-house at Clarice Way as his principal home and continues to do so. Where there is any conflict of evidence I prefer that of the plaintiffs [the respondents] and their witnesses to Mr. Swann and his witnesses."

She based that conclusion, as her judgment shows, not merely on the fact that he had purchased the property, but that he was a registered residential customer of British Telecom from March 18, 1983; there was a telephone at that address; he wrote from that address on August 25, 1983 to the Governor of the Bank of Scotland; he wrote to the Guardian Building Society on January 21, 1984 in respect of an arrears of mortgage on the house; he gave that address in letters to the Metropolitan Police in March and April 1984 as his residence; and on April 23, 1983 his firearms certificate had been changed from the address, 24 Hinchcliffe, to this address in Clarice Way and a police officer had signed to state that arrangements at the new address were satisfactory.

Mr. Swann subsequently returned to the charge with regard to his claim to buy 24 Hinchcliff Close and the respondents began once again to get out valuations. But in the meantime, another branch of the borough had discovered the position in regard to Clarice Way and a notice to quit was served upon Mr. Swann on September 29, 1983. By that time the second defendant, who is the daughter of Mr. Swann, had moved in, together with Mr. O'Brien and their two children. Mr. O'Brien has now moved out.

In answer to the respondents' claim for possession, based upon the termination of the tenancy, and their claim for non-payment of rent, Mr. Swann set up his entitlement to buy the premises and asserted that it was wholly the failure of the respondents not to have granted the long lease of the premises to him. He made various counter-claims in regard to the money he had spent on the property.

The respondent's answer to that, quite simply, was that Mr. Swann had ceased to be a secure tenant. A "secure tenant" is, under the Act, a tenant who occupies the dwelling-house as his only, or principal, home, and that, it was contended, had ceased to be the case so far as 24 Hinchcliffe Close was concerned because, of course, Clarice Way had taken its place.

In my judgment this case is simply dealt with by the following propositions.

In March 1982 Mr. Swann was entitled to serve a notice under section 5 of the Housing Act 1980, claiming the right to buy, because he was a secure tenant, and this was admitted by the notice in reply served by the respondents. The respondents provided Mr. Swann with a perfectly straight-forward offer for him to accept so the matter could proceed. He took no further step. The matter did not proceed. Accordingly, the offer which the respondents were obliged to make under the statute lapsed by efflux of time. When Mr. Swann returned to the charge a year or more later, that offer, as I have indicated, having lapsed, he was no longer a secure tenant and therefore he no longer was entitled to apply under section 5 of the Act to buy the premises.

Mr. Swann takes a point, which in fact is dealt with by the learned judge, and in my view properly dealt with by the learned judge. He submits that, given that he was a secure tenant and as such made a claim as a secure tenant in March 1982 to buy, thereafter he has a right to purchase which cannot be defeated by any change in his status; *i.e.* by his thereafter ceasing to be a secure tenant.

In regard to this, the learned judge said: "Section 16(1) to (11) set out the steps to completion of the right to buy. Section 16(1) uses the term 'secure tenant.' Section 16(2) to (10) uses the term 'landlord' and, or 'tenant.' " She then came to section 16(11) [now Housing Act 1985, s.139(2)], and I set that out in full. It reads as follows:

"On the grant to *a secure tenant* of an estate in fee simple or of a lease in pursuance of this Chapter the secure tenancy of the dwelling-house shall come to an end and, if there is then a sub-tenancy, section 139 of the Law of Property Act, 1925 shall apply as on a merger or surrender."

That section proceeds in my judgment on the assumption that, at the end of the procedure, when the various investigations have been made, the various terms spelt out and accepted, and the time for the grant comes, that grant has to be made to a secure tenant. Accordingly the status of "secure tenant" has to exist, not only at the time when the claim to buy is made, but also at the time when the grant comes to be made. If during the period between claim and grant the tenant has ceased to be a secure tenant, he is not entitled to that grant.

I therefore conclude that the learned county court judge came to the correct conclusion and I would dismiss this appeal.

Parker L.J. and Sir David Cairns agreed.

Dance v. *Welwyn Hatfield D. C.* [1990] 1 W.L.R. 1097

Nourse L.J. said (at 1099–1105):

It is natural to expect that "the right to buy," which was introduced by the Housing Act 1980 and is now governed by Part V of the Housing Act 1985, will bear a strong resemblance to an option to purchase. In some respects it does. But because it is a statutory and not a contractual right, from whose perfection the purchaser can desist at any time before he has acquired the property, the resemblance is far from complete. Furthermore, allied to the right to buy is a right to a mortgage, in exercising which the purchaser may be able to defer completion for up to three years. On the other side, the rights cannot be exercised if the purchaser is obliged, whether immediately or prospectively, to give up possession of the property under an order of the court, or if he is bankrupt or in danger of becoming so.

The interaction of these provisions and the problems to which they can give rise were considered by this court in *Enfield London Borough Council* v. *McKeon* [1986] 1 W.L.R. 1007, a decision to which close consideration must be given in this case, whose facts are not the same. Here the matter has reached the stage contemplated by section 138 of the 1985 Act (section 16 of the 1980 Act). The question is whether the defendants' duty under that section to convey the property to the plaintiffs is modified by the claim for possession which they have made, but in furtherance of which they have not obtained an order of the court. The question largely depends on whether the right to buy has by that stage been "exercised" or not.

The plaintiffs, Mr. Cyril Dance and his wife Joan, are the joint tenants of No. 29 Ravenfield Road, Welwyn Garden City, a three bedroomed house of which the landlords and freehold owners are the defendants, Welwyn Hatfield District Council. It is agreed that for the purposes of the Act of 1985 as amended the property is a dwelling-house of which the plaintiffs are the secure tenants. It is also agreed that the right to buy the property, *i.e.* to acquire the freehold of it, has arisen in their favour under section 118(1)(a) of the Act of 1985.

The material provisions of the Act of 1985 are lengthy and intricate. With two exceptions, I propose to summarise their effect as briefly as I can.

Nourse L.J. quoted section 121 (see p. 507) and continued:

Sections 122 to 125 provide for the tenant's exercise of the right to buy, for the landlord's admission or denial of the right and, where the right is established, for notice to be given of the purchase price which the landlord proposes and other matters. Section 126 to 128 provide that the purchase price shall be the equivalent of the open-market value of the dwelling-house, determined in the case of a dispute by the district valuer, less any discount to which the tenant is entitled under sections 129 to 131. Sections 132 to 137 make provision for the tenant's right to a mortgage. Section 138, so far as material, is in these terms:

"(1) Where a secure tenant has claimed to exercise the right to buy and that right has been established, then, as soon as all matters relating to the grant and to the amount to be left outstanding or advanced on the security of the dwelling-house have been agreed or determined, the landlord shall make to the tenant—

(a) if the dwelling-house is a house and the landlord owns the freehold, a grant of the dwelling-house for an estate in fee simple absolute, ... in accordance with the following provisions of this Part.

(2) If the tenant has failed to pay the rent or any other payment due from him as a tenant for a period of four weeks after it has been lawfully

demanded from him, the landlord is not bound to comply with subsection (1) while the whole or part of that payment remains outstanding.

(3) The duty imposed on the landlord by subsection (1) is enforceable by injunction."

Section 139 provides for the terms and effect of the conveyance or grant and the mortgage, if there is one. Sections 140 and 141 empower the landlord to serve two successive notices to complete on the tenant, subject to the tenant's right to defer completion, and so that if the tenant does not complete the landlord is no longer bound to do so. Section 142 provides that in a case where he is not entitled to a full mortgage the tenant is entitled to defer completion, provided that he has served an appropriate notice and deposited the sum of £150 with the landlord.

In the present case the plaintiffs' right to buy was admitted by the defendants, who proposed a price which was acceptable to the plaintiffs. The plaintiffs then claimed the right to a mortgage and they were notified of the amount which, in the opinion of the defendants, they were entitled to leave outstanding on the security of the property. That was not the full amount of the purchase price and so the plaintiffs became entitled to defer completion. By a letter date August 6, 1987 the defendants' chief legal officer informed the plaintiffs' solicitors that he had received instructions to proceed with the sale. By a notice dated September 29, 1987 the plaintiffs, within the time allowed to them, claimed the right to defer completion in accordance with section 142 of the Housing Act 1985. They also deposited the sum of £150 with the defendants. It is agreed that, by virtue of section 140(3)(c) of the Act of 1985, the effect of that was to entitle the plaintiffs to defer completion until February 5, 1990, being three years after the service of the plaintiffs' notice claiming to exercise the right to buy under section 122(1). By a letter dated October 29, 1987 the defendants' chief legal officer acknowledged that the plaintiffs had chosen to defer their purchase for three years.

The letter of October 29, 1987 also confirmed that there was no planned compulsory purchase by the defendants of any properties in Ravenfield Road. The true position was that on August 15, 1987 the defendants' housing committee had resolved to demolish all buildings in the area in order to make way for a redevelopment scheme. That was not made known to the plaintiffs until they received a letter from the defendants dated July 7, 1988, in which they were informed that the defendants intended to carry out demolition in the area and that the proposals included 29, Ravenfield Road. They were also told that it was proposed to refund their deposit of £150 to them as soon as possible. However, by a letter dated September 2, 1988 the plaintiffs' solicitors wrote to the defendants:

"We refer to previous correspondence in this matter, and our Clients would like to complete this purchase on Monday, September 26. Accordingly, we enclose herewith the Transfer duly signed by our Clients, for sealing by the Council. If this date is not convenient, please let us know as soon as possible."

On September 30, the defendants served on the plaintiffs a notice seeking possession of the property on ground 10 in Part II of Schedule 2 to the Housing Act 1985 ...

Nourse L.J. read Ground 10 (see p. 253) and continued:

No accommodation having been reached between the parties, on November 24, 1988 the plaintiffs issued proceedings in the Hertford County Court claiming an injunction pursuant to section 138(3) of the Act of 1985 directing the defendant to convey the property to them as required by subsection (1)(a) of that section. By their defence and counterclaim the defendants asserted their right to possession of the property and contended that the plaintiffs' right to buy ceased to become exercisable "if an order is made pursuant to section 121(1) of the said Act." They requested that the plaintiffs' claim for injunctive relief should be adjourned until the defendants' claim for possession had been determined.

In due course the matter came on for hearing before Judge Hamilton. On July 10, 1989 the learned judge delivered a full and careful judgment, to which this court is indebted for its consideration of the material provisions of the Act of 1985 and their bearing on the facts of this case. If left to himself, the judge would have held that the defendants' duty to convey the freehold under section 138(1)(a) had arisen. But he thought that the decision in *Enfield London Borough Council* v. *McKeon* [1986] 1 W.L.R. 1007 obliged him to decide to the contrary. In the end he acceded to the defendants' request to adjourn the plaintiffs' claim for an injunction until the merits of the defendants' claim for possession had been determined. He directed that the two claims should be heard together. The plaintiffs now appeal to this court, renewing their claim for an immediate injunction.

Enfield London Borough Council v. *McKeon* [1986] 1 W.L.R. 1007 was decided under the 1980 Act as amended by the Housing and Building Control Act 1984. For the sake of convenience, I will continue to refer to the corresponding provisions of the Housing Act 1985. The material facts of that case were these. The tenant served on the landlords a notice claiming to exercise the right to buy under section 122(1). The landlords then served a notice admitting the right to buy under section 124. The next thing which happened was that the landlords served on the tenant a notice indicating their intention to seek possession of the property on ground 16 in Part III of the Schedule 2 to the Act of 1985, namely that the accommodation was more extensive than was reasonably required by the tenant. Some seven weeks later the landlords, pursuant to the obligation imposed on them by section 125, served on the tenant a notice containing the particulars required by that section. Two months later the landlords issued proceedings, claiming possession on ground 16. Although it is not clear whether the price proposed by the landlords had been accepted by the tenant, it is, I think, clear that a stage had not been reached when, for the purposes of section 138(1), all matters relating to the grant and to the amount to be left outstanding or advance on the security of the property had been agreed or determined. The facts accordingly differed from those of the present case in an important respect.

It was argued on behalf of the tenant that the right to buy had been "exercised" for the purposes of section 121(1) when she had served her notice under section 122(1). As to that, Slade L.J., with whose judgment the other member of the court, Eastham J., agreed, said [1986] 1 W.L.R. at 1014–1015:

"According to usual legal terminology, an ordinary option to purchase is, I think, commonly regarded as being exercised at the moment when notice is first given of the donee's intention to exercise the option. Correspondingly, on a first reading of section [121(1)], I was inclined to think that the tenant's right to buy must be 'exercised' for the purposes of that subsection at the moment when he serves his notice under section [122(1)] (which is also the 'relevant time' of ascertaining the purchase price payable—see section [125(2)(a)])—and at no other time. Nevertheless, I am now satisfied that this is not the correct way to read the word 'exercised' in the particular context of section [121]. In my judgment, the right is 'exercised' each and every time when the tenant takes any step towards the implementation of his right to purchase."

Slade L.J. then said that he was particularly fortified in that conclusion by three considerations, the third of which was that, if the tenant's submissions were correct, the right to compel completion would not be affected in any way if at the date of completion a bankruptcy petition was pending against her. He continued, at 1015G:

"In my judgment, the short answer to the [tenant's] point of law is that, for the purpose of applying section [121] (on the true construction of which her case depends) the [Act of 1985] treats a tenant as purporting to exercise his right to buy at any time and from time to time when he takes steps towards implementation of that right, up to and including completion of the purchase. If, therefore, any of the circumstances set out in [section 121] subsist at any time between the time when he serves his section [122(1)] notice and completion, his right to buy ceases to be exercisable."

Mr. Haines, for the defendants, submitted that the decision in *Enfield London Borough Council* v. *McKeon* [1986] 1 W.L.R. 1007 is binding on this court and, moreover, that it is decisive of this case. He relied particularly on the view of Slade L.J. that the Housing Act 1985 treats a tenant as purporting to exercise his right to buy at any time and from time to time when he takes steps towards implementation of that right, "up to and including completion of the purchase." Although others might have preferred the simple view of section 121(1) which had been urged on Slade L.J. and Eastham J. by the tenant, we must certainly accept that their decision is binding on us. I do not, however, think that it is decisive of this case. Although the words of Slade L.J. on their face apply here, the decision is only a binding authority for cases where the facts are the same. As I have already pointed out, the facts of this case are different. Indeed, the facts of *Enfield London Borough Council* v. *McKeon* [1986] 1 W.L.R. 1007 were such that it never became necessary to consider section 138, to whose effect on the facts of this case I now turn.

By his letter of August 6, 1987 the defendants' chief legal officer informed the plaintiffs' solicitors that he had received instructions to proceed with the sale of the property. Subject perhaps to a notification by the plaintiffs that the amount to be left outstanding on the mortgage was acceptable to them, that was effectively an acknowledgement that all matters relating to the grant and to the amount to be left outstanding or advanced on the security of the dwelling-house had been agreed or determined as contemplated by section 138(1) of the Housing Act 1985. Accordingly, as recognised by that letter, the defendants had already come under a duty to convey the freehold to the plaintiffs if and when they were requested to do so. No request was made at that time, because on September 29, 1987 the plaintiffs exercised their right to defer completion. But that deferment was brought to a premature end by their solicitors' letter of September 2, 1988 requesting completion on September 26, following. At that stage, by virtue of section 138(3), the defendants' duty to convey the freehold became enforceable by injunction.

What was the effect of the coming into operation of section 138(3) of the Act 1985. There was some debate as to the intention of Parliament in making the duty to convey enforceable by injunction. It was suggested that it was in order to make good the inability of the county court to grant an order by way of mandamus. I do not think that the reason is important. What is important is that the tenant's remedy is an injunction, that is to say an order that the landlord shall convey to him the legal estate in the property. The right to an injunction in a case where there is no contract cannot be any different in its incidents from the right to an order for specific performance in a case where there is a contract; as to which I need only cite a passage from the well known judgment of Sir George Jessel M.R. in *London and South Western Railway Co.* v. *Gomm* (1882) 20 Ch.D. 562, 581:

> "The right to call for a conveyance of the land is an equitable interest or equitable estate. In the ordinary case of a contract for purchase there is no doubt about this, and an option for repurchase is not different in its nature. A person exercising the option has to do two things, he has to give notice of his intention to purchase, and to pay the purchase money; but as far as the man who is liable to convey is concerned, his estate or interest is taken away from him without his consent, and the right to take it away being vested in another, the covenant giving the option must give that other an interest in the land."

Although that was a case of a contractual option to purchase, the principle is the same. Here the equitable interest in the property is acquired by the tenant directly the landlord's duty to convey arises and becomes enforceable by injunction under section 138 of the Act of 1985. Subject to payment of the purchase price and execution of the mortgage, if there is one, by the tenant, the landlord is bound to convey to him the legal estate in the property.

Although neither section 142 nor section 140(3)(c) contains any express provision bearing on the point, it was not suggested by Mr. Haines that the three year deferment period could not be prematurely determined by the tenant. I am in no doubt that that is a correct view of the matter. I therefore conclude that as from September 2, or, at the latest, September 26, 1988 the plaintiffs, being entitled to enforce the defendants' duty by injunction, became the equitable owners of the freehold in the property. At that stage, if not beforehand, they must, on any natural use of language, have "exercised" their right to buy for the purposes of section 121(1) of the Act of 1985. At that stage there was no order of the court obliging them to give up possession of the property. Nor had any proceedings been commenced. Nor had the plaintiffs even been served with a formal notice requiring them to give up possession. In the circumstances, I do not see how section 121(1) can be said to affect the matter.

I should add that I was at one time, although I am no longer, troubled by section 122(3) of the Act of 1985, which provides that the tenant's notice claiming to exercise the right to buy under subsection (1) of that section "may be withdrawn at any time by notice in writing served on the landlord." The effect of subsection (3), as I understand it, is that the tenant may withdraw from the purchase at any time up to actual completion. It was suggested by Mr. Haines that the tenant's ability to withdraw his notice showed that the right to buy had not been exercised. I do not think that that suggestion is correct. If the right to withdraw is relied on by a tenant who has already become entitled to enforce the landlord's duty under section 138(1), admittedly the right to buy will cease to be *enforceable*. But that does not mean that it has not already been *exercised*. That is a distinction which was correctly made by Judge Hamilton.

Mr. Haines submitted that the judge's decision to adjourn the plaintiffs' claim for an injunction can in any event be supported on the ground that an injunction is a discretionary remedy. That may or may not be correct in this context, but, if it is, it is correct only to a limited extent. I have already compared the injunction which is available under section 138(3) of the Act 1985 with an order for specific performance. The comparison may or may not be exact, but the injunction cannot be less readily available than an order for specific performance, which, although it is a discretionary remedy is refused only on well settled grounds, for example hardship to the party against whom it is granted.

No such grounds are alleged by the defendants in this case. There is no ground on which the injunction can properly be refused.

I fully recognise that to distinguish this case from *Enfield London Borough Council* v. *McKeon* [1986] 1 W.L.R. 1007, will leave the law in a somewhat unsatisfactory state. It is perhaps inevitable that novel legislation of this kind will give rise to difficulties which can only be identified in a case by case process. Be that as it may, I am in no doubt that the distinction ought to be made and we in this court are in a better position to make it than was Judge Hamilton in the court below.

I would allow the appeal and make an order in a form corresponding with an order for specific performance of an uncompleted contract.

Sir Nicolas Browne-Wilkinson V.C. and McCowan L.J. agreed.

(B)   THE PRICE

Section 126 of the Housing Act 1985 lays down the formula for working out the price that the secure tenant must pay to buy his home when exercising the right to buy—namely, the value of the dwelling-house calculated by reference to section 127 less the discount to which the tenant is entitled by virtue of sections 129 to 131.

The value of the dwelling-house is the price that it would realise if sold on the open market by a willing seller, on the basis of a certain number of assumptions: that the vendor is selling the freehold with vacant possession; that neither the tenant nor a member of his family living here with him wants to buy the property; and that the property has the benefit and burden of certain rights and duties, such as rights of way.[8]

The discount to which the tenant is entitled depends on whether the dwelling-house in question is a flat or a house, and the length of the applicant's period of occupation in public sector accommodation. Section 129 of the Housing Act 1985 provides:

(1) Subject to the following provisions of this Part, a person exercising the right to buy is entitled to a discount of a percentage calculated by reference to the period which is to be taken into account in accordance with Schedule 4 (qualifying period for right to buy and discount).

(2) The discount is, subject to any order under subsection (2A)—

   (a)   in the case of a house, 32 per cent. plus one per cent. for each complete year by which the qualifying period exceeds two years, up to a maximum of 60 per cent.;

   (b)   in the case of a flat, 44 per cent. plus two per cent. for each complete year by which the qualifying period exceeds two years, up to a maximum of 70 per cent.

---

[8] Housing Act 1985, s.127(1) and (2). Where the tenant is entitled to a long lease rather than the freehold, a different set of assumptions are made: Housing Act 1985, s.127(3).

(2A) The Secretary of State may by order made with the consent of the Treasury provide that, in such cases as may be specified in the order—

(a) the minimum percentage discount,

(b) the percentage increase for each complete year of the qualifying period after the first two, or

(c) the maximum percentage discount,

shall be such percentage, higher than that specified in subsection (2), as may be specified in the order.

(2B) An order—

(a) may make different provision with respect to different cases or descriptions of case,

(b) may contain such incidental, supplementary or transitional provisions as appear to the Secretary of State to be necessary or expedient, and

(c) shall be made by statutory instrument and shall not be made unless a draft of it has been laid before and approved by resolution of each House of Parliament.

Notes

(i)   There is a statutory ceiling on the amount which can be claimed by a secure tenant by way of discount. The current limit is £50,000.[9]

(ii)   The Court of Appeal has considered the right of a secure tenant by succession to claim a discount not only on the basis of the successor's period of occupation, but also on the basis of the period of occupation by the original tenant.

McIntyre v. *Merthyr Tydfil B.C.* (1989) 21 H.L.R. 320

Lloyd L.J. said (at 321–324):

In this case we are concerned with the public sector tenant's right to buy his house. The relevant provisions were formerly to be found in Part I of the Housing Act 1980. They are now to be found in Part V of the Housing Act 1985. The particular section with which we are concerned is section 13(1) of the 1980 Act, which provides:

"Where, after a secure tenant (in this section referred to as 'the former tenant') has given a notice claiming the right to buy, another person (in this section referred to as 'the new tenant, becomes the secure tenant—

(a) under the same secure tenancy; or

(b) under a periodic tenancy arising by virtue of section 29 of this Act on the coming to an end of the secure tenancy;

---

[9] Housing Act 1985, s.131(2); Housing (Right to Buy) (Maximum Discount) Order 1989 (S.I. 1989 No. 513).

the new tenant shall be in the same position as if the notice had been given by him and he had been the secure tenant at the time it was given."

The corresponding section in the 1985 Act is section 136(1). The last two lines of the subsections, on which this case turns, are identical in both Acts.

The facts are not in dispute. Mrs. Margaret McIntyre was the tenant of a council house at 68 Aneurin Crescent, Keir Hardie Estate, Merthyr Tydfil. She had lived there with her husband since 1958. Her husband died in 1982. Mrs. McIntyre then became the secure tenant in his place.

In August 1984 she was minded to exercise her right to buy the house from the council under the provisions of the 1980 Act. She filled in Form RTB1. "RTB" stands for "right to buy."

In due course the council served a counter-notice on form RTB2, in which they admitted Mrs. McIntyre's right to buy. They indicated that the price would be based on the market value of the house on the day when they received Form RTB1, namely August 30, 1984.

On December 4, 1984, the council sent Mrs. McIntyre a further notice under section [125] of the [1985] Act, Form RTB4, in which they stated that the price at which Mrs. McIntyre was entitled to buy the house was the market value of the house on August 30, 1984 (namely, £14,000), less a discount of £7,840, based on 26 years' occupation by Mrs. McIntyre and her deceased husband.

The next stage would have been completion. But, on January 4, 1985, before the conveyance was executed, Mrs. McIntyre died. She left two children, Terence Patrick McIntyre and Paula McIntyre. It was agreed between them that Paula should succeed to the secure tenancy under the provisions of section [89] the [1985] Act.

There is a document in the bundle which might suggest that Paula has been granted a fresh tenancy from January 21, 1985. But it is common ground that that was a mistake and that Paula is the new secure tenant under the same secure tenancy within the meaning of section [136(1)].

The question we have to decide is whether Paula is entitled to the same discount as her mother or whether, as the council contends, she is entitled to a more limited discount based on her own occupation of the house since she reached the age of 16. We were told that it makes a difference of some £2,000 or £3,000, whichever view is right.

The learned assistant recorder decided in favour of the council. His reasoning is not perhaps altogether clear. He seems to have rejected the council's argument that the section is purely procedural, yet he accepted the council's conclusion. For my part, I do not find it helpful to ask whether the subsection is procedural or not. It is better to give the words their ordinary meaning, so far as one can, having due regard to the context in which the words appear.

For the applicant it was argued that the plain meaning of the words is that Paula should stand in her mother's shoes for all purposes. It cannot have been intended, it was argued, that the council should have to give a fresh notice under section [122] of the [1985] Act admitting the applicant's right to buy; and, if that is so, there would be no logic in requiring the council to serve a fresh notice under section [122] of the [1985] Act setting out the calculation of the purchase price.

For the council, it was accepted that the value at August 30, 1984, remained the relevant value for the purpose of ascertaining the purchase price under [sections 126 and 127 of the 1985 Act]. But it was argued that the council were entitled to re-calculate the other elements in the purchase price, namely the appropriate discount and to give a further notice accordingly.

Mr. Masterman for the council observed that section [136(1)] of the [1985] Act might have concluded with the simple formula that "the new tenant shall be in the same position as the former tenant." If that had been the language of the subsection, then he accepted that he would have been in difficulties. But the language is subtly different. It provides that the new tenant shall be in the same position as if he had been a secure tenant. In other words, it does not provide that he shall be in the same position as the former tenant with all the former tenant's qualities and characteristics. It provides that he shall be in the same position as if he had been the secure tenant himself with all his own qualities and characteristics.

Counsel were unable to direct us to guidance in the textbooks, save for a passage in Hill & Redman on the *Law of Landlord and Tenant* at p. D.399. That passage favours the council's construction. The editors point out that the applicant's construction could have most unjust consequences since the new tenant might be entitled to a greater discount than the former tenant. In that perhaps unlikely event, the applicant's construction would lead to injustice because the new tenant would be limited to the former tenant's discount instead of being able to rely on his own greater discount.

I find the arguments in this case evenly balanced, but in the end I have come to the conclusion that the applicant's argument should be preferred. It is not right to look on section [136(1)] as having been intended to confer a benefit on the new tenant, any more than one should look on section [137] which caters for the corresponding case of a change in the landlord after notice given, as having been intended to confer a benefit on the new landlord. No doubt that would be the effect of section [136(1)] at a time of rising property values. But it would have the opposite effect at a time of falling property values. Similarly, as Hill & Redman point out in the passage to which I have referred, tying the new tenant to the former tenant's discount would be detrimental to the new tenant if he were entitled to a greater discount. But it would be beneficial to the new tenant if, as here, he were entitled to a lesser discount. So I do not regard that approach as leading anywhere.

A better approach is to look at section [136] and section [137] as providing for the continuation of the process which starts with the tenant's original notice under section [122] and ends with completion in accordance with section [138] as if there had been no change either of the tenant or of the landlord, as the case might be. The only exception is in relation to the new tenant's right to leave part of the purchase price on mortgage—see section [136(2)]. Obviously the new tenant's financial circumstances may differ from those of the former tenant, so he is entitled to serve a new notice under section [134]. The editors of Messrs. Hill & Redman regard that as an argument in favour of the council's construction. I regard it as an argument, if anything, in favour of the applicant's construction on the principle *expressio unius est exclusio alterius*. But at best it is neutral.

For the reasons I have given I prefer the applicant's construction, and would accordingly allow this appeal.

Hollings J. agreed.

(iii) In order to prevent secure tenants taking excessive economic advantage of the discount when exercising the right to buy, it is provided that in certain circumstances the discount is repayable on sale of the dwelling-house by the former secure tenant. Section 155 of the Housing Act 1985 has the effect of requiring a former secure tenant to repay part of the discount if he sells the dwelling-house within three years of exercising the right to buy. The amount to be repaid depends on when the sale takes place: a former secure tenant who sells in the first year is required to repay the whole of the discount; if sale takes place in the second year two-thirds must be repaid; if a former secure tenant sells in the third year one-third is repayable.

The obligation to repay takes effect as if the landlord had a legal charge over the property for the amount of the discount.[10] This charge ranks in priority after any charge securing money borrowed by the tenant to finance the right to buy.[11]

(iv) There is a category of exempted disposals which do not give rise to an obligation to repay the discount. Sections 160 to 161 of the Housing Act 1985 provide:

160.—(1) A disposal is an exempted disposal for the purposes of this Part if—

(a) it is a disposal of the whole of the dwelling-house and a further conveyance of the freehold or an assignment of the lease and the persons or each of the persons to whom it is made is a qualifying person (as defined in subsection (2));

(b) it is a vesting of the whole of the dwelling-house in a person taking under a will or on an intestacy;

(c) it is a disposal of the whole of the dwelling-house in pursuance of an order made under section 24 of the Matrimonial Causes Act 1973 (property adjustment orders in connection with matrimonial proceedings) or section 2 of the Inheritance (Provisions for Family and Dependants) Act 1975 (orders as to financial provision to be made from estate);

(d) it is a compulsory disposal (as defined in section 161); or

(e) it is a disposal of property consisting of land included in the dwelling-house by virtue of section 184 (land let with or used for the purposes of the dwelling-house).

(2) For the purposes of subsection (1)(a), a person is a qualifying person in relation to a disposal if—

(a) he is the person, or one of the persons, by whom the disposal is made,

(b) he is the spouse or a former spouse of that person, or one of those persons, or

[10] s.156(1).
[11] s.156(2).

(c)   he is a member of the family of that person, or one of those persons, and has resided with him throughout the period of twelve months ending with the disposal.

161. In this Part a "compulsory disposal" means a disposal of property which is acquired compulsorily, or is acquired by a person who has made or would have made, or for whom another person has made or would have made, a compulsory purchase order authorising its compulsory purchase for the purposes for which it is acquired.

This list of exempted disposals has been construed strictly. In *R.* v. *Rushmoor B.C. ex p. Barrett*[12] a husband and wife had exercised the right to buy in 1984. The marriage was dissolved in 1985, and the following year—in the context of proceedings for financial relief—the registrar made a consent order that the matrimonial home should be sold and the proceeds divided between them. After sale of the property was completed the local authority claimed to be entitled to have the discount repaid.

The Court of Appeal held that for the purposes of section 160(1)(c) the 1985 Act exempted disposals arose where there had been an adjustment of property under section 24 of the Matrimonial Causes Act 1973, but did not extend to cases where there had been and outright sale pursuant to an order made under section 24A of the 1973 Act.

Sir Frederick Lawson said in the course of his judgment:

In this case there has been a disposal. Under what jurisdiction of the court was the order for disposal made? It was clearly made under section 24A and was not a property adjustment order under section 24. It follows that, on the face of it, it was not an exempted disposal.[13]

Accordingly, the former tenants were required to repay the discount.

(v)   In designated rural areas (in particular, National Parks and areas of outstanding natural beauty), restrictions may be imposed on a former secure tenant's right to sell the dwelling-house.[14] For example, on the transfer of a council house to a secure tenant who exercises the right to buy, a covenant may be inserted into the conveyance preventing the former tenant from selling the dwelling-house except to someone who lives or works in the area.[15]

(C)   THE PROCEDURE

The Act contains intricate provisions which lay down detailed procedures for the exercise of the right to buy.

---

[12] [1988] 2 W.L.R. 1271.
[13] At 1278.
[14] s.157.
[15] s.157(3).

The procedure is initiated by the tenant serving a notice claiming the right to buy.[16] The landlord must respond to this notice (normally within four weeks) either admitting the claim, or denying it and giving reasons.[17] If the claim is admitted by the landlord, or established by legal proceedings, the landlord must then serve another notice stating the proposed terms of sale.[18] Again, the Act lays down time limits with which the landlord must comply (eight weeks in the case of freeholds, 12 weeks in the case of leases).

One of the perceived problems from a procedural point of view is delay by local authorities. In the 1987 White Paper *Housing: The Government's Proposals* attention was drawn to the fact that in cases of delay "[t]here is already power for the government to step in and take over sales."[19] This mechanism was not thought to be sufficient since "tenants ought to have the power to take action themselves if their applications are delayed."[20]

Section 124 of the Housing Act 1988 introduced the following alteration to the right to buy procedure:

(i)   A secure tenant who has claimed to exercise the right to buy may serve on the landlord an initial notice of delay where the landlord has failed to keep to the statutory time-table.[21]

(ii)   If the landlord fails to respond to the initial notice of delay, the tenant may serve an operative notice of delay which activates section 153B.[22]

(iii)   After an operative notice of delay has been served, payments of rent by the tenant are treated as payments towards the purchase price of the dwelling-house which the tenant intends to acquire.[23] If the tenant pays rent on this basis for more than a year, the landlord is subjected to a penalty: the purchase price is reduced by 150 per cent. of the tenant's rent payments.[24]

It is worth noting that a secure tenant may withdraw his claim to exercise the right to buy at any time by giving written notice to his landlord; the tenant does not have to give reasons.[25] There is nothing to prevent a tenant who has withdrawn a claim to exercise the right to buy from starting the procedure again with a new section 122 notice at some later date.

---

[16] s.122.
[17] s.123. Disputes are determined by the county court: Housing Act 1985, s.181.
[18] s.124.
[19] para. 2.12. These powers are conferred on the Secretary of State by Housing Act 1985, ss.164 to 166. See *R.* v. *Secretary of State for the Environment ex parte Norwich C.C.* [1982] Q.B. 808.
[20] para. 2.12.
[21] s.153A(1).
[22] s.153A(4).
[23] s.153B.
[24] s.153B(3) and (4).
[25] s.122(3).

(D) RIGHT TO A MORTGAGE

A secure tenant who has the right to buy his home also has the right to obtain a mortgage to finance the purchase either from the landlord or, where the landlord is a housing association, from the Housing Corporation.[26] There are provisions regulating the amount which the secure tenant can borrow,[27] the term of the mortgage[28] and the rate of interest.[29] The 1985 Act also lays down the procedure to be followed where a secure tenant exercises his right to a mortgage.[30]

(E) SHARED OWNERSHIP LEASES

In certain circumstances, a secure tenant may have the right to be granted a shared ownership lease. The idea of the scheme established by section 143 to 153 is to provide tenants who cannot afford to purchase their homes outright with a mechanism for becoming owner-occupiers. The tenant who exercises the right to be granted a shared ownership lease starts by purchasing an initial share of a long lease of the dwelling-house. Subsequently, the tenant may purchase further shares of the long lease until eventually the tenant owns the entire lease. At that point the tenant is entitled to acquire the freehold (assuming that the dwelling-house in question is a house and the landlord owns the freehold interest). In the meantime, the rent that the tenant has to pay to the landlord is reduced according to the size of the share of the long lease which he has at that point acquired.

The right to be granted a shared ownership lease under section 143 of the Housing Act 1985 is subordinate to the right to buy, in the sense that it only arises if the tenant's right to buy has been established and the tenant's notice claiming to exercise it remains in force.[31] Furthermore, the right conferred by section 143 is dependent on the tenant having claimed to exercise the right to a mortgage, but not being entitled to a full mortgage.[32]

Broadly speaking, the procedure which applies to the exercise of the right to buy is replicated in the context of the right to be granted a shared ownership lease: the procedure is initiated by a notice served by the tenant on the landlord[33]; the landlord must in reply serve a notice either admitting or denying the claim[34]; the system of delay notices set

---

[26] s.132.
[27] s.133.
[28] Sched. 7.
[29] Sched. 16.
[30] ss. 134 and 135.
[31] s.143(1)(a).
[32] s.143(1)(b). A full mortgage (which is defined by section 133) covers the aggregate of the purchase price, the costs incurred by the tenant and the costs incurred by the landlord or the Housing Corporation.
[33] s.144.
[34] s.146.

out in section 153A and 153B applies equally to the right to be granted a shared ownership lease[34a]; the tenant is also entitled to a mortgage.

There are, however, specific provisions which result from the particular nature of the transaction. The Act lays down special formulae for working out the cost of the initial share of the tenant (which must be at least 50 per cent. and in any event a multiple of 12.5 per cent.[35]), and the discount to which the tenant is entitled.

Section 148 of the Housing Act 1985 states:

(1) The consideration for the grant of a shared ownership lease (the tenant's "initial contribution") shall be determined by the formula—

$$C = \frac{S\,(V - D)}{100}$$

and the effective discount shall be determined by the formula—

$$E = \frac{S \times D}{100}$$

where—

  C= the tenant's initial contribution,
  E= the effective discount,
  S= the tenant's initial share expressed as a percentage,
  V= the value of the dwelling-house at the relevant time, determined in accordance with section 127, and
  D= the discount which if the tenant were exercising the right to buy would be applicable under sections 129 to 131.

(2) In determining the value of the dwelling-house for the purposes of this section, the assumptions to be made under section 127 (which vary according to whether it is the freehold or a lease which is to be acquired) are those applicable in relation to the dwelling-house for the purposes of the right to buy.

There are further provisions dealing with the calculation of the rent payable by the tenant under a shared ownership lease,[36] and the price to be paid when purchasing additional shares of the lease.[37]

There is no provision in the Housing Act 1985 for the repurchase by the landlord in cases of financial hardship on the part of the former secure tenant who has exercised his right to be granted a shared ownership lease. This can work seriously to the disadvantage of the tenant, who is effectively precluded from reverting to his secured status. In *R. v. Hillingdon L.B.C. ex p. Tinn*[38] it was held that, not only are local authority landlords not required to buy back the tenant's shared ownership lease, they are not even required to accept a surrender of the

[34a] See p. 528.
[35] s.145.
[36] Sched. 8, para. 4.
[37] Sched. 8, para. 3.
[38] (1988) 20 H.L.R. 305.

shared ownership lease by the tenant. Accordingly, if the tenant cannot keep up the payments of rent and mortgage instalments the practical solution is to try to sell the lease to a third party. The problem would then be that the tenant might be regarded by the local authority as intentionally homeless with the consequence that he or she would not be entitled to be rehoused on a permanent basis by the local authority under their duties to the homeless.[39]

(F) DEFECTIVE HOUSING

During the post-war period a number of local authorities—in an attempt to alleviate the chronic housing shortage as quickly as possible—commissioned the erection of so-called "system-built" houses. These houses were built predominantly of prefabricated concrete, and many types had design defects, which have subsequently come to light. The law seeks to ensure that a secure tenant who has exercised the right to buy in relation to one of these system-built houses should not be financially prejudiced by the fact that the design defect significantly reduces the value of the house. If certain conditions are satisfied (the most important of which is that the type of house and the defect in question have been designated by the Secretary of State[40]), a former secure tenant is normally entitled to financial assistance so that the defect can be remedied—though in some cases the former landlord may be required to repurchase the property. The details of the statutory scheme are to be found in Part XVI of the 1985 Act (replacing the Housing Defects Act 1984).

The statutory scheme in relation to each type of defective property is intended to have a limited life-span: assistance in respect of the twenty-two types of prefabricated concrete house which have been designated must be sought within 10 years of the designations coming into operation.[41] This means that the latest date on which an application for assistance may be made is December 1, 1994.

(G) TENANT INCENTIVES

Section 129 of the Housing Act 1988 introduced another policy aimed at further encouraging owner-occupation:

(1) In accordance with a scheme made by a local housing authority and approved by the Secretary of State under this section, the authority may make

---

[39] See Chapter 9.
[40] Under Housing Act 1985, s.528 (replacing Housing Defects Act 1984, s.1.)
[41] Housing Defects (Prefabricated Concrete Dwellings) (England and Wales) Designations 1984 (which were made under s.1 of the Housing Defects Act 1984 and which remain in force by virtue of s.2 of the Housing (Consequential Provisions) Act 1985).

grants to or for the benefit of qualifying tenants or licensees of the authority with a view to assisting each person to whom or for whose benefit a grant is made to obtain accommodation otherwise than as a tenant or licensee of the authority either—

(a) by acquiring an interest in a dwelling-house; or

(b) by carrying out works to a dwelling-house to provide additional accommodation; or

(c) by both of those means.

(2) A scheme under this section shall contain such provisions as the local housing authority considers appropriate together with any which the Secretary of State may require as a condition of his approval and, without prejudice to the generality, a scheme may include provisions specifying, or providing for the determination of—

(a) the persons who are qualifying tenants or licensees for the purposes of the scheme;

(b) the interests which qualifying tenants or licensees may be assisted to acquire;

(c) the works for the carrying out of which grants may be made;

(d) the circumstances in which a grant may be made for the benefit of a qualifying tenant or licensee;

(e) the amount of the grant which may be made in any particular case and the terms on which it may be made;

(f) the limits on the total number and amount of grants which may be made; and

(g) the period within which the scheme is to apply.

(3) The Secretary of State may approve a scheme made by a local housing authority under this section with or without conditions and, where a scheme has been approved, the authority shall take such steps as it considers appropriate to bring the scheme to the attention of persons likely to be able to benefit from it and shall take such other steps (if any) as the Secretary of State may direct in any particular case to secure publicity for the scheme.

(4) The Secretary of State may revoke an approval of a scheme under this section by a notice given to the local housing authority concerned; and, where such a notice is given, the revocation shall not affect the operation of the scheme in relation to any grants made or agreed before the date of the notice.

Note

A system which enables a local authority to pay cash incentives to help existing tenants to buy homes of their own has certain advantages from the local authority's point of view when compared to the right to buy. If a secure tenant exercises the right to buy, the local authority's housing stock is automatically reduced. However, if a secure tenant receives assistance from the local authority under a section 129 scheme approved by the Secretary of State, the local authority's housing stock is preserved.

Approved schemes were established by 44 authorities in 1989–90, and by the end of June 1990 approval had been given to 89 authorities. The scope of these schemes is, however, limited: these various approved schemes have the potential to release only 2,597 houses. The maximum grants which can be made to individual tenants range from £6,000 to £28,000.[42]

Bibliographical note

For an overview of the law relating to the right to buy see A. Arden, *Manual of Housing Law* (4th ed., 1989, Sweet & Maxwell) paras. 4.51–4.60; D. J. Hughes, *Public Sector Housing Law* (2nd ed., 1987, Butterworths) Chapter 2; D.C. Hoath, *Public Housing Law* (1989, Sweet & Maxwell) Chapter 14.

For a full account of the background, operation and effects of the right to buy see R. Forrest & A. Murie, *Selling the Welfare State: The Privatisation of Public Housing* (1988, Routledge)

II VOLUNTARY TRANSFER

By virtue of sections 32 and 43 of the Housing Act 1985 (as amended) local authorities may, with the consent of the Secretary of State, dispose of their housing stock. It was through the precursor of section 32 (namely, section 104 of the Housing Act 1957) that local authority tenants had the opportunity of buying their homes prior to the introduction of the right to buy in 1980. As regards the sale of individual dwelling-houses the right to buy has effectively superseded the voluntary sale provisions. The importance of the voluntary transfer provisions now lies in the disposal by local authorities of sizeable blocks of council housing, or even the whole of their housing stock to private sector landlords.

32.—(1) Without prejudice to the provisions of Part V (the right to buy) and Part IV of the Housing Act 1988 (change of landlords; secure tenants), a local authority have power by this section, and not otherwise, to dispose of land held by them for the purposes of this Part.

(2) A disposal under this section may be effected in any manner but, subject to subsection (3), shall not be made without the consent of the Secretary of State.

(3) No consent is required for the letting of land under a secure tenancy or under what would be a secure tenancy but for any of paragraphs 2 to 12 of Schedule 1 (tenancies, other than long leases, which are not secure).

43.—(1) The consent of the Secretary of State is required for the disposal by a local authority, otherwise than in pursuance of Part V (the right to buy) or Part

[42] H.C. Written Answers, Vol. 174, cols. 639–641, June 21, 1990.

IV of the Housing Act 1988 (change of landlord: secure tenants), of a house belonging to the authority—

(a)   which is let on a secure tenancy, or

(b)   of which a lease has been granted in pursuance of Part V, but which has not been acquired or appropriated by the authority for the purposes of this Part.

(2) Consent may be given—

(a)   either generally to all local authorities or to any particular house or description of house,

(b)   either generally in relation to all houses or in relation to any particular house or description of house.

(3) Consent may be given subject to conditions.

(4) Consent may, in particular, be given subject to conditions as to the price, premium or rent to be obtained on a disposal of the house, including conditions as to the amount by which, on a disposal of the house by way of sale or by the grant or assignment of a lease at a premium, the price or premium is to be, or may be, discounted by the local authority.

(4A) The matters to which the Secretary of State may have regard in determining whether to give consent and, if so, to what conditions consent should be subject shall include—

(a)   the extent (if any) to which the person to whom the proposed disposal is to be made (in this subsection referred to as "the intending purchaser") is, or is likely to be, dependent upon, controlled by or subject to influence from the local authority making the disposal or any members or officers of that authority;

(b)   the extent (if any) to which the proposed disposal would result in the intending purchaser becoming the predominant or a substantial owner in any area of housing accommodation let on tenancies or subject to licences;

(c)   the terms of the proposed disposal; and

(d)   any other matters whatsoever which he considers relevant.

(5) For the purposes of this section the grant of an option to purchase the freehold of, or any other interest in, a house to which this section applies is a disposal and a consent given under this section to such a disposal extends to a disposal made in pursuance of the option.

Where a local authority intends to transfer dwellings which are subject to secure tenancies to a private sector landlord not only is the consent of the Secretary of State required, but the local authority must comply with procedures laid down by section 106A and Schedule 3A of the Housing Act 1985:

106A.—(1) The provisions of Schedule 3A have effect with respect to the duties of—

(a)   a local authority proposing to dispose of dwelling-houses subject to secure tenancies, and

(b) the Secretary of State in considering whether to give his consent to such disposal,

to have regard to the views of tenants liable as a result of the disposal to cease to be secure tenants.

(2) In relation to a disposal to which that Schedule applies, the provisions of that Schedule apply in place of the provisions of section 105 (consultation on matters of housing management).

SCHEDULE 3A

CONSULTATION BEFORE DISPOSAL TO PRIVATE SECTOR LANDLORD

Disposals to which this Schedule applies

1.—(1) This Schedule applies to the disposal by a local authority of an interest in land as a result of which a secure tenant of the authority will become the tenant of a private sector landlord.

(2) For the purposes of this Schedule the grant of an option which if exercised would result in a secure tenant of a local authority becoming the tenant of a private sector landlord shall be treated as a disposal of the interest which is the subject of the option.

(3) Where a disposal of land by a local authority is in part a disposal to which this Schedule applies, the provisions of this Schedule apply to that part as to a separate disposal.

(4) In this paragraph "private sector landlord" means a person other than an authority or body within section 80 (the landlord condition for secure tenancies).

Application for Secretary of State's consent

2.—(1) The Secretary of State shall not entertain an application for his consent to a disposal to which this Schedule applies unless the authority certify either—

(a) that the requirements of paragraph 3 as to consultation have been complied with, or

(b) that the requirements of that paragraph as to consultation have been complied with except in relation to tenants expected to have vacated the dwelling-house in question before the disposal;

and the certificate shall be accompanied by a copy of the notices given by the authority in accordance with that paragraph.

(2) Where the certificate is in the latter form, the Secretary of State shall not determine the application until the authority certify as regards the tenants not originally consulted—

(a) that they have vacated the dwelling-house in question, or

(b) that the requirements of paragraph 3 as to consultation have been complied with;

and a certificate under sub-paragraph (b) shall be accompanied by a copy of the notices given by the authority in accordance with paragraph 3.

(3) References in this Schedule to the Secretary of State's consent to a disposal are to the consent required by section 32 or 43 (general requirement of consent for disposal of houses or land held for housing purposes).

3.—(1) The requirements as to consultation referred to above are as follows.

(2) The authority shall serve notice in writing on the tenant informing him of—

(a) such details of their proposal as the authority consider appropriate, but including the identity of the person to whom the disposal is to be made,

(b) the likely consequences of the disposal for the tenant, and

(c) the effect of the provisions of this Schedule and of sections 171A to 171H (preservation of right to buy on disposal to private sector landlord),

and informing him that he may, within such reasonable period as may be specified in the notice, make representations to the authority.

(3) The authority shall consider any representations made to them within that period and shall serve a further written notice on the tenant informing him—

(a) of any significant changes in their proposal, and

(b) that he may within such period as is specified (which must be at least 28 days after the service of the notice) communicate to the Secretary of State his objection to the proposal,

and informing him of the effect of paragraph 5 (consent to be withheld if majority of tenants are opposed).

Power to require further consultation

4. The Secretary of State may require the authority to carry out such further consultation with their tenants, and to give him such information as to the results of that consultation, as he may direct.

Consent to be withheld if majority of tenants are opposed

5.—(1) The Secretary of State shall not give his consent if it appears to him that a majority of the tenants of the dwelling-houses to which the application relates do not wish the disposal to proceed; but this does not affect his general discretion to refuse consent on grounds relating to whether a disposal has the support of the tenants or on any other ground.

(2) In making his decision the Secretary of State may have regard to any information available to him; and the local authority shall give him such information as to the representations made to them by tenants and others, and other relevant matters, as he may require.

Protection of purchasers

6. The Secretary of State's consent to a disposal is not invalidated by a failure on his part or that of the local authority to comply with the requirements of this Schedule.

Note

There have been relatively few voluntary transfers of large blocks of council housing under these provisions of the Housing Act 1985. In reply to a question in Parliament it was reported on May 10, 1990 that the Secretary of State had given consent for five local authorities to dispose of the major part of their housing stock into the private sector.[43] At that time the Secretary of State was considering six applications from local authorities to transfer tenanted housing to new landlords.[44] It was further reported in August 1990 that consent had been given to three more authorities to dispose of a total of some 9,400 dwellings.[45]

The controversial sale of Rochester-upon-Medway D.C.'s housing stock (amounting to 8,000 homes) also went through in the summer of 1990. This sale was, at the time, the largest which had taken place and was significant in that it was the first sale to a private sector landlord which was not registered with the Housing Corporation.

III   TENANT'S CHOICE

The Government's 1987 White Paper set out the following proposals:

5.9 The Government intends to introduce arrangements to allow council tenants to choose to transfer to other landlords. This will offer a remedy for tenants who receive a poor service from their council. Exposing councils to healthy competition should also contribute to a better general standard of services even for tenants who do not transfer. Tenants will be able to decide, if they wish to transfer, to set the process in hand at a time of their own choosing.

5.10 Tenants who wish to transfer will need to identify a new landlord willing to take them on. Landlords will be formally approved on the basis of their suitability and viability. There will be arrangements to put tenants and prospective new landlords in touch. Many approved landlords will be established housing associations, but some will be commercial landlords. In other cases, tenants may if they wish be able to take control of their own homes by forming a cooperative with their neighbours. The legislation will give prospective

---

[43] The five authorities in question were: Broadland D.C. Chiltern D.C., Newbury D.C., Sevenoaks D.C. and Swale B.C.

[44] HC Written Answers, Vol. 172, cols. 188–189, May 10, 1990.

[45] *Inside Housing*, August 3, 1990, p. 2. The authorities in question were: Mid-Sussex, Medina and South Wight.

landlords, once they have a tenant's agreement, the right to negotiate to the transfer of the tenant's home on legally defined terms.

5.11 The position in relation to blocks of maisonettes and flats will be complex, and special arrangements of various kinds will be needed which are not needed in the case of houses. The position generally, however will be that the freehold of a block will be transferred where a majority of tenants want to do so. But although some tenants in a block may want a change of landlord, their neighbours may want to stay with the council. The legislation will therefore provide that, even where a block transfers to a new landlord, tenants can, if they wish, continue in their homes as tenants of the council.

(A)   THE SCOPE OF PART IV

The tenants' choice provisions do not apply to all property owned by all landlords listed in section 80 of the Housing Act 1985. The scope of Part IV is circumscribed in two ways.

First, the possibility of transfer under Part IV of the Housing Act 1988 applies only where property is held by a "public sector landlord" as defined by section 93(2):

The following are public sector landlords for the purposes of this Part, namely—

(a)   a local housing authority within the meaning of section 1 of the Housing Act 1985 (in this Part referred to as "the 1985 Act");
(b)   a new town corporation within the meaning of section 4(b) of that Act;
(c)   a housing action trust within the meaning of Part III of this Act; and
(d)   the Development Board for Rural Wales.

Secondly, there are restrictions on the property which can be acquired by the tenants' choice procedure. By virtue of section 93(1) of the 1988 Act the right to acquire under Part IV cannot be exercised except in relation to (a) buildings, the freehold of which is owned by the public sector landlord, and which are occupied by qualifying tenants and (b) freehold property which is reasonably required for occupation with such buildings.

According to section 93(3) of the 1988 Act a person is a qualifying tenant if he is a secure tenant holding directly from a public sector landlord. This definition is, however, subject to the exceptions contained in subsection (4) which provides that a person is not a qualifying tenant (a) if he is obliged to give up possession in pursuance of a court order, or (b) if the circumstances fall within exceptions to the right to buy contained in paragraphs 5 to 11 of Schedule 5 to the Housing Act 1985.[46]

It should also be noted that certain types of premises are excluded by section 95, notably: buildings which are not used primarily for residential purposes[47]; buildings which comprise a number of dwelling-houses and in relation to which the number of non-qualifying tenants

[46] See pp. 511–512.
[47] s.95(1).

exceeds the number of qualifying tenants[48]; and dwelling-houses which are not occupied by secure tenants.[49]

(B) OUTLINE OF THE PROCEDURE

The Housing Corporation, which plays an important role in the operation of Part IV,[50] explains the procedure—from the individual tenant's perspective—in the following terms[51]:

1 ARE YOU INTERESTED?

If tenants are interested in finding out about the scheme, they should contact the Housing Corporation ... (Alternatively, a landlord which has been approved by the Corporation can express interest in a particular house, block of flats group of dwellings or estate). In either case ...

2 WE GIVE YOU INFORMATION

The Corporation will send information about all the possible options, including various types of non-profit making housing associations, tenants' co-ops, and commercial landlords. If tenants wish, we can attend meetings on the estate and answer questions.[52] Then, if tenants wish, we will move on to Step 3 ...

3 TENANTS LOOK AT POSSIBLE LANDLORDS

If tenants are interested in particular types of landlord, we will contact alternative landlords of those types and introduce them on a no-commitment basis. We have published a leaflet on the questions you should ask possible landlords—ask for a copy. To make a fair comparison, tenants will need to ask their existing landlord the same questions. At this stage, landlords will not have enough information to be able to make detailed promises about rent and repairs etc, but tenants will be able to question them in detail about their record and policies.

Alternatively, if tenants are mainly interested in setting up a new tenant-controlled co-op or housing association, we can advise on how to do this.

4 TENANTS DECIDE

Once tenants have considered all of this, we will ask which (if any) landlord they wish to proceed further with. How we do this will vary. If for example only a small number of homes are involved, an open

[48] s.95(3).
[49] s.95(4).
[50] Housing Act 1988 established Housing for Wales (see ss.46 and 47 and Schedule 5). As regards property in Wales, functions which would have been carried out by the Housing Corporation are performed by Housing for Wales.
[51] *Tenant's Choice: How it Works* pp. 8–9. Footnotes giving references to the relevant statutory provisions have been added to the text.
[52] Housing Act 1988, s.106.

tenants' meeting might be enough. But in some cases, particularly in large estates, we may need a formal opinion survey. Often however, there will be an obvious front-runner. Only the landlord with the most tenant support will be allowed to go forward. A landlord must convince us that they have the support "in principle" of at least 10 per cent. of tenants. . . .

5 THE LANDLORD APPLIES

If an alternative landlord emerges, it can then apply formally to the existing public sector landlord to take over the housing concerned.[53] After this, exactly which property is to be included[54] and the price to be paid[55] is sorted out (with binding adjudication where disputes occur[56]). At this stage, the possible landlord will be told details of who is living on the estate, what the level of rent arrears is, etc.[57] Don't worry about confidentiality—the landlord won't be able to pass on information to anyone outside the proposed sale.[58] The landlord will also find out what repairs and improvements are needed, costs, etc. Throughout the process, the alternative landlord must keep all tenants informed of progress.

6 THE LANDLORD MAKES AN OFFER

Once it has all the information needed, the alternative landlord will write to every tenant setting out in detail what is being offered—rents, repairs, local management arrangements, and much more.[59] This offer (which we will check before it goes out to ensure that it covers all the areas that are needed) will provide the information tenants need to make a final decision. If you transfer, you will go on to a different form of tenancy. Details of this will be provided. If the transfer goes ahead, the landlord will be legally bound to keep the promises made in the offer of tenancy terms.[60] . . .

7 TENANTS VOTE

Tenants then vote on the offer.[61] An independent body (approved by us) will send a ballot paper and a Freepost return envelope, together with an explanation of the ballot, to all tenants; joint tenants will get

---

[53] Housing Act 1988, s.96.
[54] Housing Act 1988, s.98.
[55] Housing Act 1988, s.99.
[56] Housing Act 1988, s.98(5) and s.99(6).
[57] Housing Act 1988, s.97.
[58] See *Criteria for approval of a Tenants' Choice Landlord*, para. 8(8). See p. 546.
[59] Housing Act 1988, s.102; Housing (Change of Landlord) Regulations 1989 (S.I. 1989 No. 367), reg. 16 and Sched. 3.
[60] In exercise of the powers conferred by section 94 of the Housing Act 1988, the Housing Corporation has established criteria which must be satisfied by an applicant seeking approval to acquire property under Part IV of the 1988 Act. Para. 8 provides (*inter alia*):
Approval will be conditional on receipt by the Corporation of a deed being executed under the seal of the applicant that will include the following undertakings: . . .
    (7)   to abide by the terms offered to tenants during the formal consultation under Sections 102 and 103 of the Housing Act 1988;
[61] Housing Act 1988, s.102; Housing (Change of Landlord) Regulations 1989, regs. 16 and 17.

one ballot paper between them. If tenants know that they will be away from home for any reason, they can have a ballot paper sent to the address they want.[62] There will be at least three weeks to return the ballot paper. At the end of this period, the independent body will spend another three weeks following-up anyone who hasn't voted, to try to ensure that they understand the importance of the vote and to give them another chance to vote if they wish.[63]

8 THE FINAL DECISION

Once the votes have been counted, the proposed transfer can only go ahead if:
(a) at least half the tenants have voted one way or the other[64];
(b) less than half the tenants vote to remain with their existing public sector landlord.[65] It is important to realise that if you vote "yes" or do not vote at all, you will transfer to become tenants of the alternative landlord if the transfer goes ahead.[66]

If these two requirements are met, the new landlord can take over, but need not do so if, for example, it feels that there is not enough tenant support.

9 HOMES ARE TRANSFERRED

The transfer is then completed.[67] If you voted "yes" or did not vote you will transfer, but secure tenants who voted "no" will remain as tenants of the old landlord.[68] (Leaseholders[69] and business tenants[70] can also vote, but unlike secure tenants they do not get the right to stay with the old landlord if the transfer as a whole goes ahead.[71])

If you transfer, you will not be able to change your mind later.

10 THE NEW LANDLORD MUST KEEP ITS PROMISES

As already mentioned, landlords will be legally obliged to honour their promises on rents, repairs, improvements, etc.[72] All Tenants' Choice landlords must offer binding arbitration,[73] and tenants can also take landlords to court if promises are broken. If disputes arise and the case

---

[62] Housing (Change of Landlord) Regulations 1989, reg. 16(7).
[63] Housing (Change of Landlord) Regulations 1989, reg. 16(5).
[64] Housing Act 1988, s.103(2)(a).
[65] Housing Act 1988, s.103(2)(b).
[66] Housing Act 1988, s.103(6).
[67] Housing Act 1988, s.104.
[68] This results from the combined effect of Housing Act 1988, ss. 100(1)(a), 104(1) and Housing (Change of Landlord) Regulations 1989, reg. 10 and Sched. 4.
[69] Housing Act 1988, s.102(2)(a).
[70] Housing Act 1988, s.102(2)(c); Housing (Change of Landlord) Regulations 1989, reg. 15(a).
[71] Housing Act 1988, s.100; Housing (Change of Landlord) Regulations 1989, reg. 7(a).
[72] See n. 60.
[73] It appears from the legislation that applicants may choose whether or not to offer arbitration (Housing Act 1988 s.102; Housing (Change of Landlord) Regulations 1989, reg. 16 and Sched. 3, para. 3(k)). However, approval by the Housing Corporation is dependent on applicants' offering binding arbitration: *Criteria for approval of a Tenants' Choice Landlord*, para. 8(1)); *Housing Management Guidance*, para. G1(a).

raises an issue of principle or is too complicated for tenants to cope with without help, we can negotiate with the landlord and, in particular circumstances, pay for tenants' legal representation.[74]

(C) APPROVED LANDLORDS

An important feature of the tenants' choice provisions is that the right to acquire public sector housing may be exercised only by an approved landlord. Section 94 of the 1988 Act provides:

(1) The right conferred by this Part shall not be exercisable except by a person who is for the time being approved by the Corporation under this section; and neither a public sector landlord nor the council of a county nor any other body which the Corporation have reason to believe might not be independent of such a landlord or council may be approved under this section.

(2) For the purposes of subsection (1) above, a person shall not be regarded as independent of a public sector landlord or the council of a county if the body is or appears likely to be under the control of, or subject to influence from, such landlord or council or particular members or officers of such landlord or council.

(3) The Corporation shall establish (and from time to time vary) criteria to be satisfied by a person seeking approval under this section and without prejudice to subsections (1) and (2) above, in deciding whether to give such approval, the Corporation shall have regard to whether the person satisfies those criteria.

A variety of different types of landlord are eligible for approval. In principle, public sector housing may be acquired under Part IV by housing associations (either registered or non-registered), by commercial landlords (including companies, partnerships and individuals) or by the tenants collectively (through mechanisms such as tenants' co-operatives, neighbourhood housing associations, and tenant companies).

To gain approval prospective landlords must satisfy certain criteria, and one of the criteria is that the applicant must comply with the Housing Corporation's guidance on the managment by tenant's choice landlords of accommodation let on assured tenancies under the Housing Act 1988.

Criteria for Approval of a Tenants' Choice Landlord[75]

In exercise of the powers conferred by Section 94 of the Housing Act 1988, the Housing Corporation has established criteria to which the Corporation shall have regard and which must be satisfied by an applicant seeking approval to acquire property from a public sector landlord under Part IV of the Housing Act 1988. The criteria, which are

---

[74] Housing Act 1988, s.107(1).
[75] Housing Corporation, *Tenants' Choice: Criteria for Landlord Approval and Guidance Notes for Applicants* (1989), Appendix I.

effective from January 15, 1989 and may be varied by the Housing Corporation, are as follows:

1 STATUTORY REQUIREMENTS

(1) Eligibility: the following bodies are not eligible for approval:

    (a) a public sector landlord, *i.e.* a local housing authority within the meaning of Section 1 of the Housing Act 1985 or a new town corporation or a housing action trust or the Development Board for Rural Wales;

    (b) a county council;

    (c) any other body which the Corporation believes might not be independent of a public sector landlord or a county council. A body shall not be regarded as independent of a public sector landlord or a county council if the body is or appears likely to be under the control of, or subject to influence from, such a landlord or council or particular members or officers of such a landlord or council.

Other statutory requirements:

    (a) an approval shall not be given except to a person making an application accompanied by such fee as the Corporation, with the consent of the Secretary of State, may specify;

    (b) an approval may be conditional upon the person or persons concerned entering into such undertakings as may be specified by the Corporation.

2 STATUS

(1) Any incorporated or unincorporated body or individual or group of individuals may apply for approval.

(2) Unincorporated bodies which have a governing instrument and all incorporated bodies (such as a society registered under the Industrial and Provident Societies Act 1965, or a registered company) must have objects or powers which will permit the acquisition, management, repair or improvement of housing accommodation.

(3) Applicants who are unincorporated and individuals must be able to demonstrate that succession arrangements are sufficient to ensure that any tenancies acquired as a result of their Tenants' Choice landlord activity will be adequately managed in the long-term.

3 CONTROL AND ACCOUNTABILITY

(1) The applicant must be, or be under the control of, a responsible person or persons with experience and skills appropriate to the anticipated scale

and nature of its operations so that the activities of a Tenants' Choice landlord are likely to be conducted in a responsible and effective manner.

(2)   In the case of an incorporated or unincorporated body, control over its administration must be vested in a committee of management, body of trustees, board of directors or other governing body.

(3)   The applicant must declare any extent to which it is under the control of, or subject to influence which could prejudice its independence from another person or organisation, and be able to show that any such influence or control operates in the best interests of the applicant and does not prejudice the applicant's ability to enter into and continue to fulfil the criteria and conditions of approval.

4   FINANCIAL REQUIREMENTS

An applicant must be able to demonstrate that it is operating, or will operate, on a sound and proper financial basis and in particular:

(1)   It must keep accounting records, have adequate systems of control and produce annual accounts which have been audited by a properly qualified auditor or, if a newly formed organisation, demonstrate arrangements for meeting these requirements.

(2)   In order to ensure its future viability, the applicant must show that:

(a)   its current and known future capital commitments are, or can be, fully financed by loans, grants or other permanent sources of capital, and

(b)   its income will be sufficient for present circumstances and taking one year with another, to meet its outgoings and provisions.

(3)   An applicant which is a registered housing association must ensure that its overheads, *e.g.* salaries and expenses, are reasonable for its size and level of activity and are properly allocated in a consistent manner to its various functions.

5   MANAGERIAL EFFICIENCY

The Corporation will consider the applicant's skills in property acquisition, finance, housing management and maintenance. Having regard to its size, its current and intended level and nature of activity, the applicant must be able to show that it has access to professional skills and experience for the efficient acquisition, management and maintenance to a high standard, of housing either from its own staff or from other persons or organisations. These arrangements must serve the best interests of tenants and not restrict the independence of the applicant.

6   PROPOSED LEVEL AND AREA OF ACTIVITY

The Corporation will consider the applicant's intended level and areas of activity as a Tenants' Choice landlord in relation to its current size and resources, including managerial resources. The applicant's proposals for growth in levels and areas of activity should be consistent with its existing and proposed capacity without endangering, in the long term, the quality of any similar housing activities which it has already undertaken.

7 EQUAL OPPORTUNITIES

Under section 56 of the Housing Act 1988, the Corporation has the statutory duty as set out in section 71 of the Race Relations Act 1976 "to eliminate unlawful racial discrimination and to promote equality of opportunity, and good relations between persons of different racial groups." An applicant must be able to demonstrate that there will be equality of opportunity in its policies and procedures.

8 OTHER REQUIREMENTS

Application for approval must be made on the form provided by the Corporation. Approval will be conditional on receipt by the Corporation of a deed being executed under the seal of the applicant that will include the following undertakings:

(1) not to submit any application to acquire property under section 96 of the Housing Act 1988 if requested not to do so by the Corporation, because the property is covered by a resolution of a local housing authority that it intends to further consult its tenants under Schedule 3A paragraph 3(3) of the Housing Act 1985 about a proposed voluntary disposal, by a resolution of a Housing Action Trust under section 79 of the Housing Act 1988 or in the case of a planned disposal by a New Town Development Corporation or the Commission for New Towns the date of the Secretary of State's instruction to initiate disposal;

(2) not to submit any application to acquire property under section 96 of the Housing Act 1988 if requested not to do so by the Corporation, because the property is covered by a resolution of a local housing authority that it intends to consult its tenants under section 27A of the Housing Act 1985 about proposals for a management agreement with a Tenant Management Co–operative;

(3) before serving any application to acquire property under section 96 of the Housing Act 1988, to comply with the Corporation's guidance for the informal consultation of tenants to establish which of any competing applicants has the clearest support among tenants and to abide by the outcome of such informal consultation;

(4) to keep tenants and the Corporation informed at all key stages of the acquisition process, and to inform tenants, the Housing Corporation and the public sector landlord should the application be withdrawn;

(5) to submit to the Corporation the material to be given to tenants as part of the formal consultation under section 102 of the Housing Act 1988 in order to allow its consistency with the approval criteria and undertakings to be assessed;

(6) to obtain the Corporation's approval to the appointment and the terms of the contract with an independent teller to conduct and certify the outcome of the ballot required under sections 102 and 103 of the Housing Act 1988 as part of the formal consultation of tenants;

(7) to abide by the terms offered to tenants during the formal consultation under sections 102 and 103 of the Housing Act 1988;

(8) to treat in strict confidence any information obtained about tenants during the course of an application, and to disclose such information to third parties only where necessary for the purpose of pursuing the application;

(9) to retain dwellings acquired as a Tenants' Choice landlord for letting at rents within the reach of those in low-paid employment;

(10) to offer tenants rents and other charges which are consistent between properties of similar size, condition and location except where different services and amenities are to be provided;

(11) to comply with the Corporation's guidance on the management by Tenants' Choice landlords of accommodation let on assured tenancies under the Housing Act 1988 or, if appropriate, the Corporation's guidance for registered housing associations letting on assured tenancies or that for fully mutual housing co-operatives, in respect of both tenancies acquired and future lettings arising from its Tenants' Choice landlord activities;

(12) not to seek to have conveyed any houses specified for exclusion from the acquisition in a notice of intention to proceed served under section 103(4)(b) of the Housing Act 1988;

(13) not to seek possession under Ground 6 of Schedule 2 to the Housing Act 1988 of a dwelling acquired under Part IV of that Act;

(14) to validate or substantiate within a reasonable time limit any information provided on the application form and furnish any other additional information required by the Corporation;

(15) to submit within 6 months of its financial year end its audited annual accounts and an annual return relating to its activities as a Tenants' Choice landlord in such form as the Corporation may determine;

(16) to provide within a reasonable time limit any additional information regarding its activities as a Tenants' Choice landlord as required by the Corporation from time to time;

(17) to give the Corporation four weeks written notice of any proposed change in its objects and powers referred to at paragraph 2(2) of these criteria or, if required by section 19 of the Housing Associations Act 1985, to obtain the Corporation's consent to such changes; and to notify the Corporation in writing within four weeks of any changes in the membership of the governing body or in the managerial and executive staff separately identified in the application form or in the registered or correspondence address of the landlord;

(18) to ensure that the requirements of these criteria are observed at all times in the future.

9   ADDITIONAL REQUIREMENTS TO QUALIFY FOR GENERAL APPROVAL

In addition to satisfying the criteria described in 1 to 8, to qualify for general approval an applicant must be able to demonstrate that it has:

(1) not less than 2 years' experience in managing social rented housing in the manner described in the Corporation's guidance for Tenants' Choice landlords on housing management practice;

(2) a high degree of financial strength and evidence of financial stability;

(3) the managerial capacity to cope with the anticipated growth in the levels and areas of its Tenants' Choice landlord activity.

The Housing Corporation Guidance on the Management by Tenants' Choice Landlords of Accommodation let on Assured Tenancies under the Housing Act 1988[76]

A MEETING HOUSING DEMAND

A1 Tenants' Choice landlords are required to retain their housing stock for letting and to dispose of it only in particular circumstances. Disposals require the consent of the Secretary of State.

A2 In determining their priorities for the provision of accommodation and the offer of tenancies, Tenants' Choice landlords should take account of housing demand and conditions in their area. They should consult and co-operate with the local housing authority, especially about its responsibilities for homeless persons and its other statutory re-housing obligations and with other relevant public bodies such as social service departments and health authorities. They should also collaborate with these bodies and with voluntary and community organisations to make their housing service known to the relevant members of the public.

A3 Tenants' Choice landlords are expected to respond to tenants' requirements for mobility, and to participate actively in recognised national and local mobility and exchange schemes.

B ALLOCATING ACCOMMODATION ON ASSURED TENANCIES

B1 Tenants' Choice landlords are expected to have publicly available policies and procedures for selecting tenants and allocating tenancies. These should be open, fair and based on housing need.

B2.1 Tenants' Choice landlords should make publicly and freely available a summary of:

a. who is eligible for their accommodation;

b. how members of the public may apply for tenancies, including any arrangements for nominations or referrals from the local housing authority and other organisations;

---

[76] Housing Corporation, *Tenants' Choice: Criteria for Landlord Approval and Guidance Notes for Applicants* (1989), Appendix II.

    c.   their policies and procedures for deciding on priority as between applicants; and

    d.   their policies and procedures for responding to tenants wishing to move (whether or not by way of exchange of dwellings) to other dwellings let by themselves or another landlord.

B2.2   They should send a copy of this summary to the Housing Corporation, as part of their application for approval under section 94 of the Housing Act 1988 and subsequently to the local housing authority in whose area they manage or are going to manage tenanted property as a Tenants' Choice landlord. A copy should also be sent to local advice centres and other organisations advising the public on access to housing and be given to people who apply to the Tenants' Choice landlord for accommodations. Where appropriate translations should be provided.

B2.3   Larger Tenants's Choice landlords will need more detailed guidelines and procedures for their staff. These should also be available to the bodies mentioned above and to any applicants or members of the public requesting to see them.

B3.1   Tenant's Choice landlords are expected to have allocation policies which are clear. They should be based upon the severity of an applicant's housing needs. Tenants' Choice landlords are expected to pay special attention to the specific housing difficulties experienced by particular groups. These will vary from time to time and from place to place. They may include elderly people, single people, families with young children, single parent families, people from ethnic minorities, young people without family support, women suffering domestic violence, disabled people, and those who care for people who would otherwise be unable to remain in their own home, but this list is not intended to be exhaustive.

B3.2   Policies and procedures must provide equality of opportunity to all sections of society, taking particular and full account of the race relations and sex discrimination legislation. (See also section H below.)

B3.3   There should be procedures which can demonstrate that policies are objective and are properly followed. For instance, among other good practices, Tenants' Choice landlords are expected to keep records of applicants' own definition of their ethnic origin, and monitor them.

B3.4   Tenants' Choice landlords should prepare annual summaries of their lettings activities to include a report on the number and types of lettings to different types of applicant. They should make these summaries available to inquirers.

B3.5   Tenants' Choice landlords should not deter low income applicants by requiring more than one or two weeks' rent in advance, to cover the first rental period. Returnable deposits should never be required for unfurnished tenancies, and kept as low as possible even when furniture is provided. Tenants' Choice landlords should never charge premiums for assured tenancies covered by this Guidance.

C TERMS OF ASSURED TENANCIES

C1   The tenancy agreement should be in writing, and should also be explained to the tenant in clear terms. Where appropriate translations should be provided.

C2   Tenants' Choice landlords are expected to give their tenants long term security where possible and cannot offer assured shorthold tenancies to tenants in the formal consultation under section 102 of the Housing Act 1988. After transfer assured shorthold tenancies should be used only in exceptional circumstances, and most tenancies granted by a Tenants' Choice landlord should continue to be periodic assured tenancies.

C3   When offering tenancies to existing tenants of a local authority or a registered housing association, Tenants' Choice landlords should explain to them fully any differences in statutory or contractual rights and obligations which the new tenancy will entail, including the effects on their Right to Buy.

C4   Prospective tenants should be fully informed of the security of tenure they would have under the Housing Act 1988, and the specified grounds on which the courts would be able to end the tenancy, and of the right for their spouse (or person living with the tenant as husband or wife at the time of the tenant's death) to succeed to the tenancy.

C5   Tenants' Choice landlords are expected to give their assured tenants additional contractual rights within the terms of the tenancy agreement, which should include:

   a.   the right to exchange tenancies with tenants of other Tenants' Choice landlords, registered housing associations, New Towns or local authorities, subject to both landlords' agreement, which should not be unreasonably withheld.

   b.   the right to take in lodgers, or sublet part of their accommodation, (provided that the subletting attracts no security of tenure) subject to the landlord's permission which should not be unreasonably withheld.

   c.   the right to carry out improvements, with the landlord's permission, which should not be unreasonably withheld.

   d.   the right to carry out repairs and have the cost refunded in certain circumstances where the landlord has failed to carry out its repairing obligations.

   e.   the right to be consulted about housing management changes, (see also Section F), and to be informed about the landlord's management policies (see Section G).

Tenant's choice landlords should consider whether they wish to grant a right of succession to the tenancy to a member of the tenant's family who had been living with the tenant for the year before the tenant's death, and had been looking after the tenant, or had accepted responsibility for the tenant's dependents, or who would be made homeless if required to vacate the accommodation.

C6   In addition the tenancy agreement should:

   a.   state that the landlord has been approved by the Housing Corporation under section 94 of the Housing Act 1988 for the purposes of Tenants' Choice and is subject to this Guidance;

   b.   permit assignment of the tenancy only:
        —   by order of the courts under the Matrimonial Causes Act, or,
        —   by way of exchange under C5.a above.

   (Tenants' Choice landlords may also wish to grant a right of assignment to a person who would be entitled to succeed to the tenancy on the death of the tenant, subject to the landlords' consent which should not be unreasonably withheld.)

c. set out the initial rent payable, and, if a service charge is included, show it separately, and the procedure for altering it (see also Section D);

d. define clearly the landlord's statutory responsibility for repairs, and the contractual responsibilities for internal decorations and repairs (and replacement of furniture and fittings where relevant) (see also Section E).

D   PRINCIPLES UPON WHICH RENT (AND OTHER CHARGES) FOR ASSURED TENANCIES ARE TO BE DETERMINED

D1   Housing accommodation originally provided by public bodies and subsequently transferred to a Tenants' Choice landlord, is intended to be accessible to people on low incomes, whether or not they are in paid employment or in receipt of housing benefit. Tenants' Choice landlords are therefore expected to set and maintain their rents at levels within the reach of those in low paid employment. This will usually entail setting rents below market level. Tenants' Choice landlords should not discriminate in their rent setting between tenants in receipt of housing benefit and others.

D2   In addition Tenant's Choice landlords are expected to take account of the need to cover the costs (after subsidy) of loan charges, and of management and maintenance, including the requirement to make prudent provision for future repairs; and, in setting the rent for each dwelling, its size, amenities, location and condition.

D3   Tenants' Choice landlords should inform their tenants of their right to refer any proposed increases, other than those within the terms set out in the tenancy agreement, to the Rent Assessment Committee which will fix a market rent for the accommodation, above which the landlord may not increase the rent for 12 months.

D4   Where Tenants' Choice landlords require tenants to pay variable service charges they should provide those tenants with written information explaining their rights under the Landlord and Tenant Act 1985.

E   MAINTENANCE AND REPAIR

E1   Tenants' Choice landlords must meet their statutory and contractual obligations to keep their housing property fit for human habitation. They should keep it in good tenantable order, including when necessary renewals to the building fabric and landlord's fixtures and fittings.

E2   They should inspect their property to ensure that they meet these obligations, and can plan effectively, and make financial provision for, long term maintenance.

E3   Tenants' Choice landlords should provide their tenants with information in clear terms on:

a. who is responsible for which repairs, including the statutory position (*e.g.*, under sections 11–14 of the Landlord and Tenant Act 1985);

b. methods for reporting the need for repairs. These should give tenants open and easy access to their landlords;

c. how long it should take for defined categories of repairs to be carried out, taking into account the importance to tenants of speed of response;

d. how emergencies should be dealt with;

e. what tenants can do if the landlord fails to meet its repairing obligations, including the right to be paid for carrying out the repair themselves or to contact the local authority Environmental Health Officers;

f. their policy for planned maintenance, including cyclical decorations of external and common parts; and

g. their policy for improvements, including the provision of alternative or temporary accommodation, disturbance payments, compensation, and the effect on rents.

F   CONSULTATION AND TENANT INVOLVEMENT

F1 Tenants' Choice landlords should consult their tenants about proposed changes in management and maintenance policy or practice which may affect a substantial proportion or number of tenants, in particular,

a. where the landlord proposes changes in the arrangements for management or maintenance, which substantially effect tenants;

b. where physical improvements to the dwellings or environment are proposed;

c. the extent and cost of services paid for out of tenants' service charges;

and should take tenants' views into account.

In addition landlords are encouraged to consult tenants and/or their representative organisation(s) when the landlord's service is the subject of regular or serious complaint by tenants. Landlords should make a reasoned response to tenants and/or their representative organisations(s) when they approach the landlord on a matter of concern to them or on a proposal which they wish to make, including proposals for increasing tenant involvement in management.

F2 Tenants' Choice landlords should make arrangements for consultation which take into account the views of the tenants affected and the part which representative tenant organisations can play.

F3 Tenants' Choice landlords should assist representative tenant organisations to obtain reasonable facilities for meetings and for the proper conduct of their business.

F4 Tenants' Choice landlords should inform their tenants what arrangement or opportunities the landlord has to enable tenants to participate in the management or control of the landlord, or of the estate or group of dwellings of which they are tenants.

G INFORMATION TO TENANTS

G1 In addition to informing their tenants and other interested parties about their:

- policies and procedures for selecting tenants and dealing with transfer requests;
- terms of tenancy;
- principles and procedures for fixing rent and other charges;
- maintenance responsibilities and procedures; and
- arrangements for consultation and participation;

as described in previous sections of this Guidance, Tenants' Choice landlords should have policies and procedures on the following matters and should inform their tenants of them in plain terms so that tenants and other interested parties may see how individual decisions fit in with them; namely policy and procedures:

a. for dealing with complaints about the landlord's service and its treatment of tenants and applicants. This should include an appeal procedure leading to the governing body. Tenants' Choice landlords are required to offer arbitration procedures for resolving disputes between themselves and their tenants;

b. for dealing with tenants' claims for compensation for failure of services, etc;

c. for dealing with complaints about serious nuisance caused by other tenants including specific procedures for dealing with complaints of racial or other discriminatory harassment;

d. for requiring tenants to move to alternative accommodation, and the circumstances in which this might be necessary;

e. for pursuing arrears of rent and other charges, including the circumstances in which the landlord may take legal action, which should be only after full investigation and consideration of the tenants' circumstances. The use of distress without a Court Order is forbidden under section 19 of the Housing Act 1988;

f. for allowing access to personal information held by the landlord (see G3 below);

g. for meeting the requirements of tenants and members of their family who become disabled.

G2.1 Tenants' Choice landlords should offer tenants information, advice and assistance in applying for housing benefit, so that they receive their proper entitlement.

G2.2 The information in G1 and G2 should be provided in writing in plain English, and also where appropriate in other languages, or in braille or on tape. It should also be explained orally at the beginning of a tenancy and/or in meetings with tenants.

G3 The Data Protection Act gives people a statutory right (subject to certain exemptions) to see and check details about themselves which are held in the form of computerised data. Landlords should allow their tenants, former tenants, and applicants for tenancies reasonable access to other personal information held about themselves or members of their family (other than that provided in confidence by third parties).

If the tenant, former tenant or applicant considers the records inaccurate he or she should be allowed to correct, or record his/her disagreement with, the information held by the landlord.

H EQUAL OPPORTUNITIES

The Housing Corporation's commitment to equal opportunities has been strengthened by an amendment to Section 71 of the Race Relations Act 1976 which will require the Corporation to have regard to the need to eliminate unlawful racial discrimination and to promote equality of opportunity and good relations between persons of different racial groups, in the exercise of all its functions.

Tenants' Choice landlords will be required to comply with the code of practice on race relations in the field of rented housing being prepared by the Commission for Racial Equality. They should also conform with best practice to avoid any kind of discrimination and to promote equality of opportunity both in access to accommodation and the provision of services to all members of the community who may be disadvantaged by race, sex or disability.

Notes

Part IV of the Housing Act 1988 has yet to make a significant impact on the public rented sector, notwithstanding the fact that the Government spent £524,000 on a national publicity campaign in March 1989 to advertise tenants' choice.

By the spring of 1990 the Housing Corporation had approved 15 landlords for the purposes of Part IV of the 1988 Act,[77] and only 20 tenants' groups had been introduced to potential transferee landlords by the Housing Corporation.[78] It was reported to Parliament in May 1990 that there had only been one formal application under Part IV of the Housing Act 1988 to acquire public sector housing stock.[79]

As a result, the Government decided to spend a further £130,000 on local advertising of tenants' choice and to provide £120,000 to the Housing Corporation to make four videos promoting the scheme.[80]

The Government's advertising of tenants' choice has not been without its problems. The Government was effectively forced to amend the tenants' choice publicity after Kirklees Federation of Tenants and Residents Associations complained to the Advertising Standards Authority about the wording of certain posters. Following an investigation by the ASA the Government agreed that the advertising campaign in the autumn of 1990 should omit reference to tenants' changing landlord "without losing your statutory rights".[81]

---

[77] Lord Hesketh, H.L. Written Answers Vol. 518 cols. 305–306, April 20, 1990.

[78] H.C. Written Answers Vol. 168 cols. 392–393, March 2, 1990.

[79] The property in question was on the Walterton and Elgin estate, Westminster. H.C. Written Answers Vol. 172 Col. 188, May 10, 1990.

[80] See Madge & Luba, Recent developments in Housing law, (1990) Legal Action, June 1990, p. 15.

[81] Watchdog raps "misleading" tenants' choice ads (1990) 7 Inside Housing, July 6, 1990, p. 1.

(D)   TRANSFER OF NEW TOWN HOUSING STOCK

Section 172(1) of the Local Government and Housing Act 1989 provides that the Secretary of State "may by regulations make provision for requiring and authorising each new town corporation to take such steps as may be prescribed for making and giving effect to proposals for disposing of their housing stock, either by transferring it as a whole to a prescribed person or by transferring different parts to different prescribed persons." However, such transfers may only be made to the district council in whose district the dwelling is situated or a person approved by the Housing Corporation.[82] The operation of this section depends almost entirely on the regulations made under it.[82a]

IV   THE PRESERVED RIGHT TO BUY

Where dwelling-houses are transferred out of the public sector—either voluntarily or under Part IV of the 1988 Act—the tenants will cease to enjoy secure status under the Housing Act 1985. Nevertheless, it is provided that, subject to certain conditions, former secure tenants will be able to purchase their homes. By virtue of sections 171A to 171H of the Housing Act 1985 (and the Housing (Preservation of Right to Buy) Regulations 1989[83]) a former secure tenant may be entitled to exercise the preserved right to buy after the transfer of the dwelling-house to a person who is not an authority or body within section 80 of the Housing Act 1985.[84]

(A)   CONDITIONS

A person will be able to exercise the preserved right to buy if a number of conditions are satisfied. First, the tenant must be a qualifying person for the purposes of section 171B, which essentially extends to (a) the person who was a secure tenant before the disposal, (b) where the former secure tenancy was granted to joint tenants, one of the joint tenants, (c) a person who on the death of the former secure tenant succeeds to the new tenancy, and (d) a person who becomes the tenant in place of the former secure tenant by an order of the court on the breakdown of marriage.

Secondly, the case must not fall into any of the exclusions. The preserved right to buy may not be exercised by former tenants of

---

[82] subs. (2).
[82a] New Towns (Transfer of Housing Stock) Regulations 1990 (S.I. 1990 No. 1700); New Towns (Transfer of Housing Stock) (Amendment) Regulations 1990 (S.I. 1990 No. 2366).
[83] S.I 1989 No. 368.
[84] s.171A(1). For the text of s.80 see p. 177.

landlords against whom the right to buy was not exercisable[85] or in any other case provided for by the Secretary of State.[86] Thirdly, the qualifying person must continue to occupy the dwelling-house to which the right to buy relates as his only or principal home.[87]

Where a qualifying person who has the preserved right to buy subsequently becomes the tenant of other premises owned by the same landlord (or, where the landlord is a company, a connected company) the tenant may exercise the preserved right to buy in relation to the new premises.[88]

It should be noted that the preserved right to buy is a modified version of the right to buy as formulated by Part V of the Housing Act 1985.[89] For example, a tenant who exercises the preserved right to buy does not have a right to mortgage,[90] and is not entitled to claim a shared ownership lease.[91]

(B) REGISTRATION

The preserved right to buy is an interest which should be protected by registration. The proper procedures are set out in Schedule 9A to the Housing Act 1985. Once protected by registration the preserved right to buy will bind the private sector landlord to whom the dwelling-house is conveyed and will continue to be enforceable even if the new landlord subsequently disposes of the land to a third party.

If the preserved right to buy is not properly protected by registration it will be void against a purchaser of the land to which the right relates.[92] However, in these circumstances, the tenant who has lost the preserved right to buy as a result of non-registration will normally have a claim against the disposing authority for breach of statutory duty.[93]

(C) REPOSSESSION ON THE BASIS OF SUITABLE ALTERNATIVE ACCOMMODATION

In the context of private sector tenancies a landlord may apply to the court for an order of possession on the basis that suitable alternative accommodation is available—either under the Rent Act 1977[94] or the Housing Act 1988.[95] (This ground for possession is, of course, discretionary: the court may order possession only if it considers it

---

[85] Namely, charities and certain housing associations as defined by Housing Act 1985, Sched. 5, paras. 1, 2 and 3.
[86] s.171A(3).
[87] s.171B(1) and (5).
[88] s.171B(6).
[89] Housing (Preservation of Right to Buy) Regulations 1989.
[90] reg. 14.
[91] reg. 21.
[92] Housing Act 1985, Sched. 9A, para. 6.
[93] Sched. 9A, paras. 1 and 9.
[94] Rent Act 1977, s.98(1)(a).
[95] Housing Act 1988, s.7 and Sched. 2, Ground 9.

reasonable to do so.) The existence of this ground for possession against a tenant whose home has been transferred into the private sector would appear to threaten to undermine the operation of the preserved right to buy.

Section 171F of the Housing Act 1985, however, protects the former secure tenant who is entitled to exercise the preserved right to buy by stating:

The court shall not order a qualifying person to give up possession of the qualifying dwelling-house in pursuance of section 98(1)(a) of the Rent Act 1977 or on Ground 9 in Schedule 2 to the Housing Act 1988 (suitable alternative accommodation) unless the court is satisfied—

  (a) that the preserved right to buy will, by virtue of section 171B(6) (accommodation with the same landlord or connected company), continue to be exercisable in relation to the dwelling-house offered by way of alternative accommodation and that the interest of the landlord in the new dwelling-house will be—

     (i) where the new dwelling-house is a house, not less than the interest of the landlord in the existing dwelling-house, or
     (ii) where the new dwelling-house is a flat, not less than the interest of the landlord in the existing dwelling-house or a term of years of which 80 years or more remain unexpired, whichever is the less; or

  (b) that the landlord of the new dwelling-house will be an authority or body within section 80(1) (the landlord condition for secure tenancies).

V   HOUSING ACTION TRUSTS

In the White Paper which preceded the Housing Act 1988 it was noted that the general policy of encouraging the transfer of blocks of public sector housing into the private sector is dependent on the housing stock being in an appropriate condition:

[T]here are some areas of local authority housing, particularly in some of the inner urban areas, where social problems and housing disrepair are so serious that in the Government's view more direct action—involving both public and private sectors—is needed to obtain improvements over a reasonable time-scale. Unless major improvements can be made to the fabric and general environment of these areas it is unlikely that policies such as the right to transfer to other landlords would be successful there.[96]

The Government's proposals were framed in the following terms:

6.2 There are several models to follow. The work of Estate Action, and the improvements that can be made by designation of General Improvement Areas and Housing Action Areas, show that the detailed problems of bad housing are not insoluble given the will and the mechanisms. On a larger scale, the Urban

---

[96] *Housing: The Government's Proposals* (1987), para. 6.1.

Development Corporations in London and on Merseyside have shown the result that a body devoted to developing a run-down area can achieve. They have brought a new drive to their task and results have been achieved that the local authorities have not been able to achieve by themselves in the past.

6.3 The Urban Development Corporation model is not wholly appropriate as it stands for the housing field. The housing problem being tackled concerns densely developed urban areas rather than largely derelict industrial areas in need of regeneration (though the two may overlap). Different kinds of expertise and people will be needed. Different statutory powers could well be necessary. The model needs adapting. The Government therefore proposes to take powers to establish analogous bodies in designated areas to take powers to establish analogous bodies in designated areas to take over responsibility for local authority housing, renovate it, and pass it on to different forms of managemenent and ownership including housing associations, tenants' cooperatives and approved private landlords. The new bodies, to be known as Housing Action Trust (HATs), will provide scope for tenants in these areas to have a diversity of landlord and ownership. And as well as improving housing conditions, they will act as enablers and facilitators for provision of other community needs such as shops, workshops and advice centres, and for encouraging local enterprise.

6.4 The HATs will have a limited lifespan. Their remit will be to secure the improvement of the stock transferred to them in their area and then hand it over to other owners and managers. Through this process they will make use of both public and private sector resources; they will assist in the Government's aim of diversifying forms of management and ownership, in conjunction with other policies such as rent deregulation and right to transfer; and disposals by HATs will generate extra funds which can be used elsewhere.

6.5 It is too early to say how may HATs will initially be created, which areas they will tackle, or how large those areas might be. But the physical quality of the stock, the effectiveness of its management and the general environment of the area will be among the relevant considerations. Each HAT, like an Urban Development Corporation, will consist of a Chairman and members appointed by the Secretary of State; they will include people with direct experience of the area.

6.6 It will be desirable for each HAT to carry out its task in close conjunction with local authorities concerned, and with the tenants of the properties transferred to it. The maximum cooperation is needed if problems are to be successfully tackled. Tenants' interests will be deeply involved, for example in respect of refurbishment programmes and eventual disposal of property by the HAT.

6.7 The Government sees the concept of HATs as a vital part of their overall housing policy, and as a means of single-mindedly tackling some of the most difficult areas of local authority housing. Once statutory powers are available, the first HATs will be set up and the experience gained from them, and particularly their success in applying public and private sector resources to the improvement of housing and the widening of choice for local authority tenants, will provide the basis for further decisions.

These policy objectives were given statutory form in Part III of the Housing Act 1988. Section 60 empowers the Secretary of State to "designate an area for which, in his opinion, it is expedient that a corporation, known as a housing action trust ... should be established."

(A)   THE CREATION OF HOUSING ACTION TRUSTS

Although the initiative for the creation of a housing action trust must come from the Secretary of State, other interested parties must be involved in the procedure. First, the Secretary of State must consult the local housing authorities which would be affected by a designation under section 60.[97] Furthermore, and more importantly, the local tenants are given a say. The Housing Act 1988 requires the Secretary of State to conduct a ballot or poll of the tenants, and it is provided that a housing action trust cannot be set up if a majority of those tenants who express an opinion about the proposal to make a designation order are opposed to it.[98]

A housing action trust is a body corporate, which for housing purposes is to be regarded as a public sector body.[99] Tenants of housing action trusts will be secure tenants under the Housing Act 1985 (as long as the relevant conditions are satisfied[1]), and as such they will normally have security of tenure under Part IV of the Housing Act 1985, and will be entitled to exercise the right to buy as provided by Part V.

(B)   DISPOSAL BY HOUSING ACTION TRUSTS

It is the Government's intention that housing action trusts should have a limited existence.[2] Accordingly, the Act contains provision for the disposal of housing stock vested in them.

A housing action trust may seek to dispose of property occupied by secure tenants with the consent of the Secretary of State.[3] However, a housing action trust may dispose of its housing stock either to a person approved by the Housing Corporation[4] or a local housing authority.[5] Furthermore, before the Secretary of State may consent to the transfer the housing action trust must comply with the procedure laid down in section 84 of the 1988 Act. This procedure both allows local authorities to express their wish to reacquire housing stock, and—as with the procedure which must be followed by local authorities which propose to dispose of their housing stock under section 32 of the Housing Act

[97] s.61(1).
[98] s.61(2) to (4).
[99] See Housing Act 1985, s.80 as amended by Housing Act 1988 (p. 177).
[1] See pp. 175–182.
[2] See *Housing: the Government's Proposals* (1987), para. 6.4.
[3] Housing Act 1988, s.84.
[4] This requirement is similar to the restriction which applies to disposal under Part IV of the Housing Act 1988.
[5] Housing Act 1988, s.79.

1985[6]—provides a mechanism for the views of the tenants to be taken into account.

When the housing action trust has substantially fulfilled its objects, it shall so far as practicable dispose of any remaining property according to the statutory procedure laid down in the Act,[7] And submit proposals to the Secretary of State for its dissolution.[8] The Secretary of State makes the dissolution order, which provides for the disposal of any property of which the housing trust was unable to divest itself.[9]

Note

The Government initially proposed that six areas should be designated as housing action trusts under Part III of the Housing Act 1988 (Tower Hamlets, Lambeth, Southwark, Sandwell, Leeds and Sunderland) and a considerable amount of money was spent by the Department of Environment on consultants' fees and other activities preliminary to the intended designation.

Expenditure on proposed housing action trusts[10]

	(a) expenditure related to consultancies £000	(b) expenditure related to the Department's information and to ballots £000
Tower Hamlets	182	3
Lambeth	182	12
Southwark	933	12
Sandwell	191	17
Leeds	161	13
Sunderland	613	23

However, notwithstanding the commitment expressed in the White Paper, and the preliminary work undertaken by the Government, there are currently no housing action trusts in existence. Local residents have not responded positively in the consultation process. The fact that in all six areas tenants have voted against the setting up of a housing action trust may result in the scrapping of the entire housing action trust programme.

---

[6] See pp. 534–537.
[7] s.88(2)(a).
[8] s.88(2)(b).
[9] s.88(3).
[10] Source: H.C. Written Answers, Vol. 174, cols. 417–418, June 18, 1990.

CHAPTER 9

HOMELESSNESS

Introduction

Homelessness has been the subject of increasing public concern, and the statistical data available suggests that the number of people who are homeless has risen considerably in recent years.

Since 1979 the number of households which have been accepted as homeless has doubled:

Households Accepted as Homeless Under the Act: 1979–1988[1]

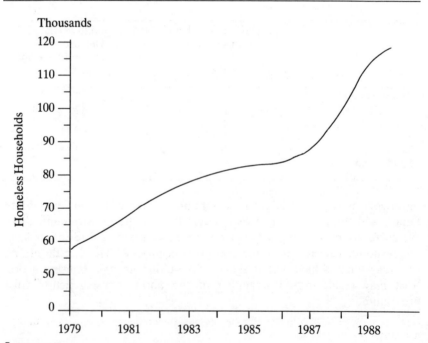

Source:
DOE "Local Authorities' Action under the Homelessness Provisions of the 1985 Housing Act: England." Quarterly Returns.

[1] *The Government's Review of the Homelessness Legislation* (1989) Figure Two, p. 5.

These figures do not, however, give a complete picture of the magnitude of the problem, since they indicate only those households who apply to local authorities and who satisfy the relevant statutory definition. It is clear that there are many people who have nowhere to live, who either make no application to the local housing authority or, if they do apply, are not accepted as homeless within the meaning of the legislation. Furthermore, there is the problem of "hidden homelessness."[2] There are many people who have a roof over their heads, but who are living in very unsatisfactory circumstances, either because the standard of accommodation is very poor, or because the accommodation is temporary, or because they require (but are unable to obtain) independent housing—for example, adult children living with their parents. It is impossible to quantify accurately how many people fall within these various categories.[3]

As regards those who are accepted as homeless by local housing authorities, *The Government's Review of the Homelessness Legislation* (1989) provides the following information:

14. In 1988, authorities recorded the following reasons given by households accepted as homeless for their difficulties (similar statistics for five years earlier are in brackets):

— parents/relatives/friends no longer able or willing to accommodate them	44%	(41%)
— relationship breakdown	19%	(19%)
— mortgage arrears	7%	(6%)
— rent arrears		
(council dwelling)	2%	(2%)
(private dwelling)	2%	(2%)
— loss of private rented dwelling	11%	(11%)
— other reason	15%	(19%)

18. The estimate is that about 50 per cent. of households go straight into permanent accommodation as soon as they are accepted as homeless. Of the remainder, perhaps 15 per cent. go into temporary family accommodation, usually leased by the council; 8 per cent.-10 per cent. go into hostels; 15 per cent.-20 per cent. are placed in bed and breakfast; and the remaining 10 per cent. or so have to stay in the accommodation they already occupy, even though it is unsatisfactory.

---

[2] See the Morris Report, Scottish Development Department, *Housing and Social Work—A Joint Approach* (1975), paras. 8.8–8.10.

[3] It has been estimated that there are at least 250,000 people without homes in England and Wales: Nuttgens, *The Home Front* (1989), p. 110.

Households Placed by Local Authorities in Bed and Breakfast and Other Temporary Accommodation. (Total Residents at Year End 1983–1988).[4]

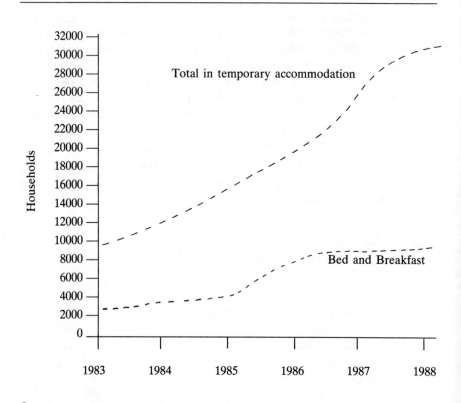

Source:
DOE "Local Authorities' Action under the Homelessness Provisions of the 1985 Housing Act: England," Quarterly Returns.

22. As the numbers of people accepted by local authorities as homeless have risen, so have the costs. The costs of temporary accommodation, however, and especially of bed and breakfast, have risen more than proportionately to the increased numbers, because the length of stay has increased as well. The identifiable "homelessness" expenditure (on temporary accommodation and administration) has risen in total from £20m in 1984–1985 to an estimated £122m in 1987–88. Temporary accommodation, at £108m (1987–88), represents the lion's share.

The inadequacy of bed and breakfast accommodation has also been noted by Nuttgens:

[4] *The Government's Review of the Homelessness Legislation* (1989) Figure three, p. 8.

More homeless households than ever before are being placed in bed and breakfast hotels. Yet bed and breakfast accommodation is a dubious solution to the problem. It has debilitating side effects. The mental and physical health of both children and adults can deteriorate.

Lord Pitt, President of the British Medical Association and Chairman of Shelter, expressed his concern about the implications of bed and breakfast accommodation.

> The experience of homeless families in the eighties is causing particular health problems among the young. A recent report has shown that approximately one third of children in bed and breakfast hotel accommodation have behavioural problems. ... Depression is endemic among the hotel homeless. Many are probably being prescribed tranquillisers. I know that in many instances doctors would prefer to prescribe new houses, not more valium. ... I, for one, am prepared to say, on the basis of present evidence, that our current housing crisis is affecting the health of a significant number of my fellow citizens.

Not only is bed and breakfast accommodation a health risk, it is also a bad economic bargain. Recent Department of the Environment figures show that it is cheaper for local authorities to refurbish or buy homes for rent than to house homeless families in hotels. The government accepts that it costs £10,950 a year to keep a family in bed and breakfast accommodation. It would cost £5,500 a year in interest payments and management costs to build a new council flat for the same family.

To rehouse everyone now living in hotels, 12,500 more decent rented homes would be needed by 1989. Government rules prevent local authorities from investing in such badly needed homes. The councils must pick up the £100 million a year hotel bill, when £56 million would provide new homes for the people now in bed and breakfast accommodation.

In Wandsworth, London, there are currently 3,400 families in bed and breakfast hotels. In order to reduce this number, the council is renting flats in the private sector to house some homeless people. Brighton currently has a total of 130 families in bed and breakfast accommodation, costing the council more than £150,000 per annum. There, however, the council has leased redundant married quarters in the local barracks, bought up some properties, leased others from private landlords, and converted an old sheltered home into single units. In co-operation with the YMCA it is setting up a purpose built hostel in the town centre. Nottingham was one of the first authorities to have a purpose built hostel for the homeless. It plans to add a second hostel shortly.[5]

I THE STATUTORY PROVISIONS

The Housing (Homeless Persons) Act 1977 introduced a new statutory scheme which imposed on local housing authorities obligations to assist and, in certain cases, to secure accommodation for the homeless. The relevant statutory provisions are now to be found in Part III of the Housing Act 1985. Before examining the duties imposed by Part III, it is important to consider the meaning of the key concepts which provide the structure of this area of the law: homelessness, priority need,

---

[5] *The Home Front* (1989), pp. 110–111.

intentionality and local connection, which are defined by sections 58 to 61 of the 1985 Act.

It should be added that there is a Code of Guidance (issued by the Secretary of State) which, to some extent, amplifies the legislative provisions.[6] Local authorities must have regard to the Code,[7] although this does not mean that they have to follow it slavishly.[8] If the Code conflicts with the terms of the legislation, then the legislation governs.[9]

The legislation has generated an enormous body of case law, the most important aspects of which are discussed in the sections which follow.

(A) HOMELESS

58.—(1) A person is homeless if he has no accommodation in England, Wales or Scotland.

(2) A person shall be treated as having no accommodation if there is no accommodation which he, together with any other person who normally resides with him as a member of his family or in circumstances in which it is reasonable for that person to reside with him—

    (a)   is entitled to occupy by virtue of an interest in it or by virtue of an order of a court, or

    (b)   has an express or implied licence to occupy, or in Scotland has a right or permission or an implied right or permission to occupy, or

    (c)   occupies as a residence by virtue of any enactment or rule of law giving him the right to remain in occupation or restricting the right of another person to recover possession.

(2A) A person shall not be treated as having accommodation unless it is accommodation which it would be reasonable for him to continue to occupy.

(2B) Regard may be had, in determining whether it would be reasonable for a person to continue to occupy accommodation, to the general circumstances prevailing in relation to housing in the district of the local housing authority to whom he has applied for accommodation or for assistance in obtaining accommodation.

(3) A person is also homeless if he has accommodation but—

    (a)   he cannot secure entry to it, or

    (b)   it is probable that occupation of it will lead to violence from some other person residing in it or to threats of violence from some other person residing in it and likely to carry out the threats, or

    (c)   it consists of a movable structure, vehicle or vessel designed or adapted for human habitation and there is no place where he is entitled or permitted both to place it and to reside in it.

---

[6] The current version of the Code of Guidance dates from 1983. However, a third edition of the Code—which is intended to be more "user friendly"—has been drafted, and should come into operation in 1991.
[7] Housing Act 1985, s.71(1).
[8] *De Falco* v. *Crawley B.C.* [1980] Q.B. 460.
[9] *R.* v. *Waveney D.C. ex p. Bowers* [1983] Q.B. 238.

(4) A person is threatened with homelessness if it is likely that he will become homeless within 28 days.

Notes

(i)   The courts have been called upon to decide whether a person who occupies short-term accommodation is homeless. In *Din* v. *Wandsworth L.B.C.* Lord Lowry said:

I consider that to be homeless and to have some temporary accommodation are not mutually inconsistent concepts. Nor does a person cease to be homeless merely by having a roof over his head or a lodging, however, precarious.[10]

In *R* v. *Ealing L.B.C. ex p. Sidhu*[11] the Court of Appeal, relying on this dictum, held that a woman who had left her husband as a result of domestic violence, could be regarded as homeless notwithstanding the fact that she had obtained temporary accommodation in a woman's aid refuge.

(ii)   Subsections (2A) and (2B) were added by section 14(1) of the Housing and Planning Act 1986 in response to the House of Lords' ruling in *R.* v. *Hillingdon L.B.C. ex p. Puhlhofer*.[12] Lord Brightman had said:

Parliament plainly, and wisely, placed no qualifying adjective before the word accommodation [in section 58(1)] and none is to be implied. The word 'appropriate' or 'reasonable' is not to be imported. Nor is accommodation not accommodation because it might in certain circumstances be unfit for human habitation ... or might involve overcrowding ... . What is properly to be regarded as accommodation is a question of fact to be decided by the local authority. There are no rules. Clearly some places in which a person might choose or be constrained to live could not properly be regarded as accommodation at all; it would be a misuse of language to describe Diogenes as having occupied accommodation within the meaning of the Act. What the local authority have to consider, in reaching a decision whether a person is homeless for the purposes of the Act, is whether he has what can properly be described as accommodation within the ordinary meaning of that word in the English language.

The significance of the amendment made by the 1986 Act has been revealed by a number of recent cases. It is particularly important to note that in considering whether it would be reasonable for the applicant to continue to occupy the accommodation in question the local authority must have regard, not only to the actual quality of the housing, but also to external factors.

---

[10] [1983] 1 A.C. 657 at 677.
[11] [1983] 2 H.L.R. 45 (Watchman, [1982] J.S.W.L. 237).
[12] [1986] A.C. 484 (Hoath, [1986] J.S.W.L. 305).

In *R. v. Kensington and Chelsea R.L.B.C. ex p. Hammell*[13] a woman had left her council flat in Scotland and come to live with her sister in London. She had left Scotland due to violence and harassment on the part of her ex-husband, who was living with another woman only a matter of 50 yards away. The applicant could not rely on subsection (3), since the violence was outside the home. Nevertheless, the Court of Appeal held that for the purposes of subsection (2A) the local authority was required to take into account the ex-husband's behaviour when considering whether it was reasonable for the applicant to continue to occupy the accommodation in Scotland.[14]

(B) PRIORITY NEED

59.—(1) The following have a priority need for accommodation—

(a) a pregnant woman or a person with whom a pregnant woman resides or might reasonably be expected to reside;

(b) a person with whom dependent children reside or might reasonably be expected to reside;

(c) a person who is vulnerable as a result of old age, mental illness or handicap or physical disability or other special reason, or with whom such a person resides or might reasonably be expected to reside;

(d) a person who is homeless or threatened with homelessness as a result of an emergency such as flood, fire or other disaster.

(2) The Secretary of State may by order made by statutory instrument—

(a) specify further descriptions of persons as having a priority need for accommodation, and

(b) amend or repeal any part of subsection (1).

(3) Before making such an order the Secretary of State shall consult such associations representing relevant authorities, and such other persons, as he considers appropriate.

(4) No order shall be made unless a draft of it has been approved by resolution of each House of Parliament.

Notes

(i) It was argued on behalf of the local authority in *R. v. Hillingdon Homeless Families Panel ex p. Islam*,[15] that where an applicant claimed to have a priority need by virtue of the fact that dependent children were living with him, the applicant also had to show that such children could reasonably be expected to live with him. This argument was

---

[13] [1989] Q.B. 518 (Walsh [1989] J.S.W.L. 177).
[14] See also *R. v. Broxbourne B.C. ex p. Willmoth* (1990) 22 H.L.R. 118; *R. v. Westminster C.C. ex p. Alouat* (1989) 21 H.L.R. 477.
[15] *The Times*, February 10, 1981.

rejected: the tests are alternative not cumulative.[16] Whether there are dependent children residing with the applicant is a question of fact, and therefore does not depend on the applicant having legal custody of the children.[17]

(ii) Section 59(1)(b) is satisfied as long as there is at least one dependent child living with the applicant. There is no requirement that the child should be wholly and exclusively dependent on and resident with the applicant.[18]

(iii) One of the most problematic aspects of section 59 is subsection (1)(c). The correct approach to this paragraph was explained in *R. v. Waveney D.C. ex p. Bowers*[19] by Waller L.J.:

The first question which has to be considered is whether or not there is vulnerability. If there is vulnerability, then does it arise from those matters which are set out within [section 59(1)(c)]? It may not arise from any single one but it may arise from a combination of these causes.[20]

As for the meaning of the term "vulnerable" a number of definitions have been suggested. In *R. v. Waveney D.C. ex p. Bowers* Waller L.J. said that vulnerable means "less able to fend for oneself so that injury or detriment will result when a less vulnerable man will be able to cope without harmful effects."[21] This was further glossed by Webster J. in *R. v. Lambeth L.B.C. ex p. Carroll* as "less able to fend for oneself when homeless or in finding and keeping accommodation."[22] Similarly, Mann J. in *R. v. Reigate & Banstead B.C. ex p. Di Domenico* stated that vulnerable means "vulnerable in the housing market,"[23] and Hodgson J. in *R. v. Bath C.C. ex p. Sangermano* indicated that "the vulnerability to be considered is vulnerability loosely in housing terms or in the context of housing."[24]

In *R. v. Bath C.C. ex p. Sangermano* having noted that the Act draws a distinction between "mental illness, that is some psychotic illness, and mental handicap" Hodgson J. concluded that the local authority had erred in law in deciding that the applicant did not have a priority need. The applicant was an Italian woman who had severe language difficulties and was of subnormal intelligence:

Looking at all the material which was before the meeting, it seems to me that had they properly instructed themselves [the local authority] could not

[16] Although the case was considered by the Court of Appeal and House of Lords (*Re Islam* [1983] 1 A.C. 688), this point was not appealed.
[17] *R. v. Ealing L.B.C. ex p. Sidhu* (1982) 2 H.L.R. 45.
[18] *R. v. Lambeth L.B.C. ex p. Vagliviello* (1990) 22 H.L.R. 392.
[19] [1983] Q.B. 238.
[20] At 245–246.
[21] At 244–245.
[22] (1988) 20 H.L.R. 142 at 146.
[23] (1988) 20 H.L.R. 153 at 158.
[24] (1984) 17 H.L.R. 94 at 97.

reasonably have come to any conclusion other than that this lady was vulnerable within the meaning of [section 59(1)(c)] of the Act—vulnerable either because of mental handicap or because of another special reason being the combination of mental handicap and extreme language difficulty.

... Clearly language difficulties on their own could not possibly amount to another special reason with [section 59(1)(c)], nor should I be seen or thought to be saying that merely because an applicant comes within the category of subnormality, as set out in the Mental Health Act, to which legislation I think plainly Parliament had regard in the framing of [section 59(1)(c)], that of itself necessarily would amount to vulnerability. I can conceive of cases where somebody, although in the medical category or the Mental Health Act category of subnormal would not in terms of [Part III of the Housing Act 1985] be vulnerable, but I have no doubt that in this case when you get a lady with her record of incompetence who is subnormal and who is incapable of, on the evidence, articulating properly either in English or indeed in Italian, then you have someone who, properly instructing itself, no local authority could, in the special circumstances of this case, come to any conclusion other than that she is vulnerable within the meaning of [section 59(1)(c)].[25]

Ultimately, decisions as to an applicant's vulnerability are questions of fact. This was made clear in *R.* v. *Wandsworth B.C. ex p. Banbury*[26] by Russell J.:

Whether grand mal epilepsy renders a person vulnerable must be at all times a question of fact and degree. Clearly if the attacks are taking place with intense regularity vulnerability would be established, and to contend otherwise would be to fly in the face of reality.[27]

(C)   INTENTIONALITY

60.—(1) A person becomes homeless intentionally if he deliberately does or fails to do anything in consequence of which he ceases to occupy accommodation which is available for his occupation and which it would have been reasonable for him to continue to occupy.

(2) A person becomes threatened with homelessness intentionally if he deliberately does or fails to do anything the likely result of which is that he will be forced to leave accommodation which is available for his occupation and which it would have been reasonable for him to continue to occupy.

(3) For the purposes of subsection (1) or (2) an act or omission in good faith on the part of a person who was unaware of any relevant fact shall not be treated as deliberate.

(4) Regard may be had, in determining whether it would have been reasonable for a person to continue to occupy accommodation, to the general circumstances prevailing in relation to housing in the district of the local housing authority to whom he applied for accommodation or for assistance in obtaining accommodation.

---

[25] (1984) 17 H.L.R. 94 at 101–102.
[26] (1986) 19 H.L.R. 76.
[27] At 83. See also *R.* v. *Reigate & Banstead B.C. ex p. Di Domenico* (1988) 20 H.L.R. 153—another case concerning an applicant who was epileptic (Walsh [1988] J.S.W.L. 285).

Notes

The overwhelming majority of homelessness cases have involved the issue of intentionality. In *R. v. Salford C.C. ex p. Davenport*[28] Fox L.J. said that a person becomes homeless intentionally if:

(i) He ceases to occupy accommodation. (ii) That accommodation was available for his occupation. (iii) It would have been reasonable for him to continue to occupy it. (iv) The person deliberately did or failed to do something in consequence of which he ceased to occupy it.

This section does not, in my opinion, require that the person should have intended to become homeless and should have done or failed to do something with the intention of becoming homeless.[29]

(i) In considering whether someone is intentionally homeless the local authority must have regard to the conduct of the applicant. In *R. v. North Devon D.C. ex p. Lewis*[30] a man left his employment as a consequence of which he lost his tied accommodation. He applied to the local authority for re-housing, but was found to be intentionally homeless. The woman who lived with him then applied in her own name. The local authority wrongly rejected her application on the basis that she was part of the same family unit. The court held that the local authority was required to consider each individual application.

However, a person may be regarded as intentionally homeless by virtue of acquiescing in the conduct of another person which leads to the loss of the accommodation.[31]

Some of the cases were discussed by Kennedy J. in *R. v. East Northamptonshire D.C. ex p. Spruce*[32] (in which the issue was whether the wife had acquiesced in the husband's rent arrears):

[Counsel for the applicant] submits that the wife's application for accommodation should be considered separately from her husband if—and he has to make this qualification in light of the authorities—there is material before the local authority to suggest that she was not a party to and had not acquiesced in, the acts or omissions of her husband which created the state of homelessness.

In support of that proposition, he invited my attention to a decision of Woolf J., as he then was, in *R. v. North Devon D.C. ex p.Lewis* [1981] 1 W.L.R. 325. The material part of this judgment is at p. 333 where the learned judge said this:

' ... as is conceded on behalf of the housing authority, there are no express words which provide that where a man and a woman are living together, if one of the couple becomes homeless intentionally, the other should be treated as being homeless intentionally ... The main argument on behalf of the

---

[28] (1983) 8 H.L.R. 54.
[29] At 62.
[30] [1981] 1 W.L.R. 328.
[31] See *R. v. Cardiff C.C. ex p. Thomas* (1983) 9 H.L.R. 64; *R. v. Salford C.C. ex p. Devenport* (1983) 8 H.L.R. 54; *R. v. Cardiff C.C. ex p. John* (1982) 9 H.L.R. 56; *R. v. Southampton C.C. ex p. Ward* (1984) 14 H.L.R. 114; *R. v. West Dorset D.C. ex p. Phillips* (1985) 17 H.L.R. 336; *R v. Penwith D.C. ex p. Trevena* (1985) 17 H.L.R. 526; *R v. Eastleigh B.C. ex p. Beattie (No. 2)* (1985) 17 H.L.R. 168; *R v. Mole Valley D.C. ex p. Burton* (1988) 20 H.L.R. 479; *R. v. Thanet D.C. ex p. Groves* (1990) 22 H.L.R. 223.
[32] (1988) 20 H.L.R. 508.

authority was that section 17' [of the 1977 Act] 'must be read as though it provided that, for the purposes of the Act, a person becomes homeless intentionally if he, or a person who resides with him or who could reasonably have been expected to reside with him, became homeless intentionally. Such a construction of section 17, in my view, is not possible ...

... the fact that the Act requires consideration of the family unit as a whole indicates that it would be perfectly proper in the ordinary case for the housing authority to look at the family as a whole and assume, in the absence of material which indicates to the contrary, where the conduct of one member of the family was such that he should be regarded as having become homeless intentionally, that was conduct to which the other members of the family were a party ... . If, however, at the end of the day *because of material put before the housing authority by the wife*' [Mr. Stoker stresses those words] 'the housing authority are not satisfied that she was a party to the decision, they would have to regard her as not having become homeless intentionally.'

In *R.* v. *Eastleigh Borough Council, ex p. Beattie* (1985) 17 H.L.R. 168, Webster J. adopted and followed that part of the decision of Woolf J., to which I have just referred. In that case, a wife had sworn an affidavit in earlier proceedings from which the housing authority should have gleaned that she was not a party to and did not acquiesce in her husband's failure to pay mortgage instalments.

In *R.* v. *West Dorset District Council, ex p. Phillips* (1985) 17 H.L.R. 336, Hodgson J. also followed the decision of Woolf J. In that case, the housing officers saw clear signs of non-acquiescence by the wife in that she actually physically attacked her husband when she learnt of the debt. It was found by the court that there was a duty on the local authority to investigate.[33]

An important point which emerges from the case law is illustrated by Kennedy J. in *R.* v. *East Northamptonshire D.C. ex p. Spruce*:

By way of example during the course of argument, I put forward the case of a wife who only finds out that her husband has failed to pay the rent or instalments of mortgage at a time when the debt has become so substantial that the couple simply cannot cope with it. In that situation, in my judgment, it would be very hard to say that simply because the wife was aware of the debt before the situation of homelessness arose, she was therefore acquiescing in the situation to such an extent that she should be regarded as being intentionally homeless.[34]

The distinction between knowledge and acquiescence has been described by Watchman and Robson as "a 'life-line' to innocent spouses and cohabitees against being found intentionally homeless because of actions of other members of the family unit."[35] They continue:

Where there is evidence that those actions were carried out in the face of opposition from other members of the family unit or that they were in no position to control the conduct of the other person or that the other members of

---

[33] At 515–516.
[34] At 518.
[35] *Homelessness and the Law in Britain* (2nd ed. 1989), p. 144.

the family unit were ignorant of the act or omission in question until it was effectively too late to do anything about it they are not to be held intentionally homeless.[36]

(iii) For a person to be intentionally homeless, the homelessness must result from a deliberate (*i.e.* voluntary) act. Accordingly, to fail deliberately to pay off mortgage arrears with the result that the mortgagee takes possession of the dwelling-house is intentional homelessness.[37] Clearly, the same applies to a tenant's failure to pay rent. An applicant who moves from settled accommodation to temporary accommodation may be regarded as having become intentionally homeless when evicted from the temporary accommodation.[38] However, the applicant may always seek to rely on subsection (3) if he did not know that the accommodation was temporary.

On the other hand, where a family unit loses accommodation on account of the woman becoming pregnant, this does not amount to intentional homelessness.[39] Similarly, a woman who leaves her accommodation because of domestic violence is generally not to be regarded as intentionally homeless. However, in *R. v. Wandsworth L.B.C. ex p. Nimako-Boateng*,[40] it was suggested that there might be circumstances where it would be reasonable for a woman to seek to remain in occupation by obtaining a court order to restrain her partner.[41]

There is also the issue whether loss of tied accommodation is deliberate. This has been discussed by the courts in a number of cases. In *R. v. Thurrock B.C. ex p. Williams*[42] it was concluded that the fact that the applicant had resigned from his job (thereby losing the tied accommodation) did not automatically lead to the conclusion that he had become homeless intention-ally. The background facts were set out by Phillips J. as follows:

Mr. Williams is a married man with a family. By trade he is a licensed house manager. For a number of years he was employed by Ind Coope, a subsidiary of Allied Breweries (UK) Limited, to manage their licensed premises known as the White Hart public house, Grays in Essex. Under his contract of employment he lived there and had tied accommodation. A letter, of February 2, 1981, purported to dismiss him on the ground, as alleged, of stock and gross profit irregularities. He was given six weeks' notice and required to quit the premises where he lived with his family by March 16, 1981, which was the date of the termination of his employment. Looking ahead, he later resigned. For the record it is right to say that he denies, and has always denied, that he has been guilty of any impropriety.[43]

---

[36] *Ibid.*
[37] *R. v. Eastleigh B.C. ex p. Beattie (No. 2)* (1985) 17 H.L.R. 168.
[38] *R. v.Wandsworth L.B.C. ex p. Rose* (1984) 11 H.L.R. 105.
[39] *R. v. Eastleigh B.C. ex p. Beattie (No. 1)* (1983) 10 H.L.R. 134.
[40] (1984) 11 H.L.R. 95.
[41] See also *R. v. Eastleigh B.C. ex p. Evans* (1984) 17 H.L.R. 515; *R. v. Purbeck D.C. ex p. Cadney* (1985) 17 H.L.R. 534.
[42] (1982) 1 H.L.R. 129.
[43] At 131.

In terms of the principles to be applied to cases involving tied accommodation Phillips J said:

It would certainly seem to be the case that if an employee occupying tied accommodation loses it through his own wilful neglect or other wrongdoing, the circumstances may be such that it is possible sensibly to say that he has deliberately done something or failed to do something else the likely result of which would be that he would be forced to leave, and therefore in the terms of the Act is intentionally homeless or threatened with homelessness. So if the employers here were right in their complaints, and it was shown that as a result Mr. Williams lost his accommodation, one could see that it would be strongly arguable, and would probably be the case, that he was intentionally homeless or threatened with homelessness. But what happened here is he does not agree that he ever misbehaved. He denies it strongly. There is therefore an issue as to whether or not the employers are right. If they are right, the homelessness is probably intentional. If they are not, the contrary would be likely to be the case.[44]

(iv) For homelessness to be intentional, not only must the applicant's conduct have been deliberate, but the homelessness must flow as a consequence of that conduct. As Arden notes: "One of the most controversial questions is just how far back an authority can look: can present homelessness be deemed intentional on account of the loss of accommodation in the past, if there has been some intervening accommodation?"[45]

Din v. *Wandsworth L.B.C.* [1983] 1 A.C. 657

Lord Wilberforce (who formed part of a 3:2 majority) said (at 665–668):

The appellants are married with four children: there is no doubt that they would fall into a potential priority class. In 1977 the whole family moved, from Croydon, into accommodation at 56, Trinity Road, Wandsworth—accommodation which was suitable for the whole family to occupy. This belonged, under a lease, together with a shop, to a relative, Mr. Jaswail. Mr. Din entered into a loose partnership with Mr. Jaswail dealing with Pakistani food, but Mr. Din retained his existing employment with the Airfix company. In April 1978 Mr. Jaswail withdrew from the business. The landlord of the premises accepted rent from Mr. Din without prejudice, but arrears of rent mounted up and Mr. Din came to be in financial difficulties. In June 1979 Mrs. Din went to the housing aid centre in Wandsworth and was put on the waiting list for accommodation. She was advised that before she could be helped she would have to wait for a court order for possession to be made against her. Mr. Din was similarly advised on July 2, 1979. On August 28, 1979, the appellants vacated the premises: no court proceedings had been initiated against them, and no demand for vacant possession had been made. I do not think that there is any doubt that this action

---

[44] At 133. See also *R.* v. *Thanet D.C. ex p. Reeve* (1982) 6 H.L.R. 31.
[45] *Manual of Housing Law* (4th ed., 1989), p. 185. In addition to the materials below, see *R.* v. *Basingstoke and Deane B.C. ex p. Bassett* (1983) 10 H.L.R. 125; *R.* v. *Christchurch B.C. ex p. Conway* (1987) 19 H.L.R. 238; *R.* v. *Merton L.B.C ex p. Ruffle* (1989) 21 H.L.R. 361 (Jones [1990] J.S.W.L. 53).

was deliberate and intentional and fell within the provisions of section [60]. They then went to live with Mr. Jaswail in a flat at Upminister: this was crowded accommodation. Mr. Din hoped to get employment with Ford Motors at Dagenham: in this he was unsuccessful. In November 1979 he returned to his previous job with Airfix and took a room in Wandsworth. In December 1979 the appellants were asked to leave the Upminster flat. On December 20, 1979, the appellants applied to the respondents as homeless persons under [Part III of the Housing Act 1985]. The respondents made appropriate inquiries and on January 4, 1980, notified the appellants that they were satisfied that the appellants' homelessness was "intentional." The reasons given were that the appellants left 56, Trinity Road after they had been advised on two occasions to remain in occupation until the owners sought a court order: they disregarded this advice and moved to 197, St. Mary's Lane, Upminster, knowing this to be only temporary accommodation ...

If one takes the words of the statute, the council has to be satisfied that the applicants became homeless intentionally (section [60]). Under section [65(3)] their duty is limited to advice and assistance if "they *are* satisfied ... that [they] *became* homeless ... intentionally." The time factors here are clearly indicated: at the time of decision (the present), the local authority must look at the time (the past) when the applicants became homeless, and consider whether their action *then* was intentional in the statutory sense. If this was the right approach there could only be one answer: when the Dins left 56, Trinity Road their action was intentional within section [60], and the council was entitled to find that it would have been reasonable for them to continue to occupy 56, Trinity Road.

The appellants' argument against this is as follows: whatever the position may have been in July 1979 when they left 56, Trinity Road, at the time of the decision in December 1979 they would have been homeless in any event: the original cause of homelessness (even if intentional) had ceased to operate. For section [60] to apply there must be a causal nexus between the intentional action and the homelessness subsisting at the time of the decision. On the facts of the case there was not, so that the decision was wrong in law. I am unable to accept this argument.

1. It cannot be reconciled with the wording of the Act. This is completely and repeatedly clear in concentrating attention on when the appellants became homeless and requiring the question of intention to be ascertained as at that time. To achieve the result desired by the appellants it is either necessary to distort the meaning of "in consequence of which he ceases to occupy" (section [60(1)] or to read in a number of words. These are difficult to devise. Donaldson L.J. suggests adding at the end of section [60(1)] "and still to occupy": the appellants, as an alternative "to the date of his application." Both are radical—and awkward—reconstructions of the section.

2. Such an interpretation, or reconstruction, of the Act is not called for by any purposive approach. As I have pointed out, the Act reflects a complex interplay of interests. It confers great benefits upon one category of persons in need of housing, to the detriment of others. This being so, it does not seem unreasonable that, in order to benefit from the priority provisions, persons in the first category should bring themselves within the plain words. Failure to do so involves, as Mr. Bruneau pointed out, greater expense for a hard pressed authority, and greater pressure on the housing stock.

3. The appellants' interpretation adds greatly to the difficulties of the local authority's task in administering this Act. It requires the authority, as well as investigating the original and actual cause of homelessness, to inquire into hypotheses—what would have happened if the appellants had not moved, hypotheses involving uncertain attitudes of landlords, rating authorities, the applicants themselves, and even intervening physical events. The difficulty of

this is well shown by the singularly imprecise and speculative evidence given as to what was likely to have happened in December 1979—see above. This approach almost invites challenge in the courts—all the more if it is open to applicants to litigate the whole state of facts with witnesses, de novo, in the county court, but still significantly if the applicants are limited to judicial review. On the other hand the respondents' contention involves a straightforward inquiry into the circumstances in which the applicants became homeless.

4. The appellants' argument is not assisted by the case of *Dyson* v. *Kerrier District Council* [1980] 1 W.L.R. 1205. There (as here) the applicant intentionally surrendered available accommodation in order to go to precarious accommodation (a "winter letting") from which she was ejected and so became homeless. It was held (in my opinion, rightly) that she had become homeless in consequence of her intentional surrender. This does not in any way support an argument that a subsequent hypothetical cause should be considered to supersede an earlier actual cause. It merely decides that a disqualification for priority by reason of an intentional surrender is not displaced by obtaining temporary accommodation. As pointed out by Ackner L.J. in the Court of Appeal, it can be displaced by obtaining "settled" accommodation.

Lambert v. *Ealing L.B.C.* [1982] 1 W.L.R. 550[46]

Lord Denning M.R. said (at 553–557):

Monsieur René Lambert is a real Frenchman. He cannot speak English. At the age of 51 he came over from France to settle in England. He previously had a good business as a bookseller in Grenoble. His wife had died, but he had three charming daughters: Véronique (aged 19) at the university; Pascalle (aged 16) and Mirelle (aged 13), both at school. Yet in the summer of 1978 he sold his business and all his possessions in France. He had £6,000 left: and he came over to England.

Previously, with his savings, he had bought a motor caravan in which he and his three daughters came to England and were on holiday here from July to August or September. Then he decided to stay. He made that decision, he says, because of his daughters: they would be better educated here than in France. This has proved true. Véronique (the eldest) is at the Queen Mary College here studying for a degree in French and Spanish. The younger two are at the Lycée Français in the Cromwell Road.

Once he had decided to stay, he had to find accommodation here for himself, his daughters, and apparently their dog. He had some savings out of the money he received from selling his business in France. So he could pay a good rent for a time. He obtained a "holiday let" at 7, St. Helen's Road, Ealing. That was for six months from September 12, 1978, until March 11, 1979. The rent was £42 a week. When that expired, he took another "holiday let" at 9, Southfield Road, W.4. The rent was £56 a week for six months from March 10, 1979, until September 10, 1979.

During this period Monsieur Lambert got a job here as a van driver for a French concern with an attractive name—Maison Bouquillon Patisserie. He has worked well for them: and they have every confidence in him.

When the second "holiday let" came to an end in September 1979 he could not find other accommodation. So a few days later, on October 9, 1979, he went to the Ealing Council and asked them to house him. Véronique went with him because her English was getting very good. He was still struggling along with

46 Watchman, [1982] J.S.W.L 233.

his bad English. They told the housing department of their difficulties. The housing department said, "Go back and await a possession order." (Housing authorities do not house people until they are actually turned out of their accommodation.)

The landlord of the "holiday let" took proceedings for possession. On February 4, 1980, the Brentford County Court made an order for Monsieur Lambert to give up possession of 9, Southfield Road on March 17, 1980. Monsieur Lambert and his family had to leave on April 14, 1980.

Monsieur Lambert then applied to be rehoused by the local authority. They decided, however, that he had become homeless intentionally. It was this decision which was being challenged.

Since our previous decision [*Youngs* v. *Thanet D.C.* (1980) 78 L.G.R. 474], there have been two cases in the House of Lords. They were decided last November. They are *Din (Taj)* v. *Wandsworth London Borough Council* [1981] 3 W.L.R. 918 and *Reg.* v. *Hillingdon London Borough Council, Ex parte Islam (Taffazul)* [1981] 3 W.L.R. 942.

Mr. Bano, on behalf of Monsieur Lambert, said that the House of Lords had put a strict construction on [Part III of the Housing Act 1985]. He urged us to do the same. He said that on the simple words of sections [58] and [60(1)] of the Act, Monsieur Lambert was homeless unintentionally. He had not done anything deliberately to make himself homeless. He had been living in England for 18 months before the possession order was obtained. He had his home here. He was then turned out by the landlord. So he became "unintentionally homeless": and the council ought to have provided permanent accommodation for him.

That simple approach, however, cannot stand. It is contrary to the decision in *De Falco* v. *Crawley Borough Council* [1980] Q.B. 460. In that case an Italian family gave up their accommodation in Naples. They were E.E.C. nationals who came to England to work. They stayed with relatives here for a few weeks, and got jobs here. Then—when the relatives would not let them stay any longer—they went to the local authority and said, "We want to be housed by you. We are unintentionally homeless. Our relatives have turned us out." But this court held—as a matter of good sense—that you have to look at the position when they left Italy. They left their home in Italy, packed up and came over here: and so became intentionally homeless in Italy. That intentional homelessness carried on when they were in England. Therefore the local authority were entitled to find that they were intentionally homeless.

The authority of that case was not shaken in the least by anything said in the House of Lords. On the contrary, it was commended. Lord Wilberforce said in *Reg.* v. *Hillingdon London Borough Council, Ex parte Islam (Taffazul)* [1981] 3 W.L.R. 942, 945:

"The difficulties of the Act are certainly diminished to some extent by the decision of the Court of Appeal in *De Falco* v. *Crawley Borough Council.* . . . But many foreseeable difficulties remain."

Lord Lowry, after pointing out the difficulties, said at p. 953: "The principle of *De Falco* . . . is the safeguard . . . " So although *De Falco* put a liberal interpretation on the statute, it was upheld by the House of Lords.

The next case is *Dyson* v. *Kerrier District Council* [1980] 1 W.L.R. 1205. A lady had a flat in Huntingdon. She left that flat and went to stay at Helston in Cornwall on a "winter let" for six months. She was turned out of the "winter let" at the end of that period. She then went to the local authority, the Kerrier District Council, and said "Please house me. I am unintentionally homeless. I have been turned out of the 'winter let.' " The Court of Appeal were faced with the literal construction of the statute; they were faced with the difficulties of interpretation; and they were faced with the fact that she had been staying at a "winter let" in Cornwall for six months. They said that nevertheless she was intentionally homeless because she had left her accommodation in Huntingdon to take on the "winter let."

Dyson v. *Kerrier District Council* was on the same lines as the *De Falco* case [1980] Q.B. 460: but it extended it a little. The lady had been living in a settled "winter let" of six months: and yet she was held to be intentionally homeless.

Now we have the case of Monsieur Lambert. He did not have just one "holiday let" in England: he had two. He started living here in September 1978: and he was not turned out of the second "holiday let" until 18 months later. After living here for 18 months, he said, "I am now homeless. I had a good home here which satisfied section [58 of the Housing Act 1985]. Now, after all that time, I am unintentionally homeless. So I ought to be housed permanently."

It seems to me that our present case is covered full square by *Dyson* v. *Kerrier District Council* [1980] 1 W.L.R. 1205. But Mr. Bano has urged us to distinguish *Dyson* v. *Kerrier District Council*. He points out that in the House of Lords in *Din (Taj)* v. *Wandsworth London Borough Council* [1981] 3 W.L.R. 918 Lord Lowry threw a great deal of doubt upon it, saying at p. 934: "I am far from satisfied that it was correctly decided."

But the other Law Lords took a different view. Lord Wilberforce said, at p. 924, that he agreed with *Dyson* v. *Kerrier District Council*: and so did Lord Fraser of Tullybelton: see p. 928. As for Lord Russell of Killowen and Lord Bridge of Harwich, they did not comment on *Dyson*: nor did they throw any doubt upon it.

On the state of the authorities, it seems to me that *Dyson* v. *Kerrier District Council* [1980] 1 W.L.R. 1205 is good law and should be followed. It comes to this. When Monsieur Lambert sold up and left France, he became homeless. He was intentionally homeless here because he had given up his home in France. That intentional homelessness was the effective cause of his becoming homeless in England. The intervening 18 months do not alter the fact that he was intentionally homeless.

In those circumstances, it seems to me that the local authority were quite right. In other cases the facts may be different. Sometimes a person will have been settled here for so long that his accommodation will be of a permanent nature. Ackner L.J. envisaged this in the *Din* case in the Court of Appeal (unreported), June 23, 1981, Court of Appeal (Civil Division) Transcript No. 372 of 1981. His words were approved by Lord Wilberforce [1981] 3 W.L.R. 918, 924G. Ackner L.J.'s words are not reported. So I will read them:

"For the sake of completeness I should perhaps add that the manner in which I have construed section [60(1)] in no way accepts the proposition—once an intentionally homeless person, always an intentionally homeless person— dramatically described by Mr. Sedley as 'the Mark of Cain.' Having become homeless intentionally a would-be applicant for local authority housing is of course at a disadvantage. So he should be, otherwise the opportunity for unfair 'queue jumping' would be increased."

Stopping there, one can well see—as May L.J. pointed out in the course of the argument—that it would be easy for a person who has secure accommodation here to think to himself, "I would like to get a council house. So I will give up that secure accommodation. I will take up a 'holiday let' for a few months. Then, when I am turned out, I will ask for a council house," and get priority over all the young married couples waiting on the housing list. That is what Ackner L.J. had in mind. If this argument were allowed to prevail, and you only looked at the last place from which the applicant was turned out, the opportunity for unfair "queue jumping" would be increased.

Ackner L.J. went on to say:

> "To remove his self-imposed disqualification, he must therefore have achieved what can be loosely described as 'a settled residence,' as opposed to what from the outset is known (as in *Dyson's* case [1980] 1 W.L.R. 1205) to be only temporary accommodation. What amounts to 'a settled residence' is a question of fact and degree depending upon the circumstances of each individual case. I can see no reason why the good sense of the local authority cannot be relied upon for making the right decision. There is always the court's supervisory jurisdiction upon which an unsuccessful applicant can, in a proper case, rely."

It seems to me that, in our present case, Monsieur Lambert and his daughters had in no sense acquired a settled residence here. It was unsettled because they were only in "holiday lets." They had nothing whatever in the sense of permanent accommodation here. They were in no way settled so as to entitle them to ignore the original cause of their homelessness. The original cause was the intentional homelessness which prevailed so as to prevent their qualifying for permanent housing under [Part III of the Housing Act 1985].

Kerr and May L.JJ. delivered brief concurring judgments.

(v) In considering the phrase "available for his occupation" reference must be had to section 75 of the Housing Act 1985 which provides:

> For the purposes of this Part accommodation shall be regarded as available for a person's occupation only if it is available for occupation both by him and by any other person who might reasonably be expected to reside with him; and references to securing accommodation for a person's occupation shall be construed accordingly.

Re Islam [1983] 1 A.C. 688[47]

Lord Wilberforce said (at 707–709):

Mr. Tafazzul Islam came to this country from Bangladesh (then East Pakistan) in 1965. He obtained employment, and from 1965 until August 1979 lived at 5 Cowley Mill Road, Uxbridge, with the right only to occupy a single room. This residence, and his place of work, were within the Borough of Hillingdon, the respondents. This borough, as is well known, includes Heathrow Airport, through which a number of persons arrive in this country who have no accommodation, so presenting great problems to the respondents, but that is quite coincidental to the present appeal. The appellant's is not an "airport" case: it could have arisen in the area of any other local authority.

In 1968 the appellant went to Bangladesh and married: his wife remained in that country, living with the appellant's parents. On four subsequent visits by

---

[47] Watchman, [1982] J.S.W.L. 101.

the appellant his wife conceived the four existing children of the family; they all lived with the appellant's parents.

In 1974 application was made for entry clearance for the appellant's wife and the then two children to come to this country to live with the appellant. It is important to appreciate that, since the appellant came to this country before 1973, this application could be made and entertained without the necessity of showing that accommodation here was available—as must be shown in post-1973 cases.

In August 1979 the appellant moved from 5 Cowley Mill Road to 120 Cowley Mill Road where he had the right to share one room with one other man.

Late in 1979 or early in 1980 the appellant's wife was issued with a Bangladeshi passport for herself and her four children and soon afterwards it was endorsed with an entry certificate: this was only valid for presentation within six months. In April 1980 the appellant heard that his wife and children were arriving in this country immediately. The appellant never had any accommodation in this country which could qualify as accommodation within the meaning of section [58] of the Act. The family spent three nights at 5 Cowley Mill Road and then some time at 120 Cowley Mill Road, until in September 1980 they were summarily evicted. The appellant then applied to the respondents for accommodation under the Act as a homeless person.

On October 2, 1980, the respondents' homeless families panel resolved as follows:

"(1) that the applicant be considered homeless, but not in priority need, as his dependent children might not reasonably be expected to reside with him having lived apart for the past seven years; (2) that, even if he were in priority need, the applicant be considered to have become homeless intentionally, having deliberately arranged for his wife and children to leave accommodation which it would have been reasonable for them to continue to occupy; (3) that accommodation continue to be secured for the applicant and his family up to and including October 16, 1980."

The appellant applied for an order for judicial review. Glidewell J., after rejecting ground (1) above (and this part of the decision has not been appealed against) held that in bringing his wife and family to England from Bangladesh without ensuring that there was permanent accommodation available to them, the appellant rendered himself, and them also, homeless "intentionally." The appellant appealed to the Court of Appeal, having obtained leave, to contend that he was not intentionally homeless because he had not left accommodation available for his occupation within the meaning of the Act.

The Court of Appeal by majority (Lord Denning M.R. and Sir Denys Buckley, Ackner L.J. dissenting) dismissed the appeal, holding that the appellant had become homeless intentionally, but the majority differed in their reasons for so holding. I regret that I am unable to agree with either of the reasons given. Lord Denning M.R. decided the case on the basis that the appellant was occupying "available" accommodation in Bangladesh. But this approach—which might be possible in some cases—is not supported by the facts. There is no finding, or evidence, that the Bangladesh accommodation was ever "available" to the applicant himself, nor that he was ever in occupation of it.

Sir Denys Buckley disagreed with this approach but held that by bringing his family here the appellant deliberately did something which had the effect of rendering the shared room at 120 Cowley Mill Road accommodation no longer available for his occupation. This, however, with respect, overlooked the provisions of section [75] which was to be read into section [60]. The room at

120 Cowley Mill Road was never accommodation (within section [58]) available for occupation by him and his family—so section [60] could not be applied to it. Sir Denys Buckley's alternative ground was that the accommodation in Uxbridge and Bangladesh taken together could constitute "available accommodation" occupied by the appellant. But I do not think that rooms in two separate continents can be combined in this way.

On the other hand, not without misgiving, but without any doubt, I have reached the conclusion that the judgment of Ackner L.J. is correct and I am glad to adopt his reasons as my own. Put very briefly, the case is four square within the Act: the appellant was "homeless": he was entitled to priority: he never had any "available accommodation" within the meaning of section [75] which he could give up: section [60] could not be applied to his case. There is no answer to his claim.

While the result in this particular case may be considered acceptable, in view of the appellant's long residence in this country and his efforts to unite his family here, and I entirely accept that immigrants as such are not intended to be excluded from the Act, I share the learned Lord Justice's misgiving whether, in relation to persons coming from overseas (whether the E.E.C. or otherwise), or indeed to some persons moving from one part of this country to another, the Act is as well considered as it is undoubtedly well intentioned.

The difficulties of the Act are certainly diminished to some extent by the decision of the Court of Appeal in *De Falco* v. *Crawley Borough Council* [1980] Q.B. 460 where a whole family was held to have deliberately left accommodation which was available to them in Italy, which, having regard to the housing situation in Crawley, it was reasonable for them to have continued to occupy. But many foreseeable difficulties remain. It would serve no purpose to anticipate them here, but I venture to suggest the need for reconsideration of the Act.

Lord Lowry said (at 715–716):

Three ways have been suggested whereby the appellant became homeless intentionally. The first was that, by bringing his family to England, he deliberately did something which rendered the Cowley Mill Road accommodation no longer available for his occupation. The inescapable flaw in this theory is that, because his family were residing with him, the Cowley Mill Road accommodation was (by reference to sections [75] and [60]) never "available," nor, of course, would it have been reasonable for the appellant (*scilicet* the family unit) to continue to occupy it: thus section [60(1)] never came into play.

The second theory was that the appellant was occupying accommodation in his father's house in Bangladesh, and again that, by sending for his family, he deliberately did something in consequence of which he and his family ceased to "occupy" accommodation in Bangladesh which was available for his and their occupation and which it would have been reasonable for him and them to occupy. I am using the words of Lord Denning M.R. *ante*, p. 695A, including the quotation marks round the word "occupy," the addition of which indicates to me that the Master of the Rolls was conscious of using the word in an artificial sense which, I very respectfully suggest, is quite inconsistent with its ordinary meaning and with the probably narrower sense in which it is used in the Act. When it speaks of occupying accommodation, the Act has in contemplation people who are residing in that accommodation (see section [58]) and residing in family units, where possible. Indeed, the Master of the Rolls truly points out, *ante*, p. 695C, that the object of the Act was "to keep the family together, so far as possible, and not separate." I also think that, on the facts proved, no one could reasonably conclude that the appellant, who had been ordinarily resident in England for 15 years and had in the past 12 years made five visits to his family in Bangladesh, was occupying in any sense recognised by our law a portion of his father's house through the agency of his wife and children. If he had ever been, at some time, ordinarily resident with his wife and children in that house since his marriage, the concept could be more easily entertained. I do not deny that, in Great Britain or elsewhere, a husband who had set up house with his wife as a family unit could later leave his wife and children at home and continue to be the legal occupier.

The third suggested method, Sir Denys Buckley's "possible alternative," contemplated occupancy both in England and in Bangladesh, but also requires the appellant to have been occupying the Bangladesh accommodation, or else he could not "cease to occupy" it. This theory is therefore open to the objections I have already stated and to those of Sir Denys Buckley at p. 700E when rejecting the view of the Master of the Rolls. *Reg.* v. *North Devon District Council, Ex parte Lewis (J.P.)* [1981] 1 W.L.R. 328 affords no help to the respondents on either the second or the third method, when its facts are examined, nor, for similar reasons, do I find it necessary to discuss *Dyson* v. *Kerrier District Council* [1980] 1 W.L.R. 1205.

My conclusion is that by no artificial or other expedient, however ingenious, can a finding of intentional homelessness be legally sustained. It is therefore idle for the respondents to suggest that your Lordships ought not to interfere with the panel's decision unless it is plainly unreasonable.

Lord Fraser, Lord Russell and Lord Bridge concurred with both speeches.[48]

(v) Finally, the local authority must consider, in the context of intentional homelessness, whether it would have been reasonable for the applicant to continue to occupy the accommodation which the applicant has given up. (This issue is also relevant to the question of homelessness within section 58(2A).)

In *R.* v. *Hammersmith & Fulham L.B.C. ex p. Duro-Rama*[49] it was held that a local authority should not confine themselves to consideration of housing circumstances, but should have regard to all the reasons for leaving the accommodation which the applicant has ceased to occupy. Woolf J. said:

What [section 60(1)] requires is that it should be shown that it was not reasonable for him to continue to occupy that accommodation. If the authority, on all the material which is before them, come to the conclusion that it would be reasonable for him to continue to occupy his previous accommodation, then they can find him homeless intentionally. In performing their task of making a decision as to this, they are fully entitled to take into account the difficulties of accommodation and the difficulties of employment in their area, and indeed in the case of someone coming from abroad the difficulties in this country in general.[50]

[48] See also *R.* v. *Westminster C.C. ex p. Ali* (1984) 11 H.L.R. 83; *R.* v. *Peterborough C.C. ex p. Carr* (1990) 22 H.L.R. 144.
[49] (1983) 81 L.G.R. 702.
[50] At 709.

As regards what is now section 60(4), Woolf J. said that it "requires the housing authority to balance the factors causing a person to cease to occupy accommodation in the area which he is leaving with factors in the area where he is applying for accommodation if he has moved from one area to another."[51]

(D) LOCAL CONNECTION

61.—(1) References in this Part to a person having a local connection with the district of a local housing authority are to his having a connection with that district—

(a) because he is, or in the past was, normally resident in that district, and that residence is or was of his own choice, or

(b) because he is employed in that district, or

(c) because of family associations, or

(d) because of social circumstances,

(2) For the purposes of this section—

(a) a person is not employed in a district if he is serving in the regular armed forces of the Crown;

(b) residence in a district is not of a person's own choice if he becomes resident in it because he, or a person who might reasonably be expected to reside with him, is serving in the regular armed forces of the Crown.

(3) Residence in a district is not of a person's own choice for the purpose of this section if he, or a person who might reasonably be expected to reside with him, became resident in it because he was detained under the authority of an Act of Parliament.

(4) The Secretary of State may by order specify other circumstances in which—

(a) a person is not to be treated for the purposes of this section as employed in a district, or

(b) residence in a district is not to be treated for those purposes as of a person's own choice.

(5) An order shall be made by statutory instrument which shall be subject to annulment in pursuance of a resolution of either House of Parliament.

Notes

(i) Part III of the Housing Act 1985 allows a housing authority to pass on the obligation of securing accommodation for homeless persons to

---

[51] At 707. See also *R.* v. *Hillingdon L.B.C. ex p. H* (1988) 20 H.L.R. 554 (Walsh [1989] J.S.W.L. 48); *R.* v. *Hammersmith L.B.C. ex p. P* (1990) 22 H.L.R. 21 (cases in which the applicant fled sectarian violence in Northern Ireland); *R.* v. *Tower Hamlets L.B. ex p. Monaf* (1988) 20 H.L.R. 529 (Walsh [1988] J.S.W.L. 125); *R.* v. *Wycombe D.C. ex p. Homes* (1990) 22 H.L.R. 150.

another housing authority if, *inter alia*, (a) the applicant does not have a local connection with the authority to which the application is made and (b) the applicant does have a local connection with the other housing authority.

The local connection provisions are only relevant if the local authority is under a duty to "secure that accommodation becomes available for [the applicant's] occupation" as provided by section 65(2).[52] The issue of local connection is not relevant for the "lesser" housing duties—namely, to provide advice and assistance[53] and to secure temporary accommodation.[54]

Section 67 of the Housing Act 1985 provides:

(1) If the local housing authority—

(a) are satisfied that an applicant is homeless and has a priority need, and are not satisfied that he became homeless intentionally, but

(b) are of opinion that the conditions are satisfied for referral of his application to another local housing authority in England, Wales and Scotland,

they may notify that other authority of the fact that his application has been made and that they are of that opinion.

(2) The conditions for referral of an application to another local housing authority are—

(a) that neither the applicant nor any person who might reasonably be expected to reside with him has a local connection with the district of the authority to whom his application was made,

(b) that the applicant or a person who might reasonably be expected to reside with him has a local connection with the district of that other authority, and

(c) that neither the applicant nor any person who might reasonably be expected to reside with him will run the risk of domestic violence in that other district.

(3) For this purpose a person runs the risk of domestic violence—

(a) if he runs the risk of violence from a person with whom, but for the risk of violence, he might reasonably be expected to reside, or from a person with whom he formerly resided, or

(b) if he runs the risk of threats of violence from such a person which are likely to be carried out.

(4) The question whether the conditions for referral of an application are satisfied shall be determined by agreement between the notifying authority and the notified authority or, in default of agreement, in accordance with such

---

[52] See p. 590.
[53] s.65(3)(b); s.65(4); s.66(3)(b). See pp. 590–591.
[54] s.63(1); s.65(3)(a). See pp. 589–590.

arrangements as the Secretary of State may direct by order made by statutory instrument.

(5) An order may direct that the arrangements shall be—

(a) those agreed by any relevant authorities or associations of relevant authorities, or

(b) in default of such agreement, such arrangements as appear to the Secretary of State to be suitable, after consultation with such associations representing relevant authorities, and such other persons, as he thinks appropriate.

(6) No order shall be made unless a draft of the order has been approved by resolution of each House of Parliament.

Re Betts [1983] 2 A.C. 613[55]

Lord Brightman said (at 619–627):

My Lords, [Part III of the Housing Act 1985] entitles a homeless person to apply to a housing authority for accommodation. If the housing authority to whom application is made considers that the applicant has no local connection with the area of that authority, the authority may be in a position to transfer the statutory responsibility to another housing authority with whose area the applicant has a local connection. The respondents to this appeal, Ronald Thomas Betts and Vivien Anne Betts, became homeless through no fault of their own at a time when they were living in the area of the appellants the Eastleigh Borough Council ("Eastleigh") in Hampshire. They applied to Eastleigh for accommodation. Mr. and Mrs. Betts had formerly lived in the area of the Blaby District Council ("Blaby") in Leicestershire. Both Eastleigh and Blaby are in agreement that the responsibility for housing Mr. and Mrs. Betts properly belongs to Blaby. Mr. and Mrs. Betts, who wish to remain in the area of Eastleigh, seek to challenge that decision by way of judicial review. They were successful before the Court of Appeal . . . .

The instant case came before the Court of Appeal [1983] 1 W.L.R. 774 in January 1983. The argument there, as also before your Lordships, was that Eastleigh could not properly transfer their responsibility to Blaby unless they were of the opinion that the applicants were not, on February 6, 1981, normally resident in the Eastleigh area; that they formed that opinion by the rigid application of a guideline that normal residence short of six months was not enough to constitute a local connection with the Eastleigh area; and that the real question for the court was the meaning in the context of the words "normally resident." After reviewing the evidence, Stephenson L.J. [1983] 1 W.L.R. 774, 783 reached the conclusion that the chief housing officer "did fetter the council's decision by a rigid application of the suggested definition of normal residence" in the Agreement of Procedures. Stephenson L.J. then considered the authorities on "ordinary residence" to which he was referred by the applicants' counsel, including not only *Shah* [1983] 2 W.L.R. 16 but also *Macrae* v. *Macrae* [1949] P. 397, 403 where Somervell L.J. pointed out, in the context of a matrimonial cause, that "Ordinary residence can be changed in a day." These authorities said the learned Lord Justice [1983] 1 W.L.R. 774, 785, showed that "a person may be normally resident where he intends to settle—not necessarily permanently or indefinitely." The judgment of Griffiths L.J. [1983] 1 W.L.R. 774, 788 was to the same effect:

[55] Watchman, [1984] J.S.W.L. 365.

" 'Normal residence' within the meaning of this Act is in my opinion to be construed in the same sense as 'ordinarily resident' was construed by the House of Lords in *Reg.* v. *Barnet London Borough Council, Ex parte Nilish Shah* [1983] 2 A.C. 309. It requires a consideration of many features of the residence and is not to be decided solely by the application of a six month rule. It follows that as the housing officer applied the six month rule to decide 'normal residence' he misdirected himself in law when forming his opinion on normal residence and thus on whether the applicants had a local connection with the local authority's area; ... "

Finally, Purchas L.J. [1983] 1 W.L.R. 774, 790:

"if the applicants had been asked by an inquirer as to where they were normally living between October 1980 and January 1981 I have little doubt that they would have answered 'in Eastleigh.' In my judgment this would be the normal reaction, as an objective test, of any person in the particular circumstances in which the applicants found themselves at that time. In the light of these authorities, the adherence to an arbitrary period of residential qualification cannot be the correct approach to section [61](1)(a)."

My Lords, in my respectful view the manner in which the applicants have approached this case, and were successful in persuading the Court of Appeal to approach it, is misconceived. Eastleigh are relieved of their obligations under section [65(2) of the Housing Act 1985] if they are "of the opinion" specified in paragraph (a) of section [67(2)]. The requisite "opinion" is that the applicants do not have (in the present tense) a local connection with the Eastleigh area but do have a local connection with the Blaby area. "Local connection" is not a defined expression in the sense that it means (inter alia) that the applicant "is or in the past was normally resident in [the area] and his residence in it is or was of his own choice." Section [61(1)] does not entitle the reader to construe section [67(2)(a)] by substituting "is or was normally resident in," or "is employed in," or "has family associations with" for the words "has a local connection with." What section [61](1) does is to say that a reference to a person having a local connection with an area is a reference to his having such a connection *because* he is, or in the past was normally resident there, or because he is employed there, or because he has family associations with that area or because there are special circumstances. Section [61] specifies those factors alone upon which the local connection is to be founded. A local connection not founded upon any of the four stated factors is irrelevant. The fundamental concept of section [67(2)(a)] is local connection, not any local connection, but a local connection having any of the origins described in section [61](1). The opinion which has to be formed by a notifying housing authority in a residence case is not whether the homeless person is now or was in the past normally resident in the area of the notifying authority, but whether the applicant has now a local connection with either area based upon the fact that he is now or was in the past normally resident in that area.

The approach of the respondents is very different. They ask the question, are they now normally resident in the Eastleigh area? They answer that question affirmatively and then claim as a result, by definition, a local connection with Eastleigh which invalidates the opinion reached by Eastleigh under section [67(2)]. The erroneous approach emerges with clarity from the terms of their notice of appeal to the Court of Appeal, the first ground of which contains the following:

"The fundamental question was what is meant in section [61](1)(a) of the said Act by the term 'normally resident.' "

Stephenson L.J. [1983] 1 W.L.R. 774 accepted that definition of the issue which was thought to be before the court when he said, at p. 780:

"The applicants' case here and below is that the council have not succeeded in transferring their responsibility to Blaby District Council. They can only do that if of opinion that the applicants were not on February 6, 1981, or before that, *normally* resident in their area."

My Lords, that is not the fundamental question. The fundamental question is the existence of a "local connection." In construing section [67(2)] it is only to be expected that the emphasis falls on "local connection," and not on past or present residence or current employment, etc. The Act is one which enables a homeless person in certain circumstances to jump over the heads of all other persons on a housing authority's waiting list, to jump the queue. One would not expect any just legislation to permit this to be done unless the applicant has in a real sense a local connection with the area in question. I accept that "residence" may be changed in a day, and that in appropriate circumstances a single day's residence may be enough to enable a person to say that he was normally resident in the area in which he arrived only yesterday. But "local connection" means far more than that. It must be built up and established; by a period of residence; or by a period of employment; or by family associations which have endured in the area; or by other special circumstances which spell out a local connection in real terms.

Subsection (2) provides, *inter alia*, that residence will not be "of choice" for the purpose of section 61(1)(a) if the applicant or a person who might reasonably be expected to reside with him is serving in the armed forces.[56]

(ii)   If an applicant does not have a local connection with any housing authority in England, Scotland or Wales, then the housing authority to which the application is made cannot divest themselves of the duties imposed by Part III of the 1985 Act.[57]

(iii)   It is important to note that homeless people are free to make their own choice about which housing authority to apply to. This fact, combined with the referral provisions, may lead to "forum shopping:"

Recent research reports have confirmed widespread inconsistencies between authorities in their interpretation and application of [Part III of the Housing Act 1985]. Not surprisingly therefore, well advised applicants are shopping around carefully for the authority likely to be most flexible in its approach. Even if they have a local connection with authority A it may be more sensible for homeless persons to apply to authority B and be accepted there. Authority B can then use the local connection provisions to refer them back to authority A for permanent

[56] See *R.* v. *Vale of White Horse D.C. ex p. Smith and Hay* (1984) 17 H.L.R. 160.
[57] *R* v. *Hillingdon L.B.C. ex p. Streeting*, [1980] 1 W.L.R. 1430.

rehousing. As the Court of Appeal confirmed in *R*. v. *Slough B.C. ex p. Ealing L.B.C.* [1981] 1 Q.B. 801, this possibility arises even if authority A has quite properly decided earlier that the applicant is intentionally homeless.[58]

In *R* v. *Slough B.C. ex p. Ealing L.B.C.*[59] the applicants (the Lynch family and Miss Jack) were former council tenants who had been evicted by the local authority (Slough B.C.). When they applied to be rehoused, Slough B.C. decided that they were intentionally homeless. The applicants then turned to Enfield L.B.C., which decided they were not intentionally homeless, and referred them back to Slough B.C..

Lord Denning M.R. said:

The law

I do not propose to analyse in detail the various sections of the Act. That would be much too tedious. I take Miss Jack's case, but the same applies to the Lynch family.

First, the Slough council were entitled to find that Miss Jack was intentionally homeless when she was removed by them from Slough into the Ealing area. But that finding was not binding on Ealing. The Ealing council were entitled to make their own inquiries and they were entitled to come to their own conclusion. They were entitled to find that Miss Jack was unintentionally homeless—even though this meant contradicting the Slough finding. Secondly, if the finding of Ealing stopped there, it would mean that Ealing was bound to house Miss Jack and her baby indefinitely under section [65(2)] of the Act. But, thirdly, Ealing was entitled to pass on *that* obligation to Slough. That follows because Miss Jack had a local connection with Slough and none with Ealing. So Ealing was the "notifying authority" and Slough the "notified authority" within section [67]. Fourthly, on being so notified, Slough came under a duty "to secure that accommodation becomes available for occupation by the person to whom the notification relates ... ": see section [68(2)]. That is the self-same duty as is imposed by section [65(2)] in the self-same words "to secure that accommodation becomes available for his occupation." It is Slough's duty to secure that accommodation is available for him indefinitely—and not merely for a short time. Fifthly, this means that Slough are bound to accept the finding of Ealing that the homelessness of Miss Jack was unintentional.

Conclusion

Each of these two families was, by long residence in Slough, the responsibility of the Slough council. Each family behaved deplorably and the Slough council were quite right to evict them for their council homes. But I am afraid that, under this statute, the Slough council cannot get rid of them by evicting them. So long as they were in Slough, each could come back at once—say they are homeless—and demand to be housed again by the Slough council indefinitely. It is an intolerable burden to put on the Slough council—and worse still on the people of the neighbourhood—who have to put up with them. Yet the statute will have it so.

In these two cases the Slough council hoped that, by moving them—or getting them to move—to adjoining areas they might shift the responsibility on to the

---

[58] Madge & Luba, Recent developments in housing law (1989) Legal Action, June, at p. 23.
[59] [1981] Q.B. 801.

adjoining local authorities. But Slough's efforts have not succeeded. The adjoining local authorities can turn round and say to Slough: "They are your responsibility. Not ours. You must have them back. You must house them indefinitely—not us."

As it happens, pending this litigation, the two families have been housed in Ealing and Hillingdon respectively at the expense of those councils. Now that we have decided that it was the responsibility of Slough to house them, Slough must bear that expense and repay Ealing and Hillingdon.[60]

Two recent cases have illustrated some of the problems to which section 67 gives rise.

In *R. v. Tower Hamlets L.B.C. ex p. Camden L.B.C.*[61] an applicant was found to be intentionally homeless by Tower Hamlets. Subsequently Camden decided that he was not intentionally homeless, and referred the applicant back to Tower Hamlets. Tower Hamlets chose not to challenge the referral in the courts, but simply ignored it. Camden then brought proceedings with a view to forcing Tower Hamlets to accept the referral.

Two important points were discussed by Henry J. First, as regards the responsibility of the second authority (in this case, Camden) he said:

They are bound to entertain all applications made to them even when such application is made by someone with no prior connection with the borough. Even when the applicant comes straight from an adverse and legally unchallengeable findings of intentional homelessness made by the borough with which he has the closest connection, the applicant can shop around and, wherever he choses to shop, that borough must make its own statutory enquiry and reach its own decision wherever he has been before and whatever the result on that occasion.[62]

Secondly, he took the view that Tower Hamlets had not acted properly in ignoring, rather than challenging, Camden's referral under section 67. He said that if the first authority "feels that it cannot accept those findings and has a case that might or might not succeed in having the finding set aside in judicial review, it seems to me that comity and good administration, and the avoidance of anarchy, all require the [first][63] borough to make a prompt challenge in those circumstances. It is quite unsatisfactory for the first borough simply to ignore a finding by the second borough which it is not prepared to challenge in the courts."[64]

A similar issue arose in *R. v. Newham L.B.C. ex p. Tower Hamlets L.B.C.* where an immigrant from Bangladesh was found to be intentionally homeless by Tower Hamlets, but was subsequently

---

[60] At 810–811.

[61] (1989) 21 H.L.R. 197 (Walsh [1989] J.S.W.L. 308).

[62] At 204.

[63] In the report the word is "second," but this does not accord with the sense of the passage. See also the headnote of the report which is to be found in the Local Government Reports: 87 L.G.R. 321.

[64] At 210.

accepted as unintentionally homeless by Newham, which then referred the applicant back to Tower Hamlets under section 67. In this case, however, rather then ignoring the referral, Tower Hamlets applied to have the referral by Newham quashed. Newham's decision to refer the applicant to Tower Hamlets was taken without reference to the refusal by Tower Hamlets to accept the applicant as unintentionally homeless on grounds which included the chronic shortage of housing in Tower Hamlets' district. On this ground, the Divisional Court quashed Newham's referral: the referring authority must have regard to the position of the local authority to whom the applicant is to be referred. The Court of Appeal dismissed Newham's appeal.[65]

(iv)   It is obvious that time consuming and expensive disputes between housing authorities as to the existence of a local connection are extremely undesirable. Lord Denning M.R., in *R.* v. *Slough B.C. ex p. Ealing L.B.C.*[66] said:

Under [Part III of the Housing Act 1985] each local authority is under a statutory duty to house the homeless persons in its area. This case raises the question: what is to happen when a person who is homeless in one housing area moves—or is moved—to another housing area and becomes homeless there? One or other local authority is bound to house him. Which is it? To us old folk this is a repeat performance of the disputes under the poor law 200 years ago. In those days each parish was responsible for the relief of those who were poor and unable to work. When a poor man moved from one parish to another, the question arose: which parish was responsible? The disputes, Blackstone tells us, "created an infinity of expensive law-suits between contending neighbourhoods, concerning those settlements and removals": see *Blackstone's Commentaries*, 17th ed. (1830), vol. I, p. 361. Many of the cases that came before Lord Mansfield were settlement cases. History tends to repeat itself. If our present cases are anything to go by, we are in for another dose of the same medicine.

However, certain steps have been taken with a view to avoiding such disputes. First, in order to facilitate agreements between notifying authorities and notified authorities—as required by section 67(4)—there is a national Agreement on Procedures for Referrals of the Homeless (which was negotiated between the Association of District Councils, the Association of Metropolitan Authorities and the London Boroughs Association). This agreement is adhered to by most housing authorities, although it is only a voluntary guideline. Secondly, by statutory instrument[67] a system of arbitration was established to deal with those cases where there is no agreement between the relevant housing authorities.

---

[65] (1991) 23 H.L.R. 62.
[66] [1981] Q.B. 801 at 807–808.
[67] Housing (Homeless Persons) (Appropriate Arrangements) Order 1978 (S.I. 1978 No. 69); Housing (Homeless Persons) (Appropriate Arrangements) (No. 2) Order 1978 (S.I. 1978 No. 661). Notwithstanding the repeal of the 1977 Act, these provisions were retained in force by the Housing (Consequential Provisions) Act 1985, s.2.

II DUTIES AND REMEDIES

(A) DUTIES TO THE HOMELESS

It would, of course, be wrong to think that local authorities have a duty to provide accommodation for everyone who is homeless. However, the legislation does require local authorities to make enquiries in any case where they have reason to believe that the applicant is homeless or threatened with homelessness. Then, depending on the circumstances, the local authority may have to take some form of action ranging from the provision of advice and assistance to the securing of permanent accommodation for the applicant.

The local authorities' duties are set out in sections 62 to 69:

62.—(1) If a person (an "applicant") applies to a local housing authority for accommodation, or for assistance in obtaining accommodation, and the authority have reason to believe that he may be homeless or threatened with homelessness, they shall make such inquiries as are necessary to satisfy themselves as to whether he is homeless or threatened with homelessness.

(2) If they are so satisfied, they shall make any further inquiries necessary to satisfy themselves as to—

(a) whether he has a priority need, and

(b) whether he became homeless or threatened with homelessness intentionally;

and if they think fit they may also make inquiries as to whether he has a local connection with the district of another local housing authority in England, Wales or Scotland.

63.—(1) If the local housing authority have reason to believe that an applicant may be homeless and have a priority need, they shall secure that accommodation is made available for his occupation pending a decision as a result of their inquiries under section 62.

(2) This duty arises irrespective of any local connection which the applicant may have with the district of another local housing authority.

64.—(1) On completing their inquiries under section 62, the local housing authority shall notify the applicant of their decision on the question whether he is homeless or threatened with homelessness.

(2) If they notify him that their decision is that he is homeless or threatened with homelessness, they shall at the same time notify him of their decision on the question whether he has a priority need.

(3) If they notify him that their decision is that he has a priority need, they shall at the same time notify him—

(a) of their decision whether he became homeless or threatened with homelessness intentionally, and

(b) whether they have notified or propose to notify another local housing authority under section 67 (referral of application on grounds of local connection).

(4) If the local housing authority notify the applicant—

(a) that they are not satisfied that he is homeless or threatened with homelessness, or

(b) that they are not satisfied that he has a priority need, or

(c) that they are satisfied that he became homeless or threatened with homelessness intentionally, or

(d) that they have notified or propose to notify another local housing authority under section 67 (referral of application on grounds of local connection),

they shall at the same time notify him of their reasons.

(5) The notice required to be given to a person under this section shall be given in writing and shall, if not received by him, be treated as having been given to him only if it is made available at the authority's office for a reasonable period for collection by him or on his behalf.

65.—(1) This section has effect as regards the duties owed by the local housing authority to an applicant where they are satisfied that he is homeless.

(2) Where they are satisfied that he has a priority need and are not satisfied that he became homeless intentionally, they shall, unless they notify another local housing authority in accordance with section 67 (referral of application on grounds of local connection), secure that accommodation becomes available for his occupation.

(3) Where they are satisfied that he has a priority need but are also satisfied that he became homeless intentionally, they shall—

(a) secure that accommodation is made available for his occupation for such period as they consider will give him a reasonable opportunity of securing accommodation for his occupation, and

(b) furnish him with advice and such assistance as they consider appropriate in the circumstances in any attempts he may make to secure that accommodation becomes available for his occupation.

(4) Where they are not satisfied that he has a priority need, they shall furnish him with advice and such assistance as they consider appropriate in the circumstances in any attempts he may make to secure that accommodation becomes available for his occupation.

66.—(1) This section has effect as regards the duties owed by the local housing authority to an applicant where they are satisfied that he is threatened with homelessness.

(2) Where they are satisfied that he has a priority need and are not satisfied that he became threatened with homelessness intentionally, they shall take reasonable steps to secure that accommodation does not cease to be available for his occupation.

(3) Where—

(a)   they are not satisfied that he has a priority need, or

(b)   they are satisfied that he has a priority need but are also satisfied that he became threatened with homelessness intentionally,

they shall furnish him with advice and such assistance as they consider appropriate in the circumstances in any attempts he may make to secure that accommodation does not cease to be available for his occupation.

(4) Subsection (2) does not affect any right of the local housing authority, whether by virtue of a contract, enactment or rule of law, to secure vacant possession of accommodation.

For the text of section 67 see pp. 582–583.

68.—(1) Where, in accordance with section 67(1), a local housing authority notify another authority of an application, the notifying authority shall secure that accommodation is available for occupation by the applicant until it is determined whether the conditions for referral of his application to the other authority are satisfied.

(2) If it is determined that the conditions for referral are satisfied, the notified authority shall secure that accommodation becomes available for occupation by the applicant; if it is determined that the conditions are not satisfied, the notifying authority shall secure that accommodation becomes available for occupation by him.

(3) When the matter has been determined, the notifying authority shall notify the applicant—

(a)   whether they or the notified authority are the authority whose duty it is to secure that accommodation becomes available for his occupation, and

(b)   of the reasons why the authority subject to that duty are subject to it.

(4) The notice required to be given to a person under subsection (3) shall be given in writing and shall, if not received by him, be treated as having been given to him only if it is made available at the authority's office for a reasonable period for collection by him or on his behalf.

69.—(1) A local housing authority may perform any duty under section 65 or 68 (duties to persons found to be homeless) to secure that accommodation becomes available for the occupation of a person—

(a)   by making available suitable accommodation held by them under Part II (provision of housing) or any enactment, or

(b)   by securing that he obtains suitable accommodation from some other person, or

(c)   by giving him such advice and assistance as will secure that he obtains suitable accommodation from some other person,

and in determining whether accommodation is suitable they shall have regard to Part IX (slum clearance), X (overcrowding) and XI (houses in multiple occupation) of this Act.

Notes

(i)   The effect of these provisions can be explained by reference to the following diagram[68]:

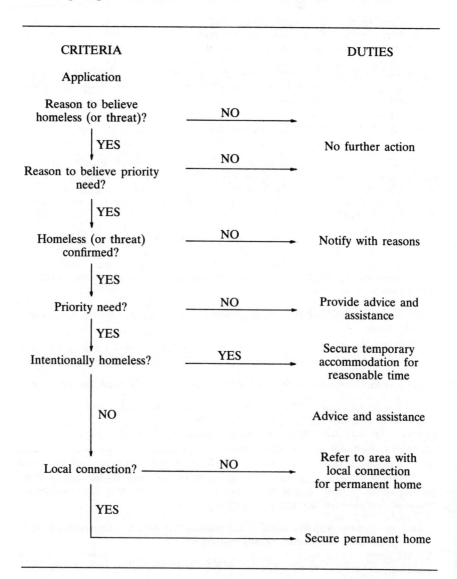

Source: *Audit Commission: "Housing the Homeless: the Local Authority Role" HMSO 1989*

---

[68] *The Government's Review of the Homelessness Legislation* (1989) Figure one, p. 3.

(ii)   The first duty of the local authority is to provide adequate facilities for receiving applications from people who are homeless.

R. v. Camden L.B.C. ex p. Gillan (1989) 21 H.L.R. 114

The facts were as follows:

The applicants, all of whom were prima facie homeless and in priority need of accommodation applied to the respondent authority for assistance pursuant to Part III of the Housing Act 1985. The respondent authority operated a service whereby persons could apply for assistance under Part III only between the hours of 9.30 a.m. and 12.30 p.m., on weekdays only. There was no provision by the authority of any service outside of those hours during weekdays or at all over weekends. At least three of the applicants had applied to the respondent authority within those hours and the authority had failed to entertain their applications. The applicants applied for judicial review of the respondent authority's failure to consider their applications.[69]

The local authority argued, *inter alia*, that as a result of rate-capping they were very short of money, and were unable to provide a more extensive service. May L.J. said (at 119):

I, for my part, agree with the submission that there is under the Act a duty on the council as a housing authority to take reasonable steps to hear and adjudicate upon applications made to them by persons who are potentially homeless. Included in that obligation is, as I think, one of making provision to receive any such applications. It is no use homeless applicants making applications for accommodation to a housing authority under the Act if their applications are not going to reach the ears of the authority to whom the application is made.

Many councils, such indeed as Camden, have separate departments to cope with those who are homeless. Others include that obligation in a branch of their general housing department. In heavily populated areas reasonable provision, in my judgment, may require some form of 24–hour cover in respect of homeless persons. As I indicated earlier, it is quite clearly the intention of Parliament that children should not sleep in the streets if it can possibly be avoided. One need only refer to occasions of domestic violence which, without seeking to be facetious, quite often happen after the public houses have closed, and you get wives or children turned out on to the streets, by those who have had rather more alcohol than has been good for them. Equally, such things as disasters by fire more often than not occur during the night, and in consequence not only may persons be killed, but certainly may a large family be rendered homeless.

In the country, where obviously different considerations apply, the necessity for this cover or that cover may of course be different. Every case must depend upon its own facts.

(iii)   When an application is received, the local authority is required by section 62(2) to make inquiries. Often, an applicant will seek to

---

[69] These facts are taken from the editor's introduction to the report: 21 H.L.R. 114, 114–115.

challenge a local authority's decision, not on the basis of an error of law as to the meaning of the fundamental concepts outlined in sections 58 to 61, but because of failure to make the necessary inquiries. As a number of recent decisions show, the cases turn on their detailed facts: sometimes the courts will regard the local authority as having taken sufficient steps[70]; sometimes the investigations undertaken by the local authority will be thought insufficient.[71]

A helpful summary of the duties of local authorities to make inquiries was given in *R. v. Gravesham B.C. ex p. Winchester* by Simon Brown J.[72]:

1. The burden lies upon the local authority to make appropriate inquiries (section [62 of the Housing Act 1985]) in a caring and sympathetic way: *R. v. West Dorset District Council ex p. Phillips* (1983) 17 H.L.R. 336. The enquiries should be pursued rigorously and fairly albeit the authority are not under a duty to conduct detailed C.I.D.-type enquiries: *Lally v. Kensington and Chelsea Royal London Borough Council, The Times*, March 27, 1980. The applicant must be given an opportunity to explain matters which the local authority is minded to regard as weighing substantially against him: *R v. Wyre Borough Council ex p. Joyce* (1983) 11 H.L.R. 75.

2. The burden is likewise upon the local authority to be satisfied that the applicant became homeless intentionally before it can reach such a conclusion; if its enquiries lead to doubt or uncertainty, the issue must be resolved in the applicant's favour: *R. v. Thurrock Borough Council ex p. Williams* (1981) 1 H.L.R. 128.

(iv) In discharging its duties to the homeless under sections 65 and 68, the local authority need only "secure that accommodation becomes available" for occupation by the applicant. The local authority does not have to provide accommodation from its own housing stock, but can fulfil its obligation by ensuring that the applicant obtains accommodation in the private or independent sectors.[73] Furthermore, where the applicant does not have a connection with the district of any housing authority in England, Scotland or Wales, the obligation may be performed by securing accommodation for the applicant abroad.

In *R. v. Bristol C.C. ex p. Browne*[74] a woman fled from her violent husband in the Republic of Ireland to Bristol. Bristol City Council considered whether or not the applicant ran the risk of further domestic violence and concluded that she did not. Accordingly, they arranged for

---

[70] See, *e.g. R. v. Kensington & Chelsea R.L.B.C. ex p. Cunha* (1989) 21 H.L.R. 16 (Walsh [1989] J.S.W.L. 180); *R. v. Nottingham C.C. ex p. Costello* (1989) 21 H.L.R. 301 (Walsh [1989] J.S.W.L. 373); *Reynolds v. Sevenoaks D.C.* (1990) 22 H.L.R. 250; *R. v. Kensington & Chelsea R.B.C. ex p. Bayani* (1990) 22 H.L.R. 406; *R. v. Barnet L.B.C. ex p. O'Connor* (1990) 22 H.L.R. 467.

[71] As in *R. v. Tower Hamlets L.B.C. ex p. Rouf* (1989) 21 H.L.R. 94 (Walsh [1989] J.S.W.L. 373); *R. v. Dacorum B.C. ex p. Brown* (1989) 21 H.L.R. 405; *R. v. Westminster C.C. ex p. Iqbal* (1990) 22 H.L.R. 215; *R. v. Swansea D.C. ex p. Evans* (1990) 22 H.L.R. 467.

[72] (1986) 18 H.L.R. 207 at 214–215.

[73] s.69.

[74] [1979] 1 W.L.R. 1437.

the local authority in her home town in the Republic of Ireland to accommodate her, and offered her assistance to return. The Divisional Court held that this was a proper discharge of the authority's duties under what are now sections 62 and 69 of the 1985 Act.

This decision does not, however, allow local authorities to avoid their responsibilities under Part III of the 1985 Act simply by finding accommodation for homeless applicants in other areas in the United Kingdom. Any accommodation secured by the local authority under Part III of the 1985 Act must be suitable—which involves location as well as size.

R v. *Wyre B.C. ex p. Parr* (1982) 2 H.L.R. 71[75]

After a period in the armed forces the applicant, who had been born in Fleetwood, lived with his family in Nottingham for three years. The family then moved back to Fleetwood—in the area of Wyre D.C.— where they lived in a caravan on the promenade. In response to the applicant's request for accommodation, Wyre D.C. sought to discharge their duty under the act by offering the applicant accommodation in Birmingham. Lord Denning M.R. said (at 76–77):

There was much discussion before us as to whether a housing authority in the North of England can fulfil its statutory duty by offering accommodation 200 miles away in Birmingham. It seems to me that, under section [67] of the Act, when a person is homeless and has a priority need, the first thing to find out is whether he has a local connection with any particular area. If he applies to a local authority with which he has a local connection, it is for them to find him accommodation. But, if he applies to a local authority with which he has no local connection, they can pass him on to some other local authority with which he has a local connection: and it is then for that other authority to find him accommodation. If there is any dispute between the two authorities, it is to be settled by arbitration.

In the present case there is no doubt that Mr. Parr's local connection—the place where he was born and bred and went to school and lived for his first 25 years of life—is Fleetwood within the Wyre local authority. That is the place where both his sisters still live. But he also has a local connection with Nottingham. That is the place where he lived for some years after he came out of the army. That is the place where his wife's sisters are still living. So Mr. Parr has a local connection with both Fleetwood and Nottingham. But the housing authority at Fleetwood did not offer him accommodation in either of those places. They offered him accommodation in Birmingham: and they said that, by making that offer, they had fulfilled their duties under the Act.

Having cited the provisions which are now section 65(2) and section 69, Lord Denning M.R. continued (at 77–79):

In this case the Wyre Borough Council say:

---

[75] Watchman, [1982] J.S.W.L. 236.

"We satisfy section [69(1)(c)]. We have secured that Mr. Parr obtains accommodation from some other person. That other person is the Birmingham housing authority."

In support of that contention they referred to *Reg.* v. *Bristol City Council* [1979] 1 W.L.R. 1437. In that case a lady came here from Tralee in Ireland to escape from her husband who was violent towards her. She came to stay in a Women's Aid hostel in Bristol. But the hostel was full. She became homeless in Bristol. The Bristol council contacted the community welfare officer in Tralee. The community welfare officer in Tralee said that he could provide the woman with accommodation where she would be safe from her husband. That offer was held to be perfectly all right. Even though the woman did not want to go back to Tralee, the Bristol City Council had fulfilled their obligations under the Act.

It is said on behalf of the Wyre Borough Council that that case is authority for the case we are considering. But I must say that that case is quite distinguishable. The accommodation in Tralee was entirely appropriate and suitable for the woman. She was found accommodation in her own home town, where she had the strongest possible local connections. In our present case Mr. Parr has no local connection with Birmingham at all.

It seems to me that the offer of Birmingham was not sufficient to satisfy the council's statutory obligations. It did not satisfy the provisions of section [69(1)(c)], "by securing that he obtains accommodation from some other person." It was agreed on all hands that the accommodation offered must be "appropriate" accommodation. That means, of course, that the house—as a dwelling—must be appropriate for a family of this size. It must have enough rooms to house his wife and five children. If it is in an area with which he has a local connection, that is good enough. He cannot reasonably refuse an offer of suitable accommodation in his own area. But it is different when the offer is only of accommodation in a far-off area with which he has no local connection. A near-by area of the same type might be appropriate. But not an area 150 miles away where his neighbours might be of a different colour and speak with a different accent and have different standards altogether. I know that beggars cannot be choosers, but they should be given some consideration—so that they are housed in a suitable environment.

In this case Mr. Parr was given no information about the accommodation in Birmingham. He was, I think, entitled to be told more about it before he could be expected to take it. Moreover, it appears that the offer was only open for a few days—until October 29. He was certainly entitled to more notice.

I would just like to say a word or two about the Code of Guidance which was referred to us. It has statutory authority. The last sentence of paragraph 2–21 deals with a case where the applicant has a local connection with two authorities. It says:

"This need [to consult other authorities] need not prevent arrangements being made, taking full account of the wishes of the applicant, for another authority to take responsibility for him."

That imports that the wishes of the applicant are to be taken into account. It comes to this: The offer of accommodation in Birmingham was too uncertain and unsatisfactory for Mr. Parr to be required to consider. It seems to me that the Wyre Borough Council have not fulfilled their obligations. I would, therefore, allow the appeal and allow mandamus to go.

Donaldson and Eveleigh L.JJ. gave concurring judgments.

Finally, it should be noted that the duty arising from section 65(2) is satisfied only if the accommodation is indefinitely available, rather than available only for a fixed period.[76]

(B) CHALLENGING LOCAL AUTHORITY DECISIONS

There is no direct form of appeal against decisions of local authorities in homelessness cases. The only possibility is for the aggrieved applicant to seek judicial review under Order 53 of the Rules of the Supreme Court.[77] The applicant must bring such an action within six months of the local authority's decision, and the court must give leave. If leave is given, then the local authority's decision may be challenged according to the principles of administrative law.

In *R.* v. *Hillingdon L.B.C. ex p. Puhlhofer* Lord Brightman said:

My Lords, I am troubled at the prolific use of judicial review for the purpose of challenging the performance by local authorities of their functions under [Part III of the Housing Act 1985]. Parliament intended the local authority to be the judge of fact. The Act abounds with the formula when, or if, the housing authority are satisfied as to this, or that, or have reason to believe this, or that. Although the action or inaction of a local authority is clearly susceptible to judicial review where they have misconstrued the Act, or abused their powers or otherwise acted perversely, I think that great restraint should be exercised in giving leave to proceed by judicial review. The plight of the homeless is a desperate one, and the plight of the applicants in the present case commands the deepest sympathy. But it is not, in my opinion, appropriate that the remedy of judicial review, which is a discretionary remedy, should be made use of to monitor the actions of local authorities under the Act save in the exceptional case. The ground upon which the courts will review the exercise of an administrative discretion is abuse of power—*e.g.* bad faith, a mistake in construing the limits of the power, a procedural irregularity, or unreasonableness in the *Wednesbury* sense—unreasonableness verging on an absurdity: see the speech of Lord Scarman in *Reg.* v. *Secretary of State for the Environment, Ex parte Nottinghamshire County Council* [1986] A.C. 240, 247–248. Where the existence or non-existence of a fact is left to the judgment and discretion of a public body and that fact involves a broad spectrum ranging from the obvious to the debatable to the just conceivable, it is the duty of the court to leave the decision of that fact to the public body to whom Parliament has entrusted the decision-making power save in a case where it is obvious that the public body, consciously or unconsciously, are acting perversely.[78]

It must be stressed that the court cannot examine the merits of the case. If the application for judicial review is successful, the court will quash the local authority's decision and send it back for reconsideration. Of course, in certain circumstances the local authority may legitimately reach the same conclusion after having reconsidered the application.

---

[76] *R.* v. *Camden L.B.C. ex p. Wait* (1986) 18 H.L.R. 434.
[77] *Cocks* v. *Thanet D.C.* [1983] 2 A.C. 286.
[78] [1986] A.C. 484 at 518.

Concluding comments

(i) The review conducted by the Government in 1989 concluded, perhaps rather complacently, that an overhaul of the legislation was not necessary:

In theory, a case can be argued for repealing the special "homelessness" legislation, since this can lead to the impression that "homelessness" is a distinct housing phenomenon, separate from the generality of housing problems. There is also the risk that the presence of such a special mechanism may discourage self reliance and personal responsibility; and, inevitably, it reduces the discretion of local authorities, and their freedom to pursue locally determined policies and priorities.

Nevertheless, the Government recognise that there remains a need for the "long stop" mechanism of the homelessness legislation to help people who are in urgent need, and cannot resolve their housing problems for themselves. They believe that the legislation has done the job that Parliament intended of it, and therefore they do not propose changes to the statutory framework.[79]

Not everyone, however, would agree with this assessment. For example, one commentator has expressed the following opinion:

At present we have an unhappy combination of legislation couched in exceedingly vague terms but fleshed out by a Code of Guidance which councils are not bound to follow, a morass of frequently confusing and sometimes contradictory case law, and no effective means of appeal for aggrieved applicants.[80]

(ii) Ultimately, the problem of homelessness cannot be resolved by imposing duties on local housing authorities. Since the principal cause of homelessness is that there is not enough accommodation available, the problem can only be resolved by attempting to satisfy the demand for housing.

There are various reasons why the supply of housing has failed to keep up with the demand. Nuttgens, writing in 1989, noted:

There has been a dramatic cut in housing expenditure. Since 1979 the amount of public money invested in housing has been cut by 40 per cent. Too few new council houses and Housing Association houses have been built for rent. Much needed repairs to the housing stock have not been carried out; the total bill for housing repairs in England is thought to be in the order of £45 billion. Above all, the decline of the rented sector has exacerbated the problem.[81]

It is the last of these factors which was been emphasised by the Government in the 1980s. According to the 1989 review of the

---

[79] paras. 46–47.
[80] Hoath, The Review of the homelessness legislation—a missed opportunity? (1990) 140 New L.J. 412 at 415.
[81] *The Home Front* (1989), p. 110.

homelessness legislation "[h]omeless figures are the acute symptoms of a long standing problem"—namely "a long-term breakdown in an effective market in rented housing."[82] The Housing Act 1988 should, therefore, be seen as an aspect of the Conservative Government's homelessness policy. It is intended that the Housing Act 1988, by abolishing rent control, will arrest the decline of the private rented sector of the housing market.

There is, however, disagreement as to the precise relationship between rent control and the supply of rented accommodation. It has been suggested that "there is little evidence to support the assertion that [the decline of the privately rented sector] is a direct result solely of rent restriction."[83] Furthermore, it has been argued that the British experience points to the "apparent paradox that the decontrol of rents leads not to the supply of more rented accommodation in the UK but to less."[84] In the context of the supply of rented housing, much depends on the relative returns from different alternative courses of action, which—in turn—depends on external economic factors, such as taxation policy. The levels of rents is only one of these external factors.

While it is far too early to evaluate the success or failure of the 1988 Act in this area, it is, perhaps, worth noting that recent surveys suggest that the effect of the Housing Act 1988 is to increase rather than decrease homelessness—by pricing prospective private sector tenants out of the market:

The 1988 Housing Act, which came into effect in January 1989, has aggravated levels of homelessness, according to a report compiled by the Nottinghamshire group of the housing charity Shelter Nottinghamshire Homeless Action. The principal finding of the report, which is based on a study carried out in Nottinghamshire since the Act came into force, is that rents in that county have risen dramatically and many more people have been priced out of the market.

The authors of the report feel, meanwhile, that the original purpose of the Act, to revitalise the private-rented sector has not been fulfilled. The report found that the average rents have increased by up to 37 per cent. in the last year and are now in the £60–90 per week range, compared with £20–40 before the Act. There is also more high-priced rented housing on the market, but fewer bedsits for single people, and most vacancies are for furnished accommodation. The authors conclude that people on low incomes will now find it more difficult to retain a private-sector tenancy than before the Act and if council rents are raised to match market rates many council tenants will face hardship. Nothing in the authors' view has been done by the legislation to reduce the incidence of homelessness or alleviate the problems faced by the homeless.[85]

Bibliographical note

The plight of the homeless prior to the introduction of the Housing (Homeless Persons) Act 1977 was well documented. See, in particular,

---

[82] para. 82.
[83] Doling & Davies, *Public Control of Privately Rented Housing* (1984), p. 134.
[84] Nevitt, *Housing, Taxation and Subsidies* (1966), p. 54.
[85] *The Times* May 1, 1990.

J. Greve, D. Page & S. Greve, *Homelessness in London* (1971, Scottish Academic Press); R. Bailey & J. Rudock, *The Grief Report* (1972, Shelter); R. Bailey, *The Squatters* (1973, Penguin); R. Bailey, *Bed and Breakfast* (1974, Shelter); R. Bailey, *The Homeless and the Empty Houses* (1977, Penguin).

There are various useful, explanatory guides to Part III of the Housing Act 1988. Note, in particular: A. Arden, *Homeless Persons*: *The Housing Act 1985 Part III* (1988, Legal Action Group); P. Q. Watchman & P. Robson, *Homelessness and the Law in Britain* (2nd ed., 1989, The Planning Exchange).

The student texts include chapters giving an outline of the working of the homelessness provisions: A. Arden, *Manual of Housing Law* (4th ed., 1989, Sweet & Maxwell) Chapter 10; D. C. Hoath, *Public Housing Law* (1987, Sweet & Maxwell) Chapters 4 to 6; D. Hughes, *Public Sector Housing Law* (2nd ed., 1987, Butterworths) Chapter 6.

Also, for a general review of the legislation see the articles by R. de Friend, The Housing (Homeless Persons) Act 1977 (1978) 41 M.L.R. 173 and P. Robson & P. Q. Watchman, The homeless persons' obstacle race [1981] J.S.W.L. 1 & 65.

There are large question-marks surrounding the effectiveness of the legislation in securing accommodation for the homeless. It has been argued that the combined effect of judicial decisions and local authority practice has been largely to reduce the extent of the duties as intended by those who proposed the legislation: P. Birkinshaw, Homelessness and the law: the effect and response to legislation (1982) 5 U.L.P. 255. This is perhaps particularly the case in the context of relationship breakdown and domestic violence. (Nearly one-fifth of applications for housing under Part III result from relationship breakdown.[86]) For an analysis of the legislation and local authority practice which indicates that Part III is very far from a comprehensive safety net for victims of domestic violence, see R. Thornton, Homelessness through relationship breakdown: the local authority response [1988] J.S.W.L. 67. See also, M. Bryan, Domestic violence: a question of housing [1984] J.S.W.L. 195.

Finally, many of the cases referred to in the preceeding pages have been the subject of academic comment. References to these casenotes are to be found in the footnotes.

---

[86] See p. 561.

INDEX

Index